THE RISE OF HEI

Where does our fascination for 'heritage' originate? This ground-breaking comparative study of preservation in France, Germany and England looks beyond national borders to reveal how the idea of heritage emerged from intense competition and collaboration in a global context. Astrid Swenson follows the 'heritage-makers' from the French Revolution to the First World War, revealing the importance of global networks driving developments in each country. Drawing on documentary, literary and visual sources, the book connects high politics and daily life and uncovers how, through travel, correspondence, world fairs and international congresses, the preservationists exchanged ideas, helped each other campaign and dreamed of establishing international institutions for the protection of heritage. Yet, these heritage-makers were also animated by fierce rivalry as international tension grew. This mixture of international collaboration and competition created the European culture of heritage, which defined preservation as integral to modernity, and still shapes current institutions and debates.

ASTRID SWENSON is Lecturer in European History at Brunel University, London. Her previous publications include *From Plunder to Preservation: Britain and the Heritage of Empire, c. 1800–1940* (co-edited with Peter Mandler, 2013).

NEW STUDIES IN EUROPEAN HISTORY

Edited by

PETER BALDWIN, University of California, Los Angeles
CHRISTOPHER CLARK, University of Cambridge
JAMES B. COLLINS, Georgetown University
MIA RODRíGUEZ-SALGADO, London School of Economics and
Political Science
LYNDAL ROPER, University of Oxford
TIMOTHY SNYDER, Yale University

The aim of this series in early modern and modern European history is to publish outstanding works of research, addressed to important themes across a wide geographical range, from southern and central Europe, to Scandinavia and Russia, from the time of the Renaissance to the Second World War. As it develops, the series will comprise focused works of wide contextual range and intellectual ambition.

A full list of titles published in the series can be found at:
www.cambridge.org/newstudiesineuropeanhistory

THE RISE OF HERITAGE

Preserving the Past in France, Germany and England, 1789–1914

ASTRID SWENSON

Brunel University

CAMBRIDGE
UNIVERSITY PRESS

CAMBRIDGE
UNIVERSITY PRESS

University Printing House, Cambridge CB2 8BS, United Kingdom

Cambridge University Press is part of the University of Cambridge.

It furthers the University's mission by disseminating knowledge in the pursuit of
education, learning and research at the highest international levels of excellence.

www.cambridge.org
Information on this title: www.cambridge.org/9781107595583

First published 2013
First paperback edition 2015

A catalogue record for this publication is available from the British Library

ISBN 978-0-521-11762-3 Hardback
ISBN 978-1-107-59558-3 Paperback

Cambridge University Press has no responsibility for the persistence or accuracy
of URLs for external or third-party internet websites referred to in this publication,
and does not guarantee that any content on such websites is, or will remain,
accurate or appropriate.

To my parents

Contents

Illustrations

Tables

Acknowledgements

I want to thank the many people who made this book possible. It started in Cambridge's wonderfully varied intellectual community, framed by debates in the History Faculty, the Heritage Research Group, St John's College, Darwin College, and in particular the Modern German History Workshop and the Cambridge Victorian Studies Group. I also owe much to the scholarly communities in Paris and Berlin and the magnificent Institute of Human Sciences in Vienna. For support and discussion during the preparation of the final manuscript, I thank my colleagues at Brunel University.

None of this would have been possible without generous financial support. In its early stages, the project was funded by the Gates Cambridge Trust, the AHRB and St John's College, Cambridge. The German Historical Institutes in London and Paris gave grants for my archival work abroad, together with their vibrant research communities. My particular thanks are to Andreas Gestrich and Werner Paravicini. The Körber-Foundation sponsored my fellowship at the Institute for Human Sciences, Vienna. I also benefited enormously from an honorary scholarship of the Studienstiftung des deutschen Volkes. The Leverhulme Trust and Darwin College, Cambridge provided me with fellowships during the second stage of the project. Brunel University and the Paul Mellon Centre for Studies in British Art helped towards the costs of image reproductions.

Permissions to use illustrations and manuscript collections are gratefully acknowledged. I am indebted to many librarians and archivists who shared their sources, knowledge and time at Cambridge University Library, St John's College Library (especially Jonathan Harrison and Pam Johnson), the Seeley Library and the Architecture and History of Art Library in Cambridge, the British Library, the German Historical Institute London, the National Archives in Kew, the Society for the Protection of Ancient Building (especially Miss Greenhill for her warm hospitality), the National Trust (especially Iain Shaw), the Archives nationales, the

Bibliothèque historique de la Ville de Paris, the Bibliothèque nationale, the Médiathèque du patrimoine, the archives of the Louvre and UNESCO's archives in Paris; the Archives departementales in Bordeaux, the Staatsbibliothek and the Geheimes Staatsarchiv Preußischer Kulturbesitz in Berlin, the Österreichische Nationalbibliothek and the Institute for Human Sciences in Vienna.

Many readers have kindly shared their expertise. Their burdens have varied from dealing with the earliest drafts to commenting on numerous chapters from the final manuscript. All have been enormously helpful. Richard Evans read the first and the last version of the entire manuscript, and many versions in between. I am thankful for many years of discussion and inspiration. Peter Mandler sharpened my understanding of both British history and the comparative perspective and inspired through his thoughtfulness and kindness. Chris Clark, David Cannadine, Indra Sengupta and the anonymous readers for the Press made very helpful suggestions on how to transform the entire manuscript. At Cambridge University Press, I am grateful to Michael Watson, Chloe Howell, Sarah Roberts and Gaia Poggiogalli for their comments throughout the process of writing and editing.

Many other friends and colleagues have helped with drafts and discussions of methodology and sources. Elisabeth Vlossak, Riccarda Torriani, Chris Warnes, Stephanie Chan, Victoria Harris, Hester Vaizey, David Motadal, Bianca Gaudenzi, Toby Simpson, Christian Wenkel, Muriel Blaive, Emilia Palonen, Harriet Larkin, Martin Worthington, Joe Devanny, Elisabeth Whitton, Heather Jones, Mirjam Brusius, Varun Uberoi, and Tamson Pietsch read chapters at various stages. I was also blessed with the wisdom of the member of the Victorian Studies Group, Sadiah Qureshi, Anna Vaninskaya, Adelene Buckland, Helen Brookman, Rachel Briand-Davies, Jocelyn Betts, David Gange, Michael Ledger-Lomas, Mary Beard, Simon Goldhill, Jim Secord, Clare Pettit. They all commented on drafts and helped me think about the experiential nature of history more broadly. I learned much from Lisa Niemeyer about historical novels during our walks in Wimpole. I am grateful to Peter Burke for discussions about conceptual history, to Robert Tombs for his insights into Anglo-French relations and Tim Blanning for his thoughts about romantic restorations. Etienne François contributed much in the early stages of the project between Paris and Berlin. I am grateful to Michel Werner for discussions on *histoire croisée*; to Françoise Haman, François Hartog, Jean-Michel Leniaud for sharing their views about French heritage and to Nabila Oulebsir, Dominique Poulot and Benedicte Savoy for reflections on the impact of borders on heritage and to Tamara van Kessel for conversations about how to write a comparative history of heritage. Melanie Hall and Chris Miele generously shared their knowledge about the National Trust and the SPAB, Philippa Levine and Chris Manias about learned societies, Elizabeth Edwards about photographic societies, and Ruth Fiori about the Amis des Monuments Parisiens and the character of the elusive Charles Normand. Discussions and teaching with Barbara Könczöl were always inspiring and shaped the twentieth-century outlook. Billie Melman, Stefan Berger and Chris Lorentz helped to sharpen ideas about popular heritage.

Various chapters were also much improved by comments at seminars and conferences and by discussions with my students at Cambridge and Brunel. I am also grateful to the many friends who provided housing and company during my archive stints, especially Christian, Pascal, Sabine and Caroline in Paris and Egon and Thomaso in Berlin.

Many of my fellow students and colleagues contributed in other ways to my life, and I felt blessed by their friendship. Thank you Anna Wolff for your laughter and for always being there, to Ralph Gäbler, Angela Johnson, Céline Beauchamp, Didier and Florence Charton-Vachet, the Breinings, Uschi and Hanno Blackert for support and true friendship. To Aldo, friend and companion, thank you for living with all things heritage. Finally, I want to thank my parents, Gisela and Eckhard Swenson, for their love and support during my entire life. Together with my grandparents and the Richardts, you ignited my interest in historical consciousness through discussions and travel to many sites, which I rediscovered during the writing as being profoundly shaped by the nineteenth-century heritage-makers. This book is for you, with love.

Abbreviations

Abg.	Abgeordneter
AN	Archives nationales, Paris
BHS	Bund Heimatschutz
BN	Bibliothèque nationale
CMH	Commission des Monuments historiques
CMN	Centre des Monument Nationaux
CPS	Commons Preservation Society
CTH	Comité des travaux historiques
CTHS	Comité des travaux historiques et scientifiques
DNB	Oxford Dictionary of National Biography
GStA PK	Geheimes Staatsarchiv Preußischer Kulturbesitz
IICI	Institut International de Co-operation Intellectuelle
JO	Journal Officiel
MAP	Médiathèque de l'architecture et du patrimoine, Paris
NT	National Trust
OED	Oxford English Dictionary
OIM	Office International des Musées
PRO	Public Record Office
SAL	Society of Antiquaries of London
SPAB	Society for the Protection of Ancient Buildings
SPPEF	Société pour la protection des paysages et de l'ésthetique de France
SPPF	Société pour la protection des paysages de France
TNA	The National Archives, London

Introduction

> The cultural heritage of a people is the memory of its living culture. It is expressed in many different forms, both tangible (monuments, landscapes, objects) and intangible (languages, knowhow, the performing arts, music, etc.). The origins of this heritage are multifarious, too. In retracing its own cultural lineage, in recognizing the many different influences that have marked its history and shaped its identity, a people is better able to build peaceful relations with other peoples, to pursue what is often an age-old dialogue and to forge its future.[1]
>
> Koïchiro Matsuura at the inauguration of the UN Year for Cultural Heritage (2002)

Following the destruction of the Bamiyan Buddhas by the Taliban in 2001, the United Nations General Assembly proclaimed 2002 as the United Nations Year for Cultural Heritage. The aim was to make public authorities, the private sector and civil society realise how cultural heritage could be an 'instrument for peace and reconciliation' and a 'factor of development'.[2] While mourning the recent destruction of heritage, the UN Year also celebrated the internationalisation of preservation since the Second World War and the thirtieth anniversary of the 1972 World Heritage Convention. As the words of former UNESCO Secretary General Koïchiro Matsuura indicate, efforts have focussed not just on increasing identification with a common world heritage or on promoting knowledge about other cultures. Additionally, care for one's own heritage is fostered as the crucial prerequisite to peaceful relations between peoples. Globally, heritage is increasingly promoted as a force of good. Preservation policies are firmly integrated into the bureaucracies of many modern states, but as local, national and international activities are seen as building upon each other they are also linked

---

[1] K. Matsuura, 'United Nations Year for Cultural Heritage', in UNESCO, 'United Nations Year for Cultural Heritage', (2002), http://portal.unesco.org/culture/en/ev.php-URL_ID=15418&URL_DO=DO_TOPIC&URL_SECTION=201.html.

[2] Ibid.

through a plethora of international and non-governmental organisations.[3] Civic engagement and heritage-related activities have also continuously been growing. For instance, across European countries, European Heritage Days are a magnet for tens of millions annual visitors.[4] In Britain, the National Trust alone has more members than all political parties put together.[5] At the beginning of the twenty-first century, the protection of one's heritage has become a quasi human right. As a result, heritage is mobilised by a variety of actors for a wide variety of purposes. It is adduced to frame the restoration of cathedrals, as well as the preservation of fox-hunting, or the marketing of local cheese, but also for the regeneration of post-industrial regions and the reconstruction of post-conflict communities.

Why did heritage become so important? Where does the belief in its potential to bring prosperity, peace and international understanding come from? Paradoxically, while heritage is used as a universal category in public discourse, the origins of international concern for heritage are perceived to be relatively recent, only dating from the post-war period. Instead, historians have sought explanations for the birth of heritage during the late eighteenth and the nineteenth century overwhelmingly in national contexts.[6] It is frequently claimed that a national 'special path' determined the appearance of heritage consciousness. This is particularly, but not solely, the case for the three European countries forming the object of this study. To put it in a stereotypical way: French heritage is often perceived as the creation of the state, in order to rally the citizens; German heritage as having been developed by the bourgeoisie as a means of self-representation, and English heritage as having been imposed by a threatened ruling class for its own protection.

Every country thus imagines it has invented heritage. But did they all magically imagine heritage at more or less the same time? And why is heritage now seen as an international phenomenon? It makes sense to go back and look at the international origins that were there all along, though for various reasons denied by actors and historians. As explanations for the emergence of heritage have been looked for in relation to the dominant questions in national historiographies, historians not only failed to consider

---

[3] On the European level see for instance Europa Nostra, www.europanostra.org.
[4] The Heritage Open Days National Partnership (2011), www.heritageopendays.org.uk.
[5] D. Cannadine, 'The First Hundred Years', in H. Newby (ed.), *The National Trust. The Next Hundred Years* (London, 1995), pp. 11–31.
[6] For a discussion of international and national approaches see D. Gillman, *The Idea of Cultural Heritage* (London, 2006), pp. 27–41.

a wider appropriation of heritage by diverse social groups in each country, but they neglected the emergence of similar ideas and practices in different national contexts and ignored the connections between them. Across countries, major developments occurred repeatedly at the same moments. First, during the French Revolution and the Napoleonic Wars, the destruction of symbols of the old order, changing ideas regarding national community, the nationalisation of property by the Revolutionary government and art looting by the French armies, led to a new notion of 'national heritage' across Europe. The 1830s and 1840s, then, saw the first Europe-wide debates about the protection of the past by the state. While history started to become established as an academic discipline, splendid restorations resurrected lost monuments and a popular culture of heritage emerged. Between 1870 and 1914, finally, modern preservationism was established. The fanciful restorations of national treasures were replaced with a new idea of authenticity emphasising the value of age. What was considered worthy of preservation also changed. The idea of heritage broadened to include vernacular alongside monumental traces, recent alongside distant pasts, nature alongside culture, and traditions alongside objects. Changing popular attitudes manifested in the foundation of a plethora of voluntary associations and meshed with growing concern on the part of the State translating into a wave of legislation.

Can these similarities be purely understood in terms of parallel, and maybe competing national developments? At first sight, it makes sense to look for national explanations, as the long nineteenth century was strongly framed by outbursts of nationalism and a disregard for foreign heritages. The period starts with a nationalist reclaiming of the past during the French Revolution, accompanied by widespread looting of art. The beginning of a new era seems succinctly captured by a petition addressed to all members of the Republic of Letters, asking them to 'stop being cosmopolitans' and restrain their 'vast affection that embraces the entire universe' and instead love their 'fatherland a little more'.[7] The end of the period is likewise dominated by war and destruction, symbolised by the burning of Louvain Library and Rheims Cathedral by the German army in 1914. However, despite this nationalist framing, one only needs to open any preservationist periodical from the nineteenth century to realise that developments across countries did not happen in isolation, but that heritage-makers from different nations were in constant touch with each other. All key moments in the conceptualisation of heritage during the long nineteenth century coincided

---

[7] C.J. Trouvé, *Le Monietuer universel*, no. 335, 5 fructidor an V (22 Aug. 1796).

with an increase in international contacts between preservationists. Personal travel and correspondence were complemented by the use of diplomatic channels and formalised exchanges between private societies. Since mid-century, the world's fairs and international congresses also provided regular venues for such exchanges. While contacts were mainly used to improve the national situations during the first two waves described above, during the third wave, internationalism became more pronounced. Heritage-makers increasingly used the transnational space not only to exchange ideas about their national situation, but also debated the creation of international institutions and the protection of a common heritage of humanity.

Hence, this book will argue that the rise of heritage cannot be understood without its transnational dimension. It shows how heritage could become an important universal category by analysing the history of heritage in France, Germany and Britain between 1789 and 1914 as an 'entangled history'. To this end it combines a comparison of the three countries with an analysis of multi-directional 'cultural transfers'.[8] It distinguishes between parallel national developments, competing, mutually induced, national developments, and developments at the international level, which had national effects. By showing which similarities and differences were due to indigenous factors, and which had broader transnational origins, it revises explanations given in the three separate national historiographies. Moreover, and perhaps more significantly, by inscribing the entanglements between the three countries into much broader interactions, the book reveals the importance of the global level for the rise of heritage.

The general benefits of comparison have often been pointed out.[9] By revealing that apparently different events can relate to similar causes and that similar events can stem from different reasons, a comparative approach can overcome what Marc Bloch labelled the explanatory lure of 'local pseudo causes'.[10] As such the 'comparative method is capable of rendering historians the most remarkable services, by introducing them to the road that can lead to the real explanations, but also, and perhaps most importantly, if we might begin with a more modest but necessary benefit, by deterring them from certain paths that are nothing but dead ends'.[11] But

[8] M. Werner and B. Zimmermann, 'Beyond Comparison. Histoire Croisée and the Challenge of Reflexivity', *History and Theory*, 45 (2006), 30–50.
[9] J. Breuilly, 'Introduction. Making Comparisons in History', in Breuilly, *Labour and Liberalism in Nineteenth-Century Europe. Essays in Comparative History* (Manchester, New York, 1992), pp. 1–5.
[10] M. Bloch, 'Pour une histoire comparée des sociétés européennes', in Bloch, *Mélanges historiques* (2 vols., Paris, 1963), I, pp. 16–40, here p. 16.
[11] Ibid., p. 24.

comparison also has its pitfalls. In particular there is a danger of constructing the entities for comparison artificially and of assuming that national cultures are distinct and closed.[12] Marc Bloch already pointed out that societies close in time and space are likely to influence each other. This inspired a school of 'cultural transfer' historians to emphasise the constant reconstruction of cultures through incorporation and 'acculturation' of foreign elements.[13] However, as most transfer studies looked only at one specific transfer, they can implicitly reintroduce the comparative element and assume transfer from one distinct national culture to another. As a result it has been suggested to combine the two interdependent approaches, looking at multinational transfers and re-transfers. Yet it remains difficult to combine comparison and transfer in writing, as one privileges synchrony and macro-history, the other diachrony and micro-history. It also remains challenging to capture all multinational transfers and re-transfers as an almost cubist perspective of simultaneity would be needed. 'Entangled history' suggests resolving the dilemma by being self-reflexive about the categories used and to emphasise asymmetries rather than glossing over them. Yet, while theoretical debates have been flourishing, empirical examples are lacking. Hence, it is one of the aims of this study to advance the debate about transnational and global history through empirical work.[14]

Heritage and history

Understanding why the transnational dimension has been written out of the history of heritage, and why different national historiographies have conceptualised this history so differently is an important prerequisite. Despite a long-established comparative angle in art-historical work,[15] and a growing

[12] Cf. M. Espagne, 'Sur les limites du comparatisme en histoire culturelle', *Genèse*, 17 (1994), 112–21. versus H.G. Haupt, J. Kocka, 'Historischer Vergleich. Methoden, Aufgaben, Probleme. Eine Einleitung', in Haupt, Kocka (eds.), *Geschichte und Vergleich*. pp. 3–45, esp. p. 10.

[13] M. Espagne and M. Werner (eds.), *Transferts. Les Relations interculturelles dans l'espace Franco-Allemand, XVIIIe-XIXe siècles* (Paris, 1988); E. François, H. Siegrist, J. Vogel (eds.), *Nation und Emotion. Deutschland und Frankreich im Vergleich, 19. und 20. Jahrhundert* (Göttingen, 1995); E. François, M.C. Hook-Demarle, R. Meyer-Kalkus, M. Werner, P. Despoix (eds.), *Marianne-Germania. Deutsch-französischer Kulturtransfer im europäischen Kontext, 1789–1914* (2 vols., Leipzig, 1998); R. Muhs, J. Paulmann, W. Steinmetz (eds.), *Aneignung und Abwehr. Interkultureller Transfer zwischen Deutschland und Großbritannien im 19. Jahrhundert* (Bodenheim, 1998); L. Jordan, B. Kortländer (eds.), *Nationale Grenzen und internationaler Austausch. Studien zum Kultur- und Wissenschaftstransfer in Europa* (Tübingen, 1995).

[14] For recent methodological reflections see G. Budde, S. Conrad, O. Janz (eds.), *Transnationale Geschichte. Themen, Tendenzen und Theorien* (Göttingen, 2006).

[15] G. Germann, *Gothic Revival in Europe and Britain. Sources, Influences and Ideas* (London, 1972); J. Jokilehto, *A History of Architectural Conservation* (Oxford, 1999); W. Denslagen, *Architectural Restoration in Western Europe. Controversy and Continuity* (Amsterdam, 1994).

concern with comparative and transnational questions more broadly,[16] the main standard works on the history of heritage have often extrapolated from national experiences under the cover of a universalist title, cherry-picking rather than comparing international examples.[17] More recently, attention has been drawn to the differences between Western and non-Western understanding of heritage, but intra-European differences and global connections are rarely highlighted.[18] The recent efforts to establish 'heritage studies' as a discipline have also not shed much light on this question, as their concern is more with heritage in the present than in the past.[19] The rich historiographies, which exist at the national level, on the other hand are often shaped by national traditions of administering heritage. Broader historical work has seen the history of heritage mainly through the lens of other dominant questions in national historiographies. Casting aside some nuances, in France, the debates about the history of heritage are still to a certain degree about assessing the legacy of the French Revolution. In Germany, the study of nineteenth-century heritage has been conducted as part of the German *Sonderweg* debate, while in Britain the 1980s 'Heritage Debate', dominated by worries about the rise of the heritage industry in relation to the decline of the industrial spirit and the revival of 'Victorian Values', has cast a long shadow.[20]

A large part of the literature on heritage is more or less openly a *littérature engagée*, using the history of preservation for particular agendas in current

---

[16] Gillman, *Idea of Cultural Heritage*. M. Hall (ed.), *Towards World Heritage. International Origins of the Preservation Movement* (Aldershot, 2011); S. Bann, *The Clothing of Clio. A Study of the Representation of History in Nineteenth-Century Britain and France* (Cambridge, 1984); S. Berger, C. Lorenz, B. Melman (eds.), *Popularizing National Pasts, 1800 to the Present* (London, 2011); B. Savoy, *Patrimoine annexé. Les biens culturels saisis par la France en Allemagne autour de 1800* (2 vols., Paris, 2003); A.S. Rolland, H. Murauskaya (eds.), *Les Musées de la Nation. Créations, transpositions, renouveau. Europe XIXe-XXe siècles* (Paris, 2009). C. Manias, 'Learned Societies and the Ancient National Past in Britain, France and Germany, 1830–1890', unpublished Ph.D. dissertation, University of London (2008); U. Protz, 'National Treasures'/'Tresor Nationaux': The control of the Export of Works of Art and the Construction of 'National Heritage'/'Patrimoine in France and the United Kingdom, 1884–1959', unpublished Ph.D. dissertation, European University Institute (2009); D. Trom, 'Natur und nationale Identität. Der Streit um den Schutz der "Natur" um die Jahrhundertwende in Deutschland und Frankreich', in François, Siegrist, Vogel (eds.), *Nation und Emotion*, pp. 147–67; A.K. Wöbse, *Weltnaturschutz. Umweltdiplomatie in Völkerbund und Vereinten Nationen 1920–1950* (Frankfurt, 2012).

[17] J.P. Babelon and A. Chastel, *La Notion de patrimoine* (Paris, 1994); F. Choay, *L'Allégorie du patrimoine* (Paris, 1992); D. Lowenthal, *The Past is a Foreign Country* (Cambridge, 1985); Lowenthal, *The Heritage Crusade and the Spoils of History* (Cambridge, 1998).

[18] L. Smith, *Uses of Heritage* (London, New York, 2006).

[19] J. Carman and M.L. Stig Sørensen (eds.), *Heritage Studies, Methods and Approaches* (London, New York, 2009).

[20] E.g. R. Hewison, *The Heritage Industry. Britain in a Climate of Decline* (London, 1987); W. Speitkamp, *Die Verwaltung der Geschichte. Denkmalpflege und Staat in Deutschland, 1871–1933* (Göttingen, 1996); D. Poulot, *Patrimoine et musées. L'institution de la culture* (Paris, 2001).

heritage politics.[21] Assumptions about heritage have also been particularly shaped by presentist concerns in the field of memory studies. Although many conceptual nuances exist between 'heritage' and 'memory', the two notions have often been used interchangeably.[22] Importantly here, the national focus of heritage studies can in part be explained by the trend towards orchestrating an explicit revival of national history through the history of memory. Especially Pierre Nora's *Lieux de mémoire* played a major role in fostering a national orientation. Whilst the idea of invented memory seemingly deconstructs nationalist assumptions, Nora presented the writing of the *Lieux de mémoire* as a patriotic endeavour to preserve vanishing memories, offering a way to reinvent the writing of national history through commemoration in a Europeanising and globalising world.[23] This appealed to other countries too and national *Lieux de mémoire* projects soon followed across Europe in the 1990s.[24] A range of scholars have since challenged the primacy of the national in studies of memory, stressing the need to pay more attention to the local context on the one hand and to European and postcolonial perspectives on the other.[25] Yet some of these attempts are no less charged with identity-building objectives. The aim of this book is not to argue that European or international origins are more enobling than national ones, but simply to open a dialogue between

[21] See J. Le Goff, 'Introduction', in Le Goff (ed.), *Patrimoine et passions identitaires. Actes des Entretiens du Patrimoine Paris 1997* (Paris, 1998), p. 13.

[22] As Pierre Nora stated in the *Lieux de mémoire*, 'Heritage [*patrimoine*]: in a sense this word could have covered this entire book'. P. Nora, Introduction to the section on 'Patrimoine', in Nora (ed.), *Les Lieux de mémoire* (7 vols., Paris, 1984–92, reprint, 3 vols., Paris, 1997), I, pp. 1429–643, here p. 1431. For similar uses see D. Sherman, *The Construction of Memory in Interwar France* (Chicago, 1999), pp. 2–3; T. Benton, 'Introduction', in Benton (ed.), *Understanding Heritage and Memory* (Manchester, 2010), p. 1.

[23] See P. Nora, 'La Nation-mémoire', in *Les Lieux de mémoire*, II, pp. 2207–16, his introductions to the different volumes of the Lieux de mémoire, as well as the revised ones in the English translation P. Nora (ed.), *Realms of Memory. Rethinking the French Past* (3 vols., New York, 1996).

[24] M. Insenghi (ed.), *I luogi della memoria* (3 vols., Rome, Bari, 1987–8); O. Feldbaek (ed.), *Dansk identiteshistorie* (Copenhagen, 1991–2); P. den Boer, W. Frijhoff (eds.), *Lieux de mémoire et identités nationales* (Amsterdam, 1993); N.C.F. van Sas (ed.), *Waar de blanke top der duinen: en andere vaderlandse herinneringen* (Amsterdam, 1995); M. Csáky (ed.), *Orte des Gedächtnisses* (Vienna, 2000); E. François and H. Schulze (eds.), *Deutsche Erinnerungsorte* (3 vols., Munich, 2001).

[25] For instance E. Apter, *Continental Drift: From National Characters to Virtual Subjects* (Chicago, 1999); Sherman, *The Construction of Memory*; E. Ezra, *The Colonial Unconscious: Race and Culture in Interwar France* (Ithaca, 2000); B. Stråth (ed.), *Myth, Memory and History in the Construction of Community. Historical Patterns in Europe and Beyond* (Brussels, 2000); 'Schwerpunktthema: Europäische lieux de mémoire?', *Jahrbuch für Europäische Geschichte*, 3 (2002); 'European Lieux de Mémoire', conference of the German Historical Institute London, Cumberland Lodge, 5–7 July 2002, report by B. Stuchtey, *German Historical Institute London Bulletin*, 24.2 (2002), pp. 121–5; 'Patrimoines de l'Europe, patrimoine européen?' 15e Entretiens du Patrimoine, 19–21 March 2007, Paris, www.culture.gouv.fr/edp2007/presentation.htm; K. Buchinger, C. Gantet, C. and J. Vogel (eds.), *Europäische Erinnerungsräume* (Frankfurt, New York, 2009).

different national and disciplinary traditions and understand how a process could simultaneously lead to different national approaches and to a
common culture of heritage. By historicising heritage in such a way, I hope
to contribute more generally to explaining the origins of many current
debates and offer a way to question hegemonic accounts of how heritage
should be interpreted.

Words and things

Despite the confident tone of some of the definitions of heritage, there is
much debate on what is meant by 'heritage' and whether it can or should be
defined at all. Designations range from enumerations of potential remains,
to defamations of heritage as 'anything that sells' or celebrations of it
as 'anything you want'. Most current definitions stress that virtually any
legacy from the past, tangible or intangible, can become heritage, as long
as a community wants to claim and transmit it.[26] This attitude is captured
in UNESCO's definition of 'heritage' as 'our legacy from the past, what we
live with today, and what we pass on to future generations',[27] and which
can be 'expressed in many different forms, both tangible (monuments,
landscapes, objects) and intangible (languages, knowhow, the performing
arts, music, etc.)'.[28] However, neither this definition nor the word heritage
itself have been used in this way for more than a few decades in English,
while other languages have different terms that do not necessarily have
the same resonances. This poses obvious problems for studying the history
of 'heritage'. Applying the word and the broad definitions of today retrospectively is anachronistic. A prospective definition is equally problematic
because a plethora of different words, ideas and movements with different
names could be taken as a starting point.

This problem of course does not just apply to heritage, but to the
history of any concept. As Jacob Burckhardt long ago observed, 'sharply
defined terminology belongs to Logic but not to History'. Whereas philosophical terminology needs to be as 'definite and compact as possible',
historical terminology needs to be 'as floating and open as possible' to take

---

[26] See J. Carman and M.L. Stig Sørensen, 'Heritage Studies. An outline', in Carman, Sørensen (eds.),
   Heritage Studies, Methods and Approaches (London, New York, 2009), pp. 11–28, here pp. 11–12;
   R. Harrison, 'What is Heritage?' in Harrison (ed.), *Understanding the Politics of Heritage* (Manchester, 2010), pp. 5–42.
[27] UNESCO, 'World Heritage', http://whc.unesco.org/en/about.
[28] Matsuura, 'United Nations Year for Cultural Heritage'.

into account the changing nature of definitions over time.[29] Moreover, a transnational approach is not only confronted with asymmetries between categories in different times but also with asymmetries between cultures which remain often untranslatable.[30] Whereas today, both English and French have generic, albeit not congruent terms (*heritage* and *patrimoine*), there is no corresponding single word in German. In addition to *Kulturerbe* a variety of expressions are needed such as *Kulturgüter* (cultural property), *Denkmal* (monument) or *Heimat* (nominally 'homeland', but carrying implications that translations are not quite able to provide). To complicate matters further, the semantic field of 'heritage' has been steadily changing and growing with the evolution of the concept. While *patrimoine* and *heritage* were already in use in the nineteenth century, at this time people referred more generally to *monuments* in all three languages. Yet a number of partial synonyms also exist in all languages, many of these come from a common Greco-Latin pool.

The scholarly vocabulary also varies, stemming from, and in turn leading to, different foci in the respective scholarly traditions. In French a number of neologisms are employed to describe the process of conceptualisation and institutionalisation which do not have an English or German equivalent, such as *patrimonialiser* (to turn something into 'heritage'), *patrimonialisation* (the process of creating (the concept of) 'heritage'), *conscience patrimoniale* ('heritage-awareness'), *champ patrimoniale* (everything that is included in the notion of 'heritage') and most recently *patrimonialisateur* ('heritage-maker'). German on the other hand has developed a number of compounds since the late nineteenth century on the basis of *Denkmal* and *Heimat*: *Denkmalpflege* (the care of monuments), *Denkmalschutz* (the legal protection of monuments), and similarly *Heimatpflege* and *Heimatschutz* (the latter had beforehand referred to the military defence of the homeland). The preservation movement is designated as *Denkmal-* and *Heimatbewegung*. '*Heimat*-"buffs"' were called *Heimatkundler* (*Heimat*-scholar), *Heimatschützer* (*Heimat*-protector) or

[29] J. Burckhard, *Über das Studium der Geschichte. Der Text der Weltgeschichtlichen Betrachtungen auf Grund der Vorarbeiten von Ernst Ziegler nach den Handschriften*, ed. P. Ganz (Munich, 1982), p. 293.
[30] See R. Koselleck, U. Spree, W. Steinmetz, 'Drei bürgerliche Welten? Zur vergleichenden Semantik der bürgerlichen Gesellschaft in Deutschland, Frankreich und England', in H.J. Puhle (ed.), *Bürger in der Gesellschaft der Neuzeit. Wirtschaft – Politik – Kultur* (Göttingen, 1991), pp. 14–58; J. Leonhard, *Liberalismus. Zur historischen Semantik eines Deutungsmusters* (Munich, 2001); B. Cassin (ed.), *Le Vocabulaire européen des philosophes. Dictionnaire des intraduisibles* (Paris, 2004); A. Gerber, 'Transnationale Geschichte "machen" – Anmerkungen zu einem möglichen Vorgehen', geschichte.transnational, 2 April 2005, http://geschichte-transnational.clio-online.net/forum/2005-04-001.

simply *Heimatler*, whereas *Denkmalpfleger* (monument-carer) increasingly designated a professional conservator. *Heimatgedanken, Heimatsinn, Heimatgefühl, Heimatliebe* (*Heimat*-thoughts, -sense, -sentiment and -love) led to all sorts of *Heimatbestrebungen* (*Heimat*-endeavours),[31] including the development of *Heimatkunst* and *Heimatstil* (*Heimat*-art and *Heimat*-style), all engendering a veritable *Denkmalcultus* (cult of monuments). The totality of all monuments was called *Denkmalbestand*. Finally there even is a word for the concept of monument: *Denkmalbegriff*.

The evolution of key words has been studied to different degrees for the respective languages,[32] but no small amount of confusion remains about why and when words evolved and replaced each other.[33] The differences in words between different cultures have also often been noticed,[34] but explanations for these differences remain unsystematic and lack a proper engagement with foreign cases.[35] For instance, Robert Hewison's assertion that *patrimoine* was derived from *patrie*, and therefore indicates a more national content of the French *patrimoine* than the English word 'heritage' with its alleged emphasis on private property, is flawed.[36] Both *patrie* (from

---

[31] C. Applegate, *A Nation of Provincials. The German Idea of Heimat* (Berkeley, Los Angeles, Oxford, 1990), pp. 3–19.

[32] On German: W. Sauerländer, 'Erweiterung des Denkmalbegriffes?', *Deutsche Kunst und Denkmalpflege*, 33 (1975), 117–30; G. Mörsch, 'Zur Differenzierbarkeit des Denkmalbegriffs', *Deutsche Kunst und Denkmalpflege*, 39 (1981), 99–108; R. Alings, *Monument und Nation. Das Bild vom Nationalstaat im Medium Denkmal* (Berlin, New York, 1996), pp. 1–15; Speitkamp, *Verwaltung der Geschichte*, pp. 83–91; Applegate, *Nation of Provincials*, pp. 3–19; R. Petri, 'Deutsche Heimat 1850–1950', *Comparativ*, 11.1 (2001), 77–127; G. Oesterle, 'Zur Historisierung des Erbebegriffes', in B. Thum (ed.), *Gegenwart als kulturelles Erbe. Ein Beitrag der Germanistik zur Kulturwissenschaft deutschsprachiger Länder* (Munich, 1985), pp. 411–51. On French: Babelon, Chastel, *La Notion de patrimoine*; A. Desvallées, 'Emergence et cheminement du mot patrimoine', *Musées et collections publiques de France*, 208.3 (1995), 6–29; Desvallées, 'A l'origine du mot "patrimoine"', in D. Poulot (ed.), *Patrimoine et modernité* (Paris, Montréal, 1998), pp. 89–105; Y. Lamy (ed.), *L'Alchimie du patrimoine. Discours et politiques* (Talence, 1996). On English: P. Berton, 'What We Mean by Heritage', *Canadian Heritage*, 7 (1981), 44; G. Davison, 'Heritage. From Patrimony to Pastiche', in G. Fairclough, R. Harrison, J.H. Jameson Jnr and J. Schofield, *The Heritage Reader* (London, New York, 2008), pp. 31–41 and S. Hall, 'Whose Heritage? Un-settling "The Heritage", Re-imagining the Post-Nation', in ibid., pp. 219–28.

[33] E.g. Choay, *L'Allégorie du patrimoine*, pp. 9–10; F. Bercé, *Dès Monuments historiques au patrimoine du XVIIIe siècle à nos jours ou 'Les égarements du coeur et de l'esprit'* (Paris, 2000), p. 7.

[34] Abdelaziz Daoust statement in 'Debat de la Matinée du 6 Janvier', in Le Goff (ed.), *Patrimoine et passions identitaires*, p. 64; J. Schofield, 'Heritage Management, Theory and Practice', in Fairclough *et al.* (eds.), *The Heritage Reader*, p. 16; Carman and Stig Sørensen (eds.), 'Heritage Studies', pp. 11–13.

[35] See for an exception, the nuanced discussion of the French and North African context: N. Oulebsir, *Les Usages du patrimoine. Monuments, musées et politiques coloniale en Algérie 1830–1930* (Paris, 2004), pp. 13–16.

[36] R. Hewison, 'La Prise de conscience du patrimoine en Grande-Bretagne', in P. Nora (ed.), *Science et conscience du patrimoine. Actes des Entretiens du Patrimoine Paris 1994* (Paris, 1997), pp. 357–63.

Latin *patria*) and *patrimoine* (from Latin *patrimonium*) are derived from the Latin word *pater*, one meaning 'fatherland', one the 'paternal heritage'.[37] In the eighteenth century *patrimoine*, like the English 'patrimony' and *patrimonium* in German, was generally applied to material and immaterial things 'inherited' from ancestors or predecessors, before coming to signify the material and immaterial 'heritage' of the nation, but also of any other community, during the course of the nineteenth and twentieth centuries in French, but rarely in English or German.[38] Interpreting the semantic development of *patrimoine* versus *heritage* as reflecting two antithetical approaches to preservation – public administration and nationalisation in France as opposed to private care for a largely privately owned 'national heritage' in Britain – too excessively relies on the notion that conceptual differences can be deduced from etymologies. This conflates word and concept in an ahistoric way.[39]

For a transnational study, the development of the vocabulary of heritage is thus crucial. Why were certain denominations chosen over others within a national context? Given that a common Greco-Latin pool existed why did we end up with such different terminologies? Did the different languages at all influence each other, and did different usages obscure cross-cultural understandings? Finally, and perhaps most problematically, do the different words always reveal differences in concepts, or are the choices also sometimes arbitrary?

Conceptual and discourse-analytical approaches assume that concepts and words are not identical, and that concepts only exist through articulation.[40] As the period during which heritage emerged as a concept was formative in the development of most modern political and social concepts, it is helpful to think about heritage's evolution in tandem with other historical concepts such as 'nation', 'culture', 'civilisation', 'time',

---

[37] 'Patrie' and 'Patrimoine', *Dictionnaire historique de la langue française* (2 vols., Paris, 1994), II, p. 1452.

[38] 'Patrimony', *OED online* (Oxford, 2004). For an early use of 'patrimony' in the French sense in English see Brown, *The Care of Ancient Monuments* (Cambridge, 1905), p. 6. For similar uses in German 'Patrimonium', *Duden, das große Wörterbuch der deutschen Sprache* (3rd edn, 10 vols., Mannheim, 1999), VI, p. 2873; however, in German *patrimonium* primarily referred to the private property of a ruler and was used in reference to feudal institutions.

[39] For other disjoint explanations see J.M. Leniaud, *L'Utopie française. Essai sur le patrimoine* (Paris, 1992), p. 1; Leniaud, *Les Archipels du passé. Le patrimoine et son histoire* (Paris, 2002), pp. 10–11.

[40] This is independent of other methodological differences. See H. Lehman, M. Richter, *The Meaning of Historical Terms and Concepts. New Studies on Begriffsgeschichte* (Washington, DC, 1996); I. Hamsher-Monk, K. Tilmans and F. van Vree (eds.), *History of Concepts. Comparative Perspectives* (Amsterdam, 1998); H. Bödeker, *Begriffsgeschichte, Diskursgeschichte, Metapherngeschichte* (Göttingen, 2003).

'property', 'progress', 'endangerment', 'art' and 'history'.[41] Methods used in studies of other concepts, such as an examination of frequency in publication titles are of limited use to understand the case of heritage because of the multitude of terms in the semantic field and the overlap with the everyday meanings of words. Patterns only acquire significance through an examination of a variety of uses in context. To understand why and how certain words were used to baptise or redefine elements of the concept, the question of agency and of conscious appropriation and transformation of a particular language, is central.[42]

Before discussing this, a word on my own linguistic choices. As it is impossible to create a meta-language for the purpose of analysis, I try to make use of the richness of analytical categories offered by the three languages, while remaining as faithful as possible to the language used in the sources, indicating the differences between historic and present English scholarly use. In the absence of a generic term, I use 'heritage' retrospectively to refer to the concept in the broad way that is indicated by UNESCO's definition. However, I use a focus on historic monuments prospectively to provide a lens for wider debates. This is not because I equate heritage with monuments – defining heritage as monuments is rightly outdated – historic monuments are only one strand of what is now called heritage, and the semantic shift from 'monument' to 'heritage' in the last decades took place in part to reflect a more inclusive, less elitist and less Eurocentric approach. Rather, this is due to my case studies surrounding debates about the built environment. In order to ground the analysis in context, a choice of focus was necessary. Given the broad current definition of heritage, other starting points could equally well have been chosen, centring for instance on languages, or the environment, or living peoples. However, while my focus is in some ways arbitrary, it is a useful one for thinking about the broader category. Historic preservation was not only one of the earliest forms of institutionalised preservation, but across languages the term 'monument' was also understood in a much wider way than it is today. It was often applied to designate tangible but also intangible remains from

---

[41] See O. Brunner, W. Conze, R. Koselleck (eds.), *Geschichtliche Grundbegriffe. Lexikon zur politisch-sozialen Sprache in Deutschland* (8 vols., 1974–97); R. Reichard, J. Lüsebrink, E. Schmitt (eds.), *Handbuch politisch-sozialer Grundbegriff in Frankreich, 1680–1820* (20 vols. to date, Munich, 1985–present); J.G.A. Pocock, 'Concepts and Discourses. A Difference in Culture? Comment on a Paper by Melvin Richter', in Lehman, Richter (eds.), *The Meaning of Historical Terms*, pp. 47–58.

[42] For a more extended discussion of methodology see A. Swenson, '"Heritage", "Patrimoine" and "Kulturerbe": Eine vergleichende historische Semantik' in D. Hemme, M. Tauschek and R. Bendix (eds.), *Prädikat Heritage. Wertschöpfungen aus kulturellen Ressourcen* (Ethnologie: Forschung und Wissenschaft 13, Müster *et al.*, 2007), pp. 53–73.

the past much like 'heritage' is now. Moreover, like present-day scholars of heritage, nineteenth-century preservationists were aware that 'monument' was a category that was difficult to define. The majority of theoretical texts, but also parliamentary debates, periodicals, and comparative studies published in the nineteenth century were constantly preoccupied with how to capture 'monument' and its relation to memory, inheritance and transmission. Through these debates one can begin to observe how attitudes to the preservation of architecture, art, texts, languages, customs, nature and living peoples were intertwined, often linking the tangible and the intangible, long before the current terms were coined.

The heritage-makers

Ideas cannot emerge independently of historical actors, but who then were the 'heritage-makers'? The question of who invented heritage is key to all three national historiographies. Although at first glance, the dominant view is that French heritage was invented by a muscular state, German heritage by the rising bourgeoisie and English heritage by the declining aristocracy, at second glance, the question of who invented heritage and whether heritage turned from a public movement into a state-controlled one or vice versa, and if so, when this occurred has received contradictory answers within each national historiography.

French historiography reflects the long standing of monument protection as a pillar of cultural policies. The focus is largely on national actors, although the need for regional studies has been stressed.[43] It is generally believed that the notion of *patrimoine* was established by a small circle of men and taken over by the state between the Revolution and the July Monarchy. Older research focussed on the establishment of the state administration. As a result the historiography often deplores the strong statist component as a form of French exceptionalism.[44] However, research on education and patriotism offers a different and more

[43] S. Gerson, 'Une France locale. The Local Past in Recent French Scholarship', *French Historical Studies*, 26.3 (2003), 539–59; Gerson, *The Pride of Place: Local Memories and Political Culture in Nineteenth-Century France* (Ithaca, NY, 2003). For local case studies see K.D. Murphy, *Memory and modernity. Viollet-le-Duc at Vézelay* (University Park, 2000); P. Poirrier (ed.), *L'Invention du patrimoine en Bourgogne* (Dijon, 2004); R. Fiori, *L'Invention du vieux Paris. Naissance d'une conscience patrimoniale dans la capital* (Paris, 2012).

[44] 'Patrimoine' in Nora (ed.), *Les Lieux de mémoire*, I, pp. 1429–643; Choay, *L'Allégorie du Patrimoine*; Leniaud, *L'Utopie française*; Babelon, Chastel, *La Notion de patrimoine*; Bercé, *Dès Monuments historiques*; Poulot, *Patrimoine et musées*; Leniaud, *Les Archipels du passé*; D. Poulot, *Une Histoire du patrimoine en Occident, XVIIIe-XXIe siècle. Du monument aux valeurs* (Paris, 2006).

participatory account,[45] as do works on learned societies, visual culture and the proliferation of collecting.[46]

Literature on the German states similarly offers different positions that engage little with each other.[47] Thomas Nipperdey's pioneering work on national monuments suggested that popular support for the idea of a national heritage was at its highest after the end of the Revolutionary Wars in 1815, when the longing for national unity manifested itself in the desire to rebuild Cologne cathedral, but that the temporary coherence of popular support was over when the cathedral was finished in 1880.[48] Rudy Koshar, in contrast, sees the beginning of a popular preservation movement only in the 1890s.[49] These different interpretations, however, in fact reveal less a hiatus in popular interest, but rather a shift in emphasis from the national to the regional level, and from monumental to vernacular definitions of heritage. Winfried Speitkamp's study offers numerous examples of how various forms of state administrations and private initiatives interacted during the *Kaiserreich*, but concludes that although the model was 'latently participatory' in the end the state came to dominate in what constitutes a particular German *Sonderweg*.[50]

[45] A.M. Thiesse, *Ils apprenaient la France. L'exaltation des régions dans le discours patriotique* (Paris, 1997).

[46] J.P. Chaline, *Sociabilité et érudition: Les sociétés savantes en France* (Paris, 1995); Gerson, *Pride of Place*; P. ten-Doesschate Chu and G.P. Weisberg (eds.), *The Popularization of Images. Visual Culture under the July Monarchy* (Princeton, 1994); T. Stammers, 'The bric-a-brac of the old regime: collecting and cultural history in post-revolutionary France', *French History*, 22.3 (2008), 295–315.

[47] As conservation is organised regionally, many studies follow administrative boundaries, e.g. R. Mohr de Pérez, *Die Anfänge der staatlichen Denkmalpflege in Preußen. Ermittlung und Erhaltung alterthümlicher Merkwürdigkeiten* (Worms, 2001); G. Dolff-Donekämpfer, *Die Entdeckung des Mittelalters. Studien zur Geschichte der Denkmalerfassung und des Denkmalschutzes in Hessen-Kassel bzw. Kurhessen im 18. und 19. Jahrhundert* (Darmstadt, Marburg, 1985); S. Dürr, *Die Anfänge der Denkmalpflege in München* (Neurid, 2001); Applegate, *Nation of Provincials*; A. Confino, *The Nation as a Local Metaphor. Würtemberg, Imperial Germany and National Memory, 1871–1918* (Chapel Hill, 1997); H. Magirius, *Geschichte der Denkmalpflege. Sachsen von den Anfängen bis zum Neubeginn 1945* (Berlin, 1989); Magirius (ed.), *Denkmalpflege in Sachsen, 1894–1994* (2 vols., Weimar, 1997), I, pp. 55–61; P. Findeisen, *Geschichte der Denkmalpflege Sachsen-Anhalt. Von den Anfängen bis in das erste Drittel des 20. Jahrhunderts* (Berlin, 1990).

[48] T. Nipperdey, 'Nationalidee und Nationaldenkmal in Deutschland im 19. Jahrhundert', in Nipperdey, *Gesellschaft, Kultur, Theorie. Gesammelte Aufsätze zur neueren Geschichte* (Göttingen, 1976), pp. 133–73; Nipperdey, 'Der Kölner Dom als Nationaldenkmal', in Nipperdey, *Nachdenken über die deutsche Geschichte* (Munich, 1986), pp. 156–71.

[49] R. Koshar, *Germany's Transient Past. Preservation and National Memory in the Twentieth Century* (Chapel Hill, 1998); Koshar, *From Monuments to Traces. Artefacts of German Memory, 1870–1990* (Berkeley, London, 2000).

[50] Speitkamp, *Verwaltung der Geschichte*, p. 401.

The fact that preservation was less centralised and state-based in Britain than in France and Germany has led to a greater focus on private and popular engagement.[51] A change of attitude towards 'heritage' is generally presumed to have taken place after 1870. But again two contrasting views exist: following Martin Wiener's critique of English backwardness which ascribed the increase in interest for national 'heritage' to the 'decline of the industrial spirit', the late Victorian years have often been portrayed as a time when the country retreated from modernity into fantasies about the national past and the rural idyll.[52] By looking at a broader public and longer period of time and relating attitudes to heritage to the wider leisure culture, however, Peter Mandler has instead suggested that the early Victorian years were characterized by a popular history boom while 'English culture became less interested in history' after 1870. Only for an aesthetic minority did heritage become more important, and it 'is this aesthetic minority's copious writings and furious activities in defence of their idea of heritage' that have been used as the evidence for a broader, and anti-modern, heritage turn in these years.[53]

The comparative perspective redresses these numerous 'special paths', showing how heritage rose everywhere through the interaction of state agencies, civil society and a broader popular culture. The Habermasian idea of the 'public sphere' remains useful to illuminate how different 'heritage-makers' interacted.[54] Although Habermas's public sphere is ideal-typical,

[51] For overviews see J. Fawcett (ed.), *The Future of the Past. Attitudes to Conservation, 1174–1974* (London, 1976); C. Dellheim, *The Face of the Past. The Preservation of the Medieval Inheritance in Victorian England* (Cambridge, 1982); M. Hunter (ed.), *Preserving the Past. The Rise of Heritage in Modern Britain* (Stroud, 1996); J. Delafons, *Politics and Preservation. A Policy History of the Built Heritage, 1882–1996* (London, 1997); B. Cowell, *The Heritage Obsession. The Battle for England's Past* (Stroud, 2008); P. Wright, *On Living in an Old Country. The National Past in Contemporary Britain* (rev. edn, 2009).

[52] M.J. Wiener, *English Culture and the Decline of the Industrial Spirit, 1850–1980* (Cambridge, 1981); R. Colls and P. Dodds (eds.), *Englishness. Politics and Culture, 1880–1920* (London, 1986); R. Samuel (ed.), *Patriotism. The Making and Unmaking of British National Identity*, Vol. 3 (London, 1989); T. Champion, 'Protecting the Monuments: Archaeological Legislation from the 1882 Act to PP16', in M. Hunter (ed.), *Preserving the Past. The Rise of Heritage in Modern Britain* (Stroud, 1996), pp. 38–56.

[53] P. Mandler, *The Fall and Rise of the Stately Home* (New Haven, CT, 1997), pp. 109–10.

[54] See J. Habermas, *The Structural Transformation of the Public Sphere. An Inquiry into a Category of Bourgeois Society* (Cambridge, 1989); C. Calhoun (ed.), *Habermas and the Public Sphere* (Cambridge, MA, London, 1992); W.J.T. Mitchell (ed.), *Art and the Public Sphere* (Chicago, 1992); J. van Horn Melton, *The Rise of the Public in Enlightenment Europe* (Cambridge, 2001); H. Barker, and S. Burrows (eds.), *Press, Politics and the Public Sphere in Europe and North America, 1760–1820* (Cambridge, 2002), T.C.W. Blanning, *The Culture of Power and the Power of Culture. Old Regime Europe, 1660–1789* (Oxford, 2002).

what is worth grasping for a better understanding of the process of heritage-making, is the idea that 'the state' and 'the public' are not mutually exclusive entities, but developed as distinct concepts together.[55] Given the ease with which historians of heritage, especially in France and Germany, attribute all kinds of motivating force to 'the state' as an independent actor, this can provide a more nuanced approach. Not only did 'the state' and members of 'the public' interact constantly in matters of heritage, but drawing a clear line between 'the state' and 'the public' is impossible given that many civil servants were also major voices in private preservation societies.

This public sphere cannot, of course, be equated with the population at large. Despite a universalist discourse, newspapers and periodicals were not read by everyone, and participation in private societies was not independent of income, rank or gender. Access to the international sphere was even more limited. However, during the course of the nineteenth century, the number of people getting involved in debates about 'heritage' steadily grew, owing partly to democratisation, better means of communication and travel. By incorporating the interaction between the preservationists and a wider leisure culture that involved a greater variety of people in heritage, but also by focussing on the interaction between the preservationists and their opponents, it is possible to draw broader conclusions about the prevalence of interest in heritage.[56] Among the multitude of actors who thus entered the stage were government officials, learned men and women, public intellectuals, lawyers, diplomats, priests, kings, feminists, socialists, novelists, landowners, cyclists, artisans, architects, town councillors, photographers and many more. Some were among the most illustrious figures of the nineteenth century and are known as a result of other areas of their life. Some are immortalised through their literary works, such as Victor Hugo or the Brothers Grimm. Some had overpowering personalities and unrivalled political influence, like Francois Guizot; some were famous for their Bohemian and radical lifestyles, like William Morris. For some, such as Millicent Fawcett, preservationism was only one issue among their many causes. Many more are only remembered through institutional records such as committee minutes, publications in learned journals, or a name in a membership list. For the vast majority of people engaged with heritage during the nineteenth century, perhaps the most vivid personal

---

[55] T. Broman, 'The Habermasian Public Sphere and "Science in the Enlightenment"', *History of Science*, 36 (1998), 123–49, esp. 126–7.

[56] For a detailed discussion see A. Swenson, 'Popular heritage and commodification debates in nineteenth- and early twentieth-century Britain, France and Germany', in Berger, Lorenz, Melman (eds.), *Popular National Histories*, pp. 102–22.

detail we can ascertain today is that they had a gigantic Victorian beard. Despite many interesting biographies among the leading preservationists, this book is not primarily about the well-known personalities, but about how and why many individuals came together as a movement and how they negotiated individual voices with collective preferences. Hence, the multiplying and increasingly unified associations and their interaction with the growing state institutions loom large in this history.[57] This does not equate the history of heritage with a history of institutions, but because institutionalisation was absolutely central to the nineteenth-century imagination, it is important to take this bias seriously in order to understand the nineteenth century in its own terms, and to comprehend the legacies for the twentieth- and twenty-first centuries. Moreover, as associations and government agencies increasingly created links within and across borders, their records and publications are key sources to trace the interaction of the local, national and international levels. Furthermore, while there is ample testimony about ordinary people's attachment to particular remains from the past, for instance through visitor statistics or the history of reading,[58] attitudinal change towards the nature of preservation usually becomes perceptible only when institutionalised. It is through the organisational press and organised action that shifts can be seen rather than through personal testimony.[59] The emphasis on institutionalisation does therefore not imply that this book is about what some scholars have called 'the authorised heritage discourse', which they define as a set of top-down texts and practices that dictate the ways in which heritage is employed within any contemporary Western society.[60] Although elites were incontestably important in the rise of heritage, their role can neither be reduced to having graciously

[57] This study focusses on those associations that were most active and influential at the national level, and at the same time interested in international developments, most importantly the Society for the Protection of Ancient Buildings (1877), *L'Ami des Monuments* (1887) and the *Tag für Denkmalpflege* (1900). To these were added firstly the major archaeological and antiquarian societies of an older pedigree, such as the Society of Antiquaries of London (1707), the *Société française pour la conservation des monuments* (1834) better known as *Société française d'archéologie* and the *Gesamtverein der Deutschen Geschichts-und Alterthumsvereine*, that linked associations all over Germany (1852); and secondly societies that combined the protection of ancient buildings with the protection of landscape, namely the National Trust (1894), the *Société pour la protection des paysages de France* (1902) and the *Bund Heimatschutz* (1904).

[58] For example, J. Rose, *The Intellectual Life of the British Working Classes* (New Haven, CT, 2001) or R. O'Connor, *The Earth on Show* (Chicago, 2007).

[59] See P. Mandler, '"The Wand of Fancy": The Historical Imagination of the Victorian Tourist', in M. Kwint, C. Breward and J. Aynsley (eds.), *Material Memories* (Oxford, New York, 1999), pp. 125–41, here pp. 126–7.

[60] L. Smith, *Uses of Heritage* (London, New York, 2006); Harrison, *Understanding the Politics of Heritage*.

educated the people about the importance of heritage (a view usually per-
petuated by histories from within preservationism) nor to exerting control
through the commodification of culture (found in a plethora of Marxist,
Foucauldian, and Gramscian approaches). Rather, the growth of heritage
in terms of ideas and institutions was more interactive, resulting from a
range of two-way exchanges between individuals and institutions, state
and civil society actors, top-down and bottom-up initiatives, producers
and consumers of historical culture.[61]

Geographies of heritage

France, Britain and Germany were of course not the only countries to think
about heritage. Yet they offer a particularly insightful comparison because
of their similarities and differences, on the one hand, and their close ties,
on the other. Firstly, the choice of France, Britain and Germany allows
relating the rise of heritage to different experiences in nation-building.
France's revolutionary upheavals and regime changes, Germany's fragmen-
tation and unification and Britain's more reform-dominated path make
for particularly effective comparison in analysing how preservation relates
to national identity. They also offer interesting differences with regard to
other factors often linked to the rise of the heritage, such as the different pace of industrialisation and urbanisation and the place of religion
with the struggle between Catholicism and anti-clericalism in France, the
Protestant-Catholic divide in Germany, and the Anglican-nonconformist
tensions in Britain. On the other hand, France, Germany and Britain make
for a good comparison as they shared the characteristic feature of having
control over their heritage without much interference from abroad, at least
during the long periods of peace. This distinguished them from the lands
of classical antiquity, especially Italy and Greece, and the growing colonial
empires, where formulating a local approach to heritage was circumscribed
by negotiations with intervening foreign powers. Instead, the fact that all
three countries were rising empires seeking global dominance meant that
they constantly observed each other. It bound them together despite the
fact that they were also in competition.

Any broad comparative study faces the danger of glossing over internal
differences, particularly regional distinctions. By focussing upon individuals and institutions that led the drive towards nationalisation and internationalisation, this study is biased towards activity in Paris, London and
Berlin and with that towards England for Britain, Prussia for Germany

---

[61] B. Melman, *The Culture of History. English Uses of the Past, 1800–1953* (Oxford, 2006), pp. 17–22.

and the capital for France. For reasons of scope, the picture is necessarily selective, and cannot address all locally and regionally specific ways in which heritage was invented. On the other hand, the transnational perspective reveals how preservationists conceptualised the links between local, national and international levels.

Although understandings of the nature of locality or regionality differed across Germany, France and Britain, within each of the three countries, competition between different localities or regions, however these were defined, was intense. Everywhere debates raged about local versus national interpretations and centralist versus regional administration. It is not possible here to go into the details of, for instance, Prussian-Bavarian, or Anglo-Scottish relations, or to address the complicated cases of borderlands such as Alsace-Lorraine. Rather the transnational perspective can show how the international realm was often used to settle battles between local actors – for instance by promoting a particular movement of merely regional importance as nationally representative. As the balance between local, national, and international levels was constantly addressed in government papers, parliamentary debates, learned publications, the press as well as in exhibitions and spectacles, it is possible to focus on how the historical actors conceptualised their relationship.

Emphasising the connections through the perspective of the actors allows us to not only go beneath but also beyond the level of the three nation states.[62] Correspondences, travel itineraries, congress attendances, world fair catalogues, and a plethora of publications with international coverage, show how on the supranational level, these particular three countries were embedded in a much wider network, a veritable 'Heritage International', which included virtually every European state, the United States of America, Japan, China, the Ottoman Empire, as well as an intense intra- and inter-imperial exchange. Hence, the history of heritage cannot be written as a narrowly defined European history, but must be understood as an entangled global history. While tracing these wider networks fully exceeds the scope of this study, showing the interaction of regional, national, European and global factors is crucial to understanding how the rise of heritage relates to changes in international relations.[63] The densening of networks,

---

[62] J. Revel (ed.), *Jeux d'échelles. La micro analyse à l'expérience* (Paris, 1996). For a more extended discussion of how regionality was conceptualised see A. Swenson, 'Zwischen Region, Nation und Internationalismus. Kulturerbekonzepte um die Jahrhundertwende in Frankreich, Deutschland und England', in D. Altenburg, L. Ehrlich and J. John, *Im Herzen Europas. Nationale Identitäten und Erinnerungskulturen* (Cologne, Weimar, Vienna, 2008), pp. 81–103.

[63] Imperial links are addressed more broadly in A. Swenson, 'The Heritage of Empire', in A. Swenson and P. Mandler (eds.), *From Plunder to Preservation, Britain and the Heritage of Empire, 1800–1950* (Proceedings of the British Academy, Oxford, 2013), pp. 3–28.

starting in the 1850s, and reaching full speed between 1870 and 1914, coincides with what economic historians have labelled the first phase of globalisation, characterised by the growth of free trade and internationalist movements and the scramble for imperial influence.[64]

It is a chief aim of this book to understand the workings of the emerging 'Heritage International'. While the book tests the hypothesis, formulated by historians of cultural transfers, that internal needs determined why certain foreign notions are perceived and transferred while others are either ignored or their import eschewed,[65] it also asks how far transfers on heritage intensified simply because of the better means of communication or whether they were much more closely related to the growing international competition, which became more and more an end in itself. Without formal international organisations, what governed this 'Heritage International'? Who was perceived as the leading nation? Did the notion of the pioneering country change over time? Or were different international role models admired across national borders? Moreover, if all of the nations recognised that they were engaged in similar tasks of preserving heritage, the question arises as to how far this international process was internationalist. Was it driven by the idea of a 'common heritage' and, if so, how was this commonality conceived? Is it possible to discern the contours of a universal culture of heritage, or was it perceived as European, Western, or Imperial?

Throughout the book the chapters interweave the vertical narratives of developments in specific states with horizontal analyses of parallels and interdependencies, and link the synchronic and macro-historical questions of comparison with the diachronic and micro-historical nature of cultural transfers; but the emphasis differs among parts. The first part explores how national preservation movements were created in parallel in France, Germany and Britain. It starts by enquiring into the origins of the heritage concept, exploring how ideological and linguistic choices can give rise to different starting points. It then examines critical moments in the formation of national heritage movements. The first chapter traces the impact of the French Revolution and the Napoleonic Wars on the three countries, showing how the years between 1789 and 1815 created a tension between national and cosmopolitan understandings of heritage. It then examines

---

[64] A. Nützenadel, 'Globalisierung und transnationale Geschichte', geschichte.transnational, 23 February 2005, http://geschichte-transnational.clio-online.net/forum/2005-02-004.

[65] J. Paulmann, 'Internationaler Vergleich und interkultureller Transfer. Zwei Forschungsansätze zur europäischen Geschichte des 18.-20. Jahrhunderts', *Historische Zeitschrift*, 267.3 (1998), 649–85, here 680.

why new international contacts created during the Revolution gave rise
to state preservation in France and several German states in the 1830s and
1840s, but not in Britain. It concludes by relating the growth of these
institutions to a nascent popular cultural across the three countries. The
second chapter focuses more closely on the actors of this historical cultural, showing why a drive towards civil society associations and a broader
understanding of heritage emerged towards the end of the century. It dis-
cusses how some associations stimulated the creation of similar bodies in
other countries and compares the increasingly dense nature of movements
in each country. Having introduced the principal actors, the analysis then
moves from an examination of the three core states to broader international interactions and highlights different uses of the international arena.
Part II examines core international meeting points. The role of restoration exhibitions at world fairs is discussed in Chapter 3, which illustrates
how these shows were both an opportunity to exchange methods and a
forum for displaying national superiority. Chapter 4 demonstrates how,
through these exhibitions, heritage-makers came together in international
congresses to elaborate international strategies and conventions, this time
using a rhetoric of international dialogue rather than national superiority.
Part III then looks at the use of these international contacts back in the
national spheres. Chapter 5 examines campaigns to save monuments in
which local preservationists received assistance from abroad and illustrates
the tension between national and universal understandings of heritage
activism. The final chapter brings national and international threads further together by scrutinising why all countries felt a desire to establish
preservation legislation. It shows how heritage-makers used allusions to
foreign practices to remedy perceived national 'inferiorities' towards other
countries, while at the same time negotiating the relationship between the
state, the Church and the individual. The story ends with the dusk of this
first phase of globalisation when war broke out in 1914 and before the dawn
of a new era of formal international protection of heritage began through
the League of Nations and UNESCO. The book concludes with an outlook on the interrelation of heritage, nationalism and internationalism in
the twentieth century, completing the circle by considering why the common history of inventing heritage is not remembered as a transnational
experience.

PART I

National heritage movements

CHAPTER I

In search of origins

In search of the origins of heritage consciousness one inevitably stumbles over foundation myths. French accounts are particularly consistent in retelling revolutionary beginnings.[1] The 'long and ardent struggle' usually starts with a few lone heroes that transformed the French Revolution from an epitome of destruction into the birthplace of preservation. Alexandre Lenoir's opposition to the revolutionary mob, rescuing statues and gravestones from the royal abbey at Saint Denis and Abbé Grégoire flaming speeches against vandalism often open the story (ill. 1.1). The Romantics' subsequent initiation of a 'necessary Revolution', led by Victor Hugo's battle cry *War on the Demolishers* is then portrayed as 'a sort of crusade', leading to the foundation of preservation societies and culminating in the government taking up the cause of national monuments. The result is a teleological story of national awakening in which conflicts and diverging ideas are left aside.[2]

The English and German foundation narratives are less strong and less consistent. They are less tied to institutional memories, and less imbued with heroism. Present day preservationists locate their foundational moments at the late nineteenth rather than the late eighteenth century. And yet this is not for want of material. An equally heroic story could have been woven out of the origins of heritage consciousness in Germany. Goethe's conversion to the beauty of Gothic Art in Strasbourg, laid down in *On German Art*, his eulogy to the architect of Strasbourg cathedral could have started a story. The curious rediscovery of the medieval plans of Cologne Cathedral during the French revolution, the formation of an opinion movement involving the Weimar Classics and the Romantic

---

[1] This is not only the case for books addressed to a broad audience, such as Bady, *Les monuments historique*, Audrerie, *La notion et la protection*, but also for academic works. See chapters on 'Patrimoine' in Nora (ed.), *Les Lieux de mémoire*, I, pp. 1429–643.

[2] J. Challamel, *Loi du 30 mars 1887 sur la conservation des monuments historiques et des objets d'art. Etude de législation comparée* (Extrait de *L'Annuaire de législation française*, Paris, 1888), pp. 1–2.

1.1 Pierre Joseph Lafontaine's engraving 'Alexandre Lenoir defends the Royal graves at
Saint Denis against the revolutionaries (1793)', like several other drawings imagining the
scene, helped to establish Lenoir as a cultivated, well dressed saviour who courageously, yet
calmly, defended the monuments of France against an enraged mob whose lack of civility
was inscribed on brutish faces.

school, the rescue of works of art from the French army by Ferdinand
Wallraf and the brothers Boisérée, the campaign to re-obtain the looted
art by the Rhenish nationalist and the brothers Grimm could have provided heroes. Two memoranda on how to protect monuments, prepared

by Goethe and Prussian star architect Karl Friedrich Schinkel's could have been early founding texts on a par with the writings of Chateaubriand and Hugo.[3] The growth of an intellectual movement later taken up by the state could have also been portrayed in a similar way as in France. However, these stories did not make it into a *lieu de mémoire*. If there is so much of a collective founding moment for today's preservationists, it is located a century later and focusses on the public debate about the restoration of Heidelberg Castle. During this debate, the prominent art historian Georg Dehio introduced an enduring caesura by rendering all earlier ways of caring for the past literally illegitimate. For him, 'nineteenth century historicism engendered not only a true daughter, *Denkmalpflege*, but also an illegitimate child: restoration. They tend to be confused, but are truly antipodal. *Denkmalpflege* tries to preserve what is there, whereas restoration wants to re-establish what does not exist.'[4]

In England, where forms of heritage consciousness could easily be found since the late eighteenth century, John Ruskin's and William Morris' attempts to rid the world of traditional restorations committed a similar act of paricide. This was eagerly fostered by the copious writings of their intellectual heirs. As a result the Manifesto of the Society for the Protection of Ancient Buildings, together with the foundation of the National Trust at the end of the nineteenth century, are the closest thing to a British foundation myth.[5]

These foundation narratives are important not just to understand why scholarly focus and public understanding of heritage has moved in different directions, but also because their creation was fundamental to redefine heritage during the late nineteenth century, as will be discussed later in this book. However, the search for the origins is also hampered by wider ideological battles, particularly in France where the revolutionary origins of heritage awareness are disputed between a republican and a royalist school of thought.[6] While the republican school claims that the Revolution

---

[3] Schinkel's role was probably most strongly emphasised in glorifying terms, e.g. Polenz, 'Zur Geschichte der Organisation der Denkmalpflege in Preußen', *Die Denkmalpflege*, 1 (1899), 37–9, 45–6; A. von Oechelhaeuser, *Wege, Ziele und Gefahren der Denkmalpflege. Festrede bei dem Feierlichen Akte des Rektoratswechsels an der Großherzoglich- Technischen Hochschule Fridericiana zu Karlsruhe am 20. November 1909* (Karslruhe, 1909), p. 7; On the legacy see Mohr de Pérez, *Denkmalpflege in Preussen.*

[4] G. Dehio, *Denkmalschutz und Denkmalpflege im Neunzehnten Jahrhundert* (Strasbourg, 1905), pp. 16.

[5] See C. Miele, 'The First Conservation Militant. William Morris and the Society for the Protection of Ancient Buildings', in Hunter (ed.), *Preserving the Past*, pp. 17–37, esp. p. 37.

[6] For a history of this dispute see D. Poulot, *Musée, nation, patrimoine, 1789–1815* (Paris, 1997), pp. 11–36; for a republican position cf. P. Léon, *La Vie des monuments français. Destruction, restaurations* (Paris, 1951); 'Patrimoine' in Nora (ed.), *Les Lieux de mémoire*, I, pp. 1429–1643; Bercé, *Dès Monuments*

engendered the very idea of *patrimoine*, Catholic and royalist writers maintain that care and transmission of the past have much older roots and that
the Republic wrongfully appropriated the idea for its own end, destroying
an organic system that took much better care of its rightful heritage than
the new order.

Further confusion is created by terminology, as the different scope of
words leads to different foci. Inside every language, terminological incon-
sistency and conflations between historic and present usages of words
create deliberate and unintended arguments. As neither *heritage*, *patrimoine*, nor *Erbe* or *Denkmalpflege* were used in a generic way during most
of the nineteenth century, how can 'heritage consciousness' *avant la lettre*
be determined? Does one speak of *heritage* and *patrimoine* with or without an epithet? It is certainly possible to discern pre-revolutionary traces
of what is now called 'cultural heritage', but what about 'national heritage'? Is interest in the past a sufficient indicator? Should a difference
be made between aesthetic, historic, learned, religious, secular or national
motivations for preservation? Should heritage consciousness be defined
by the wish to transmit past remains for their own sake without changing them or is their adaptation and transformation a necessary part of
the story? And for whom should the past be transmitted? Starting dates
will differ if we talk about transmission between individuals, families,
the aristocracy, religious communities, local communities, the nation, or
humanity. Finally, what must the nature of the community transmitting
these remains be? Is the interest of a few individuals enough or does there
have to be a mass movement (and if so, how large do 'the masses' have
to be)?

In their most general sense, memorial practices start with the dawn
of time. Ideas about restoration can be traced back at least to Alexander
the Great, who ordered the repair of the tombs of Cyrus the Great.[7]
Prohibitions against plunder and destruction were also already a concern
of the Ancients. For instance, the Greek historian Polybius called for the
protection of works of art from seizure by foreigners, while Cicero vilified
the praetor of Sicily for looting the island's treasures for his private use.[8]
Although they acknowledge the importance of antique and Renaissance
ideas for the emergence of preservation, most authors, however, suggest

---

historiques; Audrerie, *La Notion et la protection*. For an affirmation of the royalist and catholic
interpretation cf. Leniaud, *Les Archipels du passé*, esp. pp. 7–23.
[7] Jokilehto, *History of Architectural Conservation*, pp. 1–68.
[8] See Margeret M. Miles, *Art as Plunder. The Ancient Origins of Debate about Cultural Property*
(Cambridge, 2008).

later beginnings rooted in national history. For each country a variety of potential starting points has been suggested. Choice of terminology again plays an important part. To come back to the French debate: while those arguing for revolutionary beginnings speak of *patrimoine national*, those who want to free heritage from 1789 simply suppress the epithet *national* and define *patrimoine* more broadly as any mnemonic practice and thus link it to the genesis of civilisation.[9] As no German study uses the notion of *Kulturerbe* as a starting point, the focus is more narrowly on either *Nationaldenkmäler* (national monuments) or *Denkmalpflege*. Yet this does not solve the problem either. *Denkmalpflege* as a word only emerged in the late nineteenth century, but 'care for monuments' can be traced back further in time than the word.[10] As institutionalisation starts comparatively late in Britain, and the linguistic usage is much less specific than in French or German, the search for origins remains even more open.

As a result, it is tricky to determine which country was the first to possess an idea of heritage on a linguistic basis. Choosing an institutional starting point is not much more straightforward either. As German art historian and conservator Paul Clemen observed already in 1898, France had a claim to primacy due to its monument administration, yet Italy first appointed a conservator in the person of Raphael. Sweden supervised excavations since Gustavus Adolphus' time, while Greece possessed the first modern Monument Act.[11] England, on the other hand, had the first Antiquarian Society and anti-restoration was first outlined here in the eighteenth century.[12] Nineteenth-century Germans prided themselves on inventing 'historical consciousnesses'. This might be a bit exaggerated, but Germany certainly had the first nationally coordinated preservation movement.[13]

'What is found at the historical beginning of things' is thus 'not the inviolable identity of their origin, it is the dissention of other things. It is disparity.'[14] By its very nature, the search for origins needs to remain inconclusive, yet various factors indicate that enduring conceptual changes were taking place during the eighteenth century across the three countries and Europe more widely. The changing use of the term 'monument', for

---

[9] Leniaud, *Les Archipels du passé*, pp. 7–23.   [10] Wolff, *Zwischen Tradition und Neubeginn*, p. 2.

[11] P. Clemen, *Die Denkmalpflege in Frankreich* (Berlin, 1898), repr. in Clemen, *Gesammelte Aufsätze* (Düsseldorf, 1948), pp. 143–59, here p. 143.

[12] M. Hunter, 'Introduction', in Hunter (ed.), *Preserving the Past*, p. 4.

[13] F. Wolff, *Denkmalarchive. Vortrag gehalten auf dem 1. Denkmalarchivtag in Dresden am 24. September 1913* (Berlin, 1913), p. 4.

[14] M. Foucault, 'Nietzsche, Genealogy, History', in D.F. Bouchard (ed.), *Language, Counter-Memory, Practice: Selected Essays and Interviews* (1977), p. 142

instance, indicates that attitudes to the past as a whole were shifting. The word was no longer solely applied to commemorative structures, such as tombs and statues, but to old buildings, objects, texts and even practices created without memorial intentions. There also was an increased interest in the local and national past, manifest in the growth of antiquarianism and the foundation of learned societies. Moreover, conceptions about the audiences of the past changed. A new idea of the public sphere was emerging and Enlightenment demanded the opening of aristocratic collections. Public museums were created virtually everywhere in Europe, apart from France, where plans to turn the Louvre into a museum did not come to fruition before the Revolution.[15] In some states, such as Sweden, the Papal States, and in the German state of Bayreuth, limited legal provisions were put in place to protect certain monuments from destruction. Some of these ideas were later attributed to the French Revolution as part of the republican foundation myth.[16] This does not mean, however, that the French Revolution did nothing more than accelerating already existing ideas. Nor was it of relevance mainly to French heritage, as a national focus would have us believe.

The history of heritage during the French Revolution has received superb scholarly coverage, especially from a French and Franco-German angle, but it is worth re-examining the familiar story to connect events and reactions across borders.[17] The comparative and transnational perspective reveals how much the period between 1789 and 1815 established not only common concepts, but also created new foundational networks for French, German and English heritage throughout the nineteenth century. If not an absolute beginning, the Revolution marked a crucial turning point for all three countries. Its radical break with the past, its attempt to destroy century-old institutions of feudalism and get rid of everything and everybody associated with them, engendered a very new sense of time and history.[18] Although acts

---

[15] A. McClellan, *Inventing the Louvre. Art Politics and the Origins of the Modern Museum in Eighteenth-Century Paris* (1994). T. Bennett, *The Birth of the Museum. History, Theory, Politics* (London, 1995); E. Pommier (ed.), *Les musées en Europe à la veille de l'ouverture du Louvres* (Paris, 1995). J.J. Sheehan, *Museums in the German Art World. From the End of the Old Regime to the Rise of Modernism* (Oxford, 2000); R.G.W. Anderson *et al.* (eds.), *Enlightening the British. Knowledge, Discovery and the Museum in the Eighteenth Century* (London, 2003); B. Savoy (ed.), *Tempel der Kunst, Die Geburt des öffentlichen Museums in Deutschland 1701–1815* (Mainz, 2006).

[16] Savoy (ed.), *Tempel der Kunst*.

[17] See E. Pommier, *L'Art de la liberté. Doctrines et débats de la Révolution française* (Paris, 1991); Poulot, *Musée, nation, patrimoine*, Savoy, *Patrimoine annexé*.

[18] P. Fritzsche, *Stranded in the Present. Modern Time and the Melancholy of History* (Cambridge, MA, London, 2004), p. 8; F. Hartog, *Régimes d'historicité. Presentisme et expérience du temps* (Paris, 2003). R. Koselleck, *Futures Past. On the Semantics of Historical Time* (New York, 2004).

of iconoclasm had often occurred before, combining iconoclasm with the idea of national sovereignty was very new. Moreover, by turning the nation into the owner of the belongings of Church, the Crown and the émigrés, a radically different situation was created. All European elites, including the German and British ones had henceforth also to grapple with the notion that aristocratic and ecclesiastical patrimonies might be claimed as national possessions. Whether these possessions needed to be destroyed as marks of the Ancient Regime, or whether they should be preserved and reinvented as a heritage for future generations led to heated debates across Europe. As part of these debates, a new vocabulary to define heritage was created, which remains in many ways 'the surest sign that a group or society has entered into the self-conscious possession of a new concept',[19] and this new vocabulary instantly made its way across borders. As the Revolutionary Wars went on, debates about 'vandalism' and preservation intensified at a European level. New ideas about works of art and science as national possessions challenged the old Republic of Letters, but although the relation between the national and the cosmopolitan changed, exchange was enhanced rather than curtailed.

Vandals and revolutionaries

For foreign observers, it might have seemed rather counter-intuitive to associate the French Revolution with the cherishing of the past. Images of destruction, ranging from the storming of the Bastille, to the toppling of princely statues, the destruction of the royal graves at St Denis, the beheading of statues of saints (most famously at Notre Dame de Paris where the kings of the Old Testament were mistaken for the kings of France) and finally the falling of real heads under the guillotine, rather than acts of preservation come to mind.[20] Monuments provided targets for spontaneous as well as calculated anger. An apothecary from Dijon, for instance, was rumoured to have chopped off the head of a statue at the church of Notre Dame every morning before opening his business satisfied by his early morning act of patriotism. Although without documentary evidence, the persistence of the anecdote illustrates how strongly the premeditated nature of destructions was felt by future generations.[21]

[19] Q. Skinner, 'Language and Social Change', in J. Tully (ed.), *Meaning and Context. Quentin Skinner and his Critics* (Princeton, 1988), p. 120.
[20] L. Réau, *Histoire du vandalisme. Les monuments détruits de l'art français* (revised edn. Paris, 1994); Gamboni, *Destruction of Art*, pp. 13–50.
[21] E. Fyot, *L'Église Notre-Dame de Dijon* (Dijon, 1910); C. Oursel, *L'Église Notre-Dame de Dijon* (Paris, 1938).

Initially, the fate of old objects and buildings were among the lesser concern of the new revolutionary institutions. The confiscation of the belongings of the First and Second Estates, however, made the intervention of the Revolutionary government on behalf of historic buildings and objects inevitable. Deprived of their traditional guardians, it had to be decided whether these newly acquired goods should be preserved as memories of French history or jettisoned as the unwanted legs of the old order. Originally, it was decided to sell everything for the benefit of the treasury, but the committee responsible for overseeing the sale included many men with an antiquarian background who proposed instead the creation of a commission that could care for the works of art, science and literature. In the petition to the Constituent Assembly which initiated this shift, François Puthod de Maison-Rouge, a former military man who since the 1780s had devoted himself to the study of literature and the language of his local Maconnais, first introduced the expression *patrimoine national* in the sense of both 'national heritage' and 'national property'.[22] Protesting against the sale, he argued that a great opportunity would be missed if these artefacts would again be passing into private hands. Selling the objects would prevent most people from ever having access to them again. As private property, the '*patrimoine* of some' would not become the '*patrimoine* of the nation'.[23] Instead, he hoped that 'the pride of seeing a family heritage (*patrimoine de famille*) transformed into national heritage (*patrimoine national*)' could achieve a new form of patriotism and national consciousness.[24] The government took up the plea and favoured the protection of confiscated goods, but ambivalent legislation towards the arts and *monuments historique* (another new term coined by another enlightened aristocrat in the attempt to preserve historical remains) became a regular feature since 1792.[25]

The Revolutionaries' doubts that the values of the Old Regime could be eradicated without destroying their physical legacy, translated increasingly into official iconoclasm.[26] In May, a decree proclaimed the need to eliminate the marks of feudalism and the memories of despotism and later in

---

[22] See Pommier, *L'Art de la liberté*, pp. 44–5.
[23] *Les Monuments ou le pèlerinage historique*, 1 (1791), 2–17.
[24] Ibid.; Desvallées, 'Origine du mot "patrimoine"', p. 103.
[25] Coined by Aubin-Louis Millin de Grandmaison in *Antiquités nationales ou recueil de monuments pour servir à l'histoire générale et particulière de l'empire français, tel que tombeaux, inscriptions, statues, vitraux, fresques etc. tirées des abbayes, monastères, châteaux et autres lieux devenus bien nationaux* (vol. 2, Paris, 1791), p. 1., qu. in Desvallées, 'Emergence et cheminement', 8.
[26] See S. Mellon, 'Alexandre Lenoir. The Museum versus the Revolution', *Proceeding of the Consortium on Revolutionary Europe*, 8 (1979), pp. 75–88, here p. 81.

the summer, in the wake of destructions by the mob, a law was enacted to destroy all monuments containing traces of feudalism in the name of liberty and equality. At the same time, older tendencies continued and a Monuments Commission was advised to preserve monuments of particular importance for the arts. The antiquary Alexandre Lenoir picked up the pieces of destruction and slowly transformed the stored and rescued objects into the nucleus of a new historic museum.

The duality of policies continued during 1793 and 1794, but the downfall of Robespierre in July set the stage for ridding the Revolution of its violent streak. In three reports to the Convention, the Abbé Grégoire advanced the idea that iconoclasm was counter-revolutionary. A priest in the Diocese of Nancy when the Revolution started, Grégoire was amongst the first to take the oath of the Civil Constitution of the Clergy and subsequently became Constitutional Bishop of Blois, deputy of the Estates General and the Convention, a member of the Senate, and of the Institute. Best remembered for his campaigns to abolish the slave trade in the French colonies and for obtaining full rights citizenship for the Jews in France, Grégoire's interests reached from the fate of the French language, to religious history, education, agriculture, artisan traditions and antiquities.[27]

His speeches to the Convention on behalf of the latter centred on a new term: *vandalisme*.[28] The condemnation of Revolutionary iconoclasm as anti-revolutionary was not entirely new, nor was the reference to Goths and Vandals as destroyers of art. Raphael had famously used the term 'Vandal' to lament the loss of antiquities to the Roman building boom during the Renaissance.[29] Several critics of the Revolution also used the appellation.[30] However, Grégoire's coining of the noun *vandalisme* not only rang timely with the war against Germany, but was part of a much larger linguistic programme to redefine Revolutionary policies.

[27] See A. Goldstein Sepinwall, *The Abbé Grégoire and the French Revolution. The Making of Modern Universalism* (Berkeley, 2005).

[28] See his reports of 31 August 1794, 24 October 1794, and 14 December 1794: *Convention nationale. Instruction publique. Rapport sur les destructions opérées par le vandalisme, et sur les moyens de le réprimer. Par Grégoire. Séance du 14 Fructidor, l'an II* (Paris, 1794); *Convention nationale. Instruction publique. Second rapport sur le vandalisme*, 3 Brumaire, l'an III (Paris, 1794); *Convention nationale. Instruction publique. Troisième rapport sur le vandalisme. Par Grégoire. 24 Frimaire, l'an III* (Paris, 1794). Repr. in H. Grégoire, *Patrimoine et cité*, ed. D. Audrerie (Bordeaux, 1999).

[29] Pommier, *L'Art de la liberté*, p. 225; J.L. Sax, 'Heritage Preservation as a Public Duty. The Abbé Grégoire and the Origins of an Idea', *Michigan Law Review*, 88 (1990), 1142–69, here 1144–9; Poulot, *Patrimoine et musées*, p. 58; 'Vandal', *OED online* (Oxford, 2004).

[30] P. Michel, 'Barbarie, civilisation, vandalisme', in Reichard, Lüsebrink, Schmitt (eds.), *Handbuch politisch-sozialer Grundbegriffe*, VIII, pp. 7–49, here p. 31.

It was probably the most explicit speech act in the history of heritage.[31] 'I created the word to kill the thing', Grégoire wrote self-consciously in his memoirs.[32]

Earlier on, Grégoire had already spoken out against the destructions, but was labelled a fanatic who tried to save the trophies of superstition under the pretext of love for art. To avoid any such accusation, Grégoire now instead used the idea of 'vandalism' to denounce his opponents as fanatics. He identified the virtues of civilisation, education, patriotism, freedom and the Revolution itself with the 'conservation' and 'restoration' of the 'common heritage' (which he called *héritage commun* rather than *patrimoine*). Vandalism, on the contrary, he equated with irrationality, ignorance, theft, violence, counter-revolution, conspiracy, treason, fanaticism, despotism and slavery. Only 'barbarians and slaves' he claimed 'hate the sciences and destroy the monuments of art. Free men love them and conserve them.'[33] True liberty could only be based on education and monuments of art and science were needed for this project. Hence, the conservation of these 'national objects that belong to nobody and are the property of all' equalled the pursuit of freedom.[34] It would be reductive, he claimed, to see the works of art only as the possessions of feudalism, when they really were the result of the French genius because they were built by ordinary people. Preserving them would allow the citizens to reconnect with the national spirit and increase patriotism.[35] For Grégoire, the fight for liberty that underpinned the Revolution made France the natural fatherland of the arts: 'Like us, the arts are the children of freedom, like us they have a fatherland, and we will give this double heritage to posterity.'[36]

Ten thousand copies of Grégoire's first report were distributed throughout France and widely discussed in the press.[37] To no small degree, his ideas found immediate resonance because of the wider political search to end the Terror. His equation of violence with barbarity, counter-revolution and foreign influence offered a way of brandishing the bloody excesses of the Terror as alien to the Revolution and thus overcome the violence.[38] In the longer term, his ideas helped to establish a sense of historical

---

[31] A. Vidler, 'The Paradoxes of Vandalism. Henri Grégoire and the Thermidorian Discourse on Historical Monuments', in J.D. Popkin and R.H. Popkin (eds.), *The Abbé Grégoire and his World* (International Archives of the History of Ideas/Archives internationales d'histoire des idées 169, London, 2000), pp. 129–56, here p. 130; Michel, 'Barbarie, civilisation, vandalisme', pp. 7–49.

[32] H. Grégoire, *Mémoires de Grégoire, Ancien Évêque de Blois*, ed. H. Carnot (Paris, 1837), p. 345.

[33] Grégoire, *Rapport sur le vandalisme*, p. 27.   [34] Ibid., p. 26.

[35] Grégoire, *Troisième rapport sur le vandalism*, p. 18.   [36] Grégoire, *Rapport sur le vandalisme*, p. 15.

[37] Michel, 'Barbarie, civilisation, vandalisme', p. 40.

[38] B. Baczko, *Comment sortir de la Terreur* (Paris, 1989); Poulot, *Patrimoine et musées*, pp. 58–9.

heritage under the Convention and subsequently inspired the state-led first inventory projects under the Consulate and the Empire.

The idea that reinterpretation was more effective than destruction was bolstered from other directions too – in particular by Alexandre Lenoir's new Museum of French Monuments, the first historic museum. Lenoir ordered the royal funeral monuments from Saint Denis, and other objects he had salvaged according to chronology, allowing the visitor to replace their original meaning with a new narrative of a continuous national history. The museum for the first time offered the possibility to take a walk from the time of Clovis to the Revolution. To symbolise the progression from the 'dark ages' to the enlightenment, the fancifully decorated period rooms became progressively flooded with light as visitors approached the eighteenth-century rooms.[39] Yet while Lenoir shaped the viewing experience of the entire Romantic generation, the ideological and linguistic legacy left by Grégoire was arguably even more important.[40] Grégoire's rhetoric of vandalism was adapted by generations of conservators, restorers and preservers throughout the next century not just in France but across Europe.[41]

German scholars at first objected to his characterisation of their Vandal ancestors as destroyers,[42] but the label stuck, and Grégoire observed with satisfaction that his neologism was naturalised in every European language.[43] Despite qualms about the injury to ancestral memory, Grégoire's reports were received in the German press with great acclaim. The second and third reports were translated and discussed in Wieland's *Neuer Teutscher Merkur*, one of the most widely read papers in the German-speaking world. Its editor was in fact the very same Karl August Böttiger who had objected to the vilification of the ancestors in the first place.[44] Böttiger had studied theology and classical philology in Leipzig, and with Herder's support, became rector of the gymnasium in Weimar, where he was at the heart of intellectual life, advising Goethe and Schiller on philological questions. Böttinger was not only the editor of the *Neuer Teutscher Merkur* between 1794–1809, but also of the important *Journal des Luxus und*

---

[39] Mellon, 'Alexandre Lenoir'; McClellan, *Inventing the Louvre*.

[40] Poulot, *Patrimoine et musées*, p. 61.   [41] Vidler, 'Paradoxes of Vandalism', p. 137.

[42] Grégoire, *Mémoires*, I, pp. 345–8 referred to Böttiger's writings in *Neue Bibliothek der schönen Wissenschaften*, trans. in *Le Mercure allemand* in 1795; Vidler, 'Paradoxes of Vandalism', p. 138.

[43] Grégoire, *Mémoires*, I, p. 345.

[44] S. Lindinger, 'Karl August Böttiger', *Biographisch-Bibliographisches Kirchen Lexikon* (2000), XVII, cols. 143–51 (rev. 2006), www.bautz.de/bbkl/b/boetiger_k_a.shtml; G. Espagne and B. Savoy (eds.), *Aubin-Louis Millin et l'Allemagne. Le Magasin encyclopédique – les lettres à Karl August Böttiger* (Hildesheim, 2005).

der Moden (1797–1803) and *London und Paris* (1804) and had a wide network of European correspondents. As a key representative of the Weimar Enlightenment, he was a known champion of the idea of art for the public and propagated Grégoire's ideas enthusiastically.[45] Subsequently, Grégoire's reception became also very strong in territories occupied by the French. Faced with the secularisation of ecclesiastical belongings, ideas developed in France helped to rethink the fate of monuments.[46] Thomas Sanderad Müller, antiquities conservator of Trier's learned society, in particular used Grégoire's reports to act against the disfigurement of his city's antique monuments.[47]

Grégoire's reports were translated into English too and the word 'vandalism' was immediately naturalised.[48] Its use was even extended to describe not only the destruction of objects but all the horrors of Jacobinism from murder to rape.[49] While the consequences of French iconoclasm and secularisations were felt more distantly in Britain than in the disintegrating Holy Roman Empire, French vandalism was a 'proximate cause for an increasingly positive evaluation' of English, i.e. Gothic architecture in England.[50] As admiration for the Revolution's ideas turned into fear of its destructive power, the first pleas for systematic preservation appeared in the *Gentleman's Magazine* and the first widespread restoration of medieval cathedrals took place all over England, underpinned by the argument that if similar hatred against the institutions of monarchy and Church was to be avoided, their physical embodiment needed better care.[51]

---

[45] 'Zustand der Künste und Wissenschaften in Frankreich unter Robespierres Regierung (1795)', *Neuer Teutscher Merkur*, 1 (1795), 77–102; 168–92.

[46] Wolff, *Zwischen Tradition und Neubeginn*, pp. 64–70.

[47] T. Sanderad Müller, *Thomas Sanderad Müller, der freien Künste und Weltweisheit Doktors, vormaligen Biobliothekars und Lehrers der Mathematik in der Abtei Sanct Maximin, Mitglied der Gesellschaft nützlicher Untersuchungen in Trier, freundschaftlicher Vortrag über Die Mishandlung der Alterthümer, Kunstwerke und wissenschaftlicher Gegenstände* (Trier, 1808), p. 60. He referred to the original French report of 31 August 1794, not the ones reproduced in the *Neuer Teutscher Merkur*.

[48] The first mention recorded in dictionaries is Helen M. Williams' *Letter from France* in 1798, see 'Vandalism', *OED online* (Oxford, 2004), but the word was already used in 1794 in the reports on Grégoire's intervention at the Convention. See for instance, 'France, National Convention, 14 Fructidor, Sunday, Aug. 11' *Oracle and Public Advertiser*, 12 September 1794; 'Gregoir's Report on the Arts', *Oracle and Public Advertiser*, 31 January 1795; 'The Arts!!! Some Extracts from the Memorial of Gregoire on Vandalism', *Tomahawk or Censor General*, 12 December 1795 and further instalments on the 14th and 17th instant; 'France. Paris, June 22', *The Times*, 27 June 1796, p. 2.

[49] For instance, *Oracle and Public Advertiser*, 27 July 1797, 'Earl Stanhope', *Oracle and Daily Advertiser*, 25 January 1799.

[50] R. Sweet, *Antiquaries. The Discovery of the Past in Eighteenth-Century Britain* (London, 2004), pp. 297–8.

[51] Ibid.; *Gentleman's Magazine*, 67 (1797), II, pp. 927–8.

However, while interest in the roots and consequences of French icon-oclasm was high, German and English preoccupation with 'vandalism' started in earnest only when the French armies began 'repatriating' works of art from vanquished territories, allegedly 'liberating' art from the oppression of ecclesiastical and feudal patrons. What had been a deplorable, yet distant phenomenon, suddenly threatened the European cultural elites at their core.

That the winner takes the spoils for personal gain or to symbolise a *translatio imperii* was nothing new.[52] Condemnations of the victors' enrichment also had an old pedigree. Cicero's disapproval of Verres, governor of Sicily, for his rapacious collection of art from temples for his private benefit was particularly famous.[53] The translocations by the Revolutionary armies, however, both legitimised and contested spoliation in new ways as a result of the language that made vandalism the dividing criterion between civilisation and barbarity. During 1794, Parisian artistic circles not only discussed the evils of vandalism at home, but increasingly debated whether the fact that fate was turning in favour of the Revolutionary Armies should lead France to imitate the Roman looting of Greek art after a victory.[54] By declaring France to be the *patrie des arts*, Grégoire himself endorsed the seizure of works of art under way in the Low Countries and the Rhineland. Although imitating the Ancients, the Moderns were portrayed as incontestably superior: 'More than the Romans, we have the right to say that by combating the tyrants, we are protecting the arts.'[55] The aim was not to steal, but to liberate the arts from despotism, and to allow them to flourish under the reign of liberty: 'If our victorious armies invade Italy, the capture of the Apollo Belvedere and the Farnese Hercules would be the most brilliant conquest. Greece decorated Rome, but should the masterpieces of the Greek republics decorate the countries of slaves? The French Republic should be their last home.'[56] The capture of artistic and scientific treasures was therefore not seen as theft, but as an act of 'repatriation'.[57]

The first seizures took place in the Low Countries and the Rhineland. While the confiscations would become the cause of a virulent public debate twenty years later, in 1794 and 1795 they produced at best local reactions and did not find a wider echo among German Enlightened circles. It is likely

---

[52] W. Treue, *Art Plunder. The Fate of Works of Art in War, Revolution and Peace* (London, 1960).
[53] Miles, *Art as Plunder*.
[54] On the genesis of the doctrine see Pommier, *L'Art de la liberté*, pp. 209–46.
[55] Grégoire, *Rapport sur le vandalisme*, p. 22.   [56] Ibid., p. 27.
[57] Pommier, *L'Art de la liberté*, pp. 209–46.

that the confiscations were not even known beyond the Rhineland. German interest in art looting only awakened when Italian patrimony was touched in the spring of 1795. While the enlightened milieu of Weimar did not seem informed about the seizures of German art, news from Italy travelled within days, via the German artist colony in Rome and the correspondents of the *Neue Teutsche Merkur*. As Bénédicte Savoy has argued, enlightened Germany's 'Italian identity' not its 'German national feeling', was wounded.[58] Like them, humanists and cosmopolitans throughout Europe, for whom Italy was first and foremost the universal centre of the arts, and hence a denationalised space where foreign artists could find freedom away from their patrons, condemned the translocations as a crime against enlightened humanity.[59]

In France, the policy did not remain uncontested either. Polemics soared with the publication in 1796 of Quatremère de Quincy's *Letters to Miranda*, followed by the publication of a petition signed by fifty French artists protesting against the translocations, and a pro-government counter-petition. The sculptor, architect and armchair archaeologist Quatremère de Quincy had been a revolutionary heritage-maker of the first hour and was the architect responsible for transforming the Church of St Geneviève into the Panthéon. Subsequently a member of the Legislative Assembly and the Committee for Public Instruction, he got somewhat disenchanted with the Revolution when he was imprisoned under the Terror in 1794 and was nearly executed twice. Although a friend of Henri Grégoire,[60] he denounced from his prison cell the 'useless warehousing' of works from Italy and called for the restitution of the fragments to the place of their birth. His attack was two pronged. Firstly, he argued that objects needed to be preserved in situ, transporting them deprived objects of their cultural value, as the meaning of an artefact was not intrinsic but depended on its uses and its location; to move it was therefore synonymous with destruction. The appropriate setting for Italian artefacts was not the Muséum in Paris, but Italy itself, a museum without walls.[61] Secondly, he objected to the seizures as a citizen of the Republic of Letters. Love of beauty and not nationalism should be the superior social bond, as it had the power to unite and advance humanity rather than to separate and destroy it. He urged

---

Savoy, *Patrimoine annexé*, I, p. 203. The following paragraphs draws on her work.
Ibid.   [60] Vidler, 'Paradoxes of Vandalism', p. 152.
[61] A. Quatremère de Quincy, *Lettres à Miranda sur le déplacement des monuments de l'art de l'Italie*, ed. E. Pommier (Paris, 1989); R. Schneider, *Quatremère de Quincy et son intervention dans les arts* (Paris, 1910), pp. 166, 182–4; S. Lavin, *Quatremère de Quincy and the Invention of a Modern Language of Architecture* (Cambridge, MA, 1992); P. Burke, 'Context in Context', *Common Knowledge*, 8.1 (2002), 152–77.

that 'all political and philosophical efforts must be employed to maintain, strengthen and augment this community'.[62]

And employed these efforts were. The polemics travelled not only from France to England and Germany, particularly via Johann Wilhelm von Archenholz, editor in Hamburg of the journal *Minerva* – and Böttiger, who had already publicised Grégoire's reports a year earlier, but a lively exchange also started between Germany and Britain.[63] The polarised French termi-nology created by Grégoire's vandalism speeches informed the anti-looting writings in France and was translated word for word into German. The rhetoric was heightened by anthropomorphising the works of art. Qua-tremère first likened the spoliations to the dismemberment of a body. This metaphor was then enhanced and mobilised by German writers who frequently employed terms imbued with violence.[64]

The trauma of having their Italian space for artistic freedom violated clashed irreconcilably with the idea of a 'heritage of freedom' and continued to preoccupy German artists and writers from Goethe and Schiller to Schlegel. Cosmopolitan in essence, the criticism also contained anti-French tones. Using the same idea as Grégoire that destruction of the arts equated barbarism, they questioned the ability of the French nation to protect works of art, given the record of Revolutionary vandalism. If works of art were damaged 'would not the whole of Europe be in the right to have complained about the barbarity of the French, who knew how to kidnap, but not to conserve works of art'.[65]

From within the cosmopolitan elite, slowly, the idea was also raised that seizures were not only 'crimes against humanity', but that the works of art seized were a national possession whose loss must create eternal hatred and desire for revenge.[66] In the first instance, however, these ideas of the sanctity of a 'national heritage', did not lead to further debates. Although the French continued to be termed barbarians for their thieving actions, most famously in Friedrich Schiller's *Antique to Paris* from 1803, on the whole, the polemics calmed down once it became clear that the fears for the objects' destruction were unfounded. The objects were brought to Paris

---

[62] Quatremère de Quincy, *Lettres*, p. 88.

[63] See for instance 'Über Kunstplünderungen in Italien und Rom', *Neuer Teutscher Merkur*, November (1796), 249–79, and Savoy, *Patrimoine annexé*, I, p. 208. For British reactions more broadly see also D. Mackay Quynn, 'The Art Confiscations of the Napoleonic Wars', *American Historical Review*, 50.3 (1945), 437–60.

[64] Savoy, *Patrimoine annexé*, I, p. 209.   [65] *London und Paris* (1798), 7e pièce, p. 244.

[66] K.H. Heydenreich, 'Darf der Sieger einem überwundenen Volke Werke der Literatur und Kunst entreißen? Eine Völkerrechtliche Quäastion', *Deutsche Monatsschrift*, August 1898, pp. 290–5, qu. in Savoy, *Patrimoine annexé*, I, pp. 224–7.

in a triumphal procession that imitated the depiction of the looting of the Temple in Jerusalem on the Arch of Titus in a *translatio imperri*. The Minister of the Interior also used the ceremony to explain to the world the conservationist reasons for the policy and to reassure international audiences that the era of vandalism was over. As visitors flocked to Paris to see the treasures, they agreed that the objects were well looked after and admiration for the new Muséum in the Louvre was expressed by many members of the cosmopolitan classicist generation and of the younger Romantic generation from Britain and Germany.[67]

The exhibition curated by Vivant Denon was widely acclaimed. There had never been an institution like the Muséum. It was the first universal museum where it was possible to see a panorama of European Art. By decontextualising the works, the Muséum, like Lenoir's Museum of French Monuments, offered a new sense of history and art history. The juxtaposition of different national schools was formative for the rediscovery of these works. For the first time art that had been hidden away in princely collections, town halls and ecclesiastical institutions, was now accessible to the public. This engendered a new sense of viewing, challenging the preference for classical and Renaissance art. Seeing medieval and early modern art from the different German territories in Paris was particularly formative for the discovery of German art by the German Romantics.[68] During the short period of peace with the United Kingdom after the Treaty of Amiens in 1802, France was also flooded with British tourists, deploring the ruin of many churches and châteaux on the way, but also admiring the captured booty in the Louvre (see ill. 1.2).[69]

However, as Napoleon's rule of Europe was challenged, the protests began again. Their tone had changed in an important way. An aesthetic and cosmopolitan defence of the arts as a universal heritage was replaced with a more nationalist and political position. A number of factors played a role in this. The 'rediscovery' of national traditions through the exhibition in Paris themselves fostered a sense of national pride. When further waves

---

[67] 'France, Speech of Thanks of the Minister of the Interior to the Commissaries employed in Collecting the Monuments of the Arts and Sciences in Italy', *Oracle and Public Advertiser*, 17 August 1798. On the reception see also *True Briton*, 11 October 1800; *Albion and Evening Advertiser*, 16 October 1800. On German reactions see Savoy, *Patrimoine annexé*, I, pp. 212–38.

[68] Ibid. See also P. Moisy, *Les Séjours en France de Sulpice Boisserée, 1820–1825. Contribution à l'étude des relations intellectuelles franco-allemandes* (Bibliothèque de la Société des études germaniques 10, Lyon, 1956).

[69] R. and I. Tombs, *That Sweet Enemy. The French and the British from the Sun King to the Present* (London, 2006), pp. 232–3.

1.2 Benjamin Zix produced several representations of the many foreigners visiting the Louvre, here in the Salon Rond.

of art looting were executed in Germany later in the decade, now emptying the more famous princely collections and ancient libraries rather than declining monasteries, this was no longer ignored by a domestic public, but it was in the final year of Napoleon's rule that publicity took a different turn (see ills 1.3–1.4).[70] A new generation was leading the protests, no longer from enlightenment Weimar but from the Rhineland through the pen of Joseph Görres, a pro-revolutionary cosmopolitan turned German nationalist. His *Rheinischer Merkur* provided a platform for the Freiherrn vom Stein and General Blüchner against Napoleon, who allegedly considered it to be the fifth great enemy power besides Russia, Britain, Austria and Prussia.

In 1796, the *Moniteur universel* had responded to the French petition against the seizures with the appeal to 'Stop being cosmopolitans, restrain your vast affection that embraces the entire universe and try to love your fatherland a little more'.[71] To justify the return of German art to Germany,

[70] Savoy, *Patrimoine annexé*, I, pp. 230–59.
[71] C.J. Trouvé, *Le Monietuer universel*, no. 335, 5 fructidor an V (22 Aug. 1796). It was also reported in Karl August Böttiger, *Journal des Luxus und der Moden*, Nov. 1796, p. 562, see Savoy, *Patrimoine annexé*, I, p. 250. On the discrediting of the cosmopolites as enemies of the Revolution see G. van

1.3 Monsieur Denon visiting the Cabinet des Antiques Berlin in 1807, depicted by Benjamin Zix, who chronicled Napoleon's conquests travelling alongside Vivant Denon. Denon is shown examining works that might be brought to his Museum. Zix' drawing stresses the erudite and civilised nature of Denon's enterprise. He holds a tray of coins, while a man beside him peers over his shoulder and another man is seated writing. The cabinet contains mainly classical treasures, including copies of works already in the Louvre, such as the Laocoön group from the Vatican, on the cabinet to the right. On the floor are many busts and various Greek and Egyptian artefacts.

the Rhenish patriotic press, now also attacked cosmopolitanism. All those who believed that 'art belonged to a higher fatherland than the political one' were declared guilty of high treason.[72] During the second occupation of Paris in 1815, the mobilisation of the German press took an exceptional magnitude on a European scale, as:

> The recovery of these objects, which are universally regarded as inalienable national property, occupies strongly the minds of men in Germany. At the former peace of Paris they were among the number of forgotten and neglected things, but this time they have drawn early attention – a sure proof

der Heuvel, 'Cosmopolite, Cosmopoliti(ti)sme', in Reichard, Lüsebrink, Schmitt (eds.), *Handbuch politisch-sozialer Grundbegriffe*, VI, pp. 41–55, esp. 50–53.
[72] *Rheinischer Merkur*, no. 288, 24 August 1815, pp. 1–2.

1.4 The anonymous engraving 'The Berliners' Wish' from 1814 expressed the desire that Napoleon might bring back, personally and on his back, the Quadriga he took from the Brandenburg Gate.

that the public mind has in the course of this year acquired great strength, and that in matters which it seriously wills, it can no longer be resisted.[73]

[73] 'Die Zurücknahme der Kunst und wissenschaflitchen Werke', *Rheinischer Merkur*, no. 279, 6 August 1815, p. 1, trans. in 'The Restoration of Works of Art And Science [From the Rhenish Mercury.]', *The Times*, 22 August 1815, p. 3.

Görres' editorial highlights the growing importance of public opinion on a national scale and marks the subordination of aesthetic and cultural questions to the national interest. The way it was endorsed and reprinted in *The Times*, also reveals the increasing coordination of protest on a European scale. In contrast to the previous years, claims for restitution from the German and the British press,[74] together with an international petition of artists urging the return of works to Rome, 'the capital of all arts for all peoples', were now successful as they meshed with the political aims of the allied troops.[75] Returning works of art and science had not been at the forefront of concern in 1814, but as a result of Napoleon's Hundred Days, France was treated with increasing severity in 1815. Led by the British government, and agreed to by the allies, restitution was embraced, and implemented with the help of British and Prussian military power. Invading the Louvre with their bayonets,[76] the victors tried to prevent Paris from ever being 'the centre of the arts' again.[77]

The restitutions established a lasting ban on the capture of works of art and science during war in international customary law. The ban was confirmed by the allied forces' own behaviour. It was agreed that they took from France nothing more than what they had lost. However, the right to restitution remained limited to the allegedly more 'civilised nations' in the concert of Europe. Egypt in particular did not receive its antiquities back. The most precious piece of booty from Napoleon's campaign in Egypt, the Rosetta Stone, remained in Britain with the new inscription 'captured from the French' chiselled on its side. At the very moment of the restitutions, the Parthenon Marbles, which Lord Elgin had in part dismantled with the idea that this way they would not fall into French hands, were on their way to London.[78] In other ways too, Britain had been the beneficiary of French art politics, especially the breaking up of ecclesiastical and princely collections on the continent. Many continental art works that

---

[74] *The Times*, 18 July 1815, p. 3 (leader); also 25 July 1815, p. 3; 'Flanders And Hamburg Mails. Mons, July 26', *The Times*, 1 August 1815, p. 2; 'Hamburg Mail. Letter From Vienna, July 19', *The Times*, 7 August 1815, p. 3; 'Berlin July 15', *The Times*, 8 August 1815, p. 2; reporting culminated in the reproduction of Görres' article. On the German role in the redistribution of Italian art see 'Brussels Papers. Vienna, Oct. 8', *The Times*, 23 October 1815, p. 3; 'The Duke of Wellington to Lord Castelreagh relative to the Seizure of the plundered Works of Art in the Louvre by their legitimate Owners, Paris Sep. 23 1815', *Gentleman's Magazine* (1815), II, pp. 620–2.

[75] Qu. in Tombs and Tombs, *That Sweet Enemy*, p. 312; P. Mansel, *Paris between Empires, 1814–1852* (London, 2001), pp. 92–6.

[76] Savoy, *Patrimoine annéxé*, p. 189   [77] Tombs and Tombs, *That Sweet Enemy*, p. 312.

[78] Ibid., pp. 234–6; On the Elgin Marbles see M. Beard, *The Parthenon* (London, 2002); J.H. Merryman, 'Whither the Elgin Marbles?', in Merryman (ed.), *Imperialism, Art and Restitution* (Cambridge, 2006), pp. 98–113; W. St Clair, 'Imperial Appropriations of the Parthenon', pp. 65–97.

were not confiscated and sent to French museums found their way to the
art market in London and in due course became part of British 'national
heritage'.

Both 'British' and 'German' heritages were thus forged in part in opposition to a common French enemy. While the German idea of 'national
heritage' was directly created through the spoliation and return of German art, the British ideas were influenced more indirectly. The general
shift from a universal conception of art to that of a 'national heritage',
and from cosmopolitan to patriotic arguments did not, however, result in
a total end of the Republic of Letters, as has been claimed.[79] The Revolution certainly had some isolating effect. It cut the relations between
Academies and Learned Societies across Europe, and restricted travel. As a
result of war and blockade, the period between 1789 and 1815 in particular
created an English elite that travelled more at home than abroad.[80] In
other respects, however, the Revolutionary and Napoleonic years increased
exchange across Europe, not least through the emigration of many writers, artists and men of learning to England and Germany and the flow
of visitors in the other direction intent on seeing the new capital of the
arts.[81]

Moreover, the relations between foreigners involved in restitution
claims and Parisian learned circles were still dominated by enlightened
sociability.[82] When German commissioners arrived in Paris in 1814, they
soon established contact with administrators and scholars, ready to assist
them, among them Karl-Benedict Hase of the Bibliothèque nationale,
Antoine Silvestre de Sacy, the naturalist Cuvier, the antiquary Millin, the
philosophers Cabanis and Degérando and the young Francois Guizot, secretary of the Minister of the Interior. Even whilst nationalist tones were
rising, the Germans frequented the Parisian salons and personal testimonies of both French and Germans involved in the negotiations are full
of esteem for the other country's negotiators.[83] Despite the condemnation
of cosmopolitans as traitors by the press, restitution fronts transcended
nationality. Backed by Wellington, Quatremère de Quincy, who after years
of exile in Germany had risen to prominence in France again, assisted
Jacob Grimm with the Hessian restitutions, and organised the Italian

---

[79] Cf. Savoy, *Patrimoine annexé*, I, p. 260.
[80] L. Colley, *Britons. Forging the Nation, 1707–1837* (New Haven, 1992, new edn. London, 2003), pp. 172–3.
[81] J. Evans, *A History of the Society of Antiquaries* (Oxford, 1956), p. 198; Tombs and Tombs, *That Sweet Enemy*, pp. 214–17.
[82] Savoy, *Patrimoine annexé*, I, p. 172.   [83] Ibid., pp. 147–95.

claims together with another friend of more than thirty years, the Italian sculptor Antonio Canova. Cosmopolitan ties were equally strong among the 'translocation party'. For instance, Alexander von Humboldt ignored the attacks by the nationalist press and never wavered in his support for his long-time friend Vivant Denon.[84]

Overall, personal contacts and knowledge about foreign cultural policies were enhanced rather than cut. The confident cosmopolitanism of the pre-revolutionary enlightenment certainly lost its dominance, but universalist ideas did not disappear. After 1815, nationalist and international tunes had to find a way to coexist, but collaboration and cultural transfer would play a part in shaping ideas and institutions invariably. This becomes evident when looking at the generation who transformed the new ideas about national heritage into state policies in the 1830s and 1840s. They were profoundly marked by the three way exchange between France, Germany and Britain. Many of the writers and historians who came to power in the July Monarchy had lived in exile in England and were imbued with English ideas of history,[85] while the leading Prussian officials who then transferred their ideas to Germany had developed close ties to France through the coordination of restitution claims in 1815.

Historical culture and the state

In 1815, most looted works of art and science had been returned, but there was no return to pre-revelatory ideas about art and history. While the monarchies across Europe tried to re-establish a sense of god-given inheritance, continentals showed at first little interest in the fate of most pre-revolutionary monuments now in public hands. In continental Europe, monuments destroyed during the Restoration far outnumbered those destroyed during the Revolution. Ultimately, however, the new sense that nations had a heritage and that preservation was a sign of civilised governance was there to stay. It has been argued that in the decades of Restoration and new revolutionary upheaval, the elites took up the idea of a national heritage as a device of control. While it is certainly true that heritage was more and more discovered as a way to overcome political tensions, the beginnings of institutionalisation were also marked by more diverse motives and beliefs, as well as by an intensification of competition across national borders. In each country, policies were shaped by the particular legacies of the revolutionary years and by the new political developments

[84] Ibid., p. 193.   [85] Tombs and Tombs, *That Sweet Enemy*, p. 332.

brought by the 1830 and 1848 revolutions (or the absence thereof). Yet despite these differences, heritage-makers from all countries also started to debate whether the same solutions might fit into their national contexts and all encountered similar tensions between centralised structures and local interests.

In the twenty-five years after the fall of Napoleon, France managed to swap her reputation as the fatherland of vandalism for the role of vanguard in the protection of the past. The Napoleonic years engendered a corpus of literature that became widely read throughout the nineteenth century beyond France's borders. Texts ranged from Chateaubriand's *Le Genie du Christianisme*, stressing the necessity of religious feeling for the appreciation of the Middle Ages, published in 1802 after his return from England to more administrative measures, such as a circular sent by the Minister of the Interior Montalivet to all Prefects to establish a list of surviving monuments with the help of the emerging learned societies.

The years after the Congress of Vienna, on the other hand, were mostly marked by a neglect of the historic record. Some of the most visible revolutionary heritage institutions were abolished. While Quatremère de Quincy oversaw the return of art from the Louvre, and closed down Alexandre Lenoir's Museum of French Monuments, the church he had once transformed into the Panthéon was being returned to worship. Many other former churches and palaces, however, were left to be used as prisons, stables, saltpetre depots, or pulled down to make way for municipal thoroughfares – such as the great Romanesque basilica of Cluny.[86] The destruction of architecture during the Restoration was more ample than during the Revolution, but so were provincial and Parisian protests. The provincial movement was led by Norman antiquary Arcisse de Caumont. Influenced by encounters with English archaeologists, he founded the *Sociéte française pour la conservation et la description des monuments de France*, generally known as *Société française d'archéologie*, which published the first nationwide paper on monuments, the *Bulletin Monumental* and started to hold itinerant annual archaeological congresses from 1834 onwards.[87] At the same time, Parisian Romantics started to condemn the ill-treatment of historic monuments. Victor Hugo's 1825 pamphlet *War on the Demolishers* provided a first rallying cry, augmented and enhanced in his novel *Notre Dame de Paris*.

---

[86] Réau, *Histoire du vandalisme*.
[87] Chaline, *Sociabilité et erudition*, p. 394; Correspondence de Caumont and Guizot, 1833–34, AN, F 17 3090.

The 1830 Revolution finally brought a turn in heritage politics. To reconcile different groups in French politics, from Jacobins to Bonapartists, Orléonists and Royalists, the July Monarchy relied on the power of national history in which competing traditions would become merged into one unifying narrative of national grandeur. An unusually high number of historians and writers in government positions led this vision, illuminated in a series of new history paintings at the palace at Versailles. Turned from a monarchical into a national monument, Versailles allowed seeing 'the present in the past, 1789 vis-à-vis 1688, the emperor at the king's home – Napoleon at Louis XIV's'. As Victor Hugo put it, the July Monarchy gave 'to this magnificent book that is called French history this magnificent binding that is called Versailles'.[88] The arrival of Louis Philippe further saw the retransformation of the Panthéon into a national memorial, and, in time, even the return of Napoleon's Ashes to France. All over the country, France's classical and medieval architecture was brought back to life through spectacular restorations financed by the government.

Underpinned by the desire for national unity, the restorations were also animated by what was happening elsewhere in Europe. 'When Germany undertakes immense works in order to complete Cologne Cathedral: when England pours out wealth to restore its old churches – doubtless France will not remain less generous in repairing' her own monuments, argued the newly appointed Inspector of Monuments, Prosper Mérimée.[89] The leading restorationist architect Eugène Emmanuel Viollet-le-Duc chimed in that although Germany and England were ahead of France in terms of restoration, France, despite earlier negligence and wilful destruction, still possessed an architectural richness rivalling that of other European countries.[90] Hence to advance 'in this new struggle in which the magnificence of her monuments and the talent of her artists seem to provide so many advantages', Mérimée reminded the Minister of the Interior not to 'hesitate to ask the Chambers for the means to execute this great work, that is so much in the interest of our national glory' (see ill. 1.5).[91]

Inspired in part by developments abroad, the rise of history in July Monarchy France was orchestrated by the creation of an array of institutions

[88] V. Hugo, *Choses vues, 1830–1846* (Paris, 1972), I, p. 133.
[89] P. Mérimée, *Rapport au Ministre de l'Intérieur* (Paris, 1843), pp. 75–76, trans. in Murphy, *Memory and Modernity*, p. 131.
[90] E.E. Viollet-le-Duc, 'De la construction des édifices religieux depuis le commencement du christianisme jusqu'au XVIe siècle, introduction', *Annales archéologique*, 1 (1844), 334–47.
[91] Mérimée, *Rapport au Ministre de l'Intérieur*, pp. 75–76, trans. in Murphy, *Memory and Modernity*, p. 131.

1.5 The Basilica of the Madeleine in Vézelay was Viollet-le-Duc's first work of restoration for the Historic Monuments Commission. Details of the project were shown internationally to propagate French progress, for instance through this drawing by E.E. Viollet-le Duc of the restoration of statues destroyed during the Revolution. Reproduced in F. Ducuing, *L'Exposition universelle de 1867 illustrée* (Paris, 1867), I, p. 373.

that would soon become the envy of Europe. They were put in place by the leading romantic historian Guizot. Germanophile interlocutor of the German commissioners in Paris in 1815 and Anglophile historian and former Ambassador to London, he became first Minister of the Interior and then Minister of Public Instruction under Louis Philippe.[92] A General Inspector of Historical Monuments was appointed in 1830. His role was fortified by a Committee for Historic Works (*Comité des travaux historiques*) destined to publish the records of France's history in 1834. A Historic Monuments Commission (*Commission des Monuments historiques*, CMH) was created in 1837 to distribute funds and supervise the restoration of

[92] P. Rosenvallon, *Le Moment Guizot* (Paris, 1885); P. Poulot, 'The Birth of Heritage. "Le moment Guizot"', *Oxford Art Journal*, 11.2 (1988), 40–56; L. Theis, 'Guizot et les institutions de mémoire. Un historien au pouvoir', in Nora (ed.), *Les Lieux de mémoire*, I, pp. 1575–97. On Guizot's links with Germany see Savoy, *Patrimoine annexé*, I, pp. 147–95; on his English connections Tombs and Tombs, *That Sweet Enemy*, pp. 332–4.

1.6 The Historic Monuments Commission, anonymous late nineteenth-century drawing.

buildings of outstanding national importance. In a procedure known as *classement*, it could select buildings regardless of whether they were owned by the state, public corporations or private persons.[93]

From the very start the administration was staffed with true enthusiasts that possessed considerable influence. Taking over from the historian Ludovic Vitet, the writer Proper Mérimée held the post of Inspector across all political changes until his death in 1870. His friend Eugène Emmanuel Viollet-le-Duc headed the architects in charge of restorations. The research committee was shaped by intellectual heavyweights like Montalembert and Victor Hugo. The Commission recruited widely among the ranks of the cultural and political elite and included not only distinguished architects but men of affairs and deputies which ensured a strong voice in the Chamber (see ill. 1.6).

[93] Cf. Leon, *La Vie des monuments français*, pp. 125–64; F. Bercé (ed.), *Les Premiers Travaux de la Commission des Monuments historiques, 1837–1848. Procès-verbaux et relevés d'architectes* (Paris, 1979); Bercé (ed.), *La Naissance des Monuments historiques. La correspondance de Prosper Mérimée avec Ludovic Vitet, 1840–1848* (Paris, 1998); Bercé (ed.), *La Correspondance Mérimée – Viollet-le-Duc* (Paris, 2001); A. Fermigier, 'Mérimée et l'inspection des monuments historiques', in Nora (ed.), *Les Lieux de mémoire*, I, pp. 1599–1614; Ministère de la Culture et de la Communication de France, 'Prosper Mérimée 1803–1870' (2003), www.merimee.culture.fr.

Located in Paris, the Historic Monuments Commission based its decisions on the Inspector's reports and a network of local informants. In general, it first wrote to the Prefects for information on monuments, who then
relied on existing local societies or alternatively founded new bodies, such
as the Departmental Historic Monuments Commission in Bordeaux.[94] Yet
the new central institutions did not try to use the structures established by
Arcisse de Caumont. The Norman antiquary himself suggested such collaboration, as his Society, present in over thirty departments, was generally
being asked for advice on the repair of even the smallest of parish churches
and had managed to obtain the collaboration of the clergy by giving lectures
in Seminars. However, Guizot was not in favour of too much provincial
independence and aimed to put the existing learned societies under the
tutelage of the state by creating an alternative network to the provincial
congresses organised by de Caumont, offering subsidies, exchange of publications and printing of the most important contributions. Mérimée too
was not keen on provincial leadership. On the margins of a request for
a subsidy by de Caumont, he noted that the Commission should examine whether it was advisable 'to encourage a society that had exactly the
same aims as the commission. By giving even a small sum, does the Commission not resign a part of its powers?'[95] Despite statist and centralising
tendencies, however, the new organisations did not replace provincial and
private enterprises.[96] Instead two parallel, but highly intertwined structures
co-existed. As the number of provincial erudites on which all institutions
relied was limited, the same individuals often served as correspondents for
the state agencies, the *Académies*, the *Société française d'archéologie*, as well
as other national societies, such as the *Antiquaires de France*.[97]

These developments in France were closely observed in the German states.
Here too, the question of what to do about the national heritage remained
difficult after the victory in 1815. Germans did not have to overcome
the same revolutionary divisions, but if anything the approach to heritage was even more complicated: while the Wars of Liberation were

[94] The Commission that had resulted both from the efforts of the Prefect and the Learned Societies
was very active under the July Monarchy before being subsequently marginalised by the central
administration under the Second Empire and the Third Republic. See Archives Departementale de
la Gironde, Bordeaux, Serie T, 4T Commission des Monuments Historiques.
[95] MAP, Dossier 'Société pour la conservation des monuments', qu. in Bercé, 'Arcisse de Caumont',
pp. 1558–9; cf. also MAP, 80/1/124.
[96] See S. Gerson, *The Pride of Place. Local Memories and Political Culture in Nineteenth-Century France*
(Ithaca, NY, 2003).
[97] Bercé, 'Arcisse de Caumont', pp. 1556–9.

driven by, and in turn, inspired by the idea of a common national heritage, after 1815, the liberal longing for a common state with a common heritage was in stark conflict with desires of the restorative governments. The territorial states tried to create identification with the new territorial borders rather than the nation as a whole. This was particularly the case in the largest of them all, Prussia. Having been the biggest beneficiary of the territorial changes of the Peace, Prussia was composed of the most diverse and most disconnected territories. It was neither a region, nor a nation nor even a locality. The Rhineland with its history of occupation, revolutionary enthusiasm and nationalist rival, but also with its catholic and carnevalesque mentality, proved a particular challenge to integration.

Historical consciousness in Prussia, a report to King Friedrich Wilhelm IV from January 1842 concluded, compared poorly with the new developments in France. 'Preservation of historic monuments', despite efforts by the late King and Friedrich Wilhelm's own 'care for artistic monuments', was hampered by ignorance and indifference, as the 'interest in antiquities was not stimulated sufficiently in many places'.[98] The report was brought forward by *Kultusminister* Friedrich Eichhorn, who was familiar with French cultural policies since he had been subordinate to Karl von Altenstein, who supervised the restitution of art to Prussia in 1815,[99] and was based on information solicited through the Prussian Ambassador in Paris from the Head of the Historic Monument Commission, Grille de Beuzelin. It concluded that French policies should be imitated to remedy German backwardness.

During the Napoleonic Wars, Prussian officials had realised the hard way that heritage could create a bond with the state, i.e. that national feeling was superior to military drill in winning wars. Hence, the care of monuments was seen as part of a programme to remedy an underlying passivity of the people toward the state, held responsible for the defeat by French troops. It was first institutionalised as part of a reform of the administrative apparatus in 1809.[100] This beginning of a systematic policy of care for public buildings responded to calls from members of the public concerned with organising the preservation of the works of art not yet transported to the Louvre. The growing rallying around 'national monuments' and the desire to rebuild them, which awoke during the Wars

---

[98] Eichhorn to Friedrich Wilhelm IV, 5 Jan. 1842, GStA PK, I. HA Rep. 89 Geh. Zivilkabinett, jüngere Periode, Nr. 20768, fols. 9–12.
[99] Savoy, *Patrimoine annexé*, I, p. 188.
[100] Mohr de Pérez, *Anfänge der staatlichen Denkmalpflege*, p. 42.

of Liberation, was also an important driving force. Plans to complete the gothic cathedral in Cologne as a 'national monument' were hatched in the same circles that were hiding German art from French troops. Romantic enthusiasm was boosted by the rediscovery of the Cathedral's medieval plans, and was eventually turned into a political cause by the patriotic movement. While Germany also looked at several other candidates for the post of best national monument, tendencies for a broader protection emerged.[101] Two texts outlining the principles of preservation were published in 1815. Together with Boiserée, Goethe worked on a memorandum for the Prussian Chancellor Hardenberg and the Austrian Prince Metternich. Afraid that his memorandum might be taken over by nationalist circles, however, Goethe reworked it into a piece of travel writing on the Rhineland.[102] Meanwhile, the architect Karl Friedrich Schinkel was sent to this newly acquired Prussian territory, with the task of reporting on the state of public buildings. The resulting memorandum of the Office of Works outlined a proposal for the establishment of a special state organisation for the listing and conservation of valuable historic monuments, not just of buildings owned by the state.[103] The secularisation in the Rhine provinces made measures particularly urgent, as churches were dilapidated and movable works of art dispersed. The memorandum suggested establishing an inventory of buildings such as churches, chapels, cloisters and convents, castles, gates, town walls, memorial columns, public fountains, tombstones and town halls in order to plan for their conservation, with a view to increase national education and interest in the fatherland's earlier destinies.[104] The institution which was to oversee the preservation of monuments resembled that invoked by Grégoire and the plans for an inventory were similar to the one attempted by Montalivet in France in 1810. However, at a time where hate against Napoleon was growing, the memorandum did not refer to these policies, but instead denounced the French method of transporting works of art to a central museum; it asserted that in Prussia, 'in each district such property should remain as an eternal sacred object'.[105] The memorandum resulted in a number of decrees proclaiming

---

[101] Wolff, *Zwischen Tradition und Neubeginn*, pp. 41–51. Nipperdey, 'Nationalidee und Nationaldenkmal'; Nipperdey, 'Der Kölner Dom'; H. Boockmann, 'Das ehemalige Deutschordens-Schloß Marienburg, 1772–1945. Die Geschichte eines politischen Denkmals', in Boockmann *et al.* (eds.), *Geschichtswissenschaft und Vereinswesen im 19. Jahrhundert* (Göttingen, 1972), pp. 99–161; Boockmann, *Die Marienburg im 19. Jahrhundert* (Frankfurt, 1992).

[102] J.W. von Goethe, *Kunst und Alterthum am Rhein und Main*, serialised between 1816 and 1832, see Wolff, *Zwischen Tradition und Neubeginn*, pp. 89–104.

[103] Repr. in Mohr de Pérez, *Denkmalpflege in Preußen*, pp. 270–6.

[104] Schinkel, Bericht vom 18 Aug. 1815, qu. ibid., p. 274.   [105] Ibid., p. 275.

that any changes to public monuments needed the consent of the Office of Works, and protecting historic town walls, abandoned castles and convents. The proposal for a proper monument administration, however, was not pursued. Several further attempts by Hardenberg and *Kultusminister* Altenstein to establish an inventory of monuments failed too.[106] Although the 'care for the conservation of architectural monuments and ruins' was formally assigned to the *Kultusministerium* in 1835, and Friedrich Wilhelm III acknowledged the importance of monument protection, he repeatedly refused the appointment of a conservator as too costly.[107]

When Eichorn advocated in 1842 to increase popular interest and to create an administration and an inventory, the suggestions were thus not new, but they now arrived at a moment when the King prepared to appease protestant-catholic tensions and liberal national feelings by championing the completion of Cologne Cathedral as a national monument. Moreover, they had the added weight of the French example. Friedrich Wilhelm IV, read 'with great interest and approval' of the French example and thought it 'very appropriate' to have similar measures installed in his own state. He awarded a medal to Grille de Beuzelin and advised Eichorn to elaborate more detailed plans.[108] As a result, architect and Schinkel-student Ferdinand von Quast (1807–1877) was appointed as Prussia's first Conservator of Artistic Monuments in 1843.[109]

In contrast to his liberal, bourgeois, atheist French counterpart Mérimée, the landowner and Lower House member von Quast was a fervent anti-rationalist, anti-revolutionary and anti-materialist conservative, championing medieval Christianity and divine right. Convinced that historic monuments had the power to connect the people to this past in an organic way, von Quast saw their maintenance as a weapon in the conservative political struggle.[110] In a memorandum outlining his ideas on preservation in 1837 von Quast praised England as a paragon. Here, he claimed the conservation of historic buildings was underpinned by continuity and was

[106] Friedrich Wilhelm III to Alternstein, 7 Jan. 1835, GStA PK, I. HA Rep. 77 Ministerium des Inneren, Tit. 1215, Nr. 3, Beiheft, Bd.1, fol. 15.
[107] Mohr de Pérez, *Denkmalpflege in Preussen*, p. 104.
[108] Friedrich Wilhelm IV to Eichorn, 15 Jan. 1842, copy, GStA PK, I. HA Rep. 93 B Ministerium der öffentlichen Arbeiten, Nr. 2331, fol. 53.
[109] See correspondence between Eichhorn and Friedrich Wilhelm IV, 14 May 1842–14 May 1843, GStA PK, I. HA Rep. 89 Geh. Zivilkabinett, jüngere Periode, Nr. 20768, fols 14- 19 and von Quast's 'Pro-Memoria Über die beste Art und Weise zur Erhaltung der in den Königlichen Landen noch vorhandenen Alterthümer', undated 1843, fols. 20–29.
[110] F. Buch, *Studien zur Preußischen Denkmalpflege am Beispiel konservatorischer Arbeiten Ferdinand von Quasts* (Worms, 1990), pp. 212–21.

therefore also met with a true understanding by the public.[111] However, despite his Anglophilia, and regardless of his abhorrence of the revolutionary changes that had led to the awakening of heritage-consciousness in France, this country remained Prussia's main model for the care of monuments.

In 1845 von Quast must have had some animated conversations with the liberal art historian Franz Kugler, his colleague in the ministry, when both travelled to the *Congrès archéologique* in France to enquire about the operation of the French system.[112] On their return, Kugler developed a memorandum urging the formation of a commission analogous to the French Historic Monument Commission. In the attempt to optimise their administration, the ministry also sent von Quast to other German states, but the Conservator did not find examples to emulate and suggested instead to inquire again in France and Belgium. Based on a report sent by Mérimée, von Quast pleaded for a full transfer of the French system, including a yearly budget, an expropriation act, penal measures against contraventions of existing decrees, architects specialised in restoration and a network of correspondents.

Again, the weight of the French example obtained some results. A commission was appointed in 1852 and an inventory questionnaire was started. Yet in contrast to its French paragon, the Prussian commission barely survived the year, as it had neither the same decision-making competencies, nor a fixed budget at its disposal. Not only was it given fewer resources, but because of a misinterpretation of the French situation, it also had to cope with a much bigger task too. It was to inventory all monuments in the Prussian provinces and enhance interest among the population. Since the French Revolution, the belief that successful protection of monuments ought to be based on knowledge of existing stock had become deeply ingrained. The problem was that Minister Eichorn wrongly assumed that in France the general inventory was the basis for the *classement*. However, the procedure of *classement* was based on the information the Commission received through the Inspector and its correspondents. The larger inventory project was executed by the Committee for Historic Works. In fact it was abandoned as too costly after only two *départements* had been covered. Yet as functions were separate, this did not affect the work of the commission. Prussia, on the other hand, persisted with the idea of first establishing a

---

[111] Jokilehto, *History of Architectural Conservation*, p. 125.
[112] Buch, *Studien zur Preußischen Denkmalpflege*, pp. 29–30; L. Koschnik, *Franz Kugler (1808–1858) als Kunsthistoriker und Kunstpolitiker* (Berlin, 1985).

general inventory, on which a special inventory of extraordinarily important and preservation-worthy monuments should be based.

The magnitude of the task deadlocked the day-to-day working of the
commission. Moreover, Quast's scientifically oriented questionnaire was so
detailed that the original idea of sending it to clergymen and schoolteachers,
whom local associations and antiquaries should assist, proved unrealistic.
The necessary local expertise simply did not exist in most Prussian territories, especially in the agrarian areas east of the Elbe. The only successful
inventory published before the redelegation of preservation to the provinces
in 1875, was achieved in Hesse-Nassau, the former Kurhessen, a territory
with a long history of enlightened sociability, assisted by the Association
for Hessian History (*Verein für hessische Geschichte und Landeskunde*). The
ministry in Berlin had to realise that without local expertise and established
associations, its reach was limited and attempts to force the emergence of
associations had little success in areas without a long tradition of bourgeois
sociability.[113]

The beginnings of state preservation in other major German states were
similar to the Prussian experience, including the importance given to the
French model. Whilst von Quast decided that France would make a better
example than any of the (mainly north) German states he had visited,
several south German governments also followed the French developments.
Bavaria appointed a General Inspector for Fine Arts in 1835, and created
a Commission for Public Art and Monuments in 1852 for the working of
which it repeatedly enquired in France. In 1868 this led to the appointment
of a General Conservator for Monuments of Art and Antiquity.[114] In
Württemberg, the state's first Conservator adapted von Quast's inventory,
resulting in the first successful inventory project in Germany.[115] Baden
appointed a conservator around the same time (1853), but in other large
states, such as Saxony, such a position was created as late as the 1890s.

State preservation in Germany, and particularly in Prussia, thus emerged
when the initial call from members of the public for the government to
act out of artistic or patriotic motives encountered an interest in art from
members of the governing elite coupled with the desire to bind the people to
the state via the veneration of historic monuments. It was however limited

---

[113] Buch, *Studien zur Preußischen Denkmalpflege*, pp. 47–61.

[114] Bavarian Embassy to de Persigny, French Minister of the Interior, Agriculture and Commerce, 14
October 1852; Bavarian Embassy to the French Minister of Foreign Affairs, 25 July 1867, MAP,
80/1/33, Dossier 'Allemagne'; On the beginning of state preservation in Bavaria see Dürr, *Anfänge
der Denkmalpflege*.

[115] Buch, *Studien zur Preußischen Denkmalpflege*, pp. 24–35.

by the extent of private collaboration. While these factors were indigenous, all major administrative steps and concepts followed the French example.

Although Britain bypassed revolutionary vandalism, secularisation, territorial reshuffling and new revolutionary upheaval, the institutions created in France and Prussia provoked interest here too. The Royal Institute of British Architects (RIBA), a year after receiving its Royal Charter in 1837, enquired of the French Minister of the Interior, Montalivet, about the institutions recently founded by the French government, presenting its aims as similar to those of the French government agency.[116] Due to its strong interest in the 'conservation of monuments of ancient times', it asked the Minister to send the reports of the Inspectorate, the Historic Monuments Commission, and the Committee for Historic Works. Further enquiries followed.[117] The new French ways also interested MPs writing on the facilitation of public access to museums, and key documents were published for the wider public. A translation of the inventory questionnaire drawn by the *Comité des Arts et Monuments* in the *Gentleman's Magazine* later inspired the first archaeological survey in the United Kingdom.[118] The Society of Antiquaries was so impressed by the new French institutions that after having declined in 1819 an offer from the *Société des Antiquaires de France* to exchange letters and transactions and rebuild transchannel communication after the wars, it reversed its decision and started formal correspondence in 1838. It also elected Guizot an Honorary Fellow a year later.[119]

Whether the government should be responsible for the safeguarding of monuments in Britain was subsequently discussed. In 1841 a Select Committee of the House of Commons considered the protection of national monuments, which it understood primarily as memorials to illustrious individuals.[120] In the course of evidence given to the Select Committee, it was suggested that such a definition would be too narrow and that other remains such as Roman ruins and historic houses could also be national monuments. The protection of these remains was particularly recommended by the architectural writer and illustrator John Britton, a

[116] Donaldson to Comte de Montalivet, 6 November 1838; reply 12 Nov 1893, MAP, 80/1/33, Dossier 'Angleterre'.
[117] Lord Granville, British Ambassador, to Comte de Montalivet, 15 December 1838, reply 21 January 1839, MAP, 80/1/33, Dossier 'Angleterre'.
[118] See D. Murray, *An Archaeological Survey of the United Kingdom. The Preservation and Protection of Our Ancient Monuments* (Glasgow, 1896). On this transfer see Brown, *Care of Ancient Monuments*, pp. 26–7.
[119] Evans, *History of the Society of Antiquaries*, p. 226.
[120] Report of the Select Committee on National Monuments and Works of Art, *Parliamentary Papers* (1841), VI, p. 437.

leading figure of the Gothic Revival.[121] He also suggested creating a commission on the French model, but his proposal was not adopted in the Select Committee report.[122] Nevertheless, a year later, the manifesto of the new Archaeological Institute again called on the government:

> to preserve from demolition or decay works from ancient time which still exist … not merely on account of their interest as specimens of art, but respect for the great Institutions of the country, sacred and secular and a lively interest in their maintenance, must as it is apprehended, be increased in proportion to the advance of an intelligent appreciation of monuments, which are tangible evidences of the gradual establishment of these Institutions.[123]

While the nation's written records received protection by the state at that time through the foundation of the Public Record Office (PRO) in 1838,[124] calls for an equal preservation of built heritage remained unsuccessful for some time.[125] It has been argued that the relatively early protection of written records stemmed from a greater appreciation for words than visual arts in Shakespeare's country.[126] Yet the foundation of the PRO was also facilitated as it offered a practical aid for the work of civil servants, rather than mere scholarly amusement. The absence of state preservation cannot be explained simply by a lack of interest in historic monuments. Firstly, there was no complete absence of state intervention for historic monuments, as Holger Hoock has argued. The monuments in question were imperial rather than national. Since the Revolutionary Wars, the state invested considerable means, through its diplomatic service, the navy and the royal engineers in acquiring objects from across the globe for the British Museum.[127]

Secondly, the absence of state intervention for British monuments, did not necessarily equate an absence of interest in historical remains. Many contemporary French and German architects shared the view that

[121] See J.M. Crook, 'John Britton and the Genesis of the Gothic Revival', in Sir J. Summerson (ed.), *Concerning Architecture* (London, 1968), pp. 98–119.
[122] Evidence of J. Britton, question 1947, Report of the Select Committee on National Monuments and Works of Art, *Parliamentary Papers* (1841), VI, p. 97; T. Champion, 'Protecting the Monuments. Archaeological Legislation from the 1882 Act to PP16', in Hunter (ed.), *Preserving the Past*, pp. 38–56, here p. 40.
[123] A. Way, 'Introduction', *Archaeological Journal*, 1 (1845), 1–6, qu. in Champion, 'Protecting the Monuments', pp. 39–40.
[124] P. Levine, *The Amateur and the Professional. Antiquaries, Historians and Archaeologists in Victorian England, 1838–1886* (Cambridge, 1986), pp. 101–34.
[125] See *Parliamentary Debates*, Commons, 3rd Ser., 81, 27 June 1845, cols. 1329–34.
[126] For example Hunter, 'Introduction', in Hunter (ed.), *Preserving the Past*, p. 13.
[127] H. Hoock, 'The British State and the Anglo-French Wars over Antiquities, 1798–1858', *Historical Journal* 50.1 (2007), 49–72.

monuments were better cared for in England than in their own countries, as they had not recently suffered from iconoclasm and secularisation and still possessed their traditional guardians (i.e. the owners that had profited from the waves of expropriations and destructions during the Reformation and the Civil War). Continentals often praised the Anglican Church and parts of the aristocracy for actively preserving their monuments.

While state institutions were put in place in Germany by imitating French models, Britain found its own solutions. The Church of England established its own machinery, restoring thousands of medieval churches in England and Wales between 1840 and 1875.[128] The restorations were part of the religious revival that tried to counteract the rise of secularism and non-conformity and were a component of the defence against challenges to the Established Church's power and privileges. Restored churches trumpeted the message that the institution, like its buildings were 'immune to the ruinous hand of time'.[129] The work of the diocesan hierarchy was reinforced by local church-buildings societies, orchestrated by the Incorporated Church Buildings Society, the architectural branch of the Ecclesiastical Commission, delivering monetary contribution by individuals. Voluntary architectural societies bridged the gap between diocese policy and parish practice, bringing together professional architects, clergy and churchmen. Anglican architects specialised in restoration, as devotion to the religious cause met sound financial interests. In due course, the RIBA established itself as the central professional body, promoting debates, issuing guidelines for the care of old churches, founding a permanent subcommittee on the Conservation of Ancient Monuments and Remains,[130] and integrating restoration into the apprentice system.[131] Thus a system was in place for maintaining a large group of monuments without a government agency.

While the Church enhanced religious heritage as a national heritage, the aristocracy contributed to the notion of a collective heritage by opening its collections and houses to the public. As Linda Colley concluded, 'only in Great Britain did it prove possible to float the idea that aristocratic property was in some magical and strictly intangible way the

---

[128] C. Miele, '"Their Interest and Habit". Professionalism and the Restoration of Medieval Churches 1837–77', in C. Brooks, A. Saint (eds.), *The Victorian Church. Architecture and Society* (Manchester, 1995), pp. 151–72. Miele, 'The First Conservation Militant', pp. 17–18.

[129] C. Miele, '"A Small Knot of Cultivated People". William Morris and the Ideologies of Protection', *Art Journal*, 54 (1995), 73–9, here 73.

[130] Miele, 'The First Conservation Militant', pp. 23–4.

[131] Miele, '"Their Interest and Habit"', pp. 161–3.

people's property also'.[132] British historians tend to ascribe the emergence of 'heritage consciousness' to ruling-class fears about the pace of social change and the possibility of political upheaval,[133] arguing that they 'should be seen in the context of the political disturbances of the 1840s when there were widespread fears for the survival of the established institutions of royalty, aristocracy and the Church'.[134] Yet while fears of upheaval and social change drove the elaboration of policies in the 1830s and 1840s, here like on the continent, a broader perspective on the emerging historical culture shows that the idea of heritage also developed in much more diverse and interactive ways.[135]

The pleasures of the past

In all three countries, political considerations were not the only driving force behind the rise of heritage. Neither was the turn to the past driven by mere nostalgia, or some 'kind of moral malaise'.[136] The article in which Viollet-le-Duc famously defined 'restoration' as a quintessentially 'modern' word and thing also captures how the turn to the past related to the proud spirit of the age:

> Our era and our era alone, since the beginning of recorded history, has assumed toward the past a quite exceptional attitude as far as history is concerned. Our age has wished to analyse the past, classify it, compare it, and write its complete history, following step-by-step the procession, the progress, and the various transformations of humanity. A fact as novel as this new analytical attitude of our era cannot be dismissed, as some superficial observers have imagined, as merely some kind of temporary fashion, or whim or weakness on our part.[137]

The complex new phenomena related to a much broader interest in the past. It was linked to the rise of history as a discipline,[138] and to Cuvier's studies of comparative anatomy and geology, unveiling to the public 'a very long history of the world that had preceded the reign of mankind'. Philologists searched for the common source of European languages, ethnographers

[132] Colley, *Britons*, pp. 174–5; Mandler, *Stately Home*, pp. 71–106.
[133] Colley, *Britons*, pp. 147–77, esp. 174–7.   [134] Champion, 'Protecting the Monuments', p. 40.
[135] Mandler, *Stately Home*, pp. 21–69.
[136] E.E. Viollet-le-Duc, 'Restauration', in Viollet-le-Duc, *Dictionnaire raisonné de l'architecture française du XIe au XVIe siècle* (10 vols., Paris, 1854–68), repr. and trans. in Berrgy Bergdoll (ed.), Viollet-le-Duc, E.E., *The Foundations of Architecture. Selections from the Dictionnaire raisonné* (New York, 1990), p. 198; For anti-nostalgic arguments, see Mandler, *Stately Home*; D. Matless, *Landscape and Englishness* (1998) or Melman, *Culture of History*.
[137] Ibid, p. 197.   [138] See S. Bann, *Romanticism and the Rise of History* (New York, 1995).

turned to the origins of 'races', and archaeologists discovered artistic productions from Egypt to India and attempted to classify their findings according to general laws.[139]

An increasingly large public eagerly consumed these new scientific discoveries. The Revolution had left the feeling that past and present were forever disrupted. Many contemporaries describe that time accelerated continuously as a result of constant political turmoil and the mechanisation of industry.[140] The sense of displacement felt all over Europe created a hunger for experiences for recent and distant pasts from fossilised antediluvian monsters to Marie Antoinette's hair and Marat's bath.[141] The emerging historical culture engendered many competing and co-existing visions of the past. For instance, a dungeon version of Tudor history could exist alongside contemporary visions of 'merrie England' and eighteenth century 'chamber of horrors' set next to enthusiasm for the same period as an age of refinement.[142] Every new experience was immediately historicised. Already in the 1850s, the events of 1848 were the subject of 'historical novels'.[143] Alongside reflections on the recent past, tales and artefacts from the biblical lands, ancient Rome and the European Middle Ages provided entertainment, but also helped to negotiate the challenges of the present, and informed debates on topics as diverse as urban overcrowding, the crises in faith and the future of education;[144] theories of evolutionary texts and exhibitions of endangered human species also were part of this historical culture.[145] Among the multiple pasts that were of interest to nineteenth-century audiences, episodes from the national past loomed large, but they were not exclusive. Foreign histories and objects, whether imperial and European, were equally present, sometimes because they offered a different light on contemporary issues than the national past could (as in the case

---

[139] Viollet-le-Duc, 'Restauration', pp. 197–8.   [140] Fritsche, *Stranded in the Present*, pp. 52, 106.

[141] See O'Connor, *The Earth on Show*; Stammers, 'The bric-a-brac' and 'Collecting Cultures, Historical Consciousness and Artefacts of the Old Regime in Nineteenth-Century Paris', unpublished Ph.D. dissertation, University of Cambridge (2010).

[142] Melman, *Culture of History*.

[143] L. Niemeyer, 'Writing German historical fiction in an age of change, 1848–1871', unpublished Ph.D. dissertation, University of Cambridge (2011).

[144] A. Vaninskaya, C. Stray, A. Jenkins, J. A. Secord, and L. Howsam, 'What the Victorians Learned: Perspectives on Nineteenth Century Schoolbooks.' *Journal of Victorian Culture*, 12.2 (2007), 262–85; S. Goldhill, *Victorian Culture and Classical Antiquity. Art, Opera, Fiction, and the Proclamation of Modernity* (Princeton, 2011); D. Gange and M. Ledger-Lomas (eds.), *Cities of God. The Bible and Archaeology in Nineteenth-century Britain* (Cambridge, 2013); A. Buckland and S. Qureshi (eds.), *Time Travellers. Victorian Perspectives on the Past* (Chicago, forthcoming).

[145] See for example J. Secord, *Victorian Sensation. The Extraordinary Publication, Reception, and Secret Authorship of Vestiges of the Natural History of Creation* (Chicago, 2000). S. Qureshi, *Peoples on Parade. Exhibitions, Empire and Anthropology in Nineteenth-Century Britain* (Chicago, 2011).

of the French Revolution in England), but also because the productions of this emerging culture industry were frequently translated and adapted across borders.[146] The historical culture thrived not simply on ideology but on pleasure and sometimes on gore. As such, picnicking in Napoleon's Carriage at Madame Tussaud's was only surpassed by seeing the waxen effigies of revolutionary leaders, produced from their guillotined heads, in the Chamber of Horrors.[147]

All branches of art, from painting to the theatre, engaged with questions about the nature of the past, and the enthusiasm was further fed by a revolution in printing and reproduction techniques.[148] Lithographs, engravings, casts, panoramas and dioramas provided ever-larger audiences with ideas of what the past had actually looked like, and the imitation of successful foreign models assured that audiences in different countries were privy to similar visual experiences.[149]

In this historical culture, historical monuments often provided the stage design, but became also increasingly of interest in their own right. As a result, writers incorporate monuments into their stories with growing prominence. In the 1830s and 1840s, thus at the moment of beginning state intervention in preservation, historic buildings even ceased to be extras in the background, and became protagonists themselves. The first and greatest star was Victor Hugo's *Notre Dame*. The translation as *The Hunchback of Notre Dame* obscures that the story was almost more about the life of the Cathedral than Quasimodo and Esmeralda. In Fredrick Althorp Paley's *The Church Restorers*, the love story even involved the building itself. The novel follows an anthropomorphised parish church through centuries of neglect and mistreatment before she finally finds the love of her life in the figure of a dashing young restorer. Some of these tales were no literary masterpieces – Paley himself freely admitted that his novel had no 'merit whatever' 'as a story' – but he figured that the form of a tale would make a far 'less technical and tedious' medium for illustrating his points about church

---

[146] Melman, *Culture of History*.   [147] Ibid.
[148] On the technical changes facilitating this emerging consumer culture, see Mandler, *Stately Home*, pp. 22–37; for a comparison with Europe p. 28; Chu, P. ten-Doesschate, 'Pop-Culture in the Making. The Romantic Taste for History', in Chu, P. ten-Doesschate and Weisberg, G.P. (eds.), *The Popularization of Images. Visual Culture under the July Monarchy* (Princeton, 1994), pp. 166–88. On panoramas: Monod, 'Moving (Dioramic) Experiences', *All the Year Round*, March 1867, pp. 304–8; R. Hyde, *Panoramania! The Art and Entertainment of the 'All Embracing View'* (London, 1988).
[149] For example Taylor and Nodier's *Voyages pittoresques et romantiques dans l'ancienne France* (1835) was an important model for Charles Knight's *Old England. A Pictorial History of Regal, Ecclesiastical, Baronial, Municipal and Popular Antiquities* (1845).

restoration than an architectural treaty.[150] The novels were not just used by their authors to promote preservation. They were also appropriated in innovative ways by their readers to protect the newly discovered heroes. Hugo's *Notre Dame*, for instance, which popularised his declaration of *War on the Demolishers*, not only inspired Viollet-le-Duc to remodel the real cathedral according to Hugo's imagination, gargoyles and all, but it had an impact on an entire generation. Young people discovering their love of monuments while climbing up the cathedral's steps, clutching Hugo's novel in their arms, were so widespread that they became part of the French heritage foundation narrative (see ill. 1.7).[151] William H. Ainsworth's imitation, *Old Saint Paul's* published in 1841,[152] did not achieve quite the same fame, but his *Tower of London*, part guidebook, part romance about the Tudor queen of nine days Jane Grey, promoted the opening and refurbishment of the Tower's historic sections.[153] In 1850, ten years after Ainsworth's book was published, the Tower attracted 200,000 visitors per year.[154] In Germany too, the interest created by novels about the Reformation informed support of the Wartburg's and other monuments' restoration.[155] Wilhelm Hauff's *Lichtenstein* even resulted in the 'reconstruction' of the fictive ruin in the 1830s.[156]

This cultural interest forms the backdrop for the spectacular restoration campaigns and the first administrative measures for the protection of heritage. The spirit of invention that animated the resurrection of the past across Europe, captured in Viollet-le-Duc's famous definition that 'to restore an edifice is not to maintain it, repair it or remake it, it is to re-establish it in a complete state that may never have existed at a given moment', defied any easy categorisation of intentions.[157] In the process of restoration cathedrals could become a symbol of religious revival or

---

[150] F.A. Paley, *The Church Restorers: A Tale Treating of Ancient and Modern Architecture and Church Decorations* (London, 1844), p. ix.
[151] Challamel, *Loi du 30 mars 1887*, p. 1; P. Bellet, 'Promenade autour du Jardin central', in F. Ducuing (ed.), *L'Exposition universelle de 1867 illustrée* (Paris, 1868), pp. 371–4.
[152] Tombs and Tombs, *That Sweet Enemy*, p. 366.
[153] For further examples of historical novels and their influence on the opening of palaces to the public see Mandler, *Stately Home*, p. 36. On the role of *The Tower of London* in popular culture see Melman, *Culture of History*.
[154] Mandler, *Stately Home*, p. 36.
[155] Niemeyer, 'Writing German historical fiction'; François, 'Die Wartburg'.
[156] Niemeyer, personal communication. The novel written in 1826 was translated as *Lichtenstein or The outlaw of Würtemberg: A Tale of the Sixteenth Century* (London, 1861). See also M. Limlei, *Geschichte als Ort der Bewährung. Menschenbild und Gesellschaftsverständnis in den deutschen historischen Romanen, 1820–1890* (Frankfurt, 1988).
[157] Viollet-le-Duc, 'Restauration', p. 195.

NOTRE DAME DE PARIS.

Page 200.

1.7 Luc Olivier Merson, 'Notre Dame de Paris'. Illustrations of Victor Hugo's novel captured and enhanced the romanticized vision of the cathedral and its gargoyles. In Alfred Barbou, *Victor Hugo and his time* (London, 1882), p. 200.

national unity, or monuments to civic communities. Medieval castles and fortresses could be restored as symbols of military strength or promoted romantic visions of chivalry, or offer a 'blood-and-guts' enjoyment.

While the notion of 'national heritage', first conceptualised as a sign of Revolutionary freedom, was to a degree taken up for social control by governing elites in all three countries in a climate of political disturbance in the 1830s and 1840s, such schemes could only operate within a broader historical culture – and failed where a public interest in the past could not be mobilised, as the case of the inventory projects show. In all three countries, members of the public had suggested preoccupation with monuments before their cause was championed by the established order. In all three countries too, the desire to 'catch up' with other European states started to emerge as a motive for institutionalisation, albeit with varying degrees of success. The newly created institutions, although trying to establish their primacy, were not only relying on public opinion and help for their work, but their visions of heritage were continuously challenged by ever-growing parts of the population. This was first and foremost done by private societies that grew into national movements, the subject of Chapter 2.

CHAPTER 2

The heritage-makers

> He also wrote a pamphlet, addressed to the seventeen learned soci-
> eties, native and foreign, containing a repetition of the statement he
> had already made, and rather more than half intimating his opin-
> ion that the seventeen learned societies were so many 'humbugs'.
> Hereupon, the virtuous indignation of the seventeen learned societies
> being roused, several fresh pamphlets appeared; the foreign learned
> societies corresponded with the native learned societies; the native
> learned societies translated the pamphlets of the foreign learned soci-
> eties into English; the foreign learned societies translated the pam-
> phlets of the native learned societies into all sorts of languages; and
> thus commenced that celebrated scientific discussion so well known
> to all men, as the Pickwick controversy.
>
> Charles Dickens, The Pickwick Papers (London, 1837), ch. XI

The growing interest in heritage was intertwined with the emergence of
many private societies dedicated to research and preservation. Over the
course of the nineteenth century, societies with different core purposes and
varying territorial ranges appeared. Activist preservation societies, professional bodies and leisure associations subsequently supplemented the more
traditional learned societies. Counting more than half a million members
across Europe, the learned bodies are often remembered through their less
than flattering literary rendering.[1] While monuments had risen as heroes
of popular literature, those who venerated them earned mostly ridicule.
The image of the antiquary as a man incapable of abstraction in his love
of worm-eaten things was a popular stereotype in the eighteenth century.
The rest of mankind remained astonished that a typical antiquary could
not 'get over the fact that the ancients had cooking-pots, spoons, forks: in a
word that, having the same needs, they had come up with the same means

---

[1] These figures apply to all learned societies, not just monument bodies. J.P. Chaline, 'Les Sociétés
savantes en Allemagne, Italie et Royaume-Uni à la fin du XIXe siècle', *Histoire, Économie et Société*,
21.1 (2002), 87–96.

[as ourselves] for satisfying them. Presumably he was no less surprised to find they were endowed with mouths and behinds'.[2] British writers from Pope to Burns, Scott, Dickens and Hardy made fun of the Mr Oldbucks and Drs Dryasdust, Professors Snores, Dozes, and Wheezys and other 'lean and fat' antiquaries and 'learned pigs'.[3] Learned societies provided also the butt of many jokes in the tales of Balzac, Flaubert, Maupassant, Alphone Daudet and the Parisian Vaudevilles.[4] Germans even invented the term *Vereinsmeier*, which captures a whole universe of pedantry and stuffiness, to refer to a person spending a disproportionate amount of his time in associations. As a result, there was perhaps 'no class of persons, devoted to literary and scientific pursuits, who have been more abused and misunderstood',[5] and no form of sociability more ridiculed in pen and ink than that which inspired the futile gatherings of Dickens' Mudfog Society for the Advancement of Everything and his Pickwick Club (see ills. 2.1–2.3).

Antiquaries and scholars of antiquarianism have long pleaded to ignore these stereotypes and acknowledge the antiquarians' important contribution to knowledge.[6] One should likewise take seriously all those nineteenth-century authors that saw private societies not so much as stuffy bodies but 'in respect to monument conservation', 'as a sort of crystallization of public opinion, representing this at its best and keeping its machinery always in working order'.[7] Virtually every preservationist belonged to at least one, and often to several such societies, including those heritage-makers employed in the new state agencies. More crucially, the sheer number of people involved in societies preoccupied with heritage, reaching the tens or even hundreds of thousands in each country by the end of our

---

[2] J. Assézat (ed.), *Oeuvres complètes de Diderot* (Paris, 1875), p. 379, qu. in A. Schnapp, 'Introduction: Neapolitan Effervescence', *Journal of the History of Collections, Special Issue: Antiquarianism, Museums and Cultural Heritage. Collecting and its Contexts in Eighteenth-Century Naples*, 19.2 (2007), 161–4.

[3] See A. Dwight Culler, *The Victorian Mirror of History* (New Haven & London, 1985), pp. 21–2; Levine, *Amateur and Professional*, pp. 17–18; R. Sweet, *Antiquaries*, pp. xiii–xiv; Manias, 'Learned Societies', p. 99; Society of Antiquaries: 'Making History: 300 Years of Antiquaries in Britain' (2007), www.spiralscratch.info/clients/sal.

[4] Chaline, *Sociabilité*, pp. 1–14.

[5] C. Roach Smith, *Collectanea Antiqua* IV (1857) (Appendix), pp. 42–3 qu. in Manias, 'Learned Societies', pp. 99–100. Manias observes that French archaeologists were less concerned with dispelling the stereotypes (largely written by Parisian intellectuals) than their British counterparts. This is all the more interesting as the English satires depict ridiculous but also self-mocking and often harmless characters, while some of the portrayals of the provincial *homme des sociétés savantes* are much less benevolent, such as the portrayal of Dr Massarel in Maupassant's *Coup d'Etat*.

[6] Sweet, *Antiquaries*, pp. xiii–xiv; Manias, 'Learned Societies', p. 99.

[7] Brown, *Care of Ancient Monuments*, p. 34; similarly A. von Wussow, *Die Erhaltung der Denkmäler in den Kulturstaaten der Gegenwart* (2 vols., Berlin, 1885), I, pp. 41–3.

2.1 Thomas Rowlandson 1789 etching shows 'An Antiquarian' as an odd old figure.

2.2 George Cruickshank, 'The Antiquarian Society' from 1812 portrays the boisterous atmosphere of meetings.

MR. PICKWICK ADDRESSES THE CLUB

2.3 'Mr. Pickwick addresses the Club'. The etched illustration by Robert Seymour for the first edition of *The Posthumous Papers of the Pickwick Club* (1836–37) by Charles Dickens captures the male sociability of the earlier learned societies.

period, makes the societies one of the best sources through which one can capture wider participation in preservation, as opposed to mere individual interest in the past. The parodies are testament to the societies' ubiquity rather than their marginality. They also offer us, as Chesterton once

observed, 'the first of all democratic doctrines, that all men are interesting',
even if their story appears rather dull or monotonous at first sight,[8] as
so much of it is only revealed through institutional records which often
lack the 'glowing tone', 'dash of wildness, and rich vein of picturesque
interest'.[9]

At a more structural level, the international flow of letters, translations and exchanges so apparent in *The Pickwick Papers*, incites us to
refocus attention from individual groups to the interconnected nature of
the heritage movement within and across national borders. Most histories of preservation see private societies as important actors, but the time
period and the kinds of societies included vary considerably across national
historiographies. As a result, different conclusions are reached about
their and, by proxy, the heritage movement's, importance and ideological
outlook. At the extremes, one can end up with 100,000 members of a
fairly reactionary, *Heimat* movement for Germany as opposed to a mere
500, albeit quite radical preservationists for Britain. In part this is because
there is no absolute way of measuring numbers or to determine whom
to include. The many lists published during the nineteenth century vary
greatly in this respect.[10] However, comparative accounts from the *fin de
siècle* offer the useful cue that contemporaries across countries considered
not only learned and activist societies but also professional bodies and
leisure associations as part of the same movement.[11] This chapter develops a common framework for assessing the evolution of different forms
of sociability over the century across the three countries, outlining the
growth and contribution of the learned societies and professional bodies, before comparing in detail new activist preservation associations and

[8] G.K. Chesterton, *Charles Dickens* (London, 1906, 11th edn, 1917), p. 19.
[9] C. Dickens, *The Mudfog Papers* (London, 1880), pp. 48–9.
[10] For instance *Annuaire de la Société de l'Histoire de France* (Paris, 1842); *L'Annuaire des Sociétés savantes de la France et de l'Etranger, sous auspices du Ministère de l'Instruction publique* (Paris, 1846); A. Hume, *The Learned Societies and Printing Clubs of the United Kingdom* (London, 1847) re-edited by A. I. Evans, *With a Supplement Containing all the Recently-Established Societies and Printing Clubs, and their Publications to the Present Time* (London, 1853). Since 1884 *The Year Book of the Scientific and Learned Societies of Great Britain and Ireland* was published; K.A. Klüpfel, 'Die historischen Vereine und Zeitschriften Deutschlands', *Zeitschrift für Geschichtswissenschaft*, 1 (1844), 518–59; J. Müller, *Die wissenschaftlichen Vereine und Gesellschaften Deutschland im 19. Jahrhundert, Bibliographie ihrer Veröffentlichungen* (3 vols., Berlin, 1883–1908); *L'Annuaire des Sociétés savantes de la France et de l'Etranger publié sous les auspices du Ministère de l'Instruction publique* (Paris, 1846); A. d'Héricourt, *Annuaire des sociétés savantes de la France et de l'Etranger* (2 vols., Paris, 1863–4); H. Delaunay, *Annuaire international des Sociétés savantes, 1903* (Paris, 1904).
[11] Esp. Brown, *Care of Ancient Monuments*, p. 34.

connecting them to wider reform movements at the end of the century. Tracing the evolution of sociability in this way, can elucidate not just the general spread of heritage-consciousness, but the complex processes of societies' co-existence, absorption, and federation helps us to understand how different conceptualisation of heritage evolved, co-existed and competed. Across all countries, the history of sociability reveals underlying tensions between the local and the national, the private and the state, the theoretical and practical, the elitist and the popular, the amateur and the professional. It is a history full of rivalry and disagreement, in which strong personalities left their mark and in which affective links (or the absence thereof) mattered for success or failure. At the same time, it is also a history of an extraordinary will to find a common language that could transcend individual preferences and unite people across social and political differences to form a movement.

Sociability, erudition and activism

The conditions under which societies emerged, initially differed from country to country, but their development then became increasingly similar and intertwined. Before the French Revolution, historical questions were only one of many preoccupations of the learned societies and academies in France and the Holy Roman Empire.[12] Specialisation started much earlier in England, potentially as a response to the iconoclasm, secularisation and redefinition of Englishness after the Supremacy Act. The first antiquarian association, the Society of Antiquaries of London (SAL) founded in 1707 and incorporated in 1757, could trace its origins to the sixteenth century.[13] After the French Revolution, on the other hand, a plethora of specifically historical, archaeological or antiquarian societies were founded across Europe. The principal foundation waves reflect different national political contexts, peaking during the Wars of Liberation and the *Vormärz*

---

[12] J.E. III. McClellan, 'L'Europe des académies', *Dix-Huitième Siècle*, 25 (1993), 153–65; McClellan, 'Learned Societies', in A.C. Kors (ed.), *Encyclopedia of the Enlightenment* (Oxford, 2002); D. Roche, *Le Siècle des Lumières en province. Académies et académiciens provinciaux, 1680–1789* (2 vols., Paris, the Hague, 1978); J. Voss, 'Akademien, gelehrte Gesellschaften und wissenschaftliche Vereine in Deutschland, 1750–1850', in E. François (ed.), *Sociabilité et société bourgeoise en France, en Allemagne et en Suisse 1750–1850* (Paris, 1986), pp. 149–67.

[13] Evans, *Society of Antiquaries*; S. Piggot, *Ruins in a Landscape. Essays in Antiquarianism* (Edinburgh, 1976).

in Germany,[14] during the July Monarchy in France,[15] and during the ecclesiological movement in Britain.[16] Overall, however, the emergence of societies preoccupied with national history and heritage followed remarkably similar patterns, culminating in a wave of foundations after 1870. National societies were often capital-based,[17] but in all three countries provincial impetus was important.[18] While centres of enlightened learning remained the seedbeds for the formation of newer societies in the first half of the nineteenth century,[19] in the second half distribution became more widespread. By the end of the nineteenth century more than 150 major associations existed in Germany,[20] every county in England had at least one archaeological association,[21] and so did most French *départements*.[22]

Everywhere, societies started on a local level. In Germany, this was related to particularism, while in France, *ancien regime* provincialism motivated some founders to focus on the old historical provinces. The attraction of localism resided, however, mainly in its potential for sociability. Many provincials could not travel to the capital or even to larger regional centres to take part in meetings of national societies, as many English testimonies show.[23] Nevertheless, an increasing desire for national coordination was felt since the 1830s, which coincided with a greater involvement by many a society in preservation rather than pure research. National coordination was first systematised in France, fuelled by the rivalry between de Caumont and Guizot, but also inspired by models of scientific communication

[14] H. Heimpel, 'Geschichtsvereine einst und jetzt', in H. Boockmann *et al.* (ed.), *Geschichtswissenschaft und Vereinswesen im 19. Jahrhundert* (Göttingen, 1972), pp. 45–73; T. Adam, 'Rettung der Geschichte – Bewahrung der Natur. Ursprung und Entwicklung der Historischen Vereine und des Umweltschutzes in Deutschland von 1770 bis zur Gegenwart', *Blätter für deutsche Landesgeschichte*, 133 (1997), pp. 239–77; Voss, 'Akademien', pp. 160–1; G. Kunz, *Verortete Geschichte. Regionales Geschichtsbewußtsein in den Deutschen Historischen Vereinen des 19. Jahrhunderts* (Kritische Studien zur Geschichtswissenschaft 138, Göttingen, 2000), pp. 55–68.

[15] However, some of the most important national societies were founded during the Empire and the Restoration. See F. Bercé, 'Les Sociétés savantes et la protection du patrimoine monumental', in Bercé, *Les Sociétés savantes. Actes du 100e Congrès des Sociétés savantes 1975* (Paris, 1976), pp. 155–67; Bercé, 'Arcisse de Caumont'.

[16] Brown, *Care of Ancient Monuments*, pp. 34–5; J.F. White, *The Cambridge Movement: The Ecclesiologist and the Gothic Revival* (London, 1962), pp. 70–136; Levine, *Amateur and Professional*, pp. 46–7.

[17] Voss, 'Akademien', pp. 156–62; Levine, *Amateur and Professional*, p. 50.

[18] Speitkamp, *Verwaltung der Geschichte*, p. 115.

[19] J.P. Chaline, 'Sociétés savantes et académies de province en France dans la première moitié du xixe siècle', in François (ed.), *Sociabilité*, pp. 169–80, esp. map 2, p. 172.

[20] Speitkamp, *Verwaltung der Geschichte*, p. 115; on distribution within Germany: Voss, 'Akademien', pp. 156–62. Wussow, *Erhaltung der Denkmäler*, p. 41, and appendix III.

[21] Brown, *Care of Ancient Monuments*, p. 34; Levine, *Amateur and Professional*, p. 45.

[22] Chaline, *Sociabilité*, p. 292.   [23] Levine, *Amateur and Professional*, pp. 48–53.

created by Humboldt in Germany and by the British Association for the Advancement of Science.[24] In the 1840s in Britain, the Royal Archaeological Institute of Great Britain and Ireland and the British Archaeological Association,[25] started to hold itinerant annual congresses, likewise inspired not only by the British Association for the Advancement of Science,[26] but now also by the French *Congrès archéologique*. Some county societies arranged combined sessions and in 1850 the Associated Architectural Societies formalised many of the hitherto casual links, while an annual joint publication offered a voice for smaller associations. Collaboration reached new heights through the Congress of Archaeological Societies first held in 1888. Organised by the Society of Antiquaries at the demand of a large number of archaeological societies,[27] its purpose differed little from the earlier congresses, but the outcome was more successful, setting nationwide aspirations for preservation and inventories in motion.[28] Coordination took longest across the many borders of the German world. Various associations had communicated with each other since the early nineteenth century, but a national umbrella organisation only emerged after several attempts. In the wake of the 1830s revolutions, the Franconian Freiherr von Aufseß, who would later found the Germanic National Museum in Nuremberg, tried in 1832 to invite all historical and archaeological associations for a general assembly but Count Metternich's opposition to this allegedly nationalist and liberal cause put an end to the endeavour.[29] After several further failed attempts, and another failed national revolution, the *Gesamtverein der deutschen Geschichts- und Alterthumsvereine* was finally founded in 1852. This General Association of German Historical and Antiquarian Associations encouraged collaboration between societies, provided a link with the Historical Commissions that had been set up in many states and held general annual assemblies; its *Korrespondenzblatt* facilitated the exchange of information and provided intelligence regarding foreign developments. At the turn of the century, the *Gesamtverein* acted as an umbrella organisation for 162 local societies and had become the major public voice in monument protection on the national level.[30]

Much like in Dickens' Pickwick controversy, in the drive towards national coordination, actors constantly looked for models abroad in the

---

[24] Chaline, *Sociabilité*, p. 394; correspondence de Caumont and Guizot, 1833–34, AN, F 17 3090; R. Fox, *The Culture of Science in France, 1700–1900* (Aldershot, 1992), pp. 543–64.
[25] Levine, *Amateur and Professional*, p. 50.   [26] Ibid., p. 49.
[27] *Proceedings of the Society of Antiquaries*, 2nd Ser., 12 (1888), p. 233.
[28] Levine, *Amateur and Professional*, p. 53.   [29] Voss, 'Akademien', p. 162.
[30] Brown, *Care of Ancient Monuments*, p. 37.

realms of history, archaeology or science more broadly. Some contacts between former academies and societies had survived the Revolutionary period, while others were newly established.[31] Honorary foreign members were frequently appointed to increase the prestige of a society and when national congresses were founded in the 1830s, foreign delegates were immediately invited. Exchange often occurred informally, but the French government, not happy just to coordinate the French societies, also attempted to provide official links with foreign bodies. As a result, the first yearbook of learned societies published by the Committee for Historic Works, envisaged to list groups inside and outside France alike. In the end only the first volume on France was ever published, but in 1857, the new *Revue des Sociétés savantes de la France et de l'Etranger* was planned as an international liaison-organ. Particular weight was accorded to historical and archaeological concerns, and the first volume published contributions from the Society of Antiquaries of London, the British Royal Archaeological Institute and the *Gesamtverein*. Although the foreign focus of the *Revue* only lasted for two years,[32] the exchange of publication continued.[33] While the state found it hard to orchestrate international exchange in the way foreseen, private societies took over. Provincial scholars rather than the Committee for Historical Works published subsequent yearbooks on foreign societies. The relatively similar institutional developments should therefore in part be ascribed to this interest and information.

The development of associations was also shaped by the state's involvement in other ways which long preceded the nineteenth century. From the seventeenth century, learned societies delivered expertise in return for recognition, legal existence and often financial support from the state.[34] During the nineteenth century, however, state influence over the new historical societies was more extensive in France and Germany than in England. Using societies for inventory projects was practical, but also reflected an attempt to control provincial independence in France. In many German states, it was hoped to achieve identification with the new particular states after the territorial regrouping of the Napoleonic Wars, hence princes or high civil servants often instigated the foundation of societies. Here, financial support went even further than in France. Societies often had their budget approved and were obliged to fulfil the demands of the authorities.[35]

---

[31] On pre-Revolutionary contacts see McClellan, 'Learned Societies'.
[32] *Revue des Sociétés savantes de la France et de l'Etranger*, published 1857–8, thereafter it became the *Revue des Sociétés savantes des départements*, published 1859–82.
[33] AN, F 17 3016.   [34] J.E. McClellan III, 'Learned Societies'.
[35] Speitkamp, *Verwaltung der Geschichte*, pp. 116–17.

This was in part a control device, but subsidising associations was also seen as a cheaper alternative to professional monument administrations. At first sight, there was less interference from the state in English private societies. Yet most of the more influential private associations, such as the SAL, derived part of their influence from a Royal Charter and the state also facilitated and encouraged activities of learned societies by providing a common space in Burlington House. In a different fashion, private societies were tied to the established order by integration into the machinery of Church restoration particularly in the early and high Victorian years.

The background of members of historical and antiquarian associations resembled each other in France, Germany and England, although available information varies.[36] In pre-1848 Germany, members came from the different courts, the nobility, the higher civil service, notables and *Bildungsbürger* such as clergymen, professors, grammar school teachers, physicians and apothecaries. In the second half of the century, local civil servants, primary school teachers, and smaller merchants gained ground.[37] The antiquarian community in England was relatively homogenous, and mostly Oxford- and Cambridge-educated. In the architectural societies, clerical membership was particularly high, but it varied geographically and at different times.[38] In France, the number of nobles and clerics in historically orientated societies was higher than in other learned societies, especially in the provinces, where pre-Revolutionary forms of enlightened sociability continued.[39] In all three countries, notables thus dominated the societies. Among them, particularly in the first half of the century, were many whose interest in the past was linked to a desire for feudal societies and religious revival. However, in all three countries larger parts of the educated middle classes were progressively included.[40] Their growing interest is not attributable to an increased interest in the past, but also to a desire for sociability and to the fact that membership was often an entrée into educated and respectable circles.[41]

Individual experiences of the past as well as the societies' contribution to heritage discourses varied. Doing much of the first hand research

---

[36] On the difficulty of comparing the social background see Koselleck, Spree, Steinmetz, 'Drei bürgerliche Welten?', pp. 14–58.
[37] Kunz, *Verortete Geschichte*, p. 68.
[38] It ranged from almost 77 per cent in the Architectural Society of the Archdeaconry of Northampton in 1844 to 7 per cent in London and Middlesex ten years later. Ordained members made up around an average of 20 per cent of amateurs and professionals engaged in historical, archaeological and antiquarian research during the period 1838 and 1886, see Levine, *Amateur and Professional*, pp. 48, 178, 184–5.
[39] Chaline, *Sociabilité*, pp. 206–12, 218–20, 242–52. [40] Ibid., p. 271.
[41] Ibid., passim; Levine, *Amateur and Professional*, p. 40; Speitkamp, *Verwaltung der Geschichte*, p. 115.

on local monuments, archives, ethnography and language, the societies contributed crucial local expertise through inventory projects and publications. While the papers of smaller societies were generally read by members only,[42] through the exchange of publications, the transactions published by the larger societies, and the new umbrella publications, knowledge about local history and heritage was slowly diffused among each nations' educated classes. Beyond this creation and propagation of knowledge, some societies were more actively involved in the preservation of historical objects and buildings than others. Activities included the purchase and restoration of monuments, the establishment of museums, or alerting the public and the authorities to particular threats.[43] Range of activities was in part delimited by the existence of other preservation institutions. In England, members of the SAL showed comparatively early interest in the fate of historic buildings. Accordingly, the earliest pleas for a systematic preservation of buildings tried to place the SAL at the core of policies. Most involved with historic building, however, were architectural associations, seeing devotion to medieval English architecture as an expression of Christian piety. In France, the contribution of local societies in restoring monuments was considerable before the foundation of the Historic Monuments Commission.[44] Afterwards, as funds for the restoration of listed monuments were allocated by the state, the role of private societies changed. Rather than caring directly for monuments, societies now mainly alerted the authorities to threats, although some societies still looked after non-listed buildings on their own.[45] In Germany, for some historic and antiquarian associations, preservation was one of many interests, for others, it was their main preoccupation. For instance the broadly named Association for Art and Antiquities in Ulm and Upper Swabia dedicated its time mostly to the restoration and safeguarding of Ulm Cathedral.[46] By mid-century, several associations were created without a learned focus, solely dedicated to the completion or restoration of particular national monuments. The best known of these was the *Kölner Dombauverein*, the fundraising and propaganda body for the completion of Cologne Cathedral.[47]

Among the members of private societies, very different ideas of how to treat monuments existed. While many associations were occupied with the actual conservation of monuments, an example from the Palatinate shows that symbolic resurrections of heritage were sometimes more highly valued

[42] Chaline, *Sociabilité*, p. 290.   [43] For examples see ibid., pp. 313–4.
[44] Bercé, 'Sociétés savantes', pp. 155–67.   [45] MAP 80/1/124.   [46] Voss, 'Akademien', p. 161.
[47] On associations dedicated to erect new national monuments see Tacke, *Denkmal im sozialen Raum*.

than the monuments themselves. In 1872, the Historical Association of the Palatinate, in consultation with the Bavarian government had planned the restoration of the castles of Wolfenstein. Given the remoteness of the location and expected costs, association and state settled for a painting in oil or a photograph instead. While few local Pfälzer would have been able to travel to Wolfenstein, the picture could be moved to the local capital Speyer, where it was widely accessible.[48] While many local societies were involved in the day-to-day running of preservation, in general they were little preoccupied with theoretical statements on the methods of preservation, leaving this ground to larger associations, particularly the *Gesamtverein*, the *Société française d'archéologie* and the *Society of Antiquaries* – although the latter long refused to take up pleas for systematic leadership.[49] Additionally, professional bodies, especially the RIBA in Britain, became increasingly important voices in restoration techniques. Comparatively, the influence of the RIBA on restoration was stronger than that of the professional associations of architects in Germany or France, as no state administration for restoration existed in England. In Germany the professional associations of architects and engineers, the *Verband Deutscher Architekten- und Ingenieursvereine*, founded a year after German unification, also became an increasingly important voice on the care of monuments alongside the *Gesamtverein*.[50] In France, the professional body dominant in restoration was the core of architects working for the Historic Monuments Commission. However, after the death of Viollet-le-Duc, the Society of Architects also became an important player in changing ideas about restoration within the profession.

While historical, archaeological and antiquarian societies continued to increase in number, in the last third of the nineteenth century, they also got increasing competition from two sides.[51] Firstly, the professionalisation of historical sciences and of the care of monuments limited associations' influence. While research was done more and more by academic historians, the new professional bodies of architects as well as government preservation agencies increasingly assumed duties formerly performed by the historical associations. Secondly, new associative forms appeared, offering alternative forms of sociability and new approaches to heritage. These societies 'with a special view to the monument question of the day' put less emphasis on

[48] Applegate, *Nation of Provincials*, p. 47.
[49] *Gentleman's Magazine*, 58 (1788), pp. 689–91; Evans, *Society of Antiquaries*, pp. 309–12.
[50] Speitkamp, *Verwaltung der Geschichte*, p. 119.
[51] Chaline, 'Les Sociétés savantes en Allemagne, Italie et Royaume-Uni', 87.

research but privileged activism; other groups promoted the enjoyment of heritage through tourism or other leisure activities, such as photography.[52]

Many of the new preservation societies were triggered by a threat to a particular heritage, but most perceived the forces of industrialisation and capitalism more generally as a danger of an unprecedented scale:

> In this age, to a degree never before approached change moves with swift and merciless strides. Not the purging waves of Puritanic reform, not the fire and sword of civil war and revolution, nor 'the wreckful siege of battering days', not even all combined have wrought such havoc among our ancient buildings as the commercial activity and the constructive and destructive restorations of to-day.[53]

In the historiography, it is generally accepted that underlying the direct stimuli were changing ideas about the role of heritage. However, national research on the formation of these preservation organisations – unless resulting in hagiographic celebrations – is dominated by two debates on their outlook and significance. It is first of all disputed whether societies were motivated by cultural pessimism and nostalgia, propagating a return to a lost form of society or whether their desire for alternative approaches to the negative sides of progress was in effect highly modern. There is furthermore considerable debate as to whether the societies' claim to represent public opinion at large should be accepted or whether they were essentially fringe organisations. To better understand their stance towards social questions as well as their representivity, it helps to reassess the main societies on the national level in a comparative way and to place them in their wider national and international networks.

Ancient buildings and open spaces in England

Of the three countries, England not only had the earliest antiquarian society, it also possessed the first self-proclaimed preservation associations with the Common Preservation Society (CPS), founded in 1865, and the Society for the Protection of Ancient Buildings (SPAB), founded in 1877, followed by the National Trust in 1894. All have received their own histories and figure prominently in most accounts on Victorian preservation, but are often written about in isolation. It is worth re-examining their familiar histories in connection with each other to start the comparative perspective. This will reveal much more coherence within the English movement

---

[52] Brown, *Care of Ancient Monuments*, p. 34.
[53] SPAB, *Annual Report*, 20 (1897), pp. 7–8.

than usually thought. It also helps to understand why subsequently the SPAB, rather then the CPS or the Trust became an important model for continental preservation.

The Commons Preservation Society founded in 1865 by the Liberal politician George Shaw-Lefevre (later Baron Eversley), was very different from the old learned societies in purpose and activity.[54] Created to unite opposition against the enclosure of commons by landowners, it brought together anti-aristocratic Radical land reformers and more moderate Liberals motivated by their belief in the civilising and healthy impact of open spaces. At first sight, the Society's focus seemed narrow, but in time the CPS was also influential in the protection of historic monuments and landscape more broadly, as will be seen when discussing preservation legislation. Moreover, the Society, whose most prominent supporter was perhaps John Stuart Mill, was an important meeting place for future preservationists. It brought together the founders of the National Trust, Robert Hunter, Octavia Hill, Hardewicke Rawnsley and Hugh Lupus Grosvenor, Duke of Westminster. James Bryce and Charles Dilke, instrumental in setting up the CPS, were also future supporters of the Trust and the Society for the Protection of Ancient Buildings;[55] other recurrent names include Henry Fawcett, later Postmaster General, the Buxtons,[56] Thomas Huxley and Sir William Harcourt, later Chancellor of the Exchequer.[57]

While the CPS addressed a particularly British problem with its fight against enclosures, the first society claiming to champion heritage more universally was founded in England too, twelve years after the CPS.[58] Spurred to action by a call for the restoration of Tewkesbury Abbey in *The Times*, the arts and crafts designer, and recent convert to socialism, William Morris,[59] suggested the foundation of an association 'to keep watch on old monuments, to protest against all "restoration" that means more than keeping out wind and weather, and, by all means, literary and other, to awaken

---

[54] A. Warren, 'Lefevre, George John Shaw-, Baron Eversley (1831–1928)', *DNB* (online edn, 2006), www.oxforddnb.com/view/article/36055.

[55] Miele, 'First Conservation Militants', p. 26.

[56] J. Gaze, *Figures in a Landscape. A History of the National Trust* (London, 1988), p. 24.

[57] J. Jenkins, P. James, *From Acorn to Oak Tree. The Growth of the National Trust, 1895–1994* (London, 1994), p. 18.

[58] On the history of the SPAB see Miele, 'A Small Knot of Cultivated People', 73–79; Miele, 'The First Conservation Militants'; Miele, 'Morris and Conservation', in Miele (ed.), *From William Morris. Building Conservation and the Arts and Crafts Cult of Authenticity, 1877–1939* (Studies in British Art 14, New Haven, London, 2005).

[59] F. MacCarthy, 'Morris, William (1834–1896)', *DNB* (online edn, 2004), www.oxforddnb.com/view/article/19322. On Morris' broader relationship with the past see: A Vaninskaya, *William Morris and the Idea of Community: Romance, History and Propaganda 1880–1914* (Edinburgh, 2010).

a feeling that our ancient buildings are not mere ecclesiastical toys, but sacred monuments to the nation's growth and hope'.[60] In his famous letter to the *Athenaeum*, Morris denounced the existing institutions in charge of the national past. He particularly attacked clergymen and architects, as they formed an unholy alliance to restore as many churches as possible for their own financial gains, and concluded that neither group should be entrusted with the maintenance of national treasures. Conservation should instead be the responsibility of non-specialist members of the public with no vested interest.

Morris' reasoning followed John Ruskin's *The Seven Lamps of Architecture* published almost three decades earlier. Ruskin introduced the idea that buildings belonged to the past and to the future but not to the present: 'We have no right whatever to touch [old buildings]. They are not ours. They belong partly to those who built them, and partly to all the generations of mankind who are to follow us.'[61] Changing them through restoration was unforgivable, as restoration was 'a lie from beginning to end'.[62] A worn original might not be able to tell as much as the first design; yet at least it was incapable of lying. Not only was it impossible to know all the details of the original designs, Ruskin argued, the changed conditions of production also made it unfeasible to reproduce the quality of the artwork. While the medieval mason had been free and creative, the Victorian worker, alienated by a pitiless wage economy in a mass-production society, was condemned to produce lifeless work.[63] While Morris acknowledged only Ruskin as an intellectual forebear, criticism of restoration of course dated back almost a century. In the 1790s, John Carter, Richard Gough and John Milner had led early opposition to James Wyatt's cathedral restorations and the belief that restoration destroyed the authenticity of buildings had grown among the archaeological societies since the 1840s. The idea was not essentially English either, as Morris later claimed. The catchphrase 'to repair, not to restore', can be traced back to the French architectural critic Didron in the 1840s.[64] By the 1860s, the 'anti-restoration' party as the Anglican press also dubbed it, had gained some ground among architects and the Church of England.[65] However, the missionary zeal and vociferous ways of Morris'

---

[60] *The Athenaeum*, 10 March 1877, p. 326, repr. in N. Kelvin, *The Collected Letters of William Morris* (4 vols., Princeton, 1984–1996), I, no. 382, pp. 351–2; Miele 'Morris and Conservation', p. 31.

[61] J. Ruskin, *The Seven Lamps of Architecture* (repr. New York, 1989), p. 197.

[62] The manifesto was reproduced on the title page of SPAB's *Annual Report* since 1901.

[63] Miele, '"A Small Knot of Cultivated People"', 73.

[64] On the transfer of anti-restoration ideas across Europe see S. Tschudi-Madsen, *Restoration and Anti-Restoration. A Study in English Restoration Philosophy* (Oslo, 1976), pp. 63–103; Stüler, 'Über die Restauration mittelalterlicher Bauwerke', copy, GStA PK, I. HA Rep. 93 B Ministerium der öffentlichen Arbeiten, Nr. 2331, fols. 81–9.

[65] Miele, '"A Small Knot of Cultivated People"', 73.

new SPAB gave 'anti-restoration' a different notoriety on the British and international levels. Yet by turning his back on the existing lobby and by choosing an anti-architect and anti-religious tone, Morris severed the link with those his Society tried to influence most.

As Chris Miele observed, the novelty of the SPAB consisted less in its anti-restoration attitude, than in being the first aesthetes' society for aesthetes 'with no vested interest in what was being done to ancient buildings except an interest in their status as historical monuments and works of art'.[66] Lacking institutional support, the 'Anti-Scrape Society' – the pet name derived from the practice of scraping facades during restoration – set a new trend by relying on mobilising public opinion. Consequently, the first *Annual Report* noted with glee: 'The Society has already been much noticed in the Press, always with respect, and generally with unqualified approval'. It was mentioned in the *Athenaeum*, the *Globe*, the *Daily Telegraph*, the *Daily News*, the *Manchester Guardian*, the *Architect*, the *Whitehall Review*, the *Graphic*, and *Truth* and 'many of the leading country journals', and was proud that a 'clever artist in *Fun*' and the satirical magazine *Punch* had 'given us good help' through 'pen and pencil' (ills. 2.4–2.5).[67] The caricatures captured the central elements of the 'anti-restoration' discourse in a concise way. *Fun* took up Ruskin's warning from the *Lamp of Memory* that restoration was as impossible as resurrecting the ghost of the original mason. Heritage's new enemies, the 'restorers', were easily identifiable as the triumvirate of 'architect, parson and squire' denounced in Morris' writings.[68] *Punch*, on the other hand, endeared ancient buildings by likening them to the face of a beloved aging grandmother, taking up a metaphor popular with preservationists since Victor Hugo's *Notre Dame*.[69]

Despite these responses in the press, success was slow. In the first five years, the SPAB prevented restoration in just five cases. The society's record only improved when the architect Hugh Thackeray Turner (1853–1937), apprentice of the restorationist architect Sir George Gilbert Scott, took over the secretariat in 1883.[70] In addition to its publicity campaigns, the SPAB now also provided technical advice.[71] In part, the Society's early difficulties stemmed from Morris' radical ideas about how preservation could prepare

---

[66] Miele, 'The First Conservation Militant', p. 20.   [67] SPAB, *Annual Report*, 1 (1878), p. 13.

[68] See Morris' letter to *The Athenaeum*, 10 March 1877, p. 326; Miele '"A Small Knot of Cultivated People"', 75.

[69] On later recurrences, SPAB, *Annual Report*, 35 (1912), 55–63.

[70] Hugh Thackeray Turner (1853–1937), F.S.A. was in office between 1883 and 1912, see J. West, 'SPAB Committee Members: Biographical Notes', in Miele (ed.), *From William Morris*, pp. 323–35, here p. 331.

[71] Miele, 'The First Conservation Militant', pp. 33, 35–6.

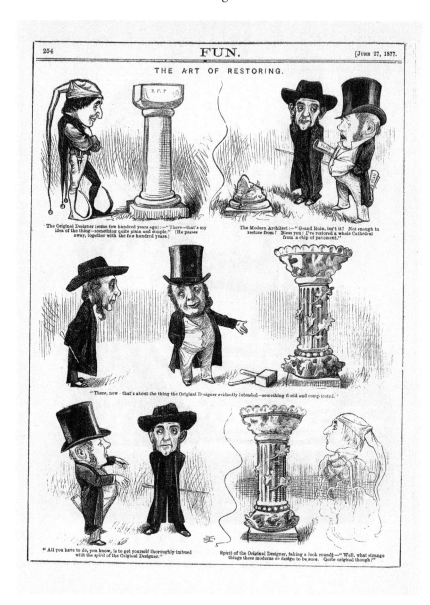

2.4 'The Art of Restoring' takes up a warning from Ruskin's *Lamp of Memory* that restoration was as impossible as resurrecting the dead and follows Morris' condemnation of architects and parsons. *Fun*, 27 June 1877, p. 254.

PUNCH'S ALMANACK FOR 1878.

THE MANIA FOR RESTORATION.

CHORUS. "{MAMMA! GRANDMAMMA! GREAT-GRAND'MA!} WHAT *HAVE* YOU BEEN DOING WITH YOURSELF? WHERE IS YOUR BEAUTIFUL WHITE HAIR, AND YOUR PRETTY CAP, AND YOUR BLACK SILK GOWN?"
Great-Grandmamma. "WELL, MY DEARS, ALL THE FINE OLD BUILDINGS ARE BEING 'RESTORED' ACCORDING TO THE ORIGINAL DESIGN. WHY SHOULDN'T FINE OLD LADIES HAVE A CHANCE AS WELL?"

2.5 The Mania for Restoration in 'Punch's Almanack for 1878' used a popular
anti-restorationist metaphor, likening old buildings to the face of a beloved mother or
grandmother. On seeing their revamped ancestor, the chorus of descendants exclaims:
"Mamma! Grandmamma! Great-Grand'ma! What have you been doing with yourself?
Where is your beautiful white hair, and your pretty cap, and your black silk gown?"
Great-Grandmamma retorts: "Well, my dears, all the fine old buildings are being 'restored'
according to the original design. Why shouldn't fine old ladies have a chance as well?"
Punch, 14 Dec. 1877.

socialism. Morris made it clear that he objected to the ownership of national
monuments by private individuals who had no obligation to save them for
the people. He repeatedly warned against capitalism's destruction of the
country's architecture and landscape.[72] On the other hand, a properly
conserved building, he reasoned, could encourage social change. Using
Ruskin's vision of a free and creative medieval mason, Morris propagated
that ancient buildings could serve as an example to revolutionaries on what
unalienated labour could accomplish. In a socialist society, they would
therefore be the seed for the rejuvenation of the arts. In the interim, they
were a way to educate and refine the nation. Therefore, those with enough
'time, money and comfort', 'a small knot of cultivated people' should

---

[72] See E.P. Thompson, *William Morris. Romantic to Revolutionary* (New York, 1976), pp. 226–42.

conserve the national monuments for the people until a classless society was achieved.[73]

Colleagues close to Morris, in particular his friend the architect Philip Webb, backroom boy of both Morris' decorative arts company and of the SPAB,[74] were alive to the fact that these views might not endear Victorian society. If the Society was to be successful, they reasoned, it was important to appeal to as broad a stratum of society as possible. Hence, the manifesto drafted by Morris, Webb and George Wardle, Morris' manager at Morris & Co, which all prospective members had to sign, was cleansed of political statements. It also did not reflect the often more creative appropriations of the past by many of the founding members from the Arts and Crafts crowd – who after all spent almost more time posing in period dress than writing petitions. Instead it adopted a language of aesthetics, summarising the SPAB's aims simply as to 'stave off decay by daily care... and resist all tampering with either fabric or ornament of the buildings as it stands'.[75]

Nonetheless Morris' time as secretary involved a number of scandals and his secular and socialist views alienated potential supporters. Many of the Society's supporters did not share his vision of preservation as a political act. After Morris proclaimed at the 1884 General Annual Meeting that only in a socialist society conservation could triumph, a wave of membership withdrawals followed. After Morris' death in 1896 several members tried to formulate a Conservative agenda, in which the Society was not to provide a public service preserving buildings for the masses, unable to appreciate the finer notions of art, but for those of 'gentle breeding' who had the 'inborn feeling of reverence'.[76] The political agendas and underlying motives for preservation of SPAB members thus had little common ground. 'Only aesthetics and a shared mistrust of professionalism permitted consensus within a Society where, otherwise, there might have been none.'[77] Consequently, the SPAB's official voice between 1883 and 1912, the architect Thackeray Turner, persistently employed a language of connoisseurship and taste.

While many well-known personalities from the art world gave their support to the Society, serving as nominal committee members, the Society's decision-making members remained essentially close friends of Morris and

---

[73] Qu. in Miele, "'A Small Knot of Cultivated People'", 73–9.
[74] See P. Burman, 'Defining a Body of Tradition. Philip Webb', in Miele (ed.), *From William Morris*, pp. 67–99.
[75] SPAB, Manifesto (1877).
[76] See H.E. Luxmoore's speech at the 1898 Annual Meeting, SPAB, *Annual Report*, 21 (1898), 61–2.
[77] Miele, "'A Small Knot of Cultivated People'", 79.

Webb from the Arts and Crafts world. Given the challenge to the professional position of architects and the secular tones with which the Society
remained associated, the number of members remained relatively small in
the early years. The first *Annual Report* of 1878 mentioned 294 members,
slowly rising to 492 by 1914. The total number of people joining between
1877 and 1918 was 1374. National in outlook, the society had half its members in the central London area, followed by the South East; 4 per cent
of the membership was foreign.[78] The largest occupational group of the
Society were artists, many from the Arts and Crafts movement, followed
by clerisy, trade and manufacture, aristocracy and landed gentry, clergymen, lawyers and to a much lesser degree schoolteachers, civil servants and
engineers.[79] The two professional groups most preoccupied with ecclesiastical architecture in Victorian and Edwardian Britain were decidedly
underrepresented, although among the Society's more active members were
many architects. Clerical membership in particular was much lower than
in the archaeological and architectural societies, although London and the
South East, where the SPAB's membership was strongest, generally had an
equally low percentage in ordained members among the learned societies.
Overall, members were well connected in the arts, politics and the court,
yet the Society lacked access to the highest circles of politics and to the
inner circles of those controlling church restoration.

Within the world of private societies, the SPAB's attempts to secure support also encountered mixed responses. In one of its earliest campaigns for
Wren's City churches, the Society collaborated successfully with the City
Church and Churchyard Protection Society, whose committee featured
many of the same names as that of the SPAB,[80] but efforts to establish
similar cooperation in rural areas were unsuccessful. Although interpersonal links existed with county societies, for instance Canon Greenwell,
FRS, FSA, and SPAB committee member since the beginning, was president of the Archaeological and Architectural Society of Durham and
Northumberland, the track had to be abandoned.[81] Possibly because of their

[78] SPAB, *Annual Report*, 37 (1914), 83–89; J. West, 'The Society for the Protection of Ancient Buildings,
1877–96, Committee, Membership and Casework', in Miele (ed.), *From William Morris*, pp. 299–
322; A. Crawford, 'Supper at Gatti's. The SPAB and the Arts and Crafts Movement', in ibid.,
pp. 101–27, here pp. 102–4.
[79] Crawford, 'Supper at Gatti's', p. 104.   [80] Miele, 'The First Conservation Militant', p. 52.
[81] SPAB Archives, 'Canon Greenwell on Restoration'; S. Huggins, 'On the So-Called Restoration of
our Cathedral and Abbey Churches', *Proceedings of the Liverpool Architectural and Archaeological
Society. Twenty Third Session. Eleventh Meeting, 5th April 1871* (Liverpool, 1871), pp. 118–31; *Opening
Address of the Section of Architecture at the Lewes Meeting August 2 1883, by J. T. Micklethwaite, F.S.A.*
Reprinted from the *Archaeological Journal*, vol. xl, p. 386, see SPAB Archives, Publications.

religious bias, many societies had different views on church restoration.[82] If not objecting to the principles expressed in the SPAB's prospectus, they objected to 'its principal originators and supporters'.[83] Cooperation with London bodies was more successful. Since 1879 the SPAB was in close contact with members of the Antiquaries, a year later the British Archaeological Association added its weight, and from the end of the 1880s the Secretary of the Royal Archaeological Institute closely collaborated with the SPAB. In order to deal with cases in the rest of the country and abroad, the SPAB employed the services of a clipping agency and used its activist members to build its own network.[84]

By the time the antagonism between the SPAB, the Church of England and the architectural profession was slowly attenuating, another preservation body with shared concerns, but a different core-purpose entered the scene: the National Trust. Established to hold 'places of historic interest or natural beauty' for the nation, it was envisaged, like the SPAB, to 'consist of men and women who should be free from the tendency to sacrifice such treasures to mercenary considerations, or to vulgarizing them in accordance with popular cries'.[85]

Its creation emerged from a longstanding collaboration between its founders, within a densening philanthropic network. The three main founders, Octavia Hill, the most important social housing reformer of her generation, Robert Hunter, solicitor for the CPS, later knighted for his work as chief solicitor of the Post Office, and Hardwicke Rawnsley, a clergyman from the Lake District, were motivated by complementary priorities.[86] Hunter championed the rights of public access against landlords. Hill viewed open spaces as fundamental for the physical and moral wellbeing of the working classes and aimed to provide 'open air

[82] Miele, 'The First Conservation Militant', p. 30.
[83] H.G. Fowler, *Church Restoration. What to do, and what to avoid by G. Hodgson Fowler, F.S.A.; F.R.I.B.A., read on February 10th 1882, Leeds Architectural Society* (Leeds, 1882), SPAB Archives, Publications.
[84] Miele, 'The First Conservation Militant', pp. 30–1.
[85] Octavia Hill, qu. in G. Darley, *Octavia Hill* (London, 1990), p. 297.
[86] G. Murphy, *Founders of the National Trust* (London, 1987); on individuals E.M. Bell, *Octavia Hill* (London, 1942); W.T. Hill, *Octavia Hill. Pioneer of the National Trust and Housing Reform* (London, 1956); Darley, *Octavia Hill*; Darley, 'Hill, Octavia (1838–1912)', *DNB* (online edn, 2004), www.oxforddnb.com/view/article/33873; Chubb, 'Hunter, Sir Robert (1844–1913)', rev. Graham Murphy, ibid., www.oxforddnb.com/view/article/34064; E. Rawnsley, *Canon Rawnsley. An Account of His Life* (Glasgow, 1923); G. Murphy, 'Rawnsley, Hardwicke Drummond (1851–1920)', *DNB* (online edn, 2004), www.oxforddnb.com/view/article/37884. On the broader epistemic community see M. Hall, 'The Politics of Collecting: The Early Aspirations of the National Trust', *Transactions of the RHS*, 13 (2003), 345–57 and A. Swenson, 'Founders of the National Trust (*act.* 1894–1895)', *DNB* (online edn, 2009), www.oxforddnb.com/view/theme/95571.

sitting rooms for the poor' (see ill. 2.6).[87] Rawnsley's fight started in the Lake District which he longed to preserve in its Wordsworthian glory.[88]

They shared many intellectual and personal influences with the founders of the SPAB, most importantly John Ruskin. Hill had met Ruskin through her activity for the Ladies' Guild and he assisted her to embark on her work as a housing reformer by lending money to buy slum properties in 1865.[89] Although they were estranged in later years, she remained deeply influenced by his ideas. The Slade Professor also introduced Hill to his Oxford pupil Hardwicke Rawnsley, who would continue his fight for the Lakes (see ill. 2.7). Long before establishing the National Trust, the three founders were linked through personal ties and common voluntary work, which also connected them to the Trust's wider epistemic community. Working in numerous areas, they were true activists, driving themselves to physical and mental exhaustion, constantly attending meetings and founding new pressure groups for a variety of purposes. Rawnsley, for example, apart from his preservationist activities, was elected to the first Cumberland County Council as an Independent Liberal, spoke all over the country on behalf of the Armenian Relief Fund, raised numerous memorials, campaigned against 'pernicious literature' and was one of three men responsible for the lighting of 2,548 bonfires throughout Britain to celebrate Queen Victoria's Diamond Jubilee.[90] Both Hunter and Hill were described as sober and constrained; 'only the clergyman looks as if he ever found life a treat'.[91] Although a minister in a remote location, he had seen more of the world than Hill or Hunter, frequently travelling in Europe, the Middle East and the United States.[92]

Collaborative work for preservation started when Hill contacted Hunter in her fight to save the fields at Swiss Cottage in relation to one of her housing projects. As a result she joined the CPS in 1875. The following year, her sister Miranda and Hunter's sister Dorothy embarked upon a common venture and created the Kyrle Society, a much forgotten, but influential headspring of the Trust. Its aim was beautifying the life of the

[87] Qu. in P. Weideger, *Gilding the Acorn. Behind the Façade of the National Trust* (London, 1994), p. 16; see O. Hill, *Our Common Land* (London, 1877); Hill, 'Natural Beauty as a National Asset', *Nineteenth Century*, 58 (1905), 935–41; R. Whelan (ed.), *Octavia Hill and the Social Housing Debate. Essays and Letters by Octavia Hill* (London, 1998).
[88] See H.D. Rawnsley, *A Nation's Heritage* (London, 1920); Cannadine, 'The First Hundred Years', p. 14.
[89] Jenkins, James, *From Acorn to Oak Tree*, p. 6.   [90] Ibid., p. 12.
[91] Weideger, *Gilding the Acorn*, p. 12.
[92] R. Fedden, *The National Trust. Past and Present* (London, 1968, revised edn, 1974), p. 21, Weideger, *Gilding the Acorn*, p. 25.

2.6 'Our Plea for Open Spaces' recognises that Octavia Hill's calls became increasingly supported, yet sadly only by the 'wise of heart and the kindly'. *Punch*, 9 June 1883, p. 266.

2.7 John Ruskin's battles against the coming of the railways in the Lake District was caricatured in Wordsworthian language. 'Lady of the Lake Loquitor', *Punch*, 5 February 1876, p. 34.

working classes. Its Open Space committee was organised by Octavia, Robert was the legal adviser, while William Morris served as a lecturer for the Society's decorative branch.[93] CPS member Hugh Lupus Grosvenor, Duke of Westminster, the future president of the National Trust, whom Octavia Hill had first met on the Committee of the Charity Organisation

[93] Jenkins, James, *From Acorn to Oak Tree*, p. 21.

Society in 1870, was president.[94] Links between the preservationists were further strengthened campaigning for particular sites, especially Hampstead Heath.

It was as the result of one such campaign, when the house of seventeenth-century diarist John Evelyn in Deptford was lost after his descendants wished to present it to the Metropolitan Board of Works, but no legal means existed for such a transaction, that Hill and Hunter grew increasingly convinced that a new kind of preservation society with the power to hold land was needed.[95] At the National Association for the Promotion of Social Science, Hunter outlined in 1884 ideas for creating such a body as a joint stock company. Hill suggested calling it a 'trust' instead of 'a company' to bring forward 'its benevolent rather than its commercial character'. Hunter tentatively pencilled '?National Trust' on her letter, but more than a decade elapsed before the society's foundation, primarily because George John Shaw-Lefevre vetoed the creation fearing it might distract from the CPS.[96]

Hill and Hunter continued their fight for open spaces, founding a range of other bodies, such as the Kent and Sussex branch of the CPS in 1888,[97] and intensified collaboration with Rawnsley, by now married to a family friend of Hill's. Rawnsley had made himself champion of the Lake District, founding several societies in the process. For instance in 1883, the year he became vicar near Keswick, he embarked on his mission to stop the railway traversing the untouched landscape. Out of a talk at the Wordsworth Society, the Lake District Defence Society was born and the Borrowdale and Derwent Water Defence Fund was established. The CPS, where Hunter was struggling to keep the railway out of Epping Forest, offered its support and throughout England people joined the eventually successful campaign. A second project against the railway touching Lake Ennerdale was subsequently won, making Rawnsley a national profile figure.[98] He went on with his local work, reviving inter alia the Keswick and District Footpath Association, during a new row in the Lakes over the enclosure of the footpath to Lattrigg and turned to the CPS again in 1893 to save the Lodore Fall south of Keswick. The failure of the latter campaign led to a revival of the idea to create a land-holding Trust, by now reinforced by fears over the effects the local government reform might have upon ancient towns and landscapes.[99] Moreover, foreign models for such

[94] Ibid., pp. 14–15.
[95] Fedden, *The National Trust*, p. 17; Jenkins, James, *From Acorn to Oak Tree*, p. 20.
[96] Octavia Hill to Robert Hunter, Feb 1885, NT Archives, Acc. 6; Jenkins, James, *From Acorn to Oak Tree*, p. 21; Fedden, *National Trust*, p. 18; Weideger, *Gilding the Acorn*, p. 28.
[97] Gaze, *Figures in a Landscape*, p. 33. [98] Weideger, *Gilding the Acorn*, p. 26.
[99] M. Hall, 'Affirming Community Life. Preservation, National Identity and the State, 1900', in Miele (ed.), *From William Morris*, pp. 129–57 and below, Chapter 6.

a Trust were by then available. Charles Eliot junior, son of the President of Harvard University, had employed Hunter's earlier ideas to found the Trustees of Public Reservations in Massachusetts in 1891, which in turn could now provide a model for the constitution of a National Trust in England.[100]

The launch of the Trust was carefully orchestrated to integrate the new body into the existing networks of Victorian philanthropy, art and politics. Hunter, Hill and Rawnsley organised a preliminary meeting at the CPS offices on 16 November 1893. In view of his active role in the Hampstead Heath Extensions Committee and the support he had given to Miranda Hill's Kyrle Society, the Duke of Westminster was invited to become the first president. As a great landowner he could inspire confidence in those who might endow the Trust with legacies. A meeting in July 1894 at Grosvenor House was held to approve the draft constitution. The fifty-member Provisional Council, which oversaw the subsequent incorporation of the Trust, included not only preservationist activists Sir John Lubbock (later first Baron Avebury), Shaw-Lefevre and Rawnsley's school friend Professor Gerald Baldwin Brown, leading expert on preservation in other countries, but many illustrious figures of Victorian politics, art and science, from the Marquess of Dufferin and Ava (the Trust's second president), the future Prime Minister Lord Rosebery, the President of the Royal Academy Sir Frederic Leighton, the scientist Thomas Henry Huxley, the Provost of Eton James John Hornby, the Master of Trinity Henry Montagu Butler, the painters William Holman Hunt and G.F. Watts, the novelist Mrs Humphry Ward, and the suffragist leader Mrs Fawcett.[101] At the first official meeting, organisations which would be useful for the Trust's purpose were also represented – among them the Linnaean Society, the Royal Academy of Arts, the Royal Botanic Society and the Trustees of Public Reservations in Massachusetts, the CPS and the Kyrle Society – and preparations had been made such that the Trust also received its first property: Dinas Oleu, a clifftop in Wales, given by Fanny Talbot, a friend of Rawnsley and Ruskin.

---

[100] NT, *Report* (1896); Gaze, *Figures in a Landscape*, p. 33, Jenkins, James, *From Acorn to Oak Tree*, p. 22; M. Waterson, *The National Trust. The First Hundred Years* (London, 1994), p. 36; M. Hall, 'Niagara Falls: Preservation and the Spectacle of Anglo-American Accord', in Hall (ed.), *Towards World Heritage*, pp. 23–43.

[101] Its Executive Committee was composed of the three founders, the Duke of Westminster, the Earl of Carlisle, the architect Alfred Waterhouse, the journalist John St Loe Strachey, CPS-member G.E. Briscoe Eyre, Philip Lyttleton Gell, Herbert Philips, Colonel Edmund Maurice, son of Frederick Denison Maurice whose Christian socialism had influenced several of the Trust founders, and Harriet Yorke Hill's companion and self-effacing fellow-worker, who remained Treasurer until 1924. NT Archives, Council and Executive Committee minutes.

Welcomed by the press as a 'Commons Preservation Society in active rather than merely advisory functions' whose existence would have spared Ruskin to write 'many a mournful page',[102] the Trust was also likened to a 'great National Gallery of natural pictures'.[103] By suggesting a solution for filling an important gap, rather than by chastising an existing system, it entered the scene in a much more consensual way than the SPAB and continuously expanded its good relations with other philanthropic and learned bodies. On top of using informal networks provided by families, friendships and cross-memberships to increase the Trust's reach, the founders also systematically formalised connections with other institutions: firstly, by choosing a number of bodies from major learned societies, museums, universities and preservation societies who would each year nominate half of the Council's effectives; secondly by collaborating with the new County Councils, to which many of the Trust's founding members also sought election. Thirdly, the Trust established a list of local correspondents and encouraged local societies to affiliate. While the SPAB had failed with a similar endeavour, thirty field clubs and archaeological societies had formally joined the Trust by 1914. It also frequently engendered new local societies, such as the Thames Preservation League.[104]

The Trust's success was helped as its public image was more gentle than the SPAB's. It avoided any presentation of itself as a partisan organisation.[105] The first promotional pamphlet mentioned a 'purely patriotic interest in those things which in the crush of our commercial enterprise and in the poverty of landholders or in the lack of local care, run the risk of passing away'.[106] Its membership has been described as a 'London Club who shared a pleasant community of interests' and 'could be relied upon to make a generous financial contribution'.[107] However, the interest in conservation was shared by a socially and ideologically quite heterogeneous group, whose motivations for preservationism had as different roots as among the SPAB membership. Politically, the majority of the early leadership was closer to the left than to the right. The Trust's early work was strongly marked by Octavia Hill's Christian-socialism. She had a certain dislike of people with money and saw preservation essentially as an extension of her social housing work and fight against deprivation. Hunter was a Liberal and

[102] *The Daily News*, 17 November 1893.   [103] *The Times*, 17 July 1894, p. 12.
[104] See NT, *Reports* 1896–1921, and NT Archives, Council and Executive Committee minutes.
[105] Mandler, *Stately Home*, p. 172.
[106] R. Hunter, *Its Aims and Its Works* (1897), NT Archives, Acc 3/2; Jenkins, James, *From Acorn to Oak Tree*, p. 28.
[107] R. Fedden, *The Continuing Purpose* (London, 1967), p. 17; Jenkins, James, *From Acorn to Oak Tree*, p. 40.

of the Provisional Council, fifteen members were either Liberal MPs or Liberal members of the House of Lords, but conservative imperialists and radical socialists were also amongst Trust supporters. Socially, middle class social reformers, dedicated to giving the people regular access to natural beauty, mingled with some of the biggest aristocratic landowners.[108] In part these differences resulted in a division of labour. While figureheads were chosen from among the aristocracy, and later the royal family, the day-to-day business was run by the founders with help from relatives and friends, like in the SPAB. A retrospective painting of a 1912 committee meeting projects the intimate, no-nonsense working atmosphere in sober upper middle class surroundings so very different from the depictions of the noisy and sociable meetings of the older learned societies (see ill. 2.8). Despite friends in high places, vigorous propaganda and effective fundraising, the Trust, however, also remained a small-scale organisation until the First World War. It had approximately 100 members in 1895, 500 in 1905 and 700 in 1915.[109] During the lifetime of the founders, it was far from obvious that the National Trust would eventually expand into 'the most important and successful voluntary society in modern Britain'.[110] It was only one of several similarly sized preservation bodies with different competences and concerns.

Because the core functions of the leading societies were different, with the CPS responsible for legal questions, the SPAB for restorations and campaigns for ancient buildings, and the Trust for landscapes and acquisitions, while a plethora of local societies championed research and particular sites, they could co-exist peacefully. Moreover, as membership and central concerns overlapped, collaborations were frequent and fruitful, creating an increasingly organised movement.[111] In particular, as it did not have enough funds or power to hold buildings itself, the SPAB saw in the Trust a source of help and often suggested buildings for acquisition. In turn, the Trust asked for conservation advice, even if it favoured more pragmatic solutions to secure access rather than following strict anti-restorationist principles.[112]

---

[108] Cannadine, 'The First Hundred Years', p. 14.

[109] Jenkins, James, *From Acorn to Oak Tree*, p. 30.

[110] Cannadine, 'The First Hundred Years', p. 11.

[111] None of the founders was originally a member of the SPAB, but Harriet Yorke, Octavia's friend and the Trust's Honorary Treasurer had joined in 1891 and Hill was given honorary membership in 1897. Other strong links were created by Ruskin, the Grosvenor family, the social reformer, Christian socialist and children's writer Thomas Hughes, the Arts and Crafts designer C.R. Ashbee, and the painter William Holman Hunt.

[112] Weideger, *Gilding the Acorn*, pp. 38–9; Gaze, *Figures in a Landscape*, pp. 31, 36, 87; Jenkins, James, *From Acorn to Oak Tree*, pp. 18–19, 29; see also Thackeray Turner to Alphone Guillon, 27 April 1894, SPAB Archives, 'Orange, Roman Theatre'.

2.8 National Trust Executive Meeting 15 April 1912. The hard working and philanthropic atmosphere depicted in this carefully composed amateur watercolour is in stark contrast to the boisterous portrayals of learned societies. Painted twelve years after the event, it offers an idealised image of the Trust's late founders. Beneath the portrait of the founder of the Commons Preservation Society Shaw-Lefevre above the mantelpiece, sits Sir Robert Hunter, while the botanist Francis Oliver stands up to speak on Blakeney Point. On Hunter's right stands Rawnsley. Octavia Hill did not attend the meeting because of severe illness but was included in the painting on the extreme right.

Unlike the CPS and the SPAB, the Trust was not primarily a propaganda machine, but a holding body, although during the early years, it regarded any issue affecting the spoliation of the countryside or of ancient build-ings as its concern and publicly intervened. This was welcome support for the CPS and the SPAB rather than competition. Thus, despite occasional disagreements, they had an excellent base for occasional collaboration, and co-existed happily, as their core activities were different.

The leadership of the main organisations moreover not only established links across the country, but sought to create contacts with preservationists across Europe and the Empire. Many shared the view pronounced by the founders of the Trust that preservation in England was important for impe-rial cohesion, as 'England, without the places of historic interest of natural beauty that are continually being threatened, would be a poorer country and less likely to attract and hold the affections of her sons who, far away are colonising the vast places of the Earth'.[113] Bryce and Rosebery, both also members of the Imperial Federation League and Rawnsley, systematically fostered the transatlantic link, while the Arts and Crafts designer C.R. Ashbee went on promotional tours to America, where a short-lived American Council of the National Trust (1901–1904) was established. The SPAB on the other hand more actively focussed on engendering European counterparts.

French friends of monuments and landscape protectors

In 1884, Morris' Society triumphantly noted that a 'French SPAB', locally known as the *Société des Amis des Monuments parisiens*, had been born with help from England.[114] Soon after its own foundation, the SPAB had started to intervene in foreign restorations, and to instigate preservation societies abroad.[115] Its manifesto was translated into French, Italian, German and Dutch, and distributed at the International Congress of Architects during the 1878 *Exposition universelle* in Paris.[116] The SPAB established correspondents in many countries, including in Italy, Holland, India, Egypt and Germany. In France, its principal correspondent was a future *Ami des Monuments*, the Parisian painter Adolphe Guillon. Having spent much time painting on the Côte d'Azure, Guillon took up residence in Vézelay in the 1850s, where his friend Viollet-le-Duc had been commissioned to restore the church.[117] Guillon continued to receive medals from the Salon in Paris, but contributed strongly to local heritage-making in Vézelay through his work as municipal councillor, the creation of a public library and a cantonal museum and through his popular paintings of landscapes and monuments. The first surviving correspondence between the SPAB and Guillon, however, did not concern English or French heritage, but a common intervention for the protection of Arab monuments in Egypt in 1880.[118] Regular correspondence on matters French and foreign followed until Guillon's death in 1896.

---

[113] NT, *Report* (1896), pp. 12–13.
[114] SPAB Archives, 5th Committee Minute Book, 24 January 1884 and 19 June 1884. SPAB, *Annual Report*, 7 (1884), 37–9. *The Builder* also reported about the foundation and George Warde sent a note to the *Athenaeum*. On the *Amis* see R. Fiori, 'La Société des amis des monuments parisiens, première société locale de sauvegarde du patrimoine à Paris', *Bulletin des amis des monuments rouennais* (2005/2006), 72–85.
[115] See below, Chapter 5.
[116] SPAB Archives, 2nd Committee Minute Book, 11 April 1878 and 3 April 1879.
[117] H. Blémont, 'Guillon, Adolphe Irenée', *Dictionnaire de Biographie Française* (vol. 17, 1989), p. 250.
[118] SPAB Archives, 3rd Committee Minute Book, 25 November 1880.

After reporting twice about the foundation of French 'SPABs' in 1879 and 1880,[119] but never mentioning them anew the SPAB's committee again discussed the possibility of instigating a sister society in 1881, but no new concrete steps were taken until two years later.[120] After reading an article by Charles Garnier in *Le Figaro* critiquing the refacing of the stonework of historic buildings in Paris, the SPAB forwarded its French manifesto to the architect of the Paris Opera, thanking him for 'furthering the views of the Society'.[121] When the SPAB learned that a preliminary meeting to found a French society would take place, a translation of the most recent *Annual Report* and copies of the English and French manifestos were also sent to Guillon 'for the consideration of the founders begging them to consider the basis this Society has found workable, before forming their own basis'.[122]

Many conscious and unconscious parallels exist between the English and French 'SPABs'. The letter that had kicked off the first was published in the *Athenaeum*, the aims of the *Société des Amis des Monuments parisiens*[123] were publicised in the bulletin of a society aspiring to be France's equivalent of the English *Athenaeum Club*,[124] the short-lived *Société historique – Cercle Saint Simon*.[125] The founding article was written by Charles Normand who would also be the principal soul and voice of this Society for the next twenty-five years. Son of the architect Alfred Normand (also a member of the new Society) Charles Normand was a government architect himself, although in the years he worked for the diverse *Amis des Monuments* organs, he dedicated himself to erudition on areas as diverse as

---

[119] At a Foreign Committee Meeting in 1879 a 'French society for the protection of ancient building' was mentioned (SPAB Archives, Foreign Committee Minute Book, 7 April 1879). To whom this referred is unclear as it was common practice to affix ones own label to foreign societies. In 1880, the *Annual Report*, 10 mentioned 'a Society having a similar aim to this has been set on foot in France, under the auspices of M. Guillon, an Honorary Member of this Society'. Again it is unclear to which Society this referred. None of these two 'French SPABs' were mentioned again.

[120] SPAB Archives, 3rd Committee Minute Book, 29 October 1881.

[121] SPAB Archives, 4th Committee Minute Book, 31 May 1883.

[122] SPAB Archives, 5th Committee Minute Book, 24 January 1884.

[123] C. Normand, 'Société des Amis des Monuments parisiens. Constituée dans le but de veiller sur les monuments d'art et sur la physionomie monumentale de Paris', *Bulletin – Cercle Saint-Simon, Société historique*, 2 (1884), 301–7.

[124] F.R. Cowell, *The Athenaeum. Club and Social Life in London, 1824–1974* (London, 1975).

[125] A number of founding members of the new preservation society, such as Eugène Münz, librarian of the *École des Beaux-arts* and Charles Normand were members or regular contributors. The *Cercle* counted among its founders such eminences as historians Monod and Lavisse and geographer Vidal de la Blache, and had a strong overlap with the *Société de l'Enseignement Superieur*, advocating university reform, see M.G. Monod, 'Rapport lu dans l'assemblée générale extraordinaire du 11 novembre', *Bulletin – Cercle Saint-Simon, Société historique*, 1 (1883), 1–12; 'Un jugement sur le Cercle Saint-Simon', *Bulletin – Cercle Saint-Simon, Société historique*, 2 (1884), 308–11.

ancient Mesopotamia and Art Nouveau, campaigning, and travel-guide-writing rather than designing buildings.[126]

Charles Normand, who shared Morris' tendency to embellish his own contribution, remained silent about the foreign impetus, so prominent in the English version of the story.[127] The reasons Normand gave for the foundation were firmly indigenous. The new body was established to find a way to reconcile the need to create healthier and more hygienic cities essential for the nation's fitness, with artistic considerations, i.e. the society's purpose was to provide an aesthetic alternative to the Haussmannisation of Paris. He also presented the destruction of the ruins of the Tuileries as a particular trigger for the Parisian society's inception.[128] As a much denser network of institutions already existed in France than in England, the article carefully marked out the Society's space within French heritage politics. Superficially, Normand stated, one might think the proposed Society had the same aims as the Historic Monuments Commission, 'the differences are however categorical and essential'.[129] As opposed to the Commission's national scope, the new Society was a local Parisian one. It was not only concerned with architecture, but with 'all branches of Art'.[130] When it referred to *monuments*, it did so in the widest possible sense, and not in the narrow one used by the state administration. It was not only concerned with past art but also with contemporary creations. Its work consisted not in distributing funds and overseeing the execution of works, but in alerting people to threats to monuments. It did not seek confrontation with the existing cultural administration, but collaboration, as roles were clearly divided: 'Sentinels at the outposts, we alert to danger, we fend off the blow, we prevent the ruin from falling down. We find the condemned, we plead their cause; others are the devout doctors who heal the fragile body parts of the beauties judged obsolete.'[131] As proof for the new society's conciliatory nature, Normand provided a support letter from a member of the Historic Monuments Commission, the late Henri Martin.[132] In contrast to

---

[126] See R. Fiori, 'Charles Normand, 1858–1934' in P. Sénéchal, C. Barbillon (eds.), *Dictionnaire critique des historiens de l'art actifs en France de la Révolution à la Première Guerre mondiale* (online edn, INHA, 2010), www.inha.fr/spip.php?article3171.

[127] SPAB, *Annual Report*, 7 (1884), 37–9.

[128] Normand, 'Société des Amis des Monuments parisiens', pp. 301–2.

[129] Ibid., p. 303.   [130] Ibid.   [131] Ibid.

[132] Bon-Louis-Henri Martin (1810–1883), worked as a notary, before concentrating upon writing novels and a prize-winning nineteen-volume *Histoire de France*. Professor at the Sorbonne for six months in 1848, he was elected to the *Académie des Sciences morales et politiques* in 1871 and to the *Académie française* in 1878. Editor for the *Siècle*, and an avowed republican, Henri Martin became mayor for the XVIᶜ arrondissement in 1870, *député* for Paris in 1871, and Senator in 1876. He was one of the founders and first president of the extreme-right *Ligue des Patriotes*, which

the British SPAB, the single largest group of members on the Society's first
committee were indeed architects restoring monuments for the Historic
Monuments Commission and the Diocesan Service.[133] The committee also
included two former Ministers of Fine Arts, Henri Wallon, perpetual secretary of the *Académie des inscriptions et belles lettres* and Antonin Proust, then
involved in rewriting a Monument Bill started under Wallon. More than
half of the remaining members worked for state art institutions as curators,
archivists or professors. The rest were architects, artists, journalists, and
politicians.[134]

From the first line of the first article, Normand linked the Society to the
history of French *patrimonialisation*, quoting Hugo's *Notre Dame de Paris*
and alluding to Montalembert's dictum that long memories make great
races. The Society also embraced a third line of tradition by electing as
first president Albert Lenoir, son of Alexandre Lenoir of the Revolutionary
Museum of French Monuments, member of the Institute and the Historic
Monuments Commission, and author of the first inventory of Parisian
historic buildings.[135] The wider membership was essentially motivated by
learned and aesthetic concerns – but while an aesthetic rhetoric served to
bridge ideological gaps among the SPAB's membership – here the founding
text used a patriotic rhetoric on top of the aesthetic one to overcome
potential divisions of faith or party:

> We want to work for the benefit of France, by trying to protect the buildings
> and artworks that create the charm and the reputation of her capital. Is it
> not through them that a constant education is provided imbuing peoples
> with the love of the forebears? Is it not a duty to transmit and accrete this
> heritage, which in countries disappeared from history still perpetuates the
> memory of the great forgotten peoples? Does not the worth of these objects
> put them above all party consideration, however strong? These examples of
> taste, elegance and grace, are they not an element of instruction nothing
> else can replace, an attraction for foreigners, a charm for all?[136]

began life as a non-partisan nationalist league calling for 'revanche'. Academie Française, www.
academie-francaise.fr/immortels/base/academiciens/fiche.asp?param=443.

[133] Normand, 'Société des Amis des Monuments parisiens', p. 307, note 1. Of the fifty-six members
of the first committee, thirteen were architects working for the CMH or the Diocesan Service.
Three further Commission members were also on the committee. See MAP, 'Biographies des
Architectes en Chef des Monuments Historiques', www.mediatheque-patrimoine.culture.gouv.fr/
fr/bibliotheque/index.html; J.M. Leniaud, 'Répertoire des architectes diocésains du XIXe siècle',
http://elec.enc.sorbonne.fr/architectes/index.php.

[134] Members included directors of major artistic periodicals with Favre (*Encyclopédie d'Architecture*),
Paul Planat (*La Semaine des Contructeurs*) and Louis Gonse (*Gazette des Beaux-Arts*).

[135] Institute National d'Histoire de l'Art (2006), 'Albert Lenoir, historien de l'architecture', www.
inha.fr/article.php3?id_article=736.

[136] Normand, 'Société des Amis des Monuments parisiens', pp. 306–7.

After having established its Parisian ground and after the foundation of a sister society in Rouen, *Les Amis des Monuments rouennais*, a nationwide *Comité des Arts et Monuments* was created.[137] Its principal task was the publication of an illustrated periodical, *L'Ami des Monuments*, as a liaison organ for monument activities in France, the French colonies and abroad.[138] Aspiring to become a platform for all societies in France, including those unable to afford their own bulletin, *L'Ami des Monuments* wished to alert the public and the state to the fate of endangered objects, buildings and landscapes in France and abroad, campaigning against the wilful destruction of modern city planning's 'holy straight line'. Like in the case of the SPAB, its aims, vigilante self-understanding and place in the heritage tradition were popularised in caricatures, most notably by one of its own members, the satirical artist Albert Robida, famous for his whimsical scenes of Paris life and his futurist cartoons (see ill. 2.9).[139]

Over the years, the ambitions and idiosyncrasies of *L'Ami des Monuments* grew, reflected in the magazine's changing subtitles.[140] When the

---

[137] 'Fondation de la Société des Amis des Monuments rouennais', *L'Ami des Monuments*, 1 (1887), p. 45; The *Bulletin des Amis des Monuments rouennais* is published 1901–present; J.P. Chaline, 'Les Amis des monuments rouennais. Naissance et évolution d'une société de sauvegarde', in *Églises, hôtels, vieilles maisons. Bulletin des Amis des Monuments rouennais, numéro spécial du Centenaire* (Rouen, 1986). On the national foundation see also SPAB, *Annual Report*, 8 (1885), 37–9.

[138] C. Normand, 'Introduction', *L'Ami des Monuments*, 1 (1887), 3–5. Published between 1887 and 1914 in 24 volumes and 135 issues. In 1890 the name was changed to *L'Ami des Monuments et des Arts*, in 1905 to *L'Ami des Monuments et des Arts parisiens et français*. Sometimes it was also referred to as *L'Ami des Monuments, des Arts et de la Curiosité*, although this title does not appear on the cover. In 1892 it absorbed the *Encyclopédie d'Architecture*; after 1900 its own parent, the *Bulletin de la Société des Amis des Monuments parisien*. As was the practice in the contemporary literature I will refer to the periodical and the national society as *L'Ami des Monuments*.

[139] From 1875 to 1879 Robida travelled around Europe and composed his series *Vieilles Villes*. In 1900, he was responsible for the design of the 'Vieux Paris' re-enactment at the *Exposition universelle*. See P. Brun, *Albert Robida (1848–1926). Sa vie, son oeuvre, suivi d'une bibliographie complète de ses écrits et dessins* (Paris, 1984). F. Hamon, 'Robida et la Vieille France', in D. Compère (ed.), *Albert Robida, du passé au future. Un auteur illustrateur sous la IIIe République* (Amiens, 2006), pp. 127–34.

[140] It started verbosely but relatively modestly with *Revue illustrée. Organe du Comité des Monuments français . . . Étude et protection des monuments d'art de la France. Physionomie des villes, défense du pittoresque et du beau. Architecture, Peinture, Sculpture, Curiosités, Souvenirs historiques, Sites pittoresques etc.* Its intellectual aspirations were stated when labelling itself *Revue des Deux Mondes* in 1890. That same year it also became the Organ of the *Comité international d'Ami des monuments* adopted by the International Congress; a year later this was changed to *Organe du Comité des Monuments français, du Comité des Monuments étrangers et de la Society for the Protection of Ancient buildings*; it further became the voice of the *Comité du Repertoire des Fouilles, découvertes et Antiquités nationals*. In 1899, the title page was labelled *Annuaire des Amateurs, Érudits et Artistes, centralisant les recherches et découvertes*. The mention of the SPAB disappeared. In 1901 it stated that it was officially adopted by the international Congress of *Art Public* and since 1903 it added *Excursions d'Erudits, d'Amateurs et d'Artistes* and called itself *Organe central de sauvegarde des monuments, de défence des sites et d'art publique*. Since 1896 the cover proudly displayed the winning of a prize of the Institute.

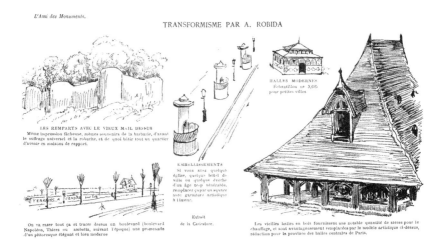

L'Ami des Monuments.

TRANSFORMISME PAR A. ROBIDA

2.9 Albert Robida's series 'Transformism' was first published in *La Caricature* and then proudly reprinted in *L'Ami des Monuments*, 2 (1888), 236 and 242–6. Robida satirises the transformation of the old towns by modern city planners. He takes up Victor Hugo's condemnation of ignorant town councils from *Guerre aux Demolisseurs*. The series culminates in an anthropomorphised 'HOLY STRAIGHT LINE', described in the text as 'Patron saint of the good city, ideal of picturesque beauty, light of the magistrates, star of local councils! Cut, destroy, erase, rake, scrap, trench, align in the name of the very holy straight line and create the modern style, the grand, delicious, superb style of the nineteenth century, or *Crétinal flamboyant*' (a wordplay with *cretin*, idiot, and *gothique flamboyant*, decorated gothic). Robida takes up Hugo's battle cry 'WAR ON THE DEMOLISHERS' and presents the saviour: 'Luckily a committee to safeguard the poor old monuments of times past, everywhere threatened, has been created to fight against the sectarians of the very demolishing and erasing straight line. The organ of the *Ami des monuments* committee has its office in the Street of Martyrs, naturally.'

SPAB's 1884 *Annual Report* welcomed the *Amis des Monuments parisiens* as a 'French SPAB', it equated the aims of both societies, as did subsequent commentators.[141] The Parisian Society, however, did not primarily start as an anti-restoration body, but as an anti-demolition society. It also tried to cooperate with the existing administration rather than confronting it; only after adopting a national perspective, the tone became more anti-Historic Monuments Commission and more anti-restorationist. Membership continued to overlap, but as will be seen in conjunction with the organisation of international congresses, the two organisations increasingly perceived each other as competitors.[142]

[141] Clemen, *Denkmalpflege in Frankreich*, pp. 143–59, here, p. 152, Brown, *Care of Ancient Monuments*, p. 53
[142] See below Chapter 4.

LES VIEILLES RUES

Conseil municipal décidant une exécution capitale au nom de la très sainte Ligne droite et une nouvelle victoire du style Crétinal flamboyant.

Dame, ce n'est pas encore le découpage en damier à l'américaine, avec des avenues à l'américaine, l'alignement est l'œuvre des siècles et non celle d'un ukase municipal. Et quels jolis noms : rue du Chat qui tourne, rue des trois Grenouilles, rue de la Truie qui file, rue du Val d'amour, rue de l'Ane qui presche, etc., etc.

2.9 (*cont.*)

From the start, *L'Ami des Monuments'* interests were much broader than the SPAB's. The pages of its publication featured a regular column on 'Vandalism in the *Départements*', on the 'Organisation of the movement against Vandalism', which praised 'Good Examples' and in time led to the foundation of a Counter-Vandalism Museum in the Hotel de Sully in Paris (see ill. 2.10). It also reported on curiosities and on the activities of other learned societies. Considerable space was moreover devoted to the history of preservation, unearthing a long history of 'friends of monuments'.[143] *L'Ami des Monuments* did not contest the Republican story, but added alternative predecessors from the Ancient Romans, to Henry IV and Jean Jacques Rousseau.[144] Although not primarily a learned publication, it featured scholarly articles on archaeological discoveries and on the history of particular monuments. It also saw the distribution of reproductions of monuments as an important contribution.[145]

[143] É. Charles, 'Le Musée du Contre-Vandalisme à l'hôtel Sully', *La Liberté*, Nr. 17013, repr. in *L'Ami des monuments*, 24 (1913), 50–5. No traces are left of this museum after Normand's death.

[144] *L'Ami des Monuments*, 21 (1907–8), 96.

[145] First as lithographs in the picturesque tradition, later as photographs. The first photograph was published in *L'Ami des Monuments*, 8 (1894), 297.

LES VIEILLES MAISONS

Partout des étages surplombants,
des tourelles et des balcons gênant
l'alignement, eau et gaz à aucun étage,
pas d'ascenseurs. Le rasoir municipal
passe dessus sans arrêt, les propriétaires amis des belles et de la saine
architecture les démolissent et font
reconstruire des *immeubles* du modèle
ci-contre à gauche, qui donneront aux
générations une haute idée de notre
superbe *style Crétinal*.

2.9 (*cont.*)

LA VIEILLE FONTAINE

Un monument tout à fait barbare des temps gothiques ; des administrateurs qui tiennent à l'élégance de la cité confiée à leurs soins intelligents ne pouvaient conserver cela, aussi l'ont-ils remplacé par la fontaine au-dessus (style Crétinal primaire) beaucoup plus ornementale.

2.9 (*cont.*)

L'ENTRÉE EN VILLE

Cette porte fortifiée, vestige des temps barbares d'avant la douce mélinite, impressionne
fâcheusement les regards de l'homme de progrès de notre siècle (le dix-neuvième comme
numéro mais le premier pour les lumières et le gaz). Et il se trouve des gens pour blâmer
notre intelligent Conseil municipal qui, se tenant toujours à l'avant-garde de la civilisation,
veut démolir ce souvenir d'un âge disparu et le remplacer par un bureau d'octroi d'une architecture beaucoup plus élégante.   (*Extrait de la Caricature.*)

2.9 (*cont.*)

TRANSFORMISME PAR ROBIDA

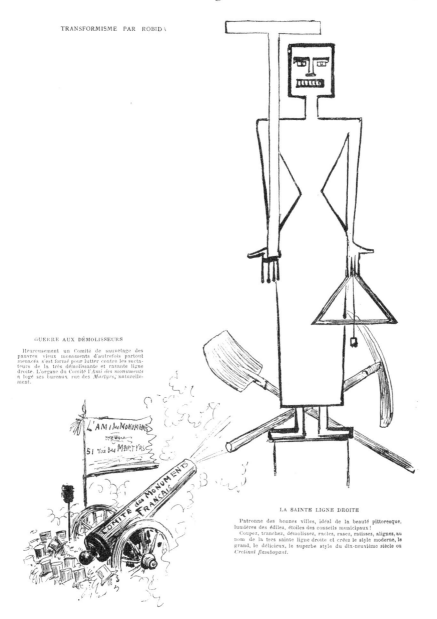

GUERRE AUX DÉMOLISSEURS

Heureusement un Comité de sauvetage des pauvres vieux monuments d'autrefois partout menacés s'est formé pour lutter contre les sectateurs de la très démolissante et rasante ligne droite. L'organe du Comité *l'Ami des monuments* a logé ses bureaux rue des *Martyrs*, naturellement.

LA SAINTE LIGNE DROITE

Patronne des bonnes villes, idéal de la beauté pittoresque, lumières des édiles, étoiles des conseils municipaux !
Coupez, tranchez, démolissez, raclez, rasez, ratissez, alignez, au nom de la très sainte ligne droite et créez le style moderne, le grand, le délicieux, le superbe style du dix-neuvième siècle ou *Crétinal flamboyant*.

2.9 (*cont.*)

PARTIE DE LA FAÇADE DU MUSEE CHARLES NORMAND
OU MUSÉE DU CONTRE-VANDALISME
PALAIS SULLY — NOUVEAU SIÉGE SOCIAL DES MEMBRES
DE L'AMI DES MONUMENTS ET DES ARTS

Cette œuvre magnifique et complète du célèbre architecte Du Cerceau, délaissée de tous
malgré sa magnificence, a été choisie en vue de sa sauvegarde par Charles Normand, pour y
installer les monuments qu'il a sauvegardés des mains des vandales et y installer le siège des
AMIS DES MONUMENTS PARISIENS.

Au premier étage, Charles Normand à la fenêtre.

5

2.10 Photograph of the 'Charles Normand Museum' or 'Museum of Counter-Vandalism'
that became the new headquarters of *L'Ami des Monuments et des Arts* in the Palais Sully.
Charles Normand looks out of the central window. By describing the museum as a safe
house for 'monuments saved from the Vandals' hands', Normand portrays himself as a
successor to the great museum founders Alexandre Lenoir and Alexandre du Sommerard.
L'Ami des Monuments, vol. 23 (1910), p. 65.

LES DISCOURS PRÈS DU MONUMENT COMMÉMORATIF DE L'EMPLACEMENT DE LA BATAILLE DE CRÉCY

2.11 Typical excursion photograph showing members of the *Amis des Monuments parisiens* listening to Charles Normand at the Monument de la Bataille de Crecy, *L'Ami des Monuments*, 20 (1906), p. 41. Institut National d'Histoire de l'Art, Bibliotheque, collection Jacques Doucet.

The publication of the periodical was the *Comité*'s highest priority, but it was also involved in petitions. The success rate is difficult to assess, as input in some successful cases was often exaggerated while many failed, but also some successful cases were not reported in *L'Ami des Monuments*.[146] In contrast to the SPAB and the Trust who did not provide sociability but concentrated on activism in their day-to-day work, activities for members included excursions to nearby monuments, and the publication of tourist guides was seen as an important 'way to assure the safeguarding of our monuments... The visit of ancient works will imbue those partaking with the taste of works of art and consequently with love to defend them' (see ills. 2.11–2.12).[147]

[146] For example on the outcome of the successful campaigns for Avignon's Town Walls discussed below in Chapter 5, nothing was reported in *L'Ami des Monument*.
[147] C. Normand, 'La Promenade des Adhérents de la Revue l'Ami des Monuments au Château de Veaux-le Praslin', *L'Ami des Monuments*, 1 (1887), 197.

NOTES SUR L'EXCURSION

DE PROVINS

PAR

CHARLES NORMAND

ous n'avons pas l'intention de faire ici une étude sur Provins ; nous voudrions seulement signaler en quelques lignes l'excursion si intéressante

L'encadrement formé par la vue de la tour dans son état actuel a été « croqué » pendant l'excursion par notre dévoué collègue *Robida*, dont nos lecteurs connaissent les spirituels volumes de voyages et le charmant numéro de la *Caricature*, dans lequel il a figuré d'une façon humoristique le but du comité et de la revue l'*Ami des Monuments*. Notre collègue M. Paul Buval, architecte à Melun, possède un relevé intéressant avec notes relatives à un projet de restauration de la tour de César conçu par M. Garrez, en novembre 1844.

LA TOUR DITE DE

CÆSAR

A PROVINS

Croquis de Robida.

2.12 Most excursions were not commemorated by photographs of the members of the party but by photographs or drawings of the sites. This typical memorial plate of *L'Ami des Monuments* excursions, drawn by Robida of the Tour de Casar illustrated Charles Normand's excursion notes. *L'Ami des Monuments*, 2 (1888), p. 192.

Statements about membership of the *Comité des Arts et Monuments* can only be approximate, as *L'Ami des Monuments* did not provide comprehensive membership data and no archives survive. A total of 194 founding members were listed in the first issue; by the end of 1888 a total of 488 individual and five corporate members had joined.[148] In 1889 a list of 'founding and committee members' was published, naming 452 individual and eleven corporate members. To this, the patronage committee of the 1889 First International Congress for the Protection of Works of Art and Monuments was added. Members were listed according to their areas of responsibility, not according to their residency. While some members were from the *département* they had under their tutelage, such as Occitan revivalist Fréderic Mistral, in other cases Parisian members were listed for different *départements*. Clusters were strongest around Paris and Rouen with their local *Amis des Monuments*. Overall, the distribution of members in charge per *département* largely overlaps with the spread of historical and archaeological societies. The majority were professional architects, museum conservators, librarians, journalists, writers, painters and local notables.[149] Numbers, as well as social and professional background thus show similarities with the SPAB's membership, including the fact that clerical membership was lower than in the learned societies and that the Society, although national in aspiration, was essentially capital-centred. Differences consisted in a much higher proportion of architects (including architects restoring buildings) among the membership and committee and a less marked overlap with social reform movements. No further membership data were published in later volumes; in a first instance it seems, however, that the enterprise gained support, and an increased membership financed larger editions and a two-colour system from 1896.

Other learned societies, especially the *Société française d'archéologie* welcomed *L'Ami des Monuments*, without giving it too much attention, not feeling their own status threatened by a newcomer with largely similar aims.[150] That the Historic Monument Commission saw the Society as a more serious rival will be illustrated through the analysis of international congresses. British or German writings on preservation in

---

[148] In 1887 a further 157 individuals and 4 corporate members subscribed, followed by another 137 individual and one corporate adhesions in 1888, *L'Ami des Monuments*, 1 (1887), 5–10, 143–45, 249–50, 345–6; *L'Ami des Monuments*, 2 (1888), 85–6, 167, 241, 319.

[149] Estimates are confirmed by membership analysis of the *Amis des Monuments rouennais* for whom longer membership records exist. Chaline, *Sociabilité*, p. 238.

[150] *Bulletin Monumental*, Ser. 6, 2 (1886), 94–5.

France around the turn of the century featured *L'Ami des Monuments* prominently thanks to its international action and energetic publishing.[151] It corresponded with several organisations abroad, including the SPAB, the RIBA and the National Trust,[152] and other ties were established with societies in Belgium, Italy and Prague. On the whole, the concept of *Ami* societies gained popularity in France and further associations were founded as local initiatives.[153] Yet by its twentieth anniversary, despite Normand's self-congratulatory tone, *L'Ami des Monuments* and the *Société des Amis des Monuments parisiens* had started to decline.[154] The *Bulletin de la Société des Amis des Monuments parisiens* ceased to exist independently in 1900 and *L'Ami des Monuments* was published less frequently from 1905, with an increasingly less varied content, before disappearing in 1914.

In part this decline can be explained through personality-related factors. The publication had increasingly become a one-man show, and when Charles Normand's health declined (he retired from public life around 1914 and died alone and forgotten in 1934) nobody was there to continue his work.[155] More structural factors were important too. Both the Parisian and the national societies were to a certain extent victims of their own successful derivatives. Members of the Parisian society had constantly fought for the foundation of the *Commission du Vieux Paris*, established in 1897.[156] This municipal commission, of which several of the most active Parisian *Amis*

[151] See for example Brown, *Care of Ancient Monuments*, p. 53; Clemen, *Die Denkmalpflege in Frankreich*, p. 152.
[152] Alphone Guillon to SPAB, 23 April 1895, SPAB Archives, 'Orange, Roman Theatre'.
[153] See *Bulletin des Amis des Monuments ornais*, published between 1901–1904; 'Société des Amis du Viel Arles', *L'Ami des Monuments*, 16 (1903), 186–7; 'Fondation des Amis des Monuments, Sites et Arts de la Côte d'Azur et Provence', *L'Ami des Monuments*, 23.2 (1912–14), 124; *L'Ami des Monument* did not comment on the foundation of the *Amis du Mont-Saint-Michel* in 1911 and the *Amis du Vieux Dieppe* in 1912, see CTHS, 'Annuaire des sociétés savantes', www.cths.fr/FICHES/Fiches_Societes/S_1763.shtm.
[154] 'Vingt ans après. Brève épître aux Amis', *L'Ami des Monuments*, 21 (1907–8), 7.
[155] It is telling that until recently, none of the standard biographical dictionaries recorded his date of death, see U. Thieme, F. Becker, *Allgemeines Lexikon der bildenden Künstler von der Antike bis zur Gegenwart* (Leipzig, 1907–50), XXV, p. 518. A. Klimt, *Saur Allgemeines Künstler Lexicon. Bio-Bibliographischer Index* (8 vols., Munich, 2000), VII. Charles Normand disappeared from the list of SPAB members in the 1926 *Annual Report*, but no obituary appeared later. Apart from the minutes of the Commission du Vieux Paris, only parish records noted his death, see Fiori, 'Charles Normand'.
[156] On the contruction of a Parisian heritage movement see, R. Fiori, *L'Invention du vieux Paris. Naissance d'une conscience patrimoniale dans la capital* (Paris, 2012). On how this triggered similar commissions in other cities see J. Davenne, 'Du Lyon Pittoresque au Secteur Sauvegarde: La constitution de la valeur patrimoniale du vieux Lyon' (Mémoire de fin d'études Institut des Etudes Poliques de Lyon, Université Lumière Lyon 2 1997), IEP Lyon, http://doc-iep.univ-lyon2.fr/Ressources/Documents/Etudiants/Memoires/MFE1997/davennej/these.html.

des Monuments became members, henceforth was responsible for Old Paris. With the care of monuments now integrated into the city's administration, the *Société* had made itself largely redundant. On a national level, *L'Ami des Monuments* had not managed to create enough of a niche for itself either. Benevolently received by other learned societies on contemporary heritage questions, it provided an overview of issues, but never became the true platform it aspired to be. While reporting on learned activities in the country, it devoted a disproportionate amount of pages to the findings of its Parisian editors and the *Bulletin Monumental* of the *Société française d'archéologie* remained the true representative of provincial erudition. It also did not provide the kind of technical advice the SPAB was able to offer. Normand therefore increasingly promoted heritage tourism by publishing excursion reports, but in this endeavour, the rapidly expanding *Touring Club*, which Normand had often assisted, attracted a substantially larger audience.[157]

While *L'Ami des Monuments* still aspired to be the umbrella organisation for all things patrimonial, several other national societies also emerged, embracing a more environmentalist, more regionalist and ultimately more political vision of heritage. They understood 'heritage' through the land (*paysage*) rather than the arts. In the founding call for another new society, 'the soil' was defined as 'the *patrimoine* we received from the past' and which 'we owe to the future'. Despite their different focus, they thus shared the idea expressed in Ruskin's anti-restorationist writings that the past is not ours and that 'every generation is really only the usufructuary' of heritage.[158]

A court case for the protection and surveillance of the sources of the river Lizon in the Doubs won by the new *Société pour la protection de l'esthétique de la France*,[159] triggered the creation of a larger, nationwide *Société pour la protection des paysages de France* (SPPF), or Society for the Protection of French Landscapes as it was known in the English-speaking world, by Nobel Laureate René Sully Prudhomme. Welcomed in the British press as the 'French National Trust',[160] it had substantially less in common with Octavia Hills's organisation, than *L'Ami des Monuments* had with the SPAB. Its eyes were turned more towards models across the

[157] C. Normand, 'Le Touring-Club visite les vestiges d'Alesia', *L'Ami des Monuments*, 21 (1907–8), 265–8, first published in *L'éclair*, no. 7124.
[158] J. Lahor, 'Une Société à créer pour la protection des paysages français', *Revue des revues*, 1 March 1901, 526–31 (emphasis added).
[159] See Leniaud, *Archipels du passé*, p. 219.
[160] 'A French "National Trust"', *The Times*, 18 April 1904, p. 11.

Rhine than across the Channel, as it was in search of models for region-
ist revival rather than the qualities of a land-holding body. It was also
more expansionist than the Trust. The SPPF was determined to claim sole
representation in landscape protection – as would its German sister organisation, the *Bund Heimatschutz* (BHS), founded in 1904.[161] Organised in
a centralist manner, the SPPF absorbed many existing associations of the
regionalist movement, creating a dense network of local and national societies whose aims, leadership and adherents overlapped. The SPPF's first
president, Charles Beauquier (1833–1916) was one of the most active figures in the regionalist movement and founder of the national movement
for decentralisation. After graduating from the *École des Chartes*, he had a
prolific career as a writer – publishing on topics as diverse as the Franco-
Prussian War, popular music and free speech – and was a deputy for his
native Doubs from 1880–1914. While the politics of the SPPF are often
characterised as conservative,[162] Beauquier, and with him French preservationism, escape any simple political categorisation in the same way as the
British societies do. Beauquier was a member of the Radical-Socialist Party,
a feminist, and fervently anti-clerical,[163] while the Deputy Secretary of the
League for Decentralisation was the extreme right nationalist Charles Maurras. The League united monarchists, moderate Republicans and Radicals
such as Maurice Faure, who also was a member of the SPPF and tireless
campaigner for the protection of landscape in the Chamber. The honorary
vice-president of the SPPF, André Theurriet was the president of the Society for National Ethnography founded in 1895 against the disappearance of
regional differences, encouraging traditional ways of life and local culture.
Another SPPF founding member was Charles-Brun, the president of the
Fédération Régionaliste Française, an agro-romanticist group, that included
leading geographers Vidal de la Blache, Foncin, and Gallois. They tried to
identify and preserve the regions as a counterweight to Parisian cen-
tralism and stop the migration into cities via a campaign for a 'return
to the land'.[164] Inspired by German regionalism, the Federation blamed
the absence of regionalism in France for the defeat of 1870 and tried to

---

[161] Trom, 'Natur und nationale Identität', p. 148.   [162] Poulot, *Patrimoine et musées*, p. 122.

[163] Leniaud, *Les Archipels du passé*, p. 220; 'Beauquier', in *Dictionnaire des Parlementaires Français* (5
vols, Paris 1889–91, repr. Ann Arbor, 1975), I, p. 226; 'Les bâtisseurs de la SPPF. Charles Beauquier
(1833–1916) Président de la "S.P.P.F" de 1901 à 1916', *Sites et Monuments* (2001), repr. SPPEF, http://
sppef.free.fr/texte/images1/biographie_beauquier.jpg.

[164] See its journal *La Réfome Sociale*. On the German equivalent, see E. Rudorff, *Der Schutz der
lanschaftlichen Natur und der geschichtlichen Denkmäler* (Berlin, 1892) and the activities and writing
of Heinrich Sohnrey, founder of the *Ausschuss für Wohlfahrspflege auf dem Lande* and BHS co-
founder.

mobilise the French regions as places of mental and physical regeneration for the fight against the German paragon and archenemy. Despite the revanchist tones, it was an equally complex body uniting members of the entire political spectrum.[165] *La Renaissance Provinciale. Société d'Etudes et de Vulgarisation des Costumes et des Arts Provinciaux*, yet another revivalist group, was also under the patronage of Beauquier and united regionalist revivalist leaders such as Nobel Laureate Mistral (also a member of *L'Ami des Monuments*) and Le Goffic (co-founder of the *Union Régionaliste Bretonne* in 1898) and revanchist nationalists, such as Maurice Barrès and Charles Maurras.[166] Other societies of the same entourage included the *Société populaire des Beaux Arts*, and the *Ligue contre la Publicité à travers les Champs*.[167] These societies shared aesthetic concerns, acknowledging their Ruskinian tradition, yet it was patriotic regionalism that provided a common ground to otherwise ideologically opposed figures as the Radicals Beauquier and Faure and leading right-wing nationalists such as Barrès and Maurras.

From the links between these societies, a complex network of formal and informal contacts, at times interwoven with the network of the older learned societies, emerged. The list of individuals and organisations joining included many local associations of natural history, history, archaeology, regional art, folklore, costumes and architecture. Civil servants, museum directors, professors, teachers, artists and writers were among the principal individual members.[168]

The protection of *paysages* was motivated by the idea of *pays*,[169] composed of naturalised cultural objects and culturalised natural objects, similar to and inspired by the German idea of *Heimat* and sometimes referred to as *petite patrie* or *matrie*.[170] Consequently, the protection of this *patrimoine du passé*, included all things connected to the *pays* from nature, to buildings, folk art, to the preservation of costumes and traditional ways of living. As such, the movement widened the established notion of heritage not only typologically, but also chronologically by including craft objects from the recent past, and geographically by focussing on

---

[165] J. Wright, *The Regionalist Movement in France 1890–1914. Jean Charles-Brun and French Political Thought* (Oxford, 2003), pp. 185–6.

[166] Trom, 'Natur und nationale Identität', pp. 154–5.   [167] Ibid., p. 151.

[168] Ibid., p. 149; C. Digeon, *La Crise allemande de la pensée française, 1870–1914* (Paris, 1959), p. 88.

[169] To find an English equivalent for *pays* is as difficult as to find a translation for *Heimat*, see E. Weber, *Peasants into Frenchmen* (Cambridge, 1976), pp. 45–6, 96; Trom, 'Natur und nationale Identität', p. 151.

[170] Ibid. and C. Beauquier, 'Séance d'ouverture', *Le Premier Congrès international pour la protection des paysages* (Paris, 1910), p. 10.

landscapes (which included villages and towns) rather than isolated monuments.[171] The SPPF tried to intervene in all these different areas. As a prerequisite for activism, members were encouraged to collect visual evidence, lithographs, photographs and postcards, which were then diffused nationally, especially in schools, to increase landscape recognition.[172] The Society frequently campaigned for the rescue of natural sites threatened by building works, industrial exploitation, railway construction or disfigured by advertisement. Beauquier and Faure, in particular, championed the legal protection of landscape and monument ensembles.

While *L'Ami des Monuments* did not establish a niche for itself among the pre-existing learned and state institutions, the SPPF moved into the hitherto uncovered space of landscape protection. Yet both circles contributed in important ways to changing the ideas of heritage. Although *L'Ami des Monuments* continued to describe 'heritage' primarily in terms of art and beauty, in contrast to the SPPF's definition in connection with the soil, both societies considerably widened the traditional French understanding of 'heritage'. Both increasingly used the term *patrimoine* to show that their definition was different from the more traditional *monuments historiques*. Each organisation was also imbedded within its own wider network: *L'Ami des Monuments* was closely intertwined with the Parisian world of arts and architecture, and the SPPF with the regionalist movement. Their aesthetic concerns and a certain personal overlap linked the two movements, and collaborations occurred on several projects. Although their spheres intertwined much less than those of the national English preservation organisations, they belie the assertion still found in most histories of heritage that the vibrant activity of private societies in the early nineteenth century was curtailed by the state under the July Monarchy, not to be resurrected again.[173]

German days for monuments and leagues for the homeland

In the decades following unification and recession interest in history and art, culture and nature met a strong longing for societal renewal in Germany

---

[171] R. de Clérmont, 'De la protection des monuments du passé, des paysages et des sites'. Supplement to the *Bulletin de l'Association Littéraire et Artistique* (1905), qu. in Trom, 'Natur und nationale Identität', pp. 158–9.

[172] On cross-fertilisation with the German *Heimtbewegung* see Trom, 'Natur und Nationale Identität', p. 160. On the hanging of photographs in schools, see H. Conwentz, *Die Heimatkunde in der Schule* (Berlin, 1904); A. Mellerio *et al.*, *L'Art et l'École* (Paris, 1907).

[173] Bercé, 'Les Sociétés savantes', 155–67; J.M. Leniaud, 'L'Etat, les sociétés savantes et les associations de défense du patrimoine: L'exception française', in Le Goff (ed.), *Patrimoine et passions identitaires*, pp. 137–54.

too. As part of a broad movement for life reform, or *Lebensreformbewegung*, the care of monuments was reconceptualised as a movement to protect the *Heimat*.[174] The old German word *Heimat* had been revived by the writers in the 1780s, as part of a drive to restore neglected words of the German language at the time of disintegrating political unity.[175] *Heimat* featured in mid-nineteenth century novels describing a nostalgic localness of the hometown, but reached general ubiquity in the years after unification, as it could bridge the 'gap between national aspiration and provincial reality'.[176] The writer and publicist Adolf Bartels promoted the concept of *Heimatkunst*, a form of art and literature to be inspired by Germany's rural regions, architects talked about establishing a distinct *Heimatstil*. An aesthetic and social movement formalised through the foundation of a plethora of local associations or *Heimatvereine*, characterised by a mixture of learned and activist interests.[177] They published periodicals and essays, wrote petitions, founded and administered museums, organised talks and architectural competitions, collected examples for preservation and new buildings projects and provided advice offices for architectural maintenance and planning. Most associations operated locally, but more and more regional societies and umbrella organisations emerged in the 1890s.[178] Notables administered most of these *Heimat* associations, and the leadership differed little from that of the older historical societies, but membership in general was more heterogeneous. While the *Heimat* movement originated 'from below', it also received considerable help 'from above'.[179] Originally the new *Heimat* associations were more independent than the historical associations, but state influence soon increased, as umbrella organisations allowed state agencies to join as corporate members. High civil servants aspired to offices in a *Heimatverein*, presidents were increasingly salaried as civil servants, and *Heimatvereine*, as their older learned counterparts, started to receive subsidies from the different states.[180] While the French regionalist movement struggled to define the territorial reach of the *pays* against the administrative structure of the Third

---

[174] See W. Krabbe, *Gesellschaftsveränderung durch Lebensreform* (Münster, 1975); Kratsch, *Kunstwart und Dürerbund*; K. Vondung (ed.), *Das wilhelminische Bildungsbürgertum* (Göttingen, 1976); M. Jefferies, 'Back to the Future? The "Heimatschutz" Movement in Wilhelmine Germany', *History*, 77.251 (1992), 411–20, here 412; Jefferies, 'Lebensreform. A Middle-Class Antidote to Wilhelminism?', in G. Eley, J. Retallack (eds.), *Wilhelminism and Its Legacies. German Modernities, Imperialism, and the Meaning of Reform 1890–1930* (Providence, Oxford, 2003), pp. 91–106.

[175] 'Heimat', in J. and W. Grimm, *Deutsches Wörterbuch* (vol. 4., Leipzig, 1877), pp. 864–6.

[176] Applegate, *Nation of Provincials*, p. 13.

[177] Speitkamp, *Verwaltung der Geschichte*, p. 121. On the related emergence of *Heimat* museums see M. Roth, *Heimatmuseum. Zur Geschichte einer deutschen Institution* (Berlin, 1990).

[178] Speitkamp, *Verwaltung der Geschichte*, p. 122.

[179] Jefferies, 'Back to the Future?', 416.   [180] Speitkamp, *Verwaltung der Geschichte*, p. 126.

Republic, the *Heimatbegriff* could simultaneously represent locality, region and nation.[181] *Heimatgefühl*, the feeling for the locality was seen as basis for national feeling, *Nationalgefühl*.[182] As such, the associations provided room to be provincial in the new nation-state. However, as the problems the *Heimat* movement attacked, such as industrialisation, modernisation, the destruction of landscapes, and a more general decline of values were perceived as nation-wide problems, leading preservationists argued that solutions also had to be sought nationally, and even internationally as shall be seen later.

As a result, three moves to unify concerns about heritage nationally occurred almost simultaneously. Starting in the domain of the care of monuments, with the creation of the periodical *Die Denkmalpflege* in 1898/1899 and the inception of the *Tag für Denkmalpflege* by the *Gesamtverein* between 1898 and 1900, the foundation of the *Bund Heimatschutz* followed in 1904. The first was a state initiative and the other two came from civil society, yet the personal and institutional overlap was again high.

To coordinate local efforts, the Prussian Conservator Reinhold Persius persuaded the *Kultusministerium* to found a nation-wide *Denkmalpflege* periodical in 1898.[183] The 'increased *Heimath-Gefühl*' after German unification had led, he argued, to a growing number of articles on *Denkmalpflege* in the press, making a national synchronisation desirable. Prussia, having just coordinated its provincial *Denkmalpflege*, should demonstrate the state's leadership in matters of preservation in a way France and Austria had indicated.[184] His was not the first attempt to create a national periodical for *Denkmalpflege* in imitation of France. Almost half a century earlier, Ferdinand von Quast had founded the *Zeitschrift für christliche Archäologie und Kunst* inspired by Didron's *Annales archéologiques*, but the enterprise was short-lived for financial reasons.[185] Possibly because an initiative of the private sector to unify *Denkmalpflege* was on its way in 1898 as well, Persius' could overcome opposition from the Ministry of

---

[181] A. Confino, 'On Localness and Nationhood', *Bulletin of the German Historical Institute London*, 23.2 (2001), 7–28, here, 9.
[182] Confino, *The Nation as a Local Metaphor*.
[183] Reinhold Persius (1835–1912), son of the renowned architect Ludwig Persius, also studied architecture in Berlin. In 1867 he became a royal architect in Potsdam, in 1872 director of the Commission for Palaces and then Prussian Conservator of Monuments between 1886 and 1901, see *Die Denkmalpflege*, 3 (1901), 33; *Die Denkmalpflege*, 14 (1912), 134.
[184] Persius, Bericht 13 Feb. 1898, GStA PK, I. HA Rep. 76 Ve Kultusministerium, Sekt. I, Abt. VI, Nr. 17, qu. in Speitkamp, *Verwaltung der Geschichte*, p. 127.
[185] Raumer 'und zugleich für den abwesenden Finanz-Minister' to Friedrich Wilhelm IV, 20 Sept. 1855, GStA PK, I. HA Rep. 89 Geh. Zivilkabinett, jüngere Periode, Nr. 20768, fols. 111–13.

Finance, ever cautious to limit expenses. As a biweekly supplement to the Office of Works' official publication, the *Centralblatt der Bauverwaltung*, *Die Denkmapflege* received a subsidy from the Prussian state. The founding editors were the Prussian civil servants Otto Sarrazin and Oscar Hoßfeld.[186] The content of *Die Denkmalpflege* was focussed on practical issues rather than theoretical debates, and was cautious in its approach to the most contentious topic of the period, anti-restoration. Although primarily an organ for civil servants, *Die Denkmalpflege* also reported news from the *Heimat* movement. More generally, a widening of focus from monumental buildings to vernacular architecture reflected the influence of *Heimat* ideas. The largely depoliticised and objectified content ensured that the periodical was soon read across state borders, and it was even recommended by the Bavarian *Kultusministerium*, otherwise unenthusiastic about Prussian attempts to dominate German preservationism.[187] Described abroad as 'the organ of the movement for the defence of the older monuments of the Fatherland which has enlisted so much public sympathy in Germany', *Die Denkmalpflege* helped to unify and professionalise the care of monuments in Germany and was regarded as the most advanced publication of this kind in Europe.[188]

While Persius prepared the launch of *Die Denkmalpflege*, the creation of the second major voice on monument care was initiated by the *Gesamtverein*. In 1898, it appointed a commission for *Denkmalpflege*, presided by Württemberg's Conservator and secretary of the main antiquarian society Eduard von Paulus.[189] The commission prepared a resolution on the future of *Denkmalpflege*, to be submitted to all German states, approved by the 1899 general assembly of the *Gesamtverein*. Here, the commission was restructured and fortified and Hugo Loersch, professor of legal history in Bonn, expert for monument law and co-founder of several historical associations, was chosen as president.[190] It included the art history professor and Rhenish Provincial Conservator Paul Clemen – who 'as the chief conservator of monuments for the Rhineland' had 'more fine medieval buildings under his care than any other man in Europe' and was perhaps the single most influential conservator in German history.

[186] Speitkamp, *Verwaltung der Geschichte*, pp. 127–8. On the recurrent opposition from the Ministry of Finance to Prussian *Denkmalschutz* see below Chapter 6.
[187] Ibid. and below Chapter 6.
[188] Brown, *Care of Ancient Monuments*, pp. 38–9. See also H.H. Möller, 'Zur Entstehung und Geschichte der deutschen Denkmalpflegezeitschriften', in M.F. Fischer (ed.), *Zeitschriften deutscher Denkmalpflege 1899–1933. Register* (s.l., 1991), pp. 5–12.
[189] On Paulus (1837–1907) see *Die Denkmalpflege*, 9 (1907), 48.
[190] G. Droege, 'Hugo Loersch', *Neue Deutsche Biographie* (21 vols., Berlin, 1953–present), xv, p. 58.

He was the first conservator of the Rhine Province from 1893 to 1911, then head of the provincial monument commission. He also founded Bonn University's Art History Institute and was the first Visiting Professor to the Germanic Museum at Harvard University. He was Germany's leading expert on preservation in France, and wrote the first monograph in German on Ruskin. During the First World War he became an eager propagandist for the war effort, organising the *Kunstschutz* programme. Clemen continuously adapted his *Denkmalbegriff* to the political order of the Monarchy, the Weimar Republic, Third Reich and the Allied Powers, when he re-established German preservation in the Rhineland after the Second World War.[191] Other well-known professionals included the Bavarian architect and art historian Gustav von Bezold, Berlin archivist Paul Bailleu and architect Peter Wallé.[192] With the backing of the *Gesamtverein*, they prepared the coming of independence of a new organisation that first met under the name *Tag für Denkmalpflege* in 1900. The *Denkmaltag*, as the new congress was also called informally, aimed to give 'all those involved, government representatives, organs of *Denkmalpflege*, architects and artists, archaeologists and art historians, and all adherents to the cause, the possibility of free exchange and unobstructed debates'.[193] The congress met annually until 1913, and from 1907 every second event was organised in conjunction with the *Bund Heimatschutz*.[194] The Monument Days evolved around six themes: the principles of *Denkmalpflege*; the relation of *Denkmalpflege* to modern art; legal and organisational structures; education and vulgarisation of *Denkmalpflege*; practical and technical aspects including controversial restorations; and new *Denkmal* categories. Its stenographic reports were distributed among all state administrations. Off-prints of particular articles were further spread by societies such as

---

[191] Qu. Brown, *Care of Ancient Monuments*, pp. 54–5. See also Clemen, *Gesammelte Aufsätze;* Hilger, 'Paul Clemen und die Denkmäler-Inventarisation in den Rheinlanden', in E. Mai, S. Waetzold (eds.), *Kunstverwaltung, Bau-und Denkmal-Politik im Kaiserreich* (Kunst, Kultur, und Politik im deutschen Kaiserreich 1, Berlin, 1981), pp. 383–98; G. Goldman, *A History of the Germanic Museum at Harvard* (Cambridge, MA, 1989), p. 11; R. Koshar, *Germany's Transient Pasts. Preservation and National Memory in the Twentieth Century* (Chapel Hill, 1998), p. 39.

[192] On Bezold (1848–1934) who had started the inventory of monuments in Bavaria with the *Bayrischer Architekten-und Ingenieurverein* and edited with Georg Dehio the *Handbuch der Kunstdenkmäler*, see *Die Denkmalpflege*, 4 (1902), 79. On Bailleu (1853–1922) see *Deutsches Biographisches Jahrbuch* (10 vols., Berlin 1925–8) IV, pp. 3–10; on Wallé (1845–1904), see J. Kohte, 'Peter Wallé', *Die Denkmalpfelge*, 6 (1904), 99; Speitkamp, *Verwaltung der Geschichte*, p. 129, note 68.

[193] *Die Denkmalpflege*, 1 (1899), 105–7, qu. 107.

[194] See A. von Oechelhaeuser (ed.), *Denkmalpflege. Auszug aus den stenographischen Berichten des Tages für Denkmalpflege* (2 vols., Leipzig, 1910–13); M. Wohlleben (ed.), *Konservieren, nicht restaurieren. Streitschriften zur Denkmalpflege um 1900. George Dehio, Alois Riegl* (Braunschweig, 1988), pp. 37–68.

the *Dürerbund*, a group that wanted to uncover an essential and popular Germanness as the basis for art and history.[195] Contents and resolutions were also reviewed in the specialist and general press in Germany and sometimes abroad.

On a permanent basis, the *Tag für Denkmalpflege* consisted only of the committee. It was neither an umbrella organisation nor a membership association, had no regular income, and no charter. Resolutions were passed yearly by the congress that also elected the committee. Participation figures were similar to membership numbers for the SPAB, the Trust or *L'Ami des Monuments*, rising from around 150 in 1903 to around 700 in 1913.[196] Yet the *Denkmaltage* were much more than a mere congress. The committee, composed of twelve members (professional art historians, architects, conservators, and politicians from Prussia, Hesse, Baden, Saxony and Bavaria) also intervened between congresses on what it considered matters of public interest, particularly legislation and controversial restorations. The loose organisation permitted the Karlsruhe art history professor Adolf von Oechelhaeuser,[197] who headed it from 1905, and his deputy Paul Clemen to principally run business as they liked.[198] Under their leadership, the committee, initially desirous to stress close ties with the different state administrations, progressively chose a more independent tone. The different German states initially reacted benevolently to the congress, but the *Denkmaltage* were viewed with increasing concern by conservators because the resolutions taken by a group of architects, engineers, art historians and interested amateurs were increasingly seen as the public representation of *Denkmalpflege*.[199] Prussia, therefore, in 1911 established a parallel Day for Conservators, or *Konservatorentag*. The time and venue were the same as the *Tag für Denkmalpflege*, but it was closed to the public. Prussia and Bavaria, in uncharacteristic unity, also unsuccessfully tried to have the *Denkmaltag* only occurring biannually. The *Denkmaltag* committee continued to solicit official representation,[200] yet the move towards an independent position ultimately strengthened the organisation's standing and the *Tag für Denkmalpflege* became the most important

[195] G. Kratsch, *Kunstwart und Dürerbund* (Göttingen, 1969).

[196] *Die Denkmalpflege*, 6 (1904), 101; 15 (1913), 97; cf. A. von Oechelhaeuser, 'Bericht über die Tätigkeit des Tages für Denkmalpflege während des ersten Dezenniums seines Bestehens,' in A. von Oechelhaeuser (ed.), *Denkmalpflege*, I, pp. 1–12, here p. 10.

[197] *Wer ist's* (1914), p. 1210, *Wer ist's* (1922), p. 1124.

[198] Speitkamp, *Verwaltung der Geschichte*, p. 131.   [199] Ibid., pp. 131–2.

[200] For example Paul Clemen to Friedrich Schmidt-Ott, 18 Sept. 1913, GStA PK VI. HA, Rep. 92 Nl. Schmidt-Ott (M), A X 1, cf. also below Chapter 4.

independent voice on all technical and theoretical heritage questions in
Germany.[201]

The third attempt to provide a national platform for heritage concerns
emanated from *Heimat* enthusiasts, in particular Ernst Rudorff (1840–
1916). A student of Clara Schumann, and a composer himself, Rudorff was
the first professor for piano at the new Royal Conservatory for Music in
Berlin.[202] Disturbed by the transformation which 'the new time' brought
to the surroundings of his parental manor, Rudorff started to campaign in
the late 1870s against the changes that modern agriculture inflicted upon
the landscape.[203] Anticipating the Garden City movement, he suggested
to conserve inherited landscapes and called for a programme of decentralised buildings with individual access to green spaces.[204] Well-travelled,
the anti-industrialist Rudorff promoted industrial England's 'feeling for the
charm of the landscape' as the example to which Germany should aspire.[205]
Before the turn of the century, Rudorff had made several attempts to create
a national *Heimatschutz* organisation (the term that had distinct military
connotations, as it was formerly used to designate the armed defence of the
homeland)[206] but nothing came of it.[207] Only after the *Heimat* idea had
gained momentum with the foundation of several local and regional associations, did his ideas for a national movement have a chance to gain support.
Again, a concrete case helped as a trigger. In 1903/1904, the first German
mass-protest against a large engineering project in an environmentally
sensitive location received support from some of the most prominent figures in Wilhelmine intellectual life, including Friedrich Nauman, Werner

---

[201] Speitkamp, *Verwaltung der Geschichte*, p. 132.
[202] G.G. Jones, 'Rudorff, Ernst (Friedrich Karl)', *The New Grove Dictionary of Music and Musicians*
(20 vols., London, 1980), XVI, p. 316.
[203] E. Rudorff, 'Das Verhältnis des modernen Lebens zur Natur', *Preußische Jahrbücher*, 45
(1880), 261–76; on Rudorff's early writings see A. Knaut, 'Ernst Rudorff und die Anfänge der
Deutschen Heimatbewegung', in E. Klueting (ed.), *Antimodernismus und Reform. Zur Geschichte
der deutschen Heimatbewegung* (Darmstadt, 1991), pp. 20–49; Jefferies, 'Back to the Future',
412.
[204] See F. Bollerey, K. Hartmann, 'A Patriarchal Utopia. The Garden City and Housing Reform in
Germany at the Turn of the Century', in A. Sutcliffe (ed.), *The Rise of Modern Urban Planning,
1880–1914* (London, 1980), pp. 135–64.
[205] Rudorff, 'Das Verhältnis des modernen Lebens zur Natur', 276; W. Rollins, '*Heimat*, Modernity
and Nation in the early Heimatschutz Movement', in J. Hermand, J. Steakley (eds.), *Heimat,
Nation, Fatherland. The German Sense of Belonging* (New York et al., 1996), pp. 87–112, here p. 91.
[206] E. Rudorff, 'Heimatschutz', *Die Grenzboten*, 56.2 (1897), 401–14, 455–68, Rudorff, 'Abermals
Heimatschutz', *Die Grenzboten*, 56.4. (1897), 111–16, repr. in P. Schultze-Naumburg (ed.),
Heimatschutz (Berlin, 1926).
[207] R. Mielke, 'Meine Beziehung zu Ernst Rudorff und die Gründung des Bundes Heimatschutz. Zu
dem 25. Jährigen Bestehen der Bewegung', *Brandenburgia*, 38 (1929), 1–16, here 5; Knaut, 'Ernst
Rudorff', p. 37.

Sombart and Max Weber. The campaign to save the Laufenburg Rapids in Baden from a hydroelectric power scheme was ultimately unsuccessful, but public awareness was raised.[208]

Preparations to found the *Bund Heimatschutz* (BHS) had started in earnest in 1901, as a small scale, rather sectarian enterprise by Rudorff, Georg Heinrich Meyer, in whose publishing house Rudorff's works were edited and the ethnologist Robert Mielke,[209] with the support of *Die Denkmalpflege* editor Oskar Hoßfeld, who provided useful connections with state officials.[210] Mielke and Hoßfeld consulted with sympathisers of the *Heimat* and 'life reform' milieu, including Heinrich Sohnrey, founder of the *Verein für ländliche Wohlfahrtspflege* consecrated to stop the desertion of rural areas and encourage the so-called inner colonisation. Essential steps, however, were planned behind closed doors, not even integrating figures like Hugo Conwentz, director of the Westprussian Provincial Museum in Danzig, an ardent proponent of *Naturschutz*, who would in 1906 create the Office for Nature Protection in Prussia, as Rudorff and Mielke thought him too scientifically oriented for a movement that essentially tried to reform all of contemporary society.[211] The founders did not want to create a mere 'organ for nature and monument care'[212] or a kind of aesthetic police, but a movement that was centred on man as part of a *Volk* shaped by its soil and its past. Through *Heimatschutz*, the German man ('der *deutsche* Mensch') should regain 'conscious recognition of his place as member of a *Volk*'.[213] The holistic education of the league should 'encompass *all* areas of our public and private cultural and economic life, permeating all stations', in short, it should become a cultural movement.[214] While culture and nature should deserve equal protection, for practical purposes, the league's work was subdivided into six areas: *Denkmalpflege*; care of vernacular architecture and promotion of vernacular buildings styles; conservation of landscape including ruins; safeguarding of the native flora, fauna and geology; promotion of traditional arts and crafts; and preservation of customs, traditions, celebrations and costumes.[215]

---

[208] M. Jefferies, 'Heimatschutz. Environmental Activism in Wilhelmine Germany', in C. Riordan (ed.), *Green Thought in German Culture* (Cardiff, 1997), pp. 42–54, here p. 42.

[209] See R. Mielke, *Volkskunst* (Magdeburg, 1896). Like Rudorff, Miele was interested in preservation in Britain. See R. Mielke, 'Denkmalpflege in England', *Die Denkmalpflege*, 8 (1906), 42–4.

[210] Speitkamp, *Verwaltung der Geschichte*, p. 133.

[211] Mielke, 'Meine Beziehung zu Ernst Rudorff', 7.   [212] Ibid.

[213] Ibid., 7–8 (emphasis in original); Speitkamp, *Verwaltung der Geschichte*, p. 133.

[214] Ibid. (emphasis in original).

[215] *Gründungsaufruf* of the *Bund Heimatschutz* of 1904 and *Satzung des Bundes Heimatschutz*, version of 1908, qu. in Speitkamp, *Verwaltung der Geschichte*, p. 134.

Like the founders of the National Trust, the BHS founders chose the committee carefully to assure as wide an appeal as possible. The artist Paul Schultze-Naumburg became first chairman. Involved in every significant reform movement of the day from the Munich and Berlin Secessions to the *Werkbund*, he was already well known through his *Heimat*-related works in Ferdinand Avenarius' influential journal *Der Kunstwart*[216] and his *Kulturarbeiten* introduced a wide audience to questions of conservation and planning.[217] He was intended primarily as a figurehead, and Rudorff and Mielke tried to block his attempts to influence the direction of the BHS. The second chairman, the Schaumburg-Lippe Minister Friedrich Freiherr von Freilitzsch in Brückeburg, was appointed to demonstrate the involvement of the political world, yet as a representative of a small state was considered a manageable influence. Mielke was executive secretary. Many cultural politicians, artists, architects, and clerics responded to the founding call,[218] including Hermann Muthesius (a regular correspondent of the SPAB, recently returned from his post as attaché at the German Embassy in London), Munich architects and city planners Gabriel von Seidl and Theodor Fischer, a Garden City prophet, Eduard Paulus, Gustav von Bezold, the restorer of Heidelberg Castle Carl Schäfer, Paul Clemen, Hans Lutsch (Persius' successor as Prussian Conservator), Jenar art history professor and land-reformer Paul Weber,[219] Hugo Conwentz, Heinrich Sohnrey and Freiburg economist Carl Johannes Fuchs.[220] The overlap of membership with the *Tag für Denkmalpflege* and Sohnrey's *Verein für ländliche Wohlfahrtspflege* was considerable, indicating how tightly knit the network of the preservation and life reform leadership was at the turn of the century. Industry and trade were less well represented than in local or regional *Heimat* associations. To counterbalance Rudorff's extreme anti-industrialist tones, Mielke incited the cooperation of economist Fuchs to demonstrate that the movement was not against industry, only against its excrescences,[221] yet the direction the BHS should take with regard to industrialisation remained a bone of contention amongst the leadership.[222]

---

[216] See Kratsch, *Kunstwart und Dürerbund*.
[217] N. Borrmann, *Paul Schultze-Naumburg 1869–1949. Maler-Publizist-Architekt* (Essen, 1989); Jefferies, 'Heimatschutz'.
[218] Mielke, 'Meine Beziehung zu Ernst Rudorff', 6, 9–15, Speitkamp, *Verwaltung der Geschichte*, p. 134.
[219] On Paul Weber, see *Wer ist's* (1922), p. 1652; Speitkamp, *Verwaltung der Geschichte*, p. 43.
[220] Speitkamp, *Verwaltung der Geschichte*, p. 134.
[221] See C.J. Fuchs, *Heimatschutz und Volkswirtschaft* (Flugschriften des Bundes Heimatschutz 1, Halle 1905).
[222] Mielke, 'Meine Beziehung zu Ernst Rudorff', 13; *Die Denkmalpflege*, 9 (1907), 100.

Many state governments welcomed the foundation of the Bund and encouraged their civil servants to assist it.[223] Schultze-Naumburg's pamphlet *The Disfiguration of our Country* was bought with public funds in a number of districts and recommended by ministries in Prussia, Bavaria and Württemberg.[224] However, the BHS' sectarian zeal also incited ambiguous feelings. Professional *Denkmalpfleger* were not without distrust towards the *Bund*'s ideology, its professional lobbyism, and its wish to establish parallel networks.[225] This irritation was shared by some of the larger *Heimatvereine*. The BHS is often portrayed as a national umbrella organisation coordinating independent regional and local *Heimatvereine*.[226] The founders, however, did not envisage the League as a mere umbrella for existing societies, but as a membership association, and even more so as a movement, hence they encouraged the foundation of new regional branches. Although the *Bund* grew rapidly, before the First World War, primarily small associations affiliated, whereas larger ones, such as the *Rheinischer Verein für Denkmalpflege und Heimatschutz*,[227] the *Bayrische Volkskunstverein* or the *Heimatbund Mecklenburg* valued their independence. In some regions, the older historical associations also mounted opposition.[228] Due to local resistance no regional branches could be founded in Posen, West and East Prussia, Thuringia and Alsace.[229] Given the persistence of opposition, the *Bund* changed its tactics in 1908, largely relinquishing centralisation in favour of a federal structure. Some of the founders did not like this new turn, as 'uniformity in the pursuit of aims' was endangered.[230] The founders however, were losing influence themselves. In 1913, the presidency went to Karl Rehorts, Provincial Conservator of the Prussian province of Saxony. Mielke had already been replaced by Saxon-Meiningen lawyer Fritz Koch. The new leadership more strongly fostered the links with state agencies and neighbouring organisations such as the *Tag für Denkmalpflege*. The appointment of a new executive secretary, the engineer Werner Linder, was indicative of the *Bund*'s desire to shed the founders' mystical utopia in favour of becoming a 'reformist pressure-group, involved in the day-to-day problems of planning and architecture'.[231]

---

[223] Speitkamp, *Verwaltung der Geschichte*, p. 135.
[224] *Die Entstellung unseres Landes*, qu. in Jefferies, 'Heimatschutz', 49.
[225] Speitkamp, *Verwaltung der Geschichte*, p. 135.   [226] Rollins, '*Heimat*', p. 89.
[227] The *Rheinischer Verein für Denkmalpflege und Heimatschutz* focussed primarily on the saving of historic buildings, see Rheinischer Verein für Denkmalpflege und Landschaftsschutz (ed.), *Erhalten und gestalten. 75 Jahre Rheinischer Verein für Denkmalpflege und Landschaftsschutz* (Neuß, 1981); Koshar, *Germany's Transient Pasts*, p. 41.
[228] Applegate, *Nation of Provincials*, p. 88.   [229] Speitkamp, *Verwaltung der Geschichte*, p. 136.
[230] Schultze-Naumburg qu. in *Die Denkmalpflege*, 13 (1911), 108.
[231] Jefferies, 'Back to the Future', 419.

While there is considerable debate about the significance of the French and British preservation movements, it remains uncontested that the *Heimatschutz* movement was an important factor in Wilhelmine society. In 1904 the BHS counted 44 corporate and 573 personal members, and 150 corporate and more than 1,000 personal members two years later.[232] Individual membership of the *Bund* stood at around 15,000 in December 1911[233] and up to 30,000 members in 1914.[234] By 1906 already, the *Heimatschutz* movement, as a whole, rather than the BHS, claimed up to 100,000 individual and corporate members.[235] Moreover, the movement's influence among the educated classes was much wider than membership numbers suggest.[236] *Heimatschutz* attracted support from 'all sections of society', but certain professions were dominant in the operations of the movement, especially teachers, civil servants and clergymen.[237] It is often highlighted that a full quarter of the *Heimatschutz* associations' membership were civil servants and that the *Bildungsbürgertum* made up half of the membership of most associations. That 30 per cent were from commercial backgrounds is mentioned in passing,[238] yet it seemed to have been overlooked that such a large support from commercial quarters is extraordinary compared to the historical associations, as well as to the constituencies of preservation organisations in France and Britain. 'By the usual standards of cultural pressure-group the *Heimatschutz* movement was highly influential.'[239] BHS membership exceeded that of the Pan-German-League, credited with an enormous impact on Wilhelmine politics, but which never rose above 20,000 members.[240] *Heimatschützer* were probably less successful than they would have wished, but 'more successful than one could have expected'.[241]

The question is therefore less whether *Heimatschutz* was a relatively important phenomenon in Wilhelmine society, but for whom and why. While the British and French movements are generally analysed in terms of

[232] Figures provided in *Die Denkmalpflege*, 6 (1904), 44; 8 (1906), 114–15; Speitkamp, *Verwaltung der Geschichte*, p. 134.
[233] C.F. Otto, 'Modern Environment and Historical Continuity', *Art Journal*, 43.2 (1983), 148–57, here 149.
[234] Rollins, '*Heimat*', p. 89; Rollins, *A Greener Vision of Home. Cultural Politics and Environmental Reform in the German Heimatschutz Movement, 1904–1918* (Ann Arbor, 1997), p. 93. For a detailed analysis of membership see pp. 69–153.
[235] Jefferies, 'Back to the Future', 41; Jefferies, *Politics and Culture in Wilhelmine Germany. The Case of Industrial Architecture* (Oxford, 1995), p. 57; Jefferies, 'Heimatschutz', 47, note 12.
[236] Koshar, *Germany's Transient Pasts*, p. 28.
[237] Jefferies, 'Back to the Future', 414; Jefferies, *Politics and Culture*, p. 58.
[238] Rollins, '*Heimat*', pp. 92–3; Rollins, *A Greener Vision*, pp. 104–5.
[239] Jefferies, 'Back to the Future', 420.
[240] Rollins, '*Heimat*', p. 89.   [241] Jefferies, 'Back to the Future', 420.

Victorian and Third Republic history, the Wilhelmine movement is evaluated with regard to its later development under the Third Reich. Arguments have been framed by larger assumptions on a German *Sonderweg* versus a European modernity, either highlighting the unique racist nature or drawing attention to the existence of preservation movements abroad to show the modernity of *Heimatschutz*. In support of their arguments different historians have drawn on comparative reasoning. According to Jefferies, the majority of *Heimatschutz* was pragmatically oriented, 'more concerned with practical conservation than political posturing' and had much in common with the members of the National Trust.[242] Rudy Koshar, on the other hand, states that to underestimate the anti-modernist, and especially racist, elements identified by the older scholarship, 'is to misrepresent the historical specificity of the movement and its later influence on and appeal to Nazism'.[243] Both positions are one-sided. Rejecting the idea of a German *Sonderweg* by drawing attention to the fact that preservation movements were founded at the same time in France, Britain and the United States means letting the *Sonderweg* return through the back door by assuming that the British and French ways were progressive and therefore any similarities between German and other preservation movements must confirm the idea of German modernity.[244] The existence of preservation movements in other countries, however, does not necessarily make *Heimatschutz* less *völkisch*. Racist elements, moreover, were not unique to Germany, as Trom's comparison with the nature preservation movement in France has shown.[245]

When looking primarily at the critique of civilisation in theoretical writings, declaring *Heimatschutz* to be 'the strongest and safest barrier to the growing threat of the realization of the Communist-Socialist state',[246] the impression that *Heimatschutz* stemmed from an anti-modern cultural pessimism, imbued with anti-socialism and anti-Semitism is predominant.[247]

[242] Jefferies, 'Heimatschutz', 47; Jefferies, 'Back to the Future', 114; Jefferies, *Politics and Culture*, pp. 59–60; for similar tendencies A. Knaut, *Zurück zur Nature! Die Wurzeln der Ökologiebewegung* (Greven, 1993).

[243] R. Koshar, 'The Antinomies of Heimat. Homeland, History, Nazism', in Hermand, Steakley (eds.), *Heimat, Nation, Fatherland*, pp. 113–36, qu. p. 113.

[244] On the methodological problem see G. Eley, 'Deutscher Sonderweg und englisches Vorbild', in, D. Blackbourn, G. Eley (eds.), *Mythen deutscher Geschichtsschreibung. Die gescheiterte bürgerliche Revolution von 1848* (Frankfurt, 1980), pp. 7–70; R.J. Evans, *Rethinking German History. Nineteenth-Century Germany and the Origins of the Third Reich* (London, 1987).

[245] Trom, 'Natur und nationale Identität'.

[246] Sohnrey qu. in Jefferies, 'Back to the Future', 412.

[247] R.P. Sieferle, *Fortschrittsfeinde? Opposition gegen Technik und Industrie von der Romantik bis zur Gegenwart* (Munich, 1984), p. 206. For a more recent example Speitkamp, *Verwaltung der Geschichte*, p. 121.

The involvement in National Socialism of some of the key figures of the Wilhelmine *Heimatschutz* movement, such as Schultze-Naumburg, who became the principal spokesman on artistic matters for the Nazi *Kampfbund für deutsche Kultur*, and the general appropriation of *Heimat* by the Third Reich, further enhance this impression.[248] However, by differentiating between groups and ideas within the *Denkmal* and *Heimat* movement and by comparison with other European preservation movements, a more complex picture emerges. The writings of the BHS leadership cannot be considered synonymous with *Heimatbestrebungen* at large. From the difficulties in creating a centralised organisation, it becomes clear that the leadership of the *Bund Heimatschutz* had no monopoly on the definition of *Heimat*. Visions from the provinces could be quite different and were usually more practice-oriented.[249] Even within the BHS approaches to *Heimatschutz* varied, and the founders' influence was limited once an organisational framework had been established.[250] Crypto-fascists, conservative figures in provincial regimes, social liberals, Garden City activists, and other bourgeois reformists were among its supporters.[251] Like in France and Britain, the *Heimat-* and *Denkmalschutz* movement was characterised by competing views and contradictions internal to modernisation.[252] It had optimistic and pessimistic sides, idealistic and pragmatic ones. Some members opposed modernisation and industrialisation per se, but many objected only to certain aspects of the process.[253] Despite their criticism of modernity, the *Heimatbewegung* and even more so the more professionalised *Denkmalbewegung* saw their endeavours to preserve the past also as decidedly modern.[254]

It is also worth considering that from an English perspective, German preservationists, in contrast to the homegrown ones, were not 'extremist', but 'practical men who are familiar with the exigencies of modern life'.[255]

---

[248] Cf. P. Schultze-Naumburg, *Kunst und Rasse* (Munich, 1928); Schultze-Naumburg, *Kunst aus Blut und Boden* (Leipzig, 1934); Borrmann, *Paul Schulze-Naumburg*.

[249] Applegate, *A Nation of Provincials*, pp. 104–7.

[250] Jefferies, 'Back to the Future', 412–13.   [251] Koshar, *Germany's Transient Pasts*, p. 28.

[252] See more generally G. Eley, 'Die deutsche Geschichte und die Widersprüche der Moderne. Das Beispiel des Kaiserreiches', in F. Bajohr (ed.), *Zivilisation und Barberei. Die wiederspüchlichen Potentiale der Moderne. Detlev Peukert zum Gedenken* (Hamburg, 1991), pp. 17–65.

[253] Jefferies, 'Back to the Future', 414; Koshar, *Germany's Transient Pasts*, p. 21. On the uneven effect of cultural pessimism see T. Nipperdey, *Deutsche Geschichte 1866–1918* (2 vols., Munich, 1991–2), I, pp. 591–92, 821.

[254] See H.G. Andresen, 'Heimatschutzarchitektur in Lübeck. Ein vergessener Versuch des angemessenen Umgangs mit einem Stadtdenkmal', in M. Brix (ed.), *Lübeck. Die Altstadt als Denkmal* (Munich, 1975) and Jefferies, 'Back to the Future', 421. R. Koshar, *Germany's Transient Pasts*, p. 9 offers more balance. See also below Chapters 3, 4, 6.

[255] Brown, *Care of Ancient Monuments*, p. 27.

Anti-capitalists like Rudorff co-existed with economists like Fuchs, who tried to influence industrialisation rather than condemning it. Nationalism was an important element of *Heimatschutz* and *Denkmalschutz*, but it did not go unchallenged. Georg Dehio and Alois Riegl publicly debated whether importance in national life[256] or the 'value of age' was the ultimate criterion for the conservation of monuments.[257] Conserving the visual integrity of the *Heimat* did certainly intersect with attempts to conserve racial characteristics.[258] Yet while *völkisch* elements were very visible in relation to monument and landscape protection in German borderlands and became fully articulated during wartime,[259] they were not necessarily dominant in many day-to-day preservationist activities before the war.[260]

Politically, the German preservation movement was more to the right than its British or French counterparts, but attitudes to socialism were more complex than usually presumed, ranging from virulent hatred to slow rapprochement. Unlike Britain, notorious socialists like Morris were not among the leaders of the preservation movement, and unlike France, leading figures of the socialist movement, like Jean Jaurès, did not become involved in campaigns.[261] German preservationists certainly drew parallels between conservation and socialism, but it was in a conservative-national way that Dehio argued 'I know of no other name for *Denkmalpflege* than socialism', rather than a Marxist one.[262] The BHS economist Fuchs, on the other hand, argued that worker-protection laws setting limits to the exploitation of men should be extended to the protection of nature.[263] *Heimatschützer* did not simply try to erect barricades against the proletariat, but argued that *Heimatschutz* would have direct benefits for the working classes through aesthetic compensation and recreational opportunities in nature, in line with other bourgeois reform groups such as the Garden City and *Volkspark* (City Park) movements, and the founders of the

[256] Dehio, *Denkmalschutz und Denkmalpflege*, p. 9.
[257] A. Riegl, *Der moderne Denkmalkultus. Sein Wesen, seine Entstehung* (Vienna, 1903) repr. in Riegl, *Gesammelte Aufsätze* (Vienna, 1996), pp. 139–84; trans. 'The Modern Cult of Monuments. Its Character and its Origin', *Oppositions*, 25 (1982), 21–51.
[258] Koshar, *Germany's Transient Pasts*, p. 28.
[259] *Kriegstagung für Denkmalpflege. Stenographischer Bericht* (Berlin, 1915); Speitkamp, *Verwaltung der Geschichte*, p. 137.
[260] Applegate, *Nation of Provincials*, p. 86.
[261] On France see below Chapter 6. On the relationship of trade union and socialist leadership to preservationism in Germany see Koshar, *Germany's Transient Pasts*, p. 72.
[262] Dehio, *Denkmalschutz und Denkmalpflege*, p. 92, Koshar, *Germany's Transient Pasts*, p. 34.
[263] C.J. Fuchs, 'Die Ausnützung der Naturkräfte', in *Heimatschutz. Bericht über die Jahresversammlung des Bundes Heimatschutz in Goslar am 12–14. Juni 1905* (Halle, 1906), pp. 91–94, here p. 93, qu. in Rollins, '*Heimat*', p. 103.

National Trust.[264] Engagement with the Social Question does of course not equal socialist thinking, but often rather reflected the search for a third way between socialism and capitalism. However, recent research on the German bourgeoisie has shown that it was much less dominated by fear of the proletariat than sometimes argued and that in the immediate pre-war years, the German bourgeoisie, and educated, reform-minded *Bürger* in particular, tended slowly towards an understanding with the Social Democrats. On the local level, *Heimatschutz* sponsored 'schemes of municipal socialism'[265] not as 'fear-laden "rear-guard actions" against the proletarian enemy, but rather as "products" of an atmosphere in which bourgeois *Heimatschützer* saw a "profound reduction in political tensions"'.[266]

Private societies and national movements

That preservation movements existed in all three countries is not reason enough to see them as modernist and to dismiss for example the *völkisch* element of the German *Heimatbewegung*. However, preservation societies in all three countries used the past to offer an alternative route to progress. Their degrees of specialisations differed, as did visions of what should be considered 'heritage' and of the social role that preservation should perform, but if seen as movements or networks rather than as isolated societies, the concerns were relatively similar. All had an increasingly broad understanding of preservation, integrating the concern for buildings, scenic ensembles and nature. For all, preservationist activism was only one part of a larger reform agenda. Some were mostly in search of artistic reform and used the rejection of restoration to overcome historicism and refine art through the Arts and Crafts, Art Nouveau and Modernism. Others saw the preservation of the past primarily as a way to engender social reform movements offering an alternative to rampant industrialisation and capitalism. For many, the two concerns were linked in a more or less diluted form of Ruskinism that viewed artistic and natural beauty as a prerequisite for a civilised and healthy population.[267]

[264] Rollins, '*Heimat*', p. 103.
[265] Ibid., p. 103 on the basis of D. Langewiesche, 'German Liberalism in the Second Empire, 1871–1914', in K.H. Jarausch, L.E. Jones (eds.), *In Search of a Liberal Germany. Studies in the History of German Liberalism from 1789 to the Present* (New York, 1990), pp. 217–35. See also Applegate, *Nation of Provincials*, p. 83.
[266] Rollins, '*Heimat*', p. 104. The reference to reduced political tensions stems from Paul von Hedemann-Heespen, 'Sollen wir Heimatschutz erzwingen? Zur Philosophie und Taktik des Heimatschutzes', *Heimatschutz*, 6 (1910), 88.
[267] See J.K. Walton, 'The National Trust. Preservation or Provision?', in M. Wheeler (ed.), *Ruskin and the Environment. The Storm-Cloud of the Nineteenth Century* (Manchester, New York, 1995),

Underneath these general concerns, however, very different ideologies and political views co-existed not only within the preservation movements in each country, but inside every organisation. Superficially, the socialist perspective on preservation was most apparent in Britain, and the racist *völkisch* element most prominent in Germany, yet opinions expressed by different members of all societies reflected almost the full political spectrum, and were solely held together by a relatively small common ground, provided by an aesthetic and/or patriotic rhetoric of the regionalist or nationalist variety.

While ideas derived from a common pool, organisational structures were more strongly moulded into the national traditions established by learned societies, political lobbyism and charity. For most bodies, campaigning was the dominant feature. The idea of a private society as a public holding body was peculiar to England, where substantially more land was privately owned, yet at the margins of the German preservation movement, similar approaches existed too.[268]

While most of the societies discussed here still exist today, their success was not necessarily foreseeable. 'Of course it might grow' Octavia Hill had remarked less than two years after the National Trust's foundation, only to add shrewdly 'but then it might not'.[269] The sentence could be applied to any of the many voluntary preservation societies. Of the national organisations discussed here, only *L'Ami des Monuments* did not survive the period, showing that a close group of activists and plans for the succession of the founding generation were equally important as heritage concepts and a niche to be filled.

In terms of membership these new societies show common factors across the different countries, while differences are also apparent. All societies were influenced by the personalities of the founders. Highly individual figures, they might have been sceptical about progress with regard to industrialisation, but all were convinced that social progress could be furthered through voluntary endeavour. No sooner was a nuisance identified, than a new committee or society was formed to combat it.[270] However, their views did not always reflect organisational views, and within each society, a distinction must be made between nominal and active membership. Everywhere,

pp. 144–64. Ruskin's reception in France and Germany, reached its peak in the 1890s and early 1900s, see P. Clemen, *John Ruskin* (Leipzig, 1900). On the diffusion of Ruskin's ideas via international congresses see below, Chapter 4.

[268] The *Verein Naturschutzpark*, founded in 1909, purchased 4,000 hectares of land on Lüneburg Heath between 1910–20, Jefferies, 'Heimatschutz', 42.

[269] Qu. in Cannadine, 'The First Hundred Years', p. 15.

[270] Cf. Weideger, *Gilding the Acorn*, p. 22.

active membership in committees and publications rarely exceeded two dozen people at any given time.[271]

In general, the more theoretically oriented, the smaller a society remained. In Britain and France the national 'anti-restoration' societies were capital-centred secular associations that had a civic and theoretical focus, but did not provide much room for sociability. In Germany, with its plethora of *Heimatvereine*, no similar society was founded; the theoretical claims of 'anti-restoration' were represented by the sober *Tag für Denkmalpflege* committee.

Although all societies discussed aspired to national coverage, many had a distinct geographical hub. The SPAB was London and South-East centred, as was the National Trust, with a second stronghold in the Lake District. The *Comité des Arts et des Monuments* remained largely an offspring of the *Société des Amis des Monuments parisiens*; it was Paris-centred with some of its more active members in Normandy and Burgundy. The French regionalist movement ironically also had a strong capital base; the *Bund Heimatschutz*'s stronghold was in Saxony as well as in Berlin, however, the umbrella principle made distribution more equal across the country.

The social background of preservation association founders was also similar and quintessentially middle-class. Most were artists, architects, social reformers, in the legal profession or in the Church. The number of individuals working in preservation-related professions, such as architecture or art history, was higher in France and Germany than in England. This lower number in England is not only explained by Morris' alienation of architects, but by a generally higher number of preservation professionals through the various bureaucracies and state art institutions on the continent. Adorning societies with aristocratic figures remained a feature across the three countries, although the tendency was probably most notable in the National Trust. In general, the proportion of aristocratic members was higher in the two English societies analysed here, than in those of the continent, either because membership fees were higher, or because the equivalent of the middle-class provincial subscribers constituting the *Heimatbewegung* in England joined local societies, rather than national bodies. Clerical membership in the preservation societies was lower than in the old learned societies. The SPAB was made up of fewer than 10 per cent clerical members, yet this derives from its London location as much

---

[271] See for examples on the *Amis des Monuments rouennais:* Chaline, *Sociabilité*, pp. 237–8; on attendance of SPAB committees see West, 'Committee', pp. 299–310.

as from its secular stance. The membership of the *Comité des Arts et des Monuments* reflected similar trends. In Germany, clerics were absent from the leadership of the *Tag für Denkmalpflege*, but in the regional *Heimatvereine* they were well represented. While artistic professions dominated the leadership of most organisations, in German and French local and regional societies an increase in the number of secondary school teachers, doctors and officers is evident. Not least, the local associations were a method for challenging the dominance of local notables in rural communities.

In all three countries, several family members were often active in societies. This introduced an important female presence.[272] In the metaphorical realm, the more emotional aspects of 'heritage' were often identified with femininity. For example, old buildings were likened to a female face in the writings of Victor Hugo, the SPAB and *Punch*. *Heimat* ideas were also framed in a language of separate spheres, with its emphasis on the home and familial warmth.[273] The link was made probably most explicit in the proposed translations of *Heimat* into French as *matrie*.[274]

In the organisational realm, however, women had a much less prominent place. In general, the more learned a society aimed to be, the less likely women were to be present. Tellingly, women figure little in the many literary caricatures of learned societies and only occur as suffering wives, or under form of caricature, like the Pig Faced Lady in Dickens' work.[275] Many learned societies excluded women from full membership; if given, access was often limited to women with family ties to male members.[276] The preservation societies more actively recognised women as multipliers. *Heimat* theorists saw the wives of notables and middle-class professionals as their 'natural mediators',[277] while both the SPAB and the National Trust reached out explicitly to men and women,[278] and organised lectures for the Women's Institutes and women's colleges.[279] Female membership was noticeably higher in new preservation associations because of

---

[272] Little has been written on the history of gender relation and the protection of heritage. For an exception see the analysis of the relationship between feminism and the museum in Edwardian Britain in J. Bailkin, *The Culture of Property. The Crisis of Liberalism in Modern Britain* (Chicago, 2004), pp. 118–58.

[273] Koshar, *Germany's Transient Pasts*, pp. 52–4.

[274] Trom, 'Natur und nationale Identität', p. 151.   [275] Dickens, *Mudfog Papers*, pp. 77–8.

[276] Evans, *Society of Antiquaries*, p. 352, Levine, *Amateur and Professional*, p. 9, note 9; Chaline, *Sociabilité*, p. 205.

[277] O. Schwindrazheim, *Offener Brief an den Bürgermeister einer Deutschen Kleinstadt* (Leipzig 1901), qu. in Speitkamp, *Verwaltung der Geschichte*, p. 43.

[278] SPAB, *Annual Report*, 1 (1878), p. 13.

[279] SPAB Archives, 'Women's Institutes Lecture 1912'; Weideger, *Gilding the Acorn*, p. 17.

their philanthropic or leisure-oriented nature,[280] yet differences between societies and countries are noticeable. Figures were lowest in Germany, linked to the predominance of the professionalised, male-dominated discipline of architecture in preservationism. Women, as spouses, attended the *Denkmaltage*, but were not involved in its organisation or agenda. The less professionalised *Heimat* associations admitted women, yet women constituted less than 5 per cent of the membership.[281] *L'Ami des Monuments* had 1–2 per cent female subscribers in its early days. A general increase in female membership can be assumed on the basis of the figures for the *Société des Amis des Monuments rouennais*, starting also at 1 per cent and augmenting to 12.5 per cent by 1913.[282] Women constituted a quarter of the participants in *L'Ami des Monuments* excursions, but as in *Die Denkmalpflege*, no articles were contributed by women in the periodical. Characteristically, an Englishwoman, Amelia Edwards, founder of the Egypt Exploration Fund, was *L'Ami des Monuments'* most illustrious female member.[283] Only in England did women hold positions of authority, and substantially more women joined in their own right rather than as wives or daughters of male members.[284] The National Trust especially relied on women for its committee and campaign work.[285] This female presence was strongly linked to the Trust's philanthropic side. The founders' position towards female emancipation more generally were mixed. While Hunter supported women's suffrage,[286] Hill was against it.[287] Women also sat on the SPAB's general committee, although never more than three at a time,[288] and many correspondents abroad were women.[289] The number of women in the Society's general membership was comparatively high, rising from 7 per cent in 1878 to 20.5 per cent in 1914.[290] About 15 per cent were known

---

[280] Chaline, *Sociabilité*, pp. 202–5.
[281] Koshar, *Germany's Transient Pasts*, p. 40; Applegate, *Nation of Provincials*, p. 67; G.L. Dubrow, 'Restoring a Female Presence. New Goals in Historic Preservation', in E. Perry Berkeley, M. McQuaid (eds.), *Architecture. A Place for Women* (Washington, 1989), pp. 159–63. On women and local preservation: Henry Brewer to SPAB, 2 July 1884, SPAB Archives, 'Nuremberg Town Walls'.
[282] Chaline, *Sociabilité*, p. 205.
[283] On Edwards see D. Gange, 'Religion and Science in Late Nineteenth-Century British Egyptology', *Historical Journal*, 49 (2006), 1083–103.
[284] West, 'Committee', p. 310.
[285] For biographies see Fedden, *National Trust*, p. 23; Gaze, *Figures in a Landscape*, pp. 48–9; Waterson, *National Trust*, pp. 45–8.
[286] Jenkins, James, *From Acorn to Oak Tree*, p. 4.   [287] Waterson, *National Trust*, pp. 58–9.
[288] SPAB, *Annual Report*, 28 (1905), 3, *Annual Report*, 36 (1913), 7.
[289] See for examples SPAB Archives, Minute Book Restoration Committee, 13 October 1881; 3rd Committee Minute Book, 3 November 1881; 'Florence Ponte Vecchio'.
[290] SPAB, *Annual Report*, 1 (1878), 45–54. West, 'Committee', p. 307; SPAB, *Annual Report*, 37 (1914), 83–99.

in their own right, including philanthropists like Hill and Burdett-Courtts, suffrage campaigners Millicent Fawcett and Helen Taylor and artists like May Morris and Kate Faulkner.[291]

The multitude of artistic and social organisations in which the preservationists were active created a dense network of contacts and overlapping memberships between learned societies, preservation lobby groups and philanthropic organisations. Most societies attempted to claim sole representation on heritage issues, yet no single body succeeded to coordinate all heritage questions, so collaboration between different organisations was necessary. Such collaboration did not always correlate with shared ideas and could occur on single issues. Conversely, it could be refused due to personal animosities, despite conceptual agreement. The structure of networks differed, being much more informal in Britain than in Germany and France, but cross-membership and correspondence were common there too. In both France and Germany, a central periodical for the care of monuments was established, but the absence of an equivalent seems not to have been lamented in England.

The nature of membership tells as much about bourgeois structures of sociability as it does about support for preservation. Moreover, comparison of total membership figures of the preservation movements is complex. At first sight, the main preservation societies in England have the lowest membership, and the *Bund Heimatschutz* the highest, with France somewhere in the middle. However to contrast the roughly 1,200 adherents which the Trust and the SPAB had together by the eve of the First World War, with the 30,000 members of the BHS, and the alleged 100,000 adherents of the *Heimatschutz* movement, is flawed, as societies affiliated to the Trust are not included in membership counts as they are in the BHS. A more accurate picture would emerge, in terms of numbers and social background of members, if local societies, such as the Lake District Defence Society, the Keswick Footpath and Commons Society or the Hindhead Preservation Society and other conservation bodies, as well as the archaeological and architectural societies that figured so prominently in reports of campaigns in the national press were included.[292] Then, approximate numbers are in the ten thousands too. If other societies' interest in the preservation of linguistic, geological, ethnographical, biblical or imperial heritage were

---

[291] Crawford, 'Supper at Gatti's', p. 102.

[292] Hundreds of local societies feature in the pages of *The Times* in relation to collaborative projects. For an analysis of different conservation bodies see also D. Evans, *A History of Nature Conservation in Britain* (London, 1992), pp. 46–9.

included too, numbers would be even higher.[293] Thus relative numbers are not so very different in the three countries. Then again, the fact that in Germany, a larger umbrella organisation rather than societies connected through overlapping membership and shared interest existed is significant as it did give the movement a very different force as a public voice and lobby group.

However, to truly understand the extent of the nineteenth-century heritage movement, it is useful to adopt a wider gaze and to think of the 'heritage-makers' not just in terms of government agencies, professional bodies, learned societies, and preservation lobby groups, but to include those interested in heritage and active in its preservation as a result of other activities, such as rambling, cycling, automobile touring, photography or even seaside bathing.[294]

The advent of the railways and the introduction of cheap excursion trains permitted access to recreational facilities on a hitherto unknown scale, only to be augmented again by the coming of the bicycle and the motor car.[295] The preservationist elite welcomed the new heritage-lovers with mixed feelings. Although, ever since Abbé Grégoire had invented the word vandalism, nineteenth-century preservationists (and with them present-day historians) have agonised about the absence of support for their cause in the population, their writings suggest that too much popular interest was also undesired. Full of disdain for the new species of monument-loving tourist, the nationalist French writer and politician Maurice Barrès argued in a petition to the French Parliament in the 1910s, that 'not only beautiful churches' which brought money to 'the innkeeper and the driver', were worthy of being protected by a Monument Law, but also those which were 'ugly, scorned, from whom the railway can earn nothing, and which do not create a living for the innkeeper'.[296] Fears over the effects of commodification mixed with class-related anxieties.[297] By the end of the century, the dread that the solitude and quiet so central to the enjoyment of the sublime were threatened by what Henry James called the 'cockneyfication'

---

[293] On societies' interest in biblical and imperial heritage, such as the Egypt Exploration Fund, the Society for the Preservation of Egyptian Antiquities or the Palestine Exploration Fund see, D. Gange, *Dialogues with the Dead. Egyptology in British Culture and Religion, 1822–1922* (Oxford, 2013).

[294] See Dom B. Maréchaux, *Notre Dame de la Fin de Terre de Soulac* (Bordeaux, 1893, re-edited 2006), p. 1.

[295] Hunter, 'Introduction', in Hunter, *Preserving the Past*, p. 2.

[296] M. Barrès, *La Grande Pitié des églises de France* (Paris, 1914), pp. 82–3.

[297] See below Chapter 5, caricatures of 'Altheidelberg', *Simplicissimus* No. 13 (1906) and 'Neu-Heidelberg: der Ott-Heinrichsbau der Zukunft. Eine ruinierte Ruine', *Lustige Blätter*, No. 34 (1904).

of tourism, was widely echoed across Europe.[298] The greatest champion of public access, Octavia Hill, despite her publicly expressed belief that the Trust's properties belonged 'to every landless man, woman and child in England',[299] also expressed in private the view that the Trust 'by no means plans to give access to the tramp, the London rough, the noisy beanfeaster'. Instead the objective was to 'preserve land in its natural beauty for the artist, the professional man, and such of the public as appreciate and respect natural beauty'.[300] Although Hill regularly organised excursions for the tenants of London's East End, she also bitterly complained that 'picnic parties carry London noise and vulgarity out into woods and fields, giving no sense of hush or rest'.[301] But however much preservationists lamented it, heritage tourism was growing and preservationists soon discovered that referring to the numbers of tourists, and their commercial weight, could be useful to back preservationist claims.

The coming of the bicycle and the motor car led not only to unprecedented private access to sites, but also to organised activity. In all three countries, leisure societies began to outnumber the preservation lobby groups in the late nineteenth and early twentieth century. For instance, inspired by the English Cyclist Touring Club, founded in 1875 and counting more than 60,000 members before the turn of the century,[302] the *Touring Club de France* was established by Parisian notables after a trip to London in 1890. Six years later, it counted 40,000 members; 75,000 in 1900 and 100,000 in 1906. It organised excursions to historic and picturesque sites, which in turn resulted in a number of local preservation efforts. Already in 1900 it was internationally recognised for its preservationism: the English *Cycling and Moting* magazine described it as combining 'the functions of our C.T.C. [Cyclist Touring Club], the Roads Improvement Association, the Automobile and Motorcar Clubs, the Commons Preservation Society, and the National Trust Society' (see ill. 2.13).[303] A similar phenomenon can be observed in Germany, where tourism and ramblers' associations became a mass occurrence. In 1869 the Alpine Club was founded, and from 1872 onwards the Vosges Club and other regional groups followed. Their purposes included the exploration and protection of nature, ruins and castles, and the propagation of historic consciousness. Within a few years

---

[298] H. James, 'In Warwickshire', *The Galaxy*, November 1877, p. 671, qu. in Mandler '"The Wand of Fancy"', p. 127.

[299] Qu. in Weideger, *Gilding the Acorn*, p. 385.

[300] Qu. ibid., p. 66.   [301] Qu. in Waterson, *National Trust*, p. 58.

[302] W. Oakley, *Winged Wheel. The History of the First Hundred Years of the Cyclists' Touring Club* (Godalming, 1977), p. 12.

[303] 'A Few Figures', *Cycling and Moting*, 20 January 1900, p. 34.

"EVERYBODY rides a wheel. There ain't no distinction in that. Now a nice smart American buggy would let folks see you were somebody; that you ain't like other people, that you've got character and individuality. Mind, I'm offering you a bargain. Say the word, and in two days the buggy will be here."

"I don't want a buggy. And I've got no horse. I'm cycling from here to New York; therefore, what would be the use of——"

"Now look here, you're a man of sense. I know you've ridden God knows where on that wheel of yours. Have a change. Ride the rest of the way to New York in a buggy. You ain't a man with prejudices, I guess. It's mighty bad for a man to always keep in one groove, ain't it? I'm talking sense, ain't I? You can't ride your wheel when it rains. If you have a buggy what does rain matter? You get mighty tired pumping along all day. In a buggy all you've got to do is to sit at your ease, like a gentleman. Think of all the waste of tissue and energy this bicycle riding is. Now I ain't no philanthropist, but you look thin, and I tell you the Lor'-mighty's truth in making it clear to your mind, as I guess you're a sensible man, that a buggy would be a perfect God-send. An' your bicycle's near worn out. Now this buggy, when you get to England, will be——"

"I don't want a buggy!"

"Now don't get curt and snappy," continued the drummer, edging his chair nearer. "Of course you don't want one. Nobody wants anything that's good for them; that's human nature. But look here, you might trade it when you get to England. You'd get a big price for it. So you'd have the use of the buggy from here to New York, and then make a profit on it. Doesn't that appeal to you?"

"No, it doesn't. I've got my bike."

So Mr. J. F. Fraser reports a conversation with a Yankee drummer, and I must say that at present his tone towards the buggy is very much up my own towards the motorcar or motor-cycle. For years many of us have been busily engaged in preaching the benefits of cycling as an exercise, and now, because Fashion shows a tendency to coquette with the new toy, we are expected to do the same.

The improvement and lightening of the cycle have so reduced the actual exertion of propelling it at a moderate pace that the old taunt of "hard labour" is no longer applicable. Indeed the boot is on the other foot now and the cyclist, pace for pace (say, three miles cycling for one mile walking, as old standard of comparison) has the easier time of it.

In driving a motorcar there is absolutely no exercise for the body, and it is only as a means of locomotion that the horseless carriage can be in any way compared to the cycle.

"A MEMBER of the British Automobile Club is having a motor gipsy van built, and means to start from Hong Kong in it next February and to proceed to Paris and London. The car is being built in Paris, and the motive power will be ordinary paraffin. The idea of using motor gipsy vans for holiday making is likely to be considerably developed in the near future." This is an extract from the "English American." When I wrote my little article on the motorvan for our Motor Supplement I hardly expected to hear so soon of such an adventurous trip on one as this would promise to be. As Mr. Fraser and his companions found the passage of Western China on cycles impossible and

From Hong Kong to London in a Gipsy Van.

were obliged to resort to native bearers, one can hardly hope that a motorvan will be able to traverse the almost trackless mountains. I advise the prospective tourist to read Mr. Fraser's book, and, if he thinks that too amusing to be taken seriously, to get Tom Stevens' earlier work, which indulges in nothing but hard fact.

THE executive of the French Touring Club are in the habit of preparing a budget and setting it before their membership. The figures of this estimate for 1900 are rather startling; the estimated receipt, with the balance of '99, but exclusive of the reserve fund, is about £25,000; it is proposed to spend the bulk of this in the following directions: Review £6,000; handbooks £600; office expenses £4,000; Paris exhibition (pavilion, &c.), £1,000; reserve fund £800; comparatively small sums are allotted to legal expenses (£40 only), danger boards (usually provided by private members), but the very large sum of £5,000 is appropriated for road improvement and publications; £1,500 has been already or is to be given towards the new Cornice road from Cannes to St. Raphael.

A Few Figures.

This shows a large minded finance, and it is no wonder that the T.C.F. now numbers some 25,000 members; but let not anyone run away with the idea that the club is on all fours with our C.T.C. and its finance analogous with the comparatively selfish expenditure of the latter body, which spends the vast bulk of its income on its membership. The fact is that the T.C.F. is by no means strictly a cycling body (or even cycling and motoring body) pure and simple. It exists for the sake of encouraging all kinds of touring and travelling, and in that capacity is bound to assist local enterprise in districts where expenditure is needed for the development of tourist traffic. In fact, it would seem to combine the functions of our C.T.C., the Roads Improvement Association, the Automobile and Motorcar Clubs, the Commons Preservation Society, and the National Trust Society.

I HAVE sent C.T.C. forms to T. J. (Plumstead), J. H. H. (Rawdon), W. G. F. (Cheam), and Mr. C. V. B. (Barnes). The correspondent who pointed out that there was already a tunnel alongside the Atherstone level crossing may be interested to learn that it is a mere cattle creep and not adapted for ordinary traffic, though no doubt a cyclist can pass under the line comfortably. For this information I am indebted to a local rider: I believe the four miles limit only refers to level crossings near to stations.

Varia.

TOURING DISTRICTS.—The Wye Valley.

I HAVE given suggested tours in the Wye Valley before, but the following is written from a lady's point of view. As a handy guide with cycling routes, I can recommend Messrs. A. Heywood's "Wye Valley," sold at one penny, or with map, twopence. A fuller work is the "Cyclists' Guide to the West Midlands," sold by Messrs. Littlebury, Worcester, in three sections costing sixpence each.

THE TOURIST EDITOR.

FOR those cyclists who are not afraid of hills—and in these free wheel days many of us prefer them—I think there

2.13 'Our Tourist Section' in this popular cycling periodical regularly detailed the historical and natural background of attractions reachable by bicycle, as well as providing an overview of other countries. *Cycling*, 20 January 1900.

the Vosges Club thus became a serious rival for the much older Society for the Protection of Historic Monuments of Alsace. While the larger historical associations and regional *Heimatschutz* societies counted about 700–800 members, tourism associations had ten times as many adherents. The Federation of German Tourism Association united in 1883, its founding year, fifteen associations with 11,000 members; in 1890 the number had risen to forty-seven associations. Although still dominated by the middle classes, their social reach was wider than that of the learned societies or preservation lobby groups; half of the members were artisans or owned smaller businesses.[304]

Membership figures clearly reveal that societies offering leisure activities were more attractive than those whose content was more learned, theoretical, high-culture and lobby-orientated. This was also reflected in cultural representations of associative life. For instance in the world of Alphonse Daudet's humoristic figure Tartarin de Tarascon, learned societies no longer figure, but being president of the local Alpine Club suffices to satisfy the hero's longing for recognition as the local matador.[305] Yet, 'heritage-consciousness' was fostered through the encounter with monuments and nature. The impetus for joining the new leisure societies was largely the enjoyment of the outdoors; however, due to increased threats to nature, landscape- and later on monument-protection became an integral part of the associations' activities. The nature of sources makes it difficult to follow the conversion from leisure activities to preservation on a personal level, but the attitudinal change gets perceivable when institutionalised.[306] On an organisational level, the leisure aspect often was increasingly combined with an attenuated form of preservationism. Many tourism associations became increasingly aware of the dangers to the landscapes and monuments that were at the heart of their activities and subsequently became involved in alerting their members to the activities of preservationists and even in campaigning themselves.[307]

---

[304] Speitkamp, *Verwaltung der Geschichte*, pp. 25, 119–20; Koshar, *Germany's Transient Pasts*, pp. 59–68 and Koshar, *German Travel Cultures* (Oxford, 2000).

[305] See Chaline, *Sociabilité*, p. 13.

[306] On the lack of detailed personal accounts from ordinary nineteenth-century tourists and the use of alternative sources see also Mandler, '"The Wand of Fancy"', pp. 126–7.

[307] See on reports of National Trust activities and hopes for further involvement: 'Our Tourist Section', *Cycling and Moting*, 22 September 1900, p. 214 and the same column in *Cycling and Moting*, 3 November 1900, p. 343. On campaigns led by tourism associations in France see for example attempts by the *Touring Club de France* to save the Romanesque chapel in Volx in 1906: 'Lettre de M. le maire de Volx à M. le président du comité des sites et monuments pittoresques du Touring Club', *Journal des Débats*, 2 February 1906, on German examples and the involvement of the Youth Movement see Speitkamp, *Verwaltung der Geschichte*, p. 120.

2.14 'The Photographic Craze: A Village besieged' first published in *Funny Folks*, 28 May 1887 and then in *Amateur Photographer*, 10 June 1887, p. 271 mocked the popularity of recording picturesque sites and rural life.

A similar story of patrimonialisation can be told for the photographic associations. Often, the photography of monuments became linked to rambling or cycling in a 'wedding of art and athletics', leading to besieged villages up and down the country (see ill. 2.14).[308] At the beginning, architecture had been a popular object for amateur photography as its still nature allowed the photographer to train photographic skills. However, amateur photographers increasingly photographed buildings not just for their picturesque value, but to preserve a record of the vanishing past, initiating various independent photographic survey movements, first on a local and later on a national level. The survey movements tried to preserve a disappearing period not so much by campaigning for physical conservation but by establishing a systematic record that was deposited in libraries and archives for future generations.[309] In addition to their involvement

[308] 'Cycling with the Camera', *Amateur Photographer*, 2 January 1884, pp. 201–3, quote p. 202. The *Touring Club de France* in particular encouraged its members to take photographs, but also involved photographic societies to contribute to its collection through subsidies and competitions. See for example *Art et Photographie. Revue bi-mensuelle illustrée pour la diffusion pratique de l'art en photographie dédiée aux amateurs*, 15 October 1900, p. 80; *Bulletin des Sociétés photographiques du Nord de la France*, May 1910, pp. 72–3.
[309] See E. Edwards, 'Commemorating A National Past. The National Photographic Record Association, 1897–1910', *Journal of Victorian Culture* 10.1 (2005), 123–31; Edwards, *The Camera as Historian:*

in record photography, photographic societies and magazines such as the *Amateur Photographer* also alerted readers when particular buildings were threatened with demolition, inciting individuals to take photographs to preserve a memory.[310]

Tourism and photographic associations can thus help us to understand that preservationism often resulted from commodification and leisure. Some preservationist purists continued to portray tourists only as destroyers, but, like Charles Normand, many started to encourage mindful tourism and collaboration between the preservation lobby groups and the leisure societies became frequent. Tellingly, the *Touring Club de France* was among the signatories of Maurice Barrès' petition to preserve all pre-1800 churches. Barrès himself, despite his earlier attacks on the effects of tourism, described the Club as 'a grand and useful association' in the work that recounted his campaigning.[311] Moreover, many of the more theoretical ideas developed by the aesthetic fringe were spread among larger parts of the population via the leisure activities. For example, the oldest consumer weekly photographic magazine, the *Amateur Photographer*, was imbued with Ruskinian and Morrisian preservationist language. Often this was implicit rather than explicit, for instance when exposing restored architectural features as 'frauds' in travel descriptions in passing,[312] but the magazine was also directly used by preservationists to communicate 'some architectural and archaeological knowledge'. The aim was not only to improve the photographer's gaze, but to prevent him from failing

> to distinguish between genuine old work full of life and thought and individuality of the original mason or carver and the cold, lifeless imitative work of the modern restorer. Possibly he may even prefer the neater and more precise work of the latter, with all its mechanical regularity, to the

Amateur Photographers and Historical Imagination, 1885–1918 (Durham, North Carolina, 2012); J. Taylor, *A Dream of England. Landscape, Photography and the Tourist's Imagination* (Manchester and New York, 1994). On the *Touring Club* photographic archives see digitalisation by MAP (2005), 'Archives photographique – Le Touring Club de France', www.mediatheque-patrimoine. culture.gouv.fr/fr/archives_photo/visites_guidees/touring%20club%20de%20france.html. On the role of French photography in shaping heritage consciousness more generally see B.L. Grad, T.A. Riggs, *Visions of City and Country. Prints and Photographs of Nineteenth-Century France. Exhibition catalogue. Worcester Art Museum and The American Federation of Arts* (Worcester MA, New York, 1982). On the use of photography by the German Heimat movement and the French regionalist movement see Trom, 'Natur und nationale Identität', pp. 147–67.

[310] See for example notes on London buildings, *Amateur Photographer*, 19 April 1901, p. 310 and 10 May 1901, p. 385.

[311] Barrès, *La Grande Pitié*, pp. 24 and 134–5.

[312] See for instance *Amateur Photographer*, 5 December 1884, p. 135.

Rock Dwellings. Kinver. Staffordshire 1895.

2.15 Sir Benjamin Stone, 'Rock dwellings. Kinver. Staffordshire. 1895', Platinum print. The photograph of rock houses from the sixteenth century, known locally as Holy Austin Rock was part of the National Photographic Record Associations' documentation of vanishing architecture, festivals, ceremonies and customs. By the time Stone photographed the rock houses, only a couple of families still lived in them.

bolder designs and execution of the twelfth century bishop who planned the building and of the nameless monk who carved the ornament.[313]

As Reverend Perkings, author of twenty-five chapters on 'Gothic Architecture' published in the magazine, acknowledged a great many books on the topic existed 'but they probably do not find their way into the hands of the photographers, as numbers of the Amateur Photographer will do'. Publishing a series in the weekly would moreover also 'enable anyone who wishes to take up the practice of architectural photography' from scratch 'to recognise the style and determine the approximate date of any buildings that he comes across'. Ideally this would lead 'in this age

[313] Rev. T. Perkings, 'Chapter on Gothic Architecture, Introduction', *Amateur Photographer*, 30 March 1894, pp. 21–2.

La race charollaise.

IV. — CHAROLLES

LA RACE CHAROLLAISE. — Si on laisse de côté l'arrondissement de Louhans, qui présente peu de curiosités remarquables, il nous reste celui de Charolles, où le touriste trouvera quelques parties intéressantes.

Charolles est une sous-préfecture de 4,000 habitants, située dans une riante vallée, au confluent de deux ruisseaux, la Semence et l'Arconce. On y voit quelques vieilles maisons du XVᵉ siècle, et deux tours qui proviennent d'un ancien château dont on a fait l'hôtel de ville.

L'arrondissement comprend quelques parties montagneuses, de belles vallées et de riches prairies où l'on

Paray-le-Monial. — Tour Saint-Nicolas.

2.16 Photographs of Le Creusot, Charolles and Paray-le-Monial from *Sites et Monuments*: *La Bourgogne* (Paris, 1906), published by the *Touring Club de France*. Each issue of the magazine covered the sites and monuments of a different region. Photographs recorded not only historical monuments and sites of natural beauty, but also proudly showed traditional cow breeds alongside new industrial buildings as part of local heritage.

Vue générale du Creusot.

2.16 (*cont.*)

when so much that is old is rapidly disappearing from the face of England' to the taking of photographic records.[314] The popular magazine thus allowed the author to communicate the philosophy of his Society for the Protection of Ancient Buildings in a way that learned publications would not.

The traffic of ideas was not one-directional either. The socially more diverse leisure groups also contributed to a change in the elites' understanding of what could be considered as heritage. It could be suggested, although further investigation is desirable, that the more vernacular focus of many of the photographic record societies helped to incorporate ethnographic elements of the vanishing present, and even images of new industrial constructions, into a previously high art-oriented understanding of heritage (see ills. 2.15–2.16).[315] Moreover, a shift not just from monumental

[314] Ibid. This was followed by two series in twenty-five instalments until 15 May 1895, pp. 168–9 and other articles on architectural education and a series on the 'Historical Development of Sculptural Art' by A. Fisher, an associate of the Society of Antiquaries, 5 April 1895, pp. 217–19.

[315] The combination of ethnographic and monumental heritage, of ancient buildings and vanishing customs is prevalent in popular collections of the French *Touring Club* or of the British National Photographic Record Association (1897–1910) and in more top-down surveys such as the Prokudin-Gorskii Photographic Record of Imperial Russia (1909–1915) and Albert Kahn's Archives of the World (1909–1930). On the latter two collections see J. Beausoleil, P. Ory (eds.), *Albert Kahn (1860–1940). Réalités d'une utopie.* Exhibition Catalogue Musée Albert Kahn (Boulogne, 1995) and Library of Congress, 'The Empire that Was Russia: The Prokudin-Gorskii Photographic Record Recreated' www.loc.gov/exhibits/empire.

to vernacular, but from national to local importance had a crucial effect on later inventory projects and national legislation, as will be seen below.[316]

By the end of the nineteenth century, an extraordinary multitude of bodies, from the learned to the professional, the activist to the leisure-loving, had thus emerged. They needed to negotiate amongst each other and with the state apparatus and monument owners the nature of 'heritage' and its preservation. The multiplication and diversification of societies is a testament to broader changes in sociability, but also reflects an increasing differentiation in ideas about 'heritage' in relation to aesthetics, race, gender, class, localness, nation, empire, religion, socialism, liberalism and conservatism, but also pleasure and duty. As the scene of individuals and institutions involved in 'heritage' became more diverse, public discussion of foreign practices and international arenas became increasingly a means for the different parties to justify their views. The next chapters will accompany the heritage-makers to different, yet intertwined arenas of internationalism and observe how they used their international contacts.

---

[316] On debates about local access and local knowledge see Edwards, 'Commemorating A National Past', 123–31.

PART II

International meeting-points

CHAPTER 3

Exhibition mania

At the world fair, the keepers of the past were provided with a prominent international arena through the grandest celebration of modern industrial progress. At first, history and heritage entered the stage through the back door. At the Great Exhibition of 1851, the past appeared in splendid, but isolated displays, such as Henri Austin Layard's archaeological findings from Nineveh. More modestly, but more constantly, many manufacturers started displaying the history of their products in an attempt to catch customers.[1] Subsequently, history became constitutive of the most diverse parts of the exhibitions. Finally, a retrospective element was systematically introduced through fine arts pavilions, arts and crafts shows and 'history of work' exhibitions that illustrated the role of human industry as the driving force behind progress and civilisation.

These historic displays have often been interpreted as an escapist counterbalance to modernisation.[2] Yet they equally served as a background against which progress was emphasised and rendered even more spectacular.[3] They justified and propagated imperial expansion by establishing a progressivist taxonomy of goods and manufacturing processes that established a parallel between the stages of production and the relation between races and nations (ill. 3.1). In the ethnographic displays, most non-European peoples were represented as possessing only the lowest level of manufacturing skills. Orientalist exhibitions portrayed some kind of

---

[1] A. von Plato, *Präsentierte Geschichte. Ausstellungskultur und Massenpublikum im Frankreich des 19. Jahrhunderts* (Frankfurt, New York, 2001), pp. 147–8.

[2] For example M. Wörner, *Vergnügen und Belehrung. Volkskultur auf den Weltausstellungen 1851–1900* (Münster, New York, 1999), p. 118.

[3] For historiographic overviews see A.C.T. Geppert, 'Welttheater. Die Geschichte des europäischen Ausstellungswesens im 19. und 20. Jahrhundert. Ein Forschungsbericht', *Neue Politische Literatur*, 47.1 (2002); A.C.T. Geppert, J. Coffey, T. Lau, 'International Exhibitions, Expositions Universelles and World's Fairs, 1851–1951. A Bibliography' (Nov. 2006), Henry Madden Library, California State University, www.csufresno.edu/library/subjectresources/specialcollections/worldfairs/ExpoBibliography3ed.pdf.

3.1 Illustrations for the 'history of work exhibition' in 1889 juxtaposed 'negro' work with eighteen-century European craftsmanship. From L. Gonse, 'L'Exposition de l'Histoire du Travail', *Revue de l'Exposition universelle de 1889* (Paris 1889), II, pp. 13–14.

intermediate state, by showing how former greatness was followed by decadence and stasis that needed the civilising mission to be rejuvenated.[4] The way in which European historicity versus non-European a-historicity was constructed through the display of objects and peoples is crucial for the development of a European sense of heritage, yet limiting the role of the world's fairs in heritage-making to this dichotomy would be reductive. Not only did non-Europeans possess more agency than these visions allow and many used the fairs to subvert some of the imposed categories, but there are also more complex processes going on within the European displays.[5]

Rather than constituting a homogenous vision, the exhibitions provided a public space for different heritage-makers to present their version of heritage. Visitors could choose among, or combine, multiple visions of the past. At the 1889 *Exposition universelle* in Paris, for instance, which as a whole celebrated the centenary of the French Revolution, visitors who had seen paintings, sculpture and architecture in the retrospective art exhibition, could explore individual nations' idea of their heritage in fancifully constructed national sections, or view the newest sensation, a display of the entire history of human housing from the stone age to present-day Lapland (ill. 3.2).[6] They could continue with private archaeological collections, a reproduction of an Egyptian street or life-size plaster casts of Ankor Wat, the history of farriery of war-horses, or stay on to delight in falconry, past and present as well as the history of virtually every other product of human labour (ills. 3.3–3.4).[7] Returning to Paris in 1900, visitors could

[4] See T. Bennett, 'The Exhibitionary Complex', in N.B. Dirks, G. Eley, S.B. Ortner (eds.), *Culture, Power, History. A Reader in Contemporary Social Theory* (Princeton, 1994), pp. 123–54. Since the publication of P. Greenhalgh, *Ephemeral Vistas. The Expositions universelles, Great Exhibitions and World's Fairs, 1851–1939* (Manchester, New York, 1988), the exhibitions' role as imperial display has been widely analysed. On the relation between representation as a modern technique of meaning and order, and the construction of otherness so important to the colonial project see in particular T. Mitchell, 'Orientalism and the Exhibitionary Order', in N. Dirks (ed.), *Colonialism and Culture* (Ann Arbor, 1992), pp. 289–318.
[5] See for instance V. Barth, *Mensch versus Welt. Die Pariser Weltausstellung von 1867* (Darmstadt, 2007), pp. 242–9.
[6] C. Garnier, A. Ammann, *L'Habitation humaine* (Paris, 1892); P. Greenhalgh, 'Education, Entertainment and Politics: Lessons from the Great International Exhibitions', in P. Vergo, *The New Museology* (London, 1989, repr. 2000), pp. 74–98, here pp. 89–92.
[7] A. Nicaise, *Exposition universelle de 1889. Galerie des arts libéraux (Champs de Mars). Collection archéologique de M. Auguste Nicaise. Inventaire descriptif* (Châlons-sur-Marne, 1895). M. Gavin, *Exposition universelle de 1889. Compte rendu de la promenade archéologique de la Commission des antiquités et des arts du département de Seine-et-Oise à l'exposition de la maréchalerie rétrospective au palais du ministère de la Guerre (esplanade des Invalides) [La Ferrure du cheval de guerre dans l'antiquité et au moyen âge jusqu'à nos jours, d'après les conférences de MM. Mathieu et Aureggio]* (Paris, 1889). *Exposition universelle internationale de 1889 à Paris. Exposition rétrospective, section III, arts et métiers.*

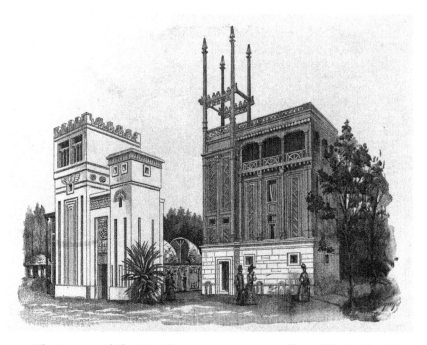

3.2 The Assyrian and Phenician Houses were among 44 pavilions of Charles Garnier's exhibition of human housing. From V. Champier, 'Les 44 Habitation Humaines construites au Champs de Mars, par M. Charles Garnier', *Revue de l'Exposition universelle de 1889* (Paris 1889), 1, p. 125.

observe how even the Eiffel Tower, attacked as the very enemy of Parisian *patrimoine* back in 1889, was already considered part of national heritage by 1900. They could visit a new edition of the old time favourite *Rue des Nations* along the Seine or relax in 'Old Paris'. This newest exhibition hit reconstructed the entire medieval city centre complete with hundreds of extras in authentic costume 'living' in the same manner as the 'inhabitants' of the many ethnographic villages (ills. 3.5–3.6).[8]

Just as exhibition organisers struggled to recreate the entire world in the space of an exhibition, drawing a complete picture of any given exhibition

Fauconnerie. Catalogue illustré par S. Arcos, Rd. Balze, Malher, Vallet etc. suivi de 'La Fauconnerie d'autrefois et la fauconnerie d'aujourd'hui' conférence faite à la Société nationale d'acclimatation, le 21 mars 1890 par M. Pierre Amédée Picho (Paris, 1890). For further examples see *Revue de l'Exposition universelle de 1889* (2 vols, Paris, 1889).

[8] On architecture built for the world exhibitions see the issue *'Identitäten, Räume, Projektionen. Weltausstellungen der Architektur* of *Wolkenkuckucksheim* 5.1 (2000), www.tu-cottbus.de/BTU/Fak2/TheoArch/Wolke/deu/Themen/themen001.html.

3.3 The Rue du Caire, one of the greatest attractions of the 1889 Paris world's fair, from Paul Bourde, 'La Rue du Caire', *Revue de l'Exposition universelle de 1889* (Paris, 1889), 1, p. 77.

3.4 A cast from Ankor. *Revue de l'Exposition universelle de 1889* (Paris 1889), 1, gravure hors texte 336 bis. In the world's fairs domestic and foreign monuments were increasingly reproduced as plaster casts to ensure a three dimensional experience.

3.5 The Rue des Nations, another exhibition favourite at the 1900 *Exposition universelle*, with the German pavilion in the centre, was frequently reproduced on postcards.

would be an undertaking of impossible magnitude.[9] As the Shah of Persia observed in 1878: 'If I wished to write a description of the Exhibition and all it contained, I should have to write from now until the closing of the Exhibition, every day for twenty-four hours, and even then I should have written only a tenth or a hundredth part. No description can give a true idea of the Exhibition; one must have seen it with one's own eyes. I left it very tired.'[10] Likewise, different aspects of the fairs provide almost limitless starting points for studying the concept of heritage.[11] Among the multitude of often-spectacular sites, this chapter focusses on the rather inconspicuous, yet highly instructive exhibitions of 'historic monuments' and restoration

[9] See Barth, *Mensch versus Welt*.
[10] Qu. in *Paris and its Exhibition: Pall Mall Gazette Extra* 49, 26 July 1889.
[11] For different approaches see for instance B. Stoklund, 'The Role of the International Exhibitions in the Construction of National Cultures in the 19th Century', *Ethnologia Europaea*, 24 (1994), 35–44; E. Fuchs, 'Nationale Repräsentation, kulturelle Identität und imperiale Hegemonie auf den Weltausstellungen: Einleitende Bemerkungen' in Fuchs (ed.), *Weltausstellungen im 19. Jahrhundert*, pp. 8–14; Wörner, *Vergnügen und Belehrung*; W. Kaiser, 'Vive la France! Vive la République? The Cultural Construction of French Identity at the World Exhibitions in Paris 1855–1900', *National Identities*, 1.3 (1999), 227–44; Plato, *Präsentierte Geschichte*.

3.6 Seductive 'inhabitants' in historic costume adorned the streets of Robida's Old Paris and posed photographs were sold as postcards and aggrandised in many books accompanying the exhibition such as L. Baschet (ed.), *Exposition Universelle 1900 (Le panorama)* (Paris, 1900).

projects.[12] Displays first in the architectural sections and then in a variety of other formats, provided not only information about what the exhibiting countries thought constituted their most representative monuments, but also demonstrated the evolving practices of their restoration and protection.

Although it is well known that world's fairs played a decisive part in the development of many modern disciplines, scholars have failed to consider the emergence of historic preservation as a movement and as a discipline in this connection. Yet, the exhibitions provided an important meeting place of national and international heritage-makers, a forum for both competition and collaboration. Most major government officials responsible for the protection of historic monuments regularly attended the world's fairs, or were informed through correspondence, as were representatives of the main private preservation associations. The exhibitions provide for more than a positivist analysis of the exchange of information. They allow examination of how the international scene was used to advance particular local agendas of different heritage-makers, notably to negotiate the role of the state and civil society. During the world's fairs, different heritage-makers had to co-exist in a shared space and could not completely avoid each other. As a result, the exhibitionary order was not only determined by ideological aims related to the representation of nation and empire or even a particular view of 'heritage', but also informed by personal rivalries and local agendas.

Historic monument exhibitions

Since fine arts sections became a regular exhibition feature through the first Parisian *Exposition universelle* in 1855, 'historical monuments' were exhibited at all major international and universal exhibitions, as well as at a number of smaller international exhibitions (table 1).[13]

---

[12] While the ephemeral architecture of the exhibitions has received much attention from A. Normand, *L'Architecture des nations étrangères. Etude sur les principales constructions du parc à l'Exposition universelle de Paris, 1867* (Paris, 1870) to T. Schriefers, 'Denkmäler mit Verfallsdatum. Zur Überwindung des traditionellen Denkmalbegriffs auf Weltausstellungen', *Wolkenkuckucksheim*, 5.1 (2000), www.tu-cottbus.de/BTU/Fak2/TheoArch/Wolke/deu/Themen/themen001.html; the architectural sections in general and the restoration studies in particular have largely escaped scholarly analysis. For an inventory of most exhibiting country's catalogues see O. Charbonneau, 'Les Monuments historiques aux expositions universelles et internationales de 1855 a 1937' (3 vols., unpublished Mémoire de Maîtrise, Université Paris-IV, 2001).

[13] On the categorisation of fairs see J.E. Findling (ed.), *Historical Dictionary of World's Fairs and Expositions, 1851–1988* (New York, Westport, London, 1990); E. Fuchs (ed.), *Weltausstellungen im 19. Jahrhundert* (Comparativ 9.5–6, Leipzig, 1999); W. Kretschmar, *Geschichte der Weltausstellungen* (Frankfurt, New York, 1999).

Table 1 *Major world exhibitions with sections on historic monuments*

1855	Paris	*Exposition universelle des produits de l'agriculture et des beaux-arts*
1862	London	International Exhibition
1867	Paris	*Exposition universelle*
1871	London	1st Annual London Exhibition
1872	London	2nd Annual London Exhibition
1873	London	3rd Annual London Exhibition
1873	Vienna	*Weltausstellung*
1874	London	4th Annual London Exhibition
1876	Philadelphia	Pennsylvania Centennial Exposition
1878	Paris	*Exposition universelle*
1889	Paris	*Exposition universelle*
1893	Chicago	World's Columbian Exposition
1900	Paris	*Exposition universelle et internationale*
1904	St Louis	Louisiana Purchase International Exposition
1915	San Francisco	Panama-Pacific International Exposition
1937	Paris	*Exposition internationale des arts et techniques dans la vie moderne*

Displays contained architectural drawings, wooden models, plaster casts and later photographs, and were complemented by written documentation relative to restorations. Initially, the French, German and British, as indeed all European as well as some non-European sections, exhibited a very high proportion of restoration studies. Housed in the architectural section of the exhibitions since 1855, the restoration studies of national architecture were mixed with depictions of Roman, Greek and Egyptian antique monuments and contemporary building projects in no particular order. However, over the course of the exhibitions, national sections began to take different paths. In the British and German sections, as in most other European countries' sections, the number of retrospective studies decreased towards the end of the century.[14] Conversely, their number gradually increased in the French

[14] On British sections see A.E. Lance, *Exposition universelle des beaux-arts. Architecture, compte-rendu par Adolphe Lance, Architecte du Gouvernement* (Paris, 1855); *London International Exhibition 1862. Official Catalogue of the Fine Art Department* (London, 1862); *Paris Universal Exhibition of 1867. Catalogue of the British Section, containing a List of the Exhibitors of the United Kingdom...* (London, 1867); *Exposition universelle de 1878 à Paris. Grande-Bretagne. Catalogue de la section des beaux-arts* (London, 1878); *Great Britain. Royal Commission for the Chicago Exhibition 1893. Official Catalogue of the British Section* (London, 1893); *Paris Exhibition, 1900. Catalogue of the British Fine Art Section* (London, 1900). On German Sections: *Visites et études de S. A. I. le prince Napoléon au Palais des beaux-arts, ou Description complète de cette exposition (peinture, sculpture, gravure, architecture) avec la liste des récompenses, les statistiques officielles et les documents et décrets faisant suite aux Visites et études au Palais de l'industrie* (Paris, 1856); *International Exhibition 1862. Special Catalogue of the Zollverein-Department* (Berlin, 1862); *Prusse et états de l'Allemagne du Nord. Catalogue spécial de l'exposition universelle de Paris en 1867 édité par la commission* (Paris, 1867); *Bericht über die Allgemeine*

section.[15] However, a common factor impinged on these divergent paths. In 1855, at the high point of the gothic revival, historicism conflated restorations and contemporary projects, hence they were exhibited together. As over the course of the century, a differentiation between authentic historic elements and new architecture was gradually developed, the exhibitions responded. Whereas the historical element became less accentuated in the British and German architectural sections, the French also acknowledged this trend by clearly separating their historical material from the modern constructions.

During the nineteenth and early twentieth century, the French developed ever more elaborate displays from the archives of the state's monument services. Already substantially represented in 1855 and 1862, works from the archives of the Historic Monuments Commission were shown as a collection in ever more splendid exhibitions in the subsequent Parisian *Expositions universelles*. They were first given separate recognition in the 1867 Exhibition of the History of Work, which systematised the idea to represent the progress of civilisation through the history of manufacture.[16] Conceptually the exhibition split not only clearly between French 'objects

---

Ausstellung zu Paris im Jahre 1867, erstattet von den für Preußen und die Norddeutschen Staaten ernannten Mitgliedern der internationalen Jury (Berlin 1868); *Wiener Weltausstellung. Amtlicher Katalog der Ausstellung des Deutschen Reiches* (Berlin, 1873); *Weltausstellung in Philadelphia 1876. Deutsche Abtheilung. Amtlicher Katalog* (Berlin, 1876); *Verzeichnis der ausgestellten Werke, Welt-Ausstellung in Paris 1878. Deutsche Abtheilung* (Berlin, 1878); W.H. Uhland (ed.), *Illustrierter Katalog der Pariser Weltausstellung von 1878 unter Mitwirkung zahlreicher Berichterstatter* (Leipzig, 1880); O.N. Witt (ed.), *Amtlicher Katalog der Ausstellung des Deutschen Reiches. Columbische Weltausstellung in Chicago* (Berlin, 1893); *Amtlicher Katalog der Ausstellung des Deutschen Reichs, Weltausstellung in Paris 1900* (Berlin, 1900); J. Lessing, *Das halbe Jahrhundert der Weltausstellungen* (Volkswirtschaftliche Zeitfragen 174, Berlin, 1900); *Photographien der deutschen Abteilung der Pariser Weltausstellung 1900* (Paris, 1900); *Weltausstellung in St Louis 1904. Amtlicher Katalog der Ausstellung des Deutschen Reichs. Hrsg. vom Reichskommissar* (Berlin, 1904). See also AN, F 21 525, Dossier 'Allemagne'.

[15] Other Mediterranean countries also continuously showed a relatively high preference for exhibiting historic monuments, but with less consistency than France. See catalogue lists reprinted in Charbonneau, 'Les Monuments historiques', II, pp. 19–92.

[16] E. du Sommerard, *Exposition universelle de 1867 à Paris. Commission de l'histoire du travail. Rapport de M. E. du Sommerard* (Paris, 1867); also published as E. du Sommerard, 'Rapport. "Commission de l'histoire du travail"', in M. Chevalier (ed.), *Rapports du jury international Exposition universelle de 1867 à Paris* (13 vols., Paris, 1868), I., pp. 139–246; *Rapport sur l'Exposition universelle de 1867, à Paris. Précis des opérations et listes des collaborateurs. Avec un appendice sur l'avenir des expositions, la statistique des opérations, les documents officiels et le plan de l'Exposition* (Paris, 1869), pp. 20–3; see also Bellet, 'Promenade', pp. 371–4; H. Dufrené, 'Histoire du travail', in E. Lacroix (ed.), *Etude sur l'Exposition de 1867. Annales et archives de l'industrie au XIXe siècle ou Nouvelle technologie des arts et métiers, de l'agriculture etc. Description générale, encyclopédique, méthodique et raisonnée de l'état actuel des arts, des sciences, de l'industrie et de l'agriculture, chez toutes les nations* (8 vols., Paris, s.d.), VI, pp. 370–88; F. Lasteyre, *De l'histoire du travail à l'Exposition universelle* (Paris, 1867); C. de Linas, *L'Histoire du travail à l'Exposition universelle de 1867* (From the *Revue de l'art chrétien*, Paris, 1867).

from the Gauls to the Revolution' and 'foreign sections', but the 300 architectural drawings of over 150 monuments which adorned the walls of
the entire French section, received their own category as 'monuments historiques'.[17] Subsequently historic monuments were then shown in even
more detail within the larger framework of retrospective art exhibitions
in 1878, 1889 and 1900, together with the restorations undertaken by the
Service for Diocesan Buildings.[18] They were also well represented at international exhibitions outside of France. Having been present in London in
1862, but prevented from participating in the first of the Annual London
Exhibitions in 1871 by the Franco-Prussian war, the Historic Monuments
Commission refrained from taking part in 1873 in London in order to
have an even ampler staging at the internationally more important Vienna
Weltausstellung the same year.[19] A year later the *monuments historiques* were
shown in London again.[20] While represented by only one drawing at the
first American world's fair in Philadelphia, considerable efforts were made
to ensure a sizeable representation in the United States in Chicago, St Louis
and San Francisco, mostly through plaster casts and photographs so as not
to endanger the drawings by sending them across the Atlantic.[21] Moreover, works from the Historic Monument Commission's archives were also
shown at exhibitions in Belgium, Denmark, Germany, Ireland, Italy, Spain,
and the Netherlands, as well as at a number of exhibitions in France.[22] In

---

[17] Sommerard, *Commission de l'histoire du travail*, pp. 66–9. On foreign sections see pp. 71–5 and
   'Architecture', in Chevalier (ed.), *Rapports du jury international Exposition universelle de 1867*, I,
   pp. 107–16. Foreign nations only exhibited objects, their architectural drawings were exhibited with
   the fine arts.

[18] *Exposition universelle de 1878 à Paris. Ministère de l'instruction publique, des cultes et des beaux-arts.
   Catalogue de l'exposition des archives de la commission des monuments historiques en France* (Paris,
   1878); *Exposition universelle internationale de 1889 à Paris. Exposition rétrospective de l'art français
   au Trocadéro* (Lille, 1889); *Exposition universelle de 1900, à Paris (Palais du Trocadéro). Catalogue
   des expositions des monuments historiques (ministère de l'instruction publique et des beaux-arts) et de
   l'exposition des édifices diocésains (ministère de l'intérieur et des cultes)* (Paris, 1900).

[19] *Exposition universelle de Vienne, 1873. France. Œuvres d'art et manufactures nationales. Commissariat
   général* (Paris, Vienna, 1873), p. 13.

[20] MAP, 80/8/5, Dossier 'Angleterre'.

[21] Sommerard to *Bureau des Monuments historiques*, 3 Dec. 1877, MAP, 80/8/7, Dossier 'Exposition uni-
   verselle de 1878'; J.A.S.M. Ozenne, E. Du Sommerard, *Expositions internationales. Section française.
   Rapport présenté au Ministre de l'agriculture et du commerce sur les expositions internationales de Londres en 1871, en 1872 et en 1874, de Vienne en 1873 et de Philadelphie en 1876, par MM. Ozenne et Du
   Sommerard* (repr. from *JO*, Paris, 1877); *Exposition internationale et universelle de Philadelphie, 1876.
   Rapport. France. Commission supérieure* (Paris, 1877), p. 55; 'Arrêté portant règlement de la section
   française de l'exposition des beaux-arts de Chicago', *JO*, 11 May 1892, 2354; 'Arrêté instituant cinq
   comités chargés de statuer sur l'admission des ouvrages d'artistes français à l'exposition de Chicago
   et nommant les membres de ces comités', *JO*, 3 June 1892, 2713; MAP, 80/8/6.

[22] MAP, 80/8/1–2; 5; AN, F 21 525, AN, F 21 4061. *Exposition de l'oeuvre de Viollet-le-Duc ouverte au
   Musée des Thermes et à l'Hôtel de Cluny* (Paris, 1880); Union centrale des arts décoratifs, *Exposition*

the major world's fairs alone, depictions of more than 500 monuments were thus displayed, with 'monographs' of a given edifice containing sometimes over twenty drawings, designs and water-colours, complemented by photographs and casts.[23]

Not only was the number of historical monuments exhibited higher than in any other national section, but the presentation was different. While exhibits in the architectural sections were classified by architect, from 1867 onwards, the French organised the likenesses of historic monuments in chronological and thematic order as a lesson in French art history. Reproductions of architecture, architectural sculpture, stained glass, wall paintings and mosaics were organised into 'Antiquity', 'Religious Architecture' (again subdivided chronologically or according to regional schools), 'Military Architecture' and 'Civil Architecture'. The art historical didactic of the exhibitions was underpinned by maps that showed the different regional architectural schools during the French Middle Ages. The main emphasis was on antique and medieval architecture, but due to the general widening of the concept of 'monument' during the course of half a century prehistoric monuments were included at later exhibitions, as was the *Ancien Regime*.

While the 1855 French section, like the British and German ones, included images of antique monuments in Italy and Greece, they were not exhibited alongside the French historic monuments in later exhibitions. These were clearly conceptualised as exhibitions of 'national art', aiming at a balanced representation of the different regions and accentuating the historical lesson with plaster casts of statues and funeral monuments of figures of representative value for French history. This vision of 'national heritage' was not confined to the contemporary territory of metropolitan France. While allusion to Alsace-Lorraine were avoided after 1871, other lost territories were incorporated, Burgundian monuments, now on Belgian territory were shown thrice, and so were newly gained heritages: antique and Arab

---

1884 Paris, Catalogue. Salons du 1er étage. Exposition forestière . . . Monuments historiques . . . Musée rétrospectif (Paris, 1884); H. Loriquet, *Préfecture du Pas-de-Calais. Commission des Monuments historiques. Catalogue de l'exposition rétrospective des arts et monuments du Pas-de-Calais, Arras, 20 mai-21 juin 1896, par Henri Loriquet* (Arras, 1896); Ministère de l'Instruction publique et des beaux-arts. Direction des Beaux-arts. Monuments historiques. Musée de Sculpture comparée, *Catalogue des moulages de sculptures appartenant aux divers centres et aux diverses époques d'art, exposés dans les galeries du Trocadéro, suivi du catalogue des dessins de Viollet-le-Duc conservés dans la bibliothèque* (Paris, 1890).

[23] See catalogues for the exhibitions in Paris 1855, London 1862, Paris 1867, Vienna 1873, London 1874, Paris 1878 and 1889, Chicago 1893, Paris 1900 quoted above, as well as reports and lists in MAP 80/8/5–7.

monuments in the new Algerian *départements* were fully integrated into
the story of national art from the 1874 exhibition onwards.[24]

The exhibitions were inspired by the chronological and national display of Alexandre Lenoir's Museum of French Monuments formative for
the organiser's generation. They were also influenced by the Musée du
Sommerard, the originally private collection of Alexandre du Sommerard, a member of the provincial administrative elite who fought in the
Revolutionary armies, and started his patronage of the arts during the
Empire. Under the Restoration he assembled one of the first collections of
medieval and Renaissance objects for which he rented the residence of the
Abbot of Cluny in Paris. After his death, it became the Museum of Cluny
under the responsibility of the French state in 1843, and housed not only
du Sommerard's collection, but the remains of the collection of Alexandre
Lenoir.[25] Its director, the founder's son Edmond was also the organiser
of the History of Work exhibition in 1867 and of subsequent historic
monuments sections in France and abroad.

The exhibitions chiefly attempted to establish a broad picture of French
monumental history, and yet, within this display the largest space was
also devoted to the Historic Monument Commission's most prominent
architects and their most spectacular restorations.[26] Of the over 500 monuments shown between 1855 and 1900, more than two-thirds were only
exhibited once, while others figured at up to eight exhibitions. Viollet-le-
Duc's restorations had particular prominence, especially the walled city of
Carcasonne, the Romanesque basilica Saint Sernin in Toulouse and Pierrefonds Castle. Other favourites were Boeswillwald's restorations of the
Ducal Palace in Nancy, Notre Dame de Laon and the Abbey of Mouzon,
Duban's work at Blois and the Sainte Chapel and Questel's Roman
restorations, especially the Pont du Gard and the Amphitheatre in Arles
(ills. 3.7–3.8).

---

[24] This nuances the argument that the French colonisers mainly tried to de-arabise the Algerian
patrimoine. See P.M.E. Lorcin, 'Rome and France in Africa: Recovering Colonial Algeria's Latin Past',
French Historical Studies, 25.2 (2002), 295–329 and C. Ford, 'Nature, Culture, and Conservation
in France and Her Colonies, 1840–1940', *Past and Present*, 183 (May 2004), 173–198. On the
patrimonialisation of the Arab architecture see Oulebsir, *Usages du patrimoine*.

[25] On the two museums see Bann, *The Clothing of Clio*, pp. 77–92; Plato, *Präsentierte Geschichte*, pp.
35–100; F. Haskell, *History and its Images. Art and the Interpretation of the Past* (New Haven, 1993),
pp. 236–52.

[26] The catalogues of 1855, 1862, 1867, 1873, 1874, 1878, 1889, 1900 mention roughly 120 different
architects and illustrators. Less than half exhibited only once, a quarter twice. The number of
architects that exhibited most constituted the core of the CMH architects, cf. *Les Architectes en
chef des Monuments historiques, centenaire du concours* (Paris, 1994); 'Biographies des Architectes en
Chef des Monuments Historiques', www.mediatheque-patrimoine.culture.gouv.fr/fr/bibliotheque/
index.html.

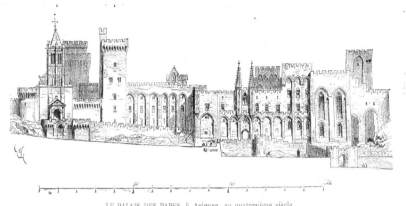

LE PALAIS DES PAPES, à Avignon, au quatorzième siècle.

3.7 A drawing of the Papal Palace, Avignon by Viollet-le-Duc shown in the History of Work Exhibition in 1867 and reproduced in *L'Exposition universelle de 1867 illustrée.* Architectural drawings of the palace were exhibited in 1862 and 1867, while restoration of the mural paintings were shown in 1874 and 1889.

The world fairs' aim to demonstrate constant progress and the formal ban on exhibiting the same works in consecutive exhibitions was thus interpreted in a rather loose way. While in the British section no historical monument, other than the restoration of Sherborne Abbey by Slater and a study of the Arch of Titus by Wyatt, were shown more than once, the organisers of the French sections argued that progress on particular restorations justified the repetition of certain monuments in the displays. However, the repeated exhibition of particular restorations and the frequency of posthumous exhibitions, make it evident that the exhibitions were less seen as progress reports, than representations of the entirety of French heritage and the work of the Historic Monuments Commission as a whole.

This singular nature of the French historic monuments exhibitions deserves explanation. Why was so much more emphasis given to historic monuments in France than in the sections of other countries? In a general way, any comparison between France, Britain and Germany is marked by the considerable asymmetries in fair organisation and participation. France was the most prolific organiser with exhibitions held in Paris in 1855, 1867, 1878, 1889 and 1900. Britain hosted the Great Exhibition in 1851 and another in 1862, but for economic reasons thereafter concentrated on international exhibitions of a less universal character. Germany made a few attempts to host an exhibition but in the end organised none. The particularist nature

3.8 Pierrefonds by E.E. Viollet-le-Duc. Pierrefonds was among the most popular monuments exhibited. As catalogues only provided lists of monuments exhibited, but no reproduction, it is uncertain which drawings exactly were shown, apart from those reproduced in illustrated reports. This drawing is from the archives of the *Commission des Monuments historiques*.

of German exhibits before unification and the German Reich's limited participation in 1878 and 1889 for political reasons further complicates comparison.[27] Given that the organising nation generally occupied about half the space of the entire exhibition, France cumulatively enjoyed more

[27] See E. Fuchs, 'Das Deutsche Reich auf den Weltausstellungen vor dem Ersten Weltkrieg', in Fuchs (ed.), *Weltausstellungen im 19. Jahrhundert*, pp. 61–88; A.C.T. Geppert, 'Ausstellungsmüde. Deutsche Grossausstellungsprojekte und ihr Scheitern, 1880–1930' and C. Cornelissen, 'Das Deutsche Reich auf den Weltausstellungen des 19. Jahrhunderts', in *Wolkenkuckucksheim*, 5.1 (2000), www.tu-cottbus.de/BTU/Fak2/TheoArch/Wolke/deu/Themen/themen001.html. On German non-participation in 1878 see AN, F 12 3265. The 1889 exhibition was boycotted by all European monarchies as it celebrated the centenary of the French Revolution.

exhibition space than any other nation.[28] Furthermore, France accorded an extraordinary place to the fine arts and was given a larger space than any other nation in most exhibitions in foreign countries.[29] Yet while this accounts for French exhibits outnumbering those of the other countries, it does not explain why such an over-proportionate part was accorded to the *monuments historiques*, while no coherent exhibitions of historic monuments were developed by the British and Germans, or other Europeans, despite their prolific restoration and preservation activities.

Entertainment and education

The content and organisational structure of the national sections suggest that, out of the three countries examined most closely, only France had a coherent vision for the exhibition of historic monuments. This sits well with France being the only country to have produced copious publications explaining the reasoning behind the exhibition of restorations. The motivation most frequently cited in the official French publications was their entertainment value. Organisers and official commentators enjoyed the certitude that the French monuments were unrivalled in their sublime beauty, variety and number and copiously quoted Viollet-le-Duc's and Mérimée's reports from the 1840s in support of their view.[30] They admitted that as a general rule 'an architectural exhibition is generally too technical to be viewed without being tiresome for a general public more in search of entertainment than education'.[31] However, the drawings held by the Commission were the 'exception to the rule'. Works of art in their own right, they were 'the object of envy of all the nations of Europe'.[32] Moreover, they were 'more pleasing to the eye than any new construction project, for they reproduce well known monuments which everybody likes to see time and again'.[33] Voices from the art establishment agreed on this point. Louis Gonse, the greatest promoter of Japanese Art in France and director of the *Gazette des Beaux Arts*, France's most important art journal, expressed the

[28] Kretschmar, *Geschichte der Weltausstellungen*, pp. 287–97.
[29] See J. Pemsel, *Die Wiener Weltausstellung von 1873. Das gründerzeitliche Wien am Wendepunkt* (Vienna, Cologne, 1989), p. 67; Michel Lagrave (Commissaire général) to *Bureau des Monuments historiques*, 6 Sep. 1903, MAP, 80/8/6, Dossier 'Exposition de St. Louis (1904)'.
[30] For example E. du Sommerard, *Exposition universelle de Vienne en 1873. Section française. Les Monuments historiques de France à l'exposition universelle de Vienne par M. E. du Sommerard* (Paris, 1876), p. 4.
[31] A. Perrault-Dabot, *Les Archives de la Commission des Monuments historiques* (Paris, 1900), p. 11.
[32] Sommerard, *Commission de l'histoire du travail*, pp. 12, 64.
[33] Perrault-Dabot, *Les Archives*, p. 11.

need for synthetic historical exhibitions addressing both specialists and as large a proportion of the general public as possible and concluded that 'the Commission only had to cull from its archives almost at random to produce a magnificent exhibition'. The drawings and the opulent plaster casts and photographers that were united in later exhibitions provided 'a unique collection of educational materials' showing better than any words 'our supremacy'. 'France is indeed the richest and vastest architectural museum in Europe.'[34] A report in one of the illustrated exhibition guides even saw the archaeological and architectural drawings as the most interesting part of the entire exhibition, 'the peach of our promenade', with which even the exotic and erotic charm of many foreign women present could not rival.[35] All reports stressed the overabundance of first-class material, subliminally regretting that it could only partially be exhibited at any given time. They assured that 'the Commission took absolutely no account of personal interests' in making the selections,[36] the choices being driven by the desire to entertain the visitors with famous monuments and familiarise them with less well known ones.[37]

Having extolled both the collection's artistic quality and its potential for entertainment, and thus alluding to the first world exhibition maxim of 'entertainment', the official commentators moved on to the second classic element of world exhibition rhetoric, the educative mission. The catalogue for the *Weltausstellung* in Vienna in 1873 outlined:

> The Commission of Historic Monuments . . . had but one aim, by responding to the call it had received; to inform about the advantages of an institution which was only founded in 1837, but which, since its creation strongly and energetically contributed to the conservation of the precious monuments of past centuries from different architectural schools which are one of the glories of our fatherland and represent the true history of our national art.[38]

In addition to the exhibition of architectural drawings, the Commission decided it was in the 'public interest' to publish some of its written records in the catalogue, the stated reason being:

---

[34] L. Gonse, 'L'Architecture', in Gonse, Alfred de Lostalot (eds.), *Exposition Universelle de 1889: Les beaux-arts et les arts decoratifs – l'art français retrospectif au Trocadero* (Paris, 1890), pp. 221–42, qu. p. 328.
[35] P. Bellet, 'Promenade autour du Jardin central', in Ducuing, F. (ed.), *L'Exposition universelle de 1867 illustrée* (Paris, 1868), pp. 371–4, qu. p. 372.
[36] Perrault-Dabot, *Les Archives*, pp. 25–30; Sommerard, *Les Monuments historiques*, pp. 1–2.
[37] Sommerard, *Commission de l'histoire du travail*, p. 63; Sommerard, *Les Monuments historiques*, p. 1.
[38] Sommerard, *Les Monuments historiques*, pp. 1–2.

Several European countries try to follow in the vein in which we preceded them. Commissions for the conservation of monuments have been
founded. Most governments are about to create similar institutions. Therefore it seemed interesting to publish the diverse documents relating to the
foundation of the Historic Monuments Commission of France, showing the
aims it pursues in the name of the Government and the means it disposes
of, as well as the results it was able to obtain.[39]

With this publication the commission addressed a real demand. Since
its foundation it had received letters from foreign government officials
enquiring about the work of the commission, as seen through the demands
from Berlin, Munich and London earlier.[40] Through the exhibitions more
generally, the French hoped to stimulate conservation abroad. For instance,
the reporter for the International Exhibition in London in 1874 suggested
that the French exhibitions of historic monuments would stimulate the
foundation, if not of a similar English commission, at least of societies
for the protection of monuments.[41] Du Sommerard's 416-page volume
on the 1873 exhibition was the most extensive monograph on the French
monuments' administration published before the First World War. Yet
the history and principles of the protection of monuments also prefaced
every exhibition catalogue and were published in the exhibitions rules, the
jury reports, and even appeared in most journalistic accounts. All French
retrospective exhibitions not only showed art but demonstrated art politics
since the French Revolution.[42] The government encouraged exhibition
publications to include studies on the work of the different state agencies,
widely diffused in France and abroad, with the aim to provide visitors
with a 'lesson on the economic administration of common goods'. As the
'social work provided by the state' steadily grew, they should illustrate the
'evolution and perfection of the different administrations'.[43]

However, the educational role of the exhibitions was seen to go even
further, as the restoration of buildings was believed to exert good influence

[39] Ibid.   [40] MAP, 80/1/32–33.
[41] E. Baumgart, *Monuments historiques. Rapport de M. Baumgart. Etabli à l'occasion de l'exposition
internationale de Londres 1874* (Paris, 1874), cf. earlier manuscript version: Baumgart, 'Rapport.
Exposition internationale. Londres 1874. Archives de la Commission des Monuments historiques',
fol. 4, MAP, 80/8/5, Dossier 'Londres'.
[42] A. Picard (ed.), *Exposition universelle internationale de 1889 à Paris. Rapport du jury international.
Groupe I – Oeuvres d'art. Classe 1 à 5 BIS* (Paris, 1890).
[43] Waldeck-Rousseau, *Président du Conseil, Ministre de l'Intérieur et des Cultes* to all *Services*, Paris
21 March 1900, copy, sent by the *Secretariat des Services des Beaux-Arts de l'Exposition Universelle de
1900* to Berr de Turique, *Chef du Service de l'Exposition des Monuments historiques en 1900*, 8 Apr.
1900, MAP 80/8/7, Dossier 'Exposition de 1900'.

on the arts and public taste.[44] Using manufactured objects from different periods to show the progress of technology and improve contemporary
industry and art was a common reasoning behind retrospective exhibitions,
but the inclusion of architectural drawings was unusual. The organisers justified it through the interdependence of architecture and manufacture and
stressed that historical monuments were first of all technical monuments.[45]
The legitimacy of historic elements in exhibitions of progress was only
explicitly questioned during the interwar years and the 1937 *Exposition
internationale* banned purely retrospective exhibits. However, even then
with the support of the General Commissioner, an ardent lover of monuments, the same old exhibition of drawings was secured by labelling them
as an exhibition about the 'use of modern technology in the conservation
of ancient monuments'.[46] The nineteenth-century exhibitions did not go
that far, but the modern side of the pursuit of restoration and appreciation
of monuments was stressed, be it out of genuine belief or simply in order to
have a pretext to include the historic monuments. Hence Viollet-le-Duc's
ideas about the modernity of restoration were taken up time and again
to underline that it 'was given to our age to understand that to conserve
buildings that tell the glory of the past is to revive one's past for the benefit
of one's present and future'.[47]

On another level, historic monuments were also portrayed as more beneficial to the nation than any other object in arts and crafts exhibitions,
as they contributed not just to rejuvenating modern industry, but could
also enable social cohesion. Du Sommerard purposefully compared works
supervised by the Historic Monuments Commission and by the Department of Public Works. As the former spent 60 per cent of its expenses on its
workforce and only 40 per cent on building materials, whereas for the latter
the opposite was true, du Sommerard concluded that the restorations were
more advantageous for the labouring classes. In contrast to the department
of Public Works, which employed itinerant workshops, alien to the locality,
the Historic Monuments Commission formed local colonies introducing
the local workforce to new standards of work. Drawing on Mérimée's
reports from the 1860s, he pointed out that the restoration work had a
moralising effect upon the workers as they were constantly faced with new

[44] Sommerard, *Les Monuments historiques*, pp. 25–31.
[45] Sommerard, *Commission de l'histoire du travail*, p. 70.
[46] E. Labbé (ed.), *Exposition internationale des Arts et Techniques à Paris en 1937, la section française,
rapport général* (5 vols., Paris, 1939), V, pp. 552–4.
[47] Sommerard, *Les Monuments historiques*, p. 3.

challenges, thus experiencing the satisfaction that comes with mastering difficulties. In contrast to contemporary projects where 'the worker is lost in ungrateful and poorly rewarded labour', on a restoration site, 'the first thing one notices is the emulation of workers, each aspiring to accomplish a difficult task and to distinguish himself by his intelligence and dexterity'. Hence, despite being unconnected to financial benefits, 'nothing is more common on our building sites than to see workers asking for more difficult tasks'.[48]

Most of the restoration sites were in small towns in the provinces and this was presented as being equally beneficial for workers and towns. For workers there was no distraction; they had to concentrate on their work, lacked opportunities of wasting money, and their 'morals' were not in danger. In return, life in the provincial cities was animated by the restorations, not least because youthful, vigorous, and passionate architects were sent from Paris to train the local workforce, invigorating remote places.[49] One might wonder whether Mérimée's and du Sommerard's positions were a response to Ruskin's *Seven Lamps of Architecture* that portrayed the status of the medieval mason as diametrically opposed to that of the contemporary building worker. While Ruskin condemned modern restorations as unbeneficial for the worker, asking for a resolution of the social question as prerequisite for artistic creation, Mérimée and du Sommerard championed architectural restoration to solve the social question. Du Sommerard saw his argument confirmed by the fact that at the end of the Italian War in 1860, Napoleon III's government allocated a part of the resources that had not been consumed by the war to the Historic Monuments Commission because of the beneficial effect the work on ancient buildings had on the 'morals of the French worker' in the hope that it might prevent upheaval at a time of growing socialist movements.[50]

The organisers of French historic monuments exhibitions thus cultivated legitimacy for them by stressing their congruence with the general aims of the world exhibitions. They were declared to be entertaining for the masses, works of art in their own right, stimulators for the arts, educators for the world, and, indirectly through the administrations' work, social and economic rejuvenants for the province and devices of social cohesion. As a consequence they were perfect weapons in the peaceful battle among nations that were the world exhibitions.

[48] Ibid., pp. 10–11.　　[49] Ibid., p. 13.　　[50] Ibid., p. 11.

A case of failed transfer?

The idea of a peaceful battle among nations was central to the world exhibitions. Announcing the 1855 *Exposition universelle*, the Napoleonic government sent a letter to potential exhibitors in all countries, explaining that the arts had for the first time been included in the exhibition of industrial progress, as the 'improvement of manufacture is closely connected with that of fine arts'.[51] The official publications also explicated that the arts, past and present, should assure France's leading international role:

> A competition of all the industries of nations was, for a first time, opened in a neighbouring and allied country, who owes her force and prosperity to industry. It is reserved to France, when she revives a Universal Exhibition of Industry, to add an exhibition of the Fine Arts, which so contribute to her glory. This innovation will be a fruitful one. We have to arrive at this peaceful battle with well-chosen arms, so that in this struggle our artists will prove themselves worthy of the other children of France who fight so valiantly the enemies of our fatherland.[52]

French official reports, guides to the exhibitions and art critics immediately responded to this battle-cry, vindicating their nation's superiority and her consequent duty to educate the world.[53] Adolphe Lance, a government architect restoring cathedrals for the Diocesan Service, who would become a member of the Historic Monuments Commission after the exhibition, hence underlined that no 'international politeness' could stop him from dismissing most of the foreign exhibits.[54] And dismissing he did. With regard to the Austrian section, Lance only hoped that the country had failed to send its best architects; his judgement of the Belgian, Dutch, Sardinian and German sections was equally devastating.[55] Lance had recently been informed about the state of restorations in the German lands in great detail by his friend Viollet-le-Duc. Viollet-le-Duc himself was rather disdainful about the artistic merit of architecture found in the German states, yet he was full of admiration for the Germans' love and care for

---

[51] Reports on the Paris Universal Exhibition, presented to both Houses of Parliament in 1856, qu. in Greenhalgh, *Ephemeral Vistas*, p. 14.
[52] *Moniteur*, 21 Mar. 1855, repr. in *Exposition universelle de 1855. Explication des ouvrages de peinture, sculpture, gravure, lithographie et architecture des artistes vivant étrangers et français, exposés au palais des beaux-arts, avenue montaigne le 15 mai 1855* (Paris, 1855); AN, F 21 519.
[53] C. Vignon (pseudonyme of M.N. Cadiot), *Exposition universelle de 1855. Beaux-arts* (Paris, 1855), p. 1
[54] Lance, *Architecture*, pp. 4–5.   [55] Ibid., pp. 14–15, 59–62.

their monuments, which he judged much superior to French attitudes.[56] However, Lance, rather than discussing Zwirner's Project for the completion of Cologne Cathedral in the Prussian section for which he might have had to find some positive words, concerned himself with the project for a thirteenth-century-style altar for the Our Lady Church in Trier by the architect Gumsheimer. Contrasting it with an altar piece from Arras restored and presented in the *Annales archéologique* by 'our skilful *confrère*' Augé de Lassus (to whom Lance owed his own commission as restorer of the Cathedral of Sens), Lance concluded that as an archaeological study, Gumsheimer's work came too late and as a sketch it lacked the necessary detail to appreciate the artist's taste and degree of creativity.[57] While not being too scathing about George Gilbert Scott's work on Ely Cathedral in his section on Britain, he generally concluded that only exceptionally talented architects could escape the fate of the English conditions that bred mediocrity.[58] Moving on to the Spanish restorations, Lance explained that Spain had only just reached the level attained by France some twenty years previously. As to the plans of restoring the Cathedral of Mallorca he cautioned that:

> When one restores a monument, one has to stay clear of ill-advised innovation ... Our Spanish brethren are not ready for the restoration of ancient monument and in the interest of Art, they should abstain from it. They have learned how to love them; they now have to learn how to respect them. To restore ancient monuments, loving them does not suffice, one has to know them well; one must imbue oneself with the spirit presiding at their construction ... Let our wrongdoings be a lesson to them.[59]

To identify this as an early statement on anti-restoration or a critique of the French Historic Monuments Commission's early work would be mistaken. When Lance spoke of the French section, he insisted on the superior quality of the drawings and restorations. He praised every single French architect for the remainder of the report and reserved the highest admiration for Viollet-le-Duc's restoration of Carcassonne.[60] Overall, the only way to receive some praise from Lance as a foreign architect was to be educated in France. Turkey received a favourable mention, thanks to work by Bilezikdji, a student of Duban's.[61] The merit thus returned again indirectly to the architects of the *Monuments historiques*. This tactic was

[56] *Lettres adressées d'Allemange à M. Adolphe Lance, architecte par M. Viollet-le-Duc* (Paris, 1856). They were first published in the *Encyclopédie d'architecture*, from October 1854 onwards.
[57] Lance, *Architecture*, pp. 63–64.   [58] Ibid., pp. 28–58.
[59] Ibid., p. 27.   [60] Ibid., p. 69.   [61] Ibid., pp. 67–8.

frequently used. For instance, in the early Third Republic, French critics often praised German art rather than denigrating it, but claimed that it was only through the reception of French art that German artists had developed.[62]

Throughout the following exhibitions 'international politeness', so disdained by Lance, improved, but this did not alter the claim to French supremacy. The art critic Bellet revelled in the exoticism of foreign exhibits, but made his article culminate in an ode to French greatness.[63] Another 'polite' nationalist was Edmond du Sommerard, who expressed himself positively about foreign participation at the History of Work Exhibition in 1867. He even inflated its extent, probably in response to his relative failure to organise a truly international exhibition. The United Kingdom had responded to his invitation with a reduced display, and the only other participants were Austria, the Netherlands, Portugal, Sweden and Norway, Romania, Spain, Egypt, and Italy. Prussia declined the invitation; Bavaria and Württemberg each contributed two single objects. Nevertheless du Sommerard affirmed that the exhibition was a success by showing the 'superiority of our country, in the past and in the present, with regard to all industries relating to taste, elegance of form, choice of material and execution of work'.[64]

While the metaphor of a battle through the arts had been expressed playfully in 1855, focussing on the rivalry with Britain, international competition and the wish to prove cultural pre-eminence both internationally and nationally played an increasingly important part after France's defeat in the Franco-Prussian War. The French regulating framework for the 1873 Vienna world's fair called explicitly for a patriotic reaction as:

> It is important that France is represented with dignity at the Universal Exhibition of Vienna, she must produce herself in a way to prove that she has not fallen from her deserved rank in the civilized world and that even on the morrow of the recent painful events, she is ready to uphold her traditional reputation with regard to the Arts, the products of the intellect and modern Science.[65]

---

[62] R. Esner, '"Art Knows No Fatherland". Internationalism and the Reception of German Art in France in the Early Third Republic', in M.H. Geyer, J. Paulmann (eds.), *The Mechanics of Internationalism. Culture, Society, and Politics from the 1840s to the First World War* (Studies of the German Historical Institute London, Oxford, 2001), pp. 357–73.

[63] Bellet, 'Promenade', pp. 372–4.

[64] Sommerard, *Commission de l'histoire du travail*, p. 63.

[65] *Exposition Universelle de Vienne, 1873. France. Œuvres d'Art et Manufactures nationales. Commissariat Général*, pp. 10–13.

The exhibition of Historic Monuments were naturally part of the larger effort to promote France as the *patrie des arts*, and the monuments administration received more than one letter from successive General Commissioners to ensure that the place which France's fine arts section received in foreign exhibitions would be suitably honoured.[66] The exhibition reports also responded to the imperative to triumph symbolically over Germany. In his report on historic monuments at the 1871 exhibition in London, Adolphe Viollet-le-Duc pointed out that Germany did not shine, despite her military success, and suggested that other countries also could not match the formidable collection of the CMH archives. France, if she had taken part in the exhibition, would have eclipsed all other architectural works.[67] The official reporter for 1873 was equally flattering about the French section and the exhibition of historical monuments especially.[68] In 1874, the reporter Baumgart commenced his account on historic monuments for the London Exhibition by quoting Adolphe Viollet-le-Duc's report on the 1871 exhibition and concluded that the comparison between France and other nations could now satisfyingly be established to France's advantage.[69] The report of the international jury for 1878 had a section tellingly entitled 'General and specific considerations on the observed tendencies – relative superiority of France, measures to maintain and enhance this supremacy'.[70] The official report for 1889 by Anatole de Baudot, Eugène-Emmanuel Viollet-le-Duc's favourite disciple, did not even bother to analyse any foreign material and only noted with regret that other nations still did not have separate sections on restoration and therefore did not deserve any comment.[71] All reporters saw the success of the exhibition further confirmed by the extraordinary number of medals French architects working for the Historic Monuments and Diocesan Services received from the international jury, both individually and collectively. They only regretted that the number of medals could

[66] MAP, 80/8/6, Dossier 'Exposition de St. Louis (1904)'.

[67] A. Viollet le Duc, Commission supérieure, *Rapport pour la France à l'exposition internationale de 1871 à Londres* (Paris, 1872), pp. 14–15.

[68] M. Cottier, *Section française, rapport sur les Beaux-Arts* (Paris, 1875), pp. 6–10.

[69] Baumgart, 'Rapport. Exposition internationale. Londres 1874. Archives de la Commission des Monuments historiques', MAP, 80/8/5, Dossier 'Londres', fol. 1.

[70] '*Considérations générales et spéciales sur les tendances observées – supériorité relative de la France, moyens de conserver cette prépondérance et de la fortifier*', in E. Vaudremer, Ministère de l'Agriculture et du Commerce, *Exposition universelle internationale de 1878 à Paris. Rapport du Jury Internationale. Groupe I, classe 4. La Section d'Architecture par M. Vaudremer, Architecture du Gouvernement et de la Ville de Paris* (Paris, 1880), p. 10.

[71] A. de Baudot, Ministère du Commerce, de l'industrie et des colonies, *Exposition universelle internationale de 1889, à Paris. Rapports du jury international. Classe 4. Dessins et modèles d'architecture. Rapport de M. de Baudot* (Paris, 1890), pp. 97–110.

have been even higher, if architects who were members of the given juries had not been ineligible for receiving honours.[72]

Apart from Baumgart's report, which extensively discussed the situation of preservation in other countries from a comparative legal perspective, most commentators were comfortable in highlighting French superiority without excessively concerning themselves with a deeper analysis of the foreign sections. The direction in which emulation should occur was framed in unilateral terms. From the exhibition reports, one might conclude that those close to the French monuments administration were convinced of their superiority and neither knew – nor felt any need to know – what was happening elsewhere in matters of preservation.[73] However, there are two twists to the story: first as will be seen later, from the early 1870s a parallel form of report emerged, mostly written by the same authors, deploring French backwardness in matters of preservation and her need to imitate foreign practices and especially legislation.[74] Secondly, it is questionable whether the exhibitions had the desired educative effect upon the international visitor. The displays were barely mentioned by foreigners and if they were, not necessarily in a favourable light.

Although many German preservationists were likely to have seen the displays, all major German preservationist papers and exhibition reports remained silent about the historic monuments exhibitions. British reactions were ample but not very favourable. While the French justified the exhibitions as being dedicated to the 'most precious specimens of our national architecture' and deplored the lack of historic monuments in the British sections,[75] the influential British architectural paper *The Builder* commented in 1855:

> Great Britain alone vindicates the actual position of her national architecture: she alone takes cognizance of the existence of iron as a building material, and it is only from the details she furnishes of executed works that any idea can be formed of the nature of the wants and tastes to which it is the duty and province of architecture to minister in the nineteenth century . . . In architecture, on the whole, we regret to say, the [French] display is inadequate to the present position of art. Although the French exhibit no less than 183 series of drawings, the whole, with two or three exceptions, may be divided into studies of existing monuments and designs for

---

[72] Sommerard, *Les Monuments historiques*, p. 3. For awards by the international juries see the reports digitilised at Conservatoire des Arts et Métiers, http://cnum.cnam.fr/RUB/fcata.html.

[73] Exceptionally, Sommerard, *Les Monuments historiques*, p. 15 briefly alluded to an Italian law that could be imitated and mentioned as one of the clinchers of the CMH its library enriched by the gifts of foreign governments.

[74] See below, Chapter 6.   [75] Bellet, 'Promenade', pp. 374.

restorations . . . and the Archives of the 'Monuments Historiques' furnish a corresponding and much more extensive collection of studies of national archaeology, representing the monuments of the country, not only as they exist [but] as they may be supposed to have existed in the days of their completeness and perfection. Each of these is certainly highly important, but neither can be accepted as an adequate illustration of the present state of architecture in France . . . France we must repeat, has not done herself justice in her Exhibition, and has missed an opportunity which may never again occur. We look in vain for any indication of the nature of those great works which have drawn upon Paris the eyes of all Europe: we recognise not a spark of that fervid imagination which has created an eclectic style of street architecture almost original. If French architects were to be judged by the present exhibition alone they would be set down as pedants, whose studies were equally laborious and barren.[76]

The statement seems to highlight fundamentally different roles attributed to the past in France and Britain. Yet it is even more revealing of the nature of the exhibition reports, which judged according to preordained national standards and freely dismissed those of others. This was magnificently caricatured by the fictional 'Angeline at the Exhibition' in *Punch*, mentioning the Trocadéro where the historic monuments were exhibited in passing:

> After lunch, Edwin met an old friend of his who lives in Paris, who told him that the British Department was the best thing in the Exhibition, and that when he had seen that he had seen everything. I quite agree with him. In duty bound we 'did' the rest of the place, but it was rather stupid. The Trocadéro contains a sort of weak imitation of the South Kensington Museum and the Foreign Courts, and the Machinery, and all those sorts of things, of course we had seen a year ago in London, Vienna and in former Expositions at Paris. But the Prince of Wales' apartments were too lovely! . . . So aesthetic and *so* English![77]

Most of the disdain for foreign exhibits by British commentators can be reduced to the same world exhibition rhetoric of national superiority employed by the French reports. Moreover, basing judgements on entirely different standards conveniently saved the French and British from having to compete directly. The different emphases within the architectural section replicated the broader idea of artistic France fighting against industrial Britain. In the same way that Napoleon III introduced the arts to compete with British industry, the International Jury for the architecture section, on which the French were comparatively overrepresented, decided to invent

---

[76] *The Builder*, 30 June 1855, pp. 301–2; see also Charbonneau, 'Les Monuments historiques', I, p. 35.
[77] 'Angelina at the Exhibition', *Punch*, 26 October 1878, p. 189.

a special category of medals for historic studies which assured that British and French architects were equally honoured, the former in the modern and the latter in the historic section.[78]

Behind these nationalist manoeuvres, far more similarities can be detected. Differences between France and Britain were less pronounced than commentators would have had themselves believe. This is particularly apparent in the actions of Henry Cole, organiser of the Great Exhibitions in 1851 and 1862 in London and of the British sections of the first two Parisian *Expositions universelles*. The head of the new South Kensington Museum was another staunch critic of the historic focus of the French exhibitions.[79] Cole at first had been keen to participate at the 'History of Work' exhibition in Paris 1867. After an Act for Facilitating the Public Exhibition of Works of Art in Certain Exhibitions was passed by Parliament in April 1866, a committee under Cole's presidency was to select the precious exhibits which private and public individuals, including the British Museum Trustees, were willing to loan.[80] However, it transpired that the substandard fire security in Paris resulted in prohibitively high insurance costs. Cole channelled his disappointment by declaring that such a historically focussed show would be misplaced in an exhibition on modern progress anyway, therefore Britain, following Prussia's example, might simply cancel her participation, or if this were too extensive a measure, the lending should be limited to metal and silver works.[81] The condemnation of the retrospective element at a progress-oriented exhibition thus simply turned a necessity into a virtue. Both Prussia and Britain had quite similar projects for applied arts museums with a historic focus, for which Prince Albert and his daughter Victoria, Crown-Princess of Prussia provided much cross-cultural support.[82] In Britain, the objects and profits from the Great Exhibition had been used immediately after the end of the show for the creation of new historic displays. Before such ventures existed in France, visitors could walk through the entire history of the inhabited

---

[78] *Rapports du jury mixte international publiés sous la dir. de S.A.I. le Prince Napoléon, président de la commission impériale* (Paris, 1856), pp. 1379–81.

[79] On Cole see E. Boynton, A. Burton, *The Great Exhibitor. The Life and Work of Henry Cole* (London, 2003); A. Burton, *Vision and Accident. The Story of the Victoria and Albert Museum* (London, 1999).

[80] Victoria and Albert Museum, Archives, Paris Exhibition 1867 [Ed84/18] Letter Book 387, 30 Dec. 1865 and 18 Feb. 1867, qu. in Plato, *Präsentierte Geschichte*, p. 173.

[81] Victoria and Albert Museum, Archives, Paris Exhibition 1867 [Ed84/18], 30 Apr. 1866 qu. ibid., cf. Sommerard, *Commission de l'histoire du travail*, pp. 63–70, 81.

[82] S. Netzer, 'Die Mediceer des deutschen Kunstgewerbes – Kronprinz Friedrich Wilhelm und Kronprinzessin Victoria', in W. Rogasch (ed.), *Victoria & Albert, Vicky & the Kaiser: ein Kapitel deutsch-englischer Familiengeschichte*. Exhibition Catalogue, Deutsches Historisches Museum Berlin, 10 Jan.–25 Mar. 1997 (Ostfildern-Ruit, 1997), www.dhm.de/ausstellungen/victalb/susi.htm.

earth at the privately rebuilt Crystal Palace in Sydenham, starting with dinosaurs in the park and slowly moving through various stages of civilization within the palace. It was even possible to supplement this experience with a visit to architectural drawing on the gallery.[83] The museology at the Great Exhibition's public successor was different, but the historic element was also important. The catalogue of Cole's first museum in Marlborough House, opened immediately after the Great Exhibition before the collection moved to its South Kensington location, already stated that objects had been chosen not only for their artistic and technical quality, but also to show their historic development.[84] As the director of Berlin's Arts and Crafts Museums, Julius Lessing observed, the South Kensington Museum became 'a model for hundreds of institutions with similar aims in the Old and New World'.[85] It was emulated not only in Berlin but also in Paris, where it inspired the Historic Monuments Commission and the National Conservatory for Arts and Crafts alike.[86] The historic displays of the 1857 Manchester Art Exhibition and the cast collections at the Crystal Palace too were the envy of the proud French heritage-makers. During their entire career in preservation, leading voices including Mérimée and Viollet-le-Duc looked with jealousy across the Channel, but also across the Rhine to the New Museum in Berlin and the Germanic Museum in Nuremberg, and frequently invoked these models in their attempts to create a cast museum to educate architects and the public in Paris.[87] In turn, Cole and Prince Albert used new developments in Berlin and Paris for their conception of the South Kensington Museum as an educational institution. Last but not least, while being snooty about the History of Works exhibition in 1867, Cole also used the British section of the exhibition to promote an international convention for the exchange of works of art through means of reproduction

---

[83] S. Phillips, *Guide to the Crystal Palace and Park* (London, 1854); J.R. Piggott, *Palace of the People. The Crystal Palace at Sydenham 1854–1936* (Madison, 2004).

[84] T. Barringer, 'Die Gründung von "Albertopolis", Prinz Albert und die frühen Jahre des South Kensington Museums', in Rogasch (ed.), *Victoria & Albert*, www.dhm.de/ausstellungen/victalb/barri.htm.

[85] Lessing, *Das halbe Jahrhundert*, p. 12.

[86] The *Commission des Monuments historiques* acquired several South Kensington catalogues for its library, *Ministère de l'instruction publique, des cultes et des beaux-arts. Catalogue de la bibliothèque de la commission des monuments historiques* (Paris, 1875); MAP, 80/1/61; B. Robertson, 'The South Kensington Museum in Context. An Alternative History', *Museum and Society*, 2.1 (2004), 1–14, here 5.

[87] See P. Mérimée, 'Les Beaux-Arts en Angleterre', *Revue des Deux Mondes*, 15 octobre 1857, 866–880 ; L. Pressouyre, 'Un grand musée en quête de sens', in Pressouyre (ed.), *Le Musée des Monuments français* (Paris, 2007), pp. 8–53; A. Swenson, 'Musées de moulages et protection du patrimoine', in Rolland, Murauskaya (eds.), *Les Musées de la Nation*, pp. 205–19.

with the aim to facilitate the creation of such historic exhibitions in all countries.[88]

Beyond the disapproving accounts, which can be explained in terms of winning the 'peaceful battle' among nations with the means of the arts, other statements, demonstrating the usefulness of the 'historic monuments' exhibitions in advancing matters of preservation, appeared in the most prominent British architectural papers and the official organ of the RIBA.[89] Even the SPAB, whose members had visited previous exhibitions in Paris, acknowledged in 1889, despite disagreeing vehemently with the restorationist ways of the Historic Monuments Commission that 'the utility of preserving an accurate record of the condition of buildings placed under their care and the practice might very well be imitated in this country'.[90] Whereas in Germany, a superabundance of specialist reports demonstrates interest in general art and crafts exhibitions, and contemporary architectural projects, explicit reference to the exhibitions of historic monuments did not appear anywhere.[91] However, it is possible that German preservationists' insistence on imitating the French in archiving the history and restoration of historic monuments derived from their observance of the French exhibitions.[92] The reception appears somewhat less negative if one moves away from the Anglo-French and Franco-German battle lines. More

[88] See Sir H. Cole, *Fifty Years of Public Work* (2 vols., London, 1884), 1, p. 260; Cole, *Memorandum upon the formation, arrangement and administration of the South Kensington Museum* (London, 1879); Boynton, Burton, *The Great Exhibitor*, pp. 231–2.

[89] *The Builder*, 23 Nov. 1889, p. 371–2; B. Fletcher, 'French Drawings', *Royal Institute of British Architects. Journal of Proceedings*, New Ser., 6 (1890), 23 Jan. 1890, p. 134; 'The Paris Exhibition 1900: Mr Ernest George's Report upon Architectural Exhibits', *Journal of the RIBA*, 3rd Ser., 8 (1901), 433–4.

[90] SPAB, *Annual Report*, 13 (1890), 63. *The Builder* reported favourably on a lecture by Perrauld-Dabot on 12 July on the archives of the Commission: 'Letter from Paris,' 4 Aug. 1900, p. 97. See also 'An Exhibition of French and English Books', *The Times*, 18 November 1908, p. 12.

[91] *Kunst und Kunstinudstrie auf der Weltausstellung von 1867. Pariser Briefe von Friedrich Pecht* (Leipzig, 1867); J. Falke, *Die Kunstindustrie der Gegenwart. Studien auf der Pariser Weltausstellung i.J. 1867* (Leipzig, 1868); *Österreich-Ungarn. Central-Comité der Weltausstellung zu Paris 1867, Die Kunstwerke und die Histoire du travail. Instrumente für Kunst und Wissenschaft* (Vienna, 1869); C. von Lützow, H. Auer, B. Bucher, R. von Eitelsberger, *Kunst und Kunstgewerbe auf der Wiener Weltausstellung 1873* (Vienna, 1873); J. Lessing, *Das Kunstgewerbe auf der Wiener Weltausstellung 1873*, in Lessing, *Berichte von der Pariser Weltausstellung 1878* (Berlin, 1878); H. Frauberger, *Die Kunstindustrie auf der Pariser Weltausstellung 1878* (Leipzig, 1879); F. Pecht, *Kunst und Kunstindustrie auf der Pariser Weltausstellung 1878* (Stuttgart, 1878); L. Gmelin, *German Artistical Handicraft at the Time of the World's-Exhibition in Chicago 1893* (Munich, 1893).

[92] F. Wolff, *Denkmalarchive. Vortrag gehalten auf dem 1. Denkmalarchivtag in Dresden am 24. September 1913* (Berlin, 1913), p. 4 deplored German backwardness and described the archives of the Historic Monuments Commission at length without alluding to the exhibitions, but mentioning the *Musée de Sculpture Comparée*. As Alsacian Conservator, Wolff was familiar with the French system. C. F. Wolff, *Einrichtungen und Tätigkeit der staatlichen Denkmalpflege im Elsaß in den Jahren 1899–1909* (Veröffentlichungen des Kaiserlichen Denkmal-Archivs zu Straßburg i.E. 10, Strasbourg, 1909).

positive reactions to the French exhibitions come in Europe for instance from Belgium and Austria, while several major American Museums, including the Metropolitan Museum of Arts, asked to obtain the architectural casts exhibited in the French section in Chicago, and in 1915 the City of San Francisco wished to be offered the photographs from the French historic monuments section.[93]

Personalities and politics

The relatively disappointing international response was not unique to the historic monuments exhibition, but a problem for the French fine arts sections more broadly: 'the whole world was prepared to see Paris as the supreme art centre, yet organisers and juries persistently failed to show off the art which earned that status.'[94] What was more, the national reaction also did not correspond to the enthusiastic expectations in the official reports. Within the historically minded elite, exhibitions found some resonance. The publishing house Hachette wished to reproduce exhibits for Lavisse's widely read *History of France*, and some leading art critics such as Louis Gonse expressed a relatively positive attitude, but the main preservationist periodicals like the *Bulletin Monumental* and *L'Ami des Monuments* ignored them completely.[95] Although the exhibitions figured in some of the broadly read exhibition periodicals, most reports were written by heritage officials, and the conclusion seems to be that they were mostly relevant to a more specific professional audience. One article claimed that to enjoy the retrospective art exhibitions, 'one needs to come in the morning, the time for the artist, learned men, men of letters, historian, and lover – by which I mean amateur', as the 'afternoon belongs to the crowd'.[96]

[93] Médiathèque, 80/8/5, Dossier 'Belgique'; Lucien Paté, 'Rapport à Monsieur le Ministre de l'Instruction publique et des Beaux-Arts', 15 Nov. 1882, MAP, 80/8/5 Dossier 'Autriche'; Jefferson Coolidge, *Ministre des Etats Unis à Paris*, to *Ministre des Affaires Étrangères*, 29 July 1892; Halsey. C. Ives to Bartelemy, 11 Aug. 1892 and *Bureau des Monuments historiques* to Edward Robinson, Director of Acquisition at the Metropolitan Museum, New York, 31 Aug. 1892; MAP, 80/8/6, Dossier 'Exposition de Chicago (1893)'; *Travaux d'Art etc* to *Bureau des Monuments historiques*, 2 Oct. 1915, MAP, 80/8/6, Dossier 'Exposition de San Francisco 1915. Participation du Service des M.H.' Likewise casts from the German sections were used to build American collections, see P. Nisbet, E. Norris, *The Busch-Reisinger Museum. History and Holdings* (Cambridge, MA, 1991), pp. 18–20, 42.
[94] Greenhalgh, *Ephemeral Vistas*, p. 207.
[95] G. Bréton, Librarie Hachette to *Bureau des Monuments historiques*, 10 Oct. 1889, see also *Président du Conseil Municipal* to *Monsieur le Ministre*, Jan. 1900, MAP, 80/8/7, Dossier 'Exposition rétrospective d'objets d'Art. Affaires générales'; press cuttings in MAP, 80/8/7.
[96] E. Bonnaffé, 'Exposition rétrospective de l'art français au Trocadéro', in Gonse, de Lostalot (eds.), *L'art français retrospectif*, pp. 511–18, qu. p. 512.

However, despite the insistence of French official reports on the aesthetic appeal of architectural drawings, the format seems to have been not especially interesting for a larger audience. In the exhibitions the drawings were overshadowed by objects (ill. 3.9).[97] Moreover, the displays were off the beaten track. While some visitors were willing to make the long and arduous journey, at the end of which nothing awaited them in terms of 'music, female dancers, or Cairo street entertainments', admission to fine arts pavilions was prohibitively expensive for a working-class audience.[98] Most visitors preferred to experience the more popular representations offered by national pavilions, human habitation, medieval city centres and foreign streets which could be enjoyed in three dimensions and with human animation.

Initially, one attraction of exhibiting material from the Historic Monument Commission's archives lay in the low costs, as the only expenses occurring related to the framing of drawings. The collection of the Commission was, moreover, readily available since it was not part of a public museum or library, which had to be left intact during the *Expositions universelles*, to ensure that the exhibitionary experience could be carried beyond the confines of the ephemeral structures and into the permanence of the city.[99] However, subsequently, the commissioning of hundreds of new photographs and plaster casts turned the *monuments historiques* into one of the most expensive elements of the French Fine Arts section.[100] In 1893, these costs provoked considerable hostility from other departments as well as from the press, despite the fact that the largest part of the expenses were borne by the American organisers.[101]

Given that the depictions of monuments were not nearly as popular as claimed, that ticket prices rendered them inaccessible to the masses, and

[97] Perrauld-Dabauld, *Les Archives*.
[98] Bonnaffé, 'Exposition rétrospective', 512. On visitor numbers Plato, *Präsentierte Geschichte*, pp. 107–20, cf. AN, F 21 519, Dossier 'Statistique' on the Fine Art Pavillion.
[99] See Sommerard, *Commission de l'histoire du travail*, pp. 74–5. On the whole city as experience see Barth, *Mensch versus Welt*.
[100] On a discussion of the costs of 1867, 1873, 1874, 1876 see du Sommerard to *Bureau des Monuments historiques*, 3 Dec. 1877, MAP, 80/8/7, Dossier 'Exposition universelle de 1878'; Correspondence between *Monuments historique* and *Commission générale*, MAP, 80/8/7, Dossier 'Exposition universelle de 1878'; on 1889 and 1900 see Berr de Turique, *Secrétaire adjoints de la Commission des Monuments Historiques, chargé de l'organisation de l'Exposition des Monuments historique en 1900*, to *Directeur des Beaux Arts*, 8 June 1900, MAP, 80/8/7, Dossier 'Exposition 1900, Decisions de principe'.
[101] L. Pons, 'Le Palais des beaux-arts à Chicago (section francaise)', *Le Figaro*, 27 Aug. 1892; see also AN F21 4061, Dossier: 'Coupure de Presse'; 'Note pour le Bureau des Travaux-d'art, Musée et exposition', 7 Feb. 1893, MAP, 80/8/6, Dossier 'Exposition de Chicago (1893)'; 'Rapport de M. le Commissaire Principal sur sa mission à Chicago', 6 July 1893 AN, F 21 4061, Dossier 'Exposition universelle de Chicago 1893; Correspondence diverse juillet 1891–fevrier 1895'.

3.9 The 'history of work' exhibition at the *Exposition universelle* (Paris, 1867). The drawing dramatised the presence of the past, creating a sense of abundance through the frame, but a glimpse at the centre of the illustration offers a more sober impression of the visitor's experience. Historic objects were exhibited in the glass cases, the walls were adorned with over 300 drawings from the archives of the Historic Monuments Commission. M. Lancelot. 'Musée rétrospectiv – Gallerie du Travail', in F. Ducuing, *L'Exposition universelle de 1867 illustrée* (Paris, 1867), II, p. 120.

that they were increasingly attacked on financial grounds, what were the motivations behind the ever more extensive displays? To explain the unusual diffusion of historical monuments in the French sections, it is helpful to examine the composition of general commissions, admission and award juries. In 1855, membership of Mérimée and of prominent restoration architect Vaudoyer in the Imperial Commission provided a jump start for the *monuments historiques* at the highest level. In the admission jury for the architectural section, in which French outnumbered foreign members, six out of twelve members were architects or even members of the Historic Monuments Commission.[102] Its head, the Comte de Nieuwerkerke was jury president, and two further members, Arcisse de Caumont and Albert Lenoir had a proven personal interest in historic monuments as well, while Mérimée and Vaudoyer were *ex officio* members. The awards jury offered a similar picture. The architectural section had only three foreign members, two Britons, the collector Sidney Cockerell and Sir Charles Barry of the Royal Academy, and Strack, architectural adviser to the Prussian court, compared to seven French members, who were all in some way connected to the institutions of historic preservation.[103] In the next half century this arrangement only changed through members' deaths and consequent replacement by their equivalents in a younger generation.[104] Members and architects of the Historic Monuments Commission and the Diocesan Buildings Service, the directors of national museums, and in particular of the *Musée de Cluny* and the *Musée du Trocadéro* occupied the most prominent places in juries and organising committees. Despite political changes, the people connected to the *monuments historiques* remained the

---

[102] These were Caristie, Duban, Labrouse, Lassus, Lenormant, Viollet-le-Duc. Among the foreign commissioners and delegates were Henry Cole for Britain, and Viebhan and Dielitz for Prussia.

[103] See AN 21 519; *Exposition universelle de 1855. Explication des ouvrages de peinture, sculpture, gravure, lithographie et architecture des artistes vivants étrangers et français, exposé au palais des Beaux-arts*, pp. xxxii–xxxvi for the *Jury d'Admission*; for the *Jury des Récompenses* see *Moniteur* 25 March 1855 and *Rapport sur l'exposition universelle de 1855, présenté à l'Empereur par S.A.I. le Prince Napoléon, président de la commission*, pp. 80–108; *Rapports du jury mixte international publiés sous la dir. de S.A.I. le Prince Napoléon, président de la commission impériale* (Paris, 1856), Classe 30, Architecture, pp. 1379–883.

[104] AN F21 525, Dossier 'III Angleterre', Sous-Chemise 'Exposition internationale de Londres en 1871'; 'Décrets en date des 4 mars, 5 avril et 2 juillet 1870', in *Exposition Universelle de Vienne, 1873. France. Oeuvres d'Art et Manufactures nationales. Commissariat Général; Exposition internationale et universelle de Philadelphie, 1876. Rapport. France. Commission supérieure* (Paris, 1877); Vaudremer, *Rapport du Jury Internationale. La Section d'Architecture*, p. 1; *Exposition universelle internationale de 1889 à Paris. Exposition rétrospective de l'art français au Trocadéro*, pp. 1–9; *JO*, 3 June 1892, 2713–14; *Exposition universelle de 1900, à Paris (Palais du Trocadéro). Catalogue des expositions des monuments historiques*; *Ministère de l'Instruction publique et des beaux arts. Exposition universelle internationale de 1900. Groupe II, Beaux arts. Extrait du décret du 4 août 1894 portant règlement général pour l'Exposition universelle de 1900* (Paris, 1899); Letter from Secrétariat du Service des Beaux Arts de l'Exposition universelle de 1900 to Paté, *Chef du Service des Monuments historiques*, 12 Mar. 1898, MAP, 80/8/7, Dossier 'Exposition 1900'.

same. Even the generational change that took place after Mérimée's and Viollet-le-Duc's death in the late nineteenth century was not accompanied by a noticeable conceptual change. As an article in *Le Figaro* complained justifiably, the same jury members sent always the same works of art, while Antonin Proust, former Arts Minister and founder of the plaster cast museum at the Trocadéro, who was in charge of the retrospective exhibitions during the world's fairs indulged in his predilections with 'paternal jealousy'.[105] Though explicitly denying any 'personal interest' in favour of the constantly emphasised 'public interest', the exhibitions not only served the interests of the ascending bourgeoisie in a general way, as has been suggested by Paul Greenhalgh. Personal preferences and vanities were an important driving force. The award of exhibition medals often led to decoration as a member of the Legion of Honour. For some, the exhibitions also were an opportunity of including a private vision in the greater narrative of the *patrimonialisation*, as in the case of Edmond du Sommerard who used the exhibition to incorporate his father's life story and the foundation of the *Musée de Cluny* into the founding narrative.[106]

The exhibitions moreover addressed a range of domestic interests of the CMH and its architects as a group. The early fairs served as a battlefield in the quarrel between the architects around Viollet-le-Duc, proponents of the gothic revival, and the Institute, responsible for teaching the fine arts in France and proclaiming the superiority of a classicist style. The exhibitions offered the medievalists the possibility to show their own works, to criticise the style of the Institute in exhibition reports, and to obtain as many medals from the international jury as possible to shift the balance of power between two rival architectural schools.[107]

---

[105] L. Pons, 'Le Palais des beaux-arts à Chicago (section francaise)', *Le Figaro*, 27 August 1892. Antonin Proust, painter and friend of Edouard Manet, journalist and *député* for the Deux-Sèvres, was Secretary of Gambetta and founder of the journal *La République*. He became the first *Ministre des Arts* under Gambetta in 1881 and created in 1882 the École du Louvre. In 1884, Proust organised an important restrospective exhibition of Manet's work, before becoming *Commissaire de l'Exposition universelle* of 1889. See *Dictionnaire des Parlémentaires Français* (5 vols., Paris, 1889–91, repr. 1975), v, pp. 53–4. On the use of the exhibitions to create his museum see Archives des Musées nationaux, 5HH Musée de Sculpture comparée, boite 1 and Swenson, 'Musées de moulages'.

[106] On broader use for social advancement see Greenhalgh, *Ephemeral Vistas*; AN, F 21 526, Dossier 'Autriche: Exposition internationale 1872–1873. Vienne': 'Liste des Récompenses décernées aux Exposants Français par le Jury International. Exposition Universelle de Vienne 1873', and 'Exposition universelle de Vienne 1873. Affaires diverses'; MAP, 80/8/7, Dossier 'Exposition universelle de 1878'.

[107] See for instance Vaudremer, *Rapport du Jury Internationale. La Section d'Architecture*; Charbonneau, 'Les Monuments historiques', pp. 45–7; on the broader battle between schools see E.E. Viollet-le-Duc, G. Viollet-le-Duc, *Esthétique appliquée à l'histoire de l'art par Eugène Viollet le Duc. Suivi de Viollet-le-Duc et l'Ecole des beaux-arts: la bataille de 1863–64* (Paris, 1994). On how the glorification of Viollet-le-Duc rubbed off on general journalistic accounts see Bellet, 'Promenades', pp. 373–4.

3.10 Inauguration of the Musée de Sculpture comparée. Drawing by Navellier Narcisse. Paris.

Furthermore, the exhibitions were not as much a means of pleasing the masses as of swaying the political elite to the cause of preservation. In the first instance, the exhibitions of the work of the CMH were a means of raising funds. Exhibition catalogues mentioned in the most detailed way the evolution of the budget for the historic monuments administration, and highlighted the need to increase it if France's unique richness in monuments was to be preserved.[108] The exhibitions were also used to lobby for further educational institutions, in particular a Museum of Comparative Sculpture at the Trocadéro to teach architects and the public. Mérimée and Viollet-le-Duc had unsuccessfully championed a cast museum since the 1840s. The exhibitions could create such a museum in an ephemeral way, before finally providing both the rooms and the nucleus of a collection through the casts made for the historic monuments exhibitions (see ill. 3.10).[109] Detailing the history of preservation, as a most heroic struggle of the forebears through the exhibitions and catalogues, also helped the Commission to promote a

[108] *Exposition universelle de 1878 à Paris. Ministère de l'instruction publique, des cultes et des beaux-arts. Catalogue de l'exposition des archives de la commission des Monuments historiques en France*, pp. 3–4; Perrault-Dabot, *Les Archives de la Commission des Monuments historiques*, p. 11.
[109] See Swenson, 'Musées de moulages'.

Monument Bill. The exhibition catalogues were not the most aggressive place to ask for legislation, but the point was stressed explicitly from the early 1870s onwards, and Baumgart's report on the 1874 London Exhibition was one of the very first comparative studies of legislation.[110]

Finally, the exhibitions aimed to affirm the primacy of the state in matters of preservation within France. The repeated telling of the history of *patrimonialisation* as culminating in the Historic Monuments Commission's work largely edited out the old learned societies.[111] However, the exhibitions were even more important to fight the new private anti-restoration movement, which increasingly attacked the very principles on which the work of the state services was based. As will be seen in the next chapter, *L'Ami des Monuments* also used the international exhibitions to diffuse its ideas and increase its profile through the congress format. Architects and artists close to the movement created the most popular historic displays in the later Parisian fairs: the crowd puller of 1889, the 'history of human habitation' was the brain child of Charles Garnier, co-founder of *Les Amis des monuments parisiens* and president of the Congress of Architects and of the First International Congress for the Protection of Monuments and Works of Art, organised by *L'Ami des Monuments*. Its imaginative rather than archaeologically accurate character made the 'history of human habitation' hardly a serious venture in the eyes of professionals, but even those critical thought it formidably entertaining (ill. 3.11).[112] All others, including 'Viollet-le-duc himself – the educator par excellence' would have failed where Garnier shone in marrying propaganda and popularisation.[113] The biggest historic attraction of the 1900 fair, the recreation of Old Paris, also brought a smile to people's face and was invented by Albert Robida, *L'Ami des Monuments'* brilliant caricaturist, who not only entertained foreigners with his medieval streets, but helped to create a considerable civic interest in a much more intimately defined heritage than the national monuments championed by the state administration (see illustration on cover).[114]

[110] See Sommerard, *Les Monuments historiques*, p. 18; Baumgart, 'Rapport. Exposition internationale. Londres 1874. Archives de la Commission des Monuments historiques' in MAP, 80/8/5, Dossier 'Londres', fols. 6–12.

[111] Sommerard, *Les Monuments historiques*, pp. 2, 5.

[112] E. Goudeau, 'L'Histoire de l'Habitation', *Revue de l'Exposition universelle de 1889*, 1, 78–85; V. Champier, 'Les 44 Habitation Humaines construites au Champs de Mars par M. Charles Garnier', *Revue de l'Exposition universelle de 1889*, 115–25.

[113] V. Champier, 'Exposition des habitations humaines reconstituées par M. Charles Garnier', in Emile Monod (ed.), *L'Exposition Universelle de 1889: Grand ouvrage illustré, historique, encyclopédique, descriptif* (3 vols., Paris, 1890), 1, pp. 158–62.

[114] See E. Emery, 'Protecting the past: Albert Robida and the Vieux Paris exhibit at the 1900 World's Fair', *Journal of European Studies*, 35.1 (2005), 65.

3.11. Caricature of Garnier's exhibition of human habitation featuring the architect at every stop. *Revue de l'Exposition universelle de 1889* (Paris 1889), 1, p. 196.

Much ado about nothing?

Through their relative marginality, the historic monuments exhibitions shed an instructive light on the dynamics of heritage-making on the international scene. Throughout the entire period, the exhibitions of monuments and restoration studies took place within an international framework, but they were not in the least internationalist in outlook.[115] Instead of aspiring to peace and goodwill among nations, a 'peaceful battle' was fought with all possible means. Reading the catalogues and reports in isolation, one could believe that every country thought itself superior to any other nation; so superior that no apparent notice needed to be taken of the foreign parts of exhibitions. And yet the exhibitions were more than a case of an over-stated sense of mission. In combination with the parallel congresses, studied in the following chapter, the exhibitions provided room for sociability and discussion, and inevitably increased knowledge about each other's methods and attitudes with regard to restoration, museologie and organisational structures.[116] The dismissive attitude towards foreign contributions can be largely attributed to the wider world exhibition discourse striving to prove national superiority.

Viewed from this perspective, the diametric opposition between attitudes of artistic France and industrial Britain to the role of the past in exhibitions must be qualified. Certainly, the displays of the architectural exhibitions show different preferences, but the preponderance of historic monuments in the French section was first and foremost caused by the strength of historic monument lobbies in state administration and exhibition organisation. During the same period, a similar group of people involved with preservation and linked with exhibition organisation did not exist in Britain and Germany. The Royal Commissions on the Ancient and Historic Monuments of England, Wales and Scotland were only founded in 1908. In Prussia, the Commission appointed in 1853 had barely survived the year. Yet even after the appointment in 1891 of Provincial Commissions and Conservators, a similar display was not discussed for the *Exposition universelle* in 1900, most likely because of the lack of a similar archival collection. Beyond these institutional differences, the underlying ideas of the benefit of past art for contemporary arts and industry was shared

---

[115] See for a different, decisively internationalist tone the inaugural speech of the historic monuments section in 1937, *Exposition internationale des Arts et Technique à Paris en 1937, la section française, rapport général*, V, p. 553.

[116] On the perceived advantage of bringing architects interested in restoration together during the exhibitions see for example a report on a meeting organised by the Ecclesiological Society in London during the 1862 exhibition, 'The Ecclesiological Society', *The Times*, 2 July 1862, p. 9.

between exhibitions organisers and museum directors, such as Edmond du Sommerard in Paris, Henry Cole in London, and Julius Lessing in Berlin.

The case study moreover, and perhaps more importantly, sheds light on the importance of the international arena for domestic agendas. Apart from increasing their personal status, the makers of the historic monuments exhibitions used the fairs to present their particular vision of preservation, obtain funds, open permanent museums and install legislation. They were not successful in dominating the public vision of heritage as other heritage-makers also used the same space for their own ends and the sheer multiplicity of historic exhibits, as well as the viewers' agency, defied any such purpose, but the makers of the historic monument exhibitions were doing well in using the fairs to push their other agendas.

Finally, the case of these exhibitions also draws attention to another more general point, by showing how the legitimisation of the protection of monuments was articulated in a circumstantial way. The exhibitions of historic monuments maintained the elitist romantic presentation of history propounded in the Museum of French Monuments and the *Musée du Sommerard* in the early nineteenth century. The heirs of Lenoir and du Sommerard however, adapted their own discourse to that of the world exhibitions, stressing the attraction of the exhibitions for a mass audience, and defining their role through the maxims of entertainment and education. In contrast to other situations heritage was not defined through the condition of endangerment – the vandal and demolisher are largely absent as heritage's constant counterparts. The exhibition-makers also rarely allude to heritage's almost metaphysical capabilities to unite the nation by bending the time space continuum. Instead they used a practical, rational and progressivist language, by stressing the unifying effect upon the nation that building sites could have on the workers. Exhibition organisers further established modern credentials for heritage, by praising the uniqueness of the present time, and Western civilisation, in valuing its historic monuments. Likewise, by using a rhetoric of national superiority they tuned into the broader language of the exhibition frameworks and reports. Just how much this use was circumstantial becomes apparent when one follows the preservationists from the exhibition to the congress halls, where they shed their claims of national superiority to celebrate international understanding.

CHAPTER 4

'Peace and goodwill among nations'

'International Congresses for *Heimatschutz* – do these words not contain an internal contradiction? Can something as national in essence as *Heimatschutz* be approached internationally?'[1] The question puzzled the more than 500 delegates at an international congress in Stuttgart in 1912, but their answer was an emphatic yes. They would have been astonished that the Athens Conference, organised by the League of Nations in 1931, is now generally portrayed as the earliest international conference on the conservation of artistic and historic monuments. Nor was it then that historic monuments were considered for the first time as a 'common heritage of mankind'.[2] International congresses on the protection of heritage existed much earlier.[3] The participation of international delegates and the international distribution of publications had already lent an international resonance to the national congresses of learned societies in the 1830s. However, the era of meetings, which could truly be considered international in both membership and subject matter started in the last third of the nineteenth century. These congresses were highly significant not only for spreading ideas about preservation across national borders, but for developing ideas of a common heritage of mankind and for forging an enduring discursive link between love for heritage and international understanding.

These congresses assumed a multitude of overlapping and sometimes rival forms, reflective of the diversity of professions and associations engaged in the care of monuments (see table 2). Preservation was first discussed in a professional setting at the regular International Congress of

---

[1] *Heimatschutz*, 8.2–3 (1912), 58.
[2] See F. Choay (ed.), *La Conférence d'Athènes sur la conservation artistique et historique des monuments, 1931* (Paris, 2002), pp. 7–9. On the development of interwar conferences: UNESCO Archives, OIM VI.I; OIM VI.17.
[3] Usually only the diplomatic conferences at Brussels and the Hague are discussed as precursors, see for instance Jokilehto, *History of Architectural Conservation*, pp. 245–94.

187

Table 2 *World exhibitions, international congresses and conferences*

Year	World's Fairs	Architects Congress	Monument Congress	Public Art Congress	*Heimat* Congress	Peace Conference	Other relevant congresses
1867	Paris	1 Paris					Prehistoric Archaeology, Norwich
1873	Vienna						1 Orientalist Paris
1874						Brussels	
1878	Paris	2 Paris					
1889	Paris	3 Paris	1 Paris				
1897	Brussels	4 Brussels		1 Brussels			
1998							Restoration, St Gallen
1899						The Hague	11–12 Orientalist Rome, Paris
1900	Paris	5 Paris		2 Paris			Historic Monument Conference, Paris
							Comparative History Paris
							5 Art History, Lübeck
							1 Classical Archaeology, Athens
1904	St Louis	6 Madrid					
1905		7 London					
1906				3 Liege			
1907						The Hague	
1908		8 Vienna					2 Classical Archaeology Cairo
							Drawings Paris
1910	Brussels			4 Brussels	1 Paris		
1911		9 Rome					3 Classical Archaeology
1912					2 Stuttgart		
1913							Worldnature, Bern

Architects,[4] before a multitude of ventures emerged that were organised by voluntary associations, including a First Official International Congress for the Protection of Works of Art and Monuments,[5] four International Congresses for Public Art,[6] and two landscape and *Heimatschutz* congresses.[7] Cultural heritage protection was further made a subject at congresses of new academic disciplines such as art history, anthropology, archaeology, and Orientalism.[8] Historical congresses, especially the first international

---

[4] The Congress was established in 1867 at the *Exposition universelle* in Paris. The first two sessions did not yet have panels devoted to the care of monuments, but touched upon it in connection with professional training. See Société impériale et centrale des architectes, *Conférence internationale Juillet 1867* (Paris, 1867). *Extrait du compte-rendu sténographique du congrès international des architectes, 3 août 1878* (Paris, 1881). Other regional or national congresses of architects not organised by the permanent committee also aimed to be 'international', e.g. Société des architectes et des ingénieurs des Alpes-Maritimes, *Congrès international et régional d'architectes et d'ingénieurs. Tenue à Nice en 1884. Compte-rendu* (Nice, 1885) or Congresso degli ingegneri ed architetti italiani, *Congresso settimo nazionale e primo internazionale di ingegneri ed architetti* (Palermo, 1892).

[5] C. Normand, Ministère du Commerce, de l'Industrie et des Colonies. Exposition universelle internationale de 1889. Direction générale de l'exploitation, *Congrès international pour la protection des œuvres d'art et des monuments, tenu à Paris du 24 au 29 juin 1889. Procès-verbaux sommaires. Rédigés par le secrétaire général Charles Normand, architecte diplômé par le gouvernement, directeur de l'Ami des monuments, secrétaire générale de la Société des amis des monuments parisien* (Paris, 1889).

[6] Published as *Congrès international de l'art public* and separately as *Oeuvre de l'art public. Premier Congrès international, Bruxelles, 1898* (Liège, 1898); *Troisième Congrès international de l'art public, Liège, 15–21 septembre 1905* (Brussels, 1905). See also the corresponding years of the journal *Art public* and 'Le Congrès international de l'Art public a Bruxelles', *L'Ami des Monuments*, 12 (1898), 112, 180–1, 234–7, 290–5; 'Congrès de l'art public', *L'Ami des Monuments*, 13 (1899), 26–30, 155, 308–17; 'Congrès et Exposition de l'Art public', *L'Ami des Monuments*, 14 (1900), 75, 103–10, 181–6 ; 'Congres de l'Art publique', *L'Ami des Monuments*, 15 (1901), 164; 'Letter from Paris', *The Builder*, 13 Oct. 1900, p. 308; Brown, *Care of Ancient Monuments*, p. 174.

[7] *Le Premier Congrès international pour la protection des paysages* (Paris, 1910); the entire volume of *Heimatschutz*, 6.2 (1910), 8.1 (1912), p. 1; 8.2–3 (1912), entire volume and 9.1 (1913), pp. 1–35; 'Erster internationaler Heimatschutzkongress in Paris', *Die Denkmalpflege*, 11 (1909), 132; 'Zweiter internationaler Kongress für Heimatschutz Stuttgart', *Die Denkmalpflege*, 14 (1912), 55, 64.

[8] P. Clemen, *Die Erhaltung der Kunstdenkmäler in Deutschland. Vortrag gehalten auf dem internationalen Kunsthistoriker-Kongresse 1900 zu Lübeck* (Nuremberg, 1900); 'Internationaler Kunsthistorischer Kongress in Lübeck', *Centralblatt der Bauverwaltung*, 20 (1900), 352; 'Gelegentlich des internationalen kunsthistorischen Congresses Lübeck', *Die Denkmalpflege*, 2 (1900), 79; 'Internationaler Kunsthistorischer Kongress in Lübeck', *Korrespondenzblatt des Gesamtvereins der Deutschen Geschichts- und Alterthumsvereine*, 48 (1900), 143; 'Congres pour la cinquantaine de l'Ecole française d'Athènes', *L'Ami des Monuments*, 11 (1897), 81–6; C. Normand, 'Le premier Congres international d'archéologie a Athènes', *L'Ami des Monuments*, 19 (1905), 100–16; 'Archäologischer Congress zur Feier des 50 jährigen Bestehens der Ecole française in Athen', *Centralblatt der Bauverwaltung*, 17 (1897), 68; 'Internationaler Kongress (XII.) für Prähistorie und Archäologie', *Korrespondenzblatt des Gesamtvereins der Deutschen Geschichts- und Alterthumsvereine*, 48 (1900), 95; T. Murray, 'The History, Philosophy and Sociology of Archaeology. The Case of the Ancient Monuments Protection Act 1882', in L. Pinsky, A. Wyle (eds.), *Critical Traditions in Contemporary Archaeology* (Cambridge, 1989), p. 56; C. Chippendale, 'The Making of the First Ancient Monuments Act, 1882, and its Administration under General Pitt-Rivers', *Journal of the British Archaeological Association*, 136 (1983), 1–55, here 6; M.A. Kaesar, 'L'Internationalisation de la préhistoire, une manoeuvre tactique? Les conséquences épitémologiques de la fondation des Congrès internationaux d'anthropologie et d'archéologie préhistoriques', in C. Blanckaert (ed.), *Les Politiques de l'anthropologie. Discours et*

congress for comparative history in Paris in 1900, also provided important meeting places, but the older and more textual discipline of history devoted less space to questions of preservation than the newer subjects that had a stronger focus on material sources.[9]

From yet a different perspective, the care of monuments was included in the diplomatic conferences codifying the laws of war, in Brussels in 1874 and in the Hague in 1899 and 1907.[10] Natural heritage (in which 'primitive peoples' were included) received its own diplomatic conference in Switzerland just before the war in 1913, after having been discussed at several international scientific congresses.[11] Beyond these targeted meetings, preservationists also met at international congresses on topics only loosely related to the care of monuments, such as hygiene, the teaching of drawing, the copyright of artistic property, the regulation of automobile traffic, alpinism, comparative law, and religious gatherings.[12]

Meetings attended mostly by preservationists from neighbouring countries further complemented congresses with a broad international outlook.[13]

pratiques en France, 1860–1940 (Paris, 2001), pp. 201–30; Blanckaert, 'The First Establishment of Pre-historic Science. The Shortcomings of Autonomy', in J. Callmer, M. Meyer, R. Struwe, C. Theune (eds.), Die Anfänge der ur- und frühgeschichtlichen Archäologie als akademisches Fach (1890–1930) im europäischen Vergleich (Rahden/Westf., 2006), pp. 149–60; 'L'Ami des Monuments et des Arts au Congrès des Orientalistes et la Sauvegarde des Monuments', L'Ami des Monuments, 11 (1897), 249–51; D.M. Reid, Whose Pharaohs? Archaeology, Museums and Egyptian National Identity from Napoleon to World War I (Berkeley, 2002), pp. 130–4.

9 'Internationaler Congress der vergleichenden Geschichtsforschung in Paris', Centralblatt der Bau-verwaltung, 20 (1900), 180.

10 Ministère des Affaires étrangères. Documents diplomatiques, Actes de la conférence de Bruxelles de 1874 sur le projet d'une convention internationale concernant la guerre. Protocoles des séances plénières. Protocoles de la commission déléguée par la conférence. Annexes (Paris, 1874).

11 P. Sarasin, Weltnaturschutz, Vortrag gehalten am VIII. Zoologenkongress in Graz am 16. August und an der 93. Versammlung der Schweizerischen Naturforschenden Gesellschaft in Basel am 5. September 1910 (Basel, 1910); Sarasin, Über nationalen und internationalen Vogelschutz: sowie einige anschließende Fragen des Weltnaturschutzes. Vortrag, gehalten am 12. Mai 1911 am zweiten deutschen Vogelschutztag in Stuttgart (Basel, 1911); Sarasin, Über die Aufgaben des Weltnaturschutzes, Denkschrift gelesen an der Delegiertenversammlung zur Weltnaturschutzkommission in Bern am 18.11.1913 (Basel, 1914). A. Kley, 'Die Weltnaturschutzkonferenz 1913 in Bern', Umweltrecht in der Praxis, Sonderheft zu Grundsatzfragen des Umweltrechts, Symposium vom 24.5.2007 zur Emeritierung von Prof. Dr. Heribert Rausch, 7 (2007), 685–705. Wöbse, Weltnaturschutz; P. Kupper, Wildnis schaffen: Eine transnationale Geschichte des Schweizerischen Nationalparks (Bern, 2012).

12 'International Congress on the Teaching of Drawing, Paris', The Builder, 15. Sept. 1900, p. 236; 'International Drawing Congress', Journal of the RIBA, 3rd Ser., 15 (1908), 327; C. Normand, 'Le Congrès des Arts décoratif en 1894', L'Ami des Monuments, 7 (1893), 333–6; C. Normand, 'Congrès international de la propriété artistique et littéraire à Venise', L'Ami des Monuments, 2 (1888), 233–5; Bericht über den VIII. Internationalen Architekten-Kongress, Wien 1908 (Vienna, 1909), p. 640; Ministère des Affaires Étrangères, Documents Diplomatique, Conférence internationale relative a la circulation des automobiles (Paris, 1910). 'Die Denkmalpflege auf dem Katholikentag', Die Denkmalpflege, 4 (1902), 99.

13 'Conservation et restauration des manuscrits. Conférence internationale à St. Gallen', L'Ami des Monuments, 12 (1898), 314; 'Wien, Versammlung von Fachmännern der Museums- und Naturwis-senschaften', Die Denkmalpflege, 5 (1904), 114.

Internationally attended meetings on monument care also took place during national art exhibitions and many congresses which did not explicitly call themselves 'international' often also had international delegates and resonance.[14] This was equally the case for the new Congress of Archaeological Societies, founded in 1888 in Britain, the Congress of Architects organised by the RIBA, as for the older *Congrès archéologique* and the Congress of the *sociétés savantes*.[15] Although the annual *Tag für Denkmalpflege* were frequently referred to as *Deutsche Denkmaltage*, they also had a number of international delegates and their broad comparative subject matter made them a leading international voice.[16]

Facilitated by the growing travel and communication means, these multiplying congresses derived to a certain degree from the national congresses of learned societies, but were even more closely linked to the general growth of internationalism in the second half of the nineteenth century. Inspired by the different internationalisms of free trade liberals and socialists since mid-century, virtually every activity from feminism to dog breeding had internationalised itself by the end of the century. The expansion of preservation-related congresses accords with the exponential increase of international meetings from quasi zero in the middle of the nineteenth century to almost 250 held in 1900.[17] Throughout this period, peaks of congress activity coincided with the date of world's fairs.[18] It was logical

[14] *Ministère des Affaires étrangères, sous-direction du Midi, 1er Bureau* to Jules Ferry, *Ministre de l'Instruction publique*, 20 Mar. 1880, AN, F 21 526, Dossier 'Italie', Chemise 'Turin, Italie, Exposition des beaux-arts'.

[15] For example the fifth congress, held in 1893 at Burlington House and presided over by Sir John Evans, president of the Society of Antiquaries counted several members of the *Société française d'archéologie*, including its president, the Comte de Marsy, and was observed favourably by the German press and Prussian *Kultusministerium*, see newspaper cutting without provenance, GStA PK, I. HA Rep. 76 Ve Kultusministerium, Sekt. 1, Tit. VI, No. 141. On the history of the congress see, O'Neil, B.H.St.J., 'The Congress of Archaeological Societies', *Antiquaries Journal*, 26 (1946), 61–6. See also *Journal of the RIBA*, 3rd Ser. 7 (1900), 407 and its *Congress Supplement comprising the papers read at the general congress of architects held in London, June 1900, with discussions thereon; Congrès archéologique de France. Séances générales tenues par le Société française pour la conservation des monuments historiques (puis Société française d'archéologie)*; and AN, F 17 3090 for attendance; on attendance of the Congress of the *Sociétés Savantes* by SPAB members see SPAB, *Annual Report*, 9 (1886), 57.

[16] 'Verzeichnis der Teilnehmer. Zehnter Tag für Denkmalpflege. Trier. 23. und 24. September 1909. Stenographischer Bericht' and 'Elfter Tag für Denkmalpflege. Danzig. 29. und 30. September 1910', GStA PK VI. HA, Rep. 92 Nl. Schmidt-Ott (M), A X 1, fols. 90, 186–286; Brown, *Care of Ancient Monuments*, p. VII.

[17] A. Rasmussen, 'Les Congrès internationaux liés aux Expositions universelles de Paris, 1867–1900', *Mil neuf cent. Cahiers Georges Sorel. Revue d'histoire intellectuelle*, 7 (1989), 23–44, here 23; see also statistics compiled by the Union of International Associations in *Yearbook of International Organizations* and *International Congress Calendar*.

[18] Rasmussen, 'Congrès internationaux', 24. The number of congresses and conferences at the world exhibitions increased steadily. Numbers vary in the literature depending on whether official and unofficial congresses are included, cf. Kretschmer, *Geschichte der Weltausstellungen*, pp. 287–97.

to profit from the presence of international experts at the exhibitions, yet while the association of congresses with the international exhibitions occurred spontaneously in most countries, in France, congresses were fully integrated into the *Exposition universelle* administration and depended on a *Commission supérieure*.[19] Placed loosely under the patronage of Prince Napoleon in 1867, this administrative arrangement began in earnest when in 1878 the French learned societies planned to hold their congresses during the exhibition. Just as the July Monarchy had integrated the learned societies into the state's cultural politics, the Third Republic appropriated the societies' move, installing a ministerial framework, which offered the already established societies and congresses its infrastructure, while also instigating new projects.[20] To understand the importance of international congresses for domestic heritage politics and the way heritage discourses were enduringly shaped by congress rhetoric, it is necessary to take this institutional framework into account. International meetings were conceptualised as part of the *Gesamtkunstwerk* of the *Expositions universelles*. They should be 'a universal exhibition of thought flanking the universal exhibition of products', amount to an encyclopaedic project, standardise methods across borders and unite all civilised nations in a universalist *entente* to overcome international conflict.[21] Congresses in particular were aimed at fostering debate among international experts, while conferences were held to disseminate scientific knowledge to a larger audience. To maximise impact, proceedings of conferences and congresses were sent to foreign governments, public libraries, learned societies and other institutions of education.[22]

Congress proposals had to be submitted to the *Commission supérieure*. To be judged successfully they had to fulfil specific requirements as to international content and membership that were decreed by the Minister of Commerce and Industry:

---

[19] Rasmussen, 'Congrès internationaux', 37; AN, F 12 3263; F 12 4285–6.

[20] Ministère de l'Agriculture et du Commerce, *Rapport administratif sur l'exposition universelle de 1878 à Paris* (2 vols., Paris 1881), I, pp. 226–38, II, pp. 275–84, 334–9.

[21] A. Picard, Ministère du Commerce, de l'Industrie et des Colonies, *Exposition universelle internationale de 1889 à Paris. Rapport général* (10 vols., Paris, 1891), III, p. 339, Rasmussen, 'Congrès internationaux', p. 26; 'L'Exposition. Conférences et congrès', *La France*, 11 Apr. 1878; 'Congrès et Conférences', *La Patrie*, 11 Apr. 1878, see press-clippings AN, F12 3265.

[22] C. Thirion (ed.), *Exposition internationale de 1878, à Paris. Congrès et conférences au Palais du Trocadéro. Comptes rendus sténographiques publiés sous les auspices du comité central des congrès et conférence et la direction de M. Ch. Thirion, secrétaire du comité* (3 vols., Paris, 1880–1). Due to the increasing number of congresses in 1889, only summary proceedings were published, but full accounts were often given by the organisers through inhouse publications, see 'Comptes-Rendus Stenographiques des Congrès et Conférences', AN 12 3236, Dossier 'Envoi des publications'.

Congresses must have an international character, not only through the participation of diverse countries, but also through the nature of questions that
they address and through the goal that they aim to achieve. This goal could
be either to establish a common action between various countries and to
provoke international measures, for example the standardisation of weights,
measures and coins, the application of sanitary rules, the preparation of
comparative statistics, the execution of major scientific work, or the collection of comparative indications on questions for which the differences
of climate, race or temperament do not allow to adopt uniform solutions,
or finally to assess the state of the sciences in the different parts of the
world.[23]

The commission favoured congresses that could complement the bigger
picture of the exhibition and discouraged those not conforming to its
vision. Political and religious topics had to be avoided by all official congresses, which made up about 60 to 75 per cent in Paris.[24] Rival congresses
on the same theme were also impeded.[25] If these conditions were met,
the minister decreed the composition of organisational committees, which
would develop the programme, and chose a patronage committee to gather
support for the congress.

Like the exhibitions, the congresses were a means of personal and institutional advancement. They were largely platforms for men of a certain
standing who had already been validated by the *Académie* and the *Collège
de France*. Yet while the organisation of the *Expositions universelles* was
bestowed upon members of the new elite of *politechniciens*, the congresses were a means for the traditional learned elites to compensate for a
loss of power in administration and to distinguish themselves from their
peers.[26]

A common heritage

In the same way that the organisers of historic monument exhibitions
appealed to nationalist exhibition language to propagate their cause, the
organisers of preservationist congresses phrased their purpose according
to the international aims expressed in the regulatory framework of the

[23] 'Arrêté du Ministre du commerce et de l'industrie, en date du 2 aout 1887, instituant
des congrès et conférences', repr. in Picard, *Exposition universelle internationale de 1889*. I,
pp. 326–8, qu. p. 327.
[24] Rasmussen, 'Congrès internationaux', p. 30.
[25] Picard, *Exposition universelle internationale de 1889*, III, p. 332.
[26] Rasmussen, 'Congrès internationaux', pp. 42–3; C. Charle, *Les Elites de la République, 1880–1900*
(Paris, 1987).

Expositions universelles. While the protection of monuments had been a subject at International Congresses of Architects in relation to training and education, the programme for the First International Congress for the Protection of Works of Art and Monuments in 1889 outlined a much broader concern and justified the need for a more specific congress by identifying a problem common to several countries, and by proposing a common solution:

> The protection and safeguarding of monuments . . . or more generally of works of art, which are of interest for the memories and the history of all civilised nations, is imperative to the thought of whoever knows, loves, and respects the traditions or glories of his fatherland. For some time, these preoccupations, common to all thinking minds, have been translated into administrative regulations and even legislation. Imbued by the same thinking, we want to provoke a sympathetic current, an international league that can constitute, even in the midst of the violence of war, an effective defence for the heritage [*patrimoine*] bequeathed by the past to all present generations.[27]

According to this programme, the knowledge, love and respect of heritage made it necessary to fight for its safeguarding internationally. Through a crafty use of synonyms for heritage, patriotism and internationalism were linked, with the former being declared the base for the latter. While the idea that 'the monuments of art belong to humanity as a whole'[28] was portrayed as something self-evident to all thinking minds, patriotism was acknowledged by labelling these monuments as everybody's *gloires de sa patrie*.[29] Finally the two potentially contradictory feelings were further reconciled at the end of the passage by using the term *patrimoine* in a new way without any epithet. Instead, the expression '*patrimoine légué par le passé*' turned time and not individuals or nations into the transmitter of heritage. Beyond nationality, party or confession, 'the respect for the past' could become a 'genuine religion'.[30]

This language soon became foundational. Subsequent international congresses on archaeology, public art, architecture and nature protection never saw the national and international paradigms as opposed. The international congresses of architects even described the international entanglement in familial terms: 'All want to work in a brotherly manner, hand

---

[27] Normand, *Procès-verbaux*, pp. 13–14.   [28] Normand, *Procès-verbaux*, resolution VI, p. 25.

[29] *Nos gloires* had been Viollet-le-Duc's favourite circumlocution for monuments, see A. Besnard, *Septième Congrès international des architectes. Londres, Juillet 1906. Essai sur la neuvième question du programme. De la responsabilité des gouvernements dans la conservation des monuments nationaux* (Paris, 1906), p. 40.

[30] Ibid., p. 19.

in hand, like the sons of the same golden mother: Architecture.'[31] The international congress of *Heimatschutz*, alone, devoted more attention to exploring the seeming irreconcilability of *Heimatschutz* and internationalism. Within Germany the strong nationalist and anti-socialist tendencies of many *Heimatschützer* made for frequent anti-internationalist comments. The movement's critique of the destructive forces of capitalism made it also unlikely to espouse liberal free trade internationalism, yet *Heimatschutz* nevertheless felt a need to internationalise itself. In part this had a pragmatic background. As the nationalist president of the *Bund Heimatschutz*, Paul Schulze-Naumburg, outlined in his opening speech for the second *Heimatschutz* congress, international cooperation was a way to assert a movement's importance and prestige:

> The mere fact that it was possible to unite an International Congress for *Heimatschutz* with all these representatives from Central European and even East Asian countries is a sign that the *Heimatschutz* movement has grown from its infancy into an important movement without which we could hardly imagine our modern cultural life. We need international connections to enlarge the circle of our alliances, to exchange experiences, to develop guidelines for a common international strategy and to spread our endeavours to the entire world.[32]

However, beyond these practical arguments, *Heimatschützer* also explicitly tried to reconcile the apparent paradox between an *international* congress and the essentially *national* aims of *Heimatschutz* in a more essential way. As one of the BHS's more moderate members, the economist Carl Johannes Fuchs pointed out:

> Surely, the means are in most cases different from country to country. But the underlying major problem is indeed the same in all modern civilised states [*Kulturstaaten*]. At the heart of *Heimatschutz* is the fight against a capitalism that relentlessly destroys the beauty of old [*das Gewordene*]. Therefore, all countries can only gain, despite national differences, from exchanging achievements and experiences on legal decisions and other practices. 'Marching together, fighting separately' – is the inversion of a well-known proverb. And if the *Heimatschutz* movement will undoubtedly enhance the differentiation and separations of peoples, this will in no way harm their

---

[31] J.M. Poupinel, Ministère du Commerce, de l'Industrie des Postes et des Télégraphes. Exposition universelle internationale de 1900. Direction générale de l'exploitation, *5e Congrès international des architectes, tenu à Paris du 30 Juillet au 4 août 1900. Procès-verbaux sommaires par M. J.M. Poupinel, secrétaire général du congrès* (Paris, 1901), p. 12. See also speech by the president of the *Verband deutscher Architekten* Stübben, qu. in Bohnstedt, 'Der Internationale Architekten-Congress in Paris vom 30. Juli bis 4. August 1900', *Centralblatt der Bauverwaltung*, 20 (1900), 449–51, here 449.

[32] *Heimatschutz*, 8 (1912), 57.

interrelations. For only he who loves and respects his own *Heimat* and his own ways – not in raw and arrogant chauvinism, but in sophisticated reflection and knowledge about its cultural importance – will respect the *Heimat* and ways of others. In this manner, the International Congresses for *Heimatschutz* can be an important means to foster the cultural rapprochement of peoples and to achieve the aim that the Cobden Club designated with the words: *peace and goodwill among nations*.[33] May the second congress for the protection of *Heimat* become a milestone along this path.[34]

The organisers of the international congress of *Heimatschutz* thus did not go so far as to speak of a 'common heritage of humanity', but emphasised that the love of one's own *Heimat* and one's own traditions would lead to a better understanding and peaceful relations among nations.[35]

Despite their different ideological penchants, all international congresses declared the love for 'heritage', 'monuments', or '*Heimat*' to be common to all civilised nations – or at least to all the thinking minds in these communities. The enemies against which heritage had to be defended were defined sufficiently vaguely to find a common denominator and ranged from war, modern planning, restorations, 'ruthless capitalism', the transformation of values to general ignorance.[36] Over time, in a sort of self-fulfilling prophecy, the profusion of international congresses was itself seen as proof for the existence of a common cause.[37]

Since the first international congress, most speeches were drenched in the rhetoric offered by the official regulations and reports, in which international membership and thematic content were a prerequisite, and the advancement of civilisation and international understanding the desired outcome.[38] The fostering of 'peace and goodwill among nations' was enduringly inherited from the organisers of the Great Exhibition of 1851. Likewise, the celebration of 'the glories of peace and work',[39] so important in French exhibitions from 1867 onwards,[40] remained another essential element of the heritage discourse, even after congress organisation grew increasingly independent of these administrative origins and heritage-makers

---

[33] The West London private members' club, named after philanthropist and the free trade internationalist Richard Cobden, was built in the 1870s as a venue to promote art and entertainment for the working man. On the propagation of Cobden's ideas through the great exhibition see J. Kemper, 'Internationalism and the Search for a National Identity: Britain and the Great Exhibition of 1851', 23 May 2000, Stanford University, www.stanford.edu/group/wwi/spring2000/exhibition/paper.htm.

[34] *Heimatschutz*, 8.2–3 (1912), 58–9.   [35] *Heimatschutz*, 8.2–3 (1912), 63.

[36] *Bericht über den VIII. Internationalen Architekten-Kongress*, pp. 252, 648.

[37] Besnard, *Septième Congrès international des architectes*, pp. 49–50.

[38] Picard, *Exposition universelle internationale de 1889*, III, p. 338–9.

[39] Normand, *Procès-verbaux*, p. 29.   [40] See Barth, *Mensch versus Welt*.

assembled in meetings unrelated to the exhibitions. The belief in international understanding was extolled by organisers and orators of all nationalities and irrespective of the political context. That such rhetoric was becoming topological was already noted at the time. Alfred Picard, coordinator of the 1889 and 1900 *Expositions universelles* and author of purple passages on international understanding in 1889, almost ironically admitted in his next report: 'The useful reconciliation between men and between peoples participating in international congresses, has been so often and so eloquently praised, that to repeat it here, would mean to develop a common place.'[41]

Even beyond the emphatic programmes, the congress members delighted in 'international politeness', so disdained in exhibition reports. Foreign colleagues became *concitoyens*, and as sons of the same architectural mother, members constantly called each other *confrère* – the French expression was even adopted in English.[42] Speakers took pride in showing themselves knowledgeable about their hosts' situation and achievements. The German architect Alfred Bohnstedt, for instance, ended his talk at the Congress of Architects in Paris with an allusion to Victor Hugo, crying out *'Guerre aux démolisseurs!'*[43] In a similar fashion, the Parisian architect Alfred Besnard not only opened his paper at the Congress of Architects in London with a quotation from Ruskin but also continuously referred to the superiority of British behaviour.[44] The fraternal attitude was fostered through social activities such as excursions, but did not stop after the congress banquets and was carried over to the national sphere. Virtually no negative comments were recorded; instead the specialist press abounded with glowing reports about international congresses (ill. 4.1).[45]

---

[41] A. Picard, Ministère du Commerce, de l'Industrie, des Postes et des Télégraphes. *Exposition universelle internationale de 1900 à Paris. Rapport général administratif et technique* (8 vols., Paris. 1902–3), VI, pp. 26–7.

[42] 'The Paris Congress', *RIBA Journal of Proceedings*, 4 July 1889, 2nd Ser., 5.2 (1889); R. Dircks, 'The VIII International Congress of Architects, Vienna', *Journal of the RIBA*, 3rd Ser., 15 (1908), 481. After the political entente cordial, the International Congress of Architects held in London was also dubbed an *'Entente cordiale* for foreign architects', see 'Congress Comments', *The Builder*, 28 July 1906, pp. 123–4.

[43] 'De la conservation des monuments historiques. Communication de M. Alfred Bohnstedt, conseiller d'architecture à Minden en W. Ancien attaché à l'Ambassade en France', *Congrès international des architectes. Cinquième session tenue à Paris du 29 juillet au 4 août 1900. Organisation, compte-rendu et notices* (Paris, 1906), p. 169; Bohnstedt, 'Die Denkmalpflege. Vortrag gehalten in Paris am 2. August 1900 beim V. Internationalen Architekten Congress', *Die Denkmalpflege*, 2 (1900), 97–9.

[44] Besnard, *Septième Congrès international des architectes. Londres, Juillet 1906.*

[45] The only negative comment made (in an otherwise positive account) concerned the low attendance of French government officials, see Bohnstedt, 'Der Internationale Architekten-Congress in Paris', 449–51.

DELPHES. — HOMOLLE COMMENTANT LE RÉSULTAT DES FOUILLES DE L'ÉCOLE FRANÇAISE D'ATHÈNES
EN PRÉSENCE DES MEMBRES DU 1ᵉʳ CONGRÈS INTERNATIONAL D'ARCHÉOLOGIE AU BORD DU TEMPLE D'APOLLON
PHOTOGRAPHIE INÉDITE DE CHARLES NORMAND

4.1 Sociability and excursions were an important part of all congresses. This photograph by Charles Normand of the International Congress of Archaeology in Athens 1905 was published in *L'Ami des Monument*, 20 (1906), p. 369.

'A most unpleasant competition'

Underneath the sweet tones of international unity, the congresses were, like the exhibitions, a battlefield for competing heritage-makers on the national and local level. This was particularly apparent in the circumstances that led to the First Official International Congresses for the Protection of Monument and Works of Art in Paris in 1889. Initiated by Charles Normand at a meeting of the *Amis des Monuments parisiens* in summer 1888 and seconded by the society's leading members Louis Gonse (who was by now also an honorary SPAB member) and the Parisian activists Eugène Müntz and Arthur Rhoné, the proposal was soon approved by the Minister of Commerce and Industry.[46] The organising committee, suggested by Normand, and appointed by ministerial decree included representatives from a wide variety of institutions concerned with the protection of monuments: members of the Historic Monuments Commission, architects of the Diocesan Service, members of the Institute, curators of several museums, professors

---

[46] 'Congrès international de protection des monuments en 1889', *L'Ami des Monuments*, 2 (1888), 168.

from the *École des Chartes*, and for the learned societies, the new president of the *Société française d'archéologie*, Count de Marsy. Politicians were represented by Senator Courcelle-Seneuil, who had distinguished himself in the push for preservation legislation during the previous years.[47] The organising committee thus embraced personalities from private and state institutions. Apart from Émile Boeswillwald, Mérimée's successor as Inspector for Historic Monuments, Courcelle-Seneuil, de Marsy, and Alfred Darcel, the director of the *Musée de Cluny*, all were also members of *L'Ami des Monuments*. The committee then worked to gather the greatest possible national and international cloud. It appointed Charles Garnier congress president, Boeswillwald and the journalist Auguste Vitu vice-presidents, and Charles Normand secretary-general, thus again representing state administration and the private society in the highest ranks, though the latter slightly outweighed the former. A patronage committee was created encompassing the most illustrious members from the world of French politics and the arts, ranging from Jules Ferry to Ernest Renan and Baron Alphonse de Rothschild.[48] Even Baron Haussmann, whose city planning the *Amis des Monuments parisiens* had been founded to combat, became a resident member. To draft the list of foreign members, existing contacts with foreign preservation societies, like the SPAB, were essential. The committee also drew on the international contacts of the International Congress of Architects and the network of correspondents of the Institute. The composition process reflected the membership and networks of *L'Ami des Monuments*, but the committee also tried to obtain standing through the broadest possible representation in France and a wide international reach.

Yet it made some people very unhappy. Although represented on both the organising and the patronage committee, members of the Historic Monuments Commission and other state institutions involved in the preservation of monuments and art must have felt the congress to be a challenge to their hegemony. They might also have been unhappy about the principles of anti-restoration promoted by the programme. Antonin Proust, former Minister of Arts, instigator of the Museum of Comparative Sculpture at the Trocadéro, and Commissioner for the retrospective art exhibitions in 1889, pushed for the creation of an alternative venture. He had been a founding member of the *Amis des Monuments parisiens*, but was absent from later membership lists. His letter to the Minister of Public Instruction and

---

[47] C. Normand, 'Congrès officiel international pour la protection des oeuvres d'art et des monuments', *L'Ami des Monuments*, 2 (1888), 230–2; *JO*, 18 July 1888.
[48] Ibid.

Fine Arts was a carefully crafted piece, playing with heritage semantics and wider exhibition discourses, by highlighting the importance of his own institution:

> The Museum of Comparative Sculpture, which stems from the initiative of the Historic Monuments Commission, is within the walls of the 1889 *Exposition universelle*. The Museum unites the most beautiful works of French architecture and sculpture and your department has made it the seat of the most successful French Art courses. I have the honour to suggest organising, during the Exhibition, in the room that welcomes the audience of French Art courses, a series of conference and periodical meetings to discuss questions relating to the protection of monuments of historic and artistic interest. This room contains busts of Mérimée, Vitet, Viollet-le-Duc... to which will be added the busts of Lenoir, Victor Hugo etc. in order to continue the homage France owes to all the men who paid service to the cause of French Art. Such a place is best prepared to receive the commission whose formation I have the honour to suggest to you.[49]

The stated purpose of Proust's congress was thus exactly the same as that of its rival. It was even put in the same words. Like Normand's project, the congress was to look at '*les questions qui se rattachent à la protections des monuments*', yet by specifying that these were '*monuments qui présentent un intérêt historique et artistique*', Proust also took up the language of the recently passed Monument Act to show that the meeting would chime into the administrations' wider aims. Rather than championing an international league for the *patrimoine*, Proust spoke more traditionally of a service for the cause of art.[50] The only international scheme proposed was the establishment of an international inventory of works of art. Like the content, the membership of this proposed congress was less internationally focussed than that of the Congress for the Protection of Works of Art and Monuments. The French members were chosen for their position in the French art administration rather than individual name or fame, the *Société des Antiquaires de France* being the only private partner included. The number of foreigners was greatly inferior to those of the French members, and they were organisers of the foreign fine arts sections rather than preservation specialists.

Certainly aware that the regulatory framework forbade rival congresses, Proust chose not to allude to the existence of *L'Ami des Monuments'* congress project. Rather than contesting the competitor openly, he argued

[49] Antonin Proust, *Commissaire spécial des Beaux-arts to Ministre de l'Instruction publique et des Beaux-arts* (Édouard Lockroy), 12 Feb. 1889, MAP, 80/8/7, Dossier 'Congrès des arts et de l'archéologie'.
[50] 'Congrès international de protection des monuments en 1889', *L'Ami des Monuments*, 2 (1888), 168.

in favour of a Congress for Art and Archaeology by stressing the place of his proposed congress within the established structures. Proust's insistence on holding the congress in the Museum of Comparative Sculpture did not only help the 'paternal jealousy' with which he tried to market his museum to foreign visitors. He also benefited from the fact that the congress rules prescribed that meetings had to take place on the exhibition site. As the localities in the Trocadéro were insufficient for the already approved number of congresses, the administration had to find alternative locations.[51] By indicating the availability of his own premises, Proust was able to circumvent this administrative problem. By stressing the museum's experience in holding conferences, and by referring to the pantheon of *patrimonialisateurs* assembled in the hall, he also indirectly indicated that the congress, and by association the Minister of Fine Arts, would continue the work of France's greatest heritage-makers, and no half-baked private initiative. The argument was successful. The minister, Édouard Lockroy, responded favourably to the request of his protégée Proust by return of post, instituting the Congress for Art and Archaeology,[52] although congresses normally had to be decreed by the Minister of Industry and Commerce.[53]

The rivals' reaction was not long in coming. Two weeks after the decrees were published in the *Journal official*, a furious Charles Garnier wrote to the Ministers of Industry and Commerce and of Public Instruction and Fine Arts.[54] Incidentally the creation of the rival congress had been one of Lockroy's last acts as minister. Two days later, on 14 February 1889 Floquet's government resigned as the Chamber had become ungovernable in the wake of the Panama Scandal. On 22 February 1889, under the second Tirard government, Tirard himself succeeded Legrand as Minister of Industry and Commerce and Fallière succeeded Lockroy as Minister of Public Instruction and Fine Arts. Garnier addressed the two new Ministers and recalled that the previous Minister of Commerce had installed a congress for the protection of monuments. Garnier described in great length how the committee had started its work, and how a patronage committee had

---

[51] Picard, *Exposition universelle internationale de 1889*, III, p. 334.

[52] *Ministre de l'Instruction publique et des Beaux-arts*, 'Arrêté instituant un congrès des arts et de l'archéologie à l'Exposition universelle et nommant les membres de ce congrès', MAP, 80/8/7, Dossier 'Congrès des art et de l'archéologie', published in the *JO*, 26 Feb. 1889, 998–9.

[53] 'Arrêté du Ministre du Commerce et de l'Industrie en date du 30 décembre 1887 portant règlement général des congrès et conférences.' Art. 11 and 13 repr. in Picard, *Exposition universelle internationale de 1889*, X, pp. 269–71.

[54] Charles Garnier to *Ministre de l'Instruction publique et des Beaux-arts*, 5 Mar. 1889, MAP, 80/8/7, Dossier 'Congrès des arts et de l'archéologie'.

been created containing 'the names of the highest authorities among those who are interested in art and archaeology'.[55] The new congress with the 'same aim' could only be seen as 'a sort of most unpleasant competition' interrupting the work under way. Given the presence of two 'almost identical' congresses, members of Garnier's project feared that their activities might be curtailed in favour of the younger contender. He thus asked the Minister of Public Instruction to inform him whether his congress must 'disappear', and be 'dispossessed of its initiative', or whether he was correct to think that its 'right to primacy' would be recognised.[56]

The new Minister of Public Instruction and Fine Arts, Fallières, wrote to Tirard, head of the new government and Minister of Commerce and Industry about the 'embarrassing situation'. Following a meeting with Garnier, Fallières suggested that the situation could be solved by amalgamating the two congresses, declaring the members and vice-presidents of the first to be members of the second, and the president of the first to be one of the vice-presidents of the second. According to Fallières, Garnier had found this solution agreeable and suggested that the members of the Congress of Architects, of which Garnier was also the president, would affiliate themselves to the Congress of Arts and Archaeology. At the Bureau for Historic Monuments, the members of the *Congrès pour la protection des oeuvres d'art* and the *Congrès des architectes* were added to a handwritten member list for the new congress indicating that the conviction existed that the problem was solved.[57] Whether this downgrading of the first congress in favour of the second was in Garnier's intention is doubtful. Charles Garnier's angry letter emphasised his congress's moral right to primacy and its higher quality in terms of the originality and work undertaken. A subordination of the Congress of Architects also seemed difficult given it was long established and therefore administered independently. The organising committees for Garnier's two congresses, which overlapped significantly, had explicitly coordinated to hold the two congresses only a day apart to facilitate attendance at both.[58]

In the meantime, the general political climate was further tensing as the political leaders involved had their minds on the heating up of the Boulanger Affair. Yet the interdepartmental and interpersonal rivalries persisted independent of the broader political context. The preparation for all

[55] Ibid.   [56] Ibid.

[57] *Ministère de l'Instruction publique et des Beaux-arts, Monuments historique, Exposition universelle, Congrès des arts et de l'archéologie*, 'Note pour Monsieur le Ministre, Paris, 27 juillet 1889', MAP, 80/8/7, Dossier 'Congrès des arts et de l'archéologie'.

[58] E. Müntz, *Troisième Congrès international des architectes. Paris, 17–22 juin 1889. Catalogue de l'exposition de portraits d'architectes organisée à l'École des beaux-arts à l'occasion du congrès, par Charles Lucas et Eugène Müntz* (Paris, 1889).

three congresses continued as if the quarrel had not taken place. Only at the last minute, several names were added to the patronage committee of the Congress for the Protection of Art and Monuments: Antonin Proust, the instigator of the rival congress, Viollet-le-Duc son and now head of the Bureau for Historic Monuments and the painter Lemeire, an early member of the *Amis des Monuments parisiens* and a member of the Historic Monuments Commission. French and foreign journalists and other influential foreign members were also included, both as a reward for publicity given to the congress and as an attempt to propagate it further.[59] As Tirard ignored Fallières's letter on the matter, Garnier's two congresses took place, while despite further stirrings from Proust, his congress had to be abandoned late in the day.[60]

The failed attempt to stage an alternative congress was subjected to a *damnatio memoriae* by both the monument administration for obvious reasons, and the *Amis des Monuments*, as it might have challenged their universalist ambitions. At the congress, Charles Normand only dealt with the episode in passing, wrapping it in allusions whose import would only have been apparent to insiders.[61] The Historic Monuments administration's response was to organise an even larger exhibition of historic monuments in 1900 together with a conference cycle, at which the would-have-been congress president of 1889, Viollet-le-Duc's favourite disciple Anatole de Baudot, gave the first two presentations.[62] The 1889 quarrel was also certainly the reason why in 1900 a conference cycle rather than a congress was organised despite the fact that overall the conference format had largely been abandoned by the exhibition leaders of 1900 due to its limited popularity in 1889 (ill. 4.2).[63]

The final victory of the congress of *L'Ami des Monuments* cannot solely be attributed to the superiority of its programme and the international

[59] See lists in Ministère du Commerce, de l'Industrie et des Colonies. Exposition universelle internationale de 1889. Direction générale de l'exploitation, *Congrès international pour la protection des œuvres d'art et des monuments*. Fascicule no. 1 – *Organisation du Congrès*. Mai 1889 (Paris, 1889); Fascicule no. 2 – *Organisation du Congrès* (Paris, 1889) and Normand, *Procès-verbaux sommaires*. On the inclusion of journalists see 'Discours prononcé à l'ouverture du premier congrès pour la protection des monuments et oeuvres d'art par Charles Normand', *L'Ami des Monuments*, 3 (1889), 191–3.

[60] *Ministère de l'Instruction publique et des Beaux-arts, Monuments historiques, Exposition universelle, Congrès des arts et de l'archéologie*, 'Note pour Monsieur le Ministre, Paris, 27 Juillet 1889', MAP, 80/8/7, Dossier 'Congrès des arts et de l'archéologie'. The *Rapport général* of the exhibition simply notes that 3 out of 72 congresses had to be abandoned: Picard, *Exposition universelle internationale de 1889*, III, pp. 336–8.

[61] 'Discours prononcé à l'ouverture du premier congrès pour la protection des monuments', p. 192.

[62] For organisation and proceedings see MAP, 80/8/7, Dossier 'Exposition 1900'.

[63] Picard, *Exposition universelle internationale de 1889*, III, pp. 340–1; Picard, *Exposition universelle internationale de 1900*, VI, p. 5.

4.2 Poster for the conference cycle organised by the Ministry for Public Instruction on historic monuments during the 1900 *Exposition universelle* in Paris.

radiance of its membership list, and was probably due to respect for the 'first come, first served' rule. Yet the episode has several broader implications. It shows that the private preservation movement in France seized the opportunity to establish its standing domestically through an international initiative. The affair also proves that private actions were taken seriously by the established art administration. The state administration would have been unlikely to take the initiative to create an international congress had there not been a rival. It is generally assumed that the state, after having reacted jealously to Arcisse de Caumont's initiatives by initiating parallel structures, had become less controlling over the learned societies during the Third Republic.[64] The example, however, demonstrates that the dynamics of action and reaction had changed little. At the same time, it shows that the relationship between the state and the private movements was not just about competition. While *L'Ami des Monuments* became more assertive as a civil society movement through the opposition it encountered from the cultural administration, paradoxically, the congress was also a means of securing governmental support. The label that came with being recognised through the governmental congress rules was ennobling and legitimising. Rather than choosing an openly oppositional route, like the congresses of socialists and later feminists that took place unofficially during the exhibitions, Charles Normand never tried to speak of the fact that his congress had been the first 'official' one.

The administrative framework marks this episode as typically French. Yet the underlying mechanisms were equally representative of Germany and England and indeed of countries across Europe. For subsequent congresses, recognition by government officials, be it through such a complicated administrative procedure as in the case of the French *Exposition universelles*, or through the simple participation of government officials at privately organised congresses, was keenly sought. It was seen as pivotal to the reputation of a congress and movement, both nationally and internationally. A dearth of governmental participants reduced a congress's prestige in the eyes of foreigners, as happened at the 1900 International Congress of Architects.[65] Consequently, all international congresses for the protection of heritage tried to obtain the patronage and presence of their governments, be it in France, Germany, Britain, Spain, Belgium or Italy.[66]

---

[64] Chaline, *Sociabilité*, pp. 369–72.
[65] Bohnstedt, 'Der Internationale Architekten-Congress in Paris', 449–51.
[66] Paul Clemen to Friedrich Schmidt-Ott, 18 Sept. 1913, GStA PK VI. HA, Rep. 92 Nl. Schmidt-Ott (M), A X 1, fol. 199.

Members of the royal families were also invited to increase a congress's standing. For example, all International Congresses of Architects after 1900 were held in monarchies and secured royal patronage. Yet foreign princes provided glamour in republican France too – the Brazilian Emperor for instance headed the list of honorary members at the First Official Congress. The private societies that presented themselves as independent public voices, and which often criticised the existing preservation policies, thus at the same time sought accreditation by the state and the established order.

The First Official Congress

Having caused a commotion in French cultural politics, the First Official International Congress for the Protection of Works of Arts and Monuments established an ambitious programme around the themes of legislation, education and restoration that set the agenda for international congresses for the next decades.[67] In order to improve national situations and establish international action, it was concerned to provide a basis for comparison and emulation. In addition to theoretical exposés, and broadly comparative papers, the state of affairs in China, Mexico, Brazil, Switzerland, Prussia, Britain, Belgium, Portugal and France were presented individually.

Though members of the congress universally demanded new legislation and devoted much time to papers on comparative law by leading experts, such as the French lawyer Jules Challamel and the Swiss Baron de Geymüller, they also cherished the voluntary principle and saw the need to educate the public to respect and love monuments as an even greater necessity than legislation.[68] To this end love for monuments was presented as both an eternal and an endangered human feeling: The Chinese General Tcheng Ki Tong (Chen Jitong) and Augé de Lassus, the restorer of Notre Dame and an *Ami des Monuments parisiens*, highlighted how the ancestral cult ensured the respect for traditions and monuments in China and Ancient Rome, respectively.[69] Western speakers at the congress, like the

---

[67] *Congrès international pour la protection des œuvres d'art et des monuments.* Fascicules no. 1 and 2.

[68] Normand, *Procès-verbaux*, pp. 17, 19, resolution XVIII, p. 28; J. Challamel, 'Congrès international pour la protection des œuvres d'art et des monuments. Des Législations françaises et étrangères établies pour assurer la conservation des œuvres d'art et des monuments', *L'Ami des Monuments*, 4 (1890), 285–300. For the correspondence between Geymüller and Prussian Conservator Persius in preparation for the talk see GStA, I HA Rep. 76 Ve, Sek 1, Abt. VI, Nr. 141.

[69] Général Tcheng-Ki-Tong, 'Congrès official international pour la protection des oeuvres d'art. Les Monuments de la Chine. Leur conservation', *L'Ami des Monuments*, 3 (1889), 326–8; Normand, *Procès-verbaux*, pp. 16, 19. Tcheng-Ki-Tong already drew parallels between the two forms of ancestral

Académie member and *Amis des Monuments parisiens*'s president Ravaisson, who had taken Charles Garnier's place as congress president when the latter had to step down because of faltering health, begged for France not to lag behind China's jealousy-inspiring example.[70] As the organic connection to antiquity and antiquities no longer existed in the Western world, it was deduced that education must take its place. Le Breton, president of the *Amis des Monuments rouennais*, reminiscent of Abbé Grégoire, proposed signage on all school walls of the maxim: *'Respect the monuments which are the glory of our country.* It was the people who constructed them, hence it must be in the interest of the people to be their best conservators; it is the people who must be made to contribute in a more extended way to the work of national safeguarding.'[71] Rather than sharing the more pessimistic attitude of the members of the *Service des Monuments historiques* who had little faith in the ordinary Frenchman's love for monuments, the members of the *Amis des Monuments* societies emphatically proclaimed that it would only be a matter of time to turn peasants into monument-lovers. Normand explained how easily the innate love of the people for monuments could be enhanced through proper education. Drawing on his work as president of the propaganda committee of the *Union française de la jeunesse* which organised museum tours for young apprentices and the visits of the *Amis des Monuments rouennais* to the surrounding villages he suggested:

> Peasants have a passion for the smallest of memories. It would suffice to organise *Amis des Monuments* committees everywhere, modelled on and with the help of the Parisian committee, whose guided tours have had such prodigious success. They serve not only to the participating elite, but thanks to the detailed summaries published by all well-informed papers they also contribute to the education and development of the entire nation.[72]

The congress was thus not just a way to triumph over the administration in organisational terms, but to highlight the merits of the private sector in general and in particular, by presenting the work of the Society for the Protection of Ancient Buildings, the *Société archéologie de Bruxelles*, the *Société pour la conservation de l'art historique suisse*, and above all the different French *Amis des Monuments* societies. Consequently, numerous members suggested different measures they believed would, within twenty years, create an entire generation that would know how to respect monuments. These ranged from the foundation of more societies to the installation of

cult in Tcheng-Ki-Tong, *Les Chinois paints par eux-memes* (Paris, 3rd edn, 1884) pp. 114–20 and 167–73.
[70] Normand, *Procès-verbaux*, pp. 17–18. [71] Ibid., p. 17. [72] Ibid., pp. 19–20.

explanatory plates on monuments, expositions of plaster casts (not unlike
those used in the Museum of Comparative Sculpture and the *Expositions
universelles*), guided tours, inexpensive guide books for which those edited
by Normand could serve as models, to the introduction of drawing lessons
and art courses in schools for which members of private societies could
serve as instructors.[73]

After legislation and education, the third major theme of the
1889 congress concerned the practices of restoration and documentation.
With regard to restoration, the congress clearly positioned itself on the
side of conservation over restoration. This was mainly achieved by presenting the views of the SPAB as leading international principles. While
the SPAB had distributed its manifesto at earlier Congresses of Architects,
the society was now for the first time given a broad international audience
to present its views.[74] The SPAB's French correspondent Adolphe Guillon
read a letter from Thackeray Turner expressing the principles of Ruskin
and the SPAB. In accordance with their sentiments, the congress resolved
that reparation should be limited to consolidation and in particular condemned the restoration of sculptures and paintings. Further resolutions
directly addressed the restoration practices in several countries and asked
for the professionalisation of those restoring works of art. Resolution VIII
for instance suggested that Historic Monuments Commissions be installed
in every country, but that an artist charged with the restoration of a particular work should only have consultative functions. This clearly criticised
the current state of affairs in France – where the possibility to combine the
function of architect working for the CMH while also being a member
was only discontinued in 1892 – but it also resounded with Morris' desire
to undo restoration-profiteering in Britain. In other ways, the congress was
more inspired by official French practices, stressing the need to properly
document the restoration of works of art. If the demolition of an edifice
could not be prevented, at least drawings, photographs, models and the
like should be deposited in public archives to preserve a memory.[75]

The formal lecture format was complemented by excursions. These
were not only moments of relaxation, in which ladies were allowed to join,
but an opportunity to propagate the results of previous campaigns.[76] The
congress included among other events a guided tour of Notre Dame by
Charles Normand in which the visitors were presented with his guidebook,
and a visit of the Roman Arena of Paris, for whose conservation the *Amis des*

[73] Ibid., p. 19.   [74] SPAB Archives, 2nd Committee Minute Book, 27 June 1878.
[75] Normand, *Procès-verbaux*, pp. 20–21, 24–28.
[76] *Congrès international pour la protection des œuvres d'art et des monuments.* Fascicule no. 2, p. 2.

Monuments parisiens had campaigned since their foundation.[77] Following the visit, the congress passed the resolution that the amphitheatre should be open to the public. The excursions' sociable setting was thus a further means of pursuing the aims of the conference hosts, and to throw the clout of the international audience behind particular local agendas.

While parts of the programme clearly focussed on domestic issues, the majority of resolutions aimed to secure a lasting international impact. At the suggestion of the Brazilian painter Pedro Américo Figueiredo and of José Velasco, the congress's Mexican honorary president, resolutions were communicated in printed form to the governments of all participants' home countries.[78] To confront the challenges identified by delegates, it was resolved that further congresses should be held on an annual basis. The national and international committees of the congress were merged with the *Comités nationaux et internationaux d'Ami des monuments*, and it was agreed that *L'Ami des Monuments* would be the congress's official printed voice, creating a link between artists, scholars and amateurs of all countries (ill. 4.3).[79] An international archive of architectural drawings should also be established.[80] The most ambitious international project outlined in the resolutions, however, was the foundation of a Red Cross for Monuments.

As reported to the wider world in *L'Ami des Monuments*, 'Charles Normand laid the foundation for an international entente to assure the safeguarding of works of art in time of war by a convention of the sort of the so-called Geneva Convention or of the Red Cross' (ill. 4.4).[81] When Normand put this topic on the programme, he intended to outline some ideas and leave them open to elaboration by other participants, for 'in fact everything is unknown as to the solution to the problem'. His reasons for airing these ideas at the congress did not allude to the context of international relations that might have spurred particular concern over buildings in times of war, such as the fate of the Holy Places during the Crimean War. He also did not allude to the Franco-Prussian war, the Russo-Turkish war of 1878, or the British conquest of Egypt in 1882, possibly because international congress etiquette forbade the criticising of an individual nation's behaviour. Instead Normand invoked the congress's unique potential to realise an international *entente*. This 'new and shining hope', would make them all worthy citizens of their fatherlands. The problem being outlined, the congress

---

[77] Normand, *Procès-verbaux*, p. 18. [78] Ibid., resolution XIX, p. 28.
[79] Ibid., pp. 16, 22, resolutions I, XI pp. 24, 26.
[80] Ibid., p. 21, resolution XII, adopted after de Geymüller's suggestion, p. 26.
[81] Normand, *Procès-verbaux*, p. 21. For the full text see C. Normand, 'Premières Idées sur l'organisation de la croix-rouge pour la protection des monuments en temps de guerre. Conférence faite au premier Congrès officiel international pour la protection des oeuvres d'art et monuments à l'Exposition universelle', *L'Ami des Monuments*, 3 (1889), 272–7.

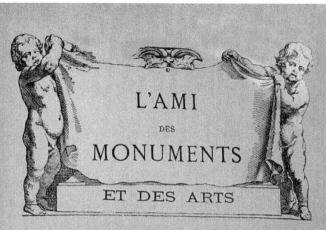

L'AMI

DES

MONUMENTS

ET DES ARTS

REVUE DES DEUX MONDES DES BEAUX-ARTS ET DE L'ARCHÉOLOGIE

ILLUSTRÉE

ORGANE DU COMITÉ DES MONUMENTS FRANÇAIS
ET DU COMITÉ INTERNATIONAL D'AMIS DES MONUMENTS

ADOPTÉE PAR LE CONGRÈS OFFICIEL INTERNATIONAL POUR LA PROTECTION DES MONUMENTS
ET ŒUVRES D'ART COMME ORGANE ENTRE LES ARTISTES, ÉRUDITS, ET AMATEURS
DE TOUS PAYS

ÉTUDE ET PROTECTION DES ŒUVRES D'ART DE LA FRANCE
REVUE DES DERNIÈRES DÉCOUVERTES DU MONDE ENTIER

FONDÉE ET DIRIGÉE PAR

CHARLES NORMAND

Architecte diplômé par le Gouvernement
Secrétaire général de la Société des Amis des Monuments parisiens
Président honoraire de la Société des Amis des Monuments rouennais

Nᵒˢ 21-22. — 4ᵉ année, 1890. — Prix de ce numéro : 12 fr.
Souscription annuelle, 25 fr. — Étranger, 30 fr.

PARIS

98, RUE DE MIROMESNIL

Autrefois, 51, rue des Martyrs

4.3 Title page for the 1890 volume of *L'Ami des Monuments* that identified the periodical as the international organ of the First Official Congress. The earlier subtitle 'Organ of the Society of Ancient Buildings' was dropped.

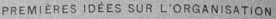

PREMIÈRES IDÉES SUR L'ORGANISATION
DE LA CROIX ROUGE

POUR LA PROTECTION DES MONUMENTS EN TEMPS DE GUERRE

Conférence faite au premier Congrès officiel international pour la protection des œuvres d'art et monuments à l'Exposition universelle,

PAR

CHARLES NORMAND

(Voir plus loin, dans le texte des vœux du Congrès, l'adoption du vœu proposé par l'auteur.)

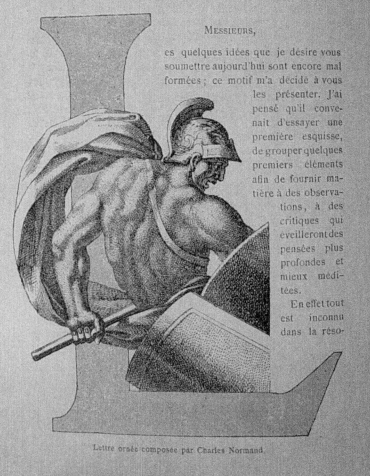

MESSIEURS,

es quelques idées que je désire vous soumettre aujourd'hui sont encore mal formées ; ce motif m'a décidé à vous les présenter. J'ai pensé qu'il convenait d'essayer une première esquisse, de grouper quelques premiers éléments afin de fournir matière à des observations, à des critiques qui eveilleront des pensées plus profondes et mieux médi- tées.

En effet tout est inconnu dans la réso-

Lettre ornée composée par Charles Normand.

4.4 First page of Charles Normand's article on a Red Cross for Monuments ornamented by the author: 'Premières Idées sur l'organisation de la croix-rouge pour la protection des monuments en temps de guerre. Conférence faite au premier Congrès officiel international pour la protection des œuvres d'art et monuments à l'Exposition universelle', *L'Ami des Monuments*, 3 (1889), pp. 272–7.

having certified its importance and public opinion having embraced it through the press, it only remained to map six steps to success. The first would be the 'platonic recognition of the principle by governments. That task should be easy, being so little troublesome.' This should be followed by the establishment of an international *classement* of buildings, which could not be touched during future wars. A state committing the 'crime' of harming them, having 'violated, both international agreement, and moral law', would suffer penalties. While efforts should be made to incessantly increase the number of listed buildings by agreements between states, such a list should only be transitory, as it is 'important to know that all monuments are worthy of solicitude'. After the end of the congress, negotiations should be started to realise the international *classement* of a first monument. 'Let us preferably choose a work situated in a country outside of future belligerent complications. Without doubt, no government would decline to support this measure, under threat of wearing in the eyes of the world and of history the stigma that marks the enemies of progress.' Any edifice would do, but preferably one outside of Europe, a lost stone in the middle of the desert, 'if you so wish, the pyramids of Egypt'. Why Normand would choose the pyramids as the first world heritage site is not hard to see, but how he could label them as 'outside future belligerent complications' might have raised a few eyebrows. For the secretary of the congress the issue seemed easy: who, he asked, could oppose such a modest request? Who on the contrary would not understand what a splendid page the people who would be the *first* to recognise this grand principle would add to its chronicle, by responding to the challenge of adopting a measure that 'is so platonic, just and compromises so little'. To achieve these aims, the present congress ought to ask for the summoning of a diplomatic congress composed of diplomats, artists and writers. To assure assistance and avoid 'deaf opposition', or 'sneering indifference', only the most influential diplomats should be chosen and those reputed for their love of beautiful things, their art collections, and scholarly contribution to history and art. If this could be achieved, next to the *Comité des Monuments Internationaux*, 'propaganda instrument of the great cause, developing the means and concepts', and the 'bristling force of peoples united towards this common end', a 'powerful influence, decisive in certain hours' would be secured in the highest ranks of politics.[82]

Inviting the floor to make further suggestions, Normand admitted that his vision was utopian but so had been the beginnings of the Geneva

---

[82] Ibid.

Convention. The delegates now had the opportunity to achieve something similar, 'save the riches of their fatherlands and their ancestors', and move 'civilisation to a new stage of progress'.[83] Convinced, the congress unanimously adopted a resolution for the constitution of a Red Cross for the protection of monuments and works of art in times of war and motioned that the different governments designate representatives to indicate the monuments that should be protected by an international convention.[84]

As such, notwithstanding the slight exaggeration of the general prevalence of its views, the 1889 Congress gave momentum to existing trends and outlined principles that remained programmatic during most of the twentieth century. Many of the opinions on preservation expressed went back to activities and publications of the SPAB and *L'Ami des Monuments*, but they had never been articulated so concisely and uncompromisingly in France or in the international arena. Moreover, the measures of international collaboration envisaged went further than any previous suggestions. Although some of the congress was tailored to a specifically French audience, most of the congress's content was formulated in a general way, and sketched a programme with the potential for universal application for generations to come. Charles Garnier noted in his opening speech that the problems the congress addressed were still far from being solved, but that a lasting solution might be found through regular international congresses. The same ideal surfaced in the closing speech of Admiral Likhatchof, delegate of the Archaeological Society of Moscow and honorary president of the congress.[85] Accordingly, the organisation of future congresses was entrusted to the newly founded permanent international committee. Unlike numerous other congresses that had the first of many sessions during an *Exposition universelle*, however, no further meetings of the International Congress for the Protection of Works of Art and Monuments were held. Instead, the heritage protection was pursued through a variety of new formats.

Continuation and elaboration

Almost a decade elapsed between the first congress of 1889 and its successors, but once successors did begin to appear, they followed thick and fast. Personal and conceptual continuities were particularly strong with the four Congresses for Public Art and the six International Congresses of Architects that took place between 1897 and 1911. The first Congress for Public

[83] Ibid.   [84] Normand, *Procès-verbaux*, p. 25.   [85] Ibid., resolution xx, p. 28.

Art was organised by the homonymous Belgium movement, with had close ties to *Art Nouveau* circles, and was concerned with the aesthetic challenges of modern city planning. The congress built on links between French and Belgium preservationists, established since 1889: the editor of *Art Public*, Eugène Broerman, praised the *Société des Ami des Monuments parisiens*, the *Commission du Vieux Paris* and the *Société centrale des Architectes français* as spiritual fathers.[86] Fittingly, the next meeting was organised in Paris in 1900 by members of the *Commission du Vieux Paris* and the *Amis des Monuments parisiens*, most notably Charles Normand and Eugène Müntz. The overarching aim was to foster 'respect for monumental ensembles or picturesque quarters of cities'.[87] Wishes of the 1889 congresses were reaffirmed, supporting conservation over restoration, penal sanctions against vandalism, documentation of demolitions, and the creation of an inventory. The means proposed to achieve these aims were also similar, including the foundation of more private associations, this time called *Sociétés d'Art public* rather than *Sociétés des Amis des Monuments*, and the organising of educational exhibitions. It was decided that the resolutions should be published in official government publications of each participating country and be sent to the mayor of every city.[88]

All pre-war International Congresses of Architects also paid specific attention to the care of monuments.[89] Like the Public Art Congresses,

[86] See the entire volume of *Art public* (1897–1998) and 'Congrès international de l'Art public', *L'Ami des Monuments*, 12 (1898), 112, 180–1, 234–7, 290–5, here 181.
[87] C. Normand, 'Le Congrès parisien, municipal, international de l'Art public ou étude des conditions de la physionomie artistique des villes', *L'Ami des Monuments*, 13 (1899), 164–8, 'Souvenir de l'Exposition: l'Art public. Voeux du Congrès de Paris, international, municipal d'art public', *L'Ami des Monuments*, 14 (1900), 211–23, qu. p. 212.
[88] Ibid., pp. 218–23.
[89] *Report upon the IV. International Congress of Architects, Brussels, 1897* (Washington, 1898); *5e Congrès international des architectes, tenu à Paris du 30 Juillet au 4 août 1900. Procès-verbaux Sommaires; Congrès international des architectes. Cinquième session tenue à Paris du 29 juillet au 4 août 1900. Organisation, compte-rendu et notices; Congrès international des architectes. Sixième session tenue à Madrid 1904. Organisation. Compte rendu et notices* (Madrid, 1906); *VIme. Congrés international des Architectes sous la haute protection de S.M. le Roi d'Espagne et le patronage du Gouvernement. Madrid. Avril 1904* (Madrid, 1904); Royal Institute of British Architects, *International Congress of Architects. Seventh session held in London 1906 under the auspices of the Royal Institute of British Architects. Transactions* (London, 1908); *Journal of the RIBA*, 3rd Ser., 13 (1906), *Congress Supplement*; Besnard, *Septième Congrès international des architectes. Londres, Juillet 1906; Bericht über den VIII. Internationalen Architekten-Kongress, Wien 1908; Congresso internazionale degli architetti. Atti del 9. Congresso internazionale degli architetti, Roma, 2–10 Ottobre 1911* (Rome, 1914). See also the reports in the organisational and specialist press. 'Internationaler Architekten Congress in Brüssel', *Centralblatt der Bauverwaltung*, 17 (1897), 238, 331, 356, 397, 416; 'Internationaler Architekten Congress in Paris', *Centralblatt der Bauverwaltung*, 20 (1900), 44, 208, 280, 286, 449–51; 'Internationaler Architekten Congress in Madrid', *Centralblatt der Bauverwaltung*, 23 (1903), 425; Bohnstedt, 'Die Denkmalpflege. Vortrag gehalten in Paris am 2. August 1900 beim v. Internationalen Architekten

they referred explicitly to many themes of the 1889 Monument Congress, discussed progress and reaffirmed resolutions. The lion's share of the discussion was taken up with comparative legislation and measures to render the public interested in preservation. Resolutions for training architects were also reaffirmed. In 1900, de Geymüller reread the suggestions he made in 1889, demanding that those wanting to receive an architectural diploma should first study the 'treasure of national heritage' (*trésor du patrimoine national*).[90] He also suggested making more use of good foreign examples and recommended that national societies of architects follow the Swiss practice of making students read the guidelines on the conservation of monuments published by the RIBA.[91] Members of the *Commission du Vieux Paris* chimed in. They had already initiated a translation of the RIBA guidelines in the *Bulletin municipal de la Ville de Paris* after the 1889 Congress.[92] Other reaffirmed aims reached from the documentation of restoration to guidelines for window restoration.[93] The emphasis on the role of the private associations remained strong and was reaffirmed through the reuse of the linguistic choices of the first congress. Both the

Congress', *Die Denkmalpflege*, 2 (1900) 93, 97–99; 'Sechster internationaler Architekten-Kongress in Madrid', *Die Denkmalpflege*, 5 (1903), 123; H. Muthesius, 'Sechster internationaler Architektenkongress in Madrid', *Die Denkmalpflege*, 6 (1904), 52; 'Internationaler Architektenkongress in Wien', *Die Denkmalpflege*, 10 (1908), 67–9. In *The Builder* see 'Congress of Architects at Paris Exhibitions', 3 Aug. 1878, p. 804 and 10. Aug 1878, p. 825; 'Congress of Architects', 6 July 1889, pp. 4–8; 'Letter from Paris', 4 Aug. 1900, p. 97, 'Paris International Congress of Architects', 11 Aug. 1900, pp. 129–30; 'International Congress of Architects', 10 Feb. 1906, p. 136; 'The International Congress of Architects', 7 July 1906, p. 7; 'Work and Play at the Architectural Congress', 14 July 1906, p. 33; 'The Congress Exhibition', 21 July 1906, pp. 67–9; 'Congress Comments', 28 July 1906, pp. 123–4; likewise 'The Paris Congress', *RIBA. Journal of Proceedings*, 2. Ser., 4 July 1889, no pagination; 'International Congress of Architects and Retrospective Exhibition of Architecture at Brussels', *Journal of the RIBA*, 3rd Ser., 4 (1897), 422; 'Chronicle. Brussels Congress', *Journal of the RIBA*, 472–4; 'The Fifth International Congress of Architects, Paris, Report of the Secretary', *Journal of the RIBA*, 7 (1900), 469–74; J.W. Locke, 'International Congress of Architects, Madrid. Report of the Secretary of the Institute', *Journal of the RIBA*, 11 (1904), 343–6; 'Seventh International Congress of Architects 1906', *Journal of the RIBA*, 11 (1904), 483, 528; 'Seventh International Congress of Architects London 1906', *Journal of the RIBA*, 13 (1906), 12, 56, 110, 129–31, 178, 193, 390, 429, 446, 500 and Congress supplement, lxii-lxvi. 'International Congress Vienna', *Journal of the RIBA*, 15 (1908), 140, 299, 328, 449–50; R. Dircks, 'The VIII International Congress of Architects, Vienna', *Journal of the RIBA*, 15 (1908), 480–81; 'Ninth International Congress of Architects at Rome', *Journal of the RIBA*, 18 (1911), 282, 314; J. Slater, 'The Ninth International Congress of Architects, Rome 1911', *Journal of the RIBA*, 19 (1912), 28–30.

90 *Congres international des architectes. Cinquième session tenue à Paris du 29 juillet au 4 août 1900. Organisation, compte-rendu et notices*, pp. 169–79.

91 Cf. RIBA, *Conservation of Ancient Monuments and Remains, General Advice to Promoters, Hints of Workmen* (London, 1865). A revised edition appeared in 1888.

92 *Congres international des architectes. Cinquième session tenue à Paris du 29 juillet au 4 août 1900. Organisation, compte-rendu et notices*, pp. 169–79.

93 Besnard, *Septième Congrès international des architectes*, p. 56.

1900 Public Art Congress and that of Architects decided to replace *monuments historiques* by the broader terms *monuments du passé* or *patrimoine* to dissociate themselves from the administrative tradition.[94]

However, as the Congress of Architects included private and government architects, papers recognised equal merits in the private and state sectors.[95] In contrast to the clearly anti-restorationist attitude of the First Congress for the Protection of Works of Arts and Monuments, the more diverse preoccupations of architects at these professional congresses led to heated debate on the merits and defects of restoration. In Brussels and Paris, debates on conservation versus restoration were animated, and because of insurmountable disagreements, no resolutions were passed.[96] Yet, a preference for conservation over restoration slowly gained support through the international discussion. At the 1904 Congress of Architects (and at the 1905 Congress of Public Art) the Belgian Professor Cloquet presented a practical solution through the theoretical distinction between 'dead monuments' whose function was now obsolete, and 'living monuments' which still served their original purpose. The first should not be restored, but prevented from decaying. The second could be restored, as utility was part of their beauty, but this should be done without demolishing parts from different periods to establish stylistic unity. Supported by the speakers of 1906, Besnard from Paris and Baldwin Brown from Edinburgh, the idea was already firmly rooted in the theoretical discourse when the president of the Austrian Association of Architects, Julius Deiniger, keynote speaker in Vienna in 1908, summarised 'the victorious advance of modern views as to the protection of monuments':[97]

> Concerning the treatment of old edifices, whether in good condition or already bearing marks of decay, the opinion that their condition should be maintained as unchanged as possible continually gains more general acceptance. This opinion applies especially to the whole beauty of the object, i.e. not to its outward formal appearance only but also to the tone the edifice may have gained through its age and history. As recently as the second half of the last century it was the almost universal endeavour to restore to an old

[94] 'Souvenir de l'Exposition: l'Art public. Ville de Paris. Congrès de l'Art public, Premier sections', *L'Ami des Monuments*, 14 (1900), 220; *Congrès international des architectes. Cinquième session tenue à Paris du 29 juillet au 4 août 1900. Organisation, compte-rendu et notices*, p. 178.
[95] Besnard, *Septième Congrès international des architectes*. Besnard gave the same paper in 1908 with a few actualisations, see *Bericht über den VIII. Internationalen Architekten-Kongress, Wien 1908*, pp. 258–312.
[96] 'Der internationale Architekten-Congress in Brüssel', *Centralblatt der Bauverwaltung* 17 (1897), 397–8; *Congrès international des architectes. Cinquième session tenue à Paris du 29 juillet au 4 août 1900. Organisation, compte-rendu et notices*.
[97] *Bericht über den VIII. Internationalen Architekten-Kongress*, p. 247, trans. p. 675.

edifice its probable original appearance. To-day this is not only considered undesirable but in some cases even reprehensible.[98]

Other congresses, like the two international congresses for landscape and *Heimatschutz* did not style themselves as heirs of the previous congress. Although some overlap in membership existed, they more strongly represented the views and networks of the organisers, namely the *Société française pour la Protection des Paysages* and the *Bund Heimatschutz*. The meetings devoted themselves to translating *Heimat, pays*, and similar local concepts for an international audience to establish a basis of comparison and collaboration. Their main reflections centred on how to deal with tourism, mountain-trains, hydropower, advertisement posters and global nature and bird protection.[99] However, in other respects important overlap also existed. The common theme which connected *Heimatschutz*, Public Art and Architects' Congresses, and which marked an important innovation vis-à-vis the 1889 congress, consisted in the strong links that were made between the protection of monuments, landscapes, and other traditions. As the survival of cultural and natural, tangible and intangible resources were increasingly seen as intertwined, a growing importance was accorded to the protection of entire ensembles rather than to individual monuments.

This new emphasis was underpinned by a discourse on hygiene.[100] Internationally, the Public Art Movement was the first to develop Ruskin's idea that artistic beauty was an important factor for public health into an aesthetic public policy.[101] It promoted the notion of combining the need for hygienic standards that had motivated the transformation and modernisation of many cities since the mid-nineteenth century with an 'aesthetic hygiene', holding that to preserve and create beauty was as important as clean water and open air to the population's well-being. More than sixty years before sector conservation became a widespread principle, its 1900 congress resolved that a *classement* should be organised for ensembles of historic or artistic interest, and that a corresponding article be added to the French Monument Act of 1887.[102] Influenced by the Public Art Congresses, and possibly through cross-fertilisation with the International

[98] Ibid.
[99] 'Dringende Fragen des Weltnaturschutzes mit besonderer Berücksichtigung der Kolonien und des Vogelschutzes', see *Heimatschutz* 8.1 (1912), 34 and 8.2–3 (1912), passim.
[100] *Heimatschutz*, 8.2–3 (1912), 83.
[101] Trom, 'Natur und nationale Identität', pp. 147–67, esp. p. 165, note 48.
[102] 'Souvenir de l'Exposition: l'Art public. Ville de Paris. Congrès de l'Art public, Premier sections', *L'Ami des Monuments*, 14 (1900), 214–15.

Congresses of Hygiene, the International Congresses of Architects also debated how Pasteur's and Koch's work could inform a new approach to preservation.[103] Architects campaigning for the preservation of historic cities emphasised that they were not fanatical traditionalists who wanted to maintain picturesque but unhealthy medieval structures. Preservation in their view was not opposed to public health, but scientific progress and the modernisation of hygienic standards had to be integrated into modern conservation policies.[104]

In addition to developing a theoretical framework, international congresses also continued to support particular national and local campaigns. For instance, the 1900 Public Art Congress used the general support for ensemble protection to promote the cause of particular sites in Paris, such as the Place des Victoires, Place des Voges, Place de la Concorde, Place Vendôme, quartier Pirouette and the Monuments des Bernardins. It also campaigned against a bridge construction project linking Venice to the Mainland.[105] Converging ideas about monument, landscape and ensemble conservation also informed a resolution by the eighth International Congress of Architects to save the Mont Saint-Michel, threatened with losing its insular character by plans to fill up the bay. The congress suggested to push for a *classement* as a natural ensemble with an artistic character under the new *Loi Beauquier*.[106] The plea bore fruit after it was taken up by the Congress of the Provincial Association of French Architects in 1908, and joined by other actors such as *L'Ami des Monuments* and the architect Corroyer, who restored the Mont Saint-Michel for the CMH.[107]

The different congresses thus thematically developed many of the notions outlined by the First International Congress for the Protection of Works of Art and Monuments, yet their multiplication also reflects that the understanding of heritage had become much broader than 'the protection of monuments and works of art' and that preservationists were in search of new formats. However, these new congresses were even more

[103] 'International Congress of Hygiene at Brussels', *Journal of the RIBA*, 3rd Ser., 11 (1904), 445.
[104] *Bericht über den VIII. Internationalen Architekten-Kongress*, pp. 253, 320–3.
[105] 'Souvenir de l'Exposition: l'Art public. Ville de Paris. Congrès de l'Art public, Premier sections', *L'Ami des Monuments*, 14 (1900), 212–13.
[106] *Bericht über den VIII. Internationalen Architekten-Kongress*, pp. 648–49.
[107] 'Vœu pour la protection du Mont Saint-Michel', *L'Ami des Monuments*, 21 (1907–8), 298–9; on Corroyer's restoration between 1878–1883, see 'Remparts au Mont-Saint-Michel', *L'Architecture* (1907), 416–18. 'Actes officiel relatif à la sauvegarde du Mont St. Michel. Decrét du classement des ramparts du mont', *L'Ami des Monuments*, 22 (1909–14), 43–4. On earlier involvement of SPAB and Guillon in the planned restoration of the church see SPAB Archives, 6th Committee Minute Book, 28 Oct. 1886; SPAB, *Annual Report*, 10 (1887), 44–5.

different from the one in 1889 in another area. While they all stressed common efforts and declared themselves bound to mutual help, the idea of an international league was hardly followed up.

Despite the profuse rhetoric of international collaboration that successor conferences inherited from the venture of 1889, it was recognised that there were limits to the possibility of internationalism. In 1900, the International Congress of Architects openly debated the effectiveness of international collaboration. The main lecturer of the panel, the German architect Bohnstedt strongly critiqued the resolutions of the 1897 congress in Brussels, which asked for standardisation of existing legislation.[108] In his opinion, such an aim was wholly unrealistic. Countries already in possession of legislation would not wish to make compromises, whereas those which had not yet passed laws would try to have more advanced ones than those already in existence abroad. Ultimately, the 1900 congress passed a very similar resolution to that of 1897, with the argument that countries already possessing legislation did not have to be concerned by it, while a resolution of an international congress at which numerous nations were represented 'can help our *confrères* in countries which don't yet have sufficient legislation to obtain a parliamentary enquiry and the passing of a law'.[109] The Russian delegate, Count Suzor, suggested that additionally the permanent committee should be in constant contact with the relevant governments to keep track of the implementation of congress resolutions, as it seemed to him that most of the resolutions were simply repetitions of older ones, which had never been implemented. At later congresses, speakers provided reports on progress in the individual countries, but no mention was made of the activities of the permanent committee. A new push for internationalisation came from another prominent architect from the Habsburg Empire, Dr Franta from Prague, who tried to instigate the foundation of an international commission for the coordination of national legislations.[110] Though Franta received lively applause, the congress eventually followed the opinion of the main speaker, Professor Deiniger, who argued that although in principle nothing would militate against such an undertaking, and that for sure 'the interest in the preservation of monuments is an international one', it seemed more realistic for individual states to first regulate according to their needs and then to look for an international agreement, than the other way round.[111]

---

[108] Qu. in *Congrès international des architectes. Cinquième session tenue à Paris du 29 juillet au 4 août 1900*, p. XLI.
[109] Ibid., p. 180.   [110] *Bericht über den VIII. Internationalen Architekten-Kongress*, p. 256.
[111] Ibid., pp. 256–7.

Despite the desirability of struggling for common aims, the time was not yet seen ripe for an international body regulating the protection of monuments and works of art. While some delegates believed that 'all political or other questions have to give way to the high interest constituted by the study of monuments of the past and we would be happy if all states represented at the congress would give precise instructions to their ambassadors',[112] the majority adhered to the recognition of immunity of national affairs. This feeling, combined with a consideration for the 'actual state of affairs',[113] ultimately only resulted in relatively vague resolutions encouraging all civilised nations to ensure the protection of their monuments.[114]

That opposition to an international body would indeed be strong became clear when the Swiss anthropologist and preservationist Paul Sarasin tried to establish one for the global protection of nature. Following his experience in the colonial sphere, Sarasin suggested to protect not just nature but also 'primitive peoples' from the encroachments of civilisation. He had aired his ideas at a variety of international congresses from zoology to *Heimatschutz* and convinced the Swiss government, keen to foster its international role, to host an international diplomatic meeting. Although seventeen governments accepted the invitation in 1913, the aim to establish an international committee was strongly opposed by many national governments, and Germany in particular instructed her representative, the head of the Prussian Commission for Nature Conservation Hugo Conwentz, to oppose any yielding of national influence. As a result, the international committee that was created in 1914 had merely advisory functions – and never took up work because of the outbreak of war.[115]

The implementation of international conventions for the protection of works of art and science, asked for since the First International Congress was therefore left to a different group of people: the diplomats about whose artistic credentials Charles Normand had been so worried.

International conventions

Many of the ideas outlined by Charles Normand in his project for a Red Cross for monuments recur in the 1899 and 1907 Hague Conventions. Drawing a direct link between the 1889 congress and the conventions is,

[112] Ibid., p. 255.   [113] Ibid., pp. 256–7.
[114] 'Angenommener Antrag des Berichterstatters Oberbaurat Julius Deininger', ibid., pp. 648, 680.
[115] Sarasin, *Über die Aufgaben des Weltnaturschutzes*; Kley, 'Weltnaturschutzkonferenz', Wöbse, *Weltnaturschutz*; Kupper, *Wildnis schaffen*.

however, difficult. Although Normand's ideas were in many ways highly original, they were not as original as he claimed. While he referred to the Geneva Convention of 1864, and modelled his ideas on the principle of the Red Cross, he did not allude to a long-established tradition in international law that dated back to at least the mid-eighteenth century.[116]

The ravaging of artistic treasures by victorious armies was first challenged by one of the fathers of international law, the Swiss jurist Emer de Vattel (1714–67) in his treaty *Le Droit des gens*, published in 1758.[117] De Vattel did not yet speak of a common heritage of humanity, but nonetheless implied that works of art belonged to mankind as a whole:

> For whatever reason a belligerent ravages a country, those edifices which do honour to human society and do not contribute to an increase in the enemy's strength should be spared: temples, tombs, public buildings, and all other works of remarkable beauty. What can be gained from their destruction? Only an enemy of mankind would deprive it happily of these monuments of art and models of taste.[118]

As seen earlier, such sentiments had had little impact on Revolutionary and Napoleonic art looting, but they did inform the restitution claims that led to the return of the works of art in 1815.[119] The theoretical principles established by de Vattel were extended during the American Civil War by Francis Lieber. His 1863 code for the government of armies influenced all later treatises. Although the victorious army had the right to appropriate all public property,

> [a]s a general rule, the property belonging to churches, to hospitals, or other establishments of an exclusively charitable character, to establishments of

---

[116] For documents see the International Committee of the Red Cross, 'International Humanitarian Law – Treaties & Documents', www.icrc.org/ihl.nsf/WebFULL?openview (English); www.icrc.org/dih.nsf/ART?OpenView&Start=1 (French). As an overview see S.E. Nahlik, 'Protection of Cultural Property', in *International Dimensions of Humanitarian Law* (Geneva, Paris, 1988); S.A. Williams, *The International and National Protection of Movable Cultural Property. A Comparative Study* (New York, 1978); Jokilehto, *History of Architectural Conservation*, pp. 245–94; R. O'Keefe, *The Protection of Cultural Property in Armed Conflict* (Cambridge, 2006).

[117] F. Bugnion, 'The Origins and Development of the Legal Protection of Cultural Property in the Event of Armed Conflict. 50th Anniversary of the 1954 Hague Convention for the Protection of Cultural Property in the Event of Armed Conflict', 14 Nov. 2004, International Red Cross, www.icrc.org/Web/Eng/siteeng0.nsf/htmlall/65SHTJ. For a broader intellectual history and the context of international relations see F.H. Hinsley, *Power and the Pursuit of Peace. Theory and Practice in the History of Relations between States* (Cambridge, 1963, repr. 1967).

[118] E. de Vattel, *Le Droit des gens, ou principes de la loi naturelle, appliqués à la conduite et aux affaires des nations et des souverains* (2 vols., London, 1758), II, p. 139. The book was translated into English and German within two years.

[119] Bugnion, 'Legal Protection of Cultural Property'; Nahlik, 'Protection of Cultural Property', p. 204; Jokilehto, *History of Architectural Conservation*, p. 282.

education, or foundations for the promotion of knowledge, whether public schools, universities, academies of learning or observatories, museums of the fine arts, or of a scientific character – such property is not to be considered public property.[120]

While national legislators everywhere tried to assert the state's right to intervene in the protection of monuments by declaring them to be public goods, Lieber conversely ensured their protection by treating them as private property, because the sanctity of private property was already firmly established, based on distinctions by de Vattel and Rousseau between military and civilian persons and objects.[121] The Lieber Code also introduced the practical suggestion that the besieged 'designate the buildings containing collections of works of art, scientific museums, astronomical observatories, or precious libraries, so that their destruction may be avoided as much as possible'.[122]

After the Franco-Prussian war brought the fear of war back to the centre of Europe, delegates from Austria-Hungary, Belgium, Denmark, France, Germany, Great Britain, Greece, Italy, the Netherlands, Russia, Spain, Sweden and Norway and Switzerland convened in Brussels in July 1874, following the initiative of Tzar Alexander II, for a new kind of international diplomatic conference. While the international system established through the concert of Europe lost stability, the private international peace movement was growing. The Brussels Conference was the first diplomatic assembly meeting in time of peace for the purpose of preserving peace, rather than concluding a war in progress.[123] Delegates were invited to examine the draft of an international agreement concerning the laws and customs of war submitted to them by the Russian government. They were chosen among the high ranks of the military and diplomatic services and among experts of international law.[124] The conference adopted the draft presented by the Russian government with slight alterations.[125] The protection of

[120] 'Instructions for the Government of Armies of the United States in the Field (Lieber Code). 24 April 1863', www.icrc.org/ihl.nsf/385ec082b509e76c41256739003e636d/c4d7fab1d847570ec125641a00581c23!OpenDocument.

[121] Bugnion, 'Legal Protection of Cultural Property', note 16.   [122] *Lieber Code*, Art. 118.

[123] Hinsley, *Power and the Pursuit of Peace*, pp. 114–49. Hinsley identifies the Hague Conferences as the first specimen, but the tribute belongs to the Brussels Conference.

[124] See Ministère des Affaires étrangères. Documents diplomatiques, *Actes de la conférence de Bruxelles de 1874 sur le projet d'une convention internationale concernant la guerre. Protocoles des séances plénières. Protocoles de la commission déléguée par la conférence* (Paris, 1874), p. 3; On biographies: B. Röben, *Johann Caspar Bluntschli, Francis Lieber und das moderne Völkerrecht 1861–1881* (Baden-Baden, 2003).

[125] *Actes de la conférence de Bruxelles*, appendices. English trans. of final declaration: 'Project of an International Declaration concerning the Laws and Customs of War. Brussels, 27 August 1874',

monuments was only a minor concern amongst the larger peacekeeping aims of the conference. The article on cultural property is now mostly presented as a transitional step to the Hague Conventions.[126] However, it was among the most hotly debated articles, and the discussion about its phrasing is instructive about the prevalence of heritage ideas outside the preservationist milieu.

During the discussion, the Belgian statesman Baron Lambermont, who would later become a leading voice in the colonial conferences of the period, pointed out that the original Russian project had included 'a clause for the protection of artistic riches', which had been 'very favourably received by public opinion'.[127] This clause had stated that the 'property of churches, charitable and educational establishments and institutions dedicated to science, the arts or philanthropy is not subjected to seizure and wilful damage of institutions of this character, historic monuments, works of art and science should be made the subject of legal proceedings by the competent authorities'.[128] In previous sessions of the conference, this original clause had been amended. Delegates had tried to improve the situation of monuments by extending the protection accorded to private property to them.[129] Lambermont objected to the privatisation of heritage which the draft embraced in the spirit of the Lieber Code. On a related point, Lambermont opposed the use of *biens des églises* with which the original *propriété des égliges* had been replaced, as in his view this expression did not properly represent the thoughts of the commission. Once destined for the priesthood, but now a lawyer and expert on foreign trade, he criticised the labelling of what he himself called *patrimoine de la religion, de l'instruction, des arts et des science* as commodities and wanted a less materialistic description, for which he used again the term *patrimoine*. This statement is all the more remarkable, as *patrimoine* was barely emerging as a generic term in preservationist discourses in the early 1870s. Other delegates also wished to enlarge the category of protected objects. The Greek Colonel Manos suggested including all works of art and not only those preserved in museums, and the Italian delegate Lanza recommended the introduction of penalties for the 'intentional destruction or degradation of artistic objects belonging

---

www.icrc.org/ihl.nsf/385ec082b509e76c41256739003e636d/a59f58bbf95aca8bc125641e003232af?
OpenDocument.

[126] Williams, *The International and National Protection*, pp. 15–17; Jokilehto, *History of Architectural Conservation*, p. 282.

[127] *Actes de la conférence de Bruxelles*, Protocole No. 18, 22 Aug. 1874, pp. 44–5.

[128] Cf. ibid., p. 56, Annexe VIII, Section I, Chapitre I, 'Nouvelle rédaction proposée par M le Président de la séance plénière du 5 août, protocole 3'.

[129] Ibid., Protocole No. 18, 22 Aug. 1874, pp. 44–5.

to the State'.[130] He pointed out that although this was already implied in the project, it would be advisable to add an explicit clause.

On the other hand, the German General Voigts-Rhetz insisted on maintaining the wording of *biens des églises* on the basis that these were indeed goods required as such by the military, e.g. for lodging and feeding armies. Despite Lambermont's retort that he was not seeking to protect monuments from military needs, that churches could still be used to tend the wounded, but that military needs had to be reconciled with 'other interests that all members of the commission cherish, without doubt, to safeguard',[131] Voigts-Rhetz refused to change the wording, but consented to the addition of a clause relating to *monuments historiques*. After the intervention of a Turkish delegate, *église* in the original draft was moreover replaced by *établissement consacré aux cultes*, to do justice to the universal, rather than purely Western and Christian claim of the declaration. The final version thus read:

> In such cases all necessary steps must be taken to spare, as far as possible, buildings dedicated to art, science, or charitable purposes, hospitals, and places where the sick and wounded are collected provided they are not being used at the time for military purposes. It is the duty of the besieged to indicate the presence of such buildings by distinctive and visible signs to be communicated to the enemy beforehand . . . The property of municipalities, that of institutions dedicated to religion, charity and education, the arts and sciences even when State property, shall be treated as private property. All seizure or destruction of, or wilful damage to, institutions of this character, historic monuments, works of art and science should be made the subject of legal proceedings by the competent authorities.[132]

Jokilehto argues that in the Brussels declaration, 'culture was declared to belong to the common heritage of mankind, artistic treasures once destroyed were irreplaceable, and their cultural worth was declared to be of value to all men, not just to the nation in whose country they were situated'.[133] This might be the underlying assumption, but, as in the Lieber Code, the motivation for the protection of cultural goods is not explicit in the convention. It does not state whether the reason for protecting cultural goods was the belief in a 'common heritage' or simply a matter of mutual convenience.

---

[130] Ibid.   [131] Ibid.
[132] Ibid., trans.: www.icrc.org/ihl.nsf/385ec082b509e76c41256739003e636d/a59f58bbf95aca8bc12564 1e003232af?OpenDocument.
[133] Jokilehto, *History of Architectural Conservation*, p. 282.

The declaration did not have an immediate effect, as it was not ratified, but it provided an important step in the movement for the codification of the laws of war. The Institute of International Law, founded in 1873 to consider ways of establishing collective scientific action for the promotion of international law, inseparable, in the opinion of its founders, from the promotion of peace, appointed a committee to study the Brussels Declaration and develop supplementary proposals. The reflections resulted in the compilation of the *Manual of the Laws and Customs of War*, adopted by the Institute of International Law at a meeting in Oxford in 1880. Assuming that since the Brussels Conference ideas had matured, and 'it seems less difficult than it did then to trace rules which would be acceptable to all peoples', but that at the same time it was premature to propose an international treaty, the authors instead offered a manual.[134]

The texts of the Brussels Conference and the *Oxford Manual* formed the basis of the two Hague Conventions. Spurred by the nascent arms race between Germany and Britain, the First Hague Peace Conference of 1899 was assembled on the initiative of Tsar Nicholas II, 'with the object of seeking the most effective means of ensuring to all peoples the benefits of a real and lasting peace, and, above all, of limiting the progressive development of existing armaments'.[135] The conference, at which twenty-six governments were represented, did not achieve its primary object of the limitation or reduction of armaments, but it nonetheless adopted three Conventions. The second included provision for the treatment of cultural property, by now an unquestioned element of international law.[136] The second peace conference, proposed in the first instance by the President of the United States of America, was convened, at the invitation of the Tsar, by the Queen of the Netherlands 'for the purpose of giving a fresh development to the humanitarian principles which served as a basis for the

---

[134] 'The Laws of War on Land. Oxford, 9 September 1880', Art. 34. www.icrc.org/ihl.nsf/ 385ec082b509e76c41256739003e636d/6a5d425d29d9d6dbc125641e0032ec97?OpenDocument.

[135] Russian note of 30 December 1898/11 January 1899, qu. in 'Final Act of the Second Peace Conference. The Hague, 18 October 1907', www.icrc.org/ihl.nsf/73cb71d18dc4372741256739003e6372/ f1de61e43d5e0f6bc12563cd002d675c?OpenDocument. See Ministère des affaires étrangères. *Conférence internationale de la paix. La Haye, 18 mai–29 juillet 1899* (The Hague, 1899); R. Shabtai (ed.), *The Hague Peace Conferences of 1899 and 1907 and International Arbitration. Reports and Documents* (The Hague, 2001). On biographical information of delegates: A. Eyffinger, *The 1899 Hague Peace Conference. 'The Parliament of Man, The Federation of the World'* (The Hague, London, Boston, 1999), pp. 125–202.

[136] 'Convention (II) concernant les lois et coutumes de la guerre sur terre et son Annexe: Règlement concernant les lois et coutumes de la guerre sur terre. La Haye, 29 juillet 1899', Art. 56. English translation: www.icrc.org/ihl.nsf/385ec082b509e76c41256739003e636d/ 81ef87b37f70d8fac125641e003513a1?OpenDocument.

work of the First Conference of 1899'. It did not add any new elements to the protection of heritage, but maintained the existing paragraphs almost without changes. While the occupying state should only be regarded as 'administrator and usufructuary of public buildings, real property, forest and agricultural works, belonging to the hostile State', the idea was carried over from the earlier documents that:

> The property of municipalities, that of institutions dedicated to religion, charity and education, the arts and sciences, even when State property, shall be treated as private property. All seizure of, destruction or wilful damage done to institutions of this character, historic monuments, works of art and science, is forbidden, and should be made the subject of legal proceedings.[137]

Throughout these conferences, Charles Normand's ideas for a Red Cross for Monuments were never alluded to. The International Museums Office in 1936 attributed the idea of a 'Croix d'Or (=croix rouge pour les monuments)'[138] to a conference held in Geneva in April 1915, while later authors credited the 1954 Hague Convention with the creation of 'La Croix-Rouge des Monuments'.[139] Those who created the international conventions of the Hague drew on the traditions established by de Vattel, the Lieber Code, the Brussels Declaration and the *Oxford Manual*, but not the preservationist congresses. The preservationists seemed to have been content with this separation of spheres. Whereas national preservation associations often petitioned their governments quoting international congress resolution to improve their national situation they were not proactive in writing to delegates of the diplomatic conferences.

Even Charles Normand himself did not pursue the idea. Certainly, *L'Ami des Monuments* continued to talk of international action, but articles under the heading 'International League against Vandalism' contained reports by foreign correspondents on their own work, but not on the work of a permanent international committee, as envisaged by the resolutions of the international congress of 1889. In 1901, a Foreign Committee

---

[137] 'Convention (IV) concernant les lois et coutumes de la guerre sur terre et son Annexe. Reglèment concernant les lois et coutumes de la guerres sur terres' (The Hague, 18 Oct. 1907), Annexe, Art. 55. English trans. www.icrc.org/ihl.nsf/385ec082b509e76c41256739003e636d/1d1726425f6955 aec125641e0038bfd6?OpenDocument; Ministère des affaires étrangères, *Deuxième conférence internationale de la paix. La Haye, 15 juin–18 octobre 1907. Actes et documents* (The Hague, 1907).

[138] Institut International de Coopération intellectuelle. Office international des Musées, *La Protection internationale des Monuments historiques et des oeuvres d'art en temps de Guerre* (Paris, 1936), p. 12, see UNESCO Archives, IICI/14/9.

[139] R.J. Wilhelm, 'La Croix-Rouge des Monuments', *Revue internationale de la Croix-Rouge*, 430 (1954), 793–815.

(*Comité des Amis des Monuments Étrangers*) was created, but its main aim was to spread knowledge about the ancient Greek, Roman and Egyptian civilisations.[140] *L'Ami des Monuments* also did not report on the two Hague Conventions. This is curious, as Charles Normand did not usually distinguish himself through his modesty. He was generally disinclined to report on initiatives to which he was not somehow connected, but he frequently reminded his readers that the original idea behind various concepts, meetings or movements had been his. However, this silence was not particular to Normand. The diplomatic conferences also did not receive attention in other preservationist journals in France, or Germany or Britain either.

This does not indicate an absence of knowledge or interest on the part of preservationists however. The reactions to the destructions at Louvain and Rheims during the First World War reveal how deeply ingrained the beliefs had become that destroying works of art contravened international and moral law.[141] The public outcry against the German destructions in the press referred explicitly to the international conventions. They likewise underpinned an international protest campaign which the SPAB asked the American Embassy to coordinate.[142] The German army reacted by creating a special service for *Kriegsdenkmalpflege*, which attached art officers to military units to identify and protect cultural property. This shows that although international conventions could not protect works of art, the principle of the sanctity of art had become so widespread that a response was necessary.[143]

---

[140] 'Albums de la Revue l'Ami des Monuments et des Arts. Fondation d'un Comité des Amis des Monuments Étrangers', *Bulletin de la Société des Amis des Monuments parisiens* (1901), Appendix.

[141] A. Kramer, *Dynamic of Destruction. Culture and Mass Killing in the First World War* (Oxford, 2007), pp. 6–30; N. Lambourne, *War Damage in Western Europe. The Destruction of Historic Monuments During the Second World War* (Edinburgh, 2001), pp. 12–39. R. Bevan, *The Destruction of Memory. Architecture at War* (London, 2006).

[142] SPAB Archives, 'War Damage Europe 1914–1915'; TNA WORK 14/137.

[143] O. Grautoff, 'Die Denkmalpflege im Urteil des Auslandes', in P. Clemen (ed.), *Kunstschutz im Kriege. Berichte über den Zustand der Kunstdenkmäler auf den verschiedenen Kriegsschauplätzen und über die deutschen und österreichischen Maßnahmen zu ihrer Erhaltung* (Leipzig, 1919), I: *Die Westfront*, pp. 111–40; C. Kott, 'Die deutsche Kunst- und Museumspolitik im besetzten Nordfrankreich im Ersten Weltkrieg zwischen Kunstrauf, Kunstschutz, Propaganda und Wissenschaft', *Kritische Berichte*, 2 (1997), 5–24; Kott, 'Kulturarbeit im Feindesland. Die deutsche Kunst- und Museumspolitik im besetzten Belgien im Ersten Weltkrieg', in R. Baumann, H. Roland (eds.), *Carl Einstein in Brüssel. Dialoge über Grenzen* (Frankfurt, Berlin, Bern, 2001), pp. 199–225; Kott, *Préserver l'art de l'ennemi? Le patrimoine artistique en Belgique et en France occupées, 1914–1918* (Brussels, 2006); on the Eastern Front see GStA PK, I. HA, Rep 76 Ve Kultusministerium, Sekt 2, Abt. VI, Nr. 22, Bd. 5; on the demolitions in the context of other atrocities see J.N. Horne, A. Kramer, *German Atrocities, 1914. A History of Denial* (New Haven, London, 2001).

Concert members

All congresses made an important contribution in spreading ideas across the world, even if the pretension of internationalism in terms of membership were as problematic as the declarations of internationalist ambitions. In many ways, the congresses' membership and audience was global. The First International Congress not only counted delegates from more than twenty countries, but underscored its internationality by electing a Chinese, two Brazilians, a Mexican, a Portuguese, a Russian and a Swiss as honorary presidents. Its Chinese honorary president, General Tcheng Ki Tong, noted, much to the satisfaction of his hosts, that by giving him the honorary presidency the congress organisers had shown that their efforts were not limited to France, to Europe or the West, but concerned with mankind as a whole.[144] Likewise, the international Congresses of Architects also had a global reach. Almost all European states were represented, as were Canada, the USA, Mexico and the French and British colonies.[145] The International congress for *Heimatschutz* attracted principally Europeans but proudly underlined the presence of a delegate of the Japanese government at the second congress in Stuttgart, while the 1913 *Weltnaturschutz* conference extended its reach from Japan to Argentina.

The pre-First World War congresses were therefore significantly more international in membership than their mid-twentieth century successors. The 1931 Athens Conference, for instance, included only European delegates. Not until the Second International Congress of Architects and Technicians of Historical Monuments in Venice in 1964, did three non-European states (Mexico, Peru and Tunisia) send official delegates, and a new era of international collaboration began.[146] Yet, the universal nature of the pre-war congresses should not be overestimated. Not only were women generally excluded from being delegates, but Europeans and non-Europeans were neither represented to the same extent nor on equal terms, as the congresses were firmly rooted in a colonial context. Large parts of the world were represented by members of the colonial administration and Westernised foreigners such as Tcheng Ki Tong. A diplomat at the Chinese embassy in Paris, he was the first francophone Chinese author, who even beat Maupassant in the race for publishing an article in the most reputed of literary journals, the *Revue des Deux Mondes*. Tcheng Ki Tong was tellingly the author of a book entitled

[144] Normand, *Procès-verbaux*, p. 23.
[145] *Bericht über den VIII. Internationalen Architekten-Kongress*, pp. 5–57.
[146] Cf. Choay (ed.), *La Conférence d'Athènes*, p. 9.

Comment devenir Parisien. The other non-European honorary presidents
of the First Congress were also strongly influenced by francophone culture.
The Brazilian painter Pedro Américo de Figueiredo for instance had studied
at the Ecole des Beaux Arts in Paris as a pupil of Jean-Auguste-Dominique
Ingres. The Eurocentric framework was moreover apparent in limiting the
reflection of the 'common heritage' to that of the 'civilised nations' or
Kulturstaaten, defined as those nations 'whose history is inscribed in its
monuments'.[147]

A certain hierarchy can also be detected among the European members,
not dissimilar to the hierarchy in the concert of Europe. Most contributions came from France, Germany, Britain, Austria-Hungary, Italy, the
Netherlands, Belgium and Switzerland and to a lesser extent from Russia,
Spain and Portugal. Certain imbalances also existed between and within
France, Germany and Britain. Many contributors intervened in the discussion only briefly, but several personalities dominated the international
conference scene. A high proportion of Frenchmen in the early congresses
was obviously linked to the impulses of the *Expositions universelles*. In Paris
and elsewhere 'natives' usually constituted about half of the membership
while international guests made up the rest. However, French delegates
and speakers remained prominent at later congresses outside of France
too. Among the most prominent voices were Charles Normand, who co-
organised the 1889 congress, the 1900 Public Art Congress and again the
First Archaeological Congress in Athens in 1905. Although he was con-
spicuously silent at congresses where he did not have the leading role, he
attended many. Several other leading members of *Les Amis des Monuments
parisiens* were also recurrent figures: Eugène Müntz of the *Commission du
Vieux Paris* propagated the 1889 ideas in the Public Art movement, Charles
Normand's father Alfred and Charles Lucas, from the same entourage,
did the job at the Congresses of Architects, before the architects Alfred
Besnard and Gaston Trélat took the lead. Preservationists connected to the
French Historic Monuments Commission attended some of the congresses
discussed, but were more prominently represented at the International
Congresses of Architects until 1889; thereafter they only really spoke at
their own conference cycle in 1900. The Comte de Marsy, head of the
Congrès archeologiques, participated at the 1889 Monument Congress and
at the English Congress of Archaeological Societies, and was a frequent
member of other international gatherings, including the First Congress of
Comparative History, but rarely appeared on the podium.

[147]   Besnard, *Septième Congrès international des architectes*, pp. 49–50.

On the British side, the RIBA offered an important pivot in international congress organisation and attendance. Its presidents, former presidents and secretaries (most notably George Aitchison and William Locke), represented the British section of the permanent committee of the architectural congresses. Subsequent RIBA leaders were also invited to the First International Congress for the Protection of Monuments, and attended the Public Art Congresses. The most prominent British speaker on the care of monuments was perhaps Gerald Baldwin Brown, an Oxford educated Londoner and Britain's first professor of Art History at the University of Edinburgh. A long-time friend of Canon Rawnsley of the National Trust, and himself member of several preservation societies, Baldwin Brown was Europe's leading comparative expert on the care of monuments. An honorary member of the RIBA, Brown was honorary vice-president of the 1897 and 1900 congresses, speaker in London in 1906, and again a congress member in Vienna in 1908.

The Society of Antiquaries was not directly engaged in international congresses on the protection of monuments, but was involved indirectly as almost all members of the RIBA on the permanent committee for the International Congress of Architects were also FSAs. The SPAB, on the other hand, made active use of the congresses in its early days to promote its principles and establish contacts. Attendance at the Congress of Architects in 1878 in Paris led to invitations to the Congress of Learned Societies and a large representation at the Monument Congress in 1889.[148] Afterwards, members continued to attend the Congress of Architects, yet apart from seizing the occasion to present the society's work at the 1906 congress in London, the SPAB did not accord much further attention to international congresses in its minutes or reports and never considered organising one itself.[149] As will be seen shortly, its international involvement was more focussed on the rescue of particular monuments in collaboration with its correspondents abroad. While Canon Rawnsley attended the First Archaeological Congress in Athens, members of the National Trust likewise rather joined international congresses in other capacities than as representatives of the institution.[150]

Germany was relatively underrepresented at the 1889 congress, with only two representatives on the patronage committee, one a French correspondent of the Institute, the other the director of the Germanic Museum in Nuremberg (and hidden in the Greek section, the discoverer of Troy,

[148] SPAB, *Annual Report*, 13 (1890), 59–61.
[149] See Lethaby's contribution, *Journal of the RIBA*, 3rd Ser. 13 (1906), Congress Supplement, pp. lxii–lxvi.
[150] On first archaeological congress see also Fedden, *National Trust*, p. 21.

Heinrich Schliemann). Instead the German situation was presented by the Swiss Geymüller. The German under-representation and relative lack of collaboration between *L'Ami des Monuments* and German preservationists may be explained by the strong anti-German feelings of leading *Amis des Monuments* such as Charles Normand and the Alsacian Eugène Müntz, veteran of the 1870 war.[151] Still, this did not prevent the Prussian Chief Conservator Rheinhold Persius from responding eagerly to Geymüller's letters to provide detailed information for his conference. The most recurrent German name at the Congresses of Architects and Public Art was Josef Stübben, president of the Federation of German Architects, who had distinguished himself through the enlargement of the City of Cologne after the medieval walls had been pulled down, and was responsible for the restoration of the remaining medieval gates. However, he rather intervened on modern architecture than *Denkmalpflege* and many of the important German preservationists were relatively absent from the congress panels. Germany hosted the 1900 session of the International Art History Congress where Paul Clemen spoke on *Denkmalschutz*, and at the end of the period the second international congress for *Heimatschutz*, but the unification of German preservationism through the *Tag für Denkmalpflege* seems to have been a more pressing need than the organisation of international congresses. On the other hand, German preservationists were enthusiastic congress participants. Paul Clemen repeatedly travelled with Friedrich Schmidt-Ott from the Prussian *Kultusministerium* to the exhibitions and congresses in Brussels 1897, Paris 1900 and Brussels 1910.[152] Hermann Muthesius, the German correspondent of the SPAB, did not intervene, but was an honorary vice president in 1904 in Madrid and reported avidly on the congress's progress on anti-restoration in the German press. The Federation of German Architects encouraged its members to attend the international congresses, even declaring attendance to be a 'duty of honour'[153] and the *Centralblatt* and *Die Denkmalpflege* proudly noted that the German delegation was consistently the largest national delegation at the Congresses of Architects.

---

[151] For instance, Müntz wrote a *revanchiste* account of the German restitution claims in 1815: 'Les Annexassions de collections d'art ou de bibliothèques et leur rôle dans les relations internationales principalement pendant la Révolution française', *Revue d'histoire diplomatique* (1894), 481–97; (1895), 375–93; (1896), 481–508; see Savoy, *Patrimoine annexe*, I, p. 290.

[152] Friedrich Schmidt-Ott (1860–1956), born as Friedrich Schmidt (he added his wife's name in 1920). After studies of law, Schmidt-Ott became assistant of Friedrich Althoff at the Prussian Kultusministerium in 1888, and his succesor as *Ministerialdirektor* in 1907 and *Kultusminister* in 1917–1918.

[153] 'Internationaler Architekten Congress in Paris', *Centralblatt der Bauverwaltung*, 20 (1900), 280.

Within the larger international exchanges, the congresses were also marked by strong bi-lateral partnerships. While the professional associations of architects in France, Germany and Britain collaborated continuously, the congress enthusiasts from *L'Ami des Monuments* primarily had contacts with Britain, Italy, Belgium and Switzerland, but not Germany. Charles Beauquier, president of the SPPF, on the other hand established persistent links between the German and French congresses, from the *Heimatschutz* meetings to the *Denkmaltage*.[154] The *Heimatschutz* congresses also welcomed the French General Inspector of Historic Monuments. Foreign partners often presented the work of a sister movement abroad. For instance at the 1889 congress Guillon reported for the SPAB. Many links between countries were also established through third parties, especially from Switzerland, Belgium and the Netherlands. The Swiss honorary president at the First International Congress for the Protection of Monuments Baron de Geymüller, served as a bridge between France, Germany and Britain at successive Public Art and architectural congresses.[155] Imbued in Germanophone, Anglophone, Francophone and Italian culture, Geymüller had studied in Lausanne, Paris and Berlin, before a long sojourn in Italy. His preservationist activities started in the 1870s, opposing him to plans for the restoration of Lausanne Cathedral, and he subsequently intervened in the restoration of the cathedral of Milan, St Peter in Rome and San Lorenzo in Florence. As an architect in Baden-Baden, he was a regular correspondent of many foreign bodies from *L'Ami des Monument* to the RIBA. Belgian preservationists, especially Cloquet, Paul Saintenoy and Charles Buls and the Dutchman de Cuypers, head of the Dutch Monument Commission founded in 1903, played an equally prominent part in acting as links between France, Germany and Britain during and beyond the congresses.[156]

Prominent congress speakers were few in number, but the congresses were significant for a larger professional and amateur crowd, composed chiefly of architects, artists, government delegates and members of learned societies. Most congresses counted between 500 and 2,000 attendees,

---

[154] 'Verzeichnis der Teilnehmer. Zehnter Tag für Denkmalpflege. Trier. 23. und 24. September 1909. Stenographischer Bericht' and 'Elfter Tag für Denkmalpflege. Danzig. 29. und 30. September 1910', GStA PK VI. HA, Rep. 92 Nl. Schmidt-Ott (M), A X 1, fols. 90, 186–286.

[155] See Leniaud, *Les Archipels du passé*, pp. 183–4; *Henri de Geymüller, architecte et historien de l'art. Un novateur dans l'approche de la restauration et de la conservation du patrimoine architectural* (Lausanne, 1995).

[156] On de Cuypers see Brown, *Care of Ancient Monuments*, p. 176.

usually a third to half were foreigners.[157] The frequent positive reports in the specialist press further disseminated results. As honorary positions were generally given to high-ranking government officials or even heads of state, sympathy in the upper echelons of society was also secured. While the preservationist congresses overlapped little with the diplomatic ones, the nature of and contributors to debates at the diplomatic conferences emphasise that knowledge about and interest in contemporary conceptual developments was not exclusive to artists, architects and state preservationists.

Congress legacies

The international congresses for the protection of heritage resulted from the conjunction of different and mutually enhancing forms of internationalism. 'Voluntary internationalism' was driven by problems which transcended the nation-state, such as the effects of modernisation and warfare. It allowed private movements to build strategic alliances with other groups abroad to invigorate their domestic position. Their interests enmeshed with the 'professional internationalism' of architects and new historic disciplines that started regular international meetings. Both were enhanced by 'institutionalised internationalism' through government involvement in periodic congresses.[158] The congresses reaffirmed and formalised existing contacts and enabled participants to create new connections. The exchange of ideas, often prolonged through epistolary correspondence, contributed to a unification of methods and, to a certain degree, a combination of forces. Differences of opinion did not generally correlate with national boundaries. The movement-based congresses of *L'Ami des Monuments*, Public Art and *Heimatschutz* united professionally diverse groups of conservation professionals, scholars, artists and amateurs, but participants shared the same values and used the congresses to exchange experiences and reaffirm theories. Conversely, discord was more pronounced at the professional congresses of architects and the diplomatic conferences where heritage concerns had to be reconciled with other needs such as urban development and military strategy.

The congresses tried to have a lasting legacy by producing a great number of resolutions. While proceedings tended to overemphasise their importance and some were never pursued, others were used in petitions for the

---

[157] 'Seventh International Congress of Architects London 1906', *Journal of the RIBA*, 3rd Ser., 13 (1906), 500.

[158] On these categories see Geyer, Paulmann (eds.), *The Mechanics of Internationalism*, p. 22.

rescue of monuments and most enduringly for legislation, as will be demonstrated more closely below. While revealing how strongly state and voluntary sectors were entangled, the congresses, like the exhibitions, helped to enhance the standing of particular movements and ideas among competing national actors. In France, preservationists, especially the *Amis des Monuments*, tried to strengthen the private movement through the organisation of an international congress. Likewise in Britain, Baldwin Brown led those who hoped that a privately organised international congress on British soil would help to bring about more involvement of the state in the care of ancient monuments.[159]

Despite the general enthusiasm for international encounters, several factors contributed to the fact that after the First Official Congress no permanent congress or organisation for the protection of monuments was installed and international collaboration instead manifested itself in a multitude of thematically and personally overlapping congresses. In France, the quarrel between the *Amis des Monuments* and the Historic Monuments Commission and consequently between two Ministries might have played a role. The organisers of the rival congresses of 1889 were not inactive in 1900, but the CMH opted for a conference cycle rather than a congress; while for the *Amis des Monuments* one congress had possibly sufficed to raise their profile. Charles Normand, the driving force behind the 1889 congress, was a somewhat volatile character, frequently changing his field of interest, and he, like other *Amis des Monuments parisiens* members were increasingly involved in the *Commission du Vieux Paris*, whose aims could be best enhanced by championing the Public Art movement with its strong municipal focus. At the International Congress of Architects in 1900, the British and German delegates added the care of monuments to the programme, but neither country organised a specific congress. The ideal organiser of an international congress in Britain would have been the SPAB, but it considered foreign restoration campaigns and the instigation of foreign preservation societies a higher priority. This is likely related to congresses not being such a favoured means of raising awareness as in France. In Germany, preservationists were preoccupied with organising collaboration at the national level. On the other hand, Belgian preservationists present at the First International Congress filled this role by internationalising the national Public Art movement in 1897.

---

[159] B. Brown, 'Government Action on the Continent in the Interest of National Monuments' *Journal of the RIBA*, 3rd Ser., 13 (1906). Congress Supplement, lxii–lxvi.

Moreover, while architects and new emerging disciplines such as art history or archaeology used the creation of one regular congress to push for professionalisation or entry into the universities, many preservationists did not have the same impulses. Professionalisation was under way, but remained in tension with the many cooperating, but also conflicting amateur movements, that used international congresses to defend their existence and to reflect about the evolving nature of their heritage concepts.

Mutual help to improve legislation and the collaborative campaigns to save particular monuments illustrate the belief in a common cause and the universal nature of heritage, but the assembled artists', architects', scholars' and government preservationists' concern with a 'common heritage of humanity' was not strong enough to campaign in the long term for its protection through international conventions. This was instead achieved by the experts of international law at diplomatic conferences. The universal dimension of the protection of a 'common heritage of humanity' was limited in other ways too. Although the endeavour was proclaimed as universal, it was at the same time reserved to 'civilised nations'. Despite the invitation of non-European members and occasional discussion of Latin American and East Asian topics, the congresses remained firmly Eurocentric, and focussed on Western culture. Organisers, speakers and causes came largely from Central and Western Europe. Despite the presence of some non-European members and delegates from the colonial administration, the treatment of heritage in the colonies was hardly mentioned at the congresses on monuments, public art, architecture, landscape or *Heimatschutz* but was left to the meetings of Orientalists, anthropologists, zoologists or again diplomats. While the rare mentions of colonial heritages, such as Normand's idea of using the Pyramids as universal rather than Egyptian monuments and the discussion on the global safeguard of birds of paradise by *Heimatschützer* are significant in the way they appropriated foreign 'heritages', the silences are even more telling. When provisions against exportation of cultural property were discussed these implicitly only ever applied to European 'heritage', i.e. objects in European possession. The legitimacy of colonising and plundering other peoples' heritage, practised by all 'civilised nations' present was never questioned. The focus on the 'civilised nations' not only enforced a Western, monumental idea of heritage, but also championed the view that modern preservation distinguished the West from 'the rest'. Even where non-European appreciation of things old was discussed in somewhat envious terms, as in the case of China, the contrast with such a presumably uninterrupted tradition, ultimately only enforced the distinctiveness of the West's preservationism as modern and progressive.

Nevertheless, the discursive link established between the protection of heritage and international understanding was probably the most lasting legacy of the congresses. Immersed in the wider rhetoric of world exhibitions and international congresses, programmes and speeches emphasised the common struggle of all civilised nations for the protection of heritage. Some desired to define strategies against a common enemy, others spoke of the defence of a 'common heritage of humanity'. It was, moreover argued that to respect a neighbour one had to love one's own heritage; love for heritage thus automatically and somewhat metaphysically stimulated peaceful relations. Through the continuous repetition at congresses, these beliefs became firm commonplaces in preservationist discourse. While the international congresses obviously did not lead to peace and goodwill among nations, and many an internationalist preservationist turned nationalist at the outbreak of the Great War, not to speak of the gravitation of some ardent proponents of international understanding from the Wilhelmine *Heimatschutz* movement towards National Socialism, the rhetoric was the congresses' enduring legacy, only enhanced through the backlash of the World Wars. As seen in the UNESCO quotation prefacing the introduction to this book, both the belief in a 'common heritage of humanity' and in the peacekeeping effect of love for one's own heritage prevailed independently of their original locus.

PART III

Transnational campaigns

CHAPTER 5

'A Morris Dance Round St Mark's'

> On a recent visit to Bergen I learnt that the German Emperor, at
> his late visit to Norway, cast longing eyes on this unique collection
> [of the Hanseatic Museum] and actually proposed to buy the house,
> transport it to Germany and there erect it again. The house as it
> stands on the quay at Bergen . . . is a relic of the highest historical,
> antiquarian, and artistic interest; removed to another site it would
> lose nearly all its value. The museum is in the hands of a private
> proprietor, whose commercial interests are stronger than his patriotic
> instincts. It is with the faint hope of arousing public interest in this
> barbarous transfer, and bringing some pressure to bear on those who
> are interested in the preservation of ancient monuments, both here
> and in Norway, that I am constrained to trouble you with this lengthy
> communication.[1]

As expressed in this letter to *The Times* by the medieval historian Ernest
H. Jacob, the international dimension of preservation also manifested itself
through efforts to change the fate of monuments in foreign countries, either
by acquiring them or by campaigning for their preservation in situ. While
the lands of classical antiquity attracted most attention, other heritages
were also increasingly appropriated, as plunder and preservation extended
to biblical lands, far away colonial possessions and traces of former 'national'
influence beyond current borders such as the Hanseatic sites around the
Baltic or the buildings left by European crusaders around the Mediterranean. The governments of France, Germany and Britain started to spend
funds and created research institutions for their investigation, preservation
and restoration. However, preservationists and the wider public were not
just interested in what could be claimed as 'their' heritage through classical,
biblical, colonial or national lineages.[2] Like national monuments, many
foreign ones progressively became better known and cherished through

---

[1] 'The Proposed Removal of the Hanseatic Museum At Bergen', *The Times*, 2 September 1890, p. 9.
[2] See Swenson, Mandler (eds.), *Plunder to Preservation*.

travel, exhibitions, literature and illustrations and their fate was eagerly followed across Europe. For instance, the completion of *the* German national monument, Cologne Cathedral, was not only helped by donations from European monarchs including the Austrian Emperor, the King of Holland and Queen Victoria, but every stone that was added to its towers between 1842 and 1880 was reported on by the British press.[3] It was also the subject of lectures at the RIBA, the British Archaeological Congress and the Royal Academy, and figured prominently in British art histories and histories of Germany. Exhibitions of a cathedral models and photographs in London received acclaim and engravings adorned the walls of London homes like they did those of Cologne burgers (ill. 5.1).[4] Greater in number, and often abandoned, many ruined fortresses in the Rhine Valley had also found English and French admirers during the Romantic era.[5] Widespread public demand for intervention in the heritage of other European countries, like that proposed in Ernest H. Jacob's letter and taken up by William Morris and the SPAB, however, was a new phenomenon and related to the emergence of private preservation lobby groups in the late nineteenth century.[6]

While some interventions were unilateral, many relied on international collaborations. Such collaborations involved diverse heritage-makers and ranged from the actions taken by international congresses seen in the last chapter, to the creation of committees staffed with Americans and Europeans for the preservation of Byzantine and Arab monuments from Istanbul to Cairo.[7] It also included transatlantic cooperation to save an Anglophone heritage, such as Shakespeare's house and Wordsworth's Lake District and cooperation soon extended to save the unspoiled beauty of

[3] Between 1803, when the cathedral was first mentioned and 1914, it featured in almost 150 articles in *The Times*. The *Illustrated London News*, and the *Quarterly Review* also regularly reported, as did specialised publications such as *The Civil Engineer and Architect's Journal* and *The Ecclesiologist*.

[4] 'Gothic Architecture In Germany', *The Times*, 23 November 1871, p. 12; 'Archaeology', *The Times*, 4 September 1877, p. 4; *The Times*, 11 December 1893, p. 9 (Leader), 'History Of Art', *The Times*, 8 February 1869, p. 4; 'The New Gallery', *The Times*, 29 September 1888, p. 6; 'The Times Column Of New Books and New Editions', *The Times*, 10 September 1891, p. 10.

[5] See R. Taylor, *The Castles of the Rhine: Recreating the Middle Ages in Modern Germany* (Waterloo, Ontario, 1998); T. Blanning, *The Romantic Revolution* (London, 2011), pp. 138–41.

[6] SPAB Archives, Bergen Hanseatic Museum; for William Morris' letter in support of E.H. Jacob: 'The Hanseatic Museum at Bergen', *The Times*, 10 September 1890, p. 12.

[7] D.M. Reid, 'Cultural Imperialism and Nationalism – the Struggle to Define and Control the Heritage of Arab Art in Egypt', *International Journal of Middle East Studies*, 24.1 (1992), 57–76; E. Goldstein, 'Redeeming Holy Wisdom: Britain and St Sophia', in Hall (ed.), *Towards World Heritage*, pp. 43–62.

5.1 'The Completion of Cologne Cathedral', *Supplement to the Illustrated London News*, 27 May 1843.

Niagara Falls and other natural sites in the United States and Canada.[8] British societies were particularly active in coordinating collaboration. Many efforts to preserve the common Anglophone heritage were championed by members of the National Trust, and the Trust also corresponded with preservationists in Europe. However, the society that organised probably the widest range of interventions across Europe and the globe was the SPAB.[9] It intervened from Egypt to India, and from Greece to Norway across several empires, areas of imperial scramble and virtually all European countries.

Since its inception, the SPAB was convinced that it should not only free England, but the entire world from restoration.[10] Consequently, it started its foreign work with an attempt to save one of Europe's best-known buildings, St Mark's in Venice.[11] After Morris received information about plans for a major restoration of the west front of St Mark's by the architect Meduna, the SPAB decided to involve the public in its protests. Letters to the press were published in all major newspapers and meetings were held throughout Britain. In the first instance, 'The Morris dance round St Mark's', as *Punch* dubbed it, easily gained momentum among the Victorian elites (ill. 5.2). The official letter of protest sent to the Italian Minister of Public Works counted more than 2,000 prominent signatories, including both Gladstone and Disraeli. The wish to save Ruskin's stones of Venice transcended party lines and many avowed opponents of the SPAB's radical philosophy also joined in. Yet, as *Punch's* uncharitable verses demonstrate, the campaign remains best remembered for its blunders. The letter of protest was sent to the wrong minister, claims of success were precipitated and the campaign had to be ended prematurely for financial

---

[8] M. Hall, 'Niagara Falls: Preservation and the Spectacle of Anglo-American Accord', in Hall (ed.), *Towards World Heritage*, pp. 23–43; Hall, 'Despoliation or Diplomacy? Britain, Canada, the United States and the Evolution of an English-Speaking Heritage', in Swenson, Mandler (eds.), *Plunder to Preservation*, pp. 241–65.

[9] See SPAB, *A School of Rational Builders. An exhibition at the Drawings Collection of the British Architectural Library, 10 March to 1 May 1892. Exhibition Catalogue* (London, 1982), pp. 19–20; F. Sharp, 'A Lesson in International Relations. Morris and the SPAB', *Journal of the William Morris Society*, 10 (1993), 9–14; Sharp, 'Exporting the Revolution. The Work of the SPAB outside Britain, 1878–1914', in Miele (ed.), *From William Morris*, pp. 187–212.

[10] SPAB Archives, 1st Committee Minute Book, 5 July 1877; 2nd Committee Minute Book, 11 April 1878.

[11] SPAB Archives, 2nd Committee Minute Book, 21 Mar. 1878–May 1880; 3rd Minute Book, 27 May 1880–Mar. 1883; and Subcommittee Minute Books, 1st Minute Book, Foreign Committee, Mar. 1879–Jul. 1879; 3rd Minute Book, Foreign Committee, Mar. 1882–May 1882; 4th Minute Book, Subcommittee on St. Mark's Venice, Nov.–Dec. 1879; case file 'St. Mark's, Venice', folder B, 1879–80; Miele, 'The First Conservation Militant', p. 27; Sharp, 'A Lesson in International Relations', pp. 9–14, Sharp, 'Exporting the Revolution', pp. 187–98.

5.2 'The Morris Dance round St Mark's', *Punch*, 10 January 1880, p. 2 shows St Mark's Venice surrounded by members of the SPAB, with Ruskin on the left side of the lion and Morris on the right.

reasons. The unsolicited interference, coupled with the patronising British demeanour, and lack of local knowledge (not even a single Italian signature was included) alienated Italian public opinion and enhanced Morris' and the Society for Ancient Buildings' image as unabashed Radicals in Britain. Consequently, the campaign failed to increase the Society's membership at home. Yet while slightly shaking the Society's belief that all publicity was good publicity, it also enhanced rather than deflated their ambition to care for heritage universally.[12]

A permanent Foreign Committee was set up, not least because 'we must consider that in trying to stimulate people elsewhere we shall get a reaction towards ourselves', but the means and extent of foreign intervention were adjusted.[13] In part the focus was redirected to cases in the British colonies. As one member, the conservative M.P. Leonard Courtney pointed out, it was unlikely that the Society would obtain the cooperation and influence of the government of countries such as France or Spain in their endeavours to put a stop to works of renovation and restoration:

> But there is a country where, if we are allowed, we may be of some assistance – in India. In one part of India there are the most wonderful works of art built under the orders of the great Mogul king. In Agra, in Delhi, and in Futtehpore Sikkri, you will find triumphs of art very different from our own, but triumphs of a very precious character, which ought to be carefully treasured.[14]

However, the constraints set by national autonomy within Europe did not lead to the SPAB abandoning the cause here either, but only to choose a more subtle mode of interaction. Instead of unilateral action, the SPAB now consulted with foreign correspondents, or asked British members abroad for their assessment of the local situation, always awaiting a local *placet* before acting. It also increasingly tried to spread its idea by stimulating the foundation of sister societies, like the various 'French SPABs'. As a result, the 1887 *Annual Report* noted that the increased interest in ancient buildings and the creation of local preservation societies 'has relieved the Society from some of the work to which it formerly devoted itself... and the Society is glad to leave the protection of foreign buildings in the hands of the local authorities whenever it is made evident that the authorities are

---

[12] See Philip Webb to Henry Brewer, 22 April 1887, SPAB Archives, 'Italian Restoration'.

[13] SPAB, *Annual Report*, 2 (1879), 23.

[14] Ibid. For major interventions see SPAB Archives, Ancient Monuments in India; Old Indian Capital of Bijpur; Arab Monuments; Cairo Coptic Churches Egypt; Ottoman Antiquities; The Dome on the Rock Jerusalem.

alive to the duties of their position as custodians of the *national monuments of the country'*.[15] Despite these changes, the number of foreign cases only temporarily decreased. Collaboration with French and German preservationists was particularly intense in the late 1890s and during the first decade of the twentieth century.[16] Foreign intervention could be triggered by reports in the press, letters by travelling SPAB affiliates or members of the public and solicitations by the Society's foreign correspondents. While only about half of all cases led to an actual intervention, those that were taken up varied greatly: famous monuments stood alongside only locally known beauties, successful cases alongside unsuccessful ones, and campaigns marking turning points in the history of preservation alongside almost unnoticed ones.

Among the multitude of international work, the many cases of collaboration between the Society for the Protection of Ancient Buildings and its French and German correspondents are particularly revealing for the processes of international cooperation and competition. Adding another layer to the understanding of the international scene for local uses, they also tell much about the relative similarity of national protest culture. The letters between preservationists of different nationalities in preparation of public campaigns moreover allow a glimpse at friendships and day-to-day interaction without the need for rhetoric so prevalent at exhibitions and congresses, yet also show in a particularly pertinent way how changing international relations affected the way notions of 'universal heritage' could be employed in public discourse.

---

[15] SPAB, *Annual Report*, 10 (1887), 44 (emphasis added).

[16] In France, SPAB discussed intervention with regard to St Maclou, Rouen (1883), St Etienne du Mont in Paris (1884), the Amphitheatres of Nimes and Arles (1884), St Julien-le Pauvre, Paris (1885) Porte de Saint Denis in Paris (1885), Mont St Michel (1886–87), Sens Cathedral (1889), Fougère Castle (1892), St Gervais, Paris (1892), the Sorbonne (1893), the Roman Theatre in Orange (1894), the Cathedral of Rouen (1895), the town walls of Avignon (1895–1901), St Wulfran, Abbeville (1896), Renaissance houses in Rouen (1897), Beauvais Cathedral (1898), St Pierre Montmartre (1896), the stained glass windows of Chartres Cathedral (1905–1906), the Pont Neuf in Cahors (1906–1907), and St Laurent, Beaulieu (1914), see eponymous files in SPAB Archives. See also on St Maclou, Rouen: 4th Committee Minute Book, Committee Meetings 4 Oct.–1 Nov. 1883 and *Annual Report*, 7 (1884), 38; St Etienne du Mont: 5th Committee Minute Book, 2 Oct. 1884; Nimes and Arles: 5th Committee Minute Book, 29 Nov. 1884; Sens Cathedral, *Annual Report*, 12 (1889), 52, Abbeville, Church of St Wulfran, *Annual Report*, 19 (1896), 15 and Beaulieu, church of St Laurent, *Annual Report*, 37 (1914), 74. In Germany campaigns focussed on Nuremberg Town Walls (1879–1884), Ulm Cathedral (1883), Nuremberg St Sebald Church (1885), Brunswick Castle (1886), Frankfurt Cathedral (1900), Freiburg Cathedral (1900), Heidelberg Castle (1901–1909), Meißen Cathedral (1902), Reinfels Ruins (1903), see SPAB Archives, case files; 5th Committee Minute Book, 3 July– 4 Sep. 1884; 29 Oct. 1884.

5.3 Cahors, Pont de Cabessut, so-called Pont Neuf or Pont Henri IV by Gustave LeGray and/or Auguste Mestral. Taken during the *Mission héliographique* in 1851, for which the Historic Monuments Commission selected five photographers to make surveys of the nation's architectural heritage to aid the Paris-based commission in determining the nature and urgency of the restoration work required throughout the country.

Bilateral collaborations

Petitions to foreign authorities often emphasised that national prestige, as well as economic benefits, would suffer if a given monument were demolished or restored. For example, in collaboration with *L'Ami des Monuments*, the SPAB pleaded with the Mayor and Town Council of Cahors in South Western France to reconsider the destruction of their Pont Neuf.[17] This late medieval bridge had been noticed during the 1851 Heliographic Mission, an initiative by the French Historic Monuments Commission that sent five illustrious photographers all over France to record monuments recently restored or in need of restoration (ill. 5.3), but had since been living in the shadow of Cahors' more famous Pont Valentré, *monument classé* since 1840.

---

[17] Charles Normand to SPAB, 23 June 1906, SPAB Archives, 'Cahors, Le Pont Neuf'.

Now the town had decided that it should be replaced by a new bridge to improve circulation.[18] To prevent demolition, the SPAB wrote:

> The Society would earnestly beg that its views may be considered by your Worship and by your Town Council, for it is felt that the charming Town of Cahors would no longer have the great attraction which it at present possesses for the many Foreigners who journey there to enjoy a sight of its antiquities, if this bridge were replaced by any modern structure. Even from the low standpoint of commercial value your Town would suffer by the destruction of the Bridge, for the many Foreigners who journey to France to see its antiquities, upon learning that the Bridge no longer existed, would be deterred from visiting the Town.[19]

While the tone seems hardly less high-handed than during the St Mark's campaign, SPAB here in fact took the cue from local protesters, who likewise stressed the importance of the bridge for attracting foreign tourists in their petition to the Minister of Public Instruction. Both local and international voices were unsuccessful, and the bridge had to make way for a more traffickable one.[20] The case shows the measured interaction between the English and French sides. During the many years of collaboration between SPAB and *L'Ami des Monuments*, at times, the French society wrote to London expressing concern regarding French monuments while at others the SPAB enquired about rumours circulating requesting further information. Many cases in which members of the SPAB and *L'Ami des Monuments* (usually Alphonse Guillon, but occasionally also Charles Garnier and Charles Normand) corresponded did not result in any specific action. The SPAB was true to the publicly announced principle of leaving matters in local hands whenever possible. In the case of St Julien le Pauvre in Paris, for example, the SPAB closed the case without any interference after Charles Normand assured his English correspondents that the monument had been preoccupying the *Amis des Monuments parisiens* since their foundation.[21] In other instances, campaigning was abandoned when it became clear that concerns were based on a false alarm. In one such case, word had reached the SPAB that the Roman Theatre in Orange was going to be restored. Several SPAB members wrote to Guillon that if the rumours were true, the English society 'would be glad to associate itself with any protest that

[18] A. de Mondenard, *La Mission héliographique. Cinq photographes parcourent la France en 1851* (Paris, 2002), p. 207.
[19] The letter is undated but followed the correspondence between the SPAB and Normand in June 1906, SPAB Archives, 'Cahors, Le Pont Neuf'.
[20] See petition received on 24 Sept. 1906, MAP 81/46/8, 'Cahors Pont Neuf'.
[21] Thackeray Turner to Charles Normand, 2 Oct. 1885, SPAB Archives, 'Paris St Julien le Pauvre, France'.

your Society may have decided to make . . . as the theatre is a monument of universal interest, I hope that you will forgive me for addressing you upon the subject'.[22] After having consulted architects working for the Historic Monuments Commission, Guillon calmed his English friends that no restoration was planned; the only thing that might happen was a consolidation of some pillars for an open air theatre, but Guillon passed the letter to Charles Normand who then talked to the architect in charge.[23]

The French case that stirred most public concern in Britain concerned the plans of the municipality of Avignon to demolish the town walls to make way for Parisian-style boulevards.[24] The SPAB was flooded with letters from members asking for a campaign, it preoccupied the British press between 1895 and 1902, and became the *pièce de résistance* to demonstrate the importance of public opinion for the protection of monuments in Baldwin Brown's study on the care of ancient monuments.[25] After an article in the *Daily Chronicle* on 9 March 1895,[26] the SPAB's secretary, Thackeray Turner wrote to one of the Society's members, Helen Taylor, to supply further information and advice.[27] Taylor, a feminist, educational reformer and political activist, had been living in Avignon with her stepfather John Stuart Mill for extended periods since 1858 and retired permanently in the Vaucluse in the late 1880s.[28] A long correspondence between Turner and Taylor ensued, while further reports appeared in the press.[29] In the end, Taylor discouraged the SPAB from taking action:

> Any remonstrance from England would I fear do more harm than good. The few who complain of the destruction of Ancient Monuments are mostly (of course not all) of royalist politics; and the mass of the inhabitants really think imitations of Paris much more beautiful than the old buildings and sincerely believe that a different opinion can only arise from political prejudice. This is the real reason why the Government does not interfere. At the present day I fancy that even in dear old Avignon there are people modern enough to appreciate old buildings and if the mischief could have been stopped it would have been.[30]

[22] SPAB to Guillon, 4 April 1894, S.C. Cockerell enclosed a letter for Guillon sent by Thackeray Turner on 6 April 1894, SPAB Archives, 'Orange, Roman Theatre'.
[23] Guillon to SPAB, 23 Apr. 1894, ibid.
[24] P. Léon, *La Vie des monuments français. Destruction, restaurations* (Paris, 1951), pp. 312–13.
[25] G.B. Brown, *The Care of Ancient Monuments* (Cambridge, 1905), p. 33.
[26] See also SPAB Archives, 12th Committee Minute Book, 21 May 1895.
[27] Thackeray Turner to Helen Taylor, 29 March 1895, SPAB Archives, 'Avignon, Palace of Popes'.
[28] P. Levine, 'Taylor, Helen (1831–1907)', *DNB* (Oxford, 2004), www.oxforddnb.com/view/article/36431.
[29] *Daily Graphic*, 2 Oct. 1895, SPAB Archives, 'Avignon, Palace of Popes'.
[30] Helen Taylor to Thackeray Turner, 15 June 1898, SPAB Archives, 'Avignon, Palace of Popes'.

After a long discussion, the committee agreed that it would be unwise of the Society to take action.[31] Further articles in *The Picture Postcard* and the *St James Gazette* in early December 1900 deplored the destruction. Forwarding the articles, another member, Miss Sheelah Chichester, inquired if the Society could do anything. Thackeray Turner answered quoting the passage from Helen Taylor's letter on how harmful intervention would be. 'After this' he concluded 'especially as it was supported by other opinion, we could not act.'[32] Yet the SPAB continued to receive letters by members on the subject and the press also continued to be animated by it.

Meanwhile 'people modern enough to appreciate old buildings' did agitate. The 1900 Public Art Congress railed against the demolition on the international level.[33] Within France not only the usual suspects like *L'Ami des Monuments* worked against the planned demolition, but protests preoccupied the Academies and all the major newspapers from *Le Journal des Debats*, to *Le Temps* and *Le Petit Parisien*.[34] Across the press, the tone was fiercely critical of municipal policies and of the Historic Monuments Commission's greater support of fellow politicians than of their designated mission.[35] Local protest too grew stronger and ever more organised. Avignon's citizens created a Committee for the Conservation of Avignon's Town Walls, published memoranda on behalf of the fortifications and sent a petition by 1800 signatories, that included not just many Avignon notables, but bakers, green-grocers and many other artisans, to the Minister of Public Instruction, attacking again both municipal policy and the apathy of central government.[36]

Back in Britain, expectations grew that this public agitation might have some results. The *Daily News*, which reported regularly about the town walls, placed its hopes in a scheduled discussion in the French Chamber.[37] The *Manchester Guardian* argued that:

> Foreigners are rather apt to describe Englishmen as the modern representatives of the Vandals, and we often accept the accusation with meekness. If the warnings that have just been addressed to lovers of art and of historic places are not over-coloured, however, we have a good opportunity for retort –

[31] Thackeray Turner to Helen Taylor, 24 June 1898, SPAB Archives, 'Avignon, Palace of Popes'.

[32] Thackeray Turner to Miss Sheelah Chichester, 12 December 1900, SPAB Archives, 'Avignon, Palace of Popes'.

[33] 'Letter from Paris', *The Builder*, 13 Oct. 1900, p. 308.

[34] 'Vandalisme à Avignon', *L'Ami des Monuments*, 15 (1901), 113–16.

[35] MAP 81/84/38 'Avignon Remparts, Coupures de presse'.

[36] MAP 81/84/38 'Avignon Remparts, Menace de demolition, petition'.

[37] *Daily News*, 3 July 1901, SPAB Archives, 'Avignon, Palace of Popes'.

better even than is afforded by the paper-mill that disfigures the beautiful gorge of Vaucluse or the Bengal lights that flare nightly in the Colosseum.[38]

Distraught by the attempt 'to ruin one of the most romantic and beautiful of French towns' and 'one of the most interesting spectacles that greets the eye of the tourist in Provence', the article concluded that foreign protest should 'be strongly urged on the French Government, who have the grave responsibility of representing the most enlightened of nations in all questions of art, and who will have the sympathy of every other nation besides if they make a stand, even at the last moment against this barbarous proposition'.

The SPAB, while intervening in other French cases, still abstained from taking action for political reasons, but as Thackeray Turner informed a worried member, the Society had learned from the public press that the French Minister of Finance might stop the demolition.[39] *The Times* reported on 6 March 1902 how the government and the Historic Monuments Commission were attacked during the debate on the fine arts estimates for allowing the municipality of Avignon to demolish a section of the ramparts. During the debates it transpired, however, that:

> The portion of the fortifications demolished consists of about 1200 ft. of the wall opposite the railway station, the portion restored or rather rebuilt, by Viollet le Duc. The really historical portions of the walls of the old city of the Popes are not to be touched. As a matter of fact the whole agitation here against the action of the Avignon authorities is rather sentimental than practical and reasonable. It is unlikely that any visitor who has admired these walls in the past will, on revisiting Avignon, discover any change in the appearance of the city.

The SPAB was seriously perturbed by the prospect that all the fuss might have been over the demolition of a restoration. Thackeray Turner wrote to Helen Taylor in order to enquire whether it was true that the walls that were being demolished were actually the parts restored by Viollet-le-Duc and whether they had been restored very badly or were in an intact state.[40] For the SPAB, and the British press, the case ended here unspectacularly. The agitation of public opinion in France, and of Avignon's residents in particular, resulted, however, in the *classement* of the town walls in their integrity, thus including the Viollet-le-Ducian restorations, on 23 February 1906 (ill. 5.4).[41]

[38] *Manchester Guardian*, 29 June 1901, SPAB Archives, 'Avignon, Palace of Popes'.
[39] Thackeray Turner to Edward Greenly, 5 July 1901, SPAB Archives, 'Avignon, Palace of Popes'.
[40] 7 March (1902?), SPAB Archive, 'Avignon, Palace of Popes'.
[41] Ministère de la Culture et de la Communication, Base Mérimée, www.culture.gouv.fr/documentation/merimee/accueil.htm.

5.4 The city walls of Avignon before and after the restoration by Viollet-le-Duc. The writing on the first postcard compares the 'gayety and liveliness' of the town to the state of its dilapidated walls, while the second one is proudly imprinted with 'restored by Viollet-le-Duc'.

Apart from recording a vivid interest in foreign monuments, the articles on Avignon in the British press reveal how foreign cases were almost always used to reflect on domestic practices. This was even more apparent in the case of Rouen Cathedral. After reading an article in *The Athenaeum* on 16 February 1895, the SPAB's secretary had written a letter to Charles Normand on what could be done to prevent the restoration, while Morris sent several letters to the British press, among them the *Daily Chronicle*, which championed his cause.[42] Although the case was lost, the *Daily Chronicle* used it to alert the public to what was happening in England:

> Some months ago Mr William Morris called attention to the threatened restoration of Rouen Cathedral. We have the painful duty of announcing that the restoration has been commenced... It is almost certain however, that the most beautiful unrestored church in France is doomed. In this connection, it might be interesting to know what really is to be done at Peterborough. We believe Mr Pearson is to do it.[43]

Mr Pearson was indeed to restore Peterborough. To prevent his scheme, one of the larger British anti-restoration campaigns was mounted, that also brought German and British preservationists together.[44] The fate of the cathedral had long been on the SPAB's mind. It worriedly observed the precarious state of the west facade in 1886 and wrote to the Dean and Chapel, without obtaining any results.[45] A decade later, a storm did so much damage that intervention was imperative. Reacting to a letter to the *Daily Chronicle* from the Dean of Peterborough soliciting help for restoration, Morris wrote several epistles to the press warning that the necessary repairs should not result in '"restoration" mania'.[46] The Dean and Chapter, however, confided not in Morris, but the architect John Loughborough Pearson, who had earlier restored the central tower. Pearson certified that the northern gable needed to be dismantled and rebuilt and suggested extending the measure to the remaining two other gables. In

[42] *Daily Chronicle*, 17 Sep. 1895, repr. in N. Kelvin, *The Collected Letters of William Morris* (4 vols., Princeton, 1984–1996), IV, no. 2416, pp. 324–9; letter to the *Athenaeum*, 24 September 1895, no. 2408, pp. 320–1.
[43] *Daily Chronicle*, 12 October 1895, SPAB Archives, 'Rouen Cathedral, France'.
[44] On the history of the cathedral see L. Reilly, *An Architectural History of Peterborough Cathedral* (Oxford, 1997).
[45] SPAB, *Annual Report*, 19 (1896), 53–5. See also Morris' letter on Peterborough Cathedral, *Pall Mall Gazette*, 10 September 1889 and 20 September 1889, repr. in Kelvin (ed.), *Letters of William Morris*, III, pp. 100–2, 104.
[46] Letter to the *Daily Chronicle*, 2 April 1895, also published in the *Daily News*, *Morning Post*, *The Standard*, *The Times*, repr. in Kelvin (ed.), *Letters of William Morris*, IV, no. 2363, pp. 262–5; letter to the *Daily Chronicle*, 7 December 1895; no. 2433, pp. 342–3.

reaction, the Society of Antiquaries and the SPAB provided a counter-plan by four architects asserting that the facade could be consolidated without demolishing the northern gable.[47] A fight ensued in the columns of the major papers which the German architect Herman Muthesius, attaché to the German Embassy in London described as a controversy of 'universal interest':

> not only as indicating that a considerable portion of the population of England begins to take an interest in the preservation of its ancient buildings, but also because the programme of an 'art party' has been re-introduced and brought to the knowledge of a wider public – an 'art party', which to all appearances, will be called upon to bring about changes in the treatment of ancient buildings and monuments.[48]

Muthesius wholeheartedly embraced the cause of the SPAB and the Antiquaries and sent both of them a copy of his official report for the Embassy, partly reprinted in the *Centralblatt der Bauverwaltung* (ill. 5.5).[49] However, he cautioned a week later:

> I should not be very glad if you had the intention to make any public use of the article. My business in England connects me with Architects of every school and any direction, and in trying to obtain the objects which I have in view I am entirely dependent on their courtesy. Though I share your opinion on the preservation of old buildings and I am convinced that they will become more or less those of the future, I should not like to meddle in controversies as long as I enjoy the hospitality of this country. When I leave it again, I shall only be too glad to assist you in any way in my power, and as to my own country, it is quite a matter of course that I shall try my best to convince my people of the rightness of your views, which I have, as you see from the article, made my own.[50]

Muthesius did not exaggerate his attempts to sway German opinion. His role as a mediator was so important that Paul Schultze-Naumburg wrote in

[47] Society of Antiquaries of London, *Statement of the Action Taken by the Society for the Protection of Ancient Buildings and the Society of Antiquaries for the Preservation of the West Front of the Cathedral Church of Peterborough* (s.l.s.d.), SPAB Archives, 'Peterborough Cathedral', III. 'Signatures to Memorial'; see also SPAB, *Annual Report*, 19 (1896), 53–5; 20 (1897), 54–5.

[48] H. Muthesius, 'Die Kathedrale von Peterborough und die Denkmalpflege in England', *Centralblatt der Bauverwaltung*, 10 April 1897, pp. 164–6, qu. p. 164, trans. as 'Peterborough Cathedral and the preservation of Ancient Buildings in England from a German point of view. From a paper by Herr Muthesius in the Centralblatt der Bauverwaltung (10 April 1897) the Official Journal of the German Department of Public Works Berlin (Ministerium der öffentlichen Arbeiten)', SPAB Archives, 'Peterborough Cathedral', II, fol. 1.

[49] Muthesius to Thackeray Turner, 14 April 1897, SPAB Archives, 'Peterborough Cathedral', 1.

[50] Muthesius to Thackeray Turner, 22 May 1897, SPAB Archives, 'Peterborough Cathedral', 1.

Nr. 15. Centralblatt der Bauverwaltung. 165

Fälschungen fern. Wo in den Bestand eines alten Gebäudes eingegriffen wurde, da geschah es eben unverkennbar und in dem gerade herrschenden Stile der Zeit. Die Zuthaten und Veränderungen, die dadurch entstanden sind, sind für uns von gleicher geschichtlicher Bedeutung wie der Urbau, da in ihnen der Geist des betreffenden Zeitalters klar ausgeprägt ist. Heute gehen die Wiederhersteller so zu Werke, daß sie Ursprüngliches herunterreißen und das Gebäude angeblich dadurch in seine beste Zeit zurückführen, daß sie die Lücken so ausfüllen, wie es ihrer persönlichen Meinung nach die alten Meister gethan haben würden. Das Gebäude wird aber gerade dadurch seines geschichtlichen Werthes beraubt, und jedenfalls muß das Neue in dem Beschauer Zweifel über das Verlorengegangene und dessen Werth erregen. Es ist im höchsten Maße bedauerlich, daß die meisten größeren Kathedralen in dieser Weise behandelt worden sind, und zwar häufig gerade von Männern, deren Fähigkeiten einer besseren Beschäftigung werth gewesen wären. Für diejenigen Gebäude, und zwar aller Zeiten und Stile, welche noch unberührt übrig geblieben sind, wird die Forderung aufgestellt: Schutz an die Stelle von Wiederherstellungen treten zu lassen; dem Verfall derart zu steuern, daß nur solche Mittel angewandt werden, die augenscheinlich nur dem Zwecke der Aufrechterhaltung des Denkmals dienen, ohne auf irgend welche Kunst-Ansprüche zu machen: Gebäude, die ihrem ursprünglichen Zwecke nicht mehr genügen, lieber unbenutzt stehen zu lassen, als sie zu erweitern, in Fällen aber, wo dies nicht möglich ist, die Erweiterung so vorzunehmen, daß sie untrüglich als in der Jetztzeit hinzugethan gekennzeichnet ist; unsere alterthümlichen Gebäude als ehrwerthe Denkmäler einer vergangenen Kunst zu behandeln, die aus entschwundenen Zeiten Kunde geben, und in die unsere heutige Kunst nicht eingreifen kann, ohne sie zu zerstören; endlich uns stets der Verpflichtung bewußt zu sein, daß wir sie der Nachwelt in demselben Zustande zu übergeben haben, in der sie auf uns gekommen sind, und daß wir kein Recht haben, diesen Zustand durch unsere Eingriffe zu entstellen.

Die scharfe Fassung dieses Programms überrascht anfangs, und man ist vielleicht geneigt, in ihr zu viel Alterthümelei zu finden. Aber wenn man bedenkt, daß sich alterorten die Auffassung in Bezug auf Wiederherstellungen immer mehr von der störungslegenden Richtung abgewandt und nach der Seite sorgsamen Instandhaltens entwickelt hat, wenn man ferner bedenkt, daß man beispielsweise auch in der Bildhauerkunst von dem in früheren Jahrhunderten so beliebten Ergänzungen und Ueberarbeitungen aufgefundener antiker Standbilder gänzlich abgekommen ist, und daß in der Malerei Ueberarbeitungen oder Aufbesserungen alter Gemälde nicht mehr möglich sind, so treten auch die Forderungen des angeführten Programms in ein anderes Licht, und man kann vielleicht in ihnen das letzte Ziel der neueren Auffassung der Denkmalpflege erblicken. Eine Reihe anderer, vorwiegend archäologischer Gesellschaften theilen die Ansicht der Gesellschaft zum Schutze der Baudenkmäler und wirken im ähnlichen Sinne wie sie, allen voran die Gesellschaft der Antiquare (Society of Antiquaries). Dieser seit mehr als hundert Jahren bestehende Verein verkörpert die archäologisch-gebildete Welt Englands und genießt eine Art staatlicher Anerkennung dadurch, daß er seine miethsfreie Unterkunft in einem staatlichen Gebäude, Burlington House in Picadilly, erhalten hat.

Das Wirken beider Gesellschaften ist vielleicht gerade in England

am Platze, wo in der That schlimmes an den Denkmälern begangen worden ist. Noch in den letzten fünfzehn Jahren hat sich hier ein Ereigniß abgespielt, das durch den dabei verübten Unfug die Entrüstung jedes Kunstfreundes hervorrufen mußte. Es ist die Wiederherstellung der Kathedrale von St. Albans, 30 Kilometer nördlich von London gelegen, die ein Architektur-Dilettant, Lord Grimthorpe, deshalb vornehmen durfte, weil er alles, was er that, bezahlte. Er baute die Kathedrale nach eigenem Gutdünken und auf eigene Faust aus, nahm alte Denkmäler heraus, fügte bedeutende Theile nach eigenem Entwurfe hinzu und hinterließ der Nachwelt an einem der interessantesten Baudenkmäler Eindrücke seiner dilettantischen Hand, die zu allen Zeiten nur als Rohheiten schlimmster Art empfunden werden können. Ein von ihm gezeichnetes großes Rosenfenster ist der Gegenstand sprichwörtlichen Spottes geworden, und wie weit sein architektonisches Verständniß reicht, mag der Umstand erhellen, daß er die Decke des Querschiffes mit einem Holzgewölbe schloß, welches mitten durch die Fenster der von ihm selbst entworfenen Querschiffwand schnitt.

Den baufälligen Zustand der Westfront der Kathedrale von Peterborough hatte die Gesellschaft zum Schutze der Baudenkmäler schon seit dem Jahre 1886 im Auge gehabt und hatte sich wiederholt schriftlich deshalb an das Capitel gewandt. Dieses stand jedoch in Beziehung zu dem Architekten Pearson, der schon früher den Vierungsthurm der Kathedrale ausgebaut hatte und in dem es den besten Rathgeber zu haben glaubte. Pearson ist der bedeutendste jetzt lebende Gothiker Englands, er blickt auf eine fünfzigjährige reiche Thätigkeit zurück, und auf seinem Scheitel sind alle Ehren gehäuft, die einem Architekten zu Theil werden können. Der neuen Kirchen in England, die von seiner Hand herrühren, sind Legion, und die bedeutendsten englischen Kathedralen sind von ihm wiederhergestellt worden. Für seine Auffassung der Behandlung alter Baudenkmäler ist sein Vorschlag für den Umbau des Kreuzganges in Lincoln bezeichnend. Der nördliche Abschluß desselben war im Mittelalter unausgeführt geblieben. Im Jahre 1669 errichtete Christopher Wren, der Erbauer der Londoner Paulskirche, als Abschluß ein Gebäude in den damals üblichen Renaissanceformen, eine neue Säulenhalle, oben Räume für die Dombibliothek enthielt. Pearsons Absicht ging dahin, dieses Gebäude abzubrechen und die vierte Seite des Kreuzganges in der Art der drei übrigen zu schließen. In ähnlicher Weise beabsichtigte er bei der Wiederherstellung des Vierungsthurmes von Peterborough, den er abriß und neu aufbaute, die Vierungsbögen dem benachbarten normannischen Schiff zu Liebe rundbogig statt spitzbogig, wie sie vorher waren, zu errichten. Diese Angelegenheiten haben ihrer Zeit viel Staub aufgewirbelt*), und nur dem lebhaften öffentlichen Einspruche, nicht zum mindesten hervorgerufen durch das Wirken der Gesellschaft zum Schutze der Baudenkmäler, ist es zu verdanken, daß die betreffenden Domcapitel damals der Absicht ihres Architekten nicht willfahrteten.

Pearson verfaßte mehrere Gutachten für das Domcapitel von Peterborough und erklärte im letzten derselben, daß die nördliche der drei Giebel abgebrochen und neu aufgebaut werden müsse, ein Verfahren, was seiner Ansicht nach am besten auch zugleich auf die beiden anderen ausgedehnt würde. Dadurch war der Schlachtruf für jenen Kampf gegeben, der, eingangs erwähnt worden ist. Die Gesell-

*) Ueber den Kreuzgang von Lincoln ist Jahrg. 1892, S. 216 berichtet.

Westfront der Kathedrale von Peterborough.

5.5 Middle page of Herman Muthesius, 'Die Kathedrale von Peterborough und die Denkmalpflege in England', *Centralblatt der Bauverwaltung*, 10 April 1897, p. 165, a shorter version of his diplomatic report about the state of restoration in England.

Der Kunstwart in 1903, the last year of Muthesius' stay in London, 'Muthesius is . . . a profound connoisseur of English architecture. Most of what has
been transferred into German intellectual ownership [*Geistesbesitz*] lately,
we owe to him'.[51]

The campaign did not manage to save the gable of the cathedral, yet the
SPAB, always needing to report victories, stated in its *Annual Report* that
this should not be a reason to be dissatisfied with the discussion, 'which
has been the means of procuring it fresh adherents, and in bringing the
principles it advocates in dealing with ancient buildings more prominently
before the public'. To prove the point 'it might be sufficient as showing the
effect of this discussion to quote the following passage from an article in
the *Centralblatt der Bauverwaltung*, the official organ of the Berlin Office
of Public Works' stating that:

> The defeat of the opposing party, it must be borne in mind, is more apparent
> than real, inasmuch in the course of the controversy they have brought
> over to their side such a body of public opinion in their favour as well
> render restorations which are preceded by demolition more difficult in
> the future. The conflict has above all things, awakened public interest in
> the preservation of ancient buildings to such an extent that it is some
> compensation for the loss of the northern gable of Peterborough Cathedral.[52]

Whether Muthesius changed his mind on being publicly quoted or whether
a compromise was reached to use the weight of an opinion expressed
in an official foreign publication without mentioning his name, is not
recorded, but the successful collaboration that ensued between the SPAB
and the German architect during the following years might indicate that
the decision was taken with his consent.

The most prominent of these Anglo-German cases was the intervention
on behalf of Heidelberg Castle. The public debate on whether the ruin
should be restored, known as the *Heidelberger Schloßstreit*, was also a formative moment for the German *Denkmalbewegung*.[53] It bestowed future
preservationists with memorable quotes, most famously the Germanisation
of the maxim 'to conserve not to restore' as *'konservieren nicht restauriern'*

---

[51] *Der Kunstwart* (1903), p. 125; on Muthesius see F. Roth, *Hermann Muthesius und die Idee der
harmonischen Kultur. Kultur als Einheit des künstlerischen Stils in allen Lebensäußerungen eines
Volkes* (Berlin, 2001); on the English years see P. Alter, 'Hermann Muthesius. Die englischen
Jahre', in G. Ritter, P. Wende (eds.), *Rivalität und Partnerschaft. Studien zu den deutsch-britischen
Beziehungen im 19. und 20. Jahrhundert* (Paderborn, 1999), pp. 53–68; N. Böhnke 'Adam Gottlieb
Hermann Muthesius. Lecture on the occasion of the presentation of the brochure "Wendgräben"',
in 'Hermann Muthesius (1861–1927)' (2001), www.hermann-muthesius.de.

[52] SPAB, *Annual Report*, 20 (1897), 54–5.

[53] On earlier controversies about restorations see Koshar, *Germany's Transient Pasts*, pp. 50–9.

and marked the turn to anti-restoration.[54] At the same time, the *Schloßstreit* was shaped by conflicts between artistic sensibilities and political memory, and between national and universal ideas of heritage. Loaded with nationalist meaning in the Franco-German conflict, the ruin was at the same time a treasured landmark for many foreign visitors, writers and artists for whom it was less a German than an international monument. Erected in the fourteenth century, it was transformed in Renaissance style by the Prince Electors Ottheinrich, Friedrich IV and Friedrich V during the sixteenth and early seventeenth centuries. Destroyed during the Thirty Years' War, it was soon rebuilt, only to be destroyed once again by French troops under Louis XIV. Prince Elector Karl Theodor, while residing in nearby Schwetzingen, tried to make it habitable once again, but lightning struck in 1764, further devastating the building. When the old Kurpfalz ceased to exist in 1803, the Markgraf of Baden became the new owner of Heidelberg Castle. Heidelberg's population meanwhile used the building as quarry and rumour had it that the government in Karlsruhe signed a contract to demolish the castle to use the gardens for agriculture. However, a French émigré, Charles de Graimberg, overwhelmed by the beauty of the ruin, decided to take residence in the castle and to save it. Graimberg did numerous drawings of the castle and commissioned a first guidebook. The considerable distribution of engravings helped to bring domestic and international visitors to Heidelberg, where a nascent tourist industry awaited them, even offering the possibility to purchase cups with the image of the castle.[55] During the following decades, the ruin fascinated German and foreign Romantics alike. German writers from Goethe, Heine, Brentano, Hölderlin to Matthisson praised it in verse. In France, Victor Hugo's descriptions and drawings increased its fame.[56] For Britain William Turner's painting achieved the same and the castle subsequently became a topic for numerous English

---

[54] See *Traum & Wirklichkeit. Vergangenheit und Zukunft der Heidelberger Schlossruine.* Exhibition Catalogue, Heidelberger Schloss, Ottheinrichsbau, 16 April to 17 July 2005 (Stuttgart, 2005); M. Wohlleben, 'Vom Nutzen eines Schlosses und vom Wert einer Ruine: zur neuen Schloßdebatte nach hundert Jahren; aus Anlaß des Kolloquiums: Vergangenheit und Zukunft der Heidelberger Schloßruine im Heidelberger Schloß, 8./9. Juni 2005, und des Ausstellungskatalogs: Traum und Wirklichkeit', *Kunstchronik*, 58.11 (2005), 562–6; V. Osteneck, 'Die Debatte um das Heidelberger Schloss', in I. Scheurmann (ed.), *ZeitSchichten. Erkennen und Erhalten – Denkmalpflege in Deutschland*, Exhibition Catalogue, Residenzschloss Dresden 30 July–13 November 2005 (Dresden, 2005), pp. 108–13; F. Hepp, 'Der Heidelberger Schloss-Streit in der Karikatur: Die "Verschäferung" des Schlosses?', Kurpfälzisches Museum Heidelberg, 'Kunstwerk des Monats', March 2006 (2006), www.zum.de/Faecher/G/BW/Landeskunde/rhein/hd/km/kdm/o6/o3b.htm.
[55] F. Hepp, A.M. Roth (eds.), *Ein Franzose in Heidelberg. Stadt und Schloss im Blick des Grafen Graimberg.* Exhibition Catalogue Kurpfälzisches Museum Heidelberg (Heidelberg, 2004).
[56] V. Hugo, *Heidelberg*, ed. M. Butor (Frankfurt, 2002).

writers and a popular subject for engraving.[57] Domestic and foreign visits to Heidelberg increased even more after the city was connected to the railway network in 1840. Thousands of postcards further propagated the castle's image. In 1898, in a single season 36,000 postcards were sent, only surpassed by 148,000 from Kyphäuser, and 128,000 from the Niederwald national monument.[58]

When in 1861 works for a railway tunnel caused cracks in the fabric of the castle, the government of Baden actively embraced the idea of preservation and plans were discussed to rebuild the ruin. In the face of the completion of Cologne Cathedral, a local paper in 1868 published a call 'to all Germans' ending with the wish that 'the *Volk* will cry: Heidelberg Castle shall not remain a ruin'.[59] As a national sanctuary, the dishonour of its destruction by the French troops should be visually obliterated and militarily avenged. At the same time, the first voices could be heard asking for the conservation of the castle as a ruin. To take a decision, the Ministry of Finance of Baden appointed a commission composed of professors of architecture and art history, and of representatives of the building authorities and of the city of Heidelberg, and commissioned a structural record. As a result, the government appointed the Karlsruhe professor of architecture Carl Schäfer to restore the facade of the *Friedrichsbau* and to complete its interior. Schäfer, who in the 1880s had still pleaded against the restoration of Renaissance buildings, reconstructed the *Friedrichsbau* between 1898 and 1903 according to his own designs, provoking mixed reactions in the architectural world, but not large-scale public criticism. When however, in 1900, he was also appointed to reconstruct the *Otthein-richsbau*, a storm of protest ensued in the entire German Empire against this 'fortgesetzte Verschäferung' as the art historian Georg Dehio dubbed it in a word play on the architect's name.[60] Alumni of Heidelberg University sent a 500-signatory petition and a declaration by current academics to the Grand Duke requesting a halt to the restoration. From Dresden, Professor Cornelius Gurlitt, co-founder of the *Denkmaltage*, mobilised German

---

[57] J.M.W. Turner, Heidelberg, c. 1844–1845, Tate Britain; 'The Town And Castle Of Heidelberg', *The Times*, 11 July 1846, p. 8; on Anglophone literary imagination of Heidelberg see 'Heidelberg University's Fifth Centenary', *The Times*, 30 July 1886, p. 4 and on engravings *The Times*, 30 April 1858, p. 11 (advertisement).

[58] 'Illustrated Post-Cards In Germany', *The Times*, 12 July 1898, p. 4.

[59] *Kölnische Zeitung*, Nr. 282 (1868), qu. in *Traum und Wirklichkeit*, p. 39.

[60] G. Dehio, *Was wird aus dem Heidelberger Schloß werden?* (Strasbourg, 1901), repr. in Wohlleben (ed.), *Konservieren nicht restaurieren*, pp. 34–42; Hepp, 'Der Heidelberger Schloss-Streit in der Karikatur'.

public opinion through a postcard campaign.[61] Heidelberg's professor of art history Henry Thode published several pamphlets and Heidelberg's middle classes joined the protests through an *Alt Heidelberg Verein*. The question also intrigued officials across the German states and was a frequent topic in the national press.[62] It was seized upon for satirical plays and depictions in the major spoof papers from *Simplicissimus*, which equated the restoration with the destruction by Louis XIV's army to *Lustige Blätter* which mocked plans to 'ruin the ruin' by turning it into a palace of consumption for domestic and foreign visitors (ills. 5.6–5.7).[63]

In the middle of the *Schloßstreit*, German anti-restorationists turned to the SPAB for support. The SPAB had already considered other German cases. The first concerned the completion of Ulm Cathedral. Reacting to an article in *The Builder* which described with admiration that 'there is something characteristic in this pride taken by the Germans in the noble creations of their past – a pride which we in England may well envy our neighbours' and concluded that 'Ulm Cathedral must be completed',[64] the SPAB had consulted one of its members, the architect Henry Brewer, a specialist in German architecture, about whether anything could be done to prevent this venture.[65] It was decided not to take further action, as Brewer pointed out:

> I myself think this operation a mistake, but it would not be of the slightest use trying to prevent it as the matter is a *national* and a *religious* movement – The German Catholics having spoilt their great national cathedral, Cologne,

---

[61] Cornelius Gurlitt (1850–1938), born in Dresden, studied architecture and art history in Stuttgart and Leipzig and became an architect in Dresden and assistant at the *Kunstgewerbemuseum*. Following his *Habilitation* in Berlin, Gurlitt became a professor at the TH Dresden in 1893, of which he was to become Rektor between 1904–15. He was co-founder and president of the Federation of German Architects and one of the co-founders of the *Tag für Denkmalpflege*. He was noted for the openness with which he studied new artistic styles. He was a proponent of modernist architecture and modernist planning, as long as it fit beauty and utility, and advocated to use *Jugendstil* when repairing old buildings. See Koshar, *Germany's Transient Pasts*, p. 45; *Traum und Wirklichkeit*, p. 110; H. Magirius, 'Cornelius Gurlitt (1850–1938)' in Magirius (ed.), *Denkmalpflege in Sachsen, 1894–1994* (2 vols., Weimar, 1997), I, pp. 15–24.

[62] Heinrich Munk to Wilhelm II, 21 Jun 1906; GStA PK I HA Rep. 93 B Nr. 2337, fol. 180; on reports in *Nationalzeitung*, fol. 191.

[63] Hepp, 'Der Heidelberger Schloss-Streit in der Karikatur'; 'Neu-Heidelberg: Der Ott-Heinrichsbau der Zukunft. Eine ruinirte Ruine', *Lustige Blätter*, 34 (1904), repr. in *Traum und Wirklichkeit*, pp. 86–7.

[64] 'Ulm Cathedral and its Restoration', *The Builder*, 10 February 1883, p. 173, SPAB Archives, 'Ulm Cathedral'.

[65] Henry Brewer (1836–1903), an architectural draughtsman, illustrated mediaeval buildings of England and Germany for *The Builder*. For SPAB he designed the tabular report form for churches and undertook the survey of churches in East Anglia as well as reporting on buildings in other areas, particularly in Germany and Italy. See J. West, 'SPAB Committee Members: Biographical Notes', in Miele (ed.), *From William Morris*, p. 324; SPAB Archives, 'Italian Restorations'.

Alt=Heidelberg

(Zeichnungen von O. Gulbransson)

Das Heidelberger Schloß wurde zweimal verwüstet. Das erstemal 1689 durch General Mélac,

das zweitemal 1906 u. ff. durch Oberbaurat Schäfer.

— 216 —

5.6 Olaf Gulbransson, 'Alt Heidelberg', *Simplicissimus*, 25 June 1906, p. 216. *Simplicissimus* intervened in the *Schloßstreit* on several occasions. Here the destruction by restoration was likened to that of Louis XIV's troops. The text read: 'Heidelberg Castle was destroyed twice. The first time in 1689 by General Mélac, the second in 1906 by Oberbaurat Schäfer.'

5.7 'New Heidelberg: The Ottheinrich Palace of the Future: A Ruined Ruin', *Lustige Blätter*, 34 (1904) warned that commodification would 'ruin the ruin'. Writings on signs in English, French and German alerted to the dangers brought by international tourists.

the Protestants must of course be allowed to spoil theirs, Ulm, and the great tower is to serve as a national German memorial of '*the Reformation in the Fatherland*'. As I greatly object both to *the Reformation* and *the completion of the tower*, I should be glad to point out any action which the society might take in the matter but I fear that any thing which we might do would bring us face to face with the strong religious feelings upon the subject which exist both in Germany and in England.[66]

The situation in Heidelberg was different. Religious feelings could be discounted. National feelings were certainly in favour of the reconstruction, but the German anti-restoration movement had also gained considerable strength since the work on the cathedrals of Cologne and Ulm, and one of its most prominent voices, Georg Dehio, argued against restoration precisely on the grounds that it unpatriotically destroyed the nation's past.[67] Moreover, in the interim the SPAB had established a record in intervening concerning monuments in Nuremberg and, with more publicity, in the planned restoration of Brunswick Castle in 1886.[68] For the latter case, it managed to enlist Queen Victoria's help through her private secretary Sir Henry Ponsonby and his wife, both SPAB members, and wrote to the authorities in Brunswick with the argument that the castle, although on German soil, was also the ancestral home of Queen Victoria.[69] Afterwards, the SPAB collaborated with Muthesius on several smaller cases in Germany, but the impulse had always come from England and not Germany.[70] In the *Schloßstreit*, however, it was Muthesius who asked for help:

> As the Castle of Heidelberg is a *building of universally recognised value and far more than only German interest* it occurred to me, that this flagrant piece of insult to a masterpiece of old architecture might be a proper occasion for your Society to intervene. A protest is going on in Germany . . . and a circular has just reached me, issued by Professor Cornelius Gurlitt who is collecting signatures to protest against this intended restoration. It seems to me, however, that your Society should act independently as I am sure this would be of greater effect than to join our protest. The Castle of Heidelberg is well known to many Englishmen and English art-lovers should take a

[66] Henry Brewer to SPAB, undated (February 1883). SPAB Archives, 'Ulm Cathedral' (emphasis in original). On Brewer's previous expressions on Cologne see 'Gothic Architecture in Germany', *The Times*, 23 November 1871, p. 12.

[67] Dehio, *Denkmalschutz und Denkmalpflege*, p. 9.

[68] SPAB Archives, 5th Committee Minute Book, 3 July–4 Sep. 1884; 29 Oct. 1884; case files 'Nuremberg Town Walls'; 'Nuremberg St. Sebald Church'.

[69] Undated Letter (1886) from SPAB to unspecified recipient in Brunswick; For a similar reasoning see *The Builder*, 9 Jan. 1886, SPAB Archives, 'Brunswick Castle'; Sharp, 'Exporting the Revolution', p. 200.

[70] SPAB Archives, 'Francfort Cathedral'.

great interest in its preservation. Such a protest from your Society would only be natural. For many reasons I also think it would be better not to mention my name in connection with the matter.[71]

While explicitly soliciting help, Muthesius again did not want to be publicly connected to the collaboration, in part because of the deterioration of Anglo-German relations. In the 1880s and 1890s it was desirable to stress English opinion against restoration to convince a German audience. When the SPAB now drafted a letter to the Grand Duke of Baden against the restoration of Heidelberg Castle, outlining the principles of the Society and stressing that 'such new work does not conform to the requirement of a work of art, and in England it is now generally recognised as being devoid of art', Muthesius pointed out that:

> There is one little thing which might perhaps – considering the present position of the two countries – be altered, namely the words 'in England' in the first column of the second page. It is of course perfectly true that in England first the new views took root and I myself have constantly emphasised that. But it would perhaps nevertheless be better not to put it in the forefront at the present occasion, as it might prejudice the receiver of the letter. 'and it is now more and more recognised as being devoid of art' would perhaps do just as well.[72]

The extent to which debates regarding the reconstruction were entangled in international relations becomes further apparent when assessing French reactions. Heidelberg Castle did not always inspire universal support. Given the enthusiastic collaboration between German and English preservationists, regardless of increasingly difficult political relations between the two nations, a view towards France is illuminating in placing internationalist tones into perspective. *L'Ami des Monuments* was silent about the whole affair, possibly because of Normand's anti-German feelings, but an article from *Le Journal de Paris*, that found its way from the desk of a SPAB member to Muthesius' office, took a radically different stance than the anti-restoration front, albeit not for aesthetic reasons:

> It is proposed to re-build – not to restore – the famous castle of Heidelberg. We can only applaud this design, for when the ruins celebrated in verse by Matthisson shall have disappeared and are replaced by new buildings

---

[71] Muthesius to Thackeray Turner, 20 November 1901, SPAB Archives, 'Heidelberg Castle' (emphasis added). Muthesius provided for background information: L. Dihm, 'Zur Wiederherstellung des Heidelberger Schlosses', *Centralblatt der Bauverwaltung*, 91 (1901), 557–8; C. Gurlitt, 'Vom Heidelberger Schloß', *Frankfurter Zeitung und Handelsblatt*, 18 Nov. 1901. Nr. 320 Abendblatt.

[72] Muthesius to Thackeray Turner, 30 Nov. 1901, SPAB Archives, 'Heidelberg Castle'.

we shall no longer hear the silly stories which young and old inhabitants of the locality repeat to foreign visitors of the so-called destruction of the castle by the French soldiers. These soldiers, who by the way, were German mercenaries, in the pay of France, who being obliged in 1689, to retreat before a superior force, blew up the fortifications of the castle and of the town, in the course of which operation a certain number of other buildings were damaged, as might be expected. As to the castle, this was burned in 1764 by lightning which has been considered by the most prejudiced up to the present at least as an element essentially international.[73]

The national and international protest in 1902, however, had an immediate effect. The sum required for carrying out the works was withdrawn from the estimates before the Diet. In an attempt to market its own value, the SPAB perhaps overestimated its contribution by concluding the entry in the *Annual Report* with: 'We may add we have been informed that the Society's action had special weight in influencing the authorities.'[74] The contribution was however appreciated enough for Muthesius and Gurlitt to ask for collaboration in further cases. The *Schloßstreit* ended officially after being carried to the sixth *Tag für Denkmalpflege* in Bamberg. The convention pleaded for the conservation of the ruin as a monument of its own history and supported Dehio's motion to consolidate the ruin to prevent further destruction and to postpone the debate for fifty or a hundred years. The suggestion was taken up by the Diet of Baden in 1910 who voted to adjourn indefinitely the reconstruction of the *Ottheinrichsbau*.

The example shows how public behaviour was affected by international relations. Yet in the years before the First World War this did not affect relations between German and English preservationists. They simply continued to collaborate in a less public way. While the public was still captivated by the Heidelberg *Schloßstreit*, Muthesius wrote again to Thackeray Turner to solicit help for an internationally much less well-known building. 'The great assistance which your Society was kind enough to render us in the matter of the Otto Heinrichsbau of Heidelberg Castle encourages me to apply again for your help in another instance of an intended restoration in Germany.'[75] The restoration in question concerned the intended erection of two spires to complete the west frontage of the cathedral of Meißen in Saxony, illustrated by a postcard Muthesius annexed (ill. 5.8).

[73] Handwritten note: 'Heidelberg Castle. From *Le Journal*. Paris daily newspaper. Dec 4th 1901', SPAB Archives, 'Heidelberg Castle'. Thackeray Turner forwarded the translation to Muthesius, but neither commented on it.
[74] SPAB, *Annual Report*, 25 (1902), 50–2.
[75] Muthesius to Thackeray Turner, 7 May 1902, SPAB Archives, 'Meissen Cathedral, Saxony'.

5.8 Meißen Cathedral. Postcard sent by Muthesius to the SPAB to illustrate the changes planned.

Like the cathedrals of Cologne and Ulm, his contemporaries thought, that of Meißen was in need of 'completion'. Construction on the gothic hall church had been started in 1260. Lightning had struck only three years after the completion of the nave in 1410, caving in the west front with its two towers erected after 1315; the smaller eastern tower had remained the cathedral's only spire for centuries, until 'completion' was decided in the late nineteenth century. The architect who had won the competitions with a design for two neo-gothic spires was the same Carl Schäfer commissioned to restore the *Ottheinrichsbau* in Heidelberg. Muthesius commented on the project:

> There is a lot of controversy about what was intended in olden times and our most competent men are of the opinion that a three-spired frontage was intended. But the man who is commissioned with the design thinks that two spires are 'archeologically correct'. Apart from the frontage the whole of the interior was going to be changed and restored. In the accompanying sketch the spires are sketched into the photographic views, but it is easily to be seen, that the continuation of the front walls is drawn, much shorter than in the elevation marked with leadpencil and that the spires in reality will appear much more compact than in the sketch, where too many lights are shown.[76]

Muthesius asked whether the SPAB was inclined to take the matter up. 'I am convinced that a letter from your part would have the same good influence as undoubtedly it had at Heidelberg. The authority in question is the "Domcapitel" in Meissen, Saxony.'[77] The letter was read and discussed at the following committee meeting and it was concluded that:

> As in the case of Heidelberg Castle, the opinion was again expressed that it was very dangerous for this Society, from a national point of view, to interfere in any way with questions which interest the Society in Germany. Nevertheless the Committee is most anxious to assist you in any way, as it fully appreciates the warm support which you give to the cause which this Society advocated, and I was therefore directed to say that the Committee will take action provided that it is understood to be entirely under your guidance and my letter which the Society may send has, as in the case of Heidelberg Castle, your entire approval.[78]

In response, Muthesius provided information from the *Bauzeitung*, a book on Meißen's west front published by Cornelius Gurlitt, as well as a letter by the professor, stating that 'after having discussed the possibility of an

[76] Muthesius to Thackeray Turner, 7 May 1902, SPAB Archives, 'Meissen Cathedral Saxony'.
[77] Ibid.
[78] Thackeray Turner to Muthesius, 9 May 1902, SPAB Archives, 'Meissen Cathedral Saxony'.

English protest meeting with unkindly acceptance . . . with various persons, he has come to the conclusion, that such an acceptance should be quite out of the question and that a protest from your Society would be the most valuable help in the matter'. Moreover, as the new King of Saxony was against the restoration, it was hoped 'that your protest would only tend to confirm him in his views'.[79] In a later letter Muthesius however added again not to refer to his or Gurlitt's name, unless the SPAB thought it absolutely necessary, 'as this might possibly weaken the effect'.[80] The SPAB obliged and principally copied the letter sent to the Grand Duke of Baden to the King of Saxony.[81]

'The cathedral at Meissen, in Saxony had just escaped from a grave danger, no less than that of being restored according to the latest canons of Teutonic architecture', could be read in the *Manchester Guardian*, a year later.[82] The *Guardian*, did not attribute the saving of the cathedral to the SPAB, however, but to 'an actual intervention of Providence' at the fourth *Tag für Denkmalpflege* where the completion was put on the agenda and 'would have been agreed to there and then'. Gurlitt had used the forum to denounce the elevation of restoration to the status of science, by pointing out that in other countries, particularly in Britain, the exact opposite was believed.

> Fortunately or unfortunately, in the course of his remarks Professor Gurlitt fell foul of another authority, Herr 'Oberbaurath' Schaefer, of Carlsruhe, whom he accused of negligence, presumption, and a dismal tendency towards 'embellishing' according to his own ideas whatever was entrusted to him. The outraged 'Oberbaurath' defended himself vigorously, carrying the war into the enemy's country by the assertion that he was well aware of Professor Gurlitt's envious hatred and that he had received from a news agency 1,400 newspaper articles attacking him, all of which, as he knew by their style, had been written by the Professor himself. Great uproar arose, the assembly took sides with one another, and the Cathedral of Meissen was forgotten.[83]

The episode belied the common British belief that the manners of German preservationists tended to be more courteous than those of the English

---

[79] Muthesius to Thackeray Turner, 26 June 1902, SPAB Archives, 'Meissen Cathedral'. The supporting material was C. Gurlitt, *Die Westtürme des Meissner Domes* (Berlin, 1902); 'Die Westthürme des Meissner Domes', *Deutsche Bauzeitung*, 3 May 1902, pp. 225–30.

[80] Muthesius to Thackeray Turner, 7 July 1902, SPAB Archives, 'Meissen Cathedral'.

[81] Draft Letter from Thackeray Turner to Muthesius, 11 July 1902, SPAB Archives, 'Meissen Cathedral'.

[82] *Manchester Guardian*, 12 October 1903, cutting sent by Edward Greenly, SPAB Archives, Rheinfels Ruins.

[83] Ibid.

'extremists'.[84] Alas, the quarrel did not save the cathedral, as from the German sources a slightly different picture emerges. The report on the episode in *Die Denkmalpflege* did not record any of the vivid detail, but in its usual bureaucratic dryness reported that there were indeed three factions, rather than two: those supporting Schäfer's designs of two spires, those championing Gurlitt's three tower version and those, headed by Dehio and the historic associations, who wanted to leave the cathedral the way it was. The report concluded: 'The consultation did not lead to a result, and to obtain one, could not have been its purpose, as Schäfer's design has already been approved for execution and the entire west front has been scaffolded.'[85] Although the general mood in Germany was turning against fanciful restoration, as the many caricatures on the restoration of the Hohkönigsburg, the Kaiser's very own pet project, show, this mood swing came too late (see ill. 5.9). Unlike in the case of Heidelberg, opposition to this reconstruction had been in vain; the west front was completed between 1903 and 1909 after Schäfer's design.[86]

International competition about international collaboration

The particularly close collaboration between the SPAB and its French and German partners ended in 1914. While the war cut Anglo-German ties, SPAB's collaboration with *L'Ami des Monuments* had slowed down already after the death of its principal correspondents Guillon and Garnier in 1896 and 1898 respectively. It ended with the disappearance of the French Society in 1914.[87] The nature of foreign campaigns was changed by the new ideas of the self-determination of peoples, but interventions did not stop with the First World War. Post-1918, the SPAB became involved in the reconstruction of buildings damaged by war and collaborated with new French preservation societies. It also intervened widely across colonies and protectorates.[88] Only during decolonisation in the 1960s was the right to foreign intervention more generally questioned, however, the tradition of

---

[84] Cf. Brown, *The Care of Ancient Monuments*, p. 27.
[85] J. Kohte, 'Der vierte Tag für Denkmalpflege in Erfurt am 25. und 26. September 1903', *Die Denkmalpflege*, 5 (1903), 105–8, qu. 106.
[86] H. Magirius, 'Cornelius Gurlitt (1850–1938)', pp. 18–21.
[87] SPAB Archives, 'German Burnings 1918'; 'War Damage Europe 1914–1915'. The only file on a German building after the war was 'Cologne Cathedral' containing solely a cutting from *The Times*, 5 March 1929.
[88] SPAB Archives, 'Calais Notre Dame'; 'Calais Porte de Guise'; 'Rheims Cathedral', 'La Sauvegarde de l'Art Français'; 'France'.

München, 20. April 1908   13. Jahrgang No. 3

SIMPLICISSIMUS

Liebhaberausgabe   Herausgeber: Albert Langen   Abonnement halbjährlich 15 Mark

(Alle Rechte vorbehalten)

Der Ausbau der Toteninsel
(Zu Th. Heine)

Ein wichtiges Ergebnis der letzten Kaiserreise ist zu verzeichnen: es wurde beschlossen, das bei Korfu gelegene Vorbild von Böcklins
Toteninsel nach den Plänen der Architekten Ihne & Ebhard stilgetreu zu restaurieren.

5.9 *Simplicissimus* frequently mocked the reconstruction of the Hohkönigsburg in Alsace
which had been initiated by the Kaiser and was financed from his imperial funds. Thomas
Theodor Heine compared it to the renovation of the Island of the Dead, a famous
symbolist painting. 'Der Ausbau der Toteninsel', *Simplicissimus*, 20 April 1908, p. 41.
While Wilhelm Schulz, accredited the restoration of the Hohkönigsburg with the
seriousness of a 'Carneval in May'. *Simplicissimus*, 4 May 1908, p. 96.

Karneval im Mai

(Zeichnung von Wilhelm Schulz)

Nach der Maskerade in der Hochkönigsburg erhält Leoncavallo den Auftrag, eine neue Oper zu Dirings Kostümen zu schreiben.

— 96 —

5.9 (*cont.*)

travelling members averting the Society to buildings abroad and suggesting intervention continued until as late as the 1980s.[89]

During the nineteenth and early twentieth centuries, interest in the fate of foreign national monuments was high among the educated travelling classes and the reaction to possible destruction was often emotional. While individuals from France, Germany and Britain were involved in campaigning for monuments on foreign soil, in Britain, more than in Germany or France, members of the public expected some form of intervention. The remnants of the Grand Tour and classical education stirred a particular passion for Italian monuments, but interest in the heritage of many countries was strong, and the public saw itself as a custodian for the fate of heritage across the globe.[90] In a few cases foreign intervention was legitimised in terms of a shared heritage, such as with Brunswick Castle for Anglo-German, or with buildings in Calais for Anglo-French history.[91] In other cases the buildings' importance for literature, art and travel had fostered their status as universal monuments, such as for Heidelberg Castle or the Roman Theatre in Orange. However, intervention also occurred similarly keenly on behalf of local heritage, such as the Pont Neuf in Cahors.

While all the French, German and British cases discussed show that the protests relied primarily on strong and ever-growing local and national protest movements, the major anti-restoration and anti-demolition voices in England, France and Germany clearly all welcomed the support by foreign preservationists. Initiatives for collaboration went both ways, sometimes being offered, sometimes being solicited. Foreigners claiming they were more advanced in matters of anti-restoration might not be desired, but foreign support remained valued regardless of the state of international relations. The wisdom of international intervention was often questioned in the first instance, but after some shilly-shallying it was mostly decided to intervene. The tone of the informal communications was amicable, especially between long-term correspondents such as Thackeray Turner and Alphonse Guillon or Hermann Muthesius.

While the major collaborations between France, Germany and Britain were of a bilateral nature, the contacts between English, German and French preservationists were also used to intervene in cases in third countries, particularly in Italy and Greece which all northern Europeans

[89] SPAB Archives, 'Greece'; 'Istanbul St. Sophia Turkey'.
[90] SPAB Archives, 'Architectural Restoration in Italy'.
[91] SPAB Archives, 'Calais Notre Dame'; 'Calais Porte de Guise'.

continued to regard as their heritage.[92] Common intervention also occurred in small countries like Monaco,[93] and in European colonies and protectorates, regardless of a more general competition between European preservationists to get their hands on monuments in contested colonial spaces.[94] In many ways intervention here was easier as it could rest on the idea of the civilising mission and European custodianship, while little regard had to be paid to public opinion of the countries under question. The first recorded correspondence between the SPAB and Guillon significantly concerned Egypt two years before the start of British occupation,[95] establishing a ground for collaboration outside of national territories. On the other hand, the trust established through interactions for British and German monuments between the SPAB and Muthesius led in 1901 to a common intervention in Turkey. Unsure what to do with news about the fate of Ottoman antiquities raised by a member of the British public in *The Times* and in a letter to the SPAB, Thackeray Turner, rather than starting a British campaign, trusted in the power of German informal imperialism and asked Muthesius whether he 'might know some persons of influence interested in antiquities who would be willing to call the attention of the German Government to the matter, with a view to that Government approaching the Turkish Government with regard to the damage which is being done'.[96] Muthesius contacted the Imperial German Archaeological Institute, who then wrote to the General Consul in Beirut.[97]

Whilst backing by foreign opinion was viewed as an effective publicity stunt, making collaboration on domestic monuments known in one's own country was often seen to be rather detrimental to success and was commonly avoided. Conversely, when addressing their members it seemed important for each national movement to claim the initiative for international action as well as for the original ideas of anti-restoration. The SPAB could claim most credit by tracing its link to John Ruskin and did so constantly to enhance its profile. Yet in the German-speaking world, Dehio's famous *konservieren nicht restaurieren* was regarded as the *locus classicus* after the *Heidelberger Schloßstreit* eclipsing any earlier or foreign origins of

[92] On common intervention in Florence see Thackeray Turner to Charles Normand, 28 Oct. 1898, SPAB Archives, 'Destructive Works in Florence'. On SPAB's earlier activity see files on 'Florence Bigallo' and 'Florence Ponte Vecchio'.

[93] See for instance Guillon's interaction with the Governor-General of Monaco about the city gateway on behalf of SPAB and *L'Ami des Monuments*, SPAB, *Annual Report*, 16 (1893), 42–7.

[94] On tension between French and British preservationists in Egypt see SPAB Archives, 'Cairo Coptic Churches Egypt'; 'Arab Monuments'.

[95] SPAB Archives, 3rd Committee Minute Book, 25 November 1880.

[96] Thackeray Turner to Muthesius, 5 March 1901, SPAB Archives, 'Ottoman Antiquities'.

[97] Muthesius to Thackeray Turner, 6 May 1901, SPAB Archives, 'Ottoman Antiquities'.

the maxim.[98] The SPAB, which drew most prestige from the international action, announced it had 'reason to believe that the zeal which is now beginning to be exhibited for the preservation of national antiquities, particularly in France and Germany, has been stimulated by the action of the Society in England'[99] and more specifically claimed credit for founding its French counterpart, while *L'Ami des Monuments* tried to give the impression that SPAB was inspired by the French.[100] Charles Normand, who frequently highlighted the French origins of anti-restoration, was moreover indignant to find in a publication by the Belgian preservationist Charles Buls that the German *Denkmalbewegung* rather than his own Society was quoted favourably. Normand's foreword to the article is telling about international cooperation on the one hand and insistence on national primacy on the other:

> We never neglect to inform Europe, Africa and America about so many interesting efforts that would otherwise not exceed a local radius. If these ideas come from important personalities such as M Buls they merit special attention; one will only regret that M Buls draws his examples from Belgian or German cases; he could have found cases of much greater interest concerning France and other countries in the seventeen volumes of *L'Ami des Monuments et des Arts*, and in the sixteen volumes of the *Société des Amis des Monuments parisiens*; the authors of these articles have signalled to Europe the ideas of the present movement in favour of urban or rural sites, of monuments and memories.[101]

Part of this self-portrayal stemmed simply from the fact that the anti-restoration associations were activist groups needing to present results to their subscribers, but it also shows that a rhetoric of international collaboration and national superiority could exist simultaneously. The two opposite discourses converged when international collaboration itself became a subject of international competition.

---

[98] See Dehio, *Denkmalschutz und Denkmalpflege im Neunzehnten Jahrhundert;* M. Wohlleben (ed.), *Konservieren nicht restaurieren: Streitschriften zur Denkmalpflege um 1900* (Braunschweig, 1988), pp. 88–103.

[99] SPAB, *Annual Report*, 10 (1887), 44.   [100] *L'Ami des Monuments*, 9 (1895), 261.

[101] *L'Ami des Monuments*, 17 (1903), 178–86.

CHAPTER 6

'A yardstick for a people's cultural attainment'

All civilised countries have, at the present time, like our own, legislation that protects the monuments of the past . . . This is the case
not only in the great European states like England, Germany, Austria,
Prussia, Italy, but also in the secondary states like Portugal, Belgium,
the Netherlands, Greece, Bulgaria, Finland etc. The same applies outside of Europe. Without mentioning Algeria and Tunisia, which are
truly speaking only an extension of France, we find regulations for
the protection of ancient monuments in Egypt, in the Asian parts of
Turkey, in British India, Japan and reaching as far as China. America
did not want to stay behind. Brazil and Mexico also took preservation
measures . . . I don't have the intention, of course, to take you to all of
the countries whose name I mentioned. This would mean a complete
trip around the world and this journey would take, like Jules Verne's,
at least 80 days. You do not have 80 days that you could give me . . . If
you agree we will not leave Europe and inside Europe we will make
a choice. We will only select nations whose example can interest or
educate us.

Louis Grandjean, 'Les Monuments historiques à l'étranger'. Conference
delivered at the *Exposition universelle* in Paris in 1900.[1]

Over the course of the nineteenth century, the growing enthusiasm for
heritage acquired a complex legislative dimension. Sporadic calls for more
state intervention could be heard since the 1820s, but between 1870 and
1914 a new, almost obsessive, preoccupation with legislation emerged. Louis
Grandjean, the French Inspector of Monuments, when asked to provide
an international audience with an overview of international developments
during the *Exposition universelle* in Paris in 1900 found it hard to limit
himself to eighty minutes. Others promised similar restrain as 'laws and

---

[1] MAP, 80/1/32, Dossier 'Législation étrangère concernant les Monuments historiques'/'Les Monuments historiques à l'étranger'.

edicts are not for a June afternoon'.[2] But enraptured audiences went on virtual voyages not to see exotic curiosities but to listen to global trends in legislation, following experts and documentary evidence shipped around the globe for much longer than Phileas Fogg. Although voluntary preservationism was steadily growing, it was now widely assumed that it was not sufficient. A German preservationist spoke also for international attitudes when claiming that: 'Without misconceiving what the enthusiasm of individual persons and the activity of associations did to awake and divulge the understanding of monuments, support and care on the part of the State are, however, necessary to preserve and protect the great heritage of the past.'[3] Germans even quickly invented a new word, *Denkmalschutz*, to differentiate the legal protection of monuments from more general care, *Denkmalpflege*. Across Europe, it was assumed that the numerous state institutions already in place in most countries could not achieve their greater purpose, and that the existing royal prescripts, ministerial decrees, circulars and local by-laws protecting cultural objects were insufficiently robust, as they were spread across different areas of the law, from civil to penal codes, administrative law and buildings regulations.[4] It was generally argued that only a designated Monument Act could ensure effective protection. By establishing that heritage was a matter of national importance, it strengthened existing institutions not only through its actual provisions, but its symbolic weight. In countries without prior state preservation, on the other hand, a formal Act became seen as a most effective way to create a lasting impact. As Grandjean indicated virtually every European and a number of non-European countries shared this concern. While earlier in the century the Papal States (1820) and Greece (1834) had passed laws to prevent northern Europeans from exporting antique monuments, Monument Acts were now passed inter alia in Sweden (1867), Hungary (1881), the United Kingdom (1882, 1892, 1900, 1913), Finland (1883), Turkey (1884), Tunisia (1886), France (1887, 1914), Bulgaria (1889), Romania (1892), Greece (1899), Portugal (1901), Italy (1902, 1909) and British India (1904). In Switzerland, where legislation was in the hand of the Cantons, Vaud, Bern, Neufchatel and Tessin passed Acts between 1898 and 1907, as did the German states of Hesse (1902) and Oldenburg (1911), to which can be added various so-called 'partial laws' on aesthetic disfiguration and

[2] Stirling Maxwell, 'A Reasonable Policy for Protecting Ancient Buildings', in SPAB *Annual Report*, 31 (1908), 92.
[3] J. Kohte, *Die Pflege der Kunstdenkmäler in Italien* (Berlin, 1898), p. 1.
[4] F. Hammer, *Die geschichtliche Entwicklung des Denkmalrechts in Deutschland* (Tübingen, 1995), pp. 29–31.

prehistoric monuments in other German states, for instance in Prussia in 1902, 1907 and 1914.

On an international scale, France, Germany and Britain were thus neither the first nor the last countries to pass legislation. As such, Grandjean's 'great European states' offer not just a prism for the wider transnational exchange between all these countries but also provide insight into how particular national motives and obstacles influenced shape and success of legislation. Proponents of legislation in each country needed to tackle different levels of need and had to overcome different forms of opposition. France already possessed an elaborate administrative apparatus since the July Monarchy, albeit with little legal power over monuments. When Germany was unified, some states had a monument administration, while no provisions existed in others. In Britain, on the other hand the state was not really engaged in monument preservation at all prior to the 1870s.

For each country, a rich literature with a national focus has drawn attention to how local cases and broader national political circumstance shaped particular laws. Overwhelmingly, however, the results of legislative debates are used to prove the strength or the weakness of heritage consciousness. While some authors celebrate the growing protection of heritage, most see in the advent of legislation a defeat of the voluntary sector. Regardless of which side they are on in the State-versus-public debate, however, virtually all deplore their own country's delay with regard to the other European states.[5] These judgments draw on arguments found in late-nineteenth

---

[5] In the historiography on Britain, the Ancient Monuments Acts have a prominent place as they mark the founding moment of state preservation: N. Boulting, 'The Law's Delays. Conservationist Legislation in the British Isles', in Fawcett (ed.), *Future of the Past*, pp. 9–34; Chippendale, 'First Ancient Monuments Act', 1–55; A. Saunders, 'A Century of Ancient Monuments Legislation 1882–1992', *Antiquaries Journal*, 63 (1983), 11–33; T. Murray, 'The History, Philosophy and Sociology of Archaeology. The Case of the Ancient Monuments Protection Act 1882', in L. Pinsky, A. Wyle (eds.), *Critical Traditions in Contemporary Archaeology* (Cambridge, 1989), pp. 55–67; on the acts as proof of the strength of heritage consciouness see esp. Champion, 'Protecting the Monuments', pp. 38–56; for arguments about the weakness of 'heritage consciousness' see Mandler, *Stately Home*, pp. 153–91; Hunter, 'Introduction', in Hunter (ed.), *Preserving the Past*, pp. 1–16, esp. 8–9. In French scholarship, the treatment of heritage legislation is caught in the polemical dispute between republican and royalist/catholic interpretations. It is documented extensively in earlier research such as P. Verdier, 'Le Service des Monuments historiques. Son histoire, organisation, administration, législation (1830–1934)', *Congrès Archéologique de France 1934* (Paris, 1934), pp. 53–246; R. Brichet, *Le Régime juridique des monuments historique en France* (Paris, 1952); P. Dussaule, *La Loi et le Service des monuments historiques français* (2 vols., Paris, 1974); A. Paléologue, 'Législation des monuments historiques', *Monuments Historiques*, 169 (1990), 19–24; C. Rigambert *Le Droit de l'archéologie française* (Paris, 1996); F. Chatelain, C. Pattyn, J. Chatelain, *Oeuvres d'art et objets de collection en droit français* (Paris, 1997); *Protection du patrimoine historique et esthétique de la France* (Paris, 1997). Most recent studies discuss the laws only as a postscript to the innovations of the July Monarchy, cf. A. Chastel, 'La

and early-twentieth century sources pleading for the emulation of foreign cases to remedy national backwardness. Yet when one juxtaposes such comparative analyses from different countries and languages, it soon becomes clear that they all employed a rhetoric of national 'delay' to push for more regulation.[6] The transnational perspective thus challenges all judgements about backwardness; it also helps to shift the gaze from debates about successes and failures to broader issues. While it is certainly true that the legislative boom can in part be ascribed to a heightened heritage awareness and the wish to protect monuments, picturesque sites and landscapes against threats posed by accelerated industrialisation, building booms and exportation for a steadily developing art market, the pre-occupation with legislation also was linked to much wider social, political and economic debates. The growth of heritage legislation cannot be divided from the contemporaneous extension of state control into all kinds of hitherto private areas from education to health and maternity. Debates about cultural property were part of a profound redefinition not only of the place of the individual in relation to the state, but also about the role of the old elites and the Churches in the age of mass politics, as well as about the relation between centre and periphery in nation state and empire.[7] Finally, heritage legislation was not just the result of national debates, but was fundamentally shaped by the growing competition between states during the age of *Weltpolitik* as it was thought to contribute to the struggle for mastery.

Notion de patrimoine', in Nora (ed.), *Les Lieux de mémoire*, I, pp. 1433–69, here p. 1454, Bercé, *Dès Monuments historiques au patrimoine*, pp. 52–3, 58–60; Choay, *L'Allégorie du patrimoine*, pp. 108–11; Poulot, *Patrimoine et musées*, pp. 121–2, 132–3, while Jean-Michel Leniaud's studies on the laws' place in anti-clerical policies aim to question the legitimacy of the state's intervention: *L'Utopie française*, pp. 19–21, Leniaud, *Les Archipels du passé*, pp. 213–41. The notion of 'delay' is prominent across the board. German authors, while showing the multiplicity of reasons that helped and impeded legislation in the different German states, also insist on Germany's backwardness: Hammer, *Entwicklung des Denkmalrechts*; M. Siegel, *Denkmalpflege als öffentliche Aufgabe. Eine ökonomische, institutionelle und historische Untersuchung* (Göttingen, 1985), pp. 35–40, 291–4. A stronger contextual analysis is given in Speitkamp, *Verwaltung der Geschichte*, pp. 287–394. On eighteenth- and early nineteenth-century decrees see N. Huse (ed.), *Denkmalpflege. Deutsche Texte aus drei Jahrhunderten* (Munich, 1984), pp. 17–34.

[6] This chapter focusses largely on legislation for the protection of sites in situ. For debates about the export of movables see U. Protz, 'National Treastures'/'Tresor Nationaux': The control of the Export of Works of Art and the Construction of 'National Heritage'/Patrimoine in France and the United Kingdom, 1884–1959 (unpublished Ph.D. dissertation, European University Institute, 2009).

[7] On etatisation see Speitkamp, *Verwaltung der Geschichte*. p. 315; on links to broader debates about property, Bailkin, *The Culture of Property*.

'A primrose by a river's brim'

If all citizens were aesthetes, there would be no need for heritage legislation, or as Baldwin Brown put it: 'If we be sensible of the charm [of monuments] the question of preservation is for us settled – we would sacrifice anything rather than let these scenes and monuments be lost to modern life.'[8] In this spirit, a majority of preservation societies felt the true solution to the problem of monument protection to consist in transforming their fellow countrymen into lovers of monuments. However, they also conceded that complete public sensitization was a chimera; 'we cannot make others sensible of the charm. To the mass of mankind', like to Wordsworth's Peter Bell, '"A primrose by a river's brim" will be a yellow primrose and nothing more, and we cannot expect from them very active sympathy in this ideal presentment of the case. On the other hand there are arguments tending to the same and which are of a more practical kind.'[9]

Such arguments had to be strong enough to overcome the view of certain legislators that a Monument Act would only 'gratify the antiquarian tastes of the few at the public expense'.[10] Even more importantly, they had to demonstrate why national claims outweighed individual property rights. A minority of Radicals, especially in Britain, wanted to remedy what in their eyes had been a wrongful seizure of land and artistic treasures by the elites.[11] For them, actual preservation was a lesser priority than national reappropriation. The majority of preservationists, however, followed a more moderate line, trying to avoid harsh attacks on the rights of private property, while at the same time seeking to establish that monuments were of national concern and their preservation was of public utility.

Precedents of such beliefs were used as a first resource. In France, preservationists drew heavily on the revolutionary invention of the principle of *patrimoine national*. Bills prepared by the government, but also most other pro-legislation texts, generally opened with a teleological account of how the heroic and revolutionary history of preservation culminated in the state providing for the monuments of a unified nation.[12] Adding excerpts from Lenoir, Chateaubriand, Montalembert, Hugo, and others to the appendices of legal projects and parliamentary papers undergirded the foundation myth.[13] Proponents of monument legislation in other countries

---

[8] Brown, *Care of Ancient Monuments*, p. 28.   [9] Ibid.
[10] *Parliamentary Debates*, Lords, 273, 28 July 1882, col. 15 (Marques of Salisbury).
[11] See Bailkin, *Culture of Property*.   [12] Challamel, *Loi du 30 Mars 1887*, pp. 1–2.
[13] *Documents parlementaires*, No. 214. Sénat. Annexe au procès-verbal de la séance du 17 juin 1913. Rapport fait au nom de la commission chargée d'examiner la proposition de loi de M. Audiffred

likewise used this 'beginning of the literary propaganda'.[14] Dubbing France
the 'motherland of modern *Denkmalpflege*',[15] the deployment of fine words
in the service of monument protection was greatly admired:

> The French have . . . distinguished themselves by the truly classic expression
> they have given through the pens of some of their greatest writers to the
> principles and sentiments that underlie the modern interest in these memo-
> rials of the past. The Monuments Act of 1887 is of comparatively recent
> date but has a history behind it. It was really in preparation for fifty years
> and during this period writers like Montalembert, Chateaubriand, Guizot
> and Victor Hugo and others inspired by them, were moulding the thought
> of the time and furnishing mottoes for future works in this field in every
> land.[16]

Hence, German and British authors adopted the 'creed of this entire school',
Montalembert's '*Les longs souvenirs font des grands peuples*' as their motto.[17]
However, they also went digging for local traditions. While neither the
administrative nature of eighteenth-century German prescripts for the protection of monuments, such as those issued by the Markgraf von Bayreuth,
nor Schinkel's or von Quast's memoranda provided equal vignettes, Goethe
proved a reliable source for quotations. His words written in the context
of the protest against the French spoliation of Italian Art, were reinter-
preted to defend heritage against internal enemies: 'All works of art belong
as such to the whole of humankind and their possession entails the duty
to take care of their conservation. Whoever neglects this duty, whoever
directly or indirectly contributes to their harm or ruin, saddles barbar-
ianism upon himself and the disdain of all educated people of present
and future times will be his punishment.'[18] In Britain, Samuel Johnson

---

et plusieurs de ses collègues, tendant à la création d'une caisse des monuments historique par M.
Audiffred, sénateur, p. 35.

[14] P. Clemen, *Die Denkmalpflege in Frankreich* (Berlin, 1898), first published in *Zeitschrift für Bauwesen*
48 (1898), repr. in Clemen, *Gesammelte Aufsätze* (Düsseldorf, 1948), pp. 143–59, hereafter cited from
Gesammelte Aufsätze, qu. p. 145.

[15] A. von Oechelhaeuser, *Wege, Ziele und Gefahren der Denkmalpflege. Festrede bei dem Feierlichen
Akte des Rektoratswechsels an der Großherzoglich- Technischen Hochschule Fridericiana zu Karlsruhe
am 20. November 1909* (Karslruhe, 1909), p. 5.

[16] Brown, *Care of Ancient Monuments*, p. 74.

[17] Oechelhaeuser, *Wege, Ziele und Gefahren der Denkmalpflege*, p. 6; Brown, *Care of Ancient Monuments*
printed the quote on the title page; both H. Loersch, *Das französische Gesetz vom 30. März 1887.
Ein Beitrag zum Recht der Denkmalpflege* (Bonn, 1897) and E. Pariset, Université de France. Faculté
de droit de Lyon, *Droit romain: Dispositions de dernière volonté à Rome et dans le droit ancien. Droit
français: les Monuments historiques. Thèse pour le doctorat* (Paris, 1891) prefixed their texts with the
motto; cf. also quoted in Clemen, *Die Denkmalpflege in Frankreich*, p. 145.

[18] J.W. von Goethe, *Propyläen. Eine periodische Schrift* (Tübingen, 1799, repr. Darmstadt 1965) II., 1.
Stück, pp. 119f. On uses see Speitkamp, *Verwaltung der Geschichte*, p. 380.

could be quoted to the effect that the 'ideas which underlie' the interest in ancient monuments 'are indeed a part of the mental equipment of rational humanity'.[19]

In addition to mobilising the preservationist tradition, more intellectual substance was given to legislation through the notion of an 'ideal joint possession' that reconciled the individual or corporeal ownership with the idea that monuments were also the property of all. This was articulated within different philosophical models.[20] Some built on ideas by Abbé, Grégoire, von Quast, Ruskin and others that the spirit of the creator inhabited an object to argue that the creator's propriety right outweighed those of any current owner. Hence the present generation had collective duties as guardians rather than individual rights as owners. While in France, some also conceptualised joint possession in terms of the Rousseauiste social contract, others pushed the essentialist arguments even further by linking it to blood and soil. The authors of a Bill introduced in 1912, drew on Hippolyte Taine's *De L'Intelligence*, arguing that because the land determined the race, and the race the individual and both together the work of the intellect, one could derive 'the right of the collectivity to have these works, this common intellectual *patrimoine*, conserved'.[21] The German *Heimat-* and *Denkmalbewegung* expressed similar ideas about the connection between land, nationality, and property by using the popular idea that a 'German law' had preceded the spread of Roman Law. The 'German Law' doctrine was widely used in the Whilhelmine period to propose an alternative theoretical framework to socialism and proclaimed that both *Gemeinschaft* and *Gesellschaft* preceded individual property.[22] As it reduced the status of private ownership to usufruct, it soon permeated debates about preservationism.[23] The leader of the *Heimatschutz* movement Rudorff, for instance spoke of 'an ideal joint possession of God's earth

---

[19] Brown, *Care of Ancient Monuments*, p. 12.

[20] *Documents parlementaires*, No. 941. Chambre des députés. Annexe au procès-verbal de la 2e séance du 11 avril 1911. Premier Rapport fait au nom de la commission de l'enseignement et des beaux-arts chargée d'examiner le projet de loi relatif à la conservation des monuments et objets ayant un intérêt historique ou artistique, par M. Théodore Reinach (Savoie), député, p. 2.

[21] *Documents parlementaires*, No. 1898. Chambre des députés. Annexe au procès verbal de la séance du 23 mai 1912. Proposition de loi relative à la protection et à la conservation du patrimoine historique et artistique de la France (renvoyé à la commission de l'enseignement et des beaux-arts), présentée par M. de Chappedelaine, député, pp. 5–6.

[22] F. Endemann, *Einführung in das Studium des Bürgerlichen Gesetzbuchs. Lehrbuch des Bürgerlichen Rechts* (3rd–5th edn, Berlin, 1900), II, pp. 262–5 and even more favourably towards Germanic law Endemann. *Lehrbuch des Bürgerlichen Rechts. Einführung in das Studium des Bürgerlichen Gesetzbuchs* (8th–9th revised edn, 1905), II, p. 486.

[23] Speitkamp, *Verwaltung der Geschichte*, pp. 376–7.

that appertains to man as man'.[24] Georg Dehio defended the right of
the public to interfere with the restoration of Heidelberg Castle in 1901
on the basis that 'the entire German people is its ideal co-proprietor'.[25]
The art historian Paul Weber campaigned for a link between preservation
and land reform, when he declared at the Federal Congress of German
Landreformers that 'the general public has certain claims, in the opinion of
our time, it poses a certain right of co-propriety of the artistic heritage of
the past'.[26] Far from being considered radical, 'German Law' philosophy
was widely accepted and actively used in preparing several Monuments
Acts, especially the Hessian Monument Act (1902), a failed draft in Baden
(1913), and the Prussian Excavation Act (1914).[27]

The question whether art and monuments could be treated like any
other form of property or whether they had inherently more collective
sides engaged a variety of scholars in Britain too.[28] While links between
preservation and land reform were generally associated with Radicalism in
Britain, prominent Tories also rehearsed ideas about ideal joint-possession.
In a debate at the Lords, the former Indian Vice-Roy, great landowner and
preservationist Lord Curzon asserted that:

> We regard the national monuments to which this Bill refers as part of the
> heritage and history of the nation. They are part of the heritage of the
> nation, because every citizen feels an interest in them although he may
> not own them and they are part of the history of the nation because they
> are documents just as valuable in reading the records of the past as is any
> manuscript or parchment deed to which you can refer . . . I believe they
> [the owners] do generally recognise that they stand with regard to these
> monuments not merely in the position of private owners of property, but
> that they are owners of that which is, in a sense – a broad sense, I admit – a
> national possession, for which they are trustees to the nation at large.[29]

Having established the principle of collective 'inheritance' as a prerequisite
for legislation,[30] preservationists did not tire to find utilitarian arguments

---

[24] E. Rudorff, 'Über das Verhältnis des modernen Lebens zur Natur', *Preußische Jahrbücher*, 45 (1880), 261–76, qu. p. 275.
[25] Dehio, *Heidelberger Schloss*, p. 35.
[26] P. Weber, *Heimatschutz, Denkmalpflege und Bodenreform. Vortrag gehalten auf dem 15. Bundestag deutscher Bodenreformer zu Berlin am 4. Oktober 1905* (Berlin, 1906), pp. 8, 17.
[27] A.B. Schmidt, 'Rechtsfragen des deutschen Denkmaschutzes', in *Festgabe für Rudolfph Sohm, dargebracht zum Goldenen Doktorjubiläum* (Munich, Leipzig, 1914), pp. 143–97, here p. 172; Preußisches Herrenhaus. Sess. 1914. *Drucksachen* Nr. 9, Entwurf eines Ausgrabungsgesetzes, Anlagen; Speitkamp, *Verwaltung der Geschichte* p. 381, note 61.
[28] Bailkin, *Culture of Property*, p. 13.
[29] *Parliamentary Debates*, Lords, 5th Ser., 11, 30 April 1912, cols. 871–2.
[30] Brown, *Care of Ancient Monuments*, p. 29.

as to why heritage was not just a right and a duty, but also a benefit. German preservationists in particular highlighted how the preservation of monuments and sites would be economically beneficial for attracting tourists.[31] Others stressed the contribution of preservation for public health, showing how open spaces and clean air would contribute to the growing political preoccupation with the quantity and quality of the population and attendant demands to improve the nation's fitness for military needs.[32] Drawing on Ruskin again, they argued by analogy that cultural monuments were necessary for the spiritual well-being of the nation.[33]

To whomever this seemed stretched, or who remained worried about the negative effects upon owners, arguments about nation and empire building were presented. In both Germany and France, calls for more legislation rode on the wave of nation-building efforts after 1871. In the Third Republic's attempts to overcome political turmoil through the creation of a common history and heritage, historic monuments maintained the important place the July Monarchy had assigned to them. In Germany, where the restoration of national monuments had played such a prominent role in cultural nationalism since the Napoleonic Wars, many argued that preservation was now ever more necessary to create identification not only with an individual's locality but with the fatherland as a whole.[34] British preservationists equally adduced the benefits for community building, but their focus was less on reconciling the four nations on the archipelago, than on creating links across the entire Empire. Potential benefits for the Empire were mentioned in the first debate of the Ancient Monuments Bill in the Commons in 1875. Imperial concerns also animated the National Trust and the SPAB throughout the period and opened Baldwin Brown's seminal plea for legislation:

> Great Britain in relation to the Empire at large . . . must always remain the soil in which are rooted all the traditional memories of the race. In the tangible evidence of a storied past, this island possesses what is necessarily wanting to our colonies and to the offshoots from those colonies . . . The

[31] On the use of this argument in the Prussian Diet in defence of the Prussian Anti-Distifuration Act (1907) and its role in passing the Monument Act in Oldernburg (1911) see Speitkamp, *Verwaltung der Geschichte*, pp. 295–8.
[32] Brown, *Care of Ancient Monuments*, p. 28. On the broader context G. Bock, P. Thane (eds.), *Maternity and Gender Policies. Women and the Rise of the European Welfare States, 1880–1950s* (London, New York, 1991).
[33] Brown, *Care of Ancient Monuments*, p. 29.
[34] For instance *Verband deutscher Architekten und Ingenieur-Vereine* to *Ministerium für landwirtschaftliche Angelegenheiten zu Berlin*, Feb. 1878, GStA PK, I. HA Rep. 87 B Ministerium für Landwirtschaft, Domänen u. Forsten, Nr. 3131, fol. 4–5.

interest which these memorials excite in the minds of our kinsfolk from across the seas is very great, and will probably increase as the generations advance. The feelings thus kindled help to keep alive throughout the Empire the sense of the unity of the stock [. . . the monuments] are imperial assets, and on economic, almost on political, grounds, the duty of safeguarding them might well be recognized even by the least artistic and least antiquarian of the population.[35]

Culture wars

Yet the least artistic and least antiquarian of the population were not so easily swayed. In every country passing legislation was a long and arduous process. Paradoxically laissez-faire Britain was the first of our three countries to acquire a Monument Act, but nine years elapsed between John Lubbock's introduction of a first Ancient Monument Bill and the passing of the much watered-down Act in 1882. In France passing the first Monument Act took almost fifteen years. The first three decades after Germany's unification saw much ink spilled on drafting bills, but all ended in the shredder. Bills drafted in Prussia and Baden in the 1880s encountered so much opposition that they had to be withdrawn before even being introduced to the Diets, and repeated attempts after the turn of the century in these two German states shared the same fate. In the end, Prussia refrained from attempting to pass a comprehensive act, but focussed instead on partial aspects such as the regulation of excavations and the aesthetic appeal of historic towns through building regulations. Only two comprehensive Monument Acts were passed in German states, the first in the Grand Duchy of Hesse in 1902, the second in the Duchy of Oldenburg in 1911.

Although the least artistic and least antiquarian of the population played their part in this – in Germany they even organised themselves with the help of the German Federation of Industrialists in a commission with the ringing name *Kommission zur Beseitigung der Auswüchse der Heimtschutzbestrebungen* – 'Commission for the Abolition of the Excrescences of the Preservation Movement' – hardline philistines were in many ways not the biggest obstacle.[36] On occasion, preservationism helped to overcome political disagreements. Lubbock's Bill, for instance, was supported by a

---

[35] Brown, *Care of Ancient Monuments*, pp. 3–4, see also pp. 30–31; National Trust, *Report* (1896), pp. 12–13; see also Miss Lena Ashwell's address at the General Meeting, SPAB, *Annual Report*, 44 (1921).

[36] On this commission founded in 1911 see Speitkamp, *Verwaltung der Geschichte*, p. 372; W. Oberkrome, *Deutsche Heimat: nationale Konzeption und regionale Praxis von Naturschutz, Landschaftsgestaltung und Kulturpolitik in Westfalen-Lippe und Thüringen (1900–1960)* (Paderborn, 2004), pp. 70–1.

number of MPs across the political spectrum. The nationalist, revanchist, antisemitic and deeply catholic boulangiste député Maurice Barrès also managed to rally some of his political opponents, among them one of the authors of the Separation Law, the laïcist and pacifist activist Ferdinand Buisson and the socialist Albert Thomas, editor of *L'Humanité*.[37]

However, most of the time, debates about preservation legislation were deeply divisive. As state intervention on behalf of monuments and sites was tied up with concerns over the place of the old order in an age of mass politics, debates became caught in the major socio-political conflicts of the time, from anti-aristocratic land reform to secular–Catholic clashes.[38] Support for codification was not solely based on love for monuments, while opposition to legislation was not necessarily founded on opposition to preservation. While preservation could be considered independently of politics in the meetings of preservation associations, and to a certain extent in the general press, as Peter Mandler argues for the British case:

> Once it entered wider debate in Parliament, however, the emerging consensus among scholarly and amenity groups hit stormy water. Liberals had to decide whether they (and their voters) cared enough about castles to extend legislative protection – or perhaps whether legislative control over historic buildings was worthwhile simply as a stroke against the landowners... Tories had to decide whether they cared enough about castles to accept the infringements on private property – and more strokes against the land – that such legislation would entail.[39]

In Britain, battles over preservation legislation were largely battles over anti-aristocratic reform, although questions about the relationship between England versus the Celtic fringe also played some part.[40] In France, on the other hand, concerns about infringements on private property were less important than the 'War of the Two Frances'. The 1887 Act was not only an Act for the better protection of monuments, but also a measure to enhance a centralist approach and weaken the influence of local communities and the Catholic Church. It raised corresponding opposition. After the Separation of State and Church matters became even more complicated. While before 1905, *classement* of churches could be interpreted as an anti-clerical measure as it extended state influence over the Church, now the failure to list

---

[37] Chambre des députés, Séance du 16 janvier 1911; Leniaud, *Les Archipels du passé*, p. 233.
[38] For the broader background see C. Clark, W. Kaiser (eds.), *Culture Wars. Secular-Catholic Conflict in Nineteenth-Century Europe* (Cambridge, New York, 2003).
[39] Mandler, *Stately Home*, pp. 187–8.
[40] Bailkin, *Culture of Property*, pp. 29–117; Murray, 'Ancient Monuments Protection Act 1882', pp. 61, 64. Chippendale, 'First Ancient Monuments Act', 15.

churches also became one. To allocate tax money for church restoration could be seen as a financing of religion by the state, forbidden by the terms of the Separation. Consequently, anti-clerical preservationists had to decide whether they wanted to risk being seen as pro-clerical by financing the repair of churches. Clericals had to decide whether preservation was worth a further extension of the state's influence into the sphere of religion.[41]

In Germany, the conflicts surrounding preservation were even more multifaceted. Like in France, state preservation was to a certain degree motivated by the wish to obtain control over Churches and local communities. Consequently, in the aftermath of the *Kulturkampf*, the Catholic Church vehemently opposed any attempt by the state to control buildings through preservation and successfully impeded the earliest German attempts at legislation in the states of Baden and Prussia.[42] The mere fear of opposition sometimes prevented the introduction of a Bill. Several conservators in Germany, especially in Bavaria and Baden opposed formal legislation as they felt they had more possibilities to informally negotiate with owners and to obtain the collaboration of the Churches (both Protestant and Catholic) if no formal Monument Act was passed that might raise fears over the state's interference. Moreover, in Germany preservation got caught in the struggles about competences in a federal system. All of the many attempts to create an imperial Monument Act after 1870 failed because of the opposition of the South German states, which feared a loss of their sovereignty in cultural policies.[43]

Sometimes, these various conflicts created unlikely alliances. For instance, in the 1880s, opposition to the French Monuments Bill in the Senate temporarily united clericals such as de Gavardie worried about religious interests, and anti-clericals, such as Émile Combes, who defended provincial independence and the sanctity of private property.[44] More often, ardent preservationists from all three countries turned against preservation legislation if they feared it could endanger other political aims. In France, Charles Beauquier, initiator of several laws and constant campaigner for a broader, more local understanding of heritage, when confronted with Barrès' plea to protect all old churches by law, let his anti-clericalism (and the memories of the Dreyfus Affair) prevail over his preservationism.

---

[41] Leniaud, *Archipels*, pp. 191–241.
[42] G. Hans, *Denkmalschutz in Baden im 19. und 20. Jahrhundert* (Münster, 1985), pp. 46–69, 77–93.
[43] Speitkamp, *Verwaltung der Geschichte*, pp. 154–63.
[44] *JO*, Annexe 83, Séance du Sénat des 10 et 13 avril 1886. Première délibération, p. 608; On Combes see G. Merle, *Émile Combes* (Paris, 1995).

Despite their common patronage of regionalist societies, Beauquier interrupted Barrès several times during the debates in the Chamber and, using a Viollet-le-Ducian definition of monument, which he otherwise constantly fought to overcome, declared that only exemplary artistic value should determine the *classement*.[45] He claimed that if God existed he would take care of his churches:

> While waiting for this new progress of the laic spirit, let the clerics moan about the destruction of the vulgar temples they call 'Houses of God'. Let us simply note the failure of the faith, which we are told can 'move mountains', but which, today, cannot even move a tile on a roof through which it rains into the temple. Aren't the freemasons right to put their work under the protection of the 'Grand Architect of the Universe'? What a poor architect is he, who is not even capable of preventing a place consecrated to his cult from collapsing![46]

In Britain, fear of anti-lordism had a similarly negative effect on the preservationist feelings of many aesthete Tories.[47] Even Lord Curzon, while pushing for draconian monument legislation as Viceroy in India, was unwilling as a prominent Tory to join the Liberal drive for state control as far as English soil was concerned, and refused to have his own holdings controlled by the state.[48]

Finally, opposition came also from within 'the state'. While some government officials and civil servants championed preservation legislation to extend control over churches, local government and private associations, especially in France and Germany, 'the state' had no uniform view and in all of the three countries (i.e. for Germany in many of the individual states) some of the strongest opposition came from within the administration. Especially those in charge of the budget were continuously reluctant to face the costs that the creation of Monuments Commissions and the restoration and conservation of monuments, as well as indemnities for expropriation would entail. The fear that if preservationists were given an

---

[45] Chambre des députés, Séance du 25 novembre 1912, p. 2773.

[46] *Le Rappel*, 3 Apr. 1911, qu. in Leniaud, *Les Archipels du passé*, p. 233.

[47] Blomfield in testimony before Select Committee, *Parliamentary Papers* (1912–13), VI, 466–8 (16 Oct, 1912); Mandler, *Stately Home*, p. 189.

[48] In India, Curzon created a directorate-general of archaeology, multiplied the restoration budget by a factor of eight, and personally oversaw repairs to monuments. He rejoiced in the restoration of the Taj Mahal and the other monuments of Agra: '"If I had done nothing else in India", he told his wife, "I have written my name here"', qu. in D. Gilmour, 'Curzon, George Nathaniel, Marquess Curzon of Kedleston (1859–1925)', *DNB* (Oxford, 2004; online edn, Oct. 2005), www.oxforddnb .com/view/article/32680. On his speeches on the 1913 Ancient Monuments Bill see *Parliamentary Debates*, Lords, 5th Ser., 11, 30 April 1912, cols. 871–83; 14, 28 May 1913 cols. 446–48 and Mandler, *Stately Home*, p. 189.

inch, they might take a mile was not only brought forward by landowners in Britain, who argued that:

> perhaps it would be contended some day that because the public had been allowed to enjoy parks which private individuals had thrown open the owner ought to be restrained if they wished to close them . . . Why should they not equally provide for preservation of the mediaeval monuments – of those old abbeys and castles which were quite as interesting as the Druidical remains? And why should they stop even there? Why not impose restriction on the owners of pictures of statues which might be of great national interest? If the owner of the 'Three Marys' or of Gainsborough's 'Blue Boy' proposed to send it out of the country, were they to prevent him, on the ground that the matter was one of national concern?[49]

The fear that such legislation might represent the thin end of the wedge was shared by the Prussian Minister of Finance. Apprehensive that any concessions could endanger other state aims such as land development and economic modernisation, he warned: 'In an alarming way this would pave the way for endeavours of such circles that one-sidedly pursue the interests of *Denkmalpflege*.'[50]

The state and the public

None of the attempts to introduce legislation can be seen as purely from above. While opposition remained fierce and decisions about preservation remained contentious throughout the period, public opinion became in favour of legislation. In every country calls from members of the public to protect monuments by law preceded government initiatives often by many decades. In France, Victor Hugo had already demanded in 1825 that 'the hammer that mutilates the face of the country has to be stopped. A law would suffice. Let it be done. Whatever property rights might exist, the destruction of a historic building cannot be permitted.'[51] Montalembert chipped in, hoping that one day a 'sufficiently enlightened, sufficiently patriotic' legislator would 'ask for special dispositions for our national

---

[49] *Parliamentary Debates*, Commons, 3rd Ser., 232, 7 March 1877, cols. 1542; Lords, 3rd Ser., 251, 11 March 1880, col. 784; Mandler, *Stately Home*, p. 158.
[50] See 'Votum' of *Finanzministerium*, 6 May 1909, BAKo R 43F, Nr. 2390, fols. 159f, qu. in Speitkamp, *Verwaltung der Geschichte*, p. 454.
[51] V. Hugo, 'Guerre aux démolisseurs', written in 1925, published in *Revue de Paris* (1829), enlarged in *Revue des deux mondes* (1832), repr. in *Oeuvres complètes* (Paris, 1834), XI, pp. 155–6.

monuments'.[52] Two decades and the creation of Guizot's institutions later, the 1854 Congress of Learned Societies alleged again that the law did not provide effective protection. Although the new procedure of *classement* prescribed that nobody could touch a listed monument without prior approval by the Minister, not much could be done to prevent infractions.[53] Expropriation was possible in theory, but in practice it was troublesome and not much employed.[54] Cases in which the CMH was powerless to protect listed monuments accumulated.[55] Mérimée's ironic surprise at finding the *classement* respected to the letter in Strasbourg is most telling: 'I encountered here, to my great surprise, the well-established opinion that a scheduled building is inviolable. From the tobacco merchant to the Prefect, all are imbued with the respect for the *classement* . . . I myself start to believe in our omnipotence.'[56] Yet as the Historic Monuments Commission felt offended by what it interpreted as a critique of its work by the learned societies, it maintained that no changes were possible under the regime of the day.[57] This only changed after the events of 1871, as part of broader policies to create a unified nation through public education and a centralised vision of history.[58] As soon as it resumed meetings after the Commune, the Historic Monuments Commission set out to use legislation to strengthen its power over the owners of the majority of listed monuments, the *fabriques*, who administered the parish churches since the concordat, and the communes. Its aim was to get rid of the 'taste for local independence', and especially the 'ambitious mayor' and 'zealous priest', who considered a monument to belong to them and them alone and who cared for it with 'all the presumption that stems from ignorance'.[59] Despite being endorsed by the learned

---

[52] Qu. in S. Hellal, 'Les Études de législations comparées du patrimoine en France, 1887–1913' (unpublished Mémoire de Maîtrise, Université Paris-IV 2000), p. 6.

[53] *Documents parlementaires*, No. 1501. Chambre des députés. Annexe au procès-verbal de la séance du 31 janvier 1887. Rapport fait au nom de la commission chargée d'examiner le projet de loi adopté par le Sénat pour la conservation des monuments historiques et objets d'art ayant un intérêt historique et artistique par M. Antonin Proust, député; see also Léon, *La Vie des monuments*, pp. 132–5.

[54] Tétreau, *Légilsation relative aux monuments et objets d'arts*, p. 93; Brown, *Care of Ancient Monuments*, p. 85. Léon, *La Vie des monuments*, p. 130.

[55] MAP, 80/1/19, Dossier 'Vandalisme'.

[56] Mérimée to Vitet, 28 Apr. 1849, qu. in Léon, *La Vie des monuments*, p. 135.

[57] *Documents parlementaires*, No. 1501. Chambre des députés. Annexe au procès-verbal de la séance du 31 janvier 1887. Rapport Proust.

[58] On these broader attempts see Nora (ed.), *Les Lieux de mémoires*, I–III.

[59] 'Avant Projet Rousse', pp. 15–18, MAP, 80/1/19. On the wider construction of the language of 'enemies' see P. Sorlin, 'Words and Images of Nationhood' in R. Tombs (ed.), *Nationhood and Nationalism in France. From Boulangism to the Great War, 1889–1918* (London, New York, 1991), pp. 74–86, esp. pp. 74–5.

societies,[60] the 1887 Act was thus primarily a government-driven initiative, fortifying the power of an existing government agency, enhancing a statist, centralist approach and weakening the influence of local communities and the Church.[61] To a certain degree, it simply continued the anti-provincial and anti-clerical attitudes of Viollet-le-Duc and Mérimée, so frequently expressed since the days of the July Monarchy, but the insistence on Parisian superiority in terms of restoration and administration could also reflect an attempt to improve the capital's status after its political and symbolic downgrade through the Commune.[62] Although in the texts published in support of the legislation (as well as in the historiography) the Commune and its effects were hardly mentioned, it was present in the subtext.[63] The recent outburst of revolutionary vandalism was countered not only by rebuilding Paris from the ashes, but it fostered the wish to save whatever else was left of France's monuments and to defy the image of France as a country of Vandals.[64] As such, passing a Monument Act was a means of demonstrating strength internally and externally. How France's historic monuments were used to demonstrate cultural pre-eminence after the defeat in the Franco-Prussian War at the *Expositions universelles* has already been seen. A Monument Act was seen as vital to ensure that the monuments representing French glory would survive and to maintain her status as a leader in cultural policies.

For decades to come, the 1887 Act became indeed regarded all over Europe as a model law, confirming France's role as 'classic land of monuments'. Yet, it had left many caveats. The majority of owners did not take up the possibility to have their properties listed. Most shared the opinion of a baker from a village in the Auvergne, who wrote to the Minister of Fine

---

[60] The *sociétés savantes* endorsed the bill, without getting futher involved. See for example 'Loi sur la conservation des monuments historiques', *Bulletin Monumental*, 6th Ser., 2 (1886), 204–9.

[61] In addition to unskillful restorations, alienations of works of art were a strong concern. *Fabriques* and communes often sold them (mostly to Germany, Britain and America) to obtain money for other projects. In theory, all objects already located inside an edifice when it was rendered to the Church through the concordat, belonged to the state, but in practice, the jurisprudence was sketchy and ineffective. See Ministère de l'Instruction publique et des Beaux-Arts, *Documents à l'appui du projet de loi pour la conservation des monuments historiques et des objets d'art. Projet présenté à la Chambre des députés et observations de la commission des monuments historiques sur ce projet* (Paris, 1879), p. 6; 'Avant Projet Rousse', pp. 19–20, MAP, 80/1/19; on court cases see *Procès-verbaux du Conseil supérieur des beaux-arts*, pp. 5–6.

[62] On the loss of Paris' status see R. Tombs, *The Paris Commune 1871* (London, New York, 1999), pp. 186–8.

[63] The same was true for many other areas of cultural life. For example, with regard to modern art, Albert Boime has suggested that the Commune was visually obliterated in impressionist paintings, yet intellectually formative for the movement. A. Boime, *Art and the French Commune. Imagining Paris after War and Revolution* (Princeton, 1995).

[64] Tombs, *The Paris Commune*, p. 187.

Arts: 'I don't like it if there are several masters in the same house'.[65] The opposition to legislation also had meant that historic or artistic interest was not enough to protect a building. Only outstanding monuments of 'national importance' were entitled to legal protection. 'For the conservation of the largest part of monuments and for objects of secondary interest, one has to count on the work of individuals and enlightened societies, on progress and on the force of public opinion.'[66]

The individuals and private societies caring for these monuments, however, were not happy to be the sole guardians and campaigned for a broader protection on the part of the state. As a result, the years 1905 to 1914 saw an accelerated concern with the legal protection of heritage. In contrast to the government-initiated Act of 1887, schemes now stemmed from different and sometimes mutually hostile quarters. Despite ideological differences, however, all drafts tried to get away from a narrow Viollet-le-Ducian definition of *monuments historiques* and suggested broader participatory models of care. Charles Beauquier, in particular, spearheaded the fight for the legal protection of landscapes and picturesque sites, supported by several national societies from the *Société pour la protection de l'esthétique de la France* to *L'Ami des Monuments*.[67] His *Loi sur la protection des monuments et des sites naturels d'intérêt artistique* (also called *Loi Beauquier* after its author) extended the state's protection to sites and monuments of artistic character, but adopting a much more decentralised character.[68] As soon as it was adopted in 1906, Beauquier initiated another Act prohibiting the affixing of advertisements on and around any *monument classé* or sites recognised by the 1906 Act.[69] The same year he deposited a further, but unsuccessful Bill, to regulate urban expansion in an aesthetic way.[70] Meanwhile the Separation of State and Church unsettled the mechanisms for the

---

[65] Qu. in Léon, *La Vie des monuments*, 146.

[66] *Documents parlementaires*, Conseil d'État, Annexe au no. 364, Rapport Courcelle-Seneuil, 28 février 1881; Poulot, *Patrimoine et musées*, p. 121.

[67] C. Beauquier, 'Proposition de Loi, ayant pour objet de protéger les sites pittoresques, historiques ou légendaires de France', *L'Ami des Monuments*, 17 (1903), 21–8. 'Texte officiel de la loi de protection des sites', *L'Ami des Monuments*, 21 (1907), 109.

[68] MAP, 80/1/28.

[69] P. Veitl, 'L'Étatisation du paysage français. La loi du 21 avril 1906 pour la "protection des sites et des monuments naturel de caractère artistique"', in M. Kaluszinki, S. Wahnich (eds.), *L'État contre la politique. Les expressions historiques de l'étatisation* (Paris, 1998), pp. 55–68; Trom, 'Natur und nationale Identität', pp. 147–67.

[70] *Documents parlementaires*, No. 263. Chambre des députés. Rapport fait (au cours de la précédente législature) au nom de la commission de l'administration générale, départementale et communale, des cultes et de la décentralisation, sur la proposition de loi de M. Charles Beauquier ayant pour objet d'imposer aux villes l'obligation de dresser des plans d'extension et d'embellissement . . . Repris le 5 juillet 1910.

preservation of religious architecture and art established by the 1887 Act.[71] The budget of the *Monuments historiques* had always been reserved for *monuments classés*, defined by their 'national importance'. In 1905 only about 909 churches were listed, out of a total of more than 45,000;[72] work on all unlisted churches was co-financed by the state, the communes and the *fabriques*. After the Separation, the Historic Monuments Service was given the part of the budget hitherto reserved for the maintenance of cathedrals, but the majority of the money formerly destined for church repairs went to the communes for unrelated projects.[73] Members of the CMH and of preservation associations campaigned for an article to be added to the Law of the Separation, proscribing that churches which were of public interest from a historic or artistic point of view, could also be listed.[74] As a result, the years between 1905 and 1913 witnessed the same number of inscriptions as the previous sixty-eight years together.[75] While the number of listed churches thus doubled, with regard to the total quantity of ecclesiastical buildings, it was small.[76] Repairs, restorations, as well as profanisations of church buildings remained central battlegrounds in villages and towns across the country in the war about the place of religion.[77] Intervening in this fight over whether the religious heritage was also the heritage of

[71] On the grass route conflict see J. McMillan, 'Priest hits Girl'. On the Front Line in the 'War of the two Frances', in Clark, Kaiser (eds.), *Culture Wars*, pp. 77–101, here p. 90.
[72] Cf. Leniaud, *Les Archipels du passé*, p. 225. A Bill from 1907, however, mentions 69,000 *établissements ecclésiastiques* rather than the 45,000 suggested by Leniaud, see *Documents parlementaires*, No. 1127. Chambre des députés. Annexe au procès-verbal de la séance du 28 juin 1907. Projet de loi tendant à modifier les articles 6, 9, 10, 14 de la loi du 9 décembre 1905 sur la Séparation des Eglises et de l'Etat. (Renvoyé à la Commission de la réforme judiciaire et de la législation civile et criminelle) présenté au nom de M. Armand Fallières, Président de la République française, M. Aristide Briand, Ministre de l'Instruction publique et des Beaux-Arts et des Cultes, et par M. Caillaux, Ministre des Finances, p. 3.
[73] Cf. Leniaud, *Les Archipels du passé*, p. 226.
[74] 'La Conservation des monuments et le texte officiel de la Loi de séparation des Eglises et de l'Etat', *L'Ami des Monuments*, 19 (1905), 330; 20 (1906), 27–32; 'La Loi de séparation dans ses rapports avec la conservation des monuments', 20 (1906), 82; 'Texte officiel de décret relatifs à la réunions du service de conservation des édifices cultuels a celui des monuments historiques', 20 (1906), 364–8; 21 (1907), 42–8.
[75] Léon, *La Vie des monuments*, p. 141.
[76] On a failed attempt to redistribute money see *Documents parlementaires*, No. 1127. Chambre des députés. Annexe au procès-verbal de la séance du 28 juin 1907; *Documents parlementaires*, No. 2213. Chambre des députés. Annexe au procès-verbal de la séance du 23 Décembre 1908. Projet de loi relative à une nouvelle répartition entre les communes des sommes rendues disponible par suite de la supression du budget des cultes (renvoyé à la commission du budget) présenté au nom de M. Armand Fallières, Président de la République française, par George Clemenceau, Président du Conseil, Ministre de l'Intérieur, Aristide Briand, Garde des Sceaux, Ministre de la Justice, Joseph Caillaux, Ministre des Finances.
[77] Leniaud, *Les Archipels du passé*, p. 229; *L'Univers*, the Catholic organ par excellence, featured a regular column on 'La démolition des églises de France'.

the nation, Maurice Barrès vigorously attacked the Historic Monuments Commission's principle of protecting only exemplary monuments. What, he exclaimed, was the preservation of a church in Toulouse to him, if that of his native village was destroyed? Protection should not be the privy of beauty, but be extended to 'all those humble churches maybe without style, but full of charm and moving memories which constitute the architectural physiognomy, the physical and moral face of the French soil'.[78] Hence the law should protect all churches built before 1800.[79] Barrès toured the country and mobilised public opinion by circulating a petition among 'artists and writers of all faiths and regardless of political allegiances, who found such emotion and artistic sensation through the modest sanctuaries, to ask from Parliament that a similar protection to that for historic monuments, picturesque sites and artistic reserves should be extended to them'. He presented it to the Chamber on 9 March 1911, signed by professional corporations, learned societies, provincial academies and the Institute.[80] Although the proposition as such led to heavy polemics, many suggestions made by Barrès and other members of the public were taken into account when the Fine Arts administration drafted a new Monument Act. The representative for Savoy, Theodor Reinach, an eminent philologist, numismatist, epigraphist and archaeologist who came from a family of preservationists, was charged to also integrate suggestions from other private members' bills and law project by private preservation associations, as well as failed drafts by the administration.[81] These had been produced with increasing frequency to overcome the problems created by the Separation, and to include wider categories of monuments, and prevent French Art from disappearing abroad.[82] The resulting Act of 1913, which still forms the basis of monument legislation in France, incorporated the growing demand

---

[78] Barrès, *La Grande Pitié*, pp. 82–3.   [79] Barrès, *La Grande Pitié*, p. 216.

[80] Qu. in Leniaud, *Les Archipels du passé*, p. 234; Léon, *La Vie des monuments*, p. 143.

[81] His two brothers were founding members of the *Amis des Monuments parisiens*; see also H. Duchêne, *Joseph Reinach, historien de l'Affaire Dreyfus* (Paris, 2006); Duchêne, *Salomon Reinach. Cultes, mythes et religions* (Paris, 1995).

[82] See *Sous Secrétaire d'Etat des Beaux-art* to Grandjean, *Inspecteur général des Monuments historiques*, 11 Aug. 1908, MAP 80/1/32, Dossier 'Législation étrangère concernant les monuments historiques'; *Documents parlementaires*, No. 281. Sénat. Annexe au procès-verbal de la séance du 7 novembre 1911. Proposition de loi tendant à modifier l'article 11 et le deuxième paragraphe de l'articles 13 de la loi du 30 mars 1887 concernant la conservation des monuments et objets d'art ayant un intérêt historique et artistique, présenté par M. Cachet, sénateur; *Documents parlementaires*, No. 1335. Chambre des députés. Annexe du procès-verbal de la 1ère séance du 26 novembre 1907. Proposition de loi sur la protection du patrimoine national artistique, historique et archéologique de la France . . . présentée par M. Ridouard, député; *Documents parlementaires*, No. 281. Sénat. Annexe au procès-verbal de la séance du 7 novembre 1911; *Documents parlementaires*, No. 448. Chambre des députés. Annexe au procès-verbal de la séance du 11 novembre 1910, Projet de loi relatif à la conservation des monuments et objets ayant un intérêt historique et artistique présenté au nom de M. Armand Fallières, Président

for a wider definition of heritage.[83] Where formerly 'national interest' had
determined *classement*, it could now be applied to any monument of 'public
interest' and its surroundings. Nonetheless, monuments of 'purely personal
local interest' remained excluded:

> We did not grant the municipalities the power to organise the protection
> of old houses, ensembles, and 'aspects' of purely local and personal interest,
> but which give, or gave – many of our old cities their characteristic features:
> The German law, it is well known, has taken care of this by arming munic-
> ipalities with very extended regulatory powers with regard to demolitions
> and new constructions. If we did not include these and some other tempting
> suggestions, we did so in order not to overload a text that is already very
> rich with novelties.[84]

Neither Beauquier's proposals to regulate urban growth, nor Barrès' suggestions to extend protection to all churches built before 1800 was thus
applied, but some of their ideas were effectively sanctioned. A wider range
of monuments was protected through a supplementary inventory and a
participatory element was introduced. Via so-called 'Caisses', individuals
could contribute funds for preservation.[85]

Hence, the lament over the top-down nature of preservation in the
historiography is somewhat exaggerated. Although French legislation had
a strong statist component, the desire to introduce it increasingly came
from civil society. What is more, demands for the extension of control

de la République française, par M. Aristide Briand, Président du Conseil, Ministre de l'Intérieur
et des Cultes, et par M. Maurice Faure, Ministre de l'Instruction publique et des Beaux-Arts;
Documents parlementaires, No. 1898. Chambre des députés. Annexe au procès verbal de la séance
du 23 mai 1912; 'Esquisse d'un avant-projet de loi de préservation des Monuments non classés,
des Fouilles et Découvertes, des Œuvres formant point de vue dans les paysages, des Meubles et
Immeubles menacés d'exportation. Etudié par le comité de la Société des amis des monuments
parisiens', *L'Ami des Monuments*, 22 (1909–1914), 203–9; 346–50. See MAP, 80/1/126; *Documents
parlementaires*, No. 1999. Chambre des députés. Annexe au procès verbal de la séance du 14 juin
1912. Deuxième rapport fait au nom de la commission de l'enseignement et des beaux-arts . . . par
M. Théodore Reinach, pp. 1343–56; *Documents parlementaires*, No. 3203. Chambre des députés.
Annexe au procès-verbal de la deuxième séance du 13 nov. 1913. Troisième Rapport fait au nom de
la commission de l'enseignement et des beaux-arts chargée d'examiner 1ᵉ le projet de loi relatif à
la conservation des monuments et objets d'art ayant un intérêt historique et artistique (no. 448),
2ᵉ La proposition de loi adopté par le Sénat tendant à modifié l'article 11 et le 2ᵉ § de l'art. 13 de
la loi du 30 mars 1887 concernant la conservation des monuments et objets d'art ayant un intérêt
historique et artistique (no. 1824), 3ᵉ la proposition de loi de M. de Chappedellaine (no. 1898) par
M. Théodore Reinach.

[83] For the application see *JO*, 29 Mar. 1924, 2978.
[84] *Documents parlementaires*, No. 1999. Chambre des députés. Annexe au procès verbal de la séance
du 14 juin 1912. Deuxième rapport Reinach, pp. 1343–56; see also Leniaud, *Les Archipels du passé*,
p. 240.
[85] Poulot, *Patrimoine et musées*, p. 122.

went much further in the drafts developed by individuals and private associations than by those of the government.

The same was the case in Germany. Preservation provisions arguably even had an older pedigree in Germany than in France and could be traced back to the time of enlightened absolutism. Edicts from Bayreuth (1771 and 1780), and Hesse-Kassel (1780) already had characteristics of modern monument legislation, yet their practical impact was limited because of the absence of special personnel and a budget. Soon after the Wars of Liberation, we find evidence of activity in more than a quarter of the states. After the 1840s, most German states created some sort of monument administration.[86] The number of decrees relating to monuments in the different states soon became almost uncountable. The need to repeat them, however, shows again how little effect they had in actual terms. Conservators and commissions suffered from too many tasks and not enough money. This slowly changed after the unification of Germany. The imperial constitution left *Denkmalschutz*, as part of domestic cultural policy, under the jurisdiction of the different states.[87] Officially, the *Reich* was merely in charge of foreign cultural policy, which included research institutes and excavations abroad and participation in international exhibitions. In practice the *Reich* did become involved in domestic projects too, for instance by allocating permanent grants to national museums, such as the Germanic National Museum in Nuremberg or the Roman-Germanic Museum in Mainz. It also provided subsidies for the restoration of a few 'national monuments' and nationally important excavations.[88] This ambiguity was repeatedly used to call for more commitment in matters of history and heritage. It was argued that if 'monuments of a distant past and a foreign people' can be regarded as imperial business, there can be no doubt that the concern for the monuments of German art standing on our soil – one of the most precious belongings and the pride of our nation – must in the most eminent sense be seen as one'.[89] In the year of German unification,

[86] Brown, *Care of Ancient Monuments*, p. 101.

[87] See Art. 4 of the *Reichsverfassung*, repr. in E.R. Huber (ed.), *Dokumente zur deutschen Verfassungsgeschichte* (4 vols., 3rd edn, Stuttgart, 1978–92), II, p. 384–402, esp. 386; K. Asal, *Die neuen reichsrechtlichen Denkmalschutzbestimmungen* (Heidelberg, 1923), p. 6; Speitkamp, *Verwaltung der Geschichte*, p. 154. Only in the *Reichsland* Alsace, *Denkmalpflege* was an imperial matter. Over time, however, the situation increasingly resembled that of any other German state, cf. Speitkamp, *Verwaltung der Geschichte*, p. 163.

[88] Cf. K. Griewank, 'Wissenschaft und Kunst in der Politik Kaiser Wilhelms I. und Bismarcks', *Archiv für Kulturgeschichte*, 34 (1952), 228–307, esp. 301.

[89] *Verband deutscher Architekten und Ingenieur-Vereine* to *Ministerium für landwirtschaftliche Angelegenheiten zu Berlin*, Feb. 1878, GStA PK, I. HA Rep. 87 B Ministerium für Landwirtschaft, Domänen u. Forsten, Nr. 3131, fol. 4–5.

Leopold von Ranke proposed the foundation of a German Academy for History and Language to Bismarck. Four years later, the Prussian conservator von Quast attempted to instigate an imperial commission for antiquities. As he encountered too much anti-Prussian opposition,[90] his was the last state-driven attempt in Imperial Germany, but private associations did not give up so easily. In 1878, the Federation of German Architects and Engineers petitioned the German Imperial Diet and several state ministries, to implement a *Reichsdenkmalplege* and a *Reichsdenkmalgesetz*, as a 'duty of honour of the German nation'.[91] A further campaign for an imperial *Denkmalschutzgesetz* was launched by the general assembly of the *Gesamtverein* in 1892, and the Federation of German Architects and Engineers gave it another go ten years later.[92]

Even though none of them achieved any results at the imperial level, the threat of imperial intervention accelerated the modernisation and institutionalisation of *Denkmalpflege* in states that wanted to prevent imperial legislation.[93] This was further enhanced by the growth of the nation-wide preservation movement. In 1899 the *Gesamtverein* dropped the demand for an imperial law and opted to lobby for uniform principles for state legislation instead. It printed guidelines and sent them to the different state's governments, urging them that only through legal provisions the 'countless monuments, hitherto without protection, can be saved from destruction, disfigurement and dissipation'.[94] The *Gesamtverein's* guidelines, and subsequent ones by the *Denkmaltage* were positively received by most *Kultusministerien*. The annual congress and the specialist press with its constant updates on national and international trends provided important ammunition for proponents of legislation within state administrations.[95]

---

[90] Speitkamp, *Verwaltung der Geschichte*, pp. 154f.
[91] *Verband deutscher Architekten und Ingenieur-Vereine* to *Ministerium für landwirtschaftliche Angelegenheiten zu Berlin*, Feb. 1878, GStA PK, I. HA Rep. 87 B Ministerium für Landwirtschaft, Domänen u. Forsten, Nr. 3131, fol. 4–5.
[92] Petition by *Verband Deutscher Architekten- und Ingenieur-Vereine*, Jan. 1902, qu. in Speitkamp, *Verwaltung der Geschichte*, p. 156; *Verhandlungen des 27. Deutschen Juristentags* (4 vols., Berlin, 1904–5), II, pp. 3–27 and IV, pp. 88–111, qu. 625–27; GStA PK, VI. HA, Nl Schmidt-Ott (M) C 39.
[93] Speitkamp, *Verwaltung der Geschichte*, p. 156.
[94] Petition by *Gesamtverein der deutschen Geschichts- und Alterthumsvereine*, Oct. 1899. attached to a draft for a *Denkmalschutzgesetz* sent by the Prussian *Kultusminister* to other ministers, GStA PK, I. HA Rep. 77 Ministerium des Inneren, Tit. 1215, Nr. 3, Beiheft, Bd.1, fol. 10; cf. Brown, *Care of Ancient Monuments*, p. 99 for a translation of excerpts.
[95] See in *Die Denkmalpflege* on Prussia: Polenz, 'Zur Geschichte der Organisation der Denkmalpflege in Preußen', 1 (1899), 37–9, 45–6 and J. Kohte, 'Die Denkmalpflege in Preußen während der letzten Jahre', 87–8; 'Preußische Verhandlungen im Abgeordnetenhaus', 2 (1900), 31; Polenz, 'Zur Lage des Denkmalschutzes in Preußen', 4 (1902), 33–6, 66–9; 5 (1903), 17–19. 'Gesetzentwurf gegen die Verunstaltung landschaftlich hervorragender Gegenden', 4 (1902), 30, 55, 100; Polenz, 'Die

All pre-1900 drafts had only been started after substantial demands from the public. Representatives at the Prussian Diet repeatedly asked for a Monument Act, among them von Quast's son and von Reichensberger, author of the memorandum the architectural associations had sent to the Imperial Diet in support of their petitions, and were not appeased by the creation of Provincial Monuments Commissions founded in the 1890s.[96] Members of both Houses continuously asked for a *Denkmalschutzgesetz* after the turn of the century.[97] When a new *Kultusminister*, von Studt, fonder

Denkmalpflege und ihre Gestaltung in Preußen', 6 (1904), 11–12; 'Die Gefährdung der Naturdenkmäler und Vorschläge zu ihrer Erhaltung', 7 (1905), 24. On *Verunstaltungsgesetz*: 9 (1907), 38, 91, 102; 10 (1908), 14, 105; 11 (1909), 15, 22, 61, 70, 101; against advertisments: 12 (1910), 111; protection of nature: 12 (1910), 64; 14 (1912), 120; 'Ortsstatute gegen Verunstaltung', 12 (1910), 32; *Ausgrabungsgesetz*: 16 (1914), 32, 47; 'Schutz der Altstadt in Städten geschichtlicher Bedeutung, Oberverwaltungsgerichtliche Entscheidung', 16 (1914), 70; on other states see: Baden: 9 (1907), 35; 11 (1909), 65, 'Schutz durch Schenkung an Staat', 14 (1912), 21, 'Orts und Landschaftsbilder, Schutzbestimmungen durch Abänderung des Polizeistrafgesetzbuches', 16 (1914), 99; Bavaria: 'Die Denkmalpflege in Bayern', 6 (1904), 7–8; 7 (1905), 64; Bremen: 11 (1909), 72; Hamburg: 14 (1912), 118; 15 (1913), 101; Hesse: 3 (1901), 36, 40, 100, 120; 4 (1902), 46, 71, 73–6, 101, 123–4; 6 (1904), 6, 101; 7 (1905), 4, 28, 123: Mecklenburg: 6 (1904), 130. Oldenburg: 12 (1910), 24; 13 (1911), 48, 104; Saxony: 'Gesetz gegen die Verunstaltung von Stadt und Land', 11 (1909), 47, 70, 101; Saxe–Coburg: 11 (1909), 48; Würtemberg: 3 (1901), 103; 7 (1905), 7, 64; 13 (1911), 14, 120; 11 (1909), 123; 12 (1910), 112; 14 (1912), 53; 16 (1914), 32. On communal decrees: in Bavaria: 6 (1904), 7–8; Berlin: 13 (1911), 56; 15 (1913), 14, 126; Braunschweig: 4 (1902), 131; Enkirch and Mosel: 13 (1911), Hannover: 12 (1910), 88; 15 (1913), 15; Hildesheim: 11 (1909), 22.

[96] *Stenographische Bericht über die Verhandlungen des Preußischen Hauses der Abgeordneten*, Sess 1879/80, vol. 2, 12. Feb. 1880, col. 1688 (Abg. v. Quast); Sess 1880, vol. 1, 15 Dec. 1880, col. 783 (Abg. v. Quast); Sess 1881, vol. 1, 18 Mar. 1882, col. 1007 (Abg. Dr. Seelig), Sess. 1883–84., vol. 2, 8. Feb. 1884, col. 1305 (Abg. Dr. Seelig); cols. 1302, 1305 (Abg. Dr. Reichensberger and Abg. von Eynern).

[97] On demands from Lower House see: *Stenographische Bericht über die Verhandlungen des Preussischen Hauses der Abgeordneten*, Sess 1901, vol. 3, cols. 3251–4 (Abg. Seydel), 3255 (Abg. Kindler), 3258 (Abg. Szmula), Sess. 1902, vol. 3, cols. 4352–5 (Abg. Kindler), 4256 (Abg. Seydel); Sess. 1903, vol. 3, cols. 3217–18 (*Berichterstatter* Abg. Dr. Friedberg: Petition Geheimer Justizrat Prof. Dr. Loersch, Bonn, Erhöhung der Mittel für die Denkmalpflege/Erlaß eines Denkmalschutzgesetzes), 3219–20 (Abg. Seydel), 3222 (Abg. Hirt), 3232 (Abg. Dr. Dittrich); *Drucksachen*, vol. 4, Nr. 167, pp. 2411–21 (Petition des Geheimen Baurats Möbius und Gen. In Mageburg u.a.D (Architeckten und Ingenieurverine u.a.) um gesetzliche Regelung des Schutzes von Baudenkmälern). Sess. 1904–05, vol. 3, cols. 3784–5, 3795–6 (*Berichterstatter* Abg. Dr. Friedberg, Abg. Schwarze), 3796–7 (Abg. Dr. Lotichius), 3799–800 (Abg. Eickhoff), 11031–2.; Sess. 1909, vol. 4, cols. 5390 (Abg. Eickhoff), 5396 (Abg. Frhr. von Wolff-Metternich); Sess. 1910, vol. 4, cols. 5045–7, 5050–2 (Abg. Witzmann and Hammer, esp. on *Naturdenkmalschutzgesetz*). On Upper House: *Stenographischer Bericht über die Verhandlungen des Preußischen Herrenhauses*, Sess. 1902, 7 May 1902, p. 256 (Graf von Hutten-Czapski), p. 274 (Struckmann); 31 March 1903, pp. 25, 35–42; 3 April 1903 (Bericht der Kommission für Petitionen über die Petition Nr. 21 des Gemeinen Baurats Moebius), and pp. 137–9 (on prehistoric momuments), cf. for Moebius Petition, *Herrenhaus*, Sess. 1903, *Drucksachen*, Nr. 41. On discussion and responses see *Stenographische Bericht über die Verhandlungen des Preußischen Hauses der Abgeordneten*, Sess. 1901, vol. 3, col. 3254 (*Kultusminister* Dr. Studt); Sess. 1902, vol. 3, col. 3459 (*Regierungskommissar Geh. Regierungsrat* Lutsch); Sess. 1903, vol. 3, col. 3233 (*Regierungskommissar Wirkl. Geh. Oberregierungsrat* von Bremen); Sess 1904/1905, vol. 3, col. 3801 (*Regierungskommisar Ministerialdir.* D. Schwartzkopff); see also consideration of Moebius petition in *Herrenhaus*, Sess 1904 *Drucksachen*, Nr. 12; Sess. 1905–06, *Drucksachen*, Nr. 20, Nr. 155 (*Berichterstatter* Struckmann). cf. cuttings in GStA PK, 1. HA Rep. 77 Ministerium des Inneren, Tit. 1215, Nr. 3, Beiheft, Bd.1.

of *Denkmalpflege* than his immediate predecessors, came into office, he developed legislation arguing his case by drawing attention to the standing *Denkmalpflege* had gained in public opinion:[98]

> Public opinion has taken possession of the issue, in particular the congresses of historical association, which time and again asked for the enactment of a Monument Act. Last year's assembly in Strasbourg formulated the attached resolutions, which this spring, on occasion of their discussion in a newspaper article, also attracted the attention of his Majesty the *Kaiser* and King. His Majesty ordered my report on the matter, in which I explained the deficiencies of the current legislation by means of the Strasburg resolutions. His Majesty thereupon deigned to order me to engineer the remedy of the current grievances by legislative means. Accordingly, I have had a Bill drafted, whose fundamental ideas, as far as they concern the limitation of property rights and the penal clauses, gained the approval of the congress of history and monument care this September, which deliberated about the topic in great length. In the other German states the wish for a legal solution is also increasingly felt. In my opinion, Prussia must not lag behind; She also cannot stand behind other great *Kulturstaaten* which have permanently regulated on the matter.[99]

As the draft encountered too much internal opposition from other government resorts, the *Kultusministerium* thereafter abandoned the plan for a comprehensive monument act, instead pushing for more limited legislation on excavations.[100] Further legislation against disfigurement acknowledged the aesthetic demands of the *Heimatbewegung*.[101] It gave power to local authorities, and inspired a number of similar laws in other German states.[102] Yet, since only aesthetic appeal and not architectural substance

---

[98] Polenz, 'Zur Lage der Denkmalpflege in Preußen, III', *Die Denkmalpflege* (1903), 17. Konrad von Studt (1838–1921), after a law degree, embarked upon a career in the civil service. During his time as *Kultusminister* he equally fostered the care of the past and the improvement of technological sciences with the foundation of the *Technische Hochschulen*. See *Deutsche Biographische Enzyclopädie* (12 vols., Munich, 1994–2003), IX, p. 606.

[99] *Kultusminister* to *Innenminister*, 21 Dec. 1900, GStA PK, I. HA Rep. 77 Ministerium des Inneren, Tit. 1215, Nr. 3, Beiheft, Bd.1, fols. 1–2.

[100] *Kultusminister* (signed Schmidt) to 'sämtliche Herren Staatsminister'. 3 Apr. 1909, 'Votum des Ministers der geistlichen p. Angelegenheiten zu dem Votum der Herrn Finanzministers vom 23 März d.Js. – I. 4215-, betreffend den Gesetzentwurf über den Schutz frühgeschichtlicher Denkmäler sowie der Ausgrabungen und Funde von Altertümern, dem Königlichen Staatsministerium ergebenst vorzulegen', and 'Gesetzentwurf', GStA PK VI. HA, Nl Schmidt-Ott (M), C 39 'Entwurf eines Ausgrabungsgesetzes', GStA PK, I. HA Rep. 89, Geh. Zivilkabinett, jüngere Periode, Nr. 20769, fol. 37; *Herrenhaus*, Sess. 1914, *Drucksachen*, Nr. 9.

[101] See *Gesetz gegen die Verunstaltung landschaftlich hervorragender Gegenden* 2 June 1902, *Gesetzes Sammlung für die Königlich Preußischen Staaten*, p. 159, qu. in Hammer, *Entwicklung des Denkmalrechts*, p. 131; *Gesetz gegen die Verunstaltung von Ortschaften und landschaftlich hervorragenden Gegenden*, 15 July 1907, *Gesetzes Sammlung für die Königlich Preußischen Staaten*, p. 206.

[102] Saxony: *Gesetz gegen die Verunstaltung von Stadt und Land* of 1909, Coburg and Gotha passed a law the same year, and Bremen *Gesetz betreffend den Schutz von Baudenkmalern und Strassen*

was protected by the new Act, members of both houses regretted that it only touched the margins of *Denkmalschutz* and that a proper *Denkmalschutzgesetz* was still needed.[103]

The Prussian experience was in many ways representative of other larger German states too. Baden had a history of pioneering yet unsuccessful drafts that were never introduced to the Diet because of opposition from the Churches and other government departments.[104] Only some provisions on archaeological remains were translated into a decree in 1914.[105] Württemberg also had a long-established administration, but although a draft bill was at least introduced to the Diet, it likewise came to nothing.[106] Fear of opposition prevented the other two large states, Bavaria and Saxony to even draft a formal Monument Bill. Bavaria had one of the oldest monument administrations and repeatedly considered demands for legislation but no draft saw the light before 1925.[107] Saxony also developed no drafts and like its Prussian neighbour, only passed an Anti-Disfiguration Act. In 1914 the Saxon Commission for the Preservation of Artistic Monuments prepared a draft, but matters were not followed up.[108]

The first German state that acquired a Monument Act, on the other hand, not only had an art-loving head of state in Grand Duke Ernst Ludwig (1892–1918), but also an especially energetic Secretary, Freiherr von

---

und Landschaftsbildern, Oldenburg follwed in 1910, Braunschweig in 1911 (less extended acts were passed in Elsass-Lothringen, Schwarzenburg-Rudolfstadt, Schaumburg-Lippe); Hamburg's 1912 *Baupflegegesetz* applied to *Natur und Kunstdenkmälern*, cf. Bredt, *Heimatschutzgesetzgebung*, pp. 42–57.

[103] 'Bericht der XII. Kommission zur Vorberatung des Gesetzentwurfes gegen die Verunstaltung von Ortschaften und landschaftl. hervorragenden Gegenden', *Preußisches Hauses der Abgeordneten*, Sess. 1907, vol. 4, *Drucksachen*, Nr. 227, esp. pp. 2841, 2851; *Drucksachen*. Nr. 333, p. 3192: 'Der preußische Gesetzentwurf gegen die Verunstaltung von Ortschaften und landschaftlich hervorragenden Gegenden', *Die Denkmalpflege*, 8 (1906), 91. see also *Preußisches Herrenhaus*, Sess. 1907, Drucksachen, Nr. 118.

[104] G. Hans, *Denkmalschutz in Baden im 19. und 20. Jahrhundert* (Münster, 1985), pp. 46–69, 77–93; Brown, *Care of Ancient Monuments*, p. 106 paraphrases and translates parts of the 1883 draft. On later attempts see *Erster Tag für Denkmalpflege. Stenographischer Bericht* (Berlin, 1900), p. 17, reprinted as P. Clemen, 'Allgemeine Grundsätze für die Gesetzgebung', in Oechelhaeuser, *Denkmalfpelge*, I, pp. 125–38, Brown, *Care of Ancient Monuments*, p. 107; *Zweiter Tag für Denkmalpflege. Stenographischer Bericht* (Berlin, 1901), p. 1; Heyer, *Denkmalpflege*, p. 22, Schmidt, 'Rechtsfragen des deutschen Denkmaschutzes', p. 155; M. Heckel, *Staat Kirche Kunst. Rechtsfragen kirchlicher Kulturdenkmäler* (Tübingen, 1968), p. 29.

[105] Hammer, *Entwicklung des Denkmalrechts*, p. 157.

[106] *Die Denkmalpflege*, 5 (1903), 7; Brown, *Care of Ancient Monuments*, p. 105; Speitkamp, *Verwaltung der Geschichte*, p. 321, note 32, p. 453; Hammer, *Entwicklung des Denkmalrechts*, pp. 157–9.

[107] *Die Denkmalpflege*, 6 (1904), 7, 13. Brown, *Care of Ancient Monuments*, p. 103; *Zweiter Tag für Denkmalpflege. Stenographischer Bericht* (Berlin, 1901), p. 48; cf. Speitkamp, *Verwaltung der Geschichte*, pp. 363 on Bavaria in the Weimar period.

[108] Magirius, *Geschichte der Denkmalpflege*, p. 197. Brown, *Care of Ancient Monuments*, p. 105.

Biegeleben, who strategically used the growth of the preservation movement to pass the draft.[109] He presented his draft to the first meeting of
the *Denkmaltage* in 1900, just after the congress had ratified the Strasbourg
Resolutions on legislation as binding for all further actions, and had the
plenum adopt a ten-point resolution outlining basic principles for legislation. On this basis, von Biegeleben presented his draft to the Hessian
government and an inter-ministerial commission. Before it was introduced
to the Diet, he gave a report about these developments and the changes
that the draft had undergone at the next *Tag für Denkmalpflege*. Although
it had to be redrafted again after opposition from the aristocracy in the
upper house, it was finally adopted.[110] Presented again at the *Denkmaltage*
by von Biegeleben, it provided the template for the only other German
pre-war *Denkmalschutzgesetz*, passed in the Northern German Duchy of
Oldenburg.[111]

Despite the competition between conservators and public preservation
bodies observed in Chapter 2, when it came to preservation legislation, their
cooperation was strong. The leading members of the German preservation
movement were all in favour of legislation and *Die Denkmalpflege* and
the *Denkmaltage* provided unequalled means of exchange. Confronted
with opposition from other resorts, the Churches and the landowners,
conservators and *Kultusminister* welcomed this support and used it to their
advantage wherever they could.

In Britain, the initiative for legislation came almost universally from the
public. As seen above, attempts for state preservation of the built heritage long remained unsuccessful. Some legislation, however, had followed
shortly after the failed calls for a monument administration in the early
1840s, triggered by the smashing of an outstanding Roman glass vase in
the British Museum. The Protection of Works of Art and Scientific and
Literary Collections Act 1845 made it an offence to destroy any work of art,
science or literature exhibited in a museum, church or other public place.
Further acts of vandalism to royal statues in London incited the passing

[109] H. Wagner, *Die Denkmalpflege in Hessen 1818–1905, und zwar: Gesetz, den Denkmalschutz betreffend,
vom 16. Juli 1902 nebst den zugehörigen Ausführungs-Vorschriften. Amtliche Handausgabe mit Motiven,
Erläuterungen und einem Sachregister, bearb. im Auftrag Großherzogl. Ministeriums des Innern*
(Darmstadt, 1905); partially trans. in, Brown, *Care of Ancient Monuments*, pp. 108–13.
[110] E.R Hönes, '100 Jahre Denkmalschutzgesetz in Hessen', *Denkmalschutz Informationen*, 26.2
(2002), 65–82, www.nationalkomitee.de/denkmalschutz/denkmalschutzinfo_2_2002.pdf; Gesetz
den Denkmalschutz betreffend vom 16. Juli 1902, *Großherzoglich Hessisches Regierungsblatt*, Nr. 41,
18 July 1902, p. 275.
[111] *Gesetzblatt für das Herzogtum Oldenburg* (1911), p. 959.

of the Public Statues Act 1854, making the Commissioners of Works the guardian of public statues in London, and damage to any scheduled statue an offence.[112] Beyond the fifteen public statues now under the guardianship of the Treasury, a very limited number of other historic monuments was maintained by the state: some Scottish ecclesiastical sites had been in state ownership since the sixteenth century and in Ireland the government took over many ecclesiastical ruins between 1874 and 1877.[113] The Church of England had its own machinery for the maintenance of its buildings, but the preservation of most other monuments depended entirely on their owner. Although in early 1869 the Office of Works enquired upon the French Foreign Ministry about the measures adopted in France for the protection of historic monuments,[114] the drafting of the first Ancient Monuments Bill was not a government initiative, and was less obviously motivated by the political context of the post-1871 years than in the other two countries.

Instead, John Lubbock's introduction of a Private Member's Bill was inspired by the antiquarian's campaign to save the pre-historic stone circle at Avebury.[115] Lubbock was successful in preventing demolition by acquiring the monument himself, but the event convinced him that voluntary action alone was insufficient. Inspired by foreign models – especially Danish preservation of prehistoric remains – the original Bill wanted to place scheduled monuments under the guardianship of a National Monuments Commission, composed of representatives from the main antiquarian societies.[116] Limited to uninhabited pre-historic monuments, the

---

[112] Champion, 'Protecting the Monuments', p. 40.
[113] Chippendale, 'First Ancient Monuments Act', pp. 3–8. It is noteworthy that long before financing the preservation of British antiquities, the government did spend money on 'foreign heritage' through the acquisition of objects for the British Museum.
[114] *Ministère des Affaires étrangères* to Le Maréchal Vaillant, *Ministre de la Maison de l'Empereur et des Beaux-Arts*, 22 February 1869, MAP, 80/1/33, Dossier 'Angleterre'; reply 23 March 1869.
[115] Sir John Lubbock (1834–1913) was MP for Maidstone 1870–80, lost his seat in 1880, but returned in the next election as MP for the University of London, of which he had been the vice-chancellor since 1872. Upon being named to the peerage in 1900 he chose the title of Avebury after the ancient monument which he had fought to save. H.G. Hutchinson, *Life of Sir John Lubbock, Lord Avebury* (London, 1914); T.L. Alborn, 'Lubbock, John, first Baron Avebury (1834–1913)', *DNB* (Oxford, 2004), www.oxforddnb.com/view/article/34618.
[116] A Bill to provide for the Preservation of Ancient National Monuments. Prepared and brought in by Sir John Lubbock, Mr Beresford Hope, Mr Bouverie, Mr Osborne Morgan, and Mr Plunket, 7 February 1873, *Parliamentary Papers* (1873), 1, p. 25. On the role of Danish ideas see Murray, 'Ancient Monuments Protection Act 1882', p. 60; Chippendale, 'First Ancient Monuments Act', pp. 4–6; J. J. A. Worsaae, *La Conservation des antiquités et des monuments nationaux en Danemark. Rapport fait à la demande de la légation impériale et royale d'Autriche-Hongrie, à Copenhague, par J.J.A. Worsaae. Traduit par E. Beauvois* (Extrait des Mém. de la Soc. Roy. Des Anitqu. Du Nord 1877, Copenhagen, 1878), see MAP, 80/1/33, Dossier 'Danemark, Novège, Suède'.

Bill still raised fears over property rights and costs for the Treasury. Some also doubted the significance of prehistoric monuments for the nation. Why, it was asked should monuments of the barbarian and pagan ancient Celts rather than those of the more recent and more English past be preserved as national monuments?[117] The nature of the commission the Bill foresaw was particularly contentious.[118] While most landowners generally objected to government interference, the fact that the Bill was not a government initiative and that an independent commission composed of antiquaries rather than a government official should have compulsory powers, was seen as equally objectionable. If, indeed, monuments were scheduled because they were national monuments, this had to be endorsed by the government. The degree of independence such a commission would give to the Scottish Society of Antiquaries further worried English peers.[119] As a result only a much watered-down version without compulsory clauses was passed. It gave birth to an Inspectorate, but did not create a commission.

While the defence of aristocratic privilege created most opposition, matters were further hindered because antiquarians and preservationists did not form a uniform camp. The list of national institutions involved in the preparation and propagation of the Bill is long and includes the British Museum, the British Association for the Advancement of Science, the Societies of Antiquaries of London, and of Scotland, the Ethnological Society (i.e. its successor the Anthropological Institute), the British Committee of the International Congress on Prehistoric Archaeology, the Royal Archaeological Institute, the British Archaeological Association, the Royal Anthropological Institute of Great Britain and Ireland, professional associations such as the RIBA and preservationist pressure groups such as the CPS and the SPAB.[120] Yet in practice, many crucial voices did not lend full support. The SAL was less willing to help because of in-fighting between the English societies concerned with archaeology. Despite being a vice-president of the Antiquaries, Lane Fox did not manage to secure their support to establish a joint committee with the Anthropological Institute to endorse Lubbock's Bill in 1871. The Antiquaries did not object to the Bill, but refused to collaborate as they were working on a similar scheme by themselves, instigated by Sir Austen Layard who, when taking up office as First Commissioner of Works in 1868, had been shocked by the neglect of

---

[117] Murray, 'Ancient Monuments Protection Act 1882', pp. 61, 64.   [118] Ibid., pp. 60–1.
[119] Chippendale, 'First Ancient Monuments Act', p. 15.
[120] Ibid., p. 6; Murray, 'Ancient Monuments Protection Act 1882', p. 56.

the monuments of the past. This state of affairs was 'not creditable' to the country especially when compared to France,[121] so he commissioned the Antiquaries to draw up an inventory on the model of the French *classement*. The task was completed the moment Lubbock sent his Bill to the SAL. But Layard had ceased to be First Commissioner, his successor did not care for ancient monuments, and the attempt came to nothing. The Antiquaries distantly approved of Lubbock's Bill, but did not get actively involved. Instead they used their energy to convince the British government to intervene in the preservation and research of classical monuments abroad.[122] The SPAB also broadly endorsed Lubbock's Bill, but devoted its real effort to the fight against restoration. Moreover, it is debatable whether the support of the SPAB rather hindered the cause by its extremism or fostered it in the long term by publicising preservation. Lubbock had hoped from the beginning of his parliamentary campaign for the support of local antiquarian and archaeological societies, but the response was also meagre. His request for societies to petition the House of Lords in 1880 resulted only in a single petition, from the Literary and Antiquarian Society of Perthshire.[123] Outside Parliament, preservation legislation secured some prominent supporters – including Charles Dickens – and the Ancient Monuments Bill attracted considerable attention on the pages of *The Times*, but it hardly affected a wider audience.[124]

After the Act was passed, the new Inspector of Ancient Monuments, the eminent archaeologist Pitt-Rivers, a Tory MP and great landowner – experienced not only difficulties in persuading owners to put monuments under guardianship, but also in finding money for simple protective measures and repeatedly lamented the government's lack of support for his work. To the SPAB's suggestion to extend the measures of the 1892 Amendment for Ireland to the whole of the UK, he regretted to reply:

> Neither the Government [nor] Parliament have any special interest in Ancient Monuments and unless some definite fund is devoted to the purpose, as I understand is the case in Ireland, I think your proposed addition to the Act is liable to become a dead letter, if it is made dependent on an annual vote. There is a case in point; Government lately refused to accept the Ruins of Whithorn Priory, which the heritors offered, no doubt in order

---

[121] *Anthropological Review*, 7.26 (1869), 332.
[122] Chippendale, 'Making of the First Ancient Monuments Act', pp. 6–7.
[123] *Lords Journal*, 122 (1880), 43, Chippendale, 'Making of the First Ancient Monuments Act', p. 25.
[124] *All the Year Round*, 7 (1872), 294–9, qu. in Chippendale, 'First Ancient Monuments Act', p. 9. For the specialist press see: *The Builder* (1882), I, pp. 27, 192, 258, 415.

to get rid of the expense of maintaining them. Lord Bute stepped in, and at a cost of £1000 put the ruins in a condition of sufficient repair, i.e. the refusal of Government had the effect of bringing forward a private individual, who at one stroke spent more on this single building, than Government had spent on the whole of the Monuments since the Act came in force.[125]

Despite these problems, the Act did lay the foundation for subsequent legislation and introduced some key features of all later provisions.[126] In the 1880s and 1890s, the relation of politics and heritage became ever more complex, since Radicalism's anti-aristocratic policies were increasingly anti-monument politics. New Radicalism wished no longer to reclaim aristocratic heritage in order to preserve it for the nation, but to redistribute aristocratic property by means of taxation. Some – like Joseph Chamberlain, former Mayor of Birmingham, and leader of the Radicals' call for land reform, housing reform and higher taxes on the rich in the 1885 election – regretted that estates were only seen in terms of pecuniary value. He still endorsed this view for the greater good, even if this had the side-effect of leading 'to the destruction of many of the most splendid historical places in the country, and of many very old and interesting country houses which, as now maintained, were part of the tradition and the glory of the country, but which could only be maintained if a reasonable valuation were placed upon them'. In the end, the social benefits gained from taxation outweighed fears for historical preservation. Conversely, the Tory spokesman Arthur Balfour merely spoke of these houses as family homes, and avoided stressing their value as national heritage, as this might lead to claims by the state.[127] Radicals and Conservatives thus equally avoided speaking of country houses as 'national heritage', as it could only weaken arguments for or against taxation. Emphasis on the pecuniary value of family heritages further destabilised ideas of national heritage, as it legitimised and increased the sales of heirlooms. And yet, as debates continued to rage, and the idea of aristocratic custodianship on behalf of the nation resurfaced time and again, 'national and historic value' became ever more established criteria.

Opening the door for further legislation was a slow and arduous task in this political climate, but, as in the other two countries, preservationists grew more united around the turn of the century. While more far-reaching

---

[125] Pitt Rivers to Thackeray Turner, 22 January 1891, SPAB Archives, 'Ancient Monuments Acts: correspondence'.
[126] Champion, 'Protecting the Monuments', p. 39.
[127] *Parliamentary Debates*, Commons, 3rd Ser., 303, 23 March 1886, cols. 1686–7, 1696–8; Mandler, *Stately Home*, p. 162.

legislation was passed in Ireland and India, preservationists also tried different and often complementary routes to transform the movement's entirely voluntary nature into an activity under the aegis of the state. They did it first by amending the existing Ancient Monuments Acts, second by securing the position of the National Trust and third by integrating historic preservation into town and country planning legislation.

The fate of secular buildings and places of natural beauty, in particular, prompted preservationists' growing belief in the necessity of legislation. Prehistoric monuments were in a limited way protected by law, ecclesiastical buildings were preserved through the internal system of the Church of England, but secular buildings were not subject to any form of national protection. A few towns had protective legislation, but these local laws were far and few between. In the 1890s, the most extensive reform of local government since Tudor times and its changes to traditional patterns of social organisation triggered concern.[128] Preservationists from England and Scotland collaborated to convince the government of the need to protect historic buildings. In 1894 the Edinburgh-based Cockburn Association – one of Britain's oldest local preservation societies founded in 1875 – established a committee to 'watch all alterations, actual or projected in connection with the City improvements in the Old Town'[129] and invited the National Trust to send a representative to its meetings.[130] This representative was Gerald Baldwin Brown, friend of Canon Rawnsley.[131] The Trust returned the favour and Cockburn Association member Patrick Geddes joined the Council.[132] The two Edinburgh-based preservationists were to become major voices in the transition to state preservation and started to establish what models existed abroad.[133] The Society of Antiquaries took up the demand for legislation and advocated that the government should conduct its own wider survey, resulting in a White Paper in 1897. The initiatives had several immediate results. London County Council (LCC) was allowed by a private Act of 1898 to hold buildings. The Ancient Monuments Protection Act (1900), drafted by Hunter, extended the Irish measures to

[128] Hall, 'Preservation, National Identity and the State', p. 134.
[129] G. Bruce, *Some Practical Good. The Cockburn Association 1875–1975. A Hundred Years Participation in Planning in Edinburgh* (Edinburgh, 1975), p. 60; Hall, 'Preservation, National Identity and the State', p. 148.
[130] Cockburn Association, *Annual Report* (1895), p. 9, qu. in Hall, 'Preservation, National Identity and the State', p. 148.
[131] *The Care of Ancient Monuments* was dedicated to Rawnsley.
[132] NT Archives, Executive Committee Minutes, 10 June 1897.
[133] Hall, 'Preservation, National Identity and the State', p. 148. NT Archives, Council Minutes, 19 Nov. 1895; undated letter from Rawnsley to Sir John Hilbert, Sir Frederik Pollard, Lord Ihring, General Pitt-Rivers, James Bryce, Shaw-Lefevre, Sir John Lubbock, Balfour, TNA, WORK 14/132.

the whole of the UK, granted some public access to sites of guardianship, and allowed other county councils to become guardians.[134] Hunter also introduced a Private Member's Bill, resulting in the National Trust Act 1907, by which the Trust acquired a unique status as 'a Statutory body for the express purpose of preserving the beautiful and interesting places for the nation' on an inalienable basis. The Office of Works wished for the model to be widely embraced, but it was at the same time guarded against the Trust's self-portrayal as a 'national custodian' and pointed out to foreign enquiries that the Trust was not 'a public Body representing the State'.[135] Hence, from a different side, Patrick Geddes pressed ahead to integrate concerns about the 'past with its heritage of good, its burden of evil' into town and country planning, supporting the Liberal Radical MP, the President of the Local Government Board John Burn and Liberal Philip Morrell.[136] Under the 1909 Town and Country Planning Act, local author-ities were permitted to incorporate 'the preservation of objects of historical interest or natural beauty' in planning schemes. A second Act, with more extended clauses on historic preservation, followed in 1913.[137] Simultane-ously, Baldwin Brown relentlessly campaigned for an improvement of the existing legislation.[138] The Antiquaries and the SPAB took up Brown's ideas to conduct a national inventory to establish a monument commission and advisory board.[139] Other scholarly groups, but also local councils, chiefly London County Council, also increasingly put pressure on the Office of Works.[140] It was after reading Brown's work that the Secretary of State for Scotland in 1908 set up a Royal Commission to compile an inventory of ancient Scottish monuments.[141] Royal Commissions for England and Wales were founded soon after to establish an inventory of monuments.

[134] On the use by the Councils see Hall, 'Preservation, National Identity and the State', p. 149; Mandler, *Stately Home*, p. 170; C. Dellheim, *The Face of the Past. The Preservation of the Medieval Inheritance in Victorian England* (Cambridge, 1982), p. 106.

[135] Draft for a Memorandum in response to enquiries from Russia and Belgium, 11 December 1909, TNA WORK 14/134; Hall, 'Preservation, National Identity and the State', p. 151.

[136] *The Nation*, 4 May 1932, quoting Geddes, qu. in Hall, 'Preservation, National Identity and the State', p. 151.

[137] Hall, 'Preservation, National Identity and the State', pp. 151–3.

[138] He first circulated his ideas in a text entitled *The Care of Historical Cities* (Edinburgh, 1904) among Scottish preservationists and antiquaries, before presenting them to a wider audience in his seminal study on *The Care of Ancient Monuments*. For his use of congresses see Chapter 4 and on other places of publication see below.

[139] Stirling Maxwell, 'A Reasonable Policy for Protecting Ancient Buildings', 92–103; on Antiquaries see Mandler, *Stately Home*, p. 182.

[140] Clerk of the London County Council to First Commissioner of Works, 13 April 1908, TNA, WORK 14/2251.

[141] D.T. Rice, 'Brown, Gerard Baldwin (1849–1932)', rev. Anne Pimlott Baker, *DNB* (Oxford, 2004) www.oxforddnb.com/view/article/32110.

The first report convinced Lewis Harcourt, the First Commissioner of Works, to fill the position of Inspector of Ancient Monuments which had remained vacant after Pitt-Rivers' death, with C.R. Peers, Secretary of the Society of Antiquaries.[142] The report also hinted that stricter legislation was extremely urgent, but no action was taken until the 'Tattershall Castle Affair' in 1911.[143] That the owners sold the castle shamelessly bit by bit, convinced scholars and preservationists but also the Office of Works to make a push against public indifference and private greed. Like in France at the same moment, it virtually rained bills. Shaw-Lefevre, now Lord Eversley, of the Commons and Footpaths Preservation Society, was asked by the preservation societies to introduce a Bill to furnish the Office of Works with an advisory board to give guidance on the protection and compulsory purchase of monuments.[144] The Office of Works also worked on a Bill, giving itself more influence, while the New Liberal Noel Buxton suggested yet another with more draconian measures.[145] To consider these different propositions, a Joint Committee of the Commons and the Lords was established.[146] Its consultations resulted in the Ancient Monuments Consolidation and Amendment Act (1913), enlarging the categories of monuments protected, and extending compulsory powers.[147] However, in 1914, the six MPs who had formed the House of Commons side of the Joint Committee, dissatisfied with the implementation of their suggestions into the 1913 Act, introduced another Bill. Like many contemporary projects in France and Germany, it proposed that the Commissioners of Works should be given the power to schedule 'any moveable or immoveable monuments, in the widest sense of the word, whose preservation is desirable in the interests of the public on account of its importance in the history of the country, the history of civilisation, or the history of architecture or art, or on account of its aesthetic value'. It also advocated even more government control over scheduled sites and objects. As many

---

[142] G.H. Duckworth's (Chairman of the Commission) testimony to the Joint Select Committee, *Parliamentary Papers* (1912–13), VI, p. 408.

[143] See Mandler, *Stately Home*, pp. 184–7.

[144] Robert Hunter to Canon Rawnsley, 23 September 1911, NT Archives, MSS: 140, qu. in Mandler, *Stately Home*, p. 187. The CPS had merged in 1899 with the National Footpath Preservation Society (founded in 1884) and was renamed Commons and Footpaths Preservation Society.

[145] Commons Bills in *Parliamentary Papers* (1911), I, p. 81; (1912–13), I, pp. 57, 63; (1913), I, pp. 121, 143; (1914), I, 129. Lords Bills in *Lords Journal*, 143 (1911–12), 517; 144 (1912–13), 57, 71–72, 101; 145 (1913), 55.

[146] Joint Select Committee, *Parliamentary Papers* (1912–13), VI, cols. 408, 474–5, 466–8.

[147] Champion, 'Protecting the Monuments', p. 42, cf. *Parliamentary Debates*, Lords, 5th Ser., 11, 30 April 1912, cols. 871–83; 14, 28 May 1913, cols. 446–48; 24 June 1913, cols. 672–3; Commons, 5th Ser., 56, 12 August 1913, cols. 1459–60.

judged these state powers as too drastic and because more pressing political concerns were on the agenda in 1914, the Bill failed to make any progress and no new Bill was introduced until the 1930s.

Across the three countries, it is noticeable that demands from certain sectors of the public exceeded governments' willingness to legislate. As the preservation movements grew in each country, their efforts to push for legislation became also more coordinated. Having a government that felt it had something to gain from ancient monuments certainly helped, but the existence of earlier decrees, as well as the anchoring of a preservation administration within government, only had a limited impact on how far reaching later Monument Acts were. When comparing France and Britain it is tempting to conclude that the existence of the Historic Monuments Commission at the heart of the Ministry of Fine Arts in France as opposed to the absence of a Fine Arts Ministry in Britain was at least in part responsible for the greater extent of legislation in France. However, adding Germany into the equation muddies the water. Here, only those states that had neither a long established preservation institution nor a *Kultusministerium* managed to implement legislation by starting from scratch.

The power of comparison

Although the growth of preservation movements clearly pushed the drive towards legislation, this is not enough to explain how legislation could succeed in the face of the considerable opposition. For this the contribution of the international context was crucial. Confronted with massive opposition but also with problems overstepping national boundaries (such as defining heritage criteria, creating inventories and bureaucracies, and establishing indemnities and penalties), preservationists made no attempt to conceal the fact that they sought solutions in cultural transfer. It was accepted and even expected in all European countries that inspiration should be sought abroad. Every single attempt to draft bills discussed above was proceeded by the official announcement that comparative evidence would be studied.

The period of the elaboration of Monument Acts coincided with the birth of comparative legislation, but the translation and comparison of laws was not limited to the legal profession.[148] All existing transnational

---

[148] See Hellal, 'Les Études de législations comparées'. In France the *Société de legilsation comparée* was particularly active in translating foreign laws in full, for example: 'Loi hongroise du 28 mai 1881 sur la conservation des monuments d'art', *Annuaire de législation étrangère* (1882); 'Loi anglaise du

networks of preservationists were mobilised and further enhanced towards this aim. In the endeavour to remain up to date in a constantly evolving legal development, collaboration among state agencies, private associations and scholars inside and across national boundaries was intense. Although efforts to create an international committee overseeing the establishment of national legislation had failed, preservation legislation remained on the programme of virtually every international congress and guidelines and petitions attempting to establish universal principles were regularly sent to national governments. International exhibitions were likewise used to talk about the need for legislation and compile comparative texts.[149] In between international meetings, ministries, parliamentary committees, learned societies, law experts and art history professors wrote to each for information to write elaborate comparative accounts. Often they used the diplomatic services to cast the net as wide as possible.[150] The results were in turn sent across countries and continents.[151] Comparative accounts were not only published as parliamentary papers,[152] but led to elaborate

18 août 1882 sur les monuments anciens', ibid.; 'Loi du 2 avril 1882 du Grand-Duché de Finlande sur la protection et la conservation des monuments anciens', *Annuaire de législation étrangère* (1884); on Italy: 'Loi du 12 juin 1902 sur la protection et la conservation des monuments et objets ayant une valeur d'art ou d'antiquité', *Annuaire de législation étrangère* (1903); 'Loi du 27 juin 1903 prohibant temporairement l'exportation des ouvrages d'antiquité et d'art', *Annuaire de législation étrangère* (1904); 'Loi du 20 juin 1909, disposition relatives aux antiquités et beaux-arts', *Annuaire de législation étrangère* (1910).

[149] Baumgart's report on the exhibition of historic monuments in London included the first major comparative analysis for France and triggered further study, see Baumgart, *Monuments Historiques*.

[150] The material gathered by national agencies about the various and often scattered provisions on the protection of heritage in their own country, often provided the basis for comparative analysis. For France see the handwritten booklet, 'Beaux Arts Archives. Décrets et arrêtés de principes 1852–1870', MAP 80/1/31; Ministère de l'Instruction publique, des Cultes et des Beaux-arts, Direction des Beaux-arts, Commission des Monuments historiques, *Circulaires ministérielles relatives à la conservation des monuments historiques* (Paris, 1875). On Germany, esp. Prussia, mainly Wussow, *Erhaltung der Denkmäler*; F.W. Bredt, *Die Denkmalpflege und ihre Gestaltung in Preußen* (Berlin, Cologne, Leipzig, 1904); H. Lezius, *Das Recht der Denkmalpflege in Preußen. Begriff, Geschichte und Organisation der Denkmalpflege nebst sämtlichen gesetzlichen Vorschriften und Verordnungen der Verwaltungsbehörden einschließlich der Gesetzgebung gegen die Verunstaltung von Ortschaften und landschaftlich hervorragenden Gegenden (Gesetze vom 2. Juni 1902 und 15. Juli 1907). Für den praktischen Gebrauch zusammengestellt und erläutert von Dr. H. Lezius, Regierungsassessor, Hilfsarbeiter im Ministerium der geistlichen, Unterrichts und Medizinalangelegenheiten* (Berlin, 1908). For updates see GStA PK VI. HA, Rep. 92 Nl. Schmidt-Ott (M), A X, 4 and C 39. Some of these earlier German decrees are reprinted in Huse (ed.), *Denkmalpflege*; see also K. Heyer, *Denkmalpflege und Heimatschutz im deutschen Recht* (Berlin, 1912).

[151] MAP, 80/1/32–33; 80/1/61; GStA PK I. HA, Rep. 76 Ve Kultusministerium, Sekt. 1, Tit. VI, No. 141. Several folders with reports on the situation abroad were later destroyed cf GStA PK I. HA, Rep. 76 Kulturministerium, Übersicht; TNA, WORK 14/134, WORK 14/2278; SPAB Archives, 'Ancient Monuments Acts 1867–1913', 'Ancient Monuments Acts: correspondence'; List of Books in the Office.

[152] Reports from her Majesty's Representatives Abroad as to the Statutory Provisions Existing in Foreign Countries for the Preservation of Historical Buildings. Presented to the House of Commons

monographs, which discussed legislation in relation to wider attitudes towards the past. Especially the works by the Prussian civil servant von Wussow, and his Austrian colleague von Helfert, both initially compiled for internal ministerial use, and the comparative study by Edinburgh art historian Gerald Baldwin Brown, written to sway the country towards preservation, became standard works across Europe and are still often used for comparative assessments today.[153] Journals concerned with monuments, whether from a learned or a preservationist perspective, also published reports on foreign legislation. The *Korrespondenzblatt*,[154] the *Central-blatt der Bauverwaltung*,[155] *Die Denkmalpflege*,[156] teemed with comparative

by Command of Her Majesty in pursuance of their Address, 30 July 1897, *Parliamentary Papers* (1897), LXXII, p. 367; Reports Showing the Systems Adopted in Certain Foreign Countries for the Preservation of Ancient Monuments, 1912–13, *Parliamentary Papers* (1912–13), LXVIII, p. 1; Reports from his Majesty's Ambassadors at Vienna and Paris Showing the Systems Adopted in Hungary and France for the Preservation of Ancient Monuments. Presented to both Houses of Parliament by Command of His Majesty. February 1914, *Parliamentary Papers* (1914), XIV, p. 295. In France or Germany, comparative material was often annexed to the Bills.

153   von Wussow, *Erhaltung der Denkmäler*, Freiherr J.A. von Helfert, *Denkmalpflege. Öffentliche Obsorge für Gegenstände der Kunst und des Altertums nach dem neuesten Stande der Gesetzgebung in den verschiedenen Culturstaaten* (Vienna, Leipzig, 1897); Brown, *Care of Ancient Monuments*.

154   'Loi pour la conservation des monuments et objets d'art ayant un intérêt historique et artistique', 35 (1887), 147–8, as appendix to the proceedings of the annual meeting; 'Die Fürsorge des Staates für die Erhaltung von Denkmälern der Vergangenheit', 42 (1894), 93–7; 'Generalversammlung in Strassburg vom 25 bis 28. September 1899, Kommission für Denkmalschutz und Denkmalpfelge', 48 (1900), 42–4; 'Denkmalschutz in England und Irland', ibid., 140; 'Erster Tag für Denkmalpflege, Gesetzgebung zum Schutz der Denkmäler', ibid., 203–7.

155   'Deutsches bürgerliches Gesetzbuch, baurechtliche Bestimmungen', 10 (1890), 350; Bohnstedt, 'Die Denkmalpflege in Frankreich', 16 (1896), 313–14. 'Über die rechtzeitige Einholung der staatlichen Genehmigung zur Beseitigung, Veränderung und Veräußerung von Baudenkmälern und beweglichen Kunstgegenständen', 303–4, 488; 'Bücherschau: Loersch, H. Das französische Gesetz vom 30. März 1897 (sic!), ein Beitrag zur Denkmalpflege', 17 (1897), 487; J. Kohte, 'Die Pflege der Kunstdenkmäler in Italien', 18 (1898), 38.

156   'Die Hauptversammlung der deutschen Geschichts- und Alterthumsvereine', 1 (1899), 105–7; Bohn-stedt, 'Die Denkmalpflege', 2 (1900), 93–5, 97–9; Resolutions of the first *Denkmaltag*, ibid., 100–3; 'Internationaler Kunsthistoriker Kongreß', ibid. 104. On Austria and the Habsburg Monarchy: 'Gesetzentwurf betreffend den Schutz der Baudenkmäler in Oesterreich', 4 (1902), 64; 'Zur Vor-bereitung eines Gesetzes zum Schutze der Naturdenkmäler in Oesterreich', 5 (1903), 115; 6 (1904), 16, 60, Decrees in Bohemia, 13 (1911), 15, Tirol, 12 (1910), 64, archdiocese of Vienna, 14 (1912), 16. Belgium, 14 (1912), 51. England: H. Muthesius, 'Denkmalschutz und Denkmalpflege in England', 3 (1901), 52–4, and British Colonies: 'Das ägyptische Denkmalgesetz', 16 (1914), 80, 'Denkmalschutz im englischen Südafrika', ibid., 120. France: J. Kohte, 'Die Denkmalpflege in Frankreich von Dr. Paul Clemen', 1 (1899), 44. Russia: 3 (1901), 104. Greece: P. Clemen, 'Die Fürsorge für die mittelalterlichen Denkmäler in Griechenland', 1 (1899), 31–3; 'Denkmalpflege in Griechenland', 4 (1902), 47. Italy: 1 (1899), 20; 2 (1900), 120, 'Das Italienische Gesetz über den Denkmalschutz', 5 (1903), 31–2, F. Brundswick, 'Denkmalpflege in Italien', 6 (1904), 117–18; 9 (1907), 4, 14; 10 (1908), 52, 80. Switzerland: E. Probst, 'Zur Geschichte der Denkmalpflege in der Schweiz', 1 (1899), 53–4; Bern: 2 (1900), 120; 3 (1901), 56, 7 (1905), 39; Neuenburg: 4 (1902), 124; Wallis: 6 (1904), 123; 9 (1907), 108; Tessin: 7 (1905), 24. 'Der Rechtliche Heimatschutz in der Schweiz', 12 (1910), 126; Sweden and Norway: 14 (1912), 120. The more legislation evolved in Germany, the fewer reports about the developments abroad were printed. Between 1912–14, the reports of German laws were plentiful, but the new laws in France and Britain were no longer reported on.

articles, which spilled over to the general press.[157] In France, *L'Ami des Monuments*, the *Bulletin Monumental* and the *Gazette des Beaux-Arts* commented on legislation from a comparative angle and published accounts of progress in foreign countries.[158] Although no specialist journal existed in Britain, comparative accounts, often from the pen of Baldwin Brown, were printed in *The Quarterly Review, The Builder* and the *Journal of the RIBA*, as well as the international congress papers and reports discussed above.[159] The subject was also taken up in national gatherings from the German *Denkmaltage* to the annual meetings of the Society of Antiquaries, the National Trust and the SPAB.[160] Further *loci* of publication included doctoral dissertations, memorial lectures, and scholarly articles on subjects from law to history.[161] Like never before, or after, articles in the main encyclopaedias from *Mayers Großes Konversations-Lexicon* to the *Encyclopaedia*

[157] Press cuttings, GStA PK VI. HA, Rep. 92 Nl. Schmidt-Ott (M), A X 1; 'Die Fürsorge des Staates für die Erhaltung von Denkmälern der Vergangenheit', *Korrespondenzblatt der Geschichts- und Alterthumsvereine*, 42 (1894), 93–7 also summarised an article comparing the legislation in different European states by the Royal Saxon Archivist Dr. H. Ermisch in the 'Wissenschaftliche Beilage zur Leipziger Zeitung'.

[158] Challamel, 'Exposition universelle de 1889. Premier congrès international officiel pour la protection des monuments et oeuvres d'art. Des législation françaises et étrangères établies pour assurer la conservation des oeuvres d'art et des monuments', *L'Ami des Monuments*, 4 (1890), 225–300; 'Chronique, Application de la loi de conservation des monuments – Italie: abrogation de l'édit de Pacca', ibid., 5 (1991), 49; A. Audollent, 'La Question des antiquités et des beaux-arts en Italie', ibid., 6 (1892), 20–34; A.C.A. Marsy, 'De la législation danoise sur la conservation des monuments historiques et des antiquités nationales', *Bulletin Monumental* (1878), 572–84; P. Gout, 'La Conservation et la restauration des monuments historiques', *Gazette des Beaux-Arts* (1881), 297–307, 411–19.

[159] Cf. Brown, *Care of Ancient Monuments*, p. 148.

[160] See A. von Oechelhaeuser, *Denkmalpflege. Auszug aus den stenographischen Berichten des Tages für Denkmalpflege* (2 vols., Leipzig, 1910–13), I, Part III: 'Gesetzliche Denkmalpflege', pp. 125–324; *Memorandum as to the Steps taken in various Countries for the Preservation of Historic Monuments and Places of Beauty*. Appendix by Sir Robert Hunter to NT, *Annual Report* (1897); Hunter, *The Preservation of Places of Interest or Beauty. A lecture delivered at the University on Tuesday, January 29th, 1907* (Manchester, 1907); Sir J. Stirling Maxwell, 'A Reasonable Policy for Protecting Ancient Buildings', SPAB, *Annual Report*, 31 (1908); A.C. Benson, 'The Ancient Monuments Consolidation and Amendment Act', *Annual Report*, 37 (1914), 12–15, as well as 15 (1892), 36; 23 (1900), 38; 24 (1901), 12; 36 (1913), 3, 18. On colonial legislation in British Honduras cf. *Annual Report*, 17 (1894), 56–7.

[161] Pariset, *Les Monuments historiques*; L. Tétreau, Faculté de droit de Paris, *Législation relative aux monuments et objets d'art dont la conservation présente un intérêt national au point de vue de l'histoire ou de l'art. Thèse pour le doctorat* (Paris, 1896); J. Constans, Université de Montpellier. Faculté de droit. *Monuments historiques et objets d'art: loi du 30 mars 1887 et décrets du 3 janvier 1889 relatifs à la conservation des monuments et objets d'art ayant un intérêt historique ou artistique. Thèse pour le doctorat* (Montpellier, 1905); F. Cros-Mayrevieille, Université de Paris. Faculté de droit, *De la protection des monuments historiques ou artistiques, des sites et des paysages: évolution historique, restrictions à la propriété privée foncière. Thèse pour le doctorat* (Paris, 1907). Cros-Mayrevieille was one of the organisers and co-author of the proceedings of the *Premier Congrès international pour la protection des paysages*; J. Metman, Université de Dijon. Faculté de droit, *La Législation française relative à la protection des monuments historiques et des objets d'art. Thèse pour le doctorat* (Dijon, 1911); J. Marguery, Université d'Aix-Marseille. Faculté de droit d'Aix, *La Protection des objets mobiliers d'intérêt historique ou artistique, législation française et italienne. Thèse pour le doctorat*

Britannica further propagated the comparative outlook.[162] To the general comparative studies can be added studies about specific countries.[163] Even titles that indicated a treatment of the national situation often devoted considerable space to a comparative perspective or reprinted foreign laws.[164] Hence, there were virtually no purely national treatments; almost every

(sciences politiques et économiques) (Paris, 1912); R. Masson, Université de Paris. Faculté de droit. *Du Rôle de l'État par rapport à l'art. Thèse* (Paris, 1912); J. Boivin-Champeaux, Université de Paris. Faculté de droit, *Des Restrictions apportées à la propriété dans un intérêt esthétique (objets d'art, fouilles, beautés naturelles. Thèse pour le doctorat* (Paris, 1913); F. Rücker, Université de Paris. Faculté des lettres. *Les Origines de la conservation des monuments historiques en France (1790–1830). Thèse pour le doctorat d'université (lettres)* (Paris, 1913); for Germany: W. Hartung, *Die Denkmalspflege im juristischen Sinn mir spezieller Berücksichtigung Bayerns. Jur. Diss. Erlangen 1906* (Bayreuth, 1906); K. Heyer, *Denkmalpflege und Heimatschutz im Deutschen Recht, Jur. Diss. Marburg 1912* (Berlin, 1912). Festive lectures were particularly popular in Germany: G. Dehio, *Denkmalschutz und Denkmalpflege im Neunzehnten Jarhhundert. Rede zur Feier des Geburtstages Sr. Majestät des Kaisers gehalten in der Aula Kaiser-Wilhelms-Universität Strassburg am 27. Januar 1905* (Strassburg, 1905); C.A. Wieland, *Der Denkmal- und Heimatschutz in der Gesetzgebung der Gegenwart. Programm zur Rektoratsfeier der Universität Basel* (Basel, 1905); K. Lange, *Die Grundsätze der modernen Denkmalpflege. Rede zum Geburtstag Wilhelms II. von Württemberg vom 25. Februar 1906* (Tübingen, 1906); von Oechelhaeuser, *Wege, Ziele und Gefahren der Denkmalpflege.* For other scholarly work see Challamel, *Loi du 30 mars 1887 sur la conservation des monuments historiques et des objets d'art. Etude de législation comparée* (Extrait de *l'Annuaire de législation française,* Paris, 1888); Challamel, 'Commentaire sur l'ouvrage de Louis Tétreau, législation relative aux monuments et objets d'art', *Bulletin de la société de législation comparée* (1898); Lepelletier, 'Prohibition d'exporter les oeuvres d'art, législation italienne, *Journal du droit international privé et de la jurisprudence comparée* (1896), 962–81; A. Chretien, 'De la protection et de la conservation des monuments et objets précieux d'après la nouvelle loi italienne', *Journal de droit international privé et de la jurisprudence comparée* (1903), 736–60; A. Hallays, 'D'une législation à faire en France pour la protection des monuments et objets d'art, *Journal des débat,* April 1903; R. Fubini, 'Projet de loi sur la protection du patrimoine artistique en Italie', *Revue trimestrielle de droit civil* (1908); Lerebourg-Pigeonniere, Julliot de la Morandiere, 'Protection du patrimoine artistique', *Revue trimestrielle de droit civil,* April–June (1908), 404–6; M. Beakert, 'De la Préservation légale du patrimoine artistique', *Handelingen van den Geschieden Oudheidkundigen Kring von Gent / Annales du cercle historique et archéologique de Gand,* 2 (1895), 57–104.

162 'Denkmalpflege', *Mayers Großes Konversations-Lexicon* (1906), p. 614; C. Weatherly, 'Monument', *Encyclopaedia Britannica* (1911), XVIII, pp. 796–800.

163 In France, these focussed specifically on Italy and to a lesser extent Britain: W. Langhorne, *De la conservation des monuments historiques en Angleterre* (repr. from *Bulletin monumental,* Paris, 1896); P. Carpentier, *La Loi italienne du 12 juin 1912 édictant des dispositions sur la protection et la conservation des monuments et objets ayant une valeur d'art et d'antiquité* (Paris, 1902); A. Fresquet, 'Rapport sur la Conservation en Angleterre des Edifices Religieux et des Objets d'Art qui les garnisses', handwritten booklet for the *Ministre des Beaux-arts,* 14 June 1910, MAP, 80/1/32, Dossier 'Grande-Bretagne', cf. on Fresquet's visit to England TNA, WORK 14/134; in Germany French and Italian provisions were published extensively: Loersch, *Das französische Gesetz vom 30. März 1887,* Clemen, *Die Denkmalpflege in Frankreich*; Kohte, *Pflege der Kunstdenkmäler in Italien.*

164 E.g. P. Clemen, *Die Erhaltung der Kunstdenkmäler in Deutschland. Vortrag gehalten auf dem internationalen kunsthistorischen Kongress zu Lübeck am 18. September 1900. Sonderabdruck aus den Verhandlungen des Kongresses nach dem stenographischen Bericht* (Nürnberg, 1900); Bredt, *Die Denkmalpflege in Preussen*; T. Ducrocq, *La Loi de 1887 et le décret du 3 janvier 1889 sur la conservation des monuments et objets mobilier présentant un intérêt national au point de vue de l'histoire et de l'art* (Paris, 1889).

publication on legislation during the period had a comparative angle of some sort.

The exchange of information and publications not only fostered links across countries, but also promoted collaboration between private and state actors.[165] It was quite typical that the first comparative studies in Britain were initiated in the same year by two private societies, the National Trust and the Society of Antiquaries, but compiled with the help of the Foreign Office and resulting in a parliamentary enquiry.[166] Across Europe, scholars and associations addressed foreign monument administrations either directly or via the diplomatic services.[167] In turn, state agencies sent scholars abroad to consult with other members of the private sector and afterwards distributed the results of their work among civil servants.[168]

As a result, a large and complex collaborative information network emerged. It was broader than the exhibitions or congress networks and included virtually every European state and their colonial territories, North and South America, Japan, China and Siam. The material compiled led to much scholarly reflection about the merits of different national solutions and every legal project used the experiences of other countries to develop the best national solution. Moreover, and perhaps more crucially, the vast data pool offered proponents of competing ideas within each country material to bolster virtually every desired domestic policy by citing examples culled from other countries. Legislation was the area in which intercultural transfer was discussed most openly. Legislative campaigns *always* started with the announcement that the best foreign examples would be studied and they were always preceded by the claim that one needed to catch up with other countries. Significantly, this argument transcended intellectual and administrative circles. For instance, a number of regional German newspapers, reporting on the demolition of local monuments, made a comparison with foreign examples. When the *Allgemeine Zeitung* described the planned

---

[165] MAP, 80/1/61, Dossier 'Ouvrages envoyés de l'étranger'.

[166] NT, *Annual Report* (1897), Appendix; Reports from her Majesty's Representatives Abroad as to the Statutory Provisions Existing in Foreign Countries for the Preservation of Historical Buildings. Presented to the House of Commons by Command of Her Majesty in pursuance of their Address, 30 July 1897, *Parliamentary Papers* (1897), LXXII, p. 367.

[167] While an enquiry in 1838 from the RIBA upon the French Minister of Interior, had been apologetic for addressing a query from a private institution to a Minister, the tone was much more relaxed at the end of the century, see above Chapter 1.

[168] The Prussian *Kultusministerium* for instance ordered 150 copies of Paul Clemen's work *Die Denkmalpflege in Frankreich* to be distributed among its civil servants. Wilhelm Ernst und Sohn, *Verlag für Architektur und technische Wissenschaften* to *Kultusministerium*, 9 Sep. 1898, GStA PK, I. HA Rep. 76 Ve Kultusministerium, Sekt. 1, Tit. VI, No. 141; on the funding of travel expenses for scholars see correspondence Kohte and Persius 1887–1889, GStA PK, I. HA Rep. 76 Ve Kultusministerium, Sekt. 1, Tit. VI, No. 141.

destruction of a gothic townhouse in Nuremberg, it lamented that if only Germany had adopted a law of the French variety this could be prevented, and urged Germany to emulate the neighbouring country's example.[169] The argument was a potent one, as through the constant international updates, the protection of monuments was declared to be a measurement for progress and civilization: 'The care of ancient monuments, in the way we understand it today, so that it can be regarded as a yardstick of a people's cultural attainment, is a modern concept and a modern activity.'[170] While preservationists found many arguments to defend heritage, no other argument was used so often and so effectively than the need to establish credentials in terms of cultural advancement. In every country, preambles, treatises and legal comments time and again referred to superior monument legislation abroad, urging the legislator to 'catch up' with the other 'civilised countries', namely the chief European powers. Even countries advanced in legislation, such as Italy, argued that they had to further improve their system to maintain their status and provide the world with an imitable example.[171] Although:

> [t]hat other countries do a thing is no argument that we should do it but it is a fact that ours is the only civilised country in which the state has made no serious effort to protect ancient buildings. Other countries have accumulated a great deal of experience by which we may profit. Even the Balkan States in the intervals of those bloody scrimmages which the newspapers elect to describe as 'unrest' have found leisure to legislate about their ancient buildings. Our own dependencies of India and Egypt under Lord Curzon and Lord Cromer embarked on careful policies of monument preservation.[172]

To be surpassed by less civilised countries in such a civilising task was declared to be even less acceptable: the general assembly of the *Gesamtverein* expounded the necessity to improve *Denkmalschutz* in Germany, as 'with regard to the legal protection of monuments, the North African States are at the present moment way superior to Prussia, Saxony, Württemberg: that

---

[169] 'Mittheilungen und Nachrichten. Denkmalpflege in Deutschland,' *Allgemeine Zeitung*, 7 Mar. 1899, Beilage; see also newspaper clippings in GStA PK, VI. HA, Rep. 92 Nl. Schmidt-Ott (M), A X 1, fol. 2.

[170] Oechelhaeuser, *Wege, Ziele und Gefahren der Denkmalpflege*, p. 5.

[171] *Atti Parlamentari*, Camera dei Deputati, Legisl. XXIII, Sess. 1909, Documenti, Disegni di Legge e Relazioni, Nr. 61 Disegno di Legge presentato dal Ministro dell'Istruzione Pubblica (Rava), di concerto col Ministro del Tresor (Carcano) et col Ministro di Grazia e Gustizia e dei Culti (Orlando V.E.) Per le antichità et le belle arti. Seduta del 30 Marzo 1909, preamble.

[172] Stirling Maxwell, 'A Reasonable Policy for Protecting Ancient Buildings', p. 92.

is a dishonourable and untenable state of affairs'.[173] Competition worked equally well on the intra-national level. Within the German Empire, smaller states, such as Hesse, used the passing of a Monument Act to prove their modernity and fight off Prussian hegemony, whereas Prussian proponents of legislation argued that Prussia could not drop behind other European powers and smaller German states;[174] the rivalry extended even to the major cities who started outmatching each other with local legislation.[175]

The competitive need was further underpinned by the argument that the ability to connect with the past and take care of it distinguished imperial ruler from colonised subject. Greece was recognised as a European power for having claimed its ancient heritage in the struggle for independence, while Egypt's neglect to do the same was used as a reason to legitimise European tutelage.[176] To prove their worth in the imperial scramble to their imperial competitors, European governments raced each other not just to pass domestic preservation laws, but to establish colonial ones: Lord Canning, Viceroy of India, already called for more state intervention in the Jewel of the Crown in 1862 as neglecting the care of ancient monuments 'will not be to our credit as an enlightened ruling power'. For Lord Curzon, his Ancient Monuments Act for India was the greatest achievement of his Vice royalty.[177]

However, while imperial rivalry drove competition, it also complicated the argument. The view that the preservation of the nation's monuments was an index of its development conflicted with the assumption that a nation's civilisation could be measured by its protection of private property. It was remarked 'that the larger and more advanced the state the less easy is it to frame and to pass a satisfactory monument law'.[178] In order to be effective, a law had to interfere with private property rights 'and in advanced communities the individual has considerable self-assertiveness, and actively contests such proposed interference'. Consequently, 'for really

---

[173] 'Die Verhandlungen über Denkmalschutz und Denkmalpflege auf der Hauptversammlung des Gesamtvereins der deutschen Geschichts- und Alterthumsvereine in Straßburg', *Die Denkmalpflege*, 1 (1899), 106–7.

[174] *Verhandlungen der zweiten Kammer der Landstände des Großherzogtums Hessen in den Jahren 1900–1903. 31. Landtag, Protokolle*, vol. 3, Nr. 71, p. 1808 (von Biegeleben); *Stenographischer Bericht über die Verhandlungen des Preußischen Hauses der Abgeordneten, Preußisches Haus der Abgeordneten*, Sess. 1901, 12 March 1901, cols. 3253–4 (Abg. Seydel); *Herrenhaus. Session 1914, Drucksachen*, Nr. 9, Entwurf eines Ausgraungsgesetzes. esp. 'Begründung', pp. 8–17.

[175] *Dritter Tag für Denkmalpflege. Stenographischer Bericht* (Berlin, 1902), pp. 97, 113; Brown, *Care of Ancient Monuments*, pp. 114–25.

[176] D.M. Reid, *Whose Pharaohs? Archaeology, Museums and Egyptian National Identity from Napoleon to World War I* (Berkeley, 2002), p. 222.

[177] Qu. in Brown, *Care of Ancient Monuments*, pp. 232–5.   [178] Ibid., p. 44.

drastic enactments, we have to go to countries . . . where the personal rights
of the highly civilised man are almost unknown', such as in 'orientally
governed' states or the European colonies.[179]

Attempting to reduce property rights by alluding to foreign examples
could therefore also backfire. The French Senator for Charente-Inferiéure,
Émile Combes, for instance, objected to the extension of state control in
the proposed Monument Bill by attacking the choice of foreign models: 'I
must confess, gentlemen, that I am only mildly touched by the examples
borrowed from foreign countries. That Sweden and Norway, Greece and
Turkey, that Spain and Austria-Hungary . . . ' In midsentence, the former
Minister of Public Instruction Bardoux upon whose report the session
was based, interrupted shouting: 'and Italy! and England!'. Ignoring this,
Combes continued: 'From the fact, that other European states have over-
taken us on this way, that they were the first to have such an exceptional
law, I will not conclude that their behaviour imposes that we imitate
them. I won't go to the Turks or even the Spanish to look for models of
liberty.'[180]

Combes' objection to the Bill stemmed less from a general disdain for
ancient monuments than from his senatorial role as a defender of provincial interests, in this case objecting to encroachments on the authority of
provincial mayors. Somewhat unwillingly he equally protected the interest
of the Church, despite being one of the most outspoken anti-clericals of
the Third Republic. But the fact that he did so by attacking the foreign
examples brought forward by Bardoux, as well as Bardoux's interruption
of his speech to throw England and Italy into the mix is significant. It
shows that, although at the moment of elaboration the broadest possible
group of countries was compared, for public debate it was important to
choose examples not only according to the efficiency of their legislation,
but also according to the stereotypes that existed about them. Patterns of
citation of different countries varied from the private to the public, as it
was inconvenient to refer to certain countries in public debate, because
they were ranked low in terms of 'civilisation' and so could not be adduced
as examples to emulate. As a general rule, the big four in this game were
always France, Germany, Britain and Italy, with slightly different accents.
British preservationists emphasised mainly examples from their main rivals
France and Germany, Germans chose France and Italy. While some French
heritage-makers, like Beauquier with close ties to the *Heimat* movement

---

[179] Ibid. and p. 235.
[180] *JO*, Annexe 83, Séance du Sénat des 10 et 13 avril 1886. Première délibération, 599.

frequently mentioned the need to emulate German laws, most referred more rarely to the archenemy, but generally preferred Italy and England.[181]

This was especially the case when it came to defend the bone of contention of every law – the restriction of private property rights. A salient example was provided by the debates during the elaboration of the first French Monuments Act. One of the main reasons for the delay between first draft and promulgation was the interference with the rights of property, which made it a so-called 'exceptional law'. Whereas the first draft only included compulsory clauses for monuments owned by the state or by public corporations, the State-Councillor Courcelle-Seneuil, one of France's leading liberal economists, decided to include privately owned monuments in the scheme.[182] In his report to the State Council, Courcelle-Seneuil defended this choice by drawing on 'an English Act from 1880' as his only example from the comparative material at his disposition.[183] He detailed John Lubbock's project, adopted in 1880 but then rejected, presenting it erroneously as an Act that has already been passed. Lubbock's project precisely dealt with the question of the protection of private monuments against harm and foresaw a commission, composed of Trustees of the British Museum, to have authority over monuments in private hands. Yet, Courcelle-Seneuil could have invoked a much stronger Swedish Law of 1867 which limited private property rights by prohibiting owners from destroying or degrading the monuments and requested the state's permission prior to any works. However, the reporter chose the English example, as England had a particular reputation concerning the precautions that were usually taken to protect private property.[184] Hence subsequent reporters such as Proust and Bardoux followed that principle. Responding to the report of the latter at the Senate, the aforementioned Émile Combes objected again:

---

[181] See for instance *Documents parlementaires*, No. 263. Chambre des députés. Rapport fait (au cours de la précédente législature) au nom de la commission de l'administration générale, départementale et communale, des cultes et de la décentralisation, sur la proposition de loi de M. Charles Beauquier ayant pour objet d'imposer aux villes l'obligation de dresser des plans d'extension et d'embellissement . . . Repris le 5 juillet 1910.

[182] 'Avant-Projet Rousse', MAP, 80/1/19; Jean Courcelle-Seneuil (1813–1892), was a journalist, before becoming professor of political economy in Chile in 1855. After his return to France he was *Conseilleur d'Etat* in 1879 and between 1881 and 1883, *maître de conférences* for political economy at the *École Normale*. He was elected to the *Académie des sciences morales et politiques*, see *Académie des sciences morales et politiques* (2003), 'Jean Courcelle-Seneuil', www.asmp.fr/fiches_academiciens/decede/COURCELLE-SENEUIL.htm.

[183] *Documents parlementaires*, Conseil d'Etat, sections réunies de l'intérieur et de législation. Annexe au no 364 du projet de loi pour la conservation des monuments et objets d'art ayant un intérêt historique et artistique. Rapport présenté par Courcelle-Seneuil, conseiller d'Etat le 28 février 1881.

[184] Hellal, 'Les Études de législations comparées', p. 33.

The example of England suffices not to win my opinion. I will definitely not be persuaded that a nation so jealous of her rights of public and private liberties as England could voluntarily have sacrificed them in the interest of morality, of art and history, without making the act a most passionate one: for art and history have never, that I know, impassioned so sober a race as the English.[185]

However, Combes' objection did not convince the Senate to change the clause. It maintained the State Council's decision. Persuaded by Courcelle-Seneuil's report it had decided to include both public and private monuments in the *classement*.[186] It proved to be a productive misunderstanding. The presumed 'English Law' had been a rejected Bill, a rejection stemming from precisely the motives Combes had guessed out. When the Ancient Monument Act was finally voted in 1882, it included no inhabited buildings, only effectively protected prehistoric monuments and all compulsory clauses had been deleted.[187] However, the categories were subsequently widened and other types of monuments were included in the following decades. Those promoting the widening of categories in Britain, constantly quoted the French law of 1887 as a major model.[188]

This particularly fruitful misunderstanding exemplifies a much more widespread process. In the multilateral transfers and retransfers between approximately twenty countries, Bills rejected in one state often served as a model for drafts in other European countries or in the colonies, where legislation could be much stricter.[189] With a certain time-displacement, ideas were then often retransferred – frequently via another intermediate stop – to the original countries, before starting to travel again.

---

[185] *JO*, Annexe 83, Séance du Sénat des 10 et 13 avril 1886. Première délibération, 599.
[186] Hellal, 'Les Etudes de législations comparées', pp. 32–6.
[187] Chippendale, 'First Ancient Monuments Act', 1–55; Saunders, 'A Century of Ancient Monuments Legislation', pp. 11–33; see below.
[188] Reports from her Majesty's Representatives Abroad as to the Statutory Provisions Existing in Foreign Countries for the Preservation of Historical Buildings. Presented to the House of Commons by Command of Her Majesty in pursuance of their Address, 30 July 1897, *Parliamentary Papers* (1897), LXXII, p. 367, esp. 'Circular to Her Majesty's Representatives abroad', 14 May 1896. Hunter in his 1896 report for the National Trust also judged France to be the first model to imitate and Stirling Maxwell in his presentation to SPAB modelled his suggestions almost entirely upon France.
[189] Examples widely cited in comparative accounts were Curzon's 1904 Act for India, a Decree of the Bay for Tunisia in 1886 (which had been established using rejected French and Italian bills and did not require the consent of the owner for *classement*) and the colonial clauses of the French Acts of 1887 and 1913. The French Acts maintained earlier pre-colonial provisions if they were stricter than the new ones and also applied to Algeria and other colonies and protectorates a number of provisions that were stricter than metropolitan ones, to give the state pre-selective rights on any objects on or beneath the earth on territory given by the state to public corporations, private individuals or in military occupation.

'Official heritage'

The international exchange and rivalry had the effect that France, Germany and Britain followed broadly similar rhythms, drafting bills slowly at first and then with more frenzy after 1900. Probably more than any other area of preservation, legislation developed in a broad transnational framework and all laws were hybrid creatures. While some transfers remained hidden, successful emulation of countries with a high reputation in terms of civilisation was openly acknowledged. For instance, the author of a failed Prussian draft in 1887 acknowledged even fifteen years later proudly that he and his colleagues had tried to adapt the Act that had just been passed in France, 'as closely to Prussian, or German, circumstances as ever possible'.[190] That competition helped was also admitted. While it had not been possible to pass said draft, the later consent by the Prussian Ministry of Finance for the appointment of Provincial Conservators and Provincial Commissions was publicly attributed to the influence of the French Act of 1887.[191]

Overarching similarities, such as the broadening of criteria, the increase in compulsive measures, the professionalisation of conservation and the search for participatory solutions reflect the common pool of ideas. On the other hand, implementation in the different countries remained strongly shaped by pre-existing administrative structures and the political conflicts in which legislation was established. To a lesser extent, the personal preferences of activists also played a part. Consequently, provisions varied with regard to monument types (prehistoric, historic, natural, surroundings); with regard to owners concerned by legislation (the state, public corporations, private persons); with regard to the level of compulsion introduced and to the administration installed, i.e. the budget put at the disposition of said administration (see table 3).

While the legal texts codified what would thereafter be considered as 'official heritage', contemporaries were as aware as postmodern scholars about the fallacies of definition.[192] Von Wussow already argued in 1885 that 'the concept of monument cannot be defined, since the word, like an

---

[190] D. Polenz, 'Zur Geschichte der Organisation der Denkmalpflege in Preußen', *Die Denkmalpflege*, I (1899), 37–39, 45–46, here 37. See also Polenz, 'Zur Lage der Denkmalpflege in Preußen, III', *Die Denkmalpflege* (1903), 17–19; Draft, 23 May 1887, GstA Rep. 76Ve, Sekt., 1 Abt. VI, Nr. 141,

[191] *Vossische Zeitung*, Morgen Ausgabe, 19 April 1899, newspaper clipping in GStA PK VI. HA, Rep. 92 Nl. Schmidt-Ott (M), A x 1, fol 3.

[192] On the notion of official heritage, see Smith, *Uses of Heritage*.

Table 3. *Legal provisions in comparison by 1914*

Provisions	Great Britain	France	Germany		
			Prussia	Hesse	Oldenburg
Pre-existing Administration	No	Yes, 1830s	Yes, 1840s	No	No
Major Acts	1882	1887	Failed 1887	1902	1911
	1892	1906	Failed 1901		
	1900	1913	(1902 /07		
	1913		*Verunstaltungs-Gesetz)*		
			(1914 *Ausgrabungs-gesetz)*		
Prehistoric mon.	Yes (1882)	Yes	Yes (1914)	Yes	Yes
Historic mon.	(very limited,	Yes	Limited (1902)		
Natural mon.	1900)	Yes	Yes	Yes	Yes
		(1906)		Yes	Yes
Surroundings	(No)	Limited		Yes	Yes
	No	1906			
Owners concerned:					
State	Yes	Yes	No	(No)	No
Public corporations	No	Yes	Yes	Yes	Yes
Private owners	(Yes)	(Yes)	(Yes)	(Yes)	Yes
Buildings in use:					
Dwelling Houses	No	Yes	Yes	Yes	Yes
Churches	No	Yes	Yes	Yes	Yes
Compulsion	Low, 1913	High	Medium	High	High
Commission	Yes (1908)	Yes	Yes (1890)	Yes	Yes
Participatory model	No	No	Yes	Yes	Yes
Budget	Low	High	Medium	High	Low

adjective, is joined to different objects as a denomination to define their essence in a certain way'.[193] Moreover:

> If all mobile and immobile objects, which originate from an expired period of culture, are declared to be monuments, because of their special importance as characteristic emblems for their period of origin for the understanding of art and crafts and for the general historical research, as well as for their extraordinary historical interest to preserve the memory of events, the ensuing questions when applied to individual cases are already posed.

---

[193] Wussow, *Erhaltung der Denkmäler*, I, p. 1.

Which emblems are characteristic? Which events of the past are of extraordinary historical interest? Which objects do have a special importance for the remembrance of events of this kind?[194]

It was seen as an epistemological impossibility to find an objective answer. 'The only point about which disagreements are excluded is that the object defined as monument has to be from the past.'[195] British and French authors often pointed out that this understanding of the term 'monument' in German was wider than the use of the same word in their own language and increasingly tried to emulate the wider definition. They likewise adopted the German term *Stadtbild* (city image) to fight for the protection of entire ensembles. The impossibility to pick and choose monuments on the basis of any objective criteria led some authors to suggest that all remains from the past be protected by law (such as in Maurice Barrès' suggestion to protect all pre-1800 churches). Others suggested extending protection as widely as possible by emphasising the intrinsic links between local and national, and between built, natural and customary heritage. Hence a draft in Baden from 1913 even included buildings and objects, which 'give a place or landscape a special characteristic imprint'.[196] Overall, however, practicability demanded making choices. While the Viollet-le-Ducian category of 'national interest', that formed the basis of the 1887 French Law, and of all its imitators, subsequently gave way to 'public interest', 'purely local interest' remained widely excluded.[197] Some of the later German laws, especially the Hessian Act, incorporated the idea that archaeological, built and natural monuments were all interlinked, but the different ways towards legislation and the different competences needed to protect culture and nature often resulted in them being treated through different agencies and laws.

[194] Ibid., pp. 1–2.

[195] Ibid., p. 2. English speakers often noticed that in this German use of the term 'monument' was broader than the English one and suggested to follow the German definitions. A.C. Grand Duff to Sir Edward Grey, 28 Feb. 1912, report on Saxony in Reports from her Majesty's Representatives Abroad as to the Statutory Provision Existing in Foreign Countries for the Preservation of Historical Buildings. Presented to the House of Commons by Command of Her Majesty in pursuance of their Address, 30 July 1897, *Parliamentary Papers* (1897), LXXII, p. 367. Brown used definitions from a Bill of 1883–4 from Baden. *The Care of ancient monuments*, pp. 17–19.

[196] Qu. in Speitkamp, *Verwaltung der Geschichte*, p. 323.

[197] The Prussian Minister of Finance used almost the exact same words as the French in rejecting a draft's definition of a monument, deeming it unjustified to provide full protection for the majority of 'monuments of scientific, artistic and arthistorical interest, but especially of monuments of purely or primarily local or regional importance', qu. in Speitkamp, *Verwaltung der Geschichte*, p. 332. Speitkamp quotes a different version of the Bill: 'Entwurf', 21 Dec. 1900, as coming into effect on 1 April 1902, GstA PK, I. HA, Rep. 84a Nr. 10746, fols. 20–6. Votum by *Finianzminister*, 4 Feb. 1901, ibid. fols 40–44.

Beyond these broad principles, ownership was crucial in determining
what would be included. Most laws distinguished between objects and
sites owned by the state, by public corporations and private individuals.
State-owned monuments were in many ways the easiest category to include.
In France state-owned buildings were included into legislation from the
first drafts in the 1870s, as disagreements between different government
departments had caused problems in the past.[198] This was particularly
the case for buildings used for purposes other than those intended since
the Revolution, as in the case of Fontevraut Abbey (a prison and thus
under the responsibility of the Interior Ministry), or that of the Papal
Palace in Avignon (barracks under the responsibility of the Ministry of
War).[199] In Britain, the inclusion of state-property was probably the only
area that did not provoke many debates. In part, this was because only a
limited number of historic monuments was maintained by the state, such
as public statues under the guardianship of the Treasury, disused castles,
some Scottish ecclesiastical sites and ecclesiastical ruins in Ireland.[200] In
contrast to France and Britain, the inclusion of state property was more
contested in Germany. The different *Kultusministerien* generally advocated
the listing of state property, both to ensure protection and to demonstrate exemplary behaviour. However, the financial administrations and
Offices of Work responsible for the buildings resisted any curtailing of
their competences. Most drafts avoided the problem by emphasising that
the state, as initiator of the *Denkmalschutz*, would naturally protect its own
monuments, without automatically listing them. Listing of state property
was further affected by the mechanisms of the federal system, as it was a
means of affirming the culture-political sovereignty of the different states.
For instance, Hesse excluded Hessian state property, but explicitly included
monuments belonging to the *Reich* and to buildings co-owned with Prussia
in the Hessian-Prussian Railway Cooperation.[201] Conversely, in an act of
internal sovereignty, in Prussia, state property was not mentioned in order

[198] 'Avant-Projet Rousse', pp. 14–15, MAP, 80/1/19.
[199] See Bercé (ed.), *Les Premiers Travaux*, pp. 3–17; Ministère de l'Instruction publique et des Beaux-Arts, *Documents à l'appui du projet de loi pour la conservation des monuments historiques et des objets d'art. Procès-verbaux du Conseil supérieur des beaux-arts* (Paris, 1879), p. 11; while not being of primary interest to most French authors, Brown pays much more attention to inter-ministerial quarrels as reason for the Bill than to concerns over local autonomy, *Care of Ancient Monuments*, pp. 80–1.
[200] Chippendale, 'Making of the First Ancient Monuments Act', pp. 3–8.
[201] Wagner, *Denkmalpflege in Hessen*, p. 31; Speitkamp, *Verwaltung der Geschichte*, p. 326.

not to encourage provincial claims through the institutions of provincial monument care.[202]

In Germany and France, the inclusion of the properties administered by communes and Churches was most contested. In both countries, public corporations were the prime target of monument legislation. However, while every single building and objects owned by them had to be subject to an individual *classement* in France, in most German states, the state had supervisory authority over public corporations and the administration of assets of Churches and communes. Where laws were passed, this supervisory authority was used to claim control over all their movable and immovable property. The Hessian Act, for example, placed all monuments owned by public corporations automatically under the law, only private monuments had to be selected through scheduling. In contrast to France and Germany, ecclesiastical buildings in use were excluded from the listing in Britain. Unlike in France and Germany, there was also no motive to assert the state's control over a Church that was already a national institution. Even the SPAB, which repeatedly quarrelled with members of the clergy over restoration practices, subscribed to the exclusion of churches from legislation.[203]

Private property was the most contested area in Britain, hence the first Act only applied to pre-historic monuments, before categories slowly were extended to later periods. However, in a land where most of the 'national heritage' was still in private hands, dwelling houses remained excluded. In France privately owned monuments could be subject to *classement*. As so much aristocratic property had passed into public ownership during the Revolution, private property was never the primary concern of debates. However, opposition was taken into account by applying different rules to private monuments than state or corporate property: *classement* had to be subject to the owner's consent. The heavy provisions that protected movable property owned by the state or public cooperations against alienation did also not apply to those in private hands. In Germany, private property was included in most schemes, especially in the Hessian and Oldenburg Acts, but again not without resistance. In Hesse provisions had to be attenuated after deliberations and as in the French Act, listing of privately owned buildings or sites was subject to consent, and movables in private hands were excluded. The question of public access to private houses or parks was

---

[202] Speitkamp, *Verwaltung der Geschichte*, p. 327.   [203] SPAB, *Annual Report*, 37 (1914), 12–13.

raised in Germany, but attracted much less concern than in England.[204] Like in France, the relatively small proportion of important monuments in private hands meant that the issue was a relatively minor one. A survey conducted in Prussia during the Weimar period stated that only 5 to 10 per cent of all monuments were in private hands.[205]

The level of compulsion was likewise shaped by the broader conflicts. France had the highest level of compulsion which it introduced earliest. Any building and object (and later natural or picturesque sites) could be subject to a *classement* which remained valid in whoever's hands a building passed, making it impossible, or subject to heavy penalties, to destroy it. Any alterations needed ministerial authorisation. While expropriation for public use was reaffirmed, *déclassement*, or removal from the list, was also possible if demanded by the owner. Provision for movables only applied to objects owned by the state or public bodies. Those belonging to the state were inalienable, and those belonging to public bodies needed the consent of the Minister for restoration, or alienation, otherwise transactions were subject to nullity and persecution by civil tribunals.[206] Archaeological findings had to be mentioned to the authorities; if found on a private territory, the land might be expropriated for public use.

German draft Bills and Acts tried to adopt the French measures. Virtually all proscribed that the property of corporations should not be passed into private hands and corporations had the duty to maintain their property and surrounding areas.[207] Most drafts and the few full and partial Acts passed contained the possibility of expropriation, but generally indemnities were given.[208] While the various Anti-Disfigurement and Excavation Acts fixed penalties for destruction or exportation, the Hessian and Oldenburg Acts introduced clauses that made a sale or alterations subject to authorisation. Here too, excavations needed to be declared to the authorities.[209] However, in contrast to the rather top-down French approach to listing and decision-making by the Minister and the Historic Monuments Commission, Hesse and Oldenburg created Monument Councils, so called *Denkmalräte*, which were composed of representatives of the authorities, learned societies, the

[204] Kohler, 'Das Recht der Kunstwerke und Alterthümer', pp. 72–4, Kohler, 'Das Recht an Denkmälern und Altertumsfunden', cols. 771–8.

[205] Report by Prussian conservator Robert Hiecke, 7 Feb. 1929, GStA PK, I. HA Rep. 77 Ministerium des Inneren, Tit. 1215, Nr. 3, Beiheft 2, qu. in Speitkamp, *Verwaltung der Geschichte*, p. 365.

[206] Art. 2279 and 2280 of the *Code civil*. [207] Speitkamp, *Verwaltung der Geschichte*, p. 228.

[208] Prussian *Kultusministerium* to *Oberpräsident* in Kassel, 11 Nov. 1901, qu. in Speitkamp, *Verwaltung der Geschichte*, p. 329.

[209] Gesetz den Denkmalschutz betreffend vom 16. Juli 1902, *Großherzoglich Hessisches Regierungsblatt*, Nr. 41, 18 July 1902, p. 275. It became effective on 1 October 1902.

Catholic and Protestant Church and other owners and experts from the world of the arts and the sciences to reach decisions based on consent rather than compulsion.

Unsurprisingly, in Britain compulsion remained lowest. Unlike railway construction, preservation was never important enough to legitimise expropriation or compulsory purchase as in France or Germany. While the first Ancient Monuments Act contained no compulsory clauses at all, some measures were subsequently included. The Advisory Board established by the 1913 Act could schedule monuments not yet reported on by the Royal Commission. The Commissioners could issue preservation orders to stop work on a site for a period of eighteen months, if there was danger of destruction. Thereafter, confirmation was required by a Bill in Parliament. A supplementary list was established for sites that were not important enough to deserve guardianship, but 'the preservation of which is of national importance'. Owners had to give notice on alterations planned. It was made an offence to damage these sites, but the owner was exempt from this last provision, which weakened the entire stipulation.

Notwithstanding the significance of the varying levels of state control and compulsion in the three countries, it should be noted that on a broader international scale, the level of compulsion and interference remained low not just in Britain, but also Germany and France. Compared to countries such as Italy, Greece, Turkey, Tunisia, but also Hungary and Denmark, as well as the French and British colonies, provisions appear much less strict and demonstrate a strong belief in the rights of owners.

Despite the general obsession to pass formal Monument Acts, and the widespread argument that preservation could only be assured through such a provision, the presence or absence of such an Act also did not necessarily equal good or bad preservation, or even determine the leeway the authorities had over heritage. The impact of a law depended often less on the wording, but more on competent personnel, interested authorities, and enough money. This can be seen with special clarity in the German states. Although only two smaller states, as well as the Hanseatic cities passed formal Monument Acts, by 1914 nearly all German states had established preservation institutions; only Mecklenburg-Strelitz, Reuß ältere Linie, Schwarzburg-Sondershausen and Lippe-Detmold did not have any regulations at all (see ill. 6.1).[210] Despite the dearth of formal acts, the wider legal

---

[210] Speitkamp, *Verwaltung der Geschichte*, pp. 320–1, note 32, p. 453. However, in Schwarzburg-Sondershausen and Lippe-Detmold plans for a *Verunstaltungsgesetz* were also in preparation.

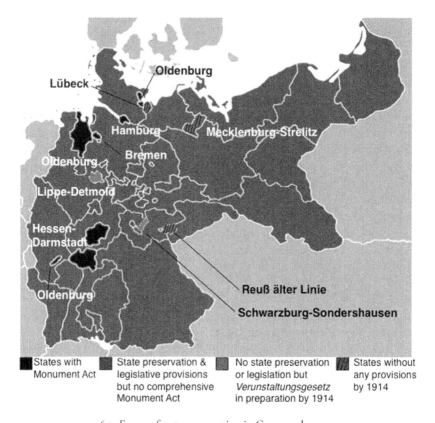

6.1. Forms of state preservation in Germany by 1914.

situation was characterised by a rapid increase and condensation of legal provision since the 1880s and the spread of these provisions over different branches of the law.[211] An imperial Monument Act never took shape, but imperial law contained a number of provisions that could be used to protect monuments. The Civil Code, which came into force in 1900, contained provision for the nullity of forbidden sales that could apply to works of art.[212] The separate law introducing and implementing the Civil Code, elaborated in the 1880s, regulated the expropriation of private land for reasons of public utility and contained building regulations relevant to preservation.[213] The Penal Code threatened any person 'who intentionally

---

[211] Ibid., p. 315.   [212] Ibid., p. 316, see § 134 *BGB.*
[213] Art. 109, 111, 119 Ziff 1 *EG zum BGB.*

and illicitly destroys or damages monuments or works of art'.[214] Even the trading regulations of 1892 demanded that trade guilds and chambers of commerce had to obtain the permission of a supervisory authority for the sale of 'objects that have a historical or scientific artistic value'.[215]

The introduction of a formal Monument Act could help to create greater cohesion, but it was not the only way. Nor was it a warrant for more preservation. It much improved the Hessian situation. A Monument Council under the presidency of von Biegeleben was immediately constituted from experts and owner's representatives. By 1912, it had listed over 2,000 buildings (something that had taken the French Monument Commission more than sixty years. At the same moment in time, France only had about twice as many monuments listed for a much bigger territory).[216] The participatory element also meant that while some proprietors had appealed against the act of *classement*, others had expressed a wish to have their monuments scheduled and most contested cases were resolved through consultation.[217] In Oldenburg, on the other hand, the Act existed mainly on paper: it was difficult to find competent personnel; implementation was left to honorary members with no budget at their disposition. As a result no systematic inventory was drawn as prescribed by the law and only those objects for which owners had asked permission to sell or repair were put on an inventory.

That the success of *Denkmalpflege* and *Denkmalschutz* rested mostly on implementation was equally true for those territories without a formal Act. Most states had a solid preservation administration, with a strong participatory element, without having a Monument Act. The situation was maybe legally unstable, yet provisions in the end were quite dense and not ineffective, especially as courts stretched the meaning of the provisions at their disposition. For instance, when a parish in the district of Aachen had secretly destroyed its Romanesque church tower despite the fact that the authorities had denied permission, the public prosecutor brought charges against the parish and secured a conviction. The parish appealed stating that in the original provision the term 'monument' only applied to statues or funeral monuments, but was rejected by the Imperial Court, because the word *Denkmal* now applied not just to public monuments but to all

---

[214] § 304 *StGB.*

[215] §§ 89b Nr. 3 103 Absatz I GewO, cf. *Gewerbeordnung für das Deutsche Reich* (21st edn, Munich 1929), pp. 50, 74.

[216] See Léon, *La Vie des monuments*, p. 141; Leniaud, *Les Archipels du passé*, p. 229.

[217] 290 remonstrances were brought forward of which 71 were withdrawn after further consultation and 191 were brought before the Ministry of the Interior, it approved of only 7; see Brown, *The Care of Ancient Monuments*, p. 113; Speitkamp, *Verwaltung der Geschichte*, p. 337.

remains of the past that had a historic, scientific or artistic importance.[218] Moreover, while the central state often refused to care for purely 'local heritage', Germany's decentralised structure and the options of local by-laws and building regulations meant that the level of protection of local monuments remained the envy of France and Britain.

It is likewise problematic to take the shape of laws as indicators for heritage consciousness at large, as debates were so tied up with broader political ends. Most of those who were against legislation were not against all forms of preservation. They simply could not reach a compromise about the importance of local, religious or familial heritages versus national and statist claims. Despite the widely diverging national problems, the role of the private preservation movement in pushing to overcome some of these debates was remarkably similar across countries. Although government agencies were a main driving force behind legislation in France and in several German states, the impetus from the private sector was even stronger. Only on one occasion did private societies object to the extension of state influence: provincial archaeological societies protested against an attempt by the French government in 1910 to prescribe that excavations on private land had to be put under the supervision of the state. The provincial societies who feared that this might end their *raison d'être* protested, the bill was rejected and withdrawn.[219] In all other cases, it is noteworthy that across the three countries demands from the public, by as ideologically opposed figures as the nationalist Barrès and the anti-clerical Beauquier, for a stronger protection of the local 'heritage', went much farther than the aims of government. While the state administration in France remained weary of many of the initiatives and tried to channel them into existing structures with varying success, different German governments viewed the campaigns by preservation associations favourably. Many a government attempting to pass legislation used the approval of the associations and the broad public support evident in the behaviour of judges and journalists, to back its schemes. The British government reacted at first with little enthusiasm to the various preservationist zealots, and those actively campaigning for legislation were fewer and more divided than in Germany. However,

---

[218] See Hammer, *Entwicklung des Denkmalrechts*, p. 182. On the use of both Imperial and Prussian law in Prussia, especially under *Kultusminister* Studt, 'Zum Schutz der Kirche Wang im Riesengebirge', *Die Denkmalpflege*, 6 (1904), 115; 7 (1905), 38. For further cases Lezius, *Das Recht der Denkmalpflege in Preußen*, pp. 65–6, 75–7; *Die Denkmalpflege*, 5 (1903), 88; Hammer, *Entwicklung des Denkmalrechts*, p. 187.

[219] See especially protests by the Société polymatique du Morbihan published in the *Revue archeologique* and then in a *Deuxième protestation contre le projet de loi relatif aux Fouilles intéressant l'archéologie et la paléontologie* (Extrait du procès verbal des la Séance du 29 Nov. 1910), MAP, 80/1/25.

it is proof of the influence of this 'small knot of cultivated people' on the political elite that legislation ultimately succeeded.

The comparative perspective finally shows that judgements on 'delay' and 'backwardness' are highly problematic, not only because the categories of 'pioneer' and 'latecomer' were subject to constant change as laws were introduced with increasing velocity.[220] Turn of the century preservationists always found elements they sincerely admired abroad and wished to emulate. Some of what they admired changed over time, but the French institutions with their level of compulsion and funding, the German definition of monuments and the German emphasis on local care, the strength of the English voluntary sector and the restoration mechanisms established by the Church of England remained constantly valued. However, and more crucially, for contemporaries, highlighting their own 'backwardness' was a rhetorical strategy used to convince opponents. It says little about actual delay, but it tells a lot about ideas about civilisation and the importance of international competition.

The question of 'failure' versus 'success' so prevalent in the secondary literature is equally tricky. If comparing original drafts with final Acts, every Act could safely be called a failure. To quote Baldwin Brown again: 'It has been pointed out already that in draft Acts we find a completeness and a logic which measures actually passed after parliamentary struggles have seldom retained.'[221] All Acts passed in Germany, France and Britain (and the rest of the countries involved in the legal race) had to make compromises with regard to property rights and budgetary constraints. Yet to interpret this as a failure of preservation would be misleading.

Despite considerable resistance from diverse opponents in all three countries, and intense battles over whether local, religious or aristocratic heritages should be seen as a national possession, the idea that such a thing as a 'national heritage' existed and that the state had to protect it was largely accepted on the eve of the First World War. At the beginning of the legal debates in the 1870s it was by no means taken for granted that 'national heritage' was more important than individual or religious heritage, or that state intervention should be the favoured course of action, not even by ardent preservationists. Yet, by 1914, it was a truth almost universally acknowledged, even by those whose interests were not particularly antiquarian. This was not least reflected in the more frequent use of the term 'heritage',

---

[220] On the problematic nature of these categories see H. Berghoff, D. Ziegler, *Pionier und Nachzügler? Vergleichende Studien zur Geschichte Großbritanniens und Deutschlands im Zeitalter der Industrialisierung. Festschrift für Sidney Pollard zum 70. Geburtstag* (Bochum, 1995), p. 28.

[221] Brown, *Care of Ancient Monuments*, p. 107.

'*patrimoine*' or '*Erbe*' in all three languages as a synonym for 'monument'.[222] 'The whole attitude of this country and of the civilized world in general has changed.' At the eve of the war, it seemed 'almost incredible... how much opposition was excited' a generation earlier.[223] Through constant international comparison, preservation, and especially formal Monument Acts, had become an attainment to define the modernity and advancement of a given state. In short, a status symbol.

---

[222] See for instance Lord Curzon's use above, or Bienvenu Martin's report for the Senate, talking of 'notre patrimoine national'. *Documents parlementaires*, No. 281. Sénat. Annexe au procès-verbal de la séance du 7 novembre 1911. Germany's wider use of monument made '*Erbe*' less of a necessity to widen categories, but here too we see it used more and more often. E.g. a conference by Oecheshaeuser first entitled 'Denkmalpflege in alter und neuer Zeit' was published under the title 'Der Väter Erbe', see Oechelhaeuser, *Wege, Ziele und Gefahren der Denkmalpflege*, p. 4. Julius Kohte and Paul Weber spoke of '*Erbe der Vergangenheit*', see *Die Pflege der Kunstdenkmäler in Italien*, p. 1 and *Heimatschutz, Denkmalpflege und Bodenreform*, 8, 17, respectively. The draft for the Prussian Excavation Law spoke of the 'national heritage of archaeological antiquities' as '*vaterländischen Erbes an Bodenaltertümern*'.

[223] *Parliamentary Debates*, Lords, 5th Ser., 11, 30 Apr. 1912, cols. 871–2.

Conclusion

'Heritage' became one of the great universalising categories of the modern era through a cross-cultural process. International collaboration and competition shaped discourses and practices, theories and institutions alike during the long nineteenth century. As inspiration was constantly sought abroad, results were a genuine mixture of ideas. Cultural transfers moulded virtually every area of heritage-making, from the creation of institutions and legislation and the foundation of a private movement, to restoration practices, exhibitionary culture, the plots of preservationist novels, and the very words used to define and defend 'heritage'. Growing international rivalry and the constant desire to 'catch up' with other countries was a decisive driving force behind the rise of preservation in individual countries. However, rivalry was intertwined with new internationalist efforts to save a common heritage and establish international conventions regulating the exportation of works of art, the preservation of nature and the protection of monuments in wartime.

Agents and networks

The transnational perspective revises both the origins of the global heritage concept, and previous nationally oriented explanations for each country. It can no longer be maintained that French heritage was created by the state, German heritage by the bourgeoisie and English heritage by an anti-modern aristocracy. Certainly, these actors did use the idea of heritage for their own benefit; however, the concept was invented and subsequently appropriated by groups that were more diverse. It developed from the interplay between civil society initiatives, emerging state administrations, monument owners, and a broader historical culture. In all three countries calls from members of the public went further than the willingness of governments to administrate, of parliaments to legislate and of owners to accept interference.

While interest in the past was fed by an increasingly varied popular culture, all three countries also witnessed a strong drive to institutionalise the protection of the past through state organisations and private bodies. Across countries, the number and diversity of people gathering to enjoy and protect heritage increased throughout the century. While notables, whose interest in the past was often related to feudal models of societies and religious revival, dominated in the early nineteenth-century, in all three countries larger parts of the educated middle-classes were progressively included. Professional bodies, activist societies with strong ties to social and artistic reform movements and leisure associations offered alternative approaches to heritage. The preservationist leadership was predominantly male, middle-class and middle-aged, but not exclusively so. While activism at the highest level was reserved to a 'small knot of cultivated people', the social and gender reach of associations and campaigns was broader. Although many different ideas about heritage existed among preservationists, a strong will was manifest to coordinate efforts at a national level. The German *Heimatbewegung* with its layers of local and regional affiliations had the largest membership and most coordinated voice, but France and England arguably had remarkably similar, if more loosely connected, movements.

By explaining the creation of these movements, the book has primarily focussed on self-proclaimed 'friends of monuments', while enemies or those merely indifferent, have mostly appeared through preservationist eyes. The history of these enemies has still to be told from their own perspective.[1] The much maligned 'demolishers', 'squires, parsons and architects', 'the zealous priests', 'ambitious mayors' and 'communes with a taste for local independence', contributed their own views on what to abandon and what to cherish. Few preservationists placed love of monument above every other consideration. Most were preservationist and destroyer in the same person, as they tried to reconcile care for the past with modernising desires of a liturgical, hygienic, democratic, commercial or artistic nature.

Everywhere, the preservationist milieu was characterised by strong interpersonal and organisational links across borders. While some organisations had particularly close ties with foreign sister bodies, members of all national preservation societies in France, Germany and England were in epistolary and often personal contact with preservationists in other countries, and so were government officials and the authors of influential theoretical texts. Contacts benefited from increasingly better means of exchange through

---

[1] See P. Mandler, 'Rethinking the "Forces of Darkness". An Anti-History of the Preservation Movement in Britain', in Hall (ed.), *Towards World Heritage*, pp. 221–39.

greater possibilities of travel, faster communication and the formalisation of internationalism through world's fairs and congresses.

The result was a dense network that stretched far beyond the three countries. Connections operated not only across the European continent and within and between empires, but straddled the entire globe. The density of links, however, was not equally distributed. Three factors seemed to determine where thick connections were established. The first connector was provided simply by familiarity with a given country, often based on historic links (be it through a common language and kinship or a belligerous history) or driven by contemporary prestige. While contemporary standing often determined how models were adduced publicly, new connections were also issue-driven. As a result, the networks connecting nature preservationists were much more oriented towards the New World than those of cultural preservationists, but here too different foci existed. Those championing historic preservation, for instance had a stronger leaning towards the lands of classical antiquity that had started to protect their monuments early on, while those focussing on pre-history were more oriented towards Northern Europe, as the field was heavily shaped in Scandinavia. Finally, personal and affective links played an important role in establishing (or preventing) particularly close connections between some countries, i.e. institutions, as the case of the links between the SPAB and *L'Ami des Monuments* or the *Bund Heimatschutz* and the SPPF indicate. Further research is necessary to map the nature and extent of heritage networks in Europe and to understand the flow of people and ideas across the globe. We need to investigate not just precisely how the respective empires were seen as a laboratory for ideas for many preservationists and how in turn foreign colonial preservation was used as a model in Europe for domestic projects, but also how indigenous ideas interacted with Western thinking and practice.[2] More needs also to be done to link in this connection interest in different forms of heritage, from textual sources to nature and living peoples, and to understand where connections were acknowledged and where they were silenced. Only then can we begin to fully grasp the mechanisms and impact of this 'First Heritage International'.

Concepts and articulations

Linguistic practice reflected the tensions between national peculiarities and the growing internationalisation. Despite the different words used to talk

[2] See Swenson and Mandler (eds.), *From Plunder to Preservation*.

about heritage, general trends manifested across languages. The substitution of the early nineteenth-century references to objects and buildings as *works of art, antiquities, antiquités* or *alterthümliche Merkwürdigkeiten* with *Heimat, matrie, patrimoine, Erbe* and *heritage* marked a desire to widen the patrimonial field to include the local alongside the national, the ordinary alongside the outstanding, nature alongside culture and traditions alongside objects. The substitutions also emotionalised preservation. Although different words remained in use synonymously, the more the preservation of the past was universalised as a moral duty, the more remains were referred to as a *heritage, patrimoine* and *Erbe*.[3]

At the same time, preservationists reflected on the different semantic dimensions of other languages. In some instances, differences were glossed over for the benefit of stressing similarities. The Society for the Protection of Ancient Buildings called various French societies 'French SPAB', the BHS spoke of the *Premier Congrès pour la protection des paysages* as *Erster International Kongreß für Heimatschutz* and *L'Ami des Monuments* re-baptised foreign societies according to its own name. In other cases, differences were highlighted, and often loan translations were proposed or words were maintained in the original language to signal the import of a superior foreign model. (Baldwin Brown's monograph, for instance, was almost more littered with German and French words than this book.)

Underneath these general developments, a variety of heritage concepts co-existed. Across national boundaries, heritage appealed to ideologically opposed figures, for which a statement by German preservationist Cornelius Gurlitt is symptomatic. Gurlitt stressed *Denkmalpflege*'s proactive drive to enhance 'social well-being', while declaring the protection of buildings to be a 'conservative practice' devoted to 'spreading beauty over the entire country with a liberal hand'.[4] 'Heritage' could be defined broadly enough or 'doctrinally void' enough, to accommodate various and often opposed aesthetic, religious and political views from proto-communist to crypto-fascist.[5] This was precisely its appeal, as it offered, like few other concepts, a language that could overcome the fractures of modernity.

Yet while a broad consensus on the benefits of heritage was developed, and preservationism could be discussed independently of politics in scholarly circles and to a certain degree in the press, once it affected social and

[3] The same principle also drove the further substitution of 'monument' by 'heritage', *patrimoine* and *Kulturerbe* since the 1970s see Swenson, 'Heritage, Patrimoine und Kulturerbe'.
[4] Gurlitt qu. in Magirius, *Geschichte der Denkmalpflege*, p. 149.
[5] For the idea of a doctrinal void see Choay, *L'Allégorie du Patrimoine*, p. 111.

political decision-making the consensus often broke down. Moreover, an examination of how the same preservationists expressed the concept in different arenas shows that discursive strategies were highly adaptable to context and addressee, and internal contradictions were frequent: preservationists condemned commercialisation and tried to employ it, they fought to preserve the past, but were desirous to abandon the past's attitude to preservation. The contingency with which heritage was defined is particularly apparent with regard to nationalism and internationalism. In the exhibition reports national superiority was claimed, at the congresses, common effort and internationalist understanding were invoked. In the legislative debate national inferiority was deplored to justify the need to introduce legislation in order to 'catch up' with other 'civilized nations'.

Competition and collaboration

The intensity of transfer produced similar ideas on a theoretic level, but practical implementation in different countries varied. The organisational form of preservation movements was shaped by traditions of sociability, activism and philanthropy. Form and degree of state preservation was influenced by factors such as the wider legal and administrative framework, the role of private property, the status of corporate bodies and the social position of monument owners. Moreover, implementation was linked to the political context. As opposition to state intervention and legislation shows, preservationist aims were at times weakened or strengthened through their association with land reform, economic development, religious revival and anti-clericalism.

It was in part because of these factors that the international arenas gained importance for the domestic agenda. Cultural transfers often served 'legitimizing one's own actions or criticizing those of others in a national debate'. Alternatively, cultural transfer helped, 'trying to find a way out of an internal political impasse by having recourse to foreign examples'.[6] In a similar way, the prestige of the international arena allowed domestic aims to be fostered. The French Historic Monuments Commission used the world's fairs to promote its own agendas; the emerging private associations used the international campaigns and congresses in the same way to increase their standing nationally. In the debate about legislation the allusion to foreign examples was the most widely used argument against opponents. While this was a general mechanism, national preferences for particular arenas

---

[6] Geyer, Paulmann (eds.), *The Mechanics of Internationalism*, p. 16.

of internal action are noticeable: *Exposition universelles* and international congresses in France, public campaigning in England, and theorising of foreign examples in scholarly publications in Germany. These different loci were chosen as they were domestically most prestigious and effective.

Beyond the utilitarian domestic use of the international scene, two souls were dwelling in most preservationists' breasts. On the one hand, the aim of most cultural transfer and international discourses was to improve the national situation, not least with the endeavour to improve one's own status and thus prestige. After the idea that certain styles corresponded to certain nations (i.e. that Germans, French and Britons had all singlehandedly invented Gothic Architecture) was challenged by the new discipline of art history, the competition of who had the most impressive national monuments was transformed into a competition about their preservation. In the first instance, European states were intent on establishing their standing as a *Kulturnation* within Europe, but this very habit of confrontation bound them together, engendering as a by-product a common culture of heritage. Yet this culture did not focus on a unified Europe, but increasingly aimed to legitimise European supremacy and expansion.

One of the most enduring discursive traditions established was the link between preservation and civilisation. Declaring preservation of monuments and non-monuments as such to be an indicator for civilisation was first employed to stop Revolutionary iconoclasm and art looting. However, in the early- to mid-nineteenth-century heritage-makers defined their countries' international standing still mostly in terms of the quality and quantity of actual monuments, in the age of imperialism, the *preservation* of heritage took predominance. The reason for this seems simple. A Herderian distinction between Europe and the 'peoples without history' was challenged in the face of majestic ancient monuments. Thus the civilisatory achievement was redefined as a European or Western ability to preserve one's own heritage and that of other parts of the world as opposed to a neglect of the ancient heritage by the 'native' population. The protection of monuments was made a yardstick for a nation's ability to rule its colonies properly.[7]

Hence, while in the early nineteenth century the success of transfer depended on a domestic need (as demonstrated by the absence of transfer of administrative measure to England in the 1840s), in the late-nineteenth and early-twentieth century, a situation of general competition between

[7] Brown, *Care of Ancient Monuments*, pp. 232–5.

countries had arisen, in which preservationism became a measurement for 'civilisation' and '*Kultur*', and foreign methods of restoration, legislation and administration were borrowed, in attempts to produce results which surpassed those of neighbouring countries.

On the other hand, a truly collaborative republic of letters existed well beyond the French Revolution. Preservationists exchanged ideas, assisted each other to save monuments across national borders, and fought to establish common standards. The period saw the first attempts to create international conventions for the protection of monuments in case of war resulting in the Hague Conventions of 1899 and 1907, based, at least in part, on the belief of a 'common cultural heritage of mankind'.

With the wisdom of hindsight we can tell that the international exchange did not lead to peace and goodwill among nations, nor did the international conventions prevent the destruction of cultural heritage in the violent conflicts of the twentieth century. Instead nationalism prevailed in the first instance, as many an internationalist preservationist turned nationalist at the outbreak of the Great War, and some ardent proponents of international understanding from the *Heimatschutz* and *Denkmalschutz* movement during the *Kaiserreich* gravitated towards National Socialism in the interwar years. Still, despite a relative failure of implementation, the rhetoric of international understanding was one of the most lasting legacies of the international congresses and only re-enhanced through the backlash of the World Wars. When international collaboration on monument protection *officially* started with the foundation of UNESCO's precursor, the 'International Committee on Intellectual Cooperation' (IICI) of the League of Nations, nationalism and universalism were further converged, 'using the protection of cultural heritage as a tool in the promotion of internationalism'. To 'counter purely nationalist interest, the League fostered the notion of common cultural heritage'.[8] The belief in a common heritage of humanity and in the peacekeeping effect of love for one's own 'heritage', i.e. the idea that 'heritage' had the power to overcome any tensions between the local, the national and the global, prevailed independent of their original locus, becoming pivots in the rhetoric of UNESCO and the EU.

---

[8] S.M. Titchen, 'On the Construction of Outstanding Universal Value. UNESCO's World Heritage Convention (Convention Concerning the Protection of the World Cultural and Natural Heritage, 1972) and the Identification and Assessment of Cultural Places for the Inclusion in the World Heritage List' (unpublished Ph.D. thesis, The Australian National University, Canberra 1995), p. 14.

Common history, divided memory

Despite this legacy, the common conceptualisation is not remembered as such and drawing direct lines between the pre-1914 exchanges and future international collaboration is not as straightforward as it seems. After 1918, references to earlier transfers were omitted by new international bodies and national agencies alike.[9]

Transfer theory assumes that a transfer process is only complete once it is forgotten. This happened with some transferred concepts before the First World War, such as the maxim *to repair not to restore*, but other transfers were publicly acknowledged and remembered, such as the imitations of the French Monument Act abroad. Further research on the transition from pre- to interwar preservation is necessary to explain this absence of remembrance, however, a number of specific factors clearly had an impact on this particular oblivion, including a generational change, the severing of contacts with German preservationists through the war, the rise of the USA as an arbiter, and the division of competences between actors in national preservation associations and international organizations in the interwar years. While national foundation myths had institutions to perpetuate them further, no organisation propagated the memory of earlier international encounters. On the contrary, the failure to achieve world peace through love of heritage might have made it desirable for the IICI to silence earlier failed attempts, in a similar way the IICI was itself forgotten once UNESCO was established and the link between 'heritage' and internationalism could be reinvented and adapted to a new international context once more.[10] But this is a different story.

---

[9] No reference to earlier encounters was made when new accounts on comparative legislation were published or when the international conferences were organised in the interwar years, see UNESCO, Archives, IICI/14/9, IICI/14/19, IICI/493, OIM.II.27, OIM.II.30, OIM.VI.1, OIM.VI.6, OIM.VI.17, OIM.VI.19, OIM.XIV.70. For national agencies: TNA, WORK 14/134, WORK 14/2278.

[10] J.J. Renoliet, *L'Unesco oubliée. La Société des nations et la coopération intellectuelle, 1919–1946* (Paris, 1999).

Glossary of foreign terms

Alterthümliche Merkwürdigkeiten, g., lit. 'antique oddities', antiquities
Antiquités, fr., antiquities
Bildungsbürger, Bildungsbürgertum, g., educated middle class
Champ patrimonial, fr., lit. 'heritage field'; everything that is considered heritage
Classement, fr., listing, scheduling of monuments
Conscience patrimoniale, fr., heritage-awareness
Denkmal, g., monument
Denkmalbegriff, g., the concept of monument
Denkmalbestand, g., all existing monuments
Denkmalbewegung, g., lit. 'monument movement'; preservation movement
Denkmalcultus, g., the cult of monuments
Denkmalpflege, g., the care of monuments
Denkmalpfleger, g., lit. 'monument-carer'; conservator
Denkmalrat, g., Monument Council
Denkmalschutz, g., the legal protection of monuments
Denkmalschutzgesetz, g., Monument Act
Erbe, g., heritage
Exposition universelle, fr., world's fair
Fabriques, fr., bodies administering the parish churches since the concordat in France
Heimat, g., home, homeland
Heimatbestrebungen, g., *Heimat*-endeavours
Heimatgedanken, g., *Heimat*-thoughts
Heimatgefühl, g., *Heimat*-sentiments
Heimatkundler, g., *Heimat*-scholar
Heimatkunst, g., *Heimat*-art
Heimatler, g., s.o. interested in the *Heimat*, a preservationist
Heimatliebe, g., *Heimat*-love

Heimatpflege, g., the care of the *Heimat*, preservation
Heimatschutz, g., the protection of the *Heimat*, preservation
Heimatschutzbewegung, g., preservation movement
Heimatschützer, g., *Heimat*-protector, preservationist
Heimatsinn, g., *Heimat*-sense
Heimatstil, g., *Heimat*-style
Heimatverein, g., *Heimat* association
Heimatbewegung, g., preservation movement
Kriegsdenkmalpflege, g., war-time preservation during the First World War
Kulturerbe, g., cultural heritage
Kulturgüter, g., cultural property
Kulturkampf, g., 'culture war' against the Catholic Church in Imperial Germany
Kultusminister, g., the secretary of the *Kultusministerium*
Kultusministerium, g. lit. department of *cult*, responsible for education, religion and culture
Kulturstaat, g., cultured or civilised state
Matrie, fr., 'mother land', '*Heimat*'
Monument historique, fr., historic monument
Nationaldenmal, g., national monument
Nationalgefühl, g., national feeling, patriotism
Naturschutz, g., nature conservation
Patrie des arts, fr., fatherland of the arts
Patrie, fr., fatherland
Patrimoine, fr., paternal heritage, inheritance, patrimony, heritage
Patrimoine du passé, fr., heritage of the past
Patrimoine national, fr., national heritage
Patrimonialisateur, fr., heritage-maker
Patrimonialisation, fr., the process of creating 'heritage'
Patrimonialiser, fr., to turn something into 'heritage'
Patrimonium, lt., paternal heritage (also used in German for patrimony)
Pays, fr., land, region, '*Heimat*'
Paysage, fr., landscape
Petite patrie, fr., lit. 'small fatherland', locality, *Heimat*
Reichsdenkmalgesetz, g., Imperial Monument Act
Reichsdenkmalplege, g., Imperial monument care
Schloßstreit, g., Debate about the restoration of Heidelberg Castle
Société Savante, fr., Learned Society
Sonderweg, g., special path
Stadtbild, g., city image

Verein, g., association, society
Vereinsmeier, g., pejorative term for member of associations
Vormärz, g., 'pre-March period' before the 1848 revolution
Weltausstellung, g., world's fair
Weltnaturschutz, g., world nature conservation

Glossary of foreign institutions

Académie des inscriptions et belles lettres, fr., Academy for Inscriptions and Letters
Bund Heimatschutz, g., Federation/League for Heimatschutz
Comité des Amis des Monuments Étrangers, fr., Foreign Committee of Friends of Monuments
Comité des Arts et Monuments, fr., Committee for Arts and Monuments, designating both the Committee founded by ministerial degree in 1837 and the Committee behind *L'Ami des Monuments*
Comité des Monuments Internationaux, fr., Committee for International Monuments
Comités nationaux et internationaux d'Ami des monuments, fr., National and International Committee of the Friends of Monuments
Commission du Vieux Paris, fr., Old Paris Commission
Comité des travaux historiques, fr., Committee for Historic Works
Congrès archéologique, fr., Archaeological Congress
Congrès des Sociétés savantes, fr., Congress of Learned Societies
Deutsche Denkmaltage, g. see *Tag für Denkmalpflege*
Dürerbund, g., artistic circle named after Albrecht Dürer
École des Chartes, fr., Grande Ecole for the training of archivists and librarians
Fédération Régionaliste Française, fr. French Regionalist Federation
Gesamtverein der deutschen Geschichts- und Alterthumsvereine, g., Federation of German Historical and Antiquarian Associations
Commission des Monuments historiques, fr., Historic Monuments Commission
Kampfbund für deutsche Kultur, g., Militant League for German Culture
Kölner Dombauverein, g., Association for the Construction of Cologne Cathedral
Kommission zur Beseitigung der Auswüchse der Heimtschutzbestrebungen, g., Commission for the Abolition of the Excrescences of the Preservation Movement
Konservatorentag, g., Day for Conservators

La Renaissance Provinciale: Société d'Etudes et de Vulgarisation des Costumes et des Arts fr., Provincial Renaissance: Society for the Study and Vulgarisation of Costumes and Arts

Les Amis des Monuments rouennais, fr., The Friends of Monuments of Rouen

Ligue contre la Publicité à travers les Champs, fr., League against Publicity in the Countryside

Ligue de decentralisation, fr., League for Decentralisation

Société archéologie de Bruxelles, fr., Archeological Society of Brussels

Société centrale des Architectes français, fr., Central Society of French Architects

Société d'Ethnographie nationale, fr., National Society for Ethnography

Société des Amis des Monuments parisiens, fr., Society of the Friends of Monuments of Paris

Société des Antiquaires de France, fr. Society of Antiquaries of France

Sociéte française, pour la conservation et la description des monuments de France aka Société française d'archéologie, fr., French Society of Archaeology

Société historique – Cercle Saint Simon, fr., Historical Society – Saint Simonian Circle

Société pour la conservation de l'art historique Suisse, fr., Swiss Society for the Conservation of Historic Art

Société pour la protection de l'esthétique de la France, fr., Society for the Protection of the Aesthetic of France

Société pour la protection des paysages de France, fr., Society for the Protection of French Landscapes

Société d'Art public, fr., Society for Public Art

Tag für Denkmalpflege, g., Day for Monument Care

Touring Club de France, fr., Touring Club of France

Union française de la jeunesse, fr., French Union for Youth

Union Régionaliste Bretonne, fr., Brittany Regionalist Union

Verband deutscher Architeken- und Ingenieur-Vereine, g., Federation of German Associations of Architects and Engineers

Verein für Kunst und Alterthum in Ulm und Oberschwaben, g., Association for Art and Antiquity in Ulm and Upper Swabia

Verein für ländliche Wohlfahrtspflege, g., Association for Rural Welfare

Werkbund, g., German Work Federation

Bibliography

ARCHIVAL SOURCES

Berlin-Dahlem, Geheimes Staatsarchiv Preußischer Kultusbesitz (GStA PK)

I. HA Rep. 76 Ve Kultusministerium

GStA PK, I. HA Rep. 76 Ve Kultusministerium, Sekt. 1, Tit. IV, Nr. 2, Bd. 2, Acta betreffend die im Jahre 1855 in Paris stattfindende Industrie und Kunstausstellung. Vol. II. von März 1855–August 1856.

GStA PK, I. HA Rep. 76 Ve Kultusministerium, Sekt. 1, Tit. IV, Nr. 2, Bd. 12, Acta betreffend die Industrie und Kunstausstellung im Auslande. Vol. XII vom Oktober 1880 bis Februar 1890.

GStA PK, I. HA Rep. 76 Ve Kultusministerium, Sekt. 1, Tit. VI, No. 141, Gesetzentwurf betr. Erhaltung der Denkmäler. Französische, englische, italienische Denkmalspflege.

GStA PK, I. HA Rep. 76 Ve Kultusministerium, Sekt. 1, Tit. VI, Nr. 2a, Acta betreffend die Sammlung der in Folge der Circular Verfügung vom 3ten Mai 1844 und 14ten März 1845 Seitens der Königlichen Regierungen erstatteten Berichte über die Inventarisation der im Preußischen Staate vorhandenen Kunstdenkmäler, sowie die zu diesem Behülf entworfenen Frage Formulare

GStA PK, I. HA Rep. 76 Ve Kultusministerium, Sekt. 1, Tit. VI, Nr. 2g, Verzeichnisse der Baudenkmäler in preußischen Provinzen

GStA PK, I. HA Rep. 76 Ve Kultusministerium, Sekt. 2, Tit. VI, Nr. 22, Bd. 5, Erhaltung der Bau und Kunstdenkmäler in der Provinz Ostpreußen. Band V. Mai 1916–1922.

I. HA Rep. 77 Ministerium des Inneren

GStA PK, I. HA Rep. 77 Ministerium des Inneren, Tit. 803, Nr. 32, Acta betr. die Erhaltung von Kunstdenkmälern

GStA PK, I. HA Rep. 77 Ministerium des Inneren, Tit. 803, Nr. 35, Acta betr. die in fremden Staaten erschienenen Bauordnungen. Vom 28. Februar 1897 bis 1918.

GStA PK, I. HA Rep. 77 Ministerium des Inneren, Tit. 1215, Nr. 3, Beiheft, Bd.1, Acta betr. den Entwurf und Gesetz über den Denkmalschutz. Vom 24 Januar 1901 bis 6. Dezember 1907.

I. HA Rep. 87 B Ministerium für Landwirtschaft, Domänen u. Forsten

GStA PK, I. HA Rep. 87 B Ministerium für Landwirtschaft, Domänen u. Forsten, Nr. 3131, Acta betreffend die Konservation von Baudenkmälern, Naturdenkmälern etc.

I. HA Rep. 89 Geh. Zivilkabinett, jüngere Periode

GStA PK, I. HA Rep. 89 Geh. Zivilkabinett, jüngere Periode, Nr. 20761, Erhaltung von Altertümern 1820, 1822, 1829.
GStA PK, I. HA. Rep. 89 Geh. Zivilkabinett, jüngere Periode, Nr. 20765, Akten betr. die Denkmäler im Auslande.
GStA PK, I. HA Rep. 89 Geh. Zivilkabinett, jüngere Periode, Nr. 20768, Acta des Königl. Geheimen Cabinets betr. die Beaufsichtigung der im Preußischen Staate befindlichen Kunstdenkmäler, 1842–1909.
GStA PK, I. HA Rep. 89, Geh. Zivilkabinett, jüngere Periode, Nr. 20769, Akten betr. die Beaufsichtigung der Kunstdenkmäler in Preußen, 1910–1918.

I. HA Rep. 90 Staats-Ministerium

GStA PK, I. HA Rep. 90 Staats-Ministerium, Nr. 1796, Akten betreffend die Maßnahmen zur Erhaltung bestehender Denkmäler und Altertümer (Denkmalspflege) im Allgemeinen. Band I von 1823–1921.

I. HA Rep. 93 B Ministerium der öffentlichen Arbeiten

GStA PK, I. HA Rep. 93 B Ministerium der öffentlichen Arbeiten, Nr. 2331, Akten betr. die Errichtung und Erhaltung der Bau-Denkmäler. Vom 27. September 1855 bis 19. Juli 1866.
GStA PK, I. HA Rep. 93 B Ministerium der öffentlichen Arbeiten, Nr. 2337, Akten betr. Bau und Kunstdenkmäler und Alterthümer im Auslande vom 31 Mai 1866 bis Ende 1910.

Nachlass Schmidt-Ott

GStA PK VI. HA, Rep. 92 Nl. Schmidt-Ott (M), A X 1, Denkmalpflege, Tagungen (Berichte)
GStA PK VI. HA, Nl Schmidt-Ott (M), A X 2, Denkmalpflege, Vermischtes
GStA PK VI. HA, Nl Schmidt-Ott (M), A X 4, Denkmalpflege

GStA PK VI. HA, Nl Schmidt-Ott (M), A X 28, Pariser Weltausstellung 1900
GStA PK VI. HA, Nl Schmidt-Ott (M), C 39, Denkmalpflege, Allgemeines

Bordeaux, Archives Departementale de la Gironde (ADG)
Serie T, 4T Commission des Monuments Historiques

Paris, Archives nationales (AN)
Sous-Série F 12 Commerce et Industrie

F 12 3263   Exposition universelle de 1878. Correspondance: fabrication des tickets, catalogue des Archives, Congrès, etc.
F 12 3265   Exposition universelle de 1878. Service de la Presse. Coupures de journaux sur l'exposition de 1878 (dossier préparé pour l'exposition de 1889)
F 12 4285–86   Exposition universelle de 1889. Service des congrès, correspondance, etc.

Sous-Série F 17 Instruction publique

F 17 3016   Sociétés savantes de France et de l'étranger. Envois de statuts, renseignements et correspondances relative à l'échange de publications entre les Sociétés savantes de France et de l' étranger
F 17 3019   Sociétés savantes de France et de l'étranger. Ministère de l'Instruction publique: Publication de la Revue des Sociétés savantes et d'une table générale des Bulletins du Comité 1848–1878. Etat des collections de la Bibliothèque des Sociétés savantes
F 17 3090   Congrès divers en France et à l'étranger. Correspondance relative à l'organisation des congrès et aux questions scientifiques traitées. Généralités. 1833–1921
F 17 3099–1   Expositions internationales et universelles. 1873–1904

Sous-Série F 21 Beaux-Arts

F 21 519   Exposition des Beaux-arts aux Exposition universelles de 1855
F 21 525–526   Exposition françaises des Beaux-arts dans les expositions étrangères: classement alphabétique des pays. 1851–1880.
F 21 565   Mémoire et projets divers, notamment sur les expositions des Beaux-arts (1858–1869). Conservation des monuments (1814–1930)

F 21 4061   Section françaises des Beaux-arts aux expositions internationales et participation française à des expositions diverses à l'étranger. 1882–1940. Exposition internationales: Classement chronologique. 1890–1899

F 21 4066   Section françaises des Beaux-arts aux expositions internationales et participation française à des expositions diverses à l'étranger. 1882–1940. Exposition universelle de 1900 à Paris. 1892–1902

Paris, Archives des Musées nationaux

5HH Musée de Sculpture comparée, boites 1–6

Paris, Médiathèque de l'Architecture et du Patrimoine

80/1 Généralités sur les monuments historiques 1808–1985

80/1/19–22   Loi du 30 mars 1887 pour la conservation des monuments et objets d'art ayant un intérêt historique et artistique et textes complémentaires, 1874–1911

80/1/23–24   Loi de séparation des Eglises et de l'Etat (9 décembre 1905)

80/1/25   Loi du 31 décembre 1913 sur les monuments historiques

80/1/26   Loi modifiant et complétant la loi du 31 décembre 1913 sur les monuments historiques

80/1/27   Législation, réglementation et projets de lois divers concernant les monuments historiques et le patrimoine en général (1914–1964)

80/1/28   Lois sur les sites et monuments naturels

80/1/31   Législation et réglementation diverse

80/1/32–33   Législation étrangère sur les monuments historiques

80/1/61   Bibliothèque du service des monuments historiques

80/1/63   Publications du Service des monuments historiques

80/1/68   Dessins

80/1/77   Musée de Sculpture Comparée

80/1/124   Sociétés savantes, associations de propriétaires de monuments historiques et de protection du patrimoine. Affaires générales

80/1/126   Association de protection du patrimoine et de propriétaires des monuments historiques

80/1/138   Coupures de presse, 1903–1907

80/8 Prêts d'objets classés

80/8/1   Prêts d'objets classés à des expositions organisées à Paris

80/8/2   Prêts d'objets classés à des expositions organisées en province

80/8/5–6   Prêts d'objets classés à des expositions organisées à l'étranger

80/8/7	Participation du Service des Monuments historiques à des expositions
81/46/8	Cahors, Pont Neuf
81/84/38	Avignon Rempart

Paris, UNESCO, Archives

AG 1. Institut International de Co-operation Intellectuelle (I.I.C.I.) 1925–1946

IICI/14/9	Publication: La Protection international des monuments historiques et des oeuvres d'art en temps de Guerre. Institut International de Coopération intellectuelle. Office international des Musées 1936
IICI/14/19	Publication: Art et Archéologie: Recueil de législation comparée et de droit international. 1939
IICI/493	Documents du C.I.C.I. Documents de l'Assemblée de la Société des Nations, 1921–1925

Office international des Musées

OIM.II.27	Recueil comparé de législation sur les antiquités et les fouilles. 1938–1940
OIM.II.30	Recueil de législation comparée et de droit international No 3
OIM.VI.1	Conservation des oeuvres d'art. Conférence de Rome. 1929–31
OIM.VI.6	Identification des oeuvres d'art. Législation internationale et nationale sur la propriété artistique
OIM.VI.17	Conservation des œuvres d'art. Architecture. Conférence d'Athènes. 1930–1933
OIM.VI.19	Conservation des œuvres d'art. Législation en vigueur dans les divers Etat sur la protection et la conservation des monuments d'art et d'histoire. 1932–1935
OIM.XIV.70	Constitution de la Commission internationale des Monuments historiques. Généralités et correspondance. 1933

London, Kew, The National Archives (TNA)

WORK: Successive Works Departments, Ancient Monuments Boards and Inspectorate

WORK 14/132	Ancient Monuments Protection Act, 1882, and Ancient Monuments Protection Amendment Bill 1892. 1882–1892
WORK 14/133	Preparation of Deed of Guardianship under the Act 1882 and 1913. 1882–1914
WORK 14/134	Enquiries from abroad on the preservation of Ancient Monuments in Great Britain. 1882–1939
WORK 14/135	Ancient Monuments Protection Act, 1900. 1899–1910

WORK 14/136   Annual reports of the Chief Inspector, 1911–1913. 1911–1924
WORK 14/137   Resolution of sympathy with France and Belgium on the destruction of their ancient monuments. 1914
WORK 14/158   Protest against proposed demolition under L.C.C. Improvement Act, 1900. 1913–1915
WORK 14/213   Stonehenge, Wiltshire: earlier discussions for possible acquisition or preservation. 1893–1915
WORK 14/2251   Royal Commission on Historical Monuments (England): appointment of Commission. 1908–1920
WORK 14/2278   Systems adopted in foreign countries for preservation of ancient monuments. 1911–1954
WORK 2470   Annual reports of the Inspectorate. 1910–1921.
WORK 2471   County correspondents organisation: appointments and duties. 1913–1964

LONDON, SOCIETY FOR THE PROTECTION OF ANCIENT BUILDINGS ARCHIVES

Administrative Records

Committee Minute Books

1st–24th Committee Minute Books. Mar. 1877–Nov. 1915

Subcommittee Minute Books

1st Minute Book, Restoration Committee, Jan. 1879–July 1880; Finance Committee, Dec. 1878–July 1882; and Foreign Committee, Mar. 1879–July 1879.
2nd Minute Book, Restoration Committee, July 1880–Nov. 1882.
3rd Minute Book, Foreign Committee, Mar. 1882–May 1882.
4th Minute Book, Miscellaneous Subcommittees; Subcommittee on City Churches, Mar. 1878; Subcommittee on St Mark's Venice, Nov.–Dec. 1879; Subcommittee appointed to arrange Annual Meeting of the Society, May 1880.

Agenda Books

1st–2nd Agenda Book Dec. 1878–Dec 1882

Case Files

Ancient Monuments Act
Ancient Monuments Acts: correspondence
Arab Monuments, Egypt

Rome, Alterations in Italy
Rouen Cathedral, France
Rouen Old Houses
Ulm Cathedral
Venice, St Mark's
War Damage, Europe 1914–1915
Women's Institutes Lecture 1912

Swindon, National Trust Archives

Council Minutes
Executive Committee Minutes
Acc. 6 Letters

PRINTED PRIMARY SOURCES

Newspapers, magazines and periodicals

Albion and Evening Advertiser
Annales archéologiques
Art et Photographie
Bulletin de la Société des Amis des Monuments parisiens
Bulletin des Amis des Monuments ornais
Bulletin des Amis des Monuments rouennais
Bulletin des Sociétés photographiques du Nord de la France
Bulletin Monumental
Centralblatt der Bauverwaltung
Congrès archéologique de France
Congrès international de l'art public
Congrès international des architectes
Cycling and Moting
Die Denkmalpflege
Fun
Gazette des Beaux-Arts
Gentleman's Magazine
Heimatschutz
Journal des Débats
Journal of the RIBA
Korrespondenzblatt des Gesamtvereins der deutschen Geschichts- und Altherthumsvereine
L'Ami des Monuments
Lustige Blätter
Mittheilungen der K.K. Zentral-Kommission zur Erforschung und Erhaltung der Kunst- und historischen Denkmale
NT Annual Reports

Oracle and Public Advertiser
Proceedings of the Society of Antiquaries
Punch
Revue de l'Exposition universelle de 1889
Revue des Sociétés savantes de la France et de l'Etranger
SPAB Annual Reports
Simplicissimus
The Amateur Photographer
The Athenaeum
The Builder
The Times (London)
The Year Book of the Scientific and Learned Societies of Great Britain and Ireland
Tomahawk or Censor General
True Briton
Zeitschrift für christliche Archäologie und Kunst

Parliamentary debates, parliamentary papers

Atti Parlamentari
Documents parlementaires
Parliamentary Debates
Parliamentary Papers
Stenographischer Bericht über die Verhandlungen des Deutschen Reichstages
Stenographischer Bericht über die Verhandlungen des Preußischen Hauses der Abgeordneten
Stenographischer Bericht über die Verhandlungen des Preußischen Herrenhauses
Verhandlungen der ersten Kammer der Landstände des Großherzogtums Hessen
Verhandlungen der zweiten Kammer der Landstände des Großherzogtums Hessen
Verhandlungen der Württembergischen Kammer der Abgeordneten

ARTICLES, BOOKS AND COLLECTIONS

'Actes officiels relatif à la sauvegarde du Mont St. Michel. Decrét du classement des ramparts du mont', *L'Ami des Monuments*, 22 (1909–1914), 43–4.
'Albums de la Revue l'Ami des Monuments et des Arts. Fondation d'un Comité des Amis des Monuments Étrangers', *Bulletin de la Société des Amis des Monuments parisiens* (1901), Appendix.
'L'Ami des Monuments et des Arts au Congrès des Orientalistes et la Sauvegarde des Monuments', *L'Ami des Monuments*, 11 (1897), 249–51.
Amtlicher Katalog der Ausstellung des Deutschen Reichs. Weltausstellung in Paris 1900 (Berlin, 1900).
Annuaire de la Société de l'Histoire de France (Paris, 1842).
'Archäologischer Congress zur Feier des 50 jährigen Bestehens der Ecole française in Athen', *Centralblatt der Bauverwaltung*, 17 (1897), 68.

Asal, K., *Die neuen reichsrechtlichen Denkmalschutzbestimmungen* (Heidelberg, 1923).

Assézat, J. (ed.), *Oeuvres complètes de Diderot* (Paris, 1875).

Audollent, A., 'La Question des antiquités et des beaux-arts en Italie', *L'Ami des Monuments*, 6 (1892), 20–34.

Barrès, M., *La Grande Pitié des église de France* (Paris, 1914).

Baschet, L. (ed.), *Exposition Universelle 1900 (Le panorama)* (Paris, 1900).

Baudot, A. de, Ministère du Commerce, de l'industrie et des colonies, *Exposition universelle internationale de 1889, à Paris. Rapports du jury international. Classe 4. Dessins et modèles d'architecture. Rapport de M. de Baudot* (Paris, 1890).

Baumgart, E., *Monuments historiques. Rapport de M. Baumgart. Etabli à l'occasion de l'exposition internationale de Londres 1874* (Paris, 1874).

Beakert, M., 'De la Préservation légale du patrimoine artistique', *Handelingen van den Geschied-en Oudheidkundigen Kring von Gent/Annales du cercle historique et archéologique de Gand*, 2 (1895), 57–104.

Beauquier, C., 'Proposition de Loi, ayant pour objet de protéger les sites pittoresques, historiques ou légendaires de France', *L'Ami des Monuments*, 17 (1903), 21–8.

'Séance d'ouverture', *Le Premier Congrès international pour la protection des paysages* (Paris, 1910), p. 10.

Bellet, P., 'Promenade autour du Jardin central', in Ducuing, F. (ed.), *L'Exposition universelle de 1867 illustrée* (Paris, 1868), pp. 371–4.

Benson, A.C., 'The Ancient Monuments Consolidation and Amendment Act', SPAB, *Annual Report*, 37 (1914), 12–15.

Bercé, F. (ed.), *La Correspondance Mérimée – Viollet-le-Duc* (Paris, 2001).

(ed.), *La Naissance des Monuments historiques. La correspondance de Prosper Mérimée avec Ludovic Vitet, 1840–1848* (Paris, 1998).

(ed.), *Les Premiers Travaux de la Commission des Monuments historiques, 1837–1848. Procès-verbaux et relevés d'architectes* (Paris, 1979).

Bericht über den VIII. Internationalen Architekten-Kongress, Wien 1908 (Vienna, 1909).

Berichte über die Allgemeine Ausstellung zu Paris im Jahre 1867, erstattet von den für Preußen und die Norddeutschen Staaten ernannten Mitglieder der internationalen Jury (Berlin, 1868).

Besnard, A., *Septième Congrès international des architectes. Londres, Juillet 1906. Essai sur la neuvième question du programme. De la responsabilité des gouvernements dans la conservation des monuments nationaux* (Paris, 1906).

Biegeleben, M. Frhr. von, 'Zum preußischen Entwurf eines Denkmalschutzgesetzes', *Kölnische Volkszeitung*, 16 June 1928.

Bohnstedt, 'Die Denkmalpflege', *Die Denkmalpflege*, 2 (1900), 93–5, 97–9.

'Die Denkmalpflege in Frankreich', *Centralblatt der Bauverwaltung*, 16 (1896), 313–14.

'Die Denkmalpflege. Vortrag gehalten in Paris am 2. August 1900 beim V. Internationalen Architekten Congress', *Die Denkmalpflege*, 2 (1900), 97–9.

'Der Internationale Architekten-Congress in Paris vom 30. Juli bis 4. August 1900', *Centralblatt der Bauverwaltung*, 20 (1900), 449–51.

Boivin-Champeaux, J., Université de Paris. Faculté de droit, *Des Restrictions apportées à la propriété dans un intérêt esthétique (objets d'art, fouilles, beautés naturelles). Thèse pour le doctorat* (Paris, 1913).

Bonnaffé, E., 'Exposition rétrospective de l'art français au Trocadero', in Louis Gonse, Alfred de Lostalot (eds.), *Exposition Universelle de 1889: Les beaux-arts et les arts decoratifs – l'art français retrospectif au Trocadéro* (Paris, 1890), pp. 511–18.

Bredt, F.W., *Die Denkmalpflege und ihre Gestaltung in Preußen* (Berlin, Cologne, Leipzig, 1904).

Brown, G.B., *The Care of Ancient Monuments. An Account of the Legislative and Other Measures Adopted in European Countries for Protecting Ancient Monuments and Objects and Scenes of Natural Beauty and for Preserving the Aspect of Historical Cities* (Cambridge, 1905).

The Care of Historical Cities (Edinburgh, 1904).

'Government Action on the Continent in the Interest of National Monuments' *Journal of the RIBA*, 3rd Ser., 13 (1906). Congress Supplement, lxii–lxvi.

Brundswick, F., 'Denkmalpflege in Italien', *Die Denkmalpflege*, 6 (1904), 117–18.

Bücherschau: Loersch, H., 'Das französische Gesetz vom 30. März 1897 (sic!), ein Beitrag zur Denkmalpflege', *Centralblatt der Bauverwaltung*, 17 (1897), 487.

Burckhard, J., *Über das Studium der Geschichte. Der Text der Westgeschichtlichen Betrachtungen auf Grund der Vorarbeiten von Ernst Ziegler nach den Handschriften*, ed. P. Ganz (Munich, 1982).

Carpentier, P., *La Loi italienne du 12 juin 1912 édictant des dispositions sur la protection et la conservation des monuments et objets ayant une valeur d'art et d'antiquité* (Paris, 1902).

Challamel, J., 'Commentaire sur l'ouvrage de Louis Tétreau, législation relative aux monuments et objets d'art', *Bulletin de la société de législation comparée* (1898).

'Congrès international pour la protection des œuvres d'art et des monuments. Des Législations françaises et étrangères établies pour assurer la conservation des œuvres d'art et des monuments', *L'Ami des Monuments*, 4 (1890), 285–300.

Loi du 30 mars 1887 sur la conservation des monuments historiques et des objets d'art. Etude de législation comparée (Extrait de *L'Annuaire de législation française*, Paris, 1888).

Champier, V., 'Les 44 Habitation Humaines construites au Champs de Mars par M. Charles Garnier', *Revue de l'Exposition universelle de 1889* (Paris 1889), I, 115–25.

'Exposition des habitations humaines reconstituées par M. Charles Garnier', in Monod, E. (ed.), *L'Exposition Universelle de 1889: Grand ouvrage illustré, historique, encyclopédique, descriptif* (3 vols., Paris, 1890), I, pp. 158–62.

Charles, É., 'Le Musée du Contre-Vandalisme à l'hôtel Sully', *La Liberté*, nr 17013, repr. in *L'Ami des monuments* 24 (1913), 50–5.

Chesterton, G.K., *Charles Dickens* (London 1906, 11th edn, 1917).

Chevalier, M. (ed.), *Rapports du jury international Exposition universelle de 1867 à Paris* (13 vols., Paris, 1868).

Choay, F. (ed.), *La Conférence d'Athènes sur la conservation artistique et historique des monuments, 1931* (Paris, 2002).

Chretien, A., 'De la protection et de la conservation des monuments et objets précieux d'après la nouvelle loi italienne', *Journal de droit international privé et de la jurisprudence comparée* (1903), 736–60.

'Chronicle. Brussels Congress', *Journal of the RIBA*, 3rd Ser., 4 (1897), 472–4.

'Chronique, Application de la loi de conservation des monuments – Italie: abrogation de l'édit de Pacca', *L'Ami des Monuments*, 5 (1991), 49.

Clemen, P., 'Allgemeine Grundsätze für die Gesetzgebung', in Oechelhaeuser, A. v. (ed.), *Denkmalpflege. Auszug aus den stenographischen Berichten des Tages für Denkmalpflege* (2 vols., Leipzig, 1910–1913), I, pp. 125–38.

Die Denkmalpflege in Frankreich (Berlin, 1898).

Die Erhaltung der Kunstdenkmäler in Deutschland. Vortrag gehalten auf dem internationalen kunsthistorischen Kongress zu Lübeck am 18. September 1900. Sonderabdruck aus den Verhandlungen des Kongresses nach dem stenographischen Bericht (Nuremberg, 1900).

'Die Fürsorge für die mittelalterlichen Denkmäler in Griechenland', *Die Denkmalpflege*, 1 (1899), 31–3.

Gesammelte Aufsätze (Düsseldorf, 1948).

John Ruskin (Leipzig, 1900).

(ed.), *Kunstschutz im Kriege. Berichte über den Zustand der Kunstdenkmäler auf den verschiedenen Kriegsschauplätzen und über die deutschen und österreichischen Maßnahmen zu ihrer Erhaltung* (Leipzig, 1919).

Cole, Sir H., *Fifty Years, of Public Work* (2 vols., London, 1884).

Memorandum upon the formation, arrangement and administration of the South Kensington Museum (London, 1879).

'Congrès de l'Art public', *L'Ami des Monuments*, 13 (1899), 26–30, 155, 308–17.

'Congrès de l'Art public', *L'Ami des Monuments*, 15 (1901), 164.

'Congrès et Exposition de l'Art public', *L'Ami des Monuments*, 14 (1900), 75, 103–10, 181–6.

'Congrès international de l'Art public', *L'Ami des Monuments*, 12 (1898), 180–181, 234–37, 290–95.

'Congrès international de protection des monuments en 1889', *L'Ami des Monuments*, 2 (1888), 168.

Congrès international des architectes. Cinquième session tenue à Paris du 29 juillet au 4 août 1900. Organisation, compte-rendu et notices (Paris, 1906).

Congrès international des architectes. Sixième session tenue à Madrid 1904. Organisation. Compte rendu et notices (Madrid, 1906).

'Congrès pour la cinquantaine de l'Ecole française d'Athènes', *L'Ami des Monuments*, 11 (1897), 81–6.

'Congress Comments', *The Builder*, 28 July 1906, pp. 123–4.

'Congress of Architects', *The Builder*, 6 July 1889, pp. 4–8.

'Congress of Architects at Paris Exhibitions', *The Builder*, 3 Aug. 1878, p. 804 and 10 Aug. 1878, p. 825.

Congresso degli ingegneri ed architetti italiani, *Congresso settimo nazionale e primo internazionale di ingegneri ed architetti* (Palermo, 1892).

Congresso internazionale degli architetti. Atti del 9. Congresso internazionale degli architetti, Roma, 2–10 Ottobre 1911 (Rome, 1914).

'Conservation et restauration des manuscrits. Conférence internationale a St. Gallen', *L'Ami des Monuments*, 12 (1898), 314.

Constans, J., Université de Montpellier. Faculté de droit. *Monuments historiques et objets d'art: loi du 30 mars 1887 et décrets du 3 janvier 1889 relatifs à la conservation des monuments et objets d'art ayant un intérêt historique ou artistique. Thèse pour le doctorat* (Montpellier, 1905).

Conwentz, H., *Die Heimatkunde in der Schule* (Berlin, 1904).

Cros-Mayrevieille, F., Université de Paris. Faculté de droit, *De la protection des monuments historiques ou artistiques, des sites et des paysages: évolution historique, restrictions à la propriété privée foncière. Thèse pour le doctorat* (Paris, 1907).

'Das ägyptische Denkmalgesetz', *Die Denkmalpflege*, 16 (1914), 80.

'Das Italienische Gesetz über den Denkmalschutz', *Die Denkmalpflege*, 5 (1903), 31–2.

Dehio, G., *Denkmalschutz und Denkmalpflege im Neunzehnten Jahrhundert. Rede zur Feier des Geburtstages Sr. Majestät des Kaisers gehalten in der Aula Kaiser-Wilhelms-Universität Strassburg am 27. Januar 1905* (Strasbourg, 1905).

Was wird aus dem Heidelberger Schloß werden? (Strasbourg, 1901).

Délaire, F., *Les Architectes élèves de l'Ecole des Beaux-Arts, 1793–1907* (2nd edn, Paris, 1907).

Delaunay, H., *Annuaire international des Sociétés savantes, 1903* (Paris, 1904).

'Denkmalpflege', *Mayers Großes Konversations-Lexicon* (1906), p. 614.

'Denkmalpflege in Griechenland', *Die Denkmalpflege*, 4 (1902), 47.

'Denkmalschutz im englischen Südafrika', *Die Denkmalpflege*, 16 (1914), 120.

'Denkmalschutz in England und Irland', *Korrespondenzblatt der Geschichts- und Alterthumsvereine*, 48 (1900), 140.

'Der preußische Gesetzentwurf gegen die Verunstaltung von Ortschaften und landschaftlich hervorragenden Gegenden', *Die Denkmalpflege*, 8 (1906), 91.

'Der Rechtliche Heimatschutz in der Schweiz', *Die Denkmalpflege*, 12 (1910), 126.

'Deutsches bürgerliches Gesetzbuch, baurechtliche Bestimmungen', *Centralblatt der Bauverwaltung*, 10 (1890), 350.

Dickens, C., *The Mudfog Papers* (London, 1880), pp. 48–9.

The Pickwick Papers (London, 1837).

'Die Denkmalpflege auf dem Katholikentag', *Die Denkmalpflege*, 4 (1902), 99.

'Die Denkmalpflege in Bayern', *Die Denkmalpflege*, 6 (1904), 7–8.

'Die Fürsorge des Staates für die Erhaltung von Denkmälern der Vergangenheit', *Korrespondenzblatt der Geschichts- und Alterthumsvereine*, 42 (1894), 93–7.

'Die Gefährdung der Naturdenkmäler und Vorschläge zu ihrer Erhaltung', *Die Denkmalpflege*, 7 (1905), 24.

'Die Hauptversammlung der deutschen Geschichts- und Alterthumsvereine', *Die Denkmalpflege*, 1 (1899), 105–7.

'Die Westthürme des Meissner Domes', *Deutsche Bauzeitung*, 3 May 1902, pp. 225–30.

Dihm, L., 'Zur Wiederherstellung des Heidelberger Schlosses', *Centralblatt der Bauverwaltung*, 91 (1901), 557–8.

Dircks, R., 'The VIII International Congress of Architects, Vienna', *Journal of the RIBA*, 3rd Ser., 15 (1908), 480–81.

'Discours prononcé à l'ouverture du premier congrès pour la protection des monuments et oeuvres d'art par Charles Normand', *L'Ami des Monuments*, 3 (1889), 191–3.

Ducrocq, T., *La Loi de 1887 et le décret du 3 janvier 1889 sur la conservation des monuments et objets mobilier présentant un intérêt national au point de vue de l'histoire et de l'art* (Paris, 1889).

Dufrené, H., 'Histoire du travail', in Lacroix, E. (ed.), *Etude sur l'Exposition de 1867. Annales et archives de l'industrie au XIXe siècle ou Nouvelle technologie des arts et métiers, de l'agriculture etc. Description générale, encyclopédique, méthodique et raisonnée de l'état actuel des arts, des sciences, de l'industrie et de l'agriculture, chez toutes les nations* (8 vols., Paris, s.d.), VI, pp. 370–88.

Endemann, F., *Einführung in das Studium des Bürgerlichen Gesetzbuchs. Lehrbuch des Bürgerlichen Rechts* (3rd–5th edn, Berlin, 1900).

Lehrbuch des Bürgerlichen Rechts. Einführung in das Studium des Bürgerlichen Gesetzbuchs (8th–9th revised edn, 1905).

'Erster internationaler Heimatschutzkongress in Paris', *Die Denkmalpflege*, 11 (1909), 132.

'Erster Tag für Denkmalpflege, Gesetzgebung zum Schutz der Denkmäler', *Korrespondenzblatt der Geschichts- und Alterthumsvereine*, 48 (1900), 203–7.

Espagne, G., Savoy, B. (eds.), *Aubin-Louis Millin et l'Allemagne. Le Magasin encyclopédique – les lettres à Karl August Böttiger* (Hildesheim, 2005).

Esquisse d'un avant-projet de loi de préservation des Monuments non classés, des Fouilles et Découvertes, des Œuvres formant point de vue dans les paysages, des Meubles et Immeubles menacés d'exportation. Etudié par le comité de la Société des amis des monuments parisiens (repr. from *L'Ami des Monuments*, 22 (1909–1914), 203–9; 346–50, Paris s.d.).

Exposition de l'oeuvre de Viollet-le-Duc ouverte au Musée des Thermes et à l'Hôtel de Cluny (Paris, 1880).

Exposition internationale et universelle de Philadelphie, 1876. Rapport. France. Commission supérieure (Paris, 1877).

Exposition universelle de 1855. Explication des ouvrages de peinture, sculpture, gravure, lithographie et architecture des artistes vivant étrangers et français, exposé au palais des beaux-arts, avenue montaigne le 15 mai 1855 (Paris, 1855).

Exposition universelle de 1878 à Paris. Grande-Bretagne. Catalogue de la section des beaux-arts (London, 1878).

Exposition universelle de 1878 à Paris. Ministère de l'instruction publique, des cultes et des beaux-arts. Catalogue de l'exposition des archives de la commission des monuments historiques en France (Paris, 1878).

Exposition universelle de 1900 à Paris (Palais du Trocadéro). Catalogue des expositions des monuments historiques (ministère de l'instruction publique et des beaux-arts) et de l'exposition des édifices diocésains (ministère de l'intérieur et des cultes) (Paris, 1900).

Exposition universelle de Vienne, 1873. France. Œuvres d'art et manufactures nationales. Commissariat général (Paris, Vienna, 1873).

Exposition universelle internationale de 1889 à Paris. Exposition rétrospective de l'art français au Trocadéro (Lille, 1889).

Exposition universelle internationale de 1889 à Paris. Exposition rétrospective, section III, arts et métiers. Fauconnerie. Catalogue illustré par S. Arcos, Rd. Balze, Malher, Vallet etc. suivi de 'La Fauconnerie d'autrefois et la fauconnerie d'aujourd'hui' conférence faite à la Société nationale d'acclimatation, le 21 mars 1890 par M. Pierre Amédée Picho (Paris, 1890).

Extrait du compte-rendu sténographique du congrès international des architectes, 3 août 1878 (Paris, 1881).

Falke, J., Die Kunsindustrie der Gegenwart. *Studien auf der Pariser Weltausstellung i.J. 1867* (Leipzig, 1868).

Fletcher, B., 'French Drawings', *Royal Institute of British Architects. Journal of Proceedings*, New Ser., 6 (1890), 23 Jan. 1890, 134.

'Fondation de la Société des Amis des Monuments rouennais', *L'Ami des Monuments*, 1 (1887), 45.

'Fondation des Amis des Monuments, Sites et Arts de la Côte d'Azur et Provence', *L'Ami des Monuments*, 23.2 (1912–14), 124.

Fowler, H.G., *Church Restoration. What to do, and what to avoid by G. Hodgson Fowler, F.S.A.; F.R.I.B.A., read on February 10th 1882, Leeds Architectural Society* (Leeds, 1882).

Frauberger, H., *Die Kunstinudstrie auf der Pariser Weltausstellung 1878* (Leipzig, 1879).

Fubini, R., 'Projet de loi sur la protection du patrimoine artistique en Italie', *Revue trimestrielle de droit civil* (1908).

Fuchs, C.J., *Heimatschutz und Volkswirtschaft* (Flugschriften des Bundes Heimatschutz 1, Halle, 1905).

Fyot, E., *L'Église Notre-Dame de Dijon* (Dijon, 1910).

Garnier, C., Ammann, A., *L'Habitation humaine* (Paris, 1892).

Gavin, M., *Exposition universelle de 1889. Compte rendu de la promenade archéologique de la Commission des antiquités et des arts du département de Seine-et-Oise à l'exposition de la maréchalerie rétrospective au palais du ministère de la Guerre (esplanade des Invalides) [La Ferrure du cheval de guerre dans l'antiquité et au moyen âge jusqu'à nos jours, d'après les conférences de MM. Mathieu et Aureggio]* (Paris, 1889).

'Gelegentlich des internationalen kunsthistorischen Congresses Lübeck', *Die Denkmalpflege*, 2 (1900), 79.

'Generalversammlung in Strassburg vom 25 bis 28. September 1899, Kommission für Denkmalschutz und Denkmalpfelge', *Korrespondenzblatt der Geschichts- und Alterthumsvereine*, 48 (1900), 42–4.

'Gesetz gegen die Verunstaltung von Stadt und Land', *Die Denkmalpflege*, 11 (1909), 47, 70, 101.

'Gesetzentwurf betreffend den Schutz der Baudenkmäler in Oesterreich', *Die Denkmalpflege*, 4 (1902), 64.

'Gesetzentwurf gegen die Verunstaltung landschaftlich hervorragender Gegenden', *Die Denkmalpflege*, 4 (1902), 30, 55, 100.

Gewerbeordnung für das Deutsche Reich (21st edn, Munich, 1929).

Gmelin, L., *Das deutsche Kunstgewerbe zur Zeit der Weltausstellung in Chicago 1893*, trans. as *German Artistical Handicraft at the time of the World's-Exhibition in Chicago 1893* (Munich, 1893).

Goethe, J.W. von, *Propyläen. Eine periodische Schrift* (Tübingen 1799, repr. Darmstadt, 1965).

Gonse, L. 'L'Architecture', in Louis Gonse, Alfred de Lostalot (eds), *Exposition Universelle de 1889*: *Les beaux-arts et les arts decoratifs – l'art francais retrospectif au Trocadero* (Paris, 1890), pp. 221–42.

L'Art japonais (Paris, 1883, repr. 2004).

Goudeau, E., 'L'Histoire de l'Habitation', *Revue de l'Exposition universelle de 1889* (Paris, 1889), I, 78–85.

Gout, P., 'La Conservation et la restauration des monuments historiques', *Gazette des Beaux-Arts* (1881), 297–307, 411–19.

Grautoff, O., 'Die Denkmalpflege im Urteil des Auslandes', in Clemen, P. (ed.), *Kunstschutz im Kriege. Berichte über den Zustand der Kunstdenkmäler auf den verschiedenen Kriegsschauplätzen und über die deutschen und österreichischen Maßnahmen zu ihrer Erhaltung* (Leipzig, 1919), I: *Die Westfront*, pp. 111–40.

Great Britain. Royal Commission for the Chicago Exhibition 1893. Official Catalogue of the British Section (London, 1893).

Grégoire, H., Convention nationale. Instruction publique. *Rapport sur les destructions opérées par le vandalisme, et sur les moyens de le réprimer. Par Grégoire. Séance du 14 Fructidor, l'an II* (Paris, 1794).

Convention nationale. Instruction publique. *Second rapport sur le vandalisme, 3 Brumaire, l'an III* (Paris, 1794).

Convention nationale. Instruction publique. *Troisième rapport sur le vandalisme. Par Grégoire. 24 Frimaire, l'an III* (Paris, 1794).

Mémoires de Grégoire, Ancien Évêque de Blois, ed. H. Carnot (2 vols., Paris, 1837).

Patrimoine et cité, ed. D. Audrerie (Bordeaux, 1999).

Grimm, J., Grimm, W., *Deutsches Wörterbuch* (vol. 4, Leipzig, 1877).

Gurlitt, C., *Die Westtürme des Meissner Domes* (Berlin, 1902).

'Vom Heidelberger Schloß', *Frankfurter Zeitung und Handelsblatt*, 18 Nov. 1901. Nr. 320 Abendblatt.

Hallays, A., 'D'une législation à faire en France pour la protection des monuments et objets d'art', *Journal des débat*, April 1903.

Hartung, W., *Die Denkmalspflege im juristischen Sinn mir spezieller Berücksichtigung Bayerns. Jur. Diss. Erlangen 1906* (Bayreuth, 1906).

Haupt, 'Die Herstellung von Kirchen und ihre verschiedenen Richtungen', *Die Denkmalpflege*, 1 (1899), 64–5; 70–2.

Helfert, J.A. Freiherr von, *Denkmalpflege. Öffentliche Obsorge für Gegenstände der Kunst und des Altertums nach dem neuesten Stande der Gesetzgebung in den verschiedenen Culturstaaten* (Vienna, Leipzig, 1897).

d'Héricourt, A., *Annuaire des sociétés savantes de la France et de l'Etranger* (2 vols., Paris, 1863–4).

Heyer, K., *Denkmalpflege und Heimatschutz im Deutschen Recht, Jur. Diss. Marburg 1912* (Berlin, 1912).

Hill, O., 'Natural Beauty as a National Asset', *Nineteenth Century*, 58 (1905), 935–41.

Our Common Land (London, 1877).

Huber, E.R. (ed.), *Dokumente zur deutschen Verfassungsgeschichte* (4 vols., 3rd edn, Stuttgart, 1978–92).

Huggins, S., 'On the So-Called Restoration of our Cathedral and Abbey Churches', *Proceedings of the Liverpool Architectural and Archaeological Society. Twenty Third Session. Eleventh Meeting*, 5 April 1871 (Liverpool, 1871), pp. 118–31.

Hugo, V., *Choses vues, 1830–1846* (Paris, 1972).

'Guerre aux démolisseurs', *Revue de Paris* (1829), reedited and enlarged in *Revue des deux mondes* (1832), repr. in *Oeuvres complètes* (Paris, 1834), XI, pp. 155–6.

Heidelberg, ed. M. Butor (Frankfurt, 2002).

Hume, A., *The Learned Societies and Printing Clubs of the United Kingdom. Being an Account of their Respective Origin, History, Objects, and Constitution. With full Details Respecting Membership, Fees, their Published Works and Transactions, Notices of their Periods and Places of Meeting, &c. and a General Introduction and a Classified Index. Compiled from official documents* (London, 1847, reedited A. I. Evans, *With a Supplement Containing all the Recently-Established Societies and Printing Clubs, and their Publications to the Present Time*, London, 1853).

Hunter, R., *The Preservation of Places of Interest or Beauty. A lecture delivered at the University on Tuesday, January 29th, 1907* (Manchester, 1907).

Hutchinson, H.G., *Life of Sir John Lubbock, Lord Avebury* (London, 1914).

Institut International de Coopération intellectuelle. Office international des Musées, *La Protection internationale des Monuments historiques et des oeuvres d'art en temps de Guerre* (Paris, 1936).

'International Congress of Architects and Retrospective Exhibition of Architecture at Brussels', *Journal of the RIBA*, 3rd Ser., 4 (1897), p. 422.

'International Congress of Architects', *The Builder*, 10 Feb. 1906, p. 136.

'International Congress of Hygiene at Brussels', *Journal of the RIBA*, 3rd Ser., 11 (1904), 445.

'International Congress on the Teaching of Drawing, Paris', *The Builder*, 15 Sept. 1900, p. 236.

'International Congress Vienna', *Journal of the RIBA*, 3rd Ser., 15 (1908), 140, 299, 328, 449–50.

'International Drawing Congress', *Journal of the RIBA*, 3rd Ser., 15 (1908), 327.

International Exhibition 1862. Special Catalogue of the Zollverein-Department (Berlin, 1862).

'Internationaler Architekten Congress in Brüssel', *Centralblatt der Bauverwaltung* (1897), 238, 331, 356, 397, 416.

'Internationaler Architekten Congress in Madrid', *Centralblatt der Bauverwaltung*, 23 (1903), 425.

'Internationaler Architekten Congress in Paris', *Centralblatt der Bauverwaltung*, 20 (1900), 44, 208, 280, 286, 449–51.

'Internationaler Architektenkongress in Wien', *Die Denkmalpflege*, 10 (1908), 67–9.

'Internationaler Congress der vergleichenden Geschichtsforschung in Paris', *Centralblatt der Bauverwaltung*, 20 (1900), 180.

'Internationaler Kongress (XII.) für Prähistorie und Archäologie', *Korrespondenzblatt des Gesamtvereins der Deutschen Geschichts- und Alterthumsvereine*, 48 (1900), 95.

'Internationaler Kunsthistoriker Kongreß', *Die Denkmalpflege*, 2 (1900), 104.

'Internationaler Kunsthistorischer Kongress in Lübeck', *Korrespondenzblatt des Gesamtvereins der Deutschen Geschichts- und Alterthumsvereine*, 48 (1900), 143.

'Internationaler Kunsthistorischer Kongress in Lübeck', *Centralblatt der Bauverwaltung*, 20 (1900), 352.

Kelvin, N. (ed.), *The Collected Letters of William Morris* (4 vols., Princeton, 1984–96).

Klüpfel, K.A., 'Die historischen Vereine und Zeitschriften Deutschlands, *Zeitschrift für Geschichtswissenschaft*, 1 (1844), 518–59.

Kohler, J., 'Das Recht an Denkmälern und Altertumsfunden', *Deutsche Juristenzeitung*, 9 (1904), cols. 771–8.

'Das Recht der Kunstwerke und Alterthümer', *Archiv für bürgerliches Recht*, 9 (1894), 56–84.

Kohte, J., 'Der vierte Tag für Denkmalpflege in Erfurt am 25. und 26. September 1903', *Die Denkmalpflege*, 5 (1903), 105–7.

'Die Denkmalpflege in Frankreich von Dr. Paul Clemen', *Die Denkmalpflege*, 1 (1899), 44.

'Die Denkmalpflege in Preußen während der letzten Jahre', *Die Denkmalpflege*, 1 (1899), 87–8.

'Peter Wallé', *Die Denkmalfpelge*, 6 (1904), 99.

Die Pflege der Kunstdenkmäler in Italien (repr. from *Centralblatt der Bauverwaltung*, 18 (1898), Berlin, 1898).

Kriegstagung für Denkmalpflege. Stenographischer Bericht (Berlin, 1915).

Kunst und Kunstindustrie auf der Weltausstellung von 1867. Pariser Briefe von Friedrich Pecht (Leipzig, 1867).

L'Annuaire des Sociétés savantes de la France et de l'Etranger, sous auspices du Ministère de l'Instruction publique (Paris, 1846).

'La Conservation des monuments et le texte officiel de la Loi de séparation des Eglises et de l'Etat', *L'Ami des Monuments*, 19 (1905), 330; 20 (1906), 27–32.

'La Loi de séparation dans ses rapports avec la conservation des monuments', *L'Ami des Monuments*, 20 (1906), 82.

Labbé, E. (ed.), *Exposition internationale des Arts et Techniques à Paris en 1937, la section française, rapport général* (5 vols., Paris, 1939).

Lahor, J., 'Une Société à créer pour la protection des paysages français', *Revue des revues*, 1 Mar. 1901, pp. 526–31.

Lance, A.E., *Exposition universelle des beaux-arts. Architecture, compte-rendu par Adolphe Lance, Architecte du Gouvernement* (Paris, 1855).

Lange, K., *Die Grundsätze der modernen Denkmalpflege. Rede zum Geburtstag Wilhelms II. von Württemberg vom 25. Februar 1906* (Tübingen, 1906).

Langhorne, W., *De la conservation des monuments historiques en Angleterre* (repr. from *Bulletin monumental*, Paris, 1896).

Lasteyre, F., *De l'histoire du travail à l'Exposition universelle* (Paris, 1867).

'Le Congres international de l'Art public a Bruxelles', *L'Ami des Monuments*, 12 (1898), 112, 180–81, 234–37, 290–95.

Le Premier Congrès international pour la protection des paysages (Paris, 1910).

Léon, P., 'La Protection des églises', *Revue de Paris*, 1 Feb. 1913, p. 21.

Lepelletier, 'Prohibition d'exporter les oeuvres d'art, législation italienne', *Journal du droit international privé et de la jurisprudence comparée* (1896), 962–81.

Lerebourg-Pigeonniere, D., Julliot de la Morandiere, L., 'Protection du patrimoine artistique', *Revue trimestrielle de droit civil*, April–June (1908), 404–6.

'Les Décrets du 3 janvier 1889 sur la conservation des monuments et objets d'art ayant un caractère historique et artistique', *Bulletin Monumental*, 6th Ser., 5 (1889), 229–41.

Lessing, J., *Berichte von der Pariser Weltausstellung 1878* (Berlin, 1878).

Das halbe Jahrhundert der Weltausstellungen (Volskwirtschaftliche Zeitfragen 174, Berlin, 1900).

Das Kunstgewerbe auf der Wiener Weltausstellung 1873, in Lessing, *Berichte von der Pariser Weltausstellung 1878* (Berlin, 1878).

'Letter from Paris,' *The Builder*, 4 Aug. 1900, p. 97.

'Letter from Paris', *The Builder*, 13 Oct. 1900, p. 308.

Lettres adressées d'Allemange à M. Adolphe Lance, architecte par M. Viollet-le-Duc (Paris, 1856).

Lezius, H., *Das Recht der Denkmalpflege in Preußen. Begriff, Geschichte und Organi-sation der Denkmalpflege nebst sämtlichen gesetzlichen Vorschriften und Verord-nungen der Verwaltungsbehörden einschließlich der Gesetzgebung gegen die Verunstaltung von Ortschaften und landschaftlich hervorragenden Gegenden (Gesetze vom 2. Juni 1902 und 15. Juli 1907). Für den praktischen Gebrauch zusammengestellt und erläutert von Dr. H. Lezius, Regierungsassessor, Hilfsar-beiter im Ministerium der geistlichen, Unterrichts und Medizinalangelegenheiten* (Berlin, 1908).

Linas, C. de, *L'Histoire du travail à l'Exposition universelle de 1867* (repr. from *Revue de l'art chrétien*, Paris, 1867).

Locke, J.W., 'International Congress of Architects, Madrid. Report of the Secretary of the Institute', *Journal of the RIBA*, 3rd Ser., 11 (1904), 343–6.

Loersch, H., *Das französische Gesetz vom 30. März 1887. Ein Beitrag zum Recht der Denkmalpflege* (Bonn, 1897).

'Loi anglaise du 18 août 1882 sur les monuments anciens', *Annuaire de législation étrangère* (1882).

'Loi du 2 avril 1882 du Grand-Duché de Finlande sur la protection et la conservation des monuments anciens', *Annuaire de législation étrangère* (1884).

'Loi du 12 juin 1902 sur la protection et la conservation des monuments et objets ayant une valeur d'art ou d'antiquité', *Annuaire de législation étrangère* (1903).

'Loi du 27 juin 1903 prohibant temporairement l'exportation des ouvrages d'antiquité et d'art', *Annuaire de législation étrangère* (1904).

'Loi du 20 juin 1909, disposition relatives aux antiquités et beaux-arts', *Annuaire de législation étrangère* (1910).

'Loi hongroise du 28 mai 1881 sur la conservation des monuments d'art', *Annuaire de législation étrangère* (1882).

'Loi pour la conservation des monuments et objets d'art ayant un intérêt historique et artistique', *Korrespondenzblatt der Geschichts- und Alterthumsvereine*, 35 (1887), 147–8.

'Loi sur la conservation des monuments historiques', *Bulletin Monumental*, 6th Ser., 2 (1886), 204–9.

London International Exhibition 1862. Official Catalogue of the Fine Art Department (London, 1862).

Loriquet, H., *Préfecture du Pas-de-Calais. Commission des Monuments historiques. Catalogue de l'exposition rétrospective des arts et monuments du Pas-de-Calais, Arras, 20 mai-21 juin 1896* (Arras, 1896).

Lützow, C. von., Auer, H., Bucher, B., Eitelsberger, R. von., *Kunst und Kunst-gewerbe auf der Wiener Weltausstellung 1873* (Vienna, 1873).

Malkowsky, G. (ed.), *Die Pariser Weltausstellung in Wort und Bild* (Berlin, 1900).

Maréchaux, Dom B. *Notre Dame de la Fin de Terre de Soulac* (Bordeaux, 1893, repr. 2006).

Marguery, J., Université d'Aix-Marseille. Faculté de droit d'Aix, *La Protection des objets mobiliers d'intérêt historique ou artistique, législation française et italienne. Thèse pour le doctorat (sciences politiques et économiques)* (Paris, 1912).

Marsy, A.C.A., 'De la législation danoise sur la conservation des monuments historiques et des antiquités nationales', *Bulletin Monumental* (1878), pp. 572–84.

Masson, R., Université de Paris. Faculté de droit. *Du Rôle de l'État par rapport à l'art. Thèse* (Paris, 1912).

Mellerio, A. *et al.*, *L'Art et l'École* (Paris, 1907).

Mérimée, P., 'Les Beaux-Arts en Angleterre', *Revue des Deux Mondes*, 15 Oct. 1857, pp. 866–880.

Rapport au Ministre de l'Intérieur (Paris, 1843).

Metman, J., Université de Dijon. Faculté de droit, *La Législation française relative à la protection des monuments historiques et des objets d'art. Thèse pour le doctorat* (Dijon, 1911).

Mielke, R., 'Denkmalpflege in England', *Die Denkmalpflege*, 8 (1906), 42–4.

'Meine Beziehung zu Ernst Rudorff und die Gründung des Bundes Heimatschutz. Zu dem 25. Jährigen Bestehen der Bewegung', *Brandenburgia*, 38 (1929), 1–16.

Volkskunst (Magdeburg, 1896).

Ministère de l'Instruction publique et des Beaux-arts, *Direction des Beaux-arts. Monuments historiques. Musée de Sculpture comparée, Catalogue des moulages de sculptures appartenant aux divers centres et aux diverses époques d'art, exposés dans les galeries du Trocadéro, suivi du catalogue des dessins de Viollet-le-Duc conservés dans la bibliothèque* (Paris, 1890).

Documents à l'appui du projet de loi pour la conservation des monuments historiques et des objets d'art. Procès-verbaux du Conseil supérieur des beaux-arts (Paris, 1879).

Documents à l'appui du projet de loi pour la conservation des monuments historiques et des objets d'art. Projet présenté à la Chambre des députés et observations de la commission des monuments historiques sur ce projet (Paris, 1879).

Exposition universelle internationale de 1900. Groupe II, Beaux arts. Extrait du décret du 4 août 1894 portant règlement général pour l'Exposition universelle de 1900 (Paris, 1899).

Ministère de l'Instruction publique, des Cultes et des Beaux-arts, Direction des Beaux-arts, Commission des Monuments historiques, *Circulaires ministérielles relatives à la conservation des monuments historiques* (Paris, 1875).

Catalogue de la bibliothèque de la commission des monuments historiques (Paris, 1875).

Ministère de l'Agriculture et du Commerce, *Rapport administratif sur l'exposition universelle de 1878 à Paris* (2 vols., Paris, 1881).

Ministère des Affaires étrangères, *Conférence internationale de la paix. La Haye, 18 mai 29 juillet 1899* (The Hague, 1899).

Deuxième conférence internationale de la paix. La Haye, 15 juin –18 octobre 1907. Actes et documents (The Hague, 1907).

Documents diplomatiques, Actes de la conférence de Bruxelles de 1874 sur le projet d'une convention internationale concernant la guerre. Protocoles des séances plénières. Protocoles de la commission déléguée par la conférence. Annexes (Paris, 1874).

Ministère du Commerce, de l'Industrie et des Colonies. Exposition universelle internationale de 1889. Direction générale de l'exploitation, *Congrès international pour la protection des œuvres d'art et des monuments*. Fascicule no 1 – *Organisation du Congrès*. Mai 1889 (Paris, 1889).

Exposition universelle internationale de 1889. Direction générale de l'exploitation, *Congrès international pour la protection des œuvres d'art et des monuments*. Fascicule no. 2 – *Organisation du Congrès* (Paris, 1889).

Monod, E. (ed.), *L'Exposition Universelle de 1889: Grand ouvrage illustré, historique, encyclopédique, descriptif* (3 vols., Paris, 1890).

Monod, M.G., 'Rapport lu dans l'assemblée générale extraordinaire du 11 novembre', *Bulletin – Cercle Saint-Simon, Société historique*, 1 (1883), 1–12.

'Moving (Dioramic) Experiences', *All the Year Round* (March 1867), 304–8.

Müller, J., *Die wissenschaftlichen Vereine und Gesellschaften Deutschland im 19. Jahrhundert, Bibliographie ihrer Veröffentlichungen* (3 vols., Berlin, 1883–1908).

Müntz, E., 'Les Annexassions de collections d'art ou de bibliothèques et leur rôle dans les relations internationales principalement pendant la Révolution française', *Revue d'histoire diplomatique* (1894), 481–97; (1895), 375–93; (1896), 481–508.

Troisième Congrès international des architectes. Paris, 17–22 juin 1889. Catalogue de l'exposition de portraits d'architectes organisée à l'École des beaux-arts à l'occasion du congrès, par Charles Lucas et Eugène Müntz (Paris, 1889).

Murray, D., *An Archaeological Survey of the United Kingdom. The Preservation and Protection of Our Ancient Monuments* (Glasgow, 1896).

Muthesius, H., 'Denkmalschutz und Denkmalpflege in England', *Die Denkmalpflege*, 3 (1901), 52–4.

'Die Kathedrale von Peterborough und die Denkmalpflege in England', *Centralblatt der Bauverwaltung*, 10 April 1897, pp. 164–6.

'Sechster internationaler Architektenkongress in Madrid', *Die Denkmalpflege*, 6 (1904), 52.

Nicaise, A., *Exposition universelle de 1889. Galerie des arts libéraux (Champs de Mars). Collection archéologique de M. Auguste Nicaise. Inventaire descriptif* (Châlons-sur-Marne, 1895).

'Ninth International Congress of Architects at Rome', *Journal of the RIBA*, 3rd Ser., 18 (1911), 282, 314.

Normand, A., *L'Architecture des nations étrangères. Etude sur les principales constructions du parc à l'Exposition universelle de Paris, 1867* (Paris, 1870).

Normand, C., 'Congrès international de la propriété artistique et littéraire à Venise', *L'Ami des Monuments*, 2 (1888), 233–5.

'Congrès officiel international pour la protection des oeuvres d'art et des monuments', *L'Ami des Monuments*, 2 (1888), 230–2.

'Introduction', *L'Ami des Monuments*, 1 (1887), 3–5.

'La Promenade des Adhérents de la Revue l'Ami des Monuments au Château de Veaux-le Praslin', *L'Ami des Monuments*, 1 (1887), 197.

'Le Congrès des Arts décoratif en 1894', *L'Ami des Monuments*, 7 (1893), 333–6.

'Le Congrès parisien, municipal, international de l'Art public ou étude des conditions de la physinomie artistique des villes', *L'Ami des Monuments*, 13 (1899), 164–8.

'Le premier Congres international d'archéologie a Athènes', *L'Ami des Monuments*, 19 (1905), 100–16.

'Le Touring-Club visite les vestiges d'Alesia', *L'Ami des Monuments*, 21 (1907–8), 265–8.

Ministère du Commerce, de l'Industrie et des Colonies. Exposition universelle internationale de 1889. Direction générale de l'exploitation, *Congrès international pour la protection des œuvres d'art et des monuments, tenu à Paris du 24 au 29 juin 1889. Procès-verbaux sommaires. Rédigés par le secrétaire général Charles Normand, architecte diplômé par le gouvernement, directeur de l'Ami des monuments, secrétaire générale de la Société des amis des monuments parisien* (Paris, 1889).

'Premières Idées sur l'organisation de la croix-rouge pour la protection des monuments en temps de guerre. Conférence faite au premier Congrès officiel international pour la protection des oeuvres d'art et monuments à l'Exposition universelle', *L'Ami des Monuments*, 3 (1889), 272–77.

'Société des Amis des Monuments parisiens. Constituée dans le but de veiller sur les monuments d'art et sur la physionomie monumentale de Paris', *Bulletin – Cercle Saint-Simon, Société historique*, 2 (1884), 301–7.

Oechelhaeuser, A. von, 'Bericht über die Tätigkeit des Tages für Denkmalpflege während des ersten Dezenniums seines Bestehens,' in Oechelhaeuser (ed.), *Denkmalpflege. Auszug aus den stenographischen Berichten des Tages für Denkmalpflege* (2 vols., Leipzig, 1910–1913), I, pp. 1–12.

(ed.), *Denkmalpflege. Auszug aus den stenographischen Berichten des Tages für Denkmalpflege* (2 vols., Leipzig, 1910–13).

Wege, Ziele und Gefahren der Denkmalpflege. Festrede bei dem Feierlichen Akte des Rektoratswechsels an der Großherzoglich-Technischen Hochschule Fridericiana zu Karlsruhe am 20. November 1909 (Karlsruhe, 1909).

Oeuvre de l'art public. Premier Congrès international, Bruxelles, 1898 (Liège, 1898).

Office international des musées, *La Conservation des monuments d'art et d'histoire* (Paris, 1933).

Oursel, C., *L'Église Notre-Dame de Dijon* (Paris, 1938).

Österreich-Ungarn. Central-Comité der Weltausstellung zu Paris 1867, Die Kunstwerke und die Histoire du travail. Instrumente für Kunst und Wissenschaft (Vienna, 1869).

Ozenne, J.A.S.M., Sommerard, E. du, *Expositions internationales. Section française. Rapport présenté au Ministre de l'agriculture et du commerce sur les expositions internationales de Londres en 1871, en 1872 et en 1874, de Vienne en 1873 et de Philadelphie en 1876, par MM. Ozenne et Du Sommerard* (repr. from *Journal Officiel*, Paris, 1877).

Paley, F.A., *The Church Restorers. A Tale Treating of Ancient and Modern Architecture and Church Decorations* (London, 1844).

Paris and its Exhibition. Pall Mall Gazette Extra 49, 26 July 1889.

Paris Exhibition, 1900. *Catalogue of the British Fine Art Section* (London, 1900).

'Paris International Congress of Architects', *The Builder,* 11 Aug. 1900, pp. 129–30.

Paris Universal Exhibition of 1867. Catalogue of the British Section, containing a List of the Exhibitors of the United Kingdom . . . in English, French, German and Italian. With Statistical Introductions and an Appendix (London, 1867).

Pariset, E., Université de France. Faculté de droit de Lyon, *Droit romain: Dispositions de dernière volonté à Rome et dans le droit ancien. Droit français: les Monuments historiques. Thèse pour le doctorat* (Paris, 1891).

Pecht, F., *Kunst und Kunstindustrie auf der Pariser* Weltausstellung 1878 (Stuttgart, 1878).

Perrault-Dabot, A., *Les Archives de la Commission des Monuments historiques* (Paris, 1900).

Perrault-Dabot, A.D.F (ed.), *Archives de la Commission des Monuments Historiques, publiées, sous le patronage de l'Administration des beaux-arts, par les soins de MM. A. de Baudot, A. Perrault-Dabot* (5 vols., Paris, s. d.).

Ministère de l'Instruction publique et des beaux-arts, *Archives de la Commission des Monuments Historiques. Catalogue des relevés, dessins et aquarelles, dressé par A. Perrault-Dabot* (Paris, 1899).

Photographien der deutschen Abteilung der Pariser Weltausstellung 1900 (Paris, 1900).

Phillips, S., *Guide to the Crystal Palace and Park* (London, 1854).

Picard, A. (ed.), *Exposition universelle internationale de 1889 à Paris. Rapport du jury international. Groupe I – Oeuvres d'art. Classe 1 à 5 BIS* (Paris, 1890).

Ministère du Commerce, de l'Industrie, des Postes et des Télégraphes. *Exposition universelle internationale de 1900 à Paris. Rapport général administratif et technique* (8 vols., Paris, 1902–3).

Ministère du Commerce, de l'Industrie et des Colonies, *Exposition universelle internationale de 1889 à Paris. Rapport général* (10 vols., Paris, 1891).

Polenz, 'Die Denkmalpflege und ihre Gestaltung in Preußen', *Die Denkmalpflege,* 6 (1904), 11–12.

'Zur Geschichte der Organisation der Denkmalpflege in Preußen', *Die Denkmalpflege,* 1 (1899), 37–9, 45–6.

'Zur Lage des Denkmalschutzes in Preußen', *Die Denkmalpflege,* 4 (1902), 33–6, 66–9; 5 (1903), 17–19.

Poupinel, J.M., Ministère du Commerce, de l'Industrie des Postes et des Télégraphes. Exposition universelle internationale de 1900. Direction générale de l'exploitation, *5e Congrès international des architectes, tenu à Paris du 30 Juillet au 4 août 1900. Procès-verbaux sommaires par M. J.M. Poupinel, secrétaire général du congrès* (Paris, 1901).

'Preußische Verhandlungen im Abgeordnetenhaus', *Die Denkmalpflege,* 2 (1900), 31.

Probst, E., 'Zur Geschichte der Denkmalpflege in der Schweiz', *Die Denkmalpflege*, 1 (1899), 53–4.

Protection du patrimoine historique et esthétique de la France (Paris, 1997).

Prusse et états de l'Allemagne du Nord. Catalogue spécial de l'exposition universelle de Paris en 1867 édité par la commission (Paris, 1867).

Quatremère de Quincy, A., *Lettres à Miranda sur le déplacement des monuments de l'art de l'Italie*, ed. E. Pommier (Paris, 1989).

Rapport sur l'Exposition universelle de 1867, à Paris. Précis des opérations et listes des collaborateurs. Avec un appendice sur l'avenir des expositions, la statistique des opérations, les documents officiels et le plan de l'Exposition (Paris, 1869).

Rapports du jury mixte international publiés sous la dir. de S.A.I. le Prince Napoléon, président de la commission impériale (Paris, 1856).

Rawnsley, H.D., *A Nation's Heritage* (London, 1920).

Redtenbacher, R., *Denkschrift über die Baudenkmäler im Deutschen Reich. Ihre Inventarisierung, Aufnahme, Erhaltung und Restauration* (Berlin, 1875).

'Remparts au Mont-Saint-Michel', *L'Architecture* (1907), 416–18.

Report upon the IV. International Congress of Architects, Brussels, 1897 (Washington, DC, 1898).

Riegl, A., 'The Modern Cult of Monuments. Its Character and its Origin', *Oppositions*, 25 (1982), 21–51.

    Der moderne Denkmalkultus. Sein Wesen, seine Entstehung (Vienna, 1903) repr. in Riegl, *Gesammelte Aufsätze* (Vienna, 1996), pp. 139–84.

Royal Institute of British Architects, *Conservation of Ancient Monuments and Remains, General Advice to Promoters, Hints to Workmen* (London, 1865).

    International Congress of Architects. Seventh session held in London 1906 under the auspices of the Royal Institute of British Architects. Transactions (London, 1908).

Rücker, F., Université de Paris. Faculté des lettres. *Les Origines de la conservation des monuments historiques en France (1790–1830). Thèse pour le doctorat d'université (lettres)* (Paris, 1913).

Rudorff, E., 'Abermals Heimatschutz', *Die Grenzboten*, 56.4. (1897), 111–16, repr. in Schultze-Naumburg, P. (ed.), *Heimatschutz* (Berlin, 1926).

    'Das Verhältnis des modernen Lebens zur Nature', *Preußische Jahrbücher*, 45 (1880), 261–76, repr. in *Heimatschutz*, 6.1 (1910), 7–21.

    Der Schutz der lanschaftlichen Natur und der geschichtlichen Denkmäler (Berlin, 1892).

    'Heimatschutz', *Die Grenzboten*, 56.2 (1897), 401–14, 455–68, repr. in Schultze-Naumburg, P. (ed.), *Heimatschutz* (Berlin, 1926).

Ruskin, J., *The Seven Lamps of Architecture* (2nd edn, Orpington 1880, repr. New York, 1989).

Sarasin, P., *Über die Aufgaben des Weltnaturschutzes, Denkschrift gelesen an der Delegiertenversammlung zur Weltnaturschutzkommission in Bern am 18.11.1913* (Basel, 1914).

Über nationalen und internationalen Vogelschutz: sowie einige anschliessende Fragen des Weltnaturschutzes. Vortrag, gehalten am 12. Mai 1911 am zweiten deutschen Vogelschutztag in Stuttgart (Basel, 1911).

Weltnaturschutz, Vortrag gehalten am VIII. Zoologenkongress in Graz am 16. August und an der 93. Versammlung der Schweizerischen Naturforschenden Gesellschaft in Basel am 5. September 1910 (Basel, 1910).

Schmidt, A.B., 'Rechtsfragen des deutschen Denkmalschutzes', in *Festgabe für Rudolph Sohm, dargebracht zum Goldenen Doktorjubiläum* (Munich, Leipzig, 1914), pp. 143–97.

Schneider, R., *Quatremère de Quincy et son intervention dans les arts* (Paris, 1910).

Schultze-Naumburg, P., *Die Entstellung unseres Landes* (3rd rev. edn, s.l., 1909).

(ed.), *Heimatschutz* (Berlin, 1926).

Kunst aus Blut und Boden (Leipzig, 1934).

Kunst und Rasse (Munich, 1928).

'Schutz der Altstadt in Städten geschichtlicher Bedeutung, Oberverwaltungsgerichtliche Entscheidung', *Die Denkmalpflege*, 16 (1914), 70.

'Sechster internationaler Architekten-Kongress in Madrid', *Die Denkmalpfleg*, 5 (1903), 123.

'Seventh International Congress of Architects 1906', *Journal of the RIBA*, 3rd Ser., 7 (1900), 483, 528.

'Seventh International Congress of Architects London 1906', *Journal of the RIBA*, 3rd Ser., 13 (1906), 129–31.

Shabtai, R. (ed.), *The Hague Peace Conferences of 1899 and 1907 and International Arbitration. Reports and Documents* (The Hague, 2001).

Slater, J., 'The Ninth International Congress of Architects, Rome 1911', *Journal of the RIBA*, 3rd Ser., 19 (1912), 28–30.

'Société des Amis du Viel Arles', *L'Ami des Monuments*, 16 (1903), 186–7.

Société des architectes et des ingénieurs des Alpes-Maritimes, *Congrès international et régional d'architectes et d'ingénieurs. Tenue à Nice en 1884. Compte-rendu* (Nice, 1885).

Société impériale et centrale des architectes, *Conférence internationale Juillet 1867* (Paris, 1867).

Society of Antiquaries of London, *Statement of the Action Taken by the Society for the Protection of Ancient Buildings and the Society of Antiquaries for the Preservation of the West Front of the Cathedral Church of Peterborough* (s.l.s.d.).

Sommerard, E. du, *Exposition universelle de 1867 à Paris. Commission de l'histoire du travail. Rapport de M. E. du Sommerard* (Paris, 1867).

Exposition universelle de Vienne en 1873. Section française. Les Monuments historiques de France à l'exposition universelle de Vienne par M. E. du Sommerard (Paris, 1876).

'Souvenir de l'Exposition: l'Art public. Voeux du Congrès de Paris, international, municipal d'art public', *L'Ami des Monuments*, 14 (1900), 211–23.

Stevenson, J.J., *Architectural Restoration. Its Principles and Practice. A paper read at the Royal Institute of British Architects on the 28th of May 1877* (London, 1877).

Stirling Maxwell, Sir J., 'A Reasonable Policy for Protecting Ancient Buildings', SPAB, *Annual Report*, 31 (1908).

Tag für Denkmalpflege. Stenographischer Bericht (Berlin, 1900–12).

Tcheng-Ki-Tong, 'Congrès official international pour la protection des oeuvres d'art. Les Monuments de la Chine. Leur conservation', *L'Ami des Monuments*, 3 (1889), 326–8.

Les Chinois paints par eux-memes (3rd edn, Paris, 1884).

Tétreau, L., Faculté de droit de Paris, *Législation relative aux monuments et objets d'art dont la conservation présente un intérêt national au point de vue de l'histoire ou de l'art. Thèse pour le doctorat* (Paris, 1896).

'Texte officiel de décret relatifs à la réunions du service de conservation des édifices culturels a celui des monuments historiques, *L'Ami des Monuments*, 20 (1906), 364–8; 21 (1907), 42–8.

'Texte officiel de la loi de protection des sites', *L'Ami des Monuments*, 21 (1907), 109.

'The Congress Exhibition', *The Builder*, 21 July 1906, pp. 67–9.

'The Fifth International Congress of Architects, Paris, Report of the Secretary', *Journal of the RIBA*, 3rd Ser., 7 (1900), 469–74.

'The International Congress of Architects', *The Builder*, 7 July 1906, p. 7.

'The Paris Congress', *RIBA Journal of Proceedings*, 4 July 1889, 2nd Ser., 5.2 (1889).

'The Paris Exhibition 1900: Mr Ernest Georges Report upon Architectural Exhibits', *Journal of the RIBA*, 3rd Ser., 8 (1901), 433–4.

Thirion, C. (ed.), *Exposition internationale de 1878, à Paris. Congrès et conférences au Palais du Trocadéro. Comptes rendus sténographiques publiés sous les auspices du comité central des congrès et conférence et la direction de M. Ch. Thirion, secrétaire du comité* (3 vols., Paris, 1880–1).

Troisième Congrès international de l'art public, Liège, 15–21 septembre 1905 (Brussels, 1905).

'Über die rechtzeitige Einholung der staatlichen Genehmigung zur Beseitigung, Veränderung und Veräußerung von Baudenkmälern und beweglichen Kunstgegenständen', *Centralblatt der Bauverwaltung*, 16 (1896), 303–4, 488.

'Über Kunstplünderungen in Italien und Rom, *Neuer Teutscher Merkur*, Nov. (1796), 249–79.

Uhland, W.H. (ed.), *Illustrierter Katalog der Pariser Weltausstellung von 1878 unter Mitwirkung zahlreicher Berichterstatter* (Leipzig, 1880).

'Ulm Cathedral and its Restoration', *The Builder*, 10 Feb. 1883.

'Un jugement sur le Cercle Saint-Simon', *Bulletin – Cercle Saint-Simon, Société historique*, 2 (1884), 308–11.

Union centrale des arts décoratifs, *Exposition 1884 Paris, Catalogue. Salons du 1er étage. Exposition forestière ... Monuments historiques ... Musée rétrospectif* (Paris, 1884).

'Vandalisme à Avignon', *L'Ami des Monuments*, 15 (1901), 113.

Vattel, E. de, *Le Droit des gens, ou principes de la loi naturelle, appliqués à la conduite et aux affaires des nations et des souverains* (2 vols., London, 1758).

Vaudremer, E., Ministère de l'Agriculture et du Commerce, *Exposition universelle internationale de 1878 à Paris. Rapport du Jury Internationale. Groupe I, classe 4. La Section d'Architecture par M. Vaudremer, Architecture du Gouvernement et de la Ville de Paris* (Paris, 1880).

Verhandlungen des 27. Deutschen Juristentags (4 vols., Berlin, 1904–5).

Verzeichnis der ausgestellten Werke, Welt-Ausstellung in Paris 1878. Deutsche Abtheilung (Berlin, 1878).

Vignon, C., *Exposition universelle de 1855. Beaux-arts* (Paris, 1855).

VIme. Congrès international des Architectes sous la haute protection de S.M. le Roi d'Espagne et le patronage du Gouvernement. Madrid. Avril 1904 (Madrid, 1904).

'Vingt ans après. Brève épître aux Amis', *L'Ami des Monuments*, 21 (1907), 7.

Viollet-le-Duc, A., Commission supérieure, *Rapport pour la France à l'exposition internationale de 1871 à Londres* (Paris, 1872).

Viollet-le-Duc, E.E, *Dictionnaire raisonné de l'architecture française du XIe au XVIe siècle* (10 vols., Paris, 1854–68).

'De la construction des édifices religieux depuis le commencement du christianisme jusqu'au XVIe siècle, introduction', *Annales archéologique*, 1 (1844), 334–47.

'Restauration', in Viollet-le-Duc, *Dictionnaire raisonné de l'architecture française du XIe au XVIe siècle* (10 vols., Paris, 1854–68), VIII, repr. and trans. in Berry Bergdoll (ed.), Viollet-le-Duc, E.E., *The Foundations of Architecture. Selections from the Dictionnaire raisonné* (New York, 1990).

Viollet-le-Duc, G., *Esthétique appliquée à l'histoire de l'art par Eugène Viollet-le-Duc. Suivi de Viollet-le-Duc et l'Ecole des beaux-arts: la bataille de 1863–64* (Paris, 1994).

Visites et études de S. A. I. le prince Napoléon au Palais des beaux-arts, ou Description complète de cette exposition (peinture, sculpture, gravure, architecture) avec la liste des récompenses, les statistiques officielles et les documents et décrets faisant suite aux 'Visites et études au Palais de l'industrie' (Paris, 1856).

'Voeu pour la protection du Mont Saint-Michel', *L'Ami des Monuments*, 21 (1907–8), 298–9.

Wagner, H., *Die Denkmalpflege in Hessen 1818–1905, und zwar: Gesetz, den Denkmalschutz betreffend, vom 16. Juli 1902 nebst den zugehörigen Ausführungs-Vorschriften. Amtliche Handausgabe mit Motiven, Erläuterungen und einem Sachregister, bearb. im Auftrag Großherzogl. Ministeriums des Innern* (Darmstadt, 1905).

Weatherly, C., 'Monument', *Encyclopaedia Britannica* (1911), XVIII, pp. 796–800.

Weber, P., *Heimatschutz, Denkmalpflege und Bodenreform. Vortrag gehalten auf dem 15. Bundestag deutscher Bodenreformer zu Berlin am 4. Oktober 1905* (Berlin, 1906).

Weltausstellung in Philadelphia 1876. Deutsche Abtheilung. Amtlicher Katalog (Berlin, 1876).

Weltausstellung in St Louis 1904. Amtlicher Katalog der Ausstellung des Deutschen Reichs. Hrsg. vom Reichskommissar (Berlin, 1904).

Whelan, R. (ed.), *Octavia Hill and the Social Housing Debate. Essays and Letters by Octavia Hill* (London, 1998).

Wieland, C.A., *Der Denkmal- und Heimatschutz in der Gesetzgebung der Gegenwart. Programm zur Rektoratsfeier der Universität Basel* (Basel, 1905).

'Wien, Versammlung von Fachmännern der Museums- und Naturwissenschaften', *Die Denkmalpflege*, 5 (1904), 114.

Wiener Weltausstellung. Amtlicher Katalog der Ausstellung des Deutschen Reiches (Berlin, 1873).

Witt, O.N. (ed.), *Amtlicher Katalog der Ausstellung des Deutschen Reiches. Columbische Weltausstellung in Chicago* (Berlin, 1893).

Wohlleben, M. (ed.), *Konservieren, nicht restaurieren. Streitschriften zur Denkmalpflege um 1900. George Dehio, Alois Riegl* (Braunschweig, 1988).

Wolff, F., *Denkmalarchive. Vortrag gehalten auf dem 1. Denkmalarchivtag in Dresden am 24. September 1913* (Berlin, 1913).

Einrichtungen und Tätigkeit der staatlichen Denkmalpflege im Elsaß in den Jahren 1899–1909 (Veröffentlichungen des Kaiserlichen Denkmal-Archivs zu Straßburg i.E. 10, Strasbourg, 1909).

'Work and Play at the Architectural Congress', *The Builder*, 14 July 1906, p. 33.

Worsaae, J.J.A., *La Conservation des antiquités et des monuments nationaux en Danemark. Rapport fait à la demande de la légation impériale et royale d'Autriche-Hongrie, à Copenhague, par J.J.A. Worsaae. Traduit par E. Beauvois* (Extrait des Mém. de la Soc. Roy. Des Antiqu. du Nord 1877, Copenhagen, 1878).

Wussow, A. von, *Die Erhaltung der Denkmäler in den Kulturstaaten der Gegenwart. Im Auftrage des Herrn Ministers der geistlichen, Unterrichts- und Medizinalangelegenheiten nach amtlichen Quellen dargestellt* (2 vols., Berlin, 1885).

'Zum Schutz der Kirche Wang im Riesengebirge', *Die Denkmalpflege*, 6 (1904), 115; 7 (1905), 38.

'Zur Vorbereitung eines Gesetzes zum Schutze der Naturdenkmäler in Oesterreich', *Die Denkmalpflege*, 5 (1903), 115; 6 (1904), 16, 60.

'Zustand der Künste und Wissenschaften in Frankreich unter Robespierres Regierung (1795)', *Neuer Teutscher Merkur*, 1 (1795), 77–102; 168–92.

'Zweiter internationaler Kongress für Heimatschutz Stuttgart', *Die Denkmalpflege*, 14 (1912) pp. 55, 64.

PRINTED SECONDARY SOURCES

Adam, T., 'Rettung der Geschichte – Bewahrung der Natur. Ursprung und Entwicklung der Historischen Vereine und des Umweltschutzes in Deutschland von 1770 bis zur Gegenwart', *Blätter für deutsche Landesgeschichte*, 133 (1997), 239–77.

Alings, R., *Monument und Nation. Das Bild vom Nationalstaat im Medium Denkmal* (Berlin, New York, 1996).

Alter, P., 'Hermann Muthesius. Die englischen Jahre', in Ritter, G., Wende, P. (eds.), *Rivalität und Partnerschaft. Studien zu den deutsch-britischen Beziehungen im 19. und 20. Jahrhundert* (Paderborn, 1999), pp. 53–68.

Anderson, R.G.W. *et al.* (eds.), *Enlightening the British. Knowledge, Discovery and the Museum in the Eighteenth Century* (London, 2003).

Andresen, H.G. 'Heimatschutzarchitektur in Lübeck. Ein vergessener Versuch des angemessenen Umgangs mit einem Stadtdenkmal', in Brix, M. (ed.), *Lübeck. Die Alstadt als Denkmal* (Munich, 1975).

Andrews, M., *The Search for the Picturesque. Landscape Aesthetics and Tourism in Britain, 1760–1800* (Aldershot, 1989).

Applegate, C., *A Nation of Provincials. The German Idea of Heimat* (Berkeley, Los Angeles, Oxford, 1990).

Apter, E., *Continental Drift. From National Characters to Virtual Subjects* (Chicago, 1999).

Assman, A., *Erinnerungsräume, Formen und Wandlungen des kulturellen Gedächtnisses* (Munich, 1999).

Assman, J., *Das kulturelle Gedächtnis. Schrift, Erinnerung und politische Identität in frühen Hochkulturen* (Munich, 1992).

Audrerie, D., *La Notion et la protection du patrimoine* (Que sais-je 3304, Paris, 1997).

Souchier, R., Vilar, L., *Le Patrimoine mondial* (Que sais-je 3436, Paris, 1998).

Babelon, J.P., Chastel, A., *La Notion de patrimoine* (Paris, 1994).

Bacher, E., 'Denkmalbegriff, Denkmälermasse und Inventar', *Deutsche Kunst und Denkmalpflege*, 38 (1980), 121–5.

Baczko, B., *Comment sortir de la Terreur* (Paris, 1989).

Bady, J.P., *Les Monuments historiques en France* (Que sais-je 2205, 2nd edn, 1998).

Bailkin, J., *The Culture of Property. The Crisis of Liberalism in Modern Britain* (Chicago, 2004).

'Bailleu', *Deutsches Biographisches Jahrbuch* (10 vols., Berlin 1925–8), IV, pp. 3–10.

Bann, S., *The Clothing of Clio. A Study of the Representation of History in Nineteenth-Century Britain and France* (Cambridge, 1984).

Romanticism and the Rise of History (New York, 1995).

Barker, H., Burrows, S. (eds.), *Press, Politics and the Public Sphere in Europe and North America, 1760–1820* (Cambridge, 2002).

Barth, V., *Mensch versus Welt. Die Pariser Weltausstellung von 1867* (Darmstadt, 2007).

Baudot, M., 'Trente ans de coordination des sociétés savantes (1830–1861)', in *Les Sociétés savantes. Actes du 100e Congrès des Sociétés savantes 1975* (Paris, 1976), pp. 8–28.

Beard, M., *The Parthenon* (London, 2002).

'Beauquier', *Dictionnaire des Parlementaires Français* (5 vols., Paris 1889–91, repr. Ann Arbor, 1975), I, p. 226.

Beausoleil, J., Ory, J. (eds.), *Albert Kahn (1860–1940). Réalités d'une utopie. Exhibition Catalogue Musée Albert Kahn* (Boulogne, 1995).

Bell, E.M., *Octavia Hill* (London, 1942).

Bennett, T., *The Birth of the Museum. History, Theory, Politics* (London, 1995).

'The Exhibitionary Complex', in Dirks, N.B., Eley, G., Ortner, S.B. (eds.), *Culture, Power, History. A Reader in Contemporary Social Theory* (Princeton, 1994), pp. 123–54.

Benton, T. (ed.), *Understanding Heritage and Memory* (Manchester, 2010).

Bercé, F., 'Arcisse de Caumont et les sociétés savantes', in Nora, P. (ed.), *Les Lieux de mémoire* (7 vols., Paris, 1984–92, repr. 3 vols., Paris, 1997), I, pp. 1545–73.

Dès Monuments historiques au patrimoine du XVIIIe siècle à nos jours ou 'Les égarements du coeur et de l'esprit' (Paris, 2000).

'Quand les Sociétés savantes découvraient le patrimoine', *Histoire*, 25 (1980), 85–7.

'Les Sociétés savantes et la protection du patrimoine monumental', *Les Sociétés savantes. Actes du 100e Congrès des Sociétés savantes 1975* (Paris, 1976), pp. 155–67.

Berger, S., Lorenz, C., Melman, B. (eds), *Popularizing National Pasts, 1800 to the Present* (London, 2011).

Berghoff, H., Ziegler, D., *Pionier und Nachzügler? Vergleichende Studien zur Geschichte Großbritanniens und Deutschlands im Zeitalter der Industrialisierung. Festschrift für Sidney Pollard zum 70. Geburtstag* (Bochum, 1995).

Berstein, S., *Édouard Herriot, ou La république en personne* (Paris, 1985).

Bertho-Lavenir, C., *La Roue et le stylo. Comment nous sommes devenus touristes* (Paris, 1999).

Berton, P., 'What We Mean by Heritage', *Canadian Heritage*, 7 (1981), 44.

Bevan, R., *The Destruction of Memory: Architecture at War* (London, 2006).

Blackbourn, D., Eley, G. (eds.), *Mythen deutscher Geschichtsschreibung. Die gescheiterte bürgerliche Revolution von 1848* (Frankfurt, 1980).

Blanckaert, C. (ed.), *Les Politiques de l'anthropologie. Discours et pratiques en France, 1860–1940* (Paris, 2001).

Blanning, T.C.W., *The Culture of Power and the Power of Culture. Old Regime Europe, 1660–1789* (Oxford, 2002).

The Romantic Revolution (London, 2011).

Blémont, H., 'Guillon, Adolphe Irenée', *Dictionnaire de Biographie Française* (vol. 17, 1989), p. 250.

Bloch, M., 'Pour une histoire comparée des sociétés européennes', in Bloch, *Mélanges historiques* (2 vols., Paris, 1963), I, pp. 16–40.

Bock, G., Thane P. (eds.), *Maternity and Gender Policies. Women and the Rise of the European Welfare States, 1880–1950s* (London, New York, 1991).

Bödeker, H., *Begriffsgeschichte, Diskursgeschichte, Metapherngeschichte* (Göttingen, 2003).

Boer, P. den, Frijhoff, W. (eds.), *Lieux de mémoire et identités nationales* (Amsterdam, 1993).

Boime, A., *Art and the French Commune. Imagining Paris after War and Revolution* (Princeton, 1995).

Bollerey, F., Hartmann, K., 'A Patriarchal Utopia. The Garden City and Housing Reform in Germany at the Turn of the Century', in Sutcliffe, A. (ed.), *The Rise of Modern Urban Planning, 1880–1914* (London, 1980), pp. 135–64.

Boockmann, H., 'Das ehemalige Deutschordens-Schloß Marienburg, 1772–1945. Die Geschichte eines politischen Denkmals', in Boockmann *et al.* (eds.), *Geschichtswissenschaft und Vereinswesen im 19. Jahrhundert* (Göttingen, 1972), pp. 99–161.

Die Marienburg im 19. Jahrhundert (Frankfurt, 1992).

Borger, H. (ed.), *Der Kölner Dom im Jahrhundert seiner Vollendung* (Cologne, 1980).

Borrmann, N., *Paul Schulze-Naumburg 1869–1949. Maler-Publizist-Architekt* (Essen, 1989).

Boulting, N., 'The Law's Delays. Conservationist Legislation in the British Isles', in Fawcett, J. (ed.), *The Future of the Past. Attitudes to Conservation, 1174–1974* (London, 1976), pp. 9–34.

Bowden, M., *Pitt-Rivers. The Life and Archaeological Work of Lieutenant-General Augustus Henry Lane Fox Pitt Rivers, DCL, FRS, FSA* (Cambridge, 1991).

Boyer, M.C., *The City of Collective Memory. Its Historical Imagery and Architectural Entertainments* (Cambridge, MA, London, 1994).

Boynton, E., Burton, A., *The Great Exhibitor. The Life and Work of Henry Cole* (London, 2003).

Breuilly, J., *Labour and Liberalism in Nineteenth-Century Europe. Essays in Comparative History* (Manchester, New York, 1992).

Brichet, R., *Le Régime juridique des monuments historiques en France* (Paris, 1952).

Broman, T., 'The Habermasian Public Sphere and "Science in the Enlightenment"', *History of Science*, 36 (1998), 123–49.

Bruce, G., *Some Practical Good. The Cockburn Association 1875–1975. A Hundred Years Participation in Planning in Edinburgh* (Edinburgh, 1975).

Brun, P., *Albert Robida (1848–1926). Sa vie, son oeuvre, suivi d'une bibliographie complète de ses écrits et dessins* (Paris, 1984).

Brunner, O., Conze, W., Koselleck, R. (eds.), *Geschichtliche Grundbegriffe. Lexikon zur politisch-sozialen Sprache in Deutschland* (8 vols., 1974–97).

Buch, F., 'Ferdinand von Quast und die Inventarisation in Preußen', in Mai, E., Waetzoldt, S. (eds.), *Kunstverwaltung, Bau- und Denkmalpolitik im Kaiserreich* (2 vols., Berlin 1981), I, pp. 361–82.

Studien zur preußischen Denkmalpflege am Beispiel konservatorischer Arbeiten Ferdinand von Quasts (Worms, 1990).

Buchinger, K., Gantet, C. and Vogel, J. (eds), *Europäische Erinnerungsräume* (Frankfurt, New York, 2009).

Buckland, A., Qureshi, S. (eds.), *Time Travellers. Victorian Perspectives on the Past* (Chicago, forthcoming).

Budde, G., Conrad, S., Janz, O. (eds.), *Transnationale Geschichte. Themen, Tendenzen und Theorien* (Göttingen, 2006).

Burke, P., 'Context in Context', *Common Knowledge*, 8.1 (2002), 152–77.

Burman, P., 'Defining a Body of Tradition. Philip Webb', in Miele, C. (ed.), *From William Morris. Building Conservation and the Arts and Crafts Cult of Authenticity, 1877–1939* (Studies in British Art 14, New Haven, London, 2005), pp. 67–99.

Burton, A., *Vision and Accident. The Story of the Victoria and Albert Museum* (London, 1999).

Calhoun, C. (ed.), *Habermas and the Public Sphere* (Cambridge, MA, London, 1992).

Callmer, J., Meyer, M., Struwe, R., Theune, C. (eds.), *Die Anfänge der ur- und frühgeschichtlichen Archäologie als akademisches Fach (1890–1930) im europäischen Vergleich* (Rahden/Westf., 2006).

Cannadine, D., *The Decline and Fall of the British Aristocracy* (New Haven, London, 1990).

‘The First Hundred Years’, in Newby, H. (ed.), *The National Trust. The Next Hundred Years* (London, 1995), pp. 11–31.

Carman, J., Stig Sørensen, M.L. (eds.), *Heritage Studies, Methods and Approaches* (London, New York, 2009).

Cassin, B. (ed.), *Le Vocabulaire européen des philosophies. Dictionnaire des intraduisibles* (Paris, 2004).

Chakrabarti, D.K., *A History of Indian Archaeology from the Beginning to 1947* (New Delhi, 1988).

Chaline, J.P., ‘Les Amis des monuments rouennais. Naissance et évolution d’une société de sauvegarde’, in *Églises, hôtels, vielles maisons. Bulletin des Amis des monuments rouennais, numéro spécial du Centenaire* (Rouen, 1986).

‘Les Sociétés savantes en Allemagne, Italie et Royaume-Uni à la fin du XIXe siècle’, *Histoire, Économie et Société*, 21.1 (2002), 87–96.

‘Sociétés savantes et académies de province en France dans la première moitié du XIXe siècle’, in François, E. (ed.), *Sociabilité et société bourgeoise en France, en Allemagne et en Suisse, 1750–1850/ Geselligkeit, Vereinswesen und bürgerliche Gesellschaft in Frankreich, Deutschland und der Schweiz, 1750–1850* (Paris, 1986), pp. 169–80.

Sociabilité et érudition. Les sociétés savantes en France (Paris, 1995).

Chamberlin, E.R., *Preserving the Past* (London, 1979).

Champion, T., ‘Protecting the Monuments. Archaeological Legislation from the 1882 Act to PP16’, in Hunter, M. (ed.), *Preserving the Past. The Rise of Heritage in Modern Britain* (Stroud, 1996), pp. 38–56.

Charle, C., *Les Elites de la République, 1880–1900* (Paris, 1987).

Chastel, A., ‘La Notion de patrimoine’, in Nora, P. (ed.), *Les Lieux de mémoire* (7 vols., Paris, 1984–92, repr. 3 vols., Paris, 1997), I, pp. 1433–69.

Chatelain, F., Pattyn, C., Chatelain, J., *Oeuvres d’art et objets de collection en droit français* (Paris, 1997).

Chippendale, C., ‘The Making of the First Ancient Monuments Act, 1882, and its Administration under General Pitt-Rivers’, *Journal of the British Archaeological Association*, 136 (1983), 1–55.

Choay, F., *L’Allégorie du Patrimoine* (Paris, 1992).

Chu, P. ten-Doesschate, ‘Pop-Culture in the Making. The Romantic Taste for History’, in Chu, Weisberg, G.P. (eds.), *The Popularization of Images. Visual Culture under the July Monarchy* (Princeton, 1994), pp. 166–88.

Clark, C., Kaiser, W. (eds.), *Culture Wars. Secular-Catholic Conflict in Nineteenth-Century Europe* (Cambridge, New York, 2003).

Clemens, G., *Sanctus Amor Patriae. Eine vergleichende Studie zu deutschen und italienischen Geschichtsvereinen im 19. Jahrhundert* (Tübingen, 2004).

Cohen, D., O'Connor, M. (eds.), *Comparison and History. Europe in Cross National Perspective* (London, 2004).

Colley, L., *Britons. Forging the Nation, 1707–1837* (New Haven, 1992, new edn. London, 2003).

Collins, M., 'English Art Magazines before 1901', *The Connoisseur* (March 1976), pp. 198–205.

Compère, D. (ed.), *Albert Robida, du passé au future. Un auteur illustrateur sous la IIIe République* (Amiens, 2006).

Confino, A., 'Collective Memory and Cultural History. Problems of Method', *American Historical Review*, 102.5 (1997), 1386–403.

'On Localness and Nationhood', *Bulletin of the German Historical Institute London*, 23.2 (2001), 7–28.

'The Nation as a Local Metaphor. Heimat, National Memory and the German Empire, 1871–1918,' *History and Memory*, 5.1 (1993), 142–86.

The Nation as a Local Metaphor. Würtemberg, Imperial Germany and National Memory, 1871–1918 (Chapel Hill, 1997).

Conrad, S., 'Entangled Memories. Versions of the past in Germany and Japan, 1945–2001', *Journal of Contemporary History*, 38 (2003), 85–99.

Cowell, B., *The Heritage Obsession. The Battle for England's Past* (Stroud, 2008).

Cowell, F.R., *The Athenaeum. Club and Social Life in London, 1824–1974* (London, 1975).

Crawford, A, 'Supper at Gatti's. The SPAB and the Arts and Crafts Movement', in Miele, C. (ed.), *From William Morris. Building Conservation and the Arts and Crafts Cult of Authenticity, 1877–1939* (Studies in British Art 14, New Haven, London, 2005), pp. 101–27.

Crook, J.M., 'John Britton and the Genesis of the Gothic Revival', in Summerson, Sir J. (ed.), *Concerning Architecture* (London, 1968), pp. 98–119.

Csáky, M. (ed.), *Orte des Gedächtnisses* (Vienna, 2000).

Darley, G., *Octavia Hill* (London, 1990).

Davison, G., 'Heritage. From Patrimony to Pastiche', in Fairclough, G., Harrison, R., Jameson Jnr, J.H., Schofield, J. (eds), *The Heritage Reader* (London, New York, 2008).

Debray, R. (ed.), *L'Abus monumental? Actes des Entretiens du Patrimoine Paris 1998* (Paris, 1999).

Delafons, J., *Politics and Preservation. A Policy History of the Built Heritage, 1882–1996* (London, 1997).

Dellheim, C., *The Face of the Past. The Preservation of the Medieval Inheritance in Victorian England* (Cambridge, 1982).

Denslagen, W., *Architectural Restoration in Western Europe. Controversy and Continuity* (Amsterdam, 1994).

Desvallées, A., 'A l'origine du mot "patrimoine"', in Poulot, D. (ed.), *Patrimoine et modernité* (Paris, Montréal, 1998), pp. 89–105.

'Emergence et cheminement du mot patrimoine', *Musées et collections publiques de France*, 208.3 (1995), 6–29.

Deutsche Biographische Enzyclopädie (12 vols., Munich, 1994–2003).

Deutsches Biographisches Jahrbuch (10 vols., Berlin, 1925–28).

Dictionnaire historique de la langue française (2 vols., Paris, 1994).

Dodd, P., 'Englishness and the National Culture', in Colls, R., Dodds, P. (eds.), *Englishness. Politics and Culture, 1880–1920* (London, 1986).

Dolff-Donekämpfer, G., *Die Entdeckung des Mittelalters. Studien zur Geschichte der Denkmalerfassung und des Denkmalschutzes in Hessen-Kassel bzw. Kurhessen im 18. und 19. Jahrhundert* (Darmstadt, Marburg, 1985).

Droege, G., 'Hugo Loersch', *Neue Deutsche Biographie* (21 vols., Berlin, 1953–present), XV, p. 58.

Dubrow, G.L., 'Restoring a Female Presence. New Goals in Historic Preservation', in Perry Berkeley, E., McQuaid, M. (eds.), *Architecture. A Place for Women* (Washington, 1989), pp. 159–63.

Duchêne, H., *Joseph Reinach, historien de l'Affaire Dreyfus* (Paris, 2006).

Salomon Reinach, Cultes, mythes et religions (Paris, 1995).

Duden, das große Wörterbuch der deutschen Sprache (3rd edn., 10 vols., Mannheim, 1999).

Dupuy, F., 'La Croyance comme monument', in Lamy, Y. (ed.), *L'Alchimie du patrimoine. Discours et politiques* (Talence, 1996), pp. 174–84.

Dürr, S., *Die Anfänge der Denkmalpflege in München* (Neurid, 2001).

Dussaule, P., *La Loi et le Service des monuments historiques français* (2 vols., Paris, 1974).

Dwight Culler, A., *The Victorian Mirror of History* (New Haven, London, 1985).

Edwards, E., 'Commemorating A National Past. The National Photographic Record Association, 1897–1910', *Journal of Victorian Culture*, 10.1 (2005), 123–31.

The Camera as Historian. Amateur Photographers and Historical Imagination, 1885–1918 (Durham, North Carolina, 2012).

Eley, G., 'Deutscher Sonderweg und englisches Vorbild', in Blackbourn, D., Eley, G. (eds.), *Mythen deutscher Geschichtsschreibung. Die gescheiterte bürgerliche Revolution von 1848* (Frankfurt, 1980), pp. 7–70.

'Die deutsche Geschichte und die Widersprüche der Moderne. Das Beispiel des Kaiserreiches', in Bajohr, F. (ed.), *Zivilisation und Barberei. Die wiederspüchlichen Potentiale der Moderne. Detlev Peukert zum Gedenken* (Hamburg, 1991), pp. 17–65.

Emery, E., 'Protecting the Past: Albert Robida and the Vieux Paris Exhibit at the 1900 World's Fair', *Journal of European Studies*, 35.1 (2005), 65.

Esner, R., '"Art Knows No Fatherland". Internationalism and the Reception of German Art in France in the Early Third Republic', in Geyer, M.H., Paulmann, J. (eds.), *The Mechanics of Internationalism. Culture, Society, and Politics from the 1840s to the First World War* (Studies of the German Historical Institute London, Oxford, 2001), pp. 357–73.

Espagne, M., 'Sur les limites du comparatisme en histoire culturelle', *Genèse*, 17 (1994), 112–21.

Werner, M. (eds.), *Transferts. Les Relations interculturelles dans l'espace Franco-Allemand, XVIIIe-XIXe siècles* (Paris, 1988).

Evans, D., *A History of Nature Conservation in Britain* (London, 1992).

Evans, J., *A History of the Society of Antiquaries* (Oxford, 1956).

Evans, R.J., *Rethinking German History. Nineteenth-Century Germany and the Origins of the Third Reich* (London, 1987).

Eyffinger, A., *The 1899 Hague Peace Conference. 'The Parliament of Man, The Federation of the World'* (The Hague, London, Boston, 1999).

Ezra, E. *The Colonial Unconscious. Race and Culture in Interwar France* (Ithaca, 2000).

Fairclough, G., Harrison, R., Jameson Jnr, J.H., Schofield, J. (eds.), *The Heritage Reader* (London, New York, 2008).

Fawcett, J. (ed.), *The Future of the Past. Attitudes to Conservation, 1174–1974* (London, 1976).

Fedden, R., *The Continuing Purpose* (London, 1967).
The National Trust. Past and Present (London, 1968, revised edn. 1974).

Fekete, J., *Denkmalpflege und Neugotik im 19. Jahrhundert. Dargestellt am Beispiel des alten Rathauses in München* (Munich, 1981).

Feldbaek, O. (ed.), *Dansk identitetshistorie* (Copenhagen, 1991–2).

Fermigier, A., 'Mérimée et l'inspection des monuments historiques', in Nora, P. (ed.), *Les Lieux de mémoire* (7 vols., Paris, 1984–92, repr. 3 vols., Paris, 1997), I, pp. 1599–1614.

Fierro, A. (ed.), *Patrimoine parisien 1789–99. Destruction, création, mutilation. Catalogue. Délégation à l'action artistique de la ville de Paris and Bibliothèque historique de la ville de Paris* (Paris, 1989).

Findeisen, P., *Geschichte der Denkmalpflege Sachsen-Anhalt. Von den Anfängen bis in das erste Drittel des 20. Jahrhunderts* (Berlin, 1990).

Findling, J.E. (ed.), *Historical Dictionary of World's Fairs and Expositions, 1851–1988* (New York, Westport, London, 1990).

Fiori, R., 'De l'histoire de la ville à la sauvegarde du patrimoine parisien, le rôle de la Société de l'histoire de Paris et de l'Île-de-France et des amis des monuments parisiens à la fin du XIXe siècle', *Bulletin de la Société de l'histoire de Paris et de l'Île-de-France* (2006), 81–112.
'La Société des amis des monuments parisiens, première société locale de sauvegarde du patrimoine à Paris', *Bulletin des amis des monuments rouennais* (2005/2006), 72–85.
L'Invention du vieux Paris. Naissance d'une conscience patrimoniale dans la capital (Paris, 2012).

Fischer, M.F. (ed.), *Zeitschriften deutscher Denkmalpflege 1899–1933. Register* (s.l., 1991).

Ford, F., 'Nature, Culture, and Conservation in France and Her Colonies, 1840–1940', *Past and Present*, 183 (2004), 173–98.

Foucard, B., 'Viollet-le-Duc et la restauration', in Nora, P. (ed.), *Les Lieux de mémoire* (7 vols., Paris, 1984–92, repr. 3 vols., Paris, 1997), I, pp. 1615–43.

Foucault, M., 'Nietzsche, Genealogy, History', in D.F. Bouchard (ed.), *Language, Counter-Memory, Practice: Selected Essays and Interviews* (1977), pp. 139–64.

Fox, R., 'Learning, Politics and Polite Culture in Provincial France. The Sociétés Savantes in the Nineteenth Century', in Fox, *The Culture of Science in France, 1700–1900* (Aldershot, 1992), pp. 543–64.

François, E. (ed.), *Lieux de mémoire, Erinnerungsorte. D'un modèle français à un projet allemand* (Berlin, 1996).

(ed.), *Sociabilité et société bourgeoise en France, en Allemagne et en Suisse, 1750–1850/ Geselligkeit, Vereinswesen und bürgerliche Gesellschaft in Frankreich, Deutschland und der Schweiz, 1750–1850* (Paris, 1986).

'Die Wartburg', in François, Schulze, H. (eds.), *Deutsche Erinnerungsorte* (3 vols., Munich, 2001), II, pp. 154–70.

Hook-Demarle, M.C., Meyer-Kalkus, R., Werner, M., Despoix, P. (eds.), *Marianne-Germania. Deutsch-französischer Kulturtransfer im europäischen Kontext, 1789–1914* (2 vols., Leipzig, 1998).

Schulze, H. (eds.), *Deutsche Erinnerungsorte* (3 vols., Munich, 2001).

Siegrist, H., Vogel, J. (eds.), *Nation und Emotion. Deutschland und Frankreich im Vergleich, 19. und 20. Jahrhundert* (Göttingen, 1995).

Fritsche, P., *Stranded in the Present. Modern Time and the Melancholy of History* (Cambridge, MA, 2004).

Fuchs, E. (ed.), *Weltausstellungen im 19. Jahrhundert* (*Comparativ* 9.5–6, Leipzig, 1999).

'Das Deutsche Reich auf den Weltausstellungen vor dem Ersten Weltkrieg', in Fuchs (ed.), *Weltausstellungen im 19. Jahrhundert* (*Comparativ* 9.5–6, Leipzig, 1999), pp. 61–88.

'Nationale Repräsentation, kulturelle Identität und imperiale Hegemonie auf den Weltausstellungen: Einleitende Bemerkungen' in Fuchs (ed.), *Weltausstellungen im 19. Jahrhundert* (*Comparativ* 9.5–6, Leipzig, 1999), pp. 8–14.

Fuhlrott, R., *Deutschsprachige Architekturzeitschriften. Entstehung und Entwicklung der Fachzeitschriften für Architektur in der Zeit von 1789–1918* (Munich, 1975).

Furet, F. (ed.), *Patrimoine, temps, espace. Patrimoine en place, patrimoine déplacé. Actes des Entretiens du Patrimoine Paris 1996* (Paris, 1997).

Gange, D., *Dialogues with the Dead. Egyptology in British Culture and Religion 1822–1922* (Oxford University Press, 2013).

'Religion and Science in Late Nineteenth-Century British Egyptology', *Historical Journal*, 49 (2006), 1083–103.

Ledger-Lomas, M. (eds.), *Cities of God: The Bible and Archaeology in Nineteenth-century Britain* (Cambridge, 2013).

Gamboni, D., *The Destruction of Art. Iconoclasm and Vandalism since the French Revolution* (London, 1997).

Gaze, J., *Figures in a Landscape. A History of the National Trust* (London, 1988).

Geppert, A.C.T., 'Welttheater. Die Geschichte des europäischen Ausstellungswesens im 19. und 20. Jarhhundert. Ein Forschungsbericht', *Neue Politische Literatur*, 47.1 (2002), 10–61.

Germann, G., *Gothic Revival in Europe and Britain. Sources, Influences and Ideas* (London, 1972).

Gerson, S., 'Une France locale. The Local Past in Recent French Scholarship', *French Historical Studies*, 26.3 (2003), 539–59.

The Pride of Place: Local Memories and Political Culture in Nineteenth-Century France (Ithaca, NY, 2003).

'Town, Nation, or Humanity? Festive Delineations of Place and Past in Northern France, ca. 1825–1865', *Journal of Modern History*, 72 (2000), 628–82.

Geyer, M.H., Paulmann, J. (eds.), *The Mechanics of Internationalism. Culture, Society, and Politics from the 1840s to the First World War* (Studies of the German Historical Institute London, Oxford, 2001).

Gißibl, B., Höhler, S., Kupper, P. (eds.), *Civilizing Nature. National Parks in Global Historical Perspective* (Oxford, 2012).

Giles, J., Middleton, T. (eds.), *Writing Englishness, 1900–1950* (London, 1995).

Gillman, D., *The Idea of Cultural Heritage* (London, 2006).

Glevarec, H., Saez, G., *Le Patrimoine saisi par les associations* (Paris, 2002).

Goldhill, S., *Victorian Culture and Classical Antiquity. Art, Opera, Fiction, and the Proclamation of Modernity* (Princeton, 2011).

Goldman, G., *A History of the Germanic Museum at Harvard* (Cambridge, MA, 1989).

Goldstein Sepinwall, A., *The Abbé Grégoire and the French Revolution. The Making of Modern Universalism* (Berkeley, CA, 2005).

Goldstein, E., 'Redeeming Holy Wisdom: Britain and St Sophia', in Hall, M. (ed.), *Towards World Heritage. International Origins of the Preservation Movement* (Aldershot, 2011), pp. 43–62.

Götz, W., *Beiträge zur Vorgeschichte der Denkmalpflege. Die Entwicklung der Denkmalpflege in Deutschland vor 1800* (Leipzig, 1956).

Grad, B.L., Riggs, T.A., *Visions of City and Country. Prints and Photographs of Nineteenth-Century France. Exhibition catalogue. Worcester Art Museum and The American Federation of Arts* (Worcester, MA, New York, 1982).

Greenhalgh, P., 'Education, Entertainment and Politics: Lessons from the Great International Exhibitions', in Vergo, P., *The New Museology* (London, 1989, rep. 2000), pp. 74–98.

Ephemeral Vistas. The Expositions universelles, Great Exhibitions and World's Fairs, 1851–1939 (Manchester, New York, 1988).

Griewank, K., 'Wissenschaft und Kunst in der Politik Kaiser Wilhelms I. und Bismarcks', *Archiv für Kulturgeschichte*, 34 (1952), 228–307.

Guha-Thakurta, T., *Monuments, Objects, Histories. Institutions of Art in Colonial and Postcolonial India* (New York, 2004).

Habermas, J., *The Structural Transformation of the Public Sphere. An Inquiry into a Category of Bourgeois Society* (Cambridge, 1989).

Halbwachs, M., *La Mémoire collective* (Paris, 1968).

Hall, M., 'Affirming Community Life. Preservation, National Identity and the State, 1900', in Miele, C. (ed.), *From William Morris. Building Conservation and the Arts and Crafts Cult of Authenticity, 1877–1939* (Studies in British Art 14, New Haven, London, 2005), pp. 129–57.

'Despoliation or Diplomacy? Britain, Canada, the United States and the Evolution of an English-Speaking Heritage', in Swenson, A., Mandler, P. (eds.), *From Plunder to Preservation, Britain and the Heritage of Empire, 1800–1950* (Proceedings of the British Academy, Oxford University Press, 2010).

'Niagara Falls: Preservation and the Spectacle of Anglo-American Accord, in Hall (ed.), *Towards World Heritage: International Origins of the Preservation Movement* (Aldershot, 2011), pp. 23–43.

'The Politics of Collecting: The Early Aspirations of the National Trust', *Transactions of the RHS*, 13 (2003), 345–57.

(ed.), *Towards World Heritage. International Origins of the Preservation Movement* (Aldershot, 2011).

Hall, S., 'Whose Heritage? Un-settling "The Heritage", re-imagining the post-nation', in Fairclough, G., Harrison, R., Jameson Jnr, J.H. and Schofield, J. (eds), *The Heritage Reader* (London, New York, 2008), pp. 219–28.

Hammer, F., *Die geschichtliche Entwicklung des Denkmalrechts in Deutschland* (Tübingen, 1995).

Hamon, F., 'Robida et la Vieille France', in Compère, D. (ed.), *Albert Robida, du passé au future. Un auteur illustrateur sous la IIIe République* (Amiens, 2006), pp. 127–34.

Hamsher-Monk, I., Tilmans, K., van Vree, F. (eds.), *History of Concepts. Comparative Perspectives* (Amsterdam, 1998).

Hans, G., *Denkmalschutz in Baden im 19. und 20. Jahrhundert* (Münster, 1985).

Hartog, F., *Régimes d'historicité. Presentisme et expérience du temps* (Paris, 2003).

'Rom und Griechenland. Die klassische Antike in Frankreich und die Rezeption von Johannes Winckelmann', in Jordan, L., Korländer, B. (eds.), *Nationale Grenzen und internationaler Austausch. Studien zum Kultur- und Wissenschaftstransfer in Europa* (Tübingen, 1995), pp. 175–99.

Harrison, R. 'What is heritage?' in Harrison (ed.), *Understanding the Politics of Heritage* (Manchester, 2010), pp. 5–42.

(ed.), *Understanding the Politics of Heritage* (Manchester, 2010), pp. 5–42.

Harvey, J., *Conservation of Buildings* (London, 1972).

Haskell, F., *The Ephemeral Museum. Old Master Paintings and the Rise of the Art Exhibition* (New Haven, London, 2000).

History and its Images. Art and the Interpretation of the Past (New Haven, 1993), pp. 236–52.

Rediscoveries in Art. Some Aspects of Taste, Fashion and Collection in England and in France (London, 1976).

Haupt, H.G., Kocka, J. (eds.), *Geschichte und Vergleich. Ansätze und Ergebnisse international vergleichender Geschichtsschreibung* (Frankfurt, New York, 1996).

Hayat, P., 'Ferdinand Buisson, militant de la laïcité et de la paix', *Revue d'Histoire et de Philosophie Religieuse*, 85.2 (2005), 235–51.

Heckel, M. 'Der Denkmalschutz an den Sakralbauten in der Bundesrepublik Deutschland. Kulturschutz und Kirchenfreiheit im säkulären Verfassungssystem', in *Denkmalpflege und Denkmalschutz an den sakralbauten in der Bundesrepublick Deutschland und in Frankreich* (Deutsch-Französische Kolloquien Kirche – Staat – Gesellschaft 7, Kehl, Strasbourg, 1987, repr. in Heckel, *Gesammelte Schriften* (2 vols., 1989)), II, pp. 1075–98.

Heimpel, H., 'Geschichtsvereine einst und jetzt', in Broockmann (ed.), *Geschichtswissenschaft und Vereinswesen im 19. Jahrhundert* (Göttingen, 1972), pp. 45–73.

Hemme, D., Tauschek, M., Bendix, R. (eds.), *Prädikat Heritage. Wertschöpfungen aus kulturellen Ressourcen* (Ethnologie: Forschung und Wissenschaft 13, Müster, 2007).

Henri de Geymüller, architecte et historien de l'art. Un novateur dans l'approche de la restauration et de la conservation du patrimoine architectural (Lausanne, 1995).

Hepp, F., Roth, A.M. (eds.), *Ein Franzose in Heidelberg. Stadt und Schloss im Blick des Grafen Graimberg. Exhibition Catalogue Kurpfälzisches Museum Heidelberg* (Heidelberg, 2004).

Hermand, J., Steakley, J. (eds.), *Heimat, Nation, Fatherland. The German Sense of Belonging* (New York, 1996).

Heuvel, G., 'Cosmopolite, Cosmopoliti(ti)sme', in Reichard, R., Lüsebrink, J., Schmitt, E. (eds.), *Handbuch politisch-sozialer Grundbegriff in Frankreich, 1680–1820* (20 vols. to date, Munich, 1985–present), VI, pp. 41–55.

Hewison, R., *The Heritage Industry. Britain in a Climate of Decline* (London, 1987). 'La Prise de conscience du patrimoine en Grande-Bretagne', in Nora, P. (ed.), *Science et conscience du patrimoine. Actes des Entretiens du Patrimoine Paris 1994* (Paris, 1997), pp. 357–63.

Hilger, 'Paul Clemen und die Denkmäler-Inventarisation in den Rheinlanden', in Mai, E., Waetzold, S. (eds.), *Kunstverwaltung, Bau-und Denkmal-Politik im Kaiserreich* (Kunst, Kultur, und Politik im deutschen Kaiserreich 1, Berlin, 1981), pp. 383–98.

Hill, W.T., *Octavia Hill. Pioneer of the National Trust and Housing Reform* (London, 1956).

Hinsley, F.H., *Power and the Pursuit of Peace. Theory and Practice in the History of Relations between States* (Cambridge, 1963, repr. 1967).

Hobsbawm, E. J., 'The Social Function of the Past. Some Questions', *Past and Present*, 55 (1972), 3–17. Ranger, T. (eds.), *The Invention of Tradition* (Cambridge, 1983).

Hoffmann, G., *Rheinische Romanik im 19. Jahrhundert. Denkmalpflege in der Preußischen Rheinprovinz* (Cologne, 1995).

Hoock, H., 'The British State and the Anglo-French Wars over Antiquities, 1798–1858', *Historical Journal* 50.1 (2007), 49–72.

Horn Melton, J. van, *The Rise of the Public in Enlightenment Europe* (Cambridge, 2001).

Horne, J.N., Kramer, A., *German Atrocities, 1914. A History of Denial* (New Haven, London, 2001).

Hounieu, J.P., 'La Syntaxe juridique de la notion de patrimoine', in Lamy, Y. (ed.), *L'Alchimie du patrimoine. Discours et politiques* (Talence, 1996), pp. 75–107.

Hunter, M., 'Bibliographical Essay', in Hunter (ed.), *Preserving the Past. The Rise of Heritage in Modern Britain* (Stroud, 1996), pp. 177–90.

Hyde, R., *Panoramania! The Art and Entertainment of the 'All Embracing View'* (London, 1988).

ICOMOS, *Revolutions and Cultural Property, 1789–1989, Congress 20–21 Nov. 1989* (Naples, 1990).

Imam, A., *Sir Alexander Cunningham and the Beginnings of Indian Archaeology* (Dacca, 1966).

Isnenghi, M. (ed.), *I luogi della memoria* (3 vols., Rome, Bari, 1987–8).

Jarausch, K.H., Jones, L.E. (eds.), *In Search of a Liberal Germany. Studies in the History of German Liberalism from 1789 to the Present* (New York, 1990).

Jeanneney, J.N., Joutard, P. (eds.), *Du Bon Usage des grands hommes en Europe* (Paris, 2003).

Jefferies, M., 'Back to the Future? The "Heimatschutz" Movement in Wilhelmine Germany', *History*, 77. 251 (1992), 411–20.

'Heimatschutz. Environmental Activism in Wilhelmine Germany', in Riordan, C. (ed.), *Green Thought in German Culture* (Cardiff, 1997), pp. 42–54.

'Lebensreform. A Middle-Class Antidote to Wilhelminism?', in Eley, G., Retallack, J. (eds.), *Wilhelminism and Its Legacies. German Modernities, Imperialism, and the Meaning of Reform 1890–1930* (Providence, Oxford, 2003), pp. 91–106.

Politics and Culture in Wilhelmine Germany. The Case of Industrial Architecture (Oxford, 1995).

Jenkins, J., James, P., *From Acorn to Oak Tree. The Growth of the National Trust, 1895–1994* (London, 1994).

Jokilehto, J., *A History of Architectural Conservation* (Oxford, 1999).

Jones, G.G., 'Rudorff, Ernst (Friedrich Karl)', *The New Grove Dictionary of Music and Musicians* (20 vols., London, 1980), XVI, p. 316.

Jordan, L., Kortländer, B. (eds.), *Nationale Grenzen und internationaler Austausch. Studien zum Kultur- und Wissenschaftstransfer in Europa* (Tübingen, 1995).

Kaesar, M.A., 'The First Establishment of Prehistoric Science. The Shortcomings of Autonomy', in Callmer, J., Meyer, M., Struwe, R., Theune, C. (eds.), *Die Anfänge der ur- und frühgeschichtlichen Archäologie als akademisches Fach (1890–1930) im europäischen Vergleich* (Rahden/Westf., 2006), pp. 149–60.

'L'Internationalisation de la préhistoire, une manoeuvre tactique? Les conséquences épitésmologiques de la fondation des Congrès internationaux d'anthropologie et d'archéologie préhistoriques', in Blanckaert, C. (ed.), *Les Politiques de l'anthropologie. Discours et pratiques en France, 1860–1940* (Paris, 2001), pp. 201–30.

Kain, R. (ed.), *Planning for Conservation* (London, 1981).

Kaiser, W., 'Cultural Transfer of Free Trade at the World Exhibitions, 1851–1862', *Journal of Modern History*, 77.3 (2005), 563–90.

'Transnational Mobilization and Cultural Representation. Political Transfer in the Age of Proto-Globalization, Democratization and Nationalism 1848–1914', *European Review of History*, 12.2 (2005), 403–24.

'Vive la France! Vive la République? The Cultural Construction of French Identity at the World Exhibitions in Paris 1855–1900', *National Identities*, 1.3 (1999), 227–44.

Kaluszinki, M., Wahnich, S. (eds.), *L'Etat contre la politique. Les expressions historiques de l'étatisation* (Paris, 1998).

Kennet, W., *Preservation* (London, 1972).

King, A., 'Architectural Journalism and the Profession. The Early Years of George Godwin', *Journal of the Society of Architectural Historians of Great Britain*, 19 (1976), 32–53.

Kirshenblatt-Gimblett, B. 'Theorizing Heritage', *Ethnomusicology*, 39 (1995), 367–380.

Kley, A., 'Die Weltnaturschutzkonferenz 1913 in Bern', *Umweltrecht in der Praxis, Sonderheft zu Grundsatzfragen des Umweltrechts, Symposium vom 24.5.2007 zur Emeritierung von Prof. Dr. Heribert Rausch*, 7 (2007), 685–705.

Klimt, A., *Saur Allgemeines Künstler Lexicon. Bio-Bibliographischer Index* (8 vols., Munich, 2000).

Klueting, E. (ed.), *Antimodernismus und Reform. Zur Geschichte der deutschen Heimatbewegung* (Darmstadt, 1991).

Knaut, A., 'Ernst Rudorff und die Anfänge der Deutschen Heimatbewegung', in Klueting, E. (ed.), *Antimodernismus und Reform. Zur Geschichte der deutschen Heimatbewegung* (Darmstadt, 1991), pp. 20–49.

Zurück zur Natur! Die Wurzeln der Ökologiebewegung (Greven, 1993).

Koschnik, L., *Franz Kugler (1808–1858) als Kunsthistoriker und Kunstpolitiker* (Berlin, 1985).

Koselleck, R., *Futures Past. On the Semantics of Historical Time* (New York, 2004).

Spree, U., Steinmetz, W., 'Drei bürgerliche Welten? Zur vergleichenden Semantik der bürgerlichen Gesellschaft in Deutschland, Frankreich und England', in Puhle, H.J. (ed.), *Bürger in der Gesellschaft der Neuzeit. Wirtschaft – Politik – Kultur* (Göttingen, 1991), pp. 14–58.

Koshar, R., 'Against the "Frightful Leveler". Historic Preservation and German Cities, 1890–1914', *Journal of Urban History*, 19.3 (1992), 7–29.

'The Antinomies of Heimat. Homeland, History, Nazism', in Hermand, J., Steakley, J. (eds.), *Heimat, Nation, Fatherland. The German Sense of Belonging* (New York, 1996), pp. 113–36.

From Monuments to Traces. Artefacts of German Memory, 1870–1990 (Berkeley, London, 2000).

German Travel Cultures (Oxford, 2000).

Germany's Transient Pasts. Preservation and National Memory in the Twentieth Century (Chapel Hill, 1998).

Kott, C., 'Die deutsche Kunst- und Museumspolitik im besetzten Nordfrankreich im Ersten Weltkrieg zwischen Kunstraub, Kunstschutz, Propaganda und Wissenschaft', *Kritische Berichte*, 2 (1997), 5–24.

'Kulturarbeit im Feindesland. Die deutsche Kunst- und Museumspolitik im besetzten Belgien im Ersten Weltkrieg', in Baumann, R., Roland, H. (eds.), *Carl Einstein in Brüssel. Dialoge über Grenzen* (Frankfurt, Berlin, Bern, 2001), pp. 199–225.

Préserver l'art de l'ennemi? Le patrimoine artistique en Belgique et en France occupées, 1914–1918 (Brussels, 2006).

Krabbe, W., *Gesellschaftsveränderung durch Lebensreform* (Münster, 1975).

Kramer, A., *Dynamic of Destruction. Culture and Mass Killing in the First World War* (Oxford, 2007).

Kratsch, G., *Kunstwart und Dürerbund* (Göttingen, 1969).

Kretschmar, W., *Geschichte der Weltausstellungen* (Frankfurt, New York, 1999).

Kunz, G., *Verortete Geschichte. Regionales Geschichtsbewußtsein in den Deutschen Historischen Vereinen des 19. Jahrhunderts* (Kritische Studien zur Geschichtswissenschaft 138, Göttingen, 2000).

Kupper, P., *Wildnis schaffen. Eine transnationale Geschichte des Schweizerischen Nationalparks* (Bern, 2012).

Labrot, V., 'L'Apport du droit international. Patrimoine commun de l'humanité et patrimoine naturel', in Lamy, Y. (ed.), *L'Alchimie du patrimoine. Discours et politiques* (Talence, 1996), pp. 109–35.

Lambourne, N., *War Damage in Western Europe: The Destruction of Historic Monuments During the Second World War* (Edinburgh, 2001).

Lamy, Y. (ed.), *L'Alchimie du patrimoine. Discours et politiques* (Talence, 1996).

'Dès Usages du mot aux syntaxes scientifiques', in Lamy (ed.), *L'Alchimie du patrimoine. Discours et politiques* (Talence, 1996), pp. 28–40.

'Le Sens d'une pratique', in Lamy (ed.), *L'Alchimie du patrimoine. Discours et politiques* (Talence, 1996), pp. 61–71.

Langewiesche, D., 'German Liberalism in the Second Empire, 1871–1914', in Jarausch, K.H., Jones, L.E. (eds.), *In Search of a Liberal Germany. Studies in the History of German Liberalism from 1789 to the Present* (New York, 1990), pp. 217–35.

Larkin, M., *Church and State after the Dreyfus Affair. The Separation Issue in France* (London, 1974).

Lavin, S., *Quatremère de Quincy and the Invention of a Modern Language of Architecture* (Cambridge, MA, 1992).

Le Goff, J. (ed.), *Patrimoine et passions identitaires. Actes des Entretiens du Patrimoine Paris 1997* (Paris, 1998).

Le Goff, J., *History and Memory*. Trans. by S. Rendall and E. Claman (New York, 1992).

Lehman, H., Richter, M., *The Meaning of Historical Terms and Concepts. New Studies on Begriffsgeschichte* (Washington, DC, 1996).

Lekan, T.M., *Imagining the Nation in Nature. Landscape Preservation and German Identity, 1885–1945* (Cambridge, MA, 2004).

Leniaud, J.M., *Les Archipels du passé. Le patrimoine et son histoire* (Paris, 2002).

Les Cathédrales au XIXe siècle. Étude du service des édifices diocésains (Paris, 1993).

'L'Etat, les sociétés savantes et les associations de défense du patrimoine. L'exception française', in Le Goff, J. (ed.), *Patrimoine et passions identitaires. Actes des Entretiens du Patrimoine Paris 1997* (Paris, 1998), pp. 137–54.

'Historicité ou perfectionnisme? Le débat sur la façade de Saint-Ouen de Rouen', *Bulletin archéologique du Comité des travaux historiques et scientifiques*, 12–13 (1976–77), 41–62.

Jean-Baptiste Lassus (1807–1857), ou le temps retrouvé des cathédrales (Paris, 1980).

Saint Denis de 1760 à nos jours (Paris, 1996).

L'Utopie française. Essai sur le patrimoine (Paris, 1992).

Léon, P., *La Vie des monuments français. Destruction, restaurations* (Paris, 1951).

Leonhard, J., *Liberalismus. Zur historischen Semantik eines Deutungsmusters* (Munich, 2001).

Les Architectes en chef des Monuments historiques, centenaire du concours (Paris, 1994).

Levine, P., *The Amateur and the Professional. Antiquaries, Historians and Archaeologists in Victorian England, 1838–1886* (Cambridge, 1986).

Limlei, M., *Geschichte als Ort der Bewährung. Menschenbild und Gesellschaftsverständnis in den deutschen historischen Romanen, 1820–1890* (Frankfurt, 1988).

Lipstadt, H., 'Early Architectural Periodicals', in Middleton, R. (ed.), *The Beaux Arts and Nineteenth-Century French Architecture* (London, 1982), pp. 50–7.

Lorcin, P.M.E., 'Rome and France in Africa: Recovering Colonial Algeria's Latin Past', *French Historical Studies*, 25.2 (2002), 295–329.

Lottes, G., 'Europäische Erinnerung und europäische Erinnerungsorte?', *Jahrbuch für Europäische Geschichte*, 3 (2002), 81–92.

Lowenthal, D., 'British National Identity and the English Landscape', *Rural History*, 2 (1991), 205–30.

The Heritage Crusade and the Spoils of History (Cambridge, 1998).

The Past is a Foreign Country (Cambridge, 1985).

Binney, M. (eds.), *Our Past Before us. Why Do we Save it?* (London, 1981).

Loyer, F. (ed.), *Ville d'hier, ville d'aujourd'hui en Europe. Actes des Entretiens du Patrimoine Paris 2000* (Paris, 2001).

Mackay Quynn, D., 'The Art Confiscations of the Napoleonic Wars', *American Historical Review*, 50.3 (1945), 437–60.

Magirius, H., 'Cornelius Gurlitt (1850–1938)' in Magirius (ed.), *Denkmalpflege in Sachsen, 1894–1994* (2 vols., Weimar, 1997), I, pp. 15–24.

(ed.), *Denkmalpflege in Sachsen, 1894–1994* (2 vols., Weimar, 1997).

Geschichte der Denkmalpflege. Sachsen von den Anfängen bis zum Neubeginn 1945 (Berlin, 1989).

'Zur Geschichte der sächsischen Denkmalpflege', in Magirius (ed.), *Denkmalpflege in Sachsen, 1894–1994* (2 vols., Weimar, 1997), I, pp. 55–61.

Mai, E., Waetzold, S. (eds.), *Kunstverwaltung, Bau-und Denkmal-Politik im Kaiserreich* (Kunst, Kultur, und Politik im deutschen Kaiserreich 1, 2 vols., Berlin, 1981).

Mandler, P., *The Fall and Rise of the Stately Home* (New Haven, London, 1997).

'"The Wand of Fancy": The Historical Imagination of the Victorian Tourist', in M. Kwint, C. Breward and J. Aynsley (eds), *Material Memories* (Oxford, New York, 1999), pp. 125–41.

'Rethinking the "Forces of Darkness". An Anti-History of the Preservation Movement in Britain', in M. Hall (ed.), *Towards World Heritage. International Origins of the Preservation Movement* (Aldershot, 2011).

Mansel, P., *Paris between Empires, 1814–1852* (London, 2001).

Marsh, J., *Back to the Land. The Pastoral Impulse in England, from 1880 to 1914* (London, 1982).

Matless, D., *Landscape and Englishness* (London, 1998).

McClellan, A., *Inventing the Louvre. Art Politics and the Origins of the Modern Museum in Eighteenth-Century Paris* (1994).

McClellan, J.E. III., 'L'Europe des académies', *Dix-Huitième Siècle*, 25 (1993), 153–65.

McManners, J., *Church and State in France, 1870–1914* (London, 1972).

McMillan, J., '"Priest hits Girl". On the Front Line in the "War of the Two Frances"', in Clark, C., Kaiser, W. (eds.), *Culture Wars. Secular-Catholic Conflict in Nineteenth-Century Europe* (Cambridge, New York, 2003), pp. 77–101.

Mellon, S., 'Alexandre Lenoir. The Museum versus the Revolution', *Proceeding of the Consortium on Revolutionary Europe*, 8 (1979), 75–88.

Melman, B., *The Culture of History. English Uses of the Past, 1800–1953* (Oxford, 2006).

Merle, G., *Emile Combes* (Paris, 1995).

Merryman, J.H. (ed.), *Imperialism, Art and Restitution* (Cambridge, 2006).

'Whither the Elgin Marbles?', in Merryman (ed.), *Imperialism, Art and Restitution* (Cambridge, 2006), pp. 98–113.

Michel, P., 'Barbarie, civilisation, vandalisme', in Reichard, R., Lüsebrink, J., Schmitt, E. (eds.), *Handbuch politisch-sozialer Grundbegriff in Frankreich, 1680–1820* (20 vols., Munich, 1985–2000), VIII, pp. 7–49.

Miele, C. (ed.), *From William Morris. Building Conservation and the Arts and Crafts Cult of Authenticity, 1877–1939* (Studies in British Art 14, New Haven, London, 2005).

'"A Small Knot of Cultivated People". William Morris and the Ideologies of Protection', *Art Journal*, 54 (1995), 73–9.

'"Their Interest and Habit". Professionalism and the Restoration of Medieval Churches 1837–77', in Brooks, C., Saint, A. (eds.), *The Victorian Church. Architecture and Society* (Manchester, 1995), pp. 151–72.

'Morris and Conservation', in Miele (ed.), *From William Morris. Building Conservation and the Arts and Crafts Cult of Authenticity, 1877–1939* (Studies in British Art 14, New Haven, London, 2005).

'The First Conservation Militant. William Morris and the Society for the Protection of Ancient Buildings', in Hunter, M. (ed.), *Preserving the Past. The Rise of Heritage in Modern Britain* (Stroud, 1996), pp. 17–37.

Miles, M., *Art as Plunder. The Ancient Origins of Debate about Cultural Property* (Cambridge, 2008).

Mitchell, T., 'Orientalism and the Exhibitionary Order', in Dirks, N. (ed.), *Colonialism and Culture* (Ann Arbor, 1992), pp. 289–318.

Mitchell. W.J.T. (ed.), *Art and the Public Sphere* (Chicago, 1992).

Mohr de Pérez, R., *Die Anfänge der staatlichen Denkmalpflege in Preußen. Ermittlung und Erhaltung alterthümlicher Merkwürdigkeiten* (Worms, 2001).

Moir, E., *The Discovery of Britain. The English Tourists, 1540–1840* (London, 1964).

Moisy, P., *Les Séjours en France de Sulpice Boisserée, 1820–1825. Contribution à l'étude des relations intellectuelles franco-allemandes* (Bibliothèque de la Société des études germaniques 10, Lyon, 1956).

Möller, H.H., 'Zur Entstehung und Geschichte der deutschen Denkmalpflegezeitschriften', in Fischer, M.F. (ed.), *Zeitschriften deutscher Denkmalpflege 1899–1933. Register* (s.l., 1991), pp. 5–12.

Mörsch, G., 'Zur Differenzierbarkeit des Denkmalbegriffs', *Deutsche Kunst und Denkmalpflege*, 39 (1981), 99–108.

Morsey, R., 'Probleme der Kulturkampf-Forschung', *Historisches Jahrbuch*, 83 (1964), 217–45.

Muhs, R., Paulmann, J., Steinmetz, W. (eds.), *Aneignung und Abwehr. Interkultureller Transfer zwischen Deutschland und Großbritannien im 19. Jahrhundert* (Bodenheim, 1998).

Murphy, G., *Founders of the National Trust* (London, 1987).

Murphy, K.D., 'Restoring Rouen. The Politics of Preservation in July Monarchy France', *Word and Image*, 2.2 (1995), 196–88.

Memory and Modernity. Viollet-le-Duc at Vézelay (University Park, 2000).

Murray, T., 'The History, Philosophy and Sociology of Archaeology. The Case of the Ancient Monuments Protection Act 1882', in Pinsky, L., Wyle, A. (eds.), *Critical Traditions in Contemporary Archaeology* (Cambridge, 1989), pp. 55–67.

Nahlik, S.E., 'Protection of Cultural Property', in *International Dimensions of Humanitarian Law* (Geneva, Paris, 1988) pp. 203–15.

Néagu, P., Chevrier, J.F., 'La Photographie d'architecture aux XIXe et XXe siècles', in *Images et imaginaire d'architecture. Centre G. Pompidou* (Paris, 1984), pp. 93–111.

Neue Deutsche Biographie (25 vols., Berlin, 1953–present).

Newby, H. (ed.), *The National Trust. The Next Hundred Years* (London, 1995).

Nipperdey, T., *Deutsche Geschichte 1866–1918* (2 vols., Munich, 1991–2).

'Der Kölner Dom als Nationaldenkmal', in Nipperdey, *Nachdenken über die deutsche Geschichte* (Munich, 1986), pp. 156–71.

'Nationalidee und Nationaldenkmal in Deutschland im 19. Jahrhundert', in Nipperdey, *Gesellschaft, Kultur, Theorie. Gesammelte Aufsätze zur neueren Geschichte* (Göttingen, 1976), pp. 133–73.

Nisbet, P., Norris, E., *The Busch-Reisinger Museum. History and Holdings* (Cambridge, MA, 1991).

Nora, P. (ed.), *Les Lieux de mémoire* (7 vols., Paris, 1984–92, reprint, 3 vols., Paris, 1997).

'La Nation-mémoire', in Nora (ed.), *Les Lieux de mémoire* (7 vols., Paris, 1984–92, reprint, 3 vols., Paris, 1997), II, pp. 2207–16.

'La Notion de 'lieu de mémoire' est-elle exportable?', in Boer, P. den, Frijhoff, W. (eds.), *Lieux de mémoire et identités nationales* (Amsterdam, 1993), pp. 3–10.

(ed.), *Realms of Memory. Rethinking the French Past* (3 vols., New York, 1996).

(ed.), *Science et conscience du patrimoine. Actes des Entretiens du Patrimoine Paris 1994* (Paris, 1997).

Nord, P., 'Social Defence and Conservative Regeneration. The National Revival, 1900–14', in Tombs, R. (ed.), *Nationhood and Nationalism in France. From Boulangism to the Great War, 1889–1918* (London, New York, 1991), pp. 210–28.

'Normand, Alfred', in Thieme, U., Becker, F., *Allgemeines Lexikon der bildenden Künstler von der Antike bis zur Gegenwart* (Leipzig, 1907–50), XXV, p. 518.

'Normand, Charles', in Klimt, A., *Saur Allgemeines Künstler Lexicon. Bio-Bibliographischer Index* (8 vols., Munich, 2000), VIII.

O'Keefe, R., *The Protection of Cultural Property in Armed Conflict* (Cambridge, 2006).

O'Neil, B.H.St.J., 'The Congress of Archaeological Societies', *Antiquaries Journal*, 26 (1946), 61–6.

Oberkrome, W., *Deutsche Heimat. Nationale Konzeption und regionale Praxis von Naturschutz, Landschaftsgestaltung und Kulturpolitik in Westfalen-Lippe und Thüringen (1900–1960)* (Paderborn, 2004).

Oakley, W., *Winged Wheel. The History of the First Hundred Years of the Cyclist's Touring Club* (Godalming, 1977).

O'Connor, R., *The Earth on Show* (Chicago, 2007).

Oesterle, G., 'Zur Historisierung des Erbebegriffes', in Thum, B. (ed.), *Gegenwart als kulturelles Erbe. Ein Beitrag der Germanistik zur Kulturwissenschaft deutschsprachiger Länder* (Munich, 1985), pp. 411–51.

Oexle, G. (ed.), *Memoria als Kultur* (Göttingen, 1995).

Offer, A., *Property and Politics, 1870–1914* (Cambridge, 1981).

Osteneck, V., 'Die Debatte um das Heidelberger Schloss', in Scheurmann, I. (ed.), *ZeitSchichten. Erkennen und Erhalten – Denkmalpflege in Deutschland, Exhibition Catalogue, Residenzschloss Dresden 30 July –13 Nov. 2005* (Dresden 2005), pp. 108–13.

Otto, C.F., 'Modern Environment and Historical Continuity', *Art Journal*, 43.2 (1983), 148–57.

Oudin, B., *Aristide Briand* (Paris, 1987).

Ousby, J., *The Englishman's England. Taste, Travel and the Rise of Tourism* (Cambridge, 1990).

Paléologue, A., 'Législation des monuments historiques', *Monuments Historiques*, 169 (1990), 19–24.

Paulmann, J., 'Internationaler Vergleich und interkultureller Transfer. Zwei Forschungsansätze zur europäischen Geschichte des 18.–20. Jahrhunderts', *Historische Zeitschrift*, 267.3 (1998), 649–85.

Pemsel, J., *Die Wiener Weltausstellung von 1873. Das gründerzeitliche Wien am Wendepunkt* (Vienna, Cologne, 1989).

Perry Berkeley, E., McQuaid, M. (eds.), *Architecture. A Place for Women* (Washington, 1989).

Petri, R., 'Deutsche Heimat 1850–1950', *Comparativ*, 11.1 (2001), 77–127.

Pevsner, Sir N., *Ruskin and Viollet-le-Duc. Englishness and Frenchness in the Appreciation of Gothic Architecture* (London, 1969).

Piggot, S., *Ruins in a Landscape. Essays in Antiquarianism* (Edinburgh, 1976).

Piggott, J.R., *Palace of the People. The Crystal Palace at Sydenham 1854–1936* (Madison, 2004).

Pimlott, J.A.R., *The Englishman's Holiday. A Social History* (London, 1947).

Plato, A. von, *Präsentierte Geschichte. Ausstellungskultur und Massenpublikum im Frankreich des 19. Jahrhunderts* (Frankfurt, New York, 2001).

Pocock, J.G.A., 'Concepts and Discourses. A Difference in Culture? Comment on a Paper by Melvin Richter', in Lehman, H., Richter, M., *The Meaning of Historical Terms and Concepts. New Studies on Begriffsgeschichte* (Washington, DC, 1996), pp. 47–58.

    Politics, Language and Time. Essays on Political Thought and History (New York, 1971).

Pointon, M. (ed.), *Art Apart. Art Institutions and Ideology across England and North America* (Manchester, 1994).

Poirrier, P. (ed.), *L'Invention du Patrimoine en Bourgogne* (Dijon, 2004).

Pommier, E., *L'Art de la liberté. Doctrines et débats de la Révolution française* (Paris, 1991).

    (ed.), *Les Musées en Europe à la veille de l'ouverture du Louvres* (Paris, 1995).

Popkin, J.D., Popkin, R.H. (eds.), *The Abbé Grégoire and his World* (International Archives of the History of Ideas/ Archives internationales d'histoire des idées 169, London, 2000).

Poulot, D., 'Alexandre Lenoir et le musée des monuments français', in Nora, P. (ed.), *Les Lieux de mémoire* (7 vols., Paris, 1984–92, reprint, 3 vols., Paris, 1997), I, pp. 1515–43.

    'The Birth of Heritage. "Le moment Guizot"', *Oxford Art Journal*, 11.2 (1988), 40–56.

    Une Histoire du patrimoine en Occident, XVIIIe–XXIe siècle. Du monument aux valeurs (Paris, 2006).

    Musée, nation, patrimoine, 1789–1815 (Paris, 1997).

    (ed.), *Patrimoine et modernité* (Paris, Montréal, 1998).

    Patrimoine et musées. L'institution de la culture (Paris, 2001).

Pressouyre, L., 'Un grand musée en quête de sens', in Pressouyre (ed.), *Le Musée des Monuments français* (Paris, 2007), pp. 8–53.

    (ed.), *Le Musée des Monuments français* (Paris, 2007).

Qureshi, S., *Peoples on Parade. Exhibitions, Empire and Anthropology in Nineteenth-Century Britain* (Chicago, 2011).

Rasmussen, A., 'Les Congrès internationaux liés aux Expositions universelles de Paris, 1867–1900', *Mil neuf cent. Cahiers Georges Sorel. Revue d'histoire intellectuelle*, 7 (1989), 23–44.

Rawnsley, E., *Canon Rawnsley. An Account of His Life* (Glasgow, 1923).

Réau, L., *Histoire du vandalisme. Les monuments détruits de l'art français* (revised edn. Paris, 1994).

Reichard, R., Lüsebrink, J., Schmitt, E. (eds.), *Handbuch politisch-sozialer Grundbegriff in Frankreich, 1680–1820* (20 vols., Munich, 1985–2000).

Reid, D.M., 'Cultural Imperialism and Nationalism – the Struggle to Define and Control the Heritage of Arab Art in Egypt', *International Journal of Middle East Studies*, 24.1 (1992), 57–76.

  Whose Pharaohs? Archaeology, Museums and Egyptian National Identity from Napoleon to World War I (Berkeley, 2002).

Reilly, L., *An Architectural History of Peterborough Cathedral* (Oxford, 1997).

Renoliet, J.J., *L'Unesco oubliée. La Société des nations et la coopération intellectuelle, 1919–1946* (Paris, 1999).

Revel, J. (ed.), *Jeux d'échelles. La micro analyse à l'expérience* (Paris, 1996).

Rheinischer Verein für Denkmalpflege und Landschaftsschutz (ed.), *Erhalten und gestalten. 75 Jahre Rheinischer Verein für Denkmalpflege und Landschaftsschutz* (Neuß, 1981).

Richter, M., 'Appreciating a Contemporary Classic. The Geschichtliche Grundbegriffe and Future Scholarship', *Finnish Yearbook of Political Thought*, 1 (1997), 25–38.

  'Towards a Lexicon of European Political and Legal Concepts. A Comparison of Begriffsgeschichte and the "Cambridge School"', *Critical Review of International Social and Political Philosophy*, 2 (2003), 91–120.

Rigambert, C., *Le Droit de l'archéologie française* (Paris, 1996).

Riordan, C. (ed.), *Green Thought in German Culture* (Cardiff, 1997).

Ritter, G., Wende, P. (eds.), *Rivalität und Partnerschaft. Studien zu den deutsch-britischen Beziehungen im 19. und 20. Jahrhundert* (Paderborn, 1999).

Röben, B., *Johann Caspar Bluntschli, Francis Lieber und das moderne Völkerrecht 1861–1881* (Baden-Baden, 2003).

Robertson, B., 'The South Kensington Museum in Context. An Alternative History', *Museum and Society*, 2.1 (2004), 1–14.

Robine, N., 'Des Usages du mot', in Lamy, Y. (ed.), *L'Alchimie du patrimoine. Discours et politiques* (Talence, 1996), pp. 44–55.

Roche, D., *Le Siècle des Lumières en province. Académies et académiciens provinciaux, 1680–1789* (2 vols., Paris, The Hague, 1978).

Rolland, A.S. and Murauskaya, H. (eds), *Les Musées de la Nation. Créations, transpositions, renouveau. Europe XIXe-XXe siècles* (Paris, 2009).

Rollins, W., *A Greener Vision of Home. Cultural Politics and Environmental Reform in the German Heimatschutz Movement, 1904–1918* (Ann Arbor, 1997).

  'Heimat, modernity and nation in the early Heimatschutz movement', in Hermand, J., Steakley, J. (eds.), *Heimat, Nation, Fatherland. The German Sense of Belonging* (New York, 1996), pp. 87–112.

Rosenvallon, P., *Le Moment Guizot* (Paris, 1885).

Roth, F., *Hermann Muthesius und die Idee der harmonischen Kultur. Kultur als Einheit des künstlerischen Stils in allen Lebensäußerungen eines Volkes* (Berlin, 2001).

Roth, M., *Heimatmuseum. Zur Geschichte einer deutschen Institution* (Berlin, 1990).

Rousso, H., *Le Regard de l'histoire. L'émergence et l'évolution de la notion de patrimoine au cours du XXe siècle en France. Actes des Entretiens du Patrimoine 2001* (Paris, 2003).

Saboya, M., *Presse et architecture au XIXe siècle. César Daly et la Revue générale de l'architecture et des travaux publiques* (Paris, 1991).

Samuel, R. (ed.), *Patriotism. The Making and Unmaking of British National Identity* (vol. 3, London, 1989).

Sas, N.C.F. van (ed.), *Waar de blanke top der duinen: en andere vaderlandse herinneringen* (Amsterdam, 1995).

Sauerländer, W., 'Erweiterung des Denkmalbegriffes?', *Deutsche Kunst und Denkmalpflege*, 33 (1975), 117–30.

Saunders, A., 'A Century of Ancient Monuments Legislation 1882–1992', *Antiquaries Journal*, 63 (1983), 11–33.

Savoy, B., *Patrimoine annexé. Les biens culturels saisis par la France en Allemagne autour de 1800* (2 vols., Paris, 2003).

(ed.), *Tempel der Kunst, Die Geburt des öffentlichen Museums in Deutschland 1701–1815* (Mainz, 2006).

Sax, J.L., 'Heritage Preservation as a Public Duty. The Abbé Grégoire and the Origins of an Idea', *Michigan Law Review*, 88 (1990), 1142–69.

Secord, J., *Victorian Sensation. The Extraordinary Publication, Reception, and Secret Authorship of Vestiges of the Natural History of Creation* (Chicago, 2000).

Sherman, D., *The Construction of Memory in Interwar France* (Chicago, 1999).

Scheurmann, I. (ed.), *ZeitSchichten. Erkennen und Erhalten – Denkmalpflege in Deutschland, Exhibition Catalogue, Residenzschloss Dresden 30 July – 13 Nov. 2005* (Dresden, 2005).

Schnapp, A., 'Introduction: Neapolitan Effervescence', *Journal of the History of Collections, Special Issue: Antiquarianism, Museums and Cultural Heritage. Collecting and its Contexts in Eighteenth-Century Naples*, 19.2 (2007), 161–4.

Schreiner, L., *Karl Friedrich Schinkel und die erste westfälische Denkmäler-Inventarisation. Festgabe zum 75. Bestehen der Denkmalpflege in Westfalen 1968* (s.l. 1968).

Sharp, F., 'A Lesson in International Relations. Morris and the SPAB', *Journal of the William Morris Society*, 10 (1993), 9–14.

'Exporting the Revolution. The Work of the SPAB outside Britain, 1878–1914', in Miele, C. (ed.), *From William Morris. Building Conservation and the Arts and Crafts Cult of Authenticity, 1877–1939* (Studies in British Art 14, New Haven, London, 2005), pp. 187–212.

Sheehan, J.J., *Museums in the German Art World. From the End of the Old Regime to the Rise of Modernism* (Oxford, 2000).

Sicard, M., 'L'Image et l'invention du monument', in Debray, R. (ed.), *L'Abus monumental? Actes des Entretiens du Patrimoine Paris 1998* (Paris, 1999), pp. 97–104.

Sieferle, R.P., *Fortschrittsfeinde? Opposition gegen Technik und Industrie von der Romantik bis zur Gegenwart* (Munich, 1984).

Siegel, M., *Denkmalpflege als öffentliche Aufgabe. Eine ökonomische, institutionelle und historische Untersuchung* (Göttingen, 1985).

Singh, U., *The Discovery of Ancient India. Early Archaeologists and the Beginnings of Archaeology* (Delhi, 2004).

Sire, A.M., *La France du patrimoine. Les choix de la mémoire* (Paris, 1996).

Skinner, Q., 'Language and Social Change', in Tully, J. (ed.), *Meaning and Context. Quentin Skinner and his Critics* (Princeton, 1988), pp. 119–32.

SKR-VKS-NIKE, *Geschichte der Restaurierung in Europa/ Histoire de la restauration en Europe. I. Congress Interlaken 1989, II. Congress Basel 1991* (2 vols., Worms, 1991–3).

Smith, L., *Uses of Heritage* (London, New York, 2006).

Sorlin, P., 'Words and Images of Nationhood' in Tombs, R. (ed.), *Nationhood and Nationalism in France. From Boulangism to the Great War, 1889–1918* (London, New York, 1991), pp. 74–86.

SPAB, *A School of Rational Builders. An exhibition at the Drawings Collection of the British Architectural Library, 10 March to 1 May 1892. Exhibition Catalogue* (London, 1982).

Speitkamp, W., 'Denkmalpflege und Heimatschutz in Deutschland zwischen Kulturkritik und Nationalsozialismus', *Archiv für Kulturgeschichte*, 70 (1988), 149–93.

'"Ein dauerndes und ehrenvolles Denkmal deutscher Kulturtätigkeit". Denkmalpflege im Kaiserreich 1871–1918', *Die Alte Stadt*, 18.2 (1991), 173–97.

'Das Erbe der Monarchie und die Denkmalpflege in der Weimarer Republik', *Deutsche Kunst und Denkmalpflege*, 50.1 (1992), 10–21.

'Die Hohkönigsburg und die Denkmalpflege im Kaiserreich', *Neue Museumskunde*, 34 (1991), 121–30.

'Kulturpolitik unter dem Einfluß der französischen Revolution. Die Anfänge der modernen Denkmalpflege in Deutschland', *Tel Aviver Jahrbuch für deutsche Geschichte*, 18 (1989), 129–59.

Die Verwaltung der Geschichte. Denkmalpflege und Staat in Deutschland, 1871–1933 (Göttingen, 1996).

Stammers, T., 'The Bric-a-Brac of the Old Regime: Collecting and Cultural History in Post-Revolutionary France', *French History*, 22.3 (2008), 295–315.

St Clair, W., 'Imperial Appropriations of the Parthenon', in Merryman, J.H. (ed.), *Imperialism, Art and Restitution* (Cambridge, 2006), pp. 65–97.

Sternhell, Z., *Maurice Barrès et le nationalisme français* (Brussels, 1985).

'The Political Culture of Nationalism', in Tombs, R. (ed.), *Nationhood and Nationalism in France. From Boulangism to the Great War, 1889–1918* (London, New York, 1991), pp. 22–38.

Stoklund, B., 'The Role of the International Exhibitions in the Construction of National Cultures in the 19th Century', *Ethnologia Europaea*, 24 (1994), 35–44.

Stråth, B. (ed.), *Myth, Memory and History in the Construction of Community. Historical Patterns in Europe and Beyond* (Brussels, 2000).

Stuchtey, B., 'European Lieux de Mémoire. German Historical Institute London Conference, held at Cumberland Lodge, Windsor Great Park, 5–7 July 2002', *German Historical Institute London Bulletin*, 24.2 (2002), 121–5.

Summerson, Sir J. (ed.), *Concerning Architecture* (London, 1968).

Sutcliffe, A. (ed.), *The Rise of Modern Urban Planning, 1880–1914* (London, 1980).

Sweet, R., *Antiquaries. The Discovery of the Past in Eighteenth-Century Britain* (London, 2004).

Swenson, A., 'Heritage, Patrimoine und Kulturerbe. Eine vergleichende historische Semantik', in Hemme, D., Tauschek, M., Bendix, R. (eds.), *Prädikat Heritage. Wertschöpfungen aus kulturellen Ressourcen* (Ethnologie: Forschung und Wissenschaft 13, Münster, 2007), pp. 53–54.

'Musées de moulages et protection du patrimoine', in Rolland, A.S., Murauskaya, H. (eds.), *Les Musées de la Nation. Créations, transpositions, renouveau. Europe XIXe-XXe siècles* (Paris, 2009), pp. 205–19.

'Popular heritage and commodification debates in nineteenth- and early twentieth-century Britain, France and Germany', in Berger, S., Lorenz, C. and Melman, B. (eds), *Popularizing National Pasts, 1800 to the Present* (London, 2011), pp. 102–22.

'The Heritage of Empire', in Swenson, A., Mandler, P. (eds.), *From Plunder to Preservation, Britain and the Heritage of Empire, 1800–1950* (Proceedings of the British Academy 187, Oxford, 2013), pp. 3–28.

'Zwischen Region, Nation und Internationalismus. Kulturerbekonzepte um die Jahrhundertwende in Frankreich, Deutschland und England, in Altenburg, D. Ehrlich, L., John, J., *Im Herzen Europas. Nationale Identitäten und Erinnerungskulturen* (Cologne, Weimar, Vienna, 2008), pp. 81–103.

Mandler, P. (eds.), *From Plunder to Preservation, Britain and the Heritage of Empire, 1800–1950* (Proceedings of the British Academy 187, Oxford, 2013).

Tacke, C., *Denkmal im sozialen Raum. Nationale Symbole in Deutschland und Frankreich im 19. Jahrhundert* (Göttingen, 1995).

Taylor, J., *A Dream of England. Landscape, Photography and the Tourist's Imagination* (Manchester and New York, 1994).

Taylor, R., *The Castles of the Rhine. Recreating the Middle Ages in Modern Germany* (Waterloo, Ontario, 1998).

Theis, L., 'Guizot et les institutions de mémoire. Un historien au pouvoir', in Nora, P. (ed.), *Les Lieux de mémoire* (7 vols., Paris, 1984–92, repr. 3 vols., Paris, 1997), I, pp. 1575–97.

Thieme, U., Becker, F., *Allgemeines Lexikon der bildenden Künstler von der Antike bis zur Gegenwart* (Leipzig, 1907–50).

Thiesse, A.M., *Ils apprenaient la France. L'exaltation des régions dans le discours patriotique* (Paris, 1997).

'Petite et grande patrie', in Le Goff, J. (ed.), *Patrimoine et passions identitaires. Actes des Entretiens du Patrimoine Paris 1997* (Paris, 1998), pp. 71–86.

Thompson, E.P., *William Morris. Romantic to Revolutionary* (New York, 1976).

Thompson, F.M.L., *Gentrification and the Enterprise Culture. Britain 1780–1980. The Ford Lectures Delivered in the University of Oxford in Hilary term 1994* (Oxford, 2001).

Tinniswood, A., *A History of Country House Visiting. Five Centuries of Tourism and Taste* (Oxford, London, 1989).

Tombs, R. (ed.), *Nationhood and Nationalism in France. From Boulongism to the Great War, 1889–1918* (London, New York, 1991).

The Paris Commune 1871 (London, New York, 1999).

Tombs, I., *That Sweet Enemy. The French and the British from the Sun King to the Present* (London, 2006).

Traum & Wirklichkeit. Vergangenheit und Zukunft der Heidelberger Schlossruine. Exhibition Catalogue, Heidelberger Schloss, Ottheinrichsbau, 16 April to 17 July 2005 (Stuttgart, 2005).

Trom, D., 'Natur und nationale Identität. Der Streit um den Schutz der "Natur" um die Jahrhundertwende in Deutschland und Frankreich', in François, E., Siegrist, H., Vogel, J. (eds.), *Nation und Emotion. Deutschland und Frankreich im Vergleich, 19. und 20. Jahrhundert* (Göttingen, 1995), pp. 147–67.

Tschudi-Madson, S., *Restoration and Anti-Restoration* (Oslo, 1976).

Vajda, S., *Maurice Barrès* (Paris, 2000).

Vallet, O., 'Les Mots du monument. Linguistique comparée', in Debray, R. (ed.), *L'Abus monumental? Actes des Entretiens du Patrimoine Paris 1998* (Paris, 1999), pp. 45–8.

Vaninskaya, A. *William Morris and the Idea of Community. Romance, History and Propaganda 1880–1914* (Edinburgh, 2010).

Vaninskaya, A., Stray, C., Jenkins, A., Secord, J.A., Howsam, L., 'What the Victorians Learned: Perspectives on Nineteenth Century Schoolbooks', *Journal of Victorian Culture*, 12.2 (2007), 262–85.

Veitl, P., 'L'Étatisation du paysage français. La loi du 21 avril 1906 pour la "protection des sites et des monuments naturel de caractère artistique"', in Kaluszinki, M., Wahnich, S. (eds.), *L'Etat contre la politique. Les expressions historiques de l'étatisation* (Paris, 1998), pp. 55–68.

Verdier, P., 'Le Service des Monuments historiques. Son histoire, organisation, administration, législation, 1830–1934', *Congrès Archéologique de France 1934* (Paris, 1934), pp. 53–246.

Vidler, A., 'The Paradoxes of Vandalism. Henri Grégoire and the Thermidorian Discourse on Historical Monuments', in Popkin, J.D., Popkin, R.H. (eds.), *The Abbé Grégoire and his World* (International Archives of the History of Ideas/ Archives internationales d'histoire des idées 169, London, 2000), pp. 129–56.

Vondung, K. (ed.), *Das wilhelminische Bildungsbürgertum* (Göttingen, 1976).

Voss, J., 'Akademien, gelehrte Gesellschaften und wissenschaftliche Vereine in Deutschland, 1750–1850', in François, E. (ed.), *Sociabilité et société bourgeoise en France, en Allemagne et en Suisse, 1750–1850/ Geselligkeit, Vereinswesen und bürgerliche Gesellschaft in Frankreich, Deutschland und der Schweiz, 1750–1850* (Paris, 1986), pp. 149–67.

Walton, J.K., 'The National Trust. Preservation or Provision?', in Wheeler, M. (ed.), *Ruskin and the Environment. The Storm-Cloud of the Nineteenth Century* (Manchester, New York, 1995).

Waterson, M., *The National Trust. The First Hundred Years* (London, 1994).

Weber E., *Peasants into Frenchmen* (Cambridge, 1976).

Weideger, P., *Gilding the Acorn. Behind the Façade of the National Trust* (London, 1994).

Wer ist's (1914, 1922).

Werner, M., Zimmermann, B. 'Beyond Comparison. Histoire Croisée and the Challenge of Reflexivity', *History and Theory*, 45 (2006), 30–50.

(eds.), *De la comparaison à l'histoire croisée* (Le Genre humain 42, Paris, 2004).

'Penser l'histoire croisée, entre empirie et réflexivité', *Annales*, 58 (2003), 7–36.

'Vergleich, Transfer, Verflechtung. Der Ansatz der Histoire croisée und die Herausforderung des Transnationalen', *Geschichte und Gesellschaft*, 28 (2002), 607–36.

West, J., 'SPAB Committee Members: Biographical Notes', in Miele, C. (ed.), *From William Morris. Building Conservation and the Arts and Crafts Cult of Authenticity, 1877–1939* (Studies in British Art 14, New Haven, London, 2005), pp. 323–35.

'The Society for the Protection of Ancient Buildings, 1877–96, Committee, Membership and Casework', in Miele, C. (ed.), *From William Morris. Building Conservation and the Arts and Crafts Cult of Authenticity, 1877–1939* (Studies in British Art 14, New Haven, London, 2005), pp. 299–322.

White, J.F., *The Cambridge Movement, the Ecclesiologists and the Gothic Revival* (Cambridge, 1962).

Wiener, M.J., *English Culture and the Decline of the Industrial Spirit, 1850–1980* (Cambridge, 1981).

Wiesand, A.J., 'La Demande sociale et les publics du patrimoine, expérience et contradiction en Allemagne', in Nora, P. (ed.), *Science et conscience du patrimoine. Actes des Entretiens du Patrimoine Paris 1994* (Paris, 1997), pp. 333–55.

Wilhelm, R.J., 'La Croix-Rouge des Monuments', *Revue internationale de la Croix-Rouge*, 430 (1954), 793–815.

Williams, S.A., *The International and National Protection of Movable Cultural Property. A Comparative Study* (New York, 1978).

Winock, M., 'Jeanne d'Arc', in Nora, P. (ed.), *Les Lieux de mémoire* (7 vols., Paris, 1984–92, repr. 3 vols., Paris, 1997), III, pp. 4427–73.

Wohlleben, M. (ed.), *Konservieren, nicht restaurieren. Streitschriften zur Denkmalpflege um 1900. George Dehio, Alois Riegl* (Braunschweig, 1988).

'Vom Nutzen eines Schlosses und vom Wert einer Ruine: zur neuen Schloßdebatte nach hundert Jahren; aus Anlaß des Kolloquiums: Vergangenheit und Zukunft der Heidelberger Schloßruine im Heidelberger Schloß, 8./9. Juni 2005, und des Ausstellungskatalogs: Traum und Wirklichkeit', *Kunstchronik*, 58.11 (2005), 562–66.

Wolff, G., *Zwischen Tradition und Neubeginn. Zur Geschichte der Denkmalpflege in der 1. Hälfte des 19. Jahrhunderts* (Frankfurt, 1992).
Wöbse, A.K., *Weltnaturschutz. Umweltdiplomatie in Völkerbund und Vereinten Nationen 1920–1950* (Frankfurt, 2012).
Wörner, M., *Vergnügen und Belehrung. Volkskultur auf den Weltausstellungen 1851–1900* (Münster, New York, 1999).
Wright, J., *The Regionalist Movement in France 1890–1914. Jean Charles-Brun and French Political Thought* (Oxford, 2003).
Wright, P., *On Living in an Old Country. The National Past in Contemporary Britain* (rev. edn, 2009).
Zanten, D. van, *Building Paris. Architectural Institutions and the Transformation of the French Capital, 1830–1870* (Cambridge, MA, 1994).

UNPUBLISHED DISSERTATIONS

Charbonneau, O., 'Les Monuments historiques aux expositions universelles et internationales de 1855 a 1937', 3 vols., unpublished Mémoire de Maîtrise, Université Paris-IV (2001).
Hellal, S., 'Les Études de législations comparées du patrimoine en France, 1887–1913', unpublished Mémoire de Maîtrise, Université Paris-IV (2000).
Manias, C., 'Learned Societies and the Ancient National Past in Britain, France and Germany, 1830–1890', unpublished Ph.D. dissertation, University of London (2008).
Niemeyer, L., 'Writing German historical fiction in an age of change, 1848–1871', unpublished Ph.D. dissertation, University of Cambridge (2011).
Protz, U., 'National Treastures'/'Tresor Nationaux': The control of the Export of Works of Art and the Construction of 'National Heritage'/'Patrimoine in France and the United Kingdom, 1884–1959', unpublished Ph.D. dissertation, European University Institute (2009).
Stammers, T., 'Collecting Cultures, Historical Consciousness and Artefacts of the Old Regime in Nineteenth-Century Paris', unpublished Ph.D. dissertation, University of Cambridge (2010).
Titchen, S.M., 'On the Construction of Outstanding Universal Value. UNESCO's World Heritage Convention (Convention Concerning the Protection of the World Cultural and Natural Heritage, 1972) and the Identification and Assessment of Cultural Places for the Inclusion in the World Heritage List', unpublished Ph.D. thesis, The Australian National University, Canberra (1995).

WEBSOURCES

Académie des sciences morales et politiques (2003), 'Jean Courcelle-Seneuil', www.asmp.fr/fiches_academiciens/decede/COURCELLE-SENEUIL.htm.
Academie Française, 'Henri Martin', www.academie-francaise.fr/immortels/base/academiciens/fiche.asp?param=443.

Alborn, T.L., 'Lubbock, John, first Baron Avebury (1834–1913)', *Oxford Dictionary of National Biography* (Oxford, 2004), www.oxforddnb.com/view/article/34618.

Archives Departementale de la Gironde (2009), 'Exposition sur la Commission des Monuments Historiques'. http://fonds-archives.gironde.fr/4T/exposition/defaut/index.jsp.

Association des Amis d'Albert Robida, www.robida.info.

Barringer, T., 'Die Gründung von "Albertopolis", Prinz Albert und die frühen Jahre des South Kensington Museums', in Rogasch, W. (ed.), Victoria & Albert, Vicky & the Kaiser: ein Kapitel deutsch-englischer Familiengeschichte. Exhibition Catalogue, Deutsches Historisches Museum Berlin, 10 Jan. – 25 Mar. 1997 (Ostfildern-Ruit, 1997), www.dhm.de/ausstellungen/victalb/barri.htm.

Bibliothèque nationale de France, 'Expositions virtuelles, Galerie des photographie, Gustave Le Gray', http://expositions.bnf.fr/legray/grand/094.htm.

Böhnke, N. (2001), 'Adam Gottlieb Hermann Muthesius. Lecture on the occasion of the presentation of the brochure "Wendgräben"', in 'Hermann Muthesius (1861–1927)', www.hermann-muthesius.de.

Bowden, M., 'Rivers, Augustus Henry Lane Fox Pitt- (1827–1900)', *Oxford Dictionary of National Biography* (Oxford, 2004), www.oxforddnb.com/view/article/22341.

Bugnion, F., 'The Origins and Development of the Legal Protection of Cultural Property in the Event of Armed Conflict. 50th Anniversary of the 1954 Hague Convention for the Protection of Cultural Property in the Event of Armed Conflict', 14 Nov. 2004, International Red Cross, www.icrc.org/Web/Eng/siteeng0.nsf/htmlall/65SHTJ.

Chubb, 'Hunter, Sir Robert (1844–1913)', rev. Graham Murphy, *Oxford Dictionary of National Biography* (Oxford, 2004), www.oxforddnb.com/view/article/34064.

Conservatoire National des Arts et Métiers (2006), 'Conservatoire Numérique des Arts et Métiers', http://cnum.cnam.fr.

Cornelissen, C., 'Das Deutsche Reich auf den Weltaussstellungen des 19. Jahrhunderts', *Wolkenkuckucksheim, Internationale Zeitschrift für Theorie und Wissenschaft der Architektur*, 5.1 (2000), www.tu-cottbus.de/BTU/Fak2/TheoArch/Wolke/deu/Themen/themen001.html.

Darley, G., 'Hill, Octavia (1838–1912)', *Oxford Dictionary of National Biography* (Oxford, 2004), www.oxforddnb.com/view/article/33873.

Davenne, J., 'Du Lyon Pittoresque au Secteur Sauvegarde: La constitution de la valeur patrimoniale du vieux Lyon' (Mémoire de fin d'études Institut des Etudes Politiques de Lyon, Université Lumière Lyon 2 1997), published by IEP Lyon, http://doc-iep.univ-lyon2.fr/Ressources/Documents/Etudiants/Memoires/MFE1997/davennej/these.html.

Europa Nostra, www.europanostra.org.

Fiori, R., 'Charles Normand, 1858–1934' in P. Sénéchal, C. Barbillon (eds.), *Dictionnaire critique des historiens de l'art actifs en France de la Révolution à la Première Guerre mondiale*, online edn, INHA (2010), www.inha.fr/spip.php?article3171.

Geppert, A.C.T., 'Ausstellungsmüde. Deutsche Grossausstellungsprojekte und ihr Scheitern, 1880–1930', *Wolkenkuckucksheim, Internationale Zeitschrift für Theorie und Wissenschaft der Architektur*, 5.1 (2000), www.tu-cottbus.de/BTU/Fak2/TheoArch/Wolke/deu/Themen/themen001.html.

Coffey, J., Lau, T., 'International Exhibitions, Expositions Universelles and World's Fairs, 1851–1951. A Bibliography', *Wolkenkuckucksheim. Internationale Zeitschrift für Theorie und Wissenschaft der Architektur* (Special Issue 2000), Technische Universität Cottbus (2000), www.tu-cottbus.de/BTU/Fak2/TheoArch/Wolke/eng/Bibliography/ExpoBibliography.htm, last update (Nov. 2006) published at Henry Madden Library, California State University www.csufresno.edu/library/subjectresources/specialcollections/worldfairs/ExpoBibliography3ed.pdf.

Gerber, A. (2005), 'Transnationale Geschichte "machen" – Anmerkungen zu einem möglichen Vorgehen', geschichte.transnational, Fachforum zur Geschichte des kulturellen Transfers und der transnationalen Verflechtungen in Europa und der Welt, 2 April 2005, http://geschichte-transnational.clio-online.net/forum/2005-04-001.

Gilmour, D., 'Curzon, George Nathaniel, Marquess Curzon of Kedleston (1859–1925)', *Oxford Dictionary of National Biography* (Oxford 2004; online edn. Oct 2005), www.oxforddnb.com/view/article/32680.

Hepp, F. (2006), 'Der Heidelberger Schloss-Streit in der Karikatur: Die "Verschäferung" des Schlosses?', Kurpfälzisches Museum Heidelberg, 'Kunstwerk des Monats', Mar. 2006, www.zum.de/Faecher/G/BW/Landeskunde/rhein/hd/km/kdm/06/03b.htm.

The Heritage Open Days National Partnership (2011), www.heritageopendays.org.uk.

H-German, 'Forum, Transnationalism, Introduction' (Jan. 2006), www.h-net.org/~german/discuss/Trans/forum_trans_index.htm.

Hönes, E.R., '100 Jahre Denkmalschutzgesetz in Hessen', *Denkmalschutz Informationen*, 26.2 (2002), pp. 65–82, www.nationalkomitee.de/denkmalschutz/denkmalschutzinfo_2_2002.pdf.

Institute National d'Histoire de l'Art (2006), 'Albert Lenoir, historien de l'architecture', www.inha.fr/article.php3?id_article=736.

International Council on Monuments and Sites (ICOMOS), 'ICOMOS Charters and other Standards', 'Athens Charter for the Restoration of Historic Monuments', www.icomos.org/docs/athens_charter.html.

Kaelble, H. (2004), 'Die Debatte über Vergleich und Transfer und was jetzt?', geschichte.transnational, Fachforum zur Geschichte des kulturellen Transfers und der transnationalen Verflechtungen in Europa und der Welt, 8 Feb. 2005, http://geschichte-transnational.clio-online.net/forum/2005-02-002.

Kemper, J., 'Internationalism and the Search for a National Identity: Britain and the Great Exhibition of 1851', 23 May 2000, Stanford University, www.stanford.edu/group/ww1/spring2000/exhibition/paper.htm.

Leniaud, J.M., 'Répertoire des architectes diocésains du XIXe siècle', http://elec.enc.sorbonne.fr/architectes/index.php.

Levine, P., 'Taylor, Helen (1831–1907)', *Oxford Dictionary of National Biography* (Oxford, 2004), www.oxforddnb.com/view/article/36431.

Library of Congress, 'The Empire that Was Russia: The Prokudin-Gorskii Photographic Record Recreated', www.loc.gov/exhibits/empire/.

Lindinger, S., 'Karl August Böttiger', *Biographisch-Bibliographisches Kirchen Lexikon* (2000), XVII, cols. 143–51, updated (2006), www.bautz.de/bbkl/b/boetiger_k_a.shtml.

MacCarthy, F., 'Morris, William (1834–1896)', *Oxford Dictionary of National Biography* (Oxford, 2004), www.oxforddnb.com/view/article/19322.

Matsuura, K. 'United Nations Year for Cultural Heritage', in UNESCO, 'United Nations Year for Cultural Heritage' (2002), http://portal.unesco.org/culture/en/ev.php-URL_ID=15418&URL_DO=DO_TOPIC&URL_SECTION=201.html.

McClellan, J.E. III., 'Learned Societies', in Kors, A. C. (ed.), *Encyclopedia of the Enlightenment* (Oxford, 2002), www.oup.com/us/pdf/enlightenment/learned.pdf.

Médiathèque du patrimioine (June 2005), 'Archives photographique – Le Touring Club de France', www.mediatheque-patrimoine.culture.gouv.fr/fr/archives_photo/visites_guidees/touring%20club%20de%20france.html.

'Biographies des Architectes en Chef des Monuments Historiques' www.mediatheque-patrimoine.culture.gouv.fr/fr/bibliotheque/index.html.

Mezer-Künzel, M., 'Welt-Stadt-Ausstellung. Chancen und Probleme für die Stadtentwicklung der Veranstaltungsorte', *Wolkenkuckucksheim, Internationale Zeitschrift für Theorie und Wissenschaft der Architektur*, 5.1 (2000), www.tu-cottbus.de/BTU/Fak2/TheoArch/Wolke/deu/Themen/themen001.html.

Ministère de la Culture et de la Communication de France, 'Base Mérimée', www.culture.gouv.fr/documentation/merimee/accueil.htm.

(2003), 'Prosper Mérimée 1803–1870', www.merimee.culture.fr.

Murphy, G., 'Rawnsley, Hardwicke Drummond (1851–1920)', *Oxford Dictionary of National Biography* (Oxford, 2004), www.oxforddnb.com/view/article/37884.

Netzer, S., 'Die Mediceer des deutschen Kunstgewerbes – Kronprinz Friedrich Wilhelm und Kronprinzessin Victoria', in Rogasch, W. (ed.), Victoria & Albert, Vicky & the Kaiser: ein Kapitel deutsch-englischer Familiengeschichte. Exhibition Catalogue, Deutsches Historisches Museum Berlin, 10 Jan.–25 Mar. 1997 (Ostfildern-Ruit, 1997), www.dhm.de/ausstellungen/victalb/susi.htm.

Nützenadel, A. (2005), 'Globalisierung und transnationale Geschichte', geschichte.transnational, Fachforum zur Geschichte des kulturellen Transfers und der transnationalen Verflechtungen in Europa und der Welt, 23 Feb. 2005 http://geschichte-transnational.clio-online.net/forum/2005-02-004.

Oxford English Dictionary Online (Oxford, 2004), www.oed.com.

Rice, D.T., 'Brown, Gerard Baldwin (1849–1932)', rev. Anne Pimlott Baker, *Oxford Dictionary of National Biography* (Oxford, 2004) www.oxforddnb.com/view/article/32110.

Rogasch, W. (ed.), Victoria & Albert, Vicky & the Kaiser: ein Kapitel deutsch-englischer Familiengeschichte. Exhibition Catalogue, Deutsches Historisches

Museum Berlin, 10 Jan.–25 Mar. 1997 (Ostfildern-Ruit, 1997), www.dhm.de/ausstellungen/victalb/inhalt.htm.

Schriefers, T., 'Denkmäler mit Verfallsdatum. Zur Überwindung des traditionellen Denkmalbegriffs auf Weltausstellungen', *Wolkenkuckucksheim, Internationale Zeitschrift für Theorie und Wissenschaft der Architektur*, 5.1 (2000), www.tu-cottbus.de/BTU/Fak2/TheoArch/Wolke/deu/Themen/themen001.html.

Société pour la protection des paysages et de l'esthétique de France, 'Les bâtisseurs de la SPPEF. Charles Beauquier (1833–1916) Président de la "S.P.P.F" de 1901 à 1916', *Sites et Monuments* (2001), repr., http://sppef.free.fr/texte/images1/biographie_beauquier.jpg.

Society of Antiquaries: 'Making History: 300 years of antiquaries in Britain' (2007), www.spiralscratch.info/clients/sal.

Swenson, A., 'Founders of the National Trust (*act.* 1894–1895)', *Oxford Dictionary of National Biography* (online edn, 2009), www.oxforddnb.com/view/theme/95571.

The International Committee of the Red Cross, 'Droit International Humanitaire – Traités & textes', www.icrc.org/dih.nsf/ART?OpenView&Start=1.

'International Humanitarian Law – Treaties & Documents', www.icrc.org/ihl.nsf/WebFULL?openview.

Warren, A., 'Lefevre, George John Shaw-, Baron Eversley (1831–1928)', *Oxford Dictionary of National Biography* (Oxford 2004, online edn., 2006), www.oxforddnb.com/view/article/36055.

Index

Printed in Great Britain
by Amazon